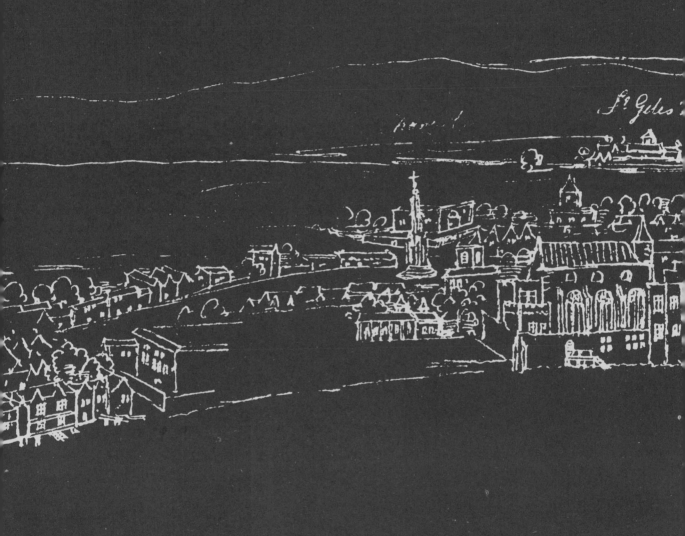

St Giles'

Proceedings in the Parliaments of Elizabeth I

VOLUME I 1558-1581

Edited by T. E. Hartley

LEICESTER
UNIVERSITY PRESS
1981

First published in 1981 by Leicester University Press
Published for the U.S. and Canada by Michael Glazier Inc.,
1210 King Street, Wilmington, Delaware 19801

Designed by Douglas Martin
Set in 'Monophoto' Poliphilus/Blado italics
Printed in Great Britain by BAS Printers Ltd
Bound by Webb Son & Co. Ltd

British Library Cataloguing in Publication Data

Proceedings in the Parliaments of Elizabeth I Vol. 1
1. England and Wales. Parliament – History
2. Great Britain – Politics and government – 1558-1603 – Sources
I. Hartley, T E
328.42'05   JN528
ISBN 0-7185-1181-6

The publication of this book has been assisted by a grant from the Twenty-Seven Foundation

Contents

The Second Parliament: Second Session, 30 September 1566-2 January 1567

The Third Parliament: 2 April-29 May 1571

The Fourth Parliament: First Session, 8 May-30 June 1572

The Fourth Parliament: Second Session, 8 February–15 March 1576

The Fourth Parliament: Third Session, 16 January–18 March 1581

Abbreviations

Add.	Additional MS (in British Library)
Ass.	*Le Livre des Assises et Pleas...* (Sawbridge, Rawlins and Roycroft, 1679)
Bede	Bede, *Ecclesiastical History*
Bracton	Henricus de Bracton, *De Legibus et Consuetudinibus Angliae*
BL	British Library
BIHR	*Bulletin of the Institute of Historical Research*
Britton	*J. Britton: an English Translation and Notes*, ed. F. M. Nichols (Washington, 1901)
Cal.	*Calendar [of Charter Rolls, of Patent Rolls, etc.]*
CJ	*Journals of the House of Commons* (1803–)
Cott.	Cottonian MS
CRO	County Record Office
D'Ewes	Simonds D'Ewes, *The Journals of all the Parliaments of Elizabeth* (1682)
DNB	*Dictionary of National Biography*
EcHR	*Economic History Review*
EHR	*English Historical Review*
EP	J. E. Neale, *Elizabeth and her Parliaments* (2 vols., 1953, 1957)
Froude	J. A. Froude, *History of England...* (1872–7 edn)
GEC	*The Complete Peerage*, ed. G. E. Cokayne (1910–59)
Hall	E. Hall, *Chronicle* (1809 edn)
Harl.	Harleian MS
HC	J. E. Neale, *The Elizabethan House of Commons* (1949)
HMC	Historical Manuscripts Commission
Holinshed	R. Holinshed, *Chronicles of England, Scotland and Ireland* (1807–8 edn)
Lansd.	Lansdowne MS
LJ	*Journals of the House of Lords* (1846)
PRO	Public Record Office
Rot.Parl.	*Rotuli Parliamentorum* (n.d.)
SP	State Papers
SR	*Statutes of the Realm* (1810–28)
TCD	Trinity College Dublin
Trans.Devons. Assoc.	*Transactions of the Devonshire Association*
TRHS	*Transactions of the Royal Historical Society*
YB	*Year Book*

Preface

This first volume of documents owes its origins to an intention, long nurtured by the late Professor Sir John Neale, to assemble in print many of the raw materials he had used in his life-long work on Elizabeth's parliaments: my greatest debt of gratitude was, and is, therefore to him for relinquishing the task to me, and having done so, for giving me every encouragement. I was fortunate enough to be allowed the use of transcripts of the manuscripts which Miss Helen Miller produced for Neale, clearly an immensely helpful concession, and I am indebted to the co-operation of Mr E. C. Mullins who gave me access to those transcripts housed in the History of Parliament Annexe of the Institute of Historical Research. Notwithstanding the transcripts I have naturally returned to the original manuscripts, and I alone remain responsible for any errors of transcription which occur.

I have generally preserved the original spelling of the manuscripts, though two cases require some comment. The lack of clear distinctions between 'u' and 'v' on the one hand, and 'i' and 'j' on the other, commonly pose problems for the transcriber, and I have followed a freer line here. My use of 'u' and 'v' is modern rather than original, though I have normally preserved the manuscripts' use of 'i' and 'i-longa'.[1] Punctuation, including capitalization, has been modernized and supplied. I have extended words appearing in common contracted forms without signifying each case; but square brackets have at other times been used to indicate that words, syllables and letters have been supplied.

Considering the large quantity of documents available for inclusion, not only in this volume, but subsequently to cover the remainder of Elizabeth's reign, it seemed to me that time imposed certain constraints upon a task which would otherwise have been of more daunting proportions: consequently, I have tried to produce a collection of 'working', rather than 'worked', documents. I have not set out to make the archives redundant in any real sense by including every variant reading from copy to copy, preferring instead to concentrate on those affecting the meaning of the material in hand; and I have refrained from exploring, except in a very broad way, all the problems of documentary provenance and authorship. This latter task, especially with regard to the diaries, is, I believe, a considerable one and deserves separate investigation and treatment on a scale which I cannot give here. I have been sparing of editorial comment and apparatus, generally attempting to provide only a brief, contextual background for the documents which stops short of lengthy

1. Cf. L. C. Hector, *The Handwriting of
English Documents* (1958), 27, 39.

analysis of their contents. There is obviously an editorial line here which may in practice be difficult to draw; and it is by no means an easy task to decide to what extent textual allusions and obscurities should be explained and commented upon. When I decided to provide comment and explanation, I was often directed to the right course as a result of discussions with colleagues and friends who were generous with both advice and knowledge. My thanks are therefore due to the following at Leicester University: Dr A. K. B. Evans, Professor G. H. Martin, and Dr A. Newman of the History Department; Mr J. D. Cloud and Dr J. H. W. G. Liebeschuetz (now Professor of Classics and Archaeology at Nottingham University) of the Classics Department; Mr J. V. Gough of the English Department; and Dr S. J. Reno (now at the Harvard Centre for the Study of World Religions) of the Religion Department. Mr J. Barton of Merton College, Oxford, was especially informative on legal matters. I am particularly indebted to Professor Joel Hurstfield, late of University College, London: it was characteristic of him that he was willing to give unstintingly of his time, encouragement and judgment.

I wish to thank the following for permission to print transcripts of manuscripts from their collections, and for the general co-operation of their staff: the British Library; the Master and Fellows of Corpus Christi College, the Master and Fellows of Gonville and Caius College, and the University Library, Cambridge; Devon Record Office; Trinity College, Dublin; House of Lords Record Office; the Inner Temple Library; Northamptonshire Record Office and the Representatives of the late Earl Fitzwilliam; the Bodleian Library and Exeter College, Oxford; the Public Record Office; and the Marquess of Salisbury.

The Research Board of the University of Leicester provided grants at various times which helped in the compilation of this edition; and the Twenty-Seven Foundation and the British Academy have both helped to finance its publication. Mrs M. Findlay of the History Department at Leicester University very patiently undertook much of the typing involved.

Since the typescript for this book was completed, signs of a vigorous re-examination of problems outlined here in the introductory material have appeared in print: I regret that I was unable to refer to them specifically at the appropriate points.

T. E. Hartley
Leicester, June 1980

Introduction

The manuscripts printed here cover the period 1559-81 and are substantially those which Professor Sir John Neale used as the basis for the first part of his study of Elizabeth's parliaments, culminating in the three volumes published between 1949 and 1957. He was probably the first – and certainly not the last – to point out that he had not made full use of his documents, that much had been put to one side as irrelevant to his purpose, and that the materials could be of use to others wishing to study Parliament from different perspectives. Many of the manuscripts had already been printed, notably by Camden, D'Ewes and Strype, though they were spread across an extensive range of publications of varying accessibility, and careless transcriptions and amendments had sometimes crept in. Neale was also aware that many of the documents existed in several versions, and that in some cases the one chosen for printing was of apparently inferior quality. So, apart from underlining the merit of making available those of the journals which had not been printed before, Neale saw the consolidation of a large quantity of materials, transcribed from their 'best' version, into one edition as an important task which would allow the kind of evidence available in the official *Journals* to be conveniently supplemented and complemented. Long before his death in 1975 he had stated his intention of producing an edition himself, but his extensive involvement with the Elizabethan section of the *History of Parliament* was largely responsible for his relinquishing any hope of realizing the plan.

Students and scholars who are familiar with *Elizabeth and her Parliaments* will know that the material divides itself into two broad categories: journals, or diaries, in the form of running accounts of proceedings in the Commons from day to day (first appearing in Elizabeth's reign in 1571), and those documents concerned with single issues, such as speeches, memoranda, petitions and so on, and conveniently described some time ago as 'separates'.[1] The very existence of all this evidence, and especially that of the journals, presents some of the most interesting, and perhaps ultimately unanswerable, questions to the historian. In his introduction to *The Elizabethan House of Commons* Neale reflected on the uneven survival of evidence through the ages, and stressed that the student of Elizabeth's parliaments inherits a documentary cornucopia: 'the evidence bursts upon us in this reign with a wealth, which however limited in comparison with the richer age to follow, is remarkable . . .'.[2] The saving clause must plainly be given full weight, as indeed should the fact that the early years of the reign offer comparatively little when set

---

1. *HC*, 369. 2. *HC*, 16-17.

against the sessions from 1571. From that time there seems to be a marked penchant for recording speeches and proceedings which emerged with considerable vigour, though it is difficult to offer satisfactory explanations for this development. Much of the evidence certainly derives from the keen interest in Elizabeth's reign and in Parliament shown by men of the early seventeenth century when there was something of a mania for copying manuscripts, and indeed the majority of the journals now exist only in copy form. In its own turn of course, a large quantity of copied material may present the historian with difficulties, the possibility of indiscernible copyists' errors and sheer fabrication being perhaps the most obvious one. Cross-checking multiple copies may reduce the problem of careless transcription, though where copies have been made from each other that safeguard vanishes; but when we can offer no contemporary Elizabethan corroboration for a speech, event, or detail offered to us in a seventeenth-century copy, we may have to face the prospect not only of dealing with the original author's own subjective interpretation, but also a latter-day reconstruction. Unless we are to be indiscriminately suspicious about their authenticity, however, we must be thankful to the many anonymous clerks who reproduced so much of what now appears to have been irredeemably lost.

The disappearance of many originals and the abundance of copies are in themselves features of the age deserving careful study. We know of considerable mobility of books and manuscripts in the sixteenth and seventeenth centuries, and though its dimensions cannot be measured accurately, some of its consequences are readily apparent. It had clearly been given impetus by the uprooting of the great monastic collections, and by the latter part of the century a number of prominent figures, both clerical and lay, had built up significant libraries of their own. Yet by no stretch of the imagination could the movement of manuscripts be described as a perfectly orderly phenomenon, and in some respects it was quite the reverse. Not only were documents likely to be subjected to unsatisfactory storage, but they were sometimes annotated and 'improved' in such a way as to distort their original form.[3] Contemporaries also became, from time to time, concerned about the apparently random manner in which important documents were circulating. State documents had probably suffered most from neglect and inadequate storage, and lack of space frequently induced state officials to transfer papers to their own households. Despite the establishment of a record office and the appointment of a keeper in 1578, papers were still finding their way into private individuals' homes, and the constitutional tussles of the early seventeenth century did nothing to reduce the interest in public documents, or prevent the state paper office lending them to individuals for their own researches.[4] One of the principal objections to the almost casual circulation of valuable documents was that it increased the chances of their being lost, either through innocent, yet careless misplacing, or through deliberate theft. Arthur Agard, keeper of the public records in James' first years, listed the perils awaiting manuscript collections: fire, water, rats and mice, misplacing, and 'the plain taking of them away'. The history of the evolution of D'Ewes' own collection of Elizabethan parliamentary papers and the value it has for so long held is in itself a comment on the situation, and Hakewell drew attention to the continuing process of copying when he referred to his own documents being 'by the length of time multiplied into very many copies'.[5]

The collectors' and copyists' contribution to this edition is plain. For example, despite Sir Robert Cotton's highly irregular approach to documentary evidence, his actively pursued antiquarian interests yielded a collection of manuscripts of great importance to his contemporaries and to scholars today. His friendship with Agard in particular, and his proximity to the parliamentary records, allowed him to produce his own copies and compilations from original documents. Cotton Titus F1 remains a valuable, and sometimes the sole, source of information on many kinds of parliamentary affairs.[6] James Ussher started his quests for books and manuscripts in England around 1602, concentrating on London, Oxford and Cambridge and encountering Cotton, Bodley and Camden as he went: this was the basis of Trinity College Dublin's library, and from it we derive the best version of the anonymous journal of 1571, and all Thomas Cromwell's diaries, one of which may in fact be Cromwell's own original manuscript.[7] William Petyt's thirst for parliamentary history allows us to supplement the relatively meagre reports of Peter Wentworth's startling speech in 1576. Later, Lansdowne acquired a large number of original Cecil papers; and Robert Harley, Speaker of the House of Commons with an extensive knowledge of procedure, not surprisingly developed a healthy appetite for books and manuscripts, and by 1705 is said to have amassed about 2,500 manuscripts, including collections of Foxe, D'Ewes and Stow. Through them we have access to the papers of Elizabethan contemporaries and Stuart commentators, and in particular, to some of the best accounts of Lord Keeper Nicholas Bacon's fine set speeches.[8] Harley 5176, like Cotton Titus F1, has been extensively used here; and, like the Cotton manuscript, it is largely a series of items copied in the clerks' hands of the period so commonly encountered, and one of the most telling symptoms of the antiquarianism already mentioned. Clearly, there was much work for the scribes, and an inscription at the foot of one folio is most probably a very practical note by one of them: '*dies* 18 at 4 howers in a day'.[9]

Even so, it does look as though there was less to copy before 1571, though the parliamentary events of the previous sessions are not obviously lacking inherent interest. We may in the end have to resort to less tangible explanations. Neale saw the emergence of parliamentary journalism and the preparation of speeches in

3. M. McKisack, *Medieval History in the Tudor Age* (1971), 34-6.

4. R. B. Wernham, 'The public records in the sixteenth and seventeenth centuries', *English Historical Scholarship in the Sixteenth and Seventeenth Centuries*, ed. L. Fox (1956), 11-30; see also, in the same book, P. Styles, 'Politics and historical research in the early seventeenth century'.

5. J. E. Neale, 'The Commons Journals of the Tudor period', *TRHS*, 4th ser., III (1920), 153-62; E. R. Foster, *Proceedings in Parliament, 1610* (1966), I. XLIIIn.

6. *DNB sub* Cotton, Robert; Neale, *art. cit.*, 156.

7. *DNB sub* Ussher, James; HMC, *Fourth Report*, 588.

8. *DNB sub* Harley, Robert; Andrew G. Watson, *The Library of Sir Simonds D'Ewes* (1966), 54-63.

9. BL Harl.5176, f. 127. As far as precise identifications are possible, the watermarks in Harl.5176 and Cott.Titus F1 lend weight to the view that much of the copying was the work of the 1610s and 1620s: E. Henwood, *Watermarks* (1950), e.g. nos. 516,608.

written form as a manifestation of a collective self-awareness and even self-confidence; and the striking dearth of supplementary Lords materials may, in itself, be corroborative evidence for that view.[10] Certainly Hooker, who came up to Parliament in 1571 and produced one of the first journals, showed a keen interest in procedure and wrote his tract on the conduct of parliamentary business at some point in the early 1570s.[11] Again, there may be some significance in the fact that the earliest known journals of Elizabeth's reign coincide with the advent of Fulk Onslow as Clerk and his more business-like approach to the Commons journals.[12] The circumstances conspiring to induce Elizabeth to summon Parliament in 1571 may in themselves have been sufficient to produce a momentous atmosphere which acted as a catalyst in the process, yet as has been noted in the past, the treasons bill and other great 'public' matters did not greatly move Hooker's pen.[13] Or, it may be that the rash of records finds a more prosaic explanation in the availability of abundant supplies of cheap paper at this time.[14] Though a lengthy study of the parliamentary journals in their own right may throw some light on the phenomenon, it must be said that some of the fundamental questions about its origins and evolution may never be answered in more than a tentative way. We do not know, for example, if there was any precise motivation for recording proceedings other than a natural, yet rather ill-defined, fascination for current affairs. But the impulse to compile personal accounts of events witnessed at first hand was probably most keenly felt by men whose involvement transcended that of the ordinary gentleman member. Cromwell's work in committees provides the most ready explanation for such a special concern, yet after 1572 when he produced his first account, it took him away from the floor of the House on many occasions and probably left him with less time to work up the kind of journal which posterity would doubtless have preferred him to write. Hooker's own eye was focussed on specific kinds of procedural detail, and his dry journal of 1571 comes as no surprise. Further, we cannot tell if the diaries were written for anyone other than their authors, to serve as enduring records of memorable weeks spent in London at a prestigious gathering of the peers, knights and burgesses of the realm, though the brevity, and sometimes elliptical nature, of the entries make this seem likely. Yet this is not to imply that the journals were hastily compiled, for the general tone of the texts suggests strongly that they were written up 'fair' subsequent to the taking of notes in the House itself.[15] There is an air of leisurely consideration of the events rather than instant recording of impressions, so that the accounts of what must have been very complex debates appear to have been well digested and epitomized.[16] Conversations with members probably helped to confirm or modify first impressions of what had been heard in the House, and if copies of speeches were available, they too were no doubt pressed into service. Equally, it is not improbable that some members had access to the Clerk's notes[17] from which they might supplement their own: in this way Cromwell may have been able to provide a good account of the bills read in the House on 23 May even though, as he said, he was away during the reading of some of them.[18] But approaches to recording parliamentary events clearly varied as did the diarists' perspectives, interests, and ability to comprehend what was before them; and invaluable as the journals are rightly judged to be, most of their limitations spring from these human considerations.

The rarity of original journals and the prevalence of copies is especially unhelpful for attempts to solve problems of authorship, for anonymous journals copied in anonymous clerks' hands have obviously been drained of the potentially illuminating hallmarks of the author's own script, and more particularly, if all other attempts to place identity have failed, we have been denied even the opportunity of determining whether the anonymous journalists of 1571 and 1572 are one and the same. It may be that painstaking and extensive textual scrutiny will in time yield a solution, and a knowledge of authorship may, or may not, add to our reading and use of them; but for the moment, the continued absence of originals allows little more than general speculation.

There does not seem to be much doubt that the journals of 1571 and 1572 were written by members of Parliament, since there are too many purely personal references placing the authors in the House for them to be mere compilations of reports made by outsiders conversing with members, or eavesdropping in meeting places where men doubtless discussed the affairs of the day. At first sight it seems unlikely that the journals are the work of one, rather than two, men since the style and approach of the two accounts are dissimilar. The 1571 journal is a carefully considered account proceeding at a steady pace, covering much ground, and showing an impressive kind of approach which presumably prompted Neale's comment that the author was 'the true pioneer of the private member's diary'.[19] The much shorter document for 1572 is a more selective, condensed account of a narrower range of topics, one of them the strictly non-parliamentary business of the Duke of Norfolk's execution. On the other hand, shifts of approach of this sort do not necessarily indicate the work of two authors. Thomas Cromwell's own journals display quite striking differences, probably occasioned by an apparently heavy involvement in the increasing amount of work undertaken in committee; and it may be that the anonymous author of 1572 himself was one of the committee concerned with the great business of the session, though there is no explicit statement that this was so.[20] There seem to be very few clues in these two accounts which could lead to a solution of the problem; and in the absence of direct references to the authors'

10. Neale, *art. cit.*, 169.

11. In this context see especially E. R. Foster, 'Speaking in the House of Commons', *BIHR*, XLIII (1970), 38 and n.

12. Neale, *art. cit.*, 136ff. Sheila Lambert suggests that Onslow's reworking of the rough notes may have been at once more complex and less consistent than Neale assumed: 'The clerks and records of the House of Commons, 1600-1640', *BIHR*, XLIII (1970), 220-1.

13. 'Hoker's Journal of the House of Commons in 1571', ed. J. B. Davidson, *Trans. Devons. Assoc.*, XI (1879), 464.

14. See for instance A. H. Shorter, *Paper Making in the British Isles, 1490-1700* (1971), 16.

15. The anonymous journalist of 1572, for example, says 'this I bare awaie' when recording the essence of part of a speech: Oxford, Bodley: Tanner 393, f.46v.

16. See Fleetwood's and Yelverton's speeches in particular.

17. Cf. Foster, *op. cit.*, I.xlv.

18. TCD MS 1045, f.36; *CJ*, I. 97. Yet see Thomas Cromwell's Diary, 1572, f.46v, for 30 May.

19. *EP*, I.184.

20. Oxford, Bodley: Tanner 393, f.59v.

constituencies, we are driven back to a close examination of the purely personal comments which occasionally appear. The author of 1571 may have been an acquaintance of Thomas Norton, for he refers to a conversation with him after a debate; but Norton's prominence and activity obviously brought him into contact with a great many men, so that the statement in itself does nothing to narrow the field of possible candidates for identification.[21] On the other hand, the journalist may not have known Norton, and their conversation may simply have been the result of his attempt to seek clarification of a point he found particularly baffling. He had already been confused on two occasions by Mr Clere of Norfolk, and his conscientious approach may have prompted him to go to Norton himself for further explanation.[22] Neale's opinion that the author was a puritan may well be correct.[23] His reporting of the attack launched by Strickland and others on the religious settlement does little to hide the author's sympathy for their point of view, but we ought perhaps ask how many members were not sympathetic, at least in some degree, to criticism of the state of the Church at this stage. It may also be safe to assume that the author enjoyed a sound command of the workings and terminology of the law, for his accounts of the legal complexities arising in debate are always succinctly perceptive and pointed, almost as though his interest had been especially caught at these moments. Indeed, the amount of space given over to the speeches of prominent lawyers may be symptomatic of the writer's professional proclivities rather than a true reflection of the balance of debate in the House. We are perhaps reading the work of a lawyer who sympathized with criticism of the Church with which Elizabeth seemed to be content; but even if this were demonstrably true, there would still be an unhelpfully large number of members who would be eligible. The limited scope of the 1572 journal in comparison with that of 1571 may mean that there are fewer clues to the identity of its author: the preoccupation is with the case against Mary Stuart as presented to a parliamentary assembly already almost wholly convinced of her guilt, and with the execution of Norfolk. The account of the preliminaries leading up to that event is so vividly written as to leave very little doubt that the author was, as he said, an eye-witness; and Cobbett long ago printed a description of the trial and execution, including a list of those present at the trial, several of whom were members of the Commons. Among them were Sir Francis Knollys, Thomas Wilson, William Fleetwood, and Thomas Norton, 'who wrote down this trial'.[24] Nothing in the journal precludes the possibility of any one of those named being its author, the fact that most of them are mentioned in the third person being no automatic disqualification. But before trying to determine which, if any, of them is likely to have been responsible for the journal, we would do well to be sure that they, and no other Commons members, were present at the execution. The author says nothing of being at the trial itself, and it is probable that an event as significant as the execution of England's only duke would have drawn more than a handful of an assembly which had been calling for his blood. It seems unlikely that the mysteries surrounding this diary, or that of 1571, can be easily resolved; yet unfortunate as this is, the evidence itself, with all its shortcomings, remains invaluable testimony of contemporary views of proceedings in two very important parliamentary sessions.

The most obvious value of the separates and journals is their usefulness in supplementing the *Commons Journals*, which have no substantial reports of speeches and debates; but it must be stressed at once that we have no certain knowledge that all the speeches printed here as separates were in fact delivered, or delivered in this form – the admittedly unusual instance of Peter Wentworth's half-heard speech in 1576 is sufficient reminder of the difference between prepared and delivered addresses. But the drafts are of great inherent interest, and it would be wrong to exclude them because there is, in some cases, no confirmation from other sources for their delivery. As far as the journals are concerned, it is easy to see how the fuller accounts provide meat for the skeletal official *Journals*, yet the detailed and comprehensive coverage of, say, the anonymous journal of 1571, or of Thomas Cromwell's of 1572, is by no means sustained, and very often pages are given over to a mere enumeration of bill readings. Because so many paper bills were destroyed in the great parliamentary fire of 1834, however, our knowledge of them consists only in their description by the Clerk and anyone else who bothered to register their existence; and the Clerk's description is invariably of the briefest nature. If we are fortunate, we have in the journals not only a confirmation of the Clerk's entry, but several two or three line reports of readings, and while this is clearly not a totally satisfactory basis for understanding legislative intentions, variations among the descriptions may add to the sum of information or reveal important shifts of interpretation and comprehension among Elizabethan observers.

Simonds D'Ewes was the most notable near-contemporary to make use of many of the materials printed here, and his edition of *The Journals of all the Parliaments of Elizabeth* became an essential source for historians. Until 1973, when the Irish University Press published a facsimile edition, his work remained relatively inaccessible, and though it is now more readily available, it is not as yet purged of the errors for which D'Ewes himself may have been responsible, or of those which Paul Bowes inflicted on the manuscript when he published it in 1682.[25] D'Ewes undoubtedly made extensive use of speeches and journals he had gathered, but the published *Journals* incorporate some errors in the dating of documents. In particular, the session of 1563 lost three items: the Lords petition of 1 February was moved forward to 1566, as was a separate version of the Queen's speech, and the fuller account of the Lord Keeper's opening speech appeared under 1572. It is arguable, however, that excisions from the source material are a more significant failing. It was probably Bowes in particular who saw no reason to allow the reader to judge for himself what was more or less interesting or important within a document, frequently adopting the editorial device of describing a bill, speech, or debate as 'of no moment', and so omitting it. While the informative journal for 1571 lay before D'Ewes, it appeared in truncated form in the printed version of his compilation. Quite remarkably, the contributions of Norton and others to the treasons debate on 9

21. TCD MS 535, f.17v.
22. *Ibid.*, fos. 8v, 12v.
23. *EP*, I.184.
24. W. Cobbett, *State Trials* (1809-24), I.958.

25. A. F. Pollard and Marjorie Blatcher, 'Hayward Townshend's Journals', *BIHR*, XII (1934-5), 4 n. 2 *et passim*.

April has been omitted, there is no record of the Treasurer's thoughts on usury, and the speeches of Popham on the Bristol Merchants and Fleetwood on the bill for coming to church have also apparently been regarded as 'of no moment'. And the list does not end here, either for 1571, or for other sessions of the reign.

In confirming or adding to what the *Commons Journals* and D'Ewes can yield, the evidence printed here may naturally provide the basis for further insights into the Elizabethan Parliament. There is perhaps a natural impulse to subject Neale's interpretation to critical analysis, as no other wholly developed thesis has appeared, in print at least, since publication. This is not the proper place for such an examination which would have to be lengthy in order to be constructive; but a general point ought to be made in anticipation of the materials which follow. There can be no doubt that Neale's work is, and will remain a successful synthesis of these contemporary accounts. On the other hand, his approach to the narration of religious and constitutional developments raises the general historical problem of bias transmitted through evidential selection. The very task of producing a readable account of parliamentary proceedings within his own declared and defined limits clearly imposed problems of organization; and the mass of evidence at his disposal compelled Neale to choose a structure for *Elizabeth I and her Parliaments* which is at once thematic and sequential.[26] One reads, for example, of the succession agitation in 1563 from start to finish and to the exclusion of all other events, moves on to other affairs in the same session, and then in due course returns to the problem again in 1566. Events have been torn from their surroundings and we have to comprehend them in their own right. The risks attendant upon this approach become more apparent when we have the fuller day-to-day running accounts of events supplied by the parliamentary diarists. If we turn to 1571 as an illustration, the Queen's message of 10 April is presented by Neale, and indeed by the anonymous journalist, as a response to Bell's speech on licences.[27] But what significance are we to attach to the fact that during the immediately preceding days the atmosphere in the House had obviously become tense on a variety of topics, not at first sight closely related?

Unless we assume that the journals and separates printed here offer a consistently inaccurate and undiscriminating picture of affairs at Westminster, then we must accept that we now have the basis for answering that question and a number of others relating to the conduct of parliamentary business. One important problem is to explain and define the concentrations of activity and influence within the Commons, to comprehend its dynamics. In the first place, the quality of royal strategy bears re-examination. Though references to individual incidents lie scattered through Neale's work, it is difficult to derive a systematic and coherent view of the conduct of privy councillors, either collectively, or individually, over the years: no sustained examination of the councillors' role has been undertaken.[28] Equally, though Elizabeth's position on state matters is well known, there is often a suggestion that royal reaction was riposte rather than carefully considered response. A careful reappraisal of the whole panoply of Lord Keeper's briefings, ministerial statements, royal messages, and crucially, the way members not only reacted to them but were able to use them, needs to be undertaken all of a piece rather than as appendages, albeit important ones, to the stories of the succession, religion and so on.[29] Another major point of interest arises from the much vaunted phenomenon of gentry invasion of borough seats, and it is worth stating an obvious point here, namely, that the mere election of droves of gentlemen for the boroughs is not necessarily synonymous with sustained energy and efficacy once inside the House. The ramifications of gentry representation of the boroughs have never been precisely charted; but whatever light is thrown on the subject here, it is clear that it must be viewed in conjunction with the role of the lawyers. We know that lawyers commonly constituted a sizeable proportion of the House, and that men like Thomas Norton were busy draughtsmen working behind the scenes to produce a stream of bills coming before the House. Norton's petition against the Duke of Norfolk in 1572 demonstrates his abilities here, for it encapsulated the essence of the more emotionally expressed complaints of Digges and Dannett within the confines of a tight formalistic and logically stated case.[30] But what the journal accounts demonstrate graphically on many occasions is the major, if not indispensable, part lawyers could play in debate. Norton himself spoke on a wide range of topics, as did his brother-in-law William Fleetwood; but they were only two of a group of legally trained and active men whose names appear with striking frequency. It is probably true that as a group lawyers were, by inclination and training, more likely to be ready speakers than many other members. It is also true that proposed legislation of a highly technical nature, for example fraudulent conveyancing or the great matter of treasons, was likely to give rise to esoteric discussions about the significance of individual words and phrases, and that in such cases the lawyers naturally became very conspicuous. These are probably some of the clearest examples, but they prompt tantalizing questions about the workings of an institution whose functions in the end were mostly legislative in the broadest sense.

Another consideration arises naturally from the focus of Neale's study, which, it must be stressed again, was never intended to be a systematic analysis of Parliament's work, only part of it. Even a cursory reading of the *Commons Journals* and D'Ewes reveals that on the periphery of Elizabeth's 'love tussles' with her Lords and Commons, business as usual continued on the floor of the House and in the committee rooms. That business was best defined by Lord Keeper Bacon's opening addresses to Parliament, repeated in a form varying only slightly each session, and then usually most obviously to accommodate the details of the particular crisis currently necessitating more taxation and special legislation. The statutory output of Elizabeth's parliaments still awaits close analysis, but the pages of *Statutes of the Realm* are telling testimony to the attention devoted to Bacon's injunction to decide which laws needed to be made, repealed, or continued. *The Elizabethan House of Commons* delineated something of the mechanism whereby this was achieved, but the materials presented here are essential aids to an understanding of the mechanism at work. We have perhaps become almost conditioned to look for innovation and

26. *EP*, I.11.
27. *EP*, I.221.
28. See *HC*, 395-6, 402-3, 411-12.
29. See, for instance, Knollys' statement on religion in 1571, and a justification for proceeding subsequently offered by a member: TCD MS 535, fos.21, 35.
30. *Archaeologia*, XXXVI (1855), 109; BL Add.48023, fos.163-4, *infra*.

political flashpoints in the record of events, and the preponderant mundaneness of the contemporary accounts may seem strangely anti-climactic, especially if there does not seem to be an intensity of feeling about incidents which we have seen as landmarks in parliamentary development. Yet it would be wrong to suppose immediately that commentators of the day lacked perception in cases of this sort, and final judgment on the quality of the journals ought to depend on our ability to comprehend the reasons for their compilation, and that is no easy task. But the journalists, who all resorted in varying degrees to merely cataloguing and describing bills before the House, were most obviously chronicling the essence of their daily business. In this sense, John Hooker's scant attention to 'the high matters of state' of his day reveals with impeccable accuracy the kernel of Parliament's role in the administration of the commonwealth.

So the journals in particular provide part of the basis for the development of a picture of parliamentary affairs more comprehensive than Neale had attempted in his own classic study. His concentration on relations between the Crown and Parliament meant that any treatment of 'commonwealth matters' as such was likely to be almost incidental (with one or two exceptions), and certainly not sustained as an integrated analysis in its own right. What the materials show is a continuing process of adjudication by the Commons on a large variety of topics initiated by themselves or by the Crown. This was an essential aspect of the life of the commonwealth which had to continue despite any intervening dramas connected with high matters of state, even if it meant extending sessions into the afternoon or taking part of the work off the floor of the House.

One of the first things to emerge from these documents, whether they deal with state, or 'commonwealth' matters, is a strong sense of the confidence and competence with which affairs were generally dispatched; yet there is rarely an impression of unseemly haste, for those debates which the diarists have chosen to relate seem invariably to have been extensive explorations of the *pros et contras* of the matter in hand. It is tempting to see in all this a measure of the sophistication which Parliament is said to have aspired to, and even attained, in the sixteenth century, but we should remember that the theory of the Commons' growing power and confidence, while generally accepted, has not received universal acclaim.[31] The problems of historical perspective inherent in the issue are indeed weighty and complex, but it is clear that an assessment of the intellectual climate in Parliament is a prerequisite for any fruitful investigation of it: assumptions, expectations and prejudices on all sides need to be recognized, for they conditioned attitudes, both during the familiar moments of friction between the Queen and the Commons, and in the handling of commonwealth matters. Opening and closing procedures were to a large extent times of introspective reflection on the functions and achievements of the estates assembled at Westminster; and though the speeches associated with these moments are permeated with staid and rigid formality, they are indispensable guides to the philosophical, and even psychological, tone of the Houses. Even the means of electing the Speaker, with its attendant paraphernalia sometimes threatening a descent into farce, gave rise to interesting, if not original, speculations about law, the commonwealth, the origins of society and Elizabeth's great historic role.

Any inclination to dismiss the accounts of these proceedings as mere formality would be misguided. In his opening speeches the Lord Keeper rehearsed the particular circumstances which had led to new financial demands; but in 1571, for instance, the anonymous diarist reported that he had gone beyond this, enlarging upon Elizabeth's achievements and in effect urging the Commons and Lords to finance a policy of peace, security and purity of religion, free from the tyranny of the 'Pope and popelings'.[32] All this deserves close examination, not least because members apparently attended closely themselves, and on several occasions men seized on their recollections of Bacon's opening addresses in order to justify subsequent stands of their own. The ostensible starting point for Wentworth's speech in 1576 was fully in accord with the Lord Keeper's general instructions, yet it developed into an argument so offensive as to prevent its full exploration. And however great or small Wentworth's claims about 'free speech' may have been, it is important to determine the origins of parliamentary unease over the matter. The term itself demands a careful definition which has not always been accorded it, and it must be said that Peter Wentworth's love of noble or emotive language, peppered with Biblical and literary allusions, seems to militate against conceptual clarity. But the problem may be alleviated, because the record usually shows how the sense in which the term was being used varied according to particular situations. Wentworth himself referred to specific circumstances in 1571 and 1572 which the journals have chronicled independently, and the earlier session of 1563 yields further clues to an understanding of a pretended confusion about the proper limits of Commons' discussions.

It may have been inevitable that matters had become complicated, because superimposed on the long-established general spheres of parliamentary activity were the special requirements of the moment. Elizabeth's accession produced a patent sense of relief, but its accompanying difficulties imbued Parliament *ab initio* with a sharp perception of the régime's fragility, only to be reinforced by the Queen's illnesses. Frequent ministerial statements of her merits, and the evolution of something akin to a theory of a divinely ordained and protected England, did nothing to assuage fears for the future. Persistent refusal to resolve doubts about the succession were not readily reconciled with Bacon's admittedly unspecific instruction to 'take order from the good of the state'; and so, amid the debates about the Queen's safety in 1572, there are signs that a doctrine of princely obligation, and indeed fallibility, was being applied pointedly to current events. There was a possibility that Elizabeth was simply unaware of the danger in which she, and therefore the nation, stood; if so, it became the Commons' duty to inform her of the

31. Roskell's remarks need close attention: J. Roskell, 'Perspectives in English parliamentary history', *Bulletin John Rylands Library*, XLVI (1963/4), 448/75. Hinton's views must be seen in the light of the considerable body of thought on law/making, and the energy with which

it was pursued, which is evident in these documents: R. W. K. Hinton, 'The decline of parliamentary government under Elizabeth I and the Early Stuarts', *Cambridge Historial Journal*, XIII (1957), 116/32.

32. TCD MS 535, f.2v.

perils.[33] But where could their theories of government lead them if this failed? 'We see not but her Majestie must needes offend in conscience before God', and if she did not ensure the subjects' safety by prolonging her life, the commons 'shal be forced to seke protection ellswhere'.[34]

There is obviously more than a hint of desperation here in Parliament's inability to provide a viable escape from the *impasse* which Elizabeth had created. There remained, of course, a deep commitment to monarchy, despite this muted and impotent infuriation with the Queen, and the reasons appear frequently in the social and political meditations in which the Speaker and others were prone to indulge, a conceptual framework being supplied by the heavily worked metaphor of the human body. It is difficult to dismiss this *tout court* as empty reiterated cant, because whenever it was used the indications are that it was regarded as a useful and significant symbol embracing a set of basic truths which would be readily understood and carry conviction. As Bacon said in 1559, the image was old and common, but no less true for being so. It appears almost *ad nauseam* in this collection, the emphasis shifting to accommodate different interests; yet there was general subscription to the basic tenet that all parts should work for the benefit of the common good. The miracle of the healthy body, as of the healthy commonwealth, lay in its achievement of a sublime harmony between its constituent parts, in the triumph of the general over the particular.

In a sense, much of the parliamentary debate of which we have evidence is an essay on this central theme. Bacon himself touched upon it in two important respects. In order to meet the growing cost of governing the realm Elizabeth had shunned frivolous expenditure for her own delight and spent her own money – a worthy example of sacrifice for the common good, and one which private men should follow.[35] More particularly, however, Bacon returned to the problem of law administration and enforcement time and again over the years. The nub of the matter was clearly stated in 1559: 'the common numbers respect themselves as private men, and not themselves as members of the whole body'. His concern as Lord Keeper was a functional one: the men who made laws in Parliament were in effect helping to unmake them when they returned home by lack of application, through lethargy or 'for favour', in the local courts. He knew the reasons, and he had a radical solution to offer; and it is to his enduring credit that in his continuing analysis of an essentially arid problem he produced some fine examples of Elizabethan prose at its best.[36] He made no obvious inroad on the task for a number of reasons, and occasionally we catch sight of the manifest suspicion of bills which proposed to strengthen sanctions against recalcitrant justices of the peace.[37] The self-interest apparent in such attitudes need not be inconsistent with the condemnation of particular interests where they conflicted with the general. Obviously, the sincerity of a declared concern for the common good may be questioned, but it may not be ignored since it provided a standard against which current practices and proposed legislation could be judged. Sometimes bills seem to have been damned not because they would benefit the few, but because in doing so the general interest would be prejudiced. For some, the Bristol Merchant Adventurers' incorporation stood or fell in this way. The speech for which Bell was reprimanded in 1571 was part of an impressive attack by lawyers on the royal financial administration, and was similarly based. The attitude persisted throughout the reign and was surely not new in 1571; but the development of an arguably peculiar Elizabethan system of licences, and an apparently full-hearted hostility to 'monopoly', make the debates of 1571 especially enlightening.

The other advantage of the head and body metaphor lay in its accommodation of the principles of social and political hierarchy. Elizabeth clearly found the comparison between herself as head of state and head of the body which directed the limbs far from odious as it was a useful standby in times of tension when the members of Parliament pressed for settlement of the succession, when the 'feet' sought to direct the head; and the retort that the head of a healthy body would not jeopardize the limbs might carry no immediate and compelling weight. The Commons' own concept of the 'feet' was probably quite different from that of the Queen's. Speaker Popham seems to have spent some time in 1581 developing the thesis which Thomas Cromwell has reported in an apparently heavily abbreviated form: here the feet are the 'common rusticall persons', implicitly inferior to those members of Parliament whom Elizabeth had once described in this way. And the assumptions and prejudices, never far below the surface here, emerge from time to time in debates, and could become part of the armoury in the attack on the system of tax-gathering.[38] The detailed consideration of the draft bill against excess in apparel, a government measure originating in the Lords, is possibly the most graphic illustration of Commons thought on this matter.[39] The implication is that any legislation which had to rely for its enforcement on the services of 'inferior persons', strengthened by authority and sanctions which might be used against members of the Commons and their kind, would have a stormy passage.

These practical applications of the metaphor of the body politic are only one example of the considerable quantity of applied political thought which lies scattered throughout parliamentary proceedings and is potentially more vividly illuminating than the somewhat arid treatises of the well-known contemporary political commentators. The notion of Elizabeth's great services to the commonwealth was, of course, well-developed, but implicit in it was the assumption that men's goods and lands would be protected, not only from the ravages of external war and internal disorder, but against maladministration, fraud, corruption and, not least, from arbitrary acts of the state. In 1571 the Speaker counted the 'equal' administration of justice as one of the Queen's major achievements, and though he was in some measure following Elizabeth's own propaganda line, he was none the less feeding the hopes of the Commons.[40] Notwithstanding the constant reiteration of loyal gratitude and appreciation for the Queen's very existence, the Commons' deliberations reveal a conscious attempt to

33. E.g. Oxford, Bodley: Tanner 393, f.56v.
34. BL Cott. Titus FI, f.172v; Add. 48023, f.162 (1572).
35. BL Harl.5176, f.91v (1563).
36. E.g. BL Harl.5176, f.112 and v (1559); Cambridge, Corpus Christi College, 543, f.24 (1571).
37. TCD MS 535, f.33v (1571); MS 1045, f.43v (1572).
38. TCD MS 535, f.8 (1571).
39. BL Sloane 326, fos. 15-18 (1576).
40. TCD MS 535, f.4v.

maintain a correct political balance between the Crown and the subject. This wariness was often based on recollections of régimes of the past, sometimes good and sometimes bad, and Elizabeth's contumacious recalcitrance in the matter of nominating an heir only seemed to stress the importance of taking heed today of the dangers which tomorrow could present should she be succeeded by a 'less gracious prince'. A natural concern, already apparent among men of property in particular, for the security of posterity became highly developed to the point where members often seem to have determined their attitudes to proposed legislation on the basis of fears of its misuse by an unwelcome future régime. The nature and extent of the royal prerogative naturally formed part of the thinking here too, and though it is true that we cannot benefit from a series of uniformly full reports on debates, there is evidence of some vigorous investigation of the problem. In 1566, Speaker Onslow voiced what was probably a widely held view when he said that the prerogative is 'not such as the prince cane take money or other thinges, or doe as he will at his own pleasure without ordere, but quietly to suffer their subiectes to enioy their owne without wrongfull suppressione.'[41] The detailed application of this blanket statement naturally proved problematic, but on a number of occasions Commons discussions have survived which make it possible to detect how far members had resolved the complexities and evolved a concept, clear in their own minds at least, of the beginnings and the end of the royal prerogative.[42]

One of the elements reinforcing the Commons' concern for the future was the lawyers' attitude to precedent and the need for careful and precise drafting of proposed legislation. Lawyers in the House never tired of citing precedents, real or imagined, as warnings, exhortations or justifications for present action, and the logical extension of the awareness of the past was a scrupulous concern for the future and the precedents which today's work might then constitute. A good lawyer would never neglect that consideration and there seemed to be times when it was markedly pertinent to the matter in hand. The commitment to the philosophy of the supremacy of statute provided the impulse toward using the available expertise in the House so as to minimize the danger of confusion, or the misinterpretation – or worse – of legislation in the law courts; and political considerations of various kinds compelled a careful analysis of legislative proposals submitted by the government, the treasons bill of 1571 and the amendments growing out of its critical examination providing the most obvious example.

Whatever the importance of Parliament's legislative work for the future, the law clearly had a large role to play in the protection of liberties and property in the present, and in order that men might in fact 'enioy their owne' for example, it was important that they should be able to establish that it was indeed their own. In a society witnessing a lively land market, the complex minefield that was the land law produced a stream of difficulties. There is doubtless a lengthy story to be told of the evolution of the land law in Elizabeth's reign, and the proceedings of 1559-81 show some of the entanglements involved. We read of fraudulent conveyances in several sessions, of fines and tenants for life, aliens' lands, corporations' conveyances and so on. In some cases the purpose of debate and legislation seems to have been to regularize and enforce a standard means of procedure, and to cut through the jungle of sharp practices which bedevilled the land market. And it must be remembered that as a high court Parliament could, and often did, take cognizance of cases of disputed title, calling witnesses and hearing counsel for the parties involved. The sheer amount of time and energy apparently devoted to all these problems demands both respect and understanding, and the record may provide varying degrees of insight into a number of problems. How far, and by what means, was the efficacy of the law advanced, and what did the lawyers themselves contribute to the process? Why did the problem of fraudulent conveyances seem to be so unmanageable? To what extent was the legislative output of the gentlemen in Parliament geared to their own interests rather than those of other elements in society, and did they subscribe to an ideal of justice, not only free from the perversions and cloggings of legalistic chicanery and wars of attrition in the courts, but readily available to all members of the commonwealth? There was one member at least who said that the law was the only fortress of the 'inferior', but what did he mean, and what support was there for his view?[43]

The evidence assembled here is no less important for an assessment of the practical nature, scope and applicability of the law in Elizabethan England, and it may incidentally shed some light on the origins of legislation for 'commonwealth matters'. How well developed, for instance, was the notion of universally and nationally valid laws which might manipulate and construct, rather than simply regulate and regularize? The old debate about usury appears to have been in part at least, concerned with seriously questioning the validity of attempting to legislate in this area, and with an investigation into the relative functions of statute, canon and civil law. And in other fields of economic and industrial control it is possible to isolate some of the lines of the arguments which shaped parliamentary action. What importance was attached to the proposal to standardize weights and measures throughout the realm; or, indeed, at a time of constructive change in the field of national defence, to a standardization of bullet production? Why did the supply of timber seem to constitute a problem, and what was offered as a solution?[44] Should Parliament seek to formulate and enforce a policy of encouraging beef production?[45]

The nature and evolution of economic regulation itself has been a continuing source of fascination, even infuriation, for economic and social historians. Industrial and craft studies, or accounts of economically regulating legislation, have necessarily concerned themselves with a number of larger questions about the role of government and policy-making. Broadly speaking, there have been two proffered solutions. On the one hand we may consider the existence of a grand strategy for the economy, masterminded by the prince and his ministers, though perhaps frustrated and transformed in transit through Parliament. Alternatively, one must accept that policy, in the sense of the implementation of plans for specific development, was to

41. BL Cott.Titus FI, f.119v.
42. E.g. TCD MS 535, fos. 34v-35 (1571).
43. *Ibid.*, f.27v (1571).
44. See G. Hammersley, 'The state and the English iron industry in the sixteenth and seventeenth centuries', *Trade, Government and the Economy in Pre-Industrial England*, ed. D. C. Coleman and A. H. John (1976), 166-86.
45. TCD MS 1045, fos.49 and v (1572).

all intents and purposes absent from contemporary, and especially government, thinking: the inspiration for legislation and other forms of regulation of the market or of production is to be found in short-term pragmatic considerations, or in ideas of internal and external security so generalized as to be common to all responsible elements of society. As far as parliamentary regulation is concerned, a basic premise common to much of the discussion is an essential dichotomy between the views and reactions of government and Parliament, particularly the Commons. It is of course regrettable that no record of debate survives on the great Statute of Artificers, and in this and other cases argument has to be constructed largely on the basis of reading the entrails of engrossed bills in the House of Lords Record Office. But an awareness of the nexus of assumptions and expectations informing members' minds whenever they came to deal with matters of this sort may help to test the appropriateness of the terms of reference usually employed in analyses of economy management. Rarely can the need to see Elizabethan problems through Elizabethan eyes have been so apparent. It may be anachronistic to seek an interventionist role for government in the sixteenth century which is more characteristic of twentieth-century industrialized and capitalized mass societies; and we may in the end have to pay closer attention to Elizabeth's dictum, namely that state affairs were not the proper sphere for parliamentary initiative, and try to determine what its implications were for commonwealth matters, which, she said, were.

The editor of a compilation of this sort is faced with a whole array of possible lines of approach, and it may be that any path which is adopted is doomed to receive less than complete support; it is probable that the methods employed here will disappoint those who have a deep and continuing commitment in other directions. There are two major choices to be made about what to include and how to present what is included. A strong case undoubtedly exists for attempting to comprehend all relevant sections of the official Lords and Commons journals, together with D'Ewes' own unique contribution. The decision to omit them is based on a number of practical and academic grounds. Both the journals and D'Ewes are already available in fairly accessible printed form, though there should be no suggestion that we must for ever be content with the editions we have. In the case of the former, we still rely on the work of eighteenth-century editors, so a revised edition, executed in accordance with present-day standards of scholarship, could supply an improved logbook of parliamentary business and its progress within and between the Houses. On the other hand, it is not at once apparent to what extent new editions of the journals would produce significant improvements on what is at present at our disposal; and the argument that the best interests of parliamentary history as a whole will be best served by a comprehensive new edition of all the official journals – rather than piecemeal sectional improvements – is not easily dismissed. Similarly, it is well known that D'Ewes' nephew did not faithfully represent his uncle's manuscript when he published it in 1682; but many of D'Ewes' sources are reproduced here in their own right as separates and journals, and so the inaccuracies and excisions which accompanied their inclusion in the edition of 1682 are readily apparent through direct comparison. Even so, an authentic rendering of the D'Ewes manuscript would be an important aid in studying Elizabethan parliaments, particularly since the Commons journals for the period 1584-1601 have disappeared subsequent to D'Ewes' use of them: it should be noted that the work has been undertaken by Miss Norah Fuidge, though it is as yet unpublished. To include D'Ewes and the relevant sections of the official journals would have substantially enlarged an already bulky project, and at the least delayed its completion. No-one knew better than did Neale that those sources, however well-produced, could only tell part of the parliamentary story, and that while the materials he assembled had yielded a great deal, they had been by no means exhausted. As the publication of his own three volumes receded into the past, albeit the recent past, he seemed to be prepared for a possible re-working of the ground he had already covered. For all these reasons he believed that an edition of the separates and the journals was an increasingly urgent priority.

The method of presenting material is in part dictated by these considerations. The integrity of all manuscripts, both separates and journals, has been preserved, even where events are common to several documents. The alternative would have been to print the record of each day's proceedings as a fusion of all the available sources. That approach has the obvious and important advantage of allowing immediate comparison of sources, an especially telling point wherever more than one journal account of proceedings has survived, but there are difficulties too. Where more than one journalist has been at work and produced what is apparently a mere daily tally of bill readings, does one shift from source to source with great rapidity in order to marry the accounts? Or does one resort to the omission of what is considered to be mere repetition? The latter course of action certainly has its pitfalls in view of what has already been said of the value of the journals; and it is clear that the task of analysing the journalists' accounts themselves would be complicated by a decision in favour of amalgamating the documents. It would be far more difficult, for example, to compare Thomas Cromwell's approach to the sessions of 1572 and 1581, or to assess his overall account of the 1572 session in relation to that of the anonymous journalist. While we may be primarily interested in parliamentary affairs as such, contemporary accounts *themselves* excite speculation and enquiry, and a printed version which dismembered them would not be the best means of satisfying legitimate interest of that sort.

My intention has been to provide for the specialist student and scholar a collection of primary sources in as straightforward a way as possible so as to minimize the risk of intruding my own views and interests. This basic consideration, and that of the great quantity of materials eventually to be included for the whole reign, has played a large part in determining the shape of the edition. Many of the documents, for instance, exist in a number of versions, and it is rarely if ever the case that any two are identical. Where significant variations exist, the policy has been to borrow words or phrases if need be from versions which at that point are superior to the main copy used: the modifications have been noted with their derivations. Similarly, significant deletions and insertions, most notably in originals rather than copies, have been represented in order to retain important elements of the evolution of the manuscript, even though this may result in a cumbersome printed version, Elizabeth's own heavily corrected drafts being the most obvious case in point.

The 'textual' footnote clearly has a place in a scheme of this sort, but the role of the elaborate machinery of supplementary information and arguments so commonly deployed at the bottom of the page is not so clear. It is partly for this reason that the intention here has been to produce a text as free as possible from extensive, often disturbing, annotation. There are arguments from convenience here as well as principle, the main one being the sheer bulk of material which militates against the kind of edition which seeks to elucidate all possible obscurities in every document. Other than this, the historian who sets out to locate all the sources in the armoury of allusions frequently employed may well find his efforts repeatedly frustrated, or only rewarded after very extensive searches in the darkest recesses of legend and mythology, especially as the approach to the classical authors, and to literature generally, as well as to legal and historical precedents, appears in some cases to have been casual to say the least. Even allowing for inaccurate reporting of speeches and faulty transcription by copyists, there is probably enough evidence here to confirm the long-held view that if there was a recognizable collective notion of the past among members of Parliament, fiction, either deliberately or innocently conjured up, played a part in it. Some attempt has been made to trace quotations tied to their authors by the speakers employing them; but members commonly resorted to Latin phrases, and it is not at once apparent if this was quotation or merely part of the veneer of culture which most lawyers and gentlemen no doubt wanted to affect.

The nature of the footnotes throughout has also been determined by the assumption that the student of parliamentary history will want a comprehensive set of documents virtually as he might find them in the archives, and that he will have at his disposal the standard printed sources for the period. It would have been possible to make a close and detailed correlation between the texts offered here and the two main alternative sources offered by the *Commons Journals* and D'Ewes' own compilation; and the commonly adopted practice of providing thumbnail sketches of each person named in the text would have added further to the bulk of the edition. The *Journals* and D'Ewes have in fact only been used to correct obvious errors and inconsistencies in the diaries, most frequently where the author has wrongly recorded the stage of a bill's progress through the House. Apparently drastic omissions may also be noted, as are those instances where the diarists have noted bills not represented in the printed official journals. And each variation between the documents common to this collection and that of D'Ewes has not been logged, though the errors of dating for which either D'Ewes himself, or his nephew, have been responsible have been recorded in the document descriptions. In view of the forthcoming Elizabethan section of the *History of Parliament* there would be little point in duplicating biographical material on the members here: the entries on the individuals which will constitute that important work of reference not only relate details of their personal background and social and political connections more fully than would have been feasible or advisable here, but attempt, where possible, to provide full details of the members' whole parliamentary career.

THE FIRST PARLIAMENT
23 JANUARY ⁄ 8 MAY 1559

Documents

Parliament was summoned for 23 January, but when the Lords and Commons assembled in the upper house they were told that the opening ceremony had been postponed for two days since Elizabeth was 'not feeling herself in good disposition of body, nor unmindful of the peril that her too much boldness by coming abroad might ensue'.[1] This message had been delivered by Sir Nicholas Bacon acting as Lord Chancellor, though enjoying the lesser rank of Lord Keeper. It was he who opened the session on 25 January, and it was he who closed it in May: the same tasks fell to him until he died in February 1579. Many of the documents covering the first session of the new reign deal with procedure rather than proceedings, illustrating the formality which was such a prominent feature of the parliamentary scene. The structure, and indeed some of the content, of Bacon's opening brief will appear again and again. After the Speaker-elect Sir Thomas Gargrave, an experienced parliamentarian and government official, had bemoaned his lack of ability, Bacon returned to reassure him that the Queen had faith in him even though he might lack it himself; and later he answered his requests for the liberties of the House.[2] And on 8 May Bacon terminated the session with a brief review of what had happened and how gratified Elizabeth had been by the help of her subjects. In this and later sessions the speeches delivered at these points often show an awareness of adhering to traditional forms, not only in the process of 'disabling' and 'enabling' the Speaker, which had, even by this time, become sheer pantomime, but in more practical and relevant matters of law enforcement, for example: 'because the aunciente order hath bene that somewhat should be sayde for your remembraunce in theis matters, therefore it is thought meete that I should trouble you with a few wordes'.[3]

But the degree of formality here must be set alongside the specific references to problems of the day and the Queen's expectations of, and reactions to, the events of the session. Bacon's opening speech is, in the broadest sense, a declaration of intent by the young Queen, not only for 1559, but for the whole reign. If religion could be established soundly, the commonwealth would have a secure foundation and so avoid continual change and alteration, 'things much to be eschewed'. Concord and unity must be everyone's target, and for her part Elizabeth promised not to be so wedded to her own fancies as to threaten the subject's freedom or provoke unrest, as had recently been the case. Though Mary was not mentioned by name, a further

1. *LJ*, I.542; *Cal. SP Venetian*, VII. 22; Neale, *EP*, I.41.
2. Gargrave (1495-1579), member for Yorkshire and member of the Council of the North, had sat in four previous parliaments.
3. BL Harl.5176, f.112.

promise not to advance the cause of a foreign power to the prejudice of native interests or lands made it clear to the assembled Lords and Commons that Elizabeth was well aware of her sister's shortcomings, especially the loss of Calais. England now found herself saddled with debts at high rates of interest, and still smarting from the loss of good men, arms and money. Elizabeth would therefore concentrate on building up her defences, a task which entailed the burden of taxation in peacetime for the sake of preventing further danger.

Unity for internal strength, garrisons for protection against European danger, subsidies for garrisons: these, along with the routine tasks of reviewing the laws and securing their enforcement, were the government's short- and long-term objectives. But in view of subsequent sensitiveness about the issues of marriage, succession and religion, it is interesting to note that pronouncements made by Bacon and Elizabeth on these issues seem to allow some flexibility to those of different persuasions. The Lord Keeper's first instruction was to legislate for a 'uniforme order of religion'. Neale stressed that this meant little, since there was no government plan for an Act of Uniformity at this stage; but that is a view of the government's plans, not of the wishes of others, and Bacon did go on to explain at some length Parliament's duty to 'conforme your selves together, usinge your whole indeavor and diligence by lawe and ordinaunce to establish that which by your learning and wisdomes shalbe thought most meete for the well performinge of this godlie purpose'.[4] In a message to the Commons later in the session, Elizabeth also failed to ban further discussion of her marriage. On Saturday 4 February a motion had been carried that she be requested to marry, a large Commons delegation had met her the following Monday afternoon, and her answer was finally delivered to the House on Friday 10 February by John Mason, member for Hampshire and diplomatic adviser to the Queen until his death in 1566.[5] The message shows already the complexity of style and argument which became so prominent a part of Elizabeth's political repertoire: she was at once content to have remained and remain unmarried, and confident that if God saw fit to change her mind he would help her make the right choice of husband. Options were left open; moreover, most contingencies were met, for she clearly envisaged the possibility of a nominated heir in the event of her not marrying, an heir who, as she acutely pointed out, could be better suited to the task of government than an heir of her own body succeeding automatically. Yet the fact that she had not set her face steadfastly against marriage, and her approval of the Commons' petition 'because that it is simple and conteineth no limytacion of place or person' defined the form future agitation might take on this issue.[6]

There are four speeches from the Lords debates on the supremacy and uniformity bills.[7] None of them is dated, and the convoluted proceedings in the supremacy bill complicate the problem of placing the contributions of Montague and Heath. Montague drew attention to the assault on the sacraments and clerical celibacy which were contained in the bill, so that it seems reasonable to suppose that the speech was drafted for the second reading debate, beginning on 13 March, on the heavily amended bill which had come up from the Commons; while Neale's inclination to place Heath's speech in the third reading debate of 18 March – when the Lords had virtually restored the bill to its original form – is unobjectionable.

Feckenham and Scot most probably registered their opposition to the uniformity bill at some point in the second and third readings of 27 and 28 April. Having said that, it must be stressed that the *Lords Journal* provides no corroborative evidence that these speeches were delivered, as opposed to bring merely prepared, though the probability must be that they were.[8]

There cannot be much doubt that the speakers were aware that the views they were putting forward were unpopular and even impolitic; and their protestations of discharging consciences in fulfilment of a duty to God, Queen and country – a duty which the Lord Keeper commonly charged the assembled estates to perform – were to be reiterated by many members in changing circumstances and on countless occasions in the sessions ahead. As steadfastly opposed as he was to Elizabeth's taking the supremacy, the most interesting aspect of Montague's speech in one sense was his treatment of precisely this point. His mind had clearly been considerably exercised by the problems inherent in offering counsel in the highest assembly in the land, and his views on the duties of members (and indeed on Elizabeth's expectations of members) in discharging those duties deserve careful scrutiny. Beyond this, the four lengthy arguments together constituted a thorough attack on the advisability of taking England into schism again, and, more fundamentally, on the propriety of such a move. The equation of Roman Catholicism with stability and unity was common, Feckenham particularly predicting imminent social and political collapse if the dangerous, and already apparent, drift to licentious Protestantism went unchecked: 'Obedience is gone . . . all degrees and kyndes of menn being desyrous of flesshelye and carnall libertie . . . the subiectes disobedient unto God and all superior powers.'[9] But important as these considerations were, the three conservative clerics were at pains to demonstrate that there could be no basis for the assumptions that parliamentary assemblies, which could not, in any case, bind their successors, might sanction a princely-held supremacy: it had no historical justification, the scriptural precepts of the Church militated against any prominent female participation, and Heath was quite confident that Parliament could produce

4. *EP*, I.42; BL Harl.5176, f.106.

5. *EP*, I.47-50; *HP sub* Mason, John.

6. BL Lansd. 94, f.29.

7. Strype printed a fifth (by Scot, on the supremacy bill), but no original has been traced. Strype claimed the existence of copies of Scot's two speeches, as well as those of Heath and Feckenham, among the Foxe MSS which were in his possession. The Harleys bought a good proportion of the Foxe MSS – Lansdowne eventually purchasing the remainder – but neither collection appears to include any of the four copies. (Harley has an incomplete copy of Scot's speech on uniformity, and of Feckenham's: it does not seem originally to have been a Foxe MS.) It may be noted that Strype's care of manuscripts was less than satisfactory, and that Robert Harley commented on the defective condition of the Foxe papers when he bought them of Strype. (*DNB sub* Foxe, John and Strype, John; J. E. Neale, 'The Elizabethan Acts of Supremacy and Uniformity', *EHR*, LXV (1950), 315.)

8. *LJ*, I.563 (Montague was one of the committees for the supremacy bill); Neale, *op. cit.*, 321; E. Jeffries Davis, 'An unpublished manuscript of the Lords' Journals for April and May, 1559', *EHR*, XXVIII (1913), 538.

9. Corpus Christi College, Cambridge, 121, 136.

no 'warrant and commission' for the action it seemed poised to take. The only proper course was to reassert clerical sovereignty, and to reject the internecine doctrinal conflicts and confusions of the Protestant divines, along with the newly proffered Prayer Book, which, in Scot's eyes, threatened not only the Mass, but the priesthood and therefore religion itself.

1. [House of Lords] Viscount Montague's speech on the supremacy bill, 13 March (?)

Text from Bodleian Library, Oxford, Eng.th.b.2, copy.
Printed. Sussex Archaeological Collections, CVIII (1970), 52⁄7.

Bodley Eng.th.b.2, pp.840⁄3

The speach of the Lord Vicount Montacute in the parliament house *anno primo Elizabethe Reginae.*

My lords, loath I am to speake and much afraide, waying reverently the matter nowe in hande, both for the weight thereof, and also remembring the person whom yt seemeth to touche therewith, not willing to impugne the judgment of others which have spoken therin whom otherwise I honour and love, considering also myne owne insufficiency in all respectes to speake in so great a matter and case of such importaunce to those in whom I doubt not either certeyne wisdome and knowledge, nor zeale to the true religion of Christe. I have therefore ernestly and hartely desyred to have beene my self excused from speaking by the declarations of others of my sorte who might, and were, able muche better to utter my mynde then my self; but seing my faithe, as I take yt, is called into question and the same impugned by others of my condition speaking as I thincke according to their consciences, and the contrarye nowe offered to be by us established by lawe, I am enforced to discharg my dutie towards God, my prynce and countrye. And nowe I might remember to your lordshipps the matter in hande, to the body wherof exhibited unto us I have to speake, and not to the particularitie of the title, which only toucheth the scripture, carying awaye by generall wordes the whole estate of Christ's religion. For as in the first parte the supremacie is only intreated of, even so in the bodie of the bill all that ever was made for the defence of the faith against the malignitie of wicked heresies are wholy repealed, and the confusion lately used in religion newely receaved and established: the masse abrogated, the sacrifice of the Churche reiected, the sacramentes prophaned, the holie aultars destroyed, temples vyolated, mariage of preistes allowed, their children made legitimate, lybertie given to them by purchase, or other meanes, to procure to their posteritie lands and hereditamentes. And thus I conceive the effect of this bill.

Therefore, nowe have I to saye that I must speake for the staye of the whole state of religion which this byll / carieth awaye dyrectly with yt; yet am I two wayes much afrayed, the one by speaking to offend those whom I most desyre to please, the other and cheife by not speaking to offend my conscience, and therby God himself. To speake therfore I am constrayned by the matter, the place, and my vocation: by the matter as touching my faithe and religion called in question; the place being a

p.841

councell, wherin all men are bounde to discharge themselves, not only by yea and naye, but also as occasion serveth to further and advaunce all those thinges that sounde to the honour of God and wealth of the realme, and to hinder, let and be against all such thinges wherin God or his Churche might bee dishonored or our countrye hyndred; thirdly, being unworthie by my vocation a member of this councell and one of you, my lords, to the which calling nothing so necessarily appertayneth as in lawes making to laye aside all affections, and nothing to doo but for conscience sake, following the rule of truthe indifferently, and justice by good deliberation before to avoide all repentaunce afterwardes. Mynding then for theis causes to speake to the whole bill and matter here being before us, I intend to professe and discharge my self with all humilitie and reverence, not condempning others, which is not my office, but leaving every man to himself without offence, as I for my parte praye and humbly require you all to shewe yourselves unto mee patiently to heare me and charitably to iudge of me, remembring the causes aforesaid which drive me, and for that I am loth to seeme unto you to frame my self a conscience, either wilfully or altogether ignorantly, I shall with your favour, as briefly as I can, render reasons why I doo for theis three causes frame myself a conscience in this matter. And here I humbly crave the priveledge of this howse, the evell observation wherof shutteth upp the mouthe of many who otherwise woulde more freely in divers matters declare their consciences if their reverend speeches were not by misreportes caried out of this House to their displeasure.

Nowe, then, to the first of my 3 causes which is the matter, and in deed, religion, the which I professed in my baptisme wher I was made a member of Christ's misticall bodie, and vowed to beleeve the holy Catholique Churche as the spowse and only beloved of Christe, by unitie in the which I am to bee saved or damned. To teache me Christe's true religion in this his Churche I learne that God hath therin appoynted neither emperour, kynge or temporall governour, but *quosdam prophetas, quosdam Apostolos, quosdam episcopos, quosdam doctores* – certeyne prophetts, certeine Apostles, certeine bishopps, certeine doctours, unto whom he hath given charge as St Paule saith[1] to the same: yet was ther never prynce nor region that durst in using this destroye the other, neither in refusing the obedience to the Pope to take to them selves the supremacie of their owne Churches, but only in this realme, neither in Germany are the more parte evill and at least gonne from the Churche of Rome, but wher the Protestantes bee, albeyt the more number in theis places resort to the assembly of that sort and sect, yet be the Churches left to such as remayne in their fathers' faithe; and in those Churches all rytes remayne invyolate, both of praying, preaching and sacrifice, and no man enforced to leave the same, which seemeth, and in deed is, contrary to nature and reason as not being offred to the Jewes, so long as they receave not faith and revolt from the same. But at Rome yt is said I did, or might, see much abomination. Truly, my lordes, I thinck I knowe that synne is greatly encreased in the whole worlde and doth in manner overflowe all nations, but if I shall saye truly I sawe no more evill there then I see in my owne countrye, saving that I did see some fewe cardynalls unworthie of the place, who to their owne shame did [blank] in the gravest councell of the rest of that sorte and number that ever I did see.[2] Thus much I have said touching my knowledg in that iourney, synce which tyme I knowe not why all that was then donne was not well donne, or why we lyve not nowe in a much better unitie then any other aucthoritie can make, saving the same that ordeyned this here those present whom God hath appoynted in this realme to teache his faithe not only affirme that we presently hold that faith and religion which pleaseth God, but, in the violating therof, wee devide our selves from the Churche and so become the vessells of the wrathe of God. If I beleeve them not, my owne bloude be uppon my owne head if I dispice them and their teaching, I dispice Christe. But why doo I beleeve them? Not for that they saye so, but because they teache me the auncient faithe of the Fathers, delivered and received from hand to hande by contynuall succession of all bishopps in the Churche of Christe, and the same wherin all the holy martyrs, patriarcks, confessours lyved and died. Wherin what cause have I to doubte if I doo not thincke thatt all the worlde is damned, saving a fewe that beleeve and professe this newe doctrine, unknowne to the Churche but by condempnation therof: in the which they never agreed among themselves, but have spent mo[re] men's lyves in their controversies, and all against the truthe of the Churche that had bene sufficient to have delyvered Greece and Constantinople from / the hands of the Turke. And as they from the first have beene, p.842 so they contynew and let not even nowe to preache before the Queene that ther be but ij sacraments, and those but [blank]. Neither maye I, therfore, nor doo knowe any cause to the contrarie, but remayne constaunt *a vita fide patrum*, and confesse God and his truthe before man, lest he deny me before his father in heaven; and so *quum veniet dies domini, peream*. At which tyme yt shall not be sufficient for me that I said nothing, and flatter myself with securitie of myne owne conscience secrete to myself; neither shall desire to please excuse me, nor feare of displeasure discharge me, no, not the thundering wordes of a preacher teaching his owne ymaginative doctrine be my warraunt, but then the worme of my owne conscience shall sting me, and God himself accuse me and saye, 'Thou hast dispiced those whom I have sent to teache thee. Thou hast denyed me thy Lord God before man. Thou hast feared man more than God. Woe be unto thee'. Being therfore thus persuaded, I rather chuse to fall into the hands of man (thoughe lately) then into the hands of God willingly; and those rather being offered, the one of two swordes, runne upon the one the healthe and end wherof I see, then on the other, to the end wherof my imagination is not able to bring mee. And therfore to this parte thus I conclude: yf we have no aucthoritie to treate uppon theis matters, yea we be utterly forbidden the same, and therfore I most humbly wishe and desyre that we entermeddle no further herein, but remayne in unitie with Christ's Churche and our neighbours.

If religion and feare of God mooved me not therin, yet am I otherwise almost as hardly driven by duty to my prynce and countrie, whom I doo (and ought to) honour, serve, and humbly obaye: and here I crave and beseech of you, my lordes, not to be noted of pride, presumption, or singularitie in that I seeme to bee fearfull of the sure and quyett estate of my soveraigne and countrye, as though the same were

---

1. Cf. Eph.4.11.
2. The reference is to Montague's visit to Rome in 1554 as representative of the nobility to sue for reconciliation (*DNB sub* Browne, Anthony).

not by your wisdomes thought on and cared for. I meane no such matter, but only to discharge my self; and in this poynte I have agayne occasion to remember my vocation and this place, the place being the highest and supreme councell of this realme of England, and I being by wrytt summoned to be present and to give counsaile in matters of waighte touching the prynce, Church, and realme of England. Wherfore now hath God placed noble men to be in dignitye before others but to this end, that they shoulde be more carefull of the honour and saftye of the prynce and countrye then others, and for any of theis to be ready and willing to sacrifice themselves. And I take God to recorde ther lyveth no subiect in this realme that with better will will put his life in adventure to serve my soveraigne Ladye then I woulde, nor woulde be more loath to offend her, nor more glad to please her Highnes. But if this matter here offred be as evill an advise as all her enemyes can imagine to give her and her realme, then I being so persuaded, ought to beware howe to agree therunto, or suffer yt to proceede if I might by my poore councell staye the same. In chaunging of religion we condempne all other nations, of whom some be our fryndes and many our enymies, open and auncyent, who long tyme have, and no doubt doo expect, an opportunitie to annoy us. If the Pope hearing us by schisme devided from the Churche doo proceede to the excommunication of the realme, which we knowe hath followed others in the like case, how enioyeth the kynge of Spaine Navarra? Ys yt not by sentence of excommunication? And therby aucthoritie given to him to possesse the same that coulde by strong hand obtayne yt? Howe came Naples from the auncyent goverment to the hands of their enemyes? Uppon such a case our own countrymen and kynge of this realme King John to what extremitie was he dryven by the like attempt in religion? This then that hath chaunced to so many maye be of right feared in our selves, being envyroned and, as yt were, set about in one of two so potent enymyes, who as you knowe would be loath to loose such opportunitie, specially remembring that if we should be devided from the universall Churche and so excommunicated (which our Lord defend), theise our neighbours, which otherwise would be most willing to assist us, neither I thincke woulde or durst give succour or helpe to us in a quarrell of faithe, the contrary wherof he so ernestly professeth, and being by the aucthoritye of the Churche restrayned, neither would of him in case by coullour wherof he enioyeth a kingdome. And ad to this our owne weaknes and povertie at home: men's myndes discontented, great somes of mony dewe, and more of necessitie demanded; and

p.843 cheifly remember the evil nature of our people that alwaies uppon a little libertie / are readie to rebell and dare doo any thinge and every man followe his owne waye, which thing if yt doo happen (as to often of late yt hath donne) who seeth not the perrill of the realme almost inevitable?

Theis thinges in my conscience I feare, and doubte, and care least of any other thing for my self, who in any of theis cases (which God keepe farr from us) will readely spend my life: but I feare my prynce's sure estate and ruyne of my native countrie. Maye I then, being her true subiect, see such perrill growe to her Highnes and agree to yt; see the daunger and losse of my countrie and, as yt were, betraye yt? *Absit.* And therfore, my lords, being moved by the zeale aforesaid, I requyre and beseeche *in visceribus Jesu Christi*, according to the nobilitie of your bloudes and auncyent fames, consider the weight of this case and by your wisdomes use yt therafter. Remember that the eyes of all Christendome be bent uppon you, doe and shall knowe what you have donne and shall doo; be not noted thus often to chaunge your faithe and religion, and with the prynce to burye your faithe: and I nothing doubt but the Queene's Maiestie, whose harte I trust is dyrected by the hande of God, of her good nature and wisdome will graciously heare and conceave your faithfull councell and advise herein, to the doing wherof we have beene all exhorted and anymated by her Maiestie, wher yt was my chaunce twise to be present when, upon occasion mynistred, her Highness declared the great confidence she reposed in her nobilitie, [and] said that she esteemed nothing so worthie praise in them as without dissimulation to advise her Highnes as they in conscience thought, without feare or desire to please; and if any should otherwise doo, she neither coulde nor would thincke well of them.

Her Maiestie therfore having thus graciously not only encouraged us to saye our consciences reverently, but also, as yt were, laying the burthen of all matters on those that should give her Highnes advise and councell, I thinke in humble declaration of the truthe we shall serve God, be faithfull to our prynce and countrie, discharge our selves of perrill that maye fall by our actes and councell, and fynally, worke the best towards God and man. And such as agree not in mynde with me herein I hartely requyre that, as I neither iudge or mislike with them, being I thincke led by conscience (as I am), even so they will thincke well of me and iudge me to speake without any other respect, but for the saving of my soule at the terrible daye of God.

2. [House of Lords] Archbishop Heath's speech on the supremacy bill, 18 March (?)

Text from Corpus Christi College, Cambridge, 121, copy.
Other MS. Oxford: Bodley, Tanner 302.
Printed. J. Strype, *Annals of the Reformation* (1824 edn), I,ii.399-407.
Somers Tracts, IX.9-16, from an untraced source said to carry the
legend: 'A tale told in Parliament. For oaths the land shall be
cloathed in mourning'.

Corpus Christi College 121, pp.137B-Cv

Spoken openly in the first session of Queene Elizabethe by th' Archbisshope of
Yorke, Dr Hethe.

My lordes all, with humble submission of my whole talke unto your wisdomes I
propose to speake to the bodye of this acte as touching the supremacie; and that the
doinges of this honorable assemble maye therin be always furthe[1] honorable, two
thinges are right necessarie of your wisdomes to be considered. First, when by the
vertue of this acte of the supremacye we muste forsake and flee from the sea of Rome,
it wold be considered of your wisdomes what matter lyeth therin, as what matter of
weight, or force, what matter of daunger or inconvenience, or els whether there be
none at all. Second, when th' intent of this act is to geve unto the Queene's Highnes
a supremacie it wold be considered of your wisdoms what this supremacie is and
whether it dothe consiste in spirituall government or temporall; if in temporall, what
further authoritye can this House geve unto her Highnes than she hathe alredy by
right and inheritance – and not by our gifte but by th' appoyntment of God – she
being our soveraigne Lord and Ladye, our King and Queen, our Emperor and
Emperesse, other kinges and princes of duetie ought to paye tribute unto her, she
being free from them all. If yow will say this supremacie doth consiste in spirituall
government, then it wold be considered what this spirituall government is, and in
what poyntes it dothe chiefly remayne; which being first agreed upon, it wold
further be considered of your wisdomes whether this House maye graunt them unto
her Highnes or not, and whether her Highnes bee an apte person to receave them or
not. And by the thoroughe examynacion of all these partes your honours shall
proceede in this matter groundlye upon throughe knowlege, and not be deceyved by
ignorance.

Nowe to the first poynt, wherein I promised to examyne this forsaking and fleing
from the sea of Rome, what matter eyther of weight, daunger or inconvenience dothe
consiste therin; and if by this our relinquishinge of the sea of Rome there were none
other matter therin then a withdrawing of our obedience from the Pope's person,

Paule the iiij^th of that name, which hathe declared himself to be a verie austere and sterne father unto us ever since his[2] first entrance into Peter's chaire, then the cause were not of suche great importance as it is in verie deede, when by the relinquishing and forsaking of the sea of Rome we muste forsake and flee from thes iiij thinges followinge. First, we muste forsake and flee from all generall councels; secondly, from all canonicall and ecclesiasticall lawes of the Churche of Christe; thirdly, from the iudgement of all other Christian princes; ffourthe and laste, we muste forsake and flee from th' unity of Christe's Churche and by leaping owt of Peter's shippe hazard ourselves to be overwhelmed and drowned in the waters of scisme, sectes and divisions.

First, touching generall councels, I shall onelie name unto you thes fowre – Nycene Councell, Constantinople, Ephesine and Calcedon Councell, whiche are approved of all men, doubted of or denyed of no man. Of the whiche iiij councels St Gregorie writeth in this wise: '*Sicut enim sancti Evangelij quatuor libros, sic hac quatuor concilia Nicenum, Constantinopolitanum, Ephesinum*[3] *suscipere me fateor ac venerari.*'[4] At Nycene Councell, the firste of these iiij, the bishoppes whiche were assembled there did write theyre epistle to Silvester, than Bishop of Rome, that theire decrees made there might be confirmed by his auctoritye. At the Councell kepte at Constantinople all the bishoppes there were obedient to Damase, then Bisshop of Rome, and he as the chief judge in that Councell did geve sentence agaynste these heretikes Macedonus, Sabellus, and Euonomius,[5] whiche Euenomius was bothe an Arrian and the first author of this heresie that onelie faythe dothe iustifye. (And heare, by the waye, it is muche to be lamented that we, th' inhabitantes of this realme, are muche more inclyned to raise up th'errours and sectes of auncient and condemned heretikes then to followe th'approved doctrine of the moste Catholique and learned fathers of Christe's Churche.) At Ephesine Councell, Nestorius the heretike was condemned by Celestine, the Bishop of Rome, he being the chief judge there. At Calcedonense all the bishoppes assembled there did write humble submission to Leo, then Bishop of Rome, wherin they did acknowlege hym to be theire chief head. Therefore, to denye th'auctoritie of the sea apostolike were to contemne and set at naughte the iudgmentes of thes foure notable councels.

Second, we muste flee from all canonicall and ecclesiasticall lawes of Christe's Churche whereunto we have allredie professed our obedience at the fonte, sayenge, '*Credo sanctam ecclesiam Catholicam*', whiche article conteyneth that we must beleve not onlye that there is an holy Catholike Churche, but that we must receave also the doctrine and sacramentes of the same Churche, obey her lawes and lyve according unto the same, which lawes do depend wholly upon th'authority of the sea apostolike. And like as it was heare openly confessed by the judges of the realme that the lawes made and agreed upon in the higher and lower house[6] of this honorable

---

1. Tanner 302 has 'founde'.
2. MS reads 'the'; this reading from Tanner 302.
3. *Sic*: Chalcedon not included.
4. Cf. St Gregory the Great, *Epistolae*, i.25; iv.38.
5. *Sic*? MS unclear; Tanner 302 has 'Euenominus.'
6. *Sic*, and in Tanner 302.

parliament be of small or of none effect before the reall assent of this king and prince be geven therunto, semblably, ecclesiasticall lawes made cannot bind th'universall Churche of Christe withowt the reall assent and confirmacion of the sea apostolike. The third, we muste forsake and flee from the iudgementes of all other Christian princes, whether they be Protestantes or Christians,[7] when none of thes do agree with these our doinges, King Henry th'Eighte being the verie first that ever toke upon him this title of supremacie. And whereas it was of late heare in this House sayd by an honorable man that the title is of right due unto a kynge for that he is a kynge, then it wold followe that Herede, being a kynge, should be supreme head of the Churche at Jerusalem, and Nero th'emperour supreme head of the Churche at Rome, they bothe being infidels and therby no membres of Christe's Churche. And if our Saviour Jesu Christe, at his departure / from this world should have lefte the spirituall government of his Churche in the handes of emperours and kynges, and not to have committed the same unto his apostles, howe negligently then should he have lefte his Churche!

p.137C[8]

It shall appeare right well by calling to your remembrance that th'Emperor Constantinus Magnus was the first Christian emperor and raigned about iij^c yeares after th'ascension of Christe. If therfore by your position Constantyne, the firste Christian emperor was the first chief head and spirituall governer of Christe's Churche throughe owt his empire, then it followeth how that our Saviour Christ for that whole tyme and space of iij^c hundred[9] yeares untill the comyng of this Constantine lefte his Churche, whiche he had so dearly bought by th'effusion of his moste precious bloud, withowt a head. And therfore how untrue the sayeng of this noble man was it shall furder appeare by th'example of King Ozias, and also of King David; for when King Ozias did take the senser to incense the altar of God the priest Azarias did resiste him and expelled him out of the temple, and sayd unto him thes wordes, '*Non est officij tui, Ozia, ut adoleas incensum Domino, sed est sacerdotum et filiorum Aaron, ad huiusmodi enim officium consecrati sunt.*'[10] Now I shall moste humbly demaund of you this question: whether he sayd trouthe or no? If ye answer that he spake the truthe, then King Ozias was not the supreme head of the churche of the Jewes. If ye shall say 'No', whye did God then plage the king withe a leprosye, and not the prieste? The priest Azarias, in resisting the kinge, did he playe the faythfull parte of a subiecte or no? If ye answer 'No', why did God then spare the priest and plage the kinge? If ye answer 'Yea', then it is moste manifeste Ozias, in that he was a kinge, could not be supreme head of the Churche. And as touching th'example of King David in bringinge home th'arke of God from the Philistians *ad civitatem* David, what supremacie and spirituall government of Godde's arke did King David there take upon him? Did he place himeself emonge the priestes, or take upon him any spirituall function to the priest apperteyninge? Did he approche neare unto th'arke, or yet presume to touche the same? No, doubtlesse, when before he sawe Ozias stroke by the hand of God for the like arrogancye and presumption. And therfore Kinge Davyd did go before th'arke of God with his harpe, making melodie, and placed him self amonges the minstrels and so humblie abased him self, beinge a kinge, as to daunce, skyp and leape before th'arke of God like as his other subiectes did, in so muche that his queene, Micholl, King Saul's daughter, beholding and seing the greate humilytie of King David did disdayne therat. Wherunto King David sayd, '*Ludam et vilior fiam plusquam factus sum coram Domino meo qui me elegit, potius quam patrem tuum, aut domum partris tui*'.[11] And wheras Queene Micholl was therfore plaged at the hand of God, *perpetua sterilitate*, King David received great praise for his humilytie.

Now, it may please your honors to consider which of bothe these kinges' examples it shalbe moste convenyent to move our Queene's Highnes to followe – th'example of the proud King Ozias and, by your persuasions and councels, to take upon her spirituall government therby adventuring yourselfes to be plaged at Godde's handes as King Ozias; or ells to followe th'example of good King David, who in refusall of all spirituall government abowt th'arke of God did humble himself as I have declared unto you? Wherunto our soveraigne ladie, the Queen's Highnes, of her owne nature verie well inclyned and bent, we maye assure ourselfes to have her Highnes as humble, as vertuous, and as godlie a mistres to raigne over us as ever had English people heare in this realme, if that her Highnes be not by our flatterie or dissimulacion seduced or begiled.

Fourthe and laste, we must forsake and flee from th'unitie of Christe's Churche, when St Ciprian, that holy martir, saith that th'unity of the Churche of Christ dothe depend of th'unity of Peter's auctority. Therfore by our leaping out of Peter's ship we must needes be overwhelmed with the waters of scisme, sectes and divisions when the same holy martir St Ciprian saythe in his epistle *ad Cornelium*[12] that all heresies, sectes and scismes to spring onelie for that men will not be obedyent to th'ead bishop of God, the Latine wherof is *neque enim aliunde haereses aborta sunt, aut nata sunt, scismata quin inde quod sacerdoti Dei non obtemperatur*. And how true this sayeng of St Ciprian is it is apparant to all men that listeth to see, bothe by th'example of the Germaynes and by us th'inhabitantes of this realme. And this our forsakeng and fleing from the unity of the Churche of Rome, this inconvenience emong manye must consequently followe therof, that either we must graunt the Churche of Rome to be of God or els a malignant churche. If ye answer it is of God, where Jesus Christe is truelie taught and all his sacramentes rightly mynistred, how then may we disburden ourselfes of forsaking and fleing from that Churche, whom we do confesse and acknowledge to be of God, when with that Churche that is of God we ought to be one, and not to admytte any separacion? If ye answer the Churche of Rome is not of God, but a malignant Churche, then it will followe that we th'inhabitantes of this realme have not as yet receaved any benefite of Christe when we have receaved none other gospell, none other doctryne, none other faythe, none other sacramentes then were sent to us from the Churche of Rome: ffirst, in Kyng Lucius' dayes, at whose humble epistle the holy martire Eleutherius, then Bishop of Rome, did send into this realme two holy monkes, Faganus and

---

7. *Sic*; Tanner 302 has 'Catholiques and Protestantes'.
8. P.137Bv has only 21 lines, unconnected with this speech.
9. *Sic.*
10. 2 Ch.26.18.

11. 2 Sam.6.20-3.
12. St Cyprian, *Epistolae*, 43; *De Catholicae Ecclesiae Unitate*, esp. ch.4; the theme is common in Cyprian's letters to Cornelius, esp.44, 45 and 52. Tanner 302 has 'his iii Epistle'.

Damianus,[13] by whose doctrine we were first put to knowlege of the faythe of Jesus Christe, of his gospells and his moste blessed sacramentes; seconde, holy St Gregorie, being Bishop of Rome, did send into this realme two other monkes, St Auguste and Melitus, to receave[14] the verie self same faythe of Jesus Christe that was before planted heare in this realme in the dayes of King Lucius; / third and laste, Paulus iij[us] being Bishop of Rome did send the Lord Cardinal Poole's good grace (by birthe a noble man of this realme) as his legate to restore us unto the same faythe that the blessed martir Eleutherius and holy St Gregory and planted heare in this realme many yeares before. If, therfore, the Churche of Rome be not of God but a malignant Churche, then we have ben deceaved all this while when the gospell, the doctrine, the faythe and sacramentes must be of the same nature that the Churche is of from whence it cam. And therfor in relinquishing and forsaking of the Churche as malignant, th'inhabitours of this realme shalbe inforced to seeke further for an other gospell of Christe, other doctryne, faythe and sacramentes then we hitherto receaved, whiche shall breed suche a scisme and error in faythe as was never in any Christian realm − and therfore of your wisdoms' worthie consideracion and maturelie to be provided for before you passe this act of supremacie. Thus muche touchinge the first chief poynt, wherin I promised to move your honours to consider what the supremacy is whiche we go about by vertue of this acte to geve unto the Queene's Highnes, and wherin it dothe consiste.

As whether in spirituall government or in temporall: yf in spirituall, like as these wordes of th'acte do importe, *scilicet*, 'suprem head of the Churche of Ingland nexte and immediatly under God', then it wold be considered of your wisdoms in what poyntes this spirituall government dothe consiste; and the poyntes being well knowne it wold be considered whether this House have authority to graunt them, and her Highnes' abilytie to receave the same. And as touching the poyntes wherin spirituall government dothe consiste, I have in reading the gospell observed these iiij[or] emonge manye, wherof the firste is to lose and bynd, when our Saviuor Christe in ordeyninge Peter to be the chief governor of his Churche sayde unto him, '*Tibi dabo claves regni celorum, quodcunque ligaveris super terram, erit ligatum et in celis, et quodcunque solveris, erit solutum et in calis.*'[15] Now it wolde be considered of your wisdomes whether ye have sufficient authoritye to graunt unto her Highnes this first poynt of spirituall government and to saye to her, '*Tibi dabimus claves regni coelorum*'. If you do saye 'Yea', then we do require the sight of the warrant and commission by the vertue of God's worde; and if ye say 'No', then ye maye be well assured and persuade your-selfes ye have insufficient authority to make her Highnes suprem head of the Churche heare in this realme.

The second poynt of spirituall government is gatherd of thes wordes of our Saviour Christe, spoke unto Peter in the xxi chapter of St John's gospell: '*Pasce, pasce, pasce*'. Now, whether your honors have authority by this High Courte of Parliament to saye unto our soveraigne Lady, '*Pasce, pasce, pasce*', yowe muste shew your warrant and commission; and further then that, her Highnes, being a woman by birthe and nature, is not qualefied by God's wordes to feede the flocke of Christe. It apperethe most playnly by St Paule in this wise, sayinge, '*Taceant in ecclesia mulieres, non enim permittitur eis loqui, sed subditas esse, sicut dicit lex*';[16] and it followethe in the

p.137Cv

same place, '*Quod turpe est mulieri loqui in ecclesiis*'; and in his first epistle to Timothe, the second chaptre saythe, '*Docere autem mulieri non permitto, neque dominari in virum, sed in silencio esse*'. Therfore it apperethe like as your honors have no authoritye to geve her Highnes this second poynt of spirituall government, to feed the flocke of Christe, so by Paule's doctrine her Highnes maye not intermedle her self in the same. Therfore she cannot be suprem head of Christe's Churche heare in this realme.

The third chief poynt of spirituall government is gatherd of thes wordes of our Saviour Jesus Christe spoken unto Peter, Luke the xxij chapter: '*Ego rogam pro te, Petre, ut non deficiat fides tua; et tu aliquando conversus confirma fratres tuos*', wherby it appearethe that one chief point of spirituall government is to confirme his brethren and ratifie them, bothe by holsome doctrine, and also admynistracion of the blessed sacramentes. But to preache or mynistre the holy sacramentes a woman maye not, neyther may she be suprem head of the Churche of Christe.

The fourthe and laste poynt of spirituall government whiche I promised to observe and note unto yow dothe consiste in excommunication and spirituall punishment of all suche as shall approve[17] themselfes not obedient children to the Churche of Christ: of the whiche authority our Saviour Christe speakethe in St Mathewe, the xviij chapter, there sayinge, '*Dic ecclesiae, si autem ecclesia[m] non audierit, sit tibi tanquam ethnieus et publicanus*'. And St Paule did excommunicate the notorius fornicator that was emonge the Corynthians by th'auctority of his apostleship, unto the whiche apostles Christe assendinge into heaven did leave the whole spirituall government of his Churche, as it apperethe by these playne wordes of Paule in his epistle to the Ephesians, the iiij[th] chapter: '*Ipse dedit ecclesia sua quosdam apostolos, alios evangelistos alios pastores, et doctores in opus ministerij in aedificationem corporis Christi.*' But a woman in the degrees of Christe's Churche is not called to be an apostle, nor evangeliste, nor to be a shepherd, neyther a doctor or preacher. Therfore, she can not be suprem head of Christe's mylitant Churche, nor yet of anie parte therof.

Thus muche I have heare said, right honorable and my verie good lordes, agaynste this acte of supremacie for the discharge of my conscience, and for the love, dread and feare that I chieflie owe unto God, and my soveraigne ladie the Queene's Highnes, and unto your lordships all; when otherwise and without mature consideracion of all these premisses your honors shalbe never able to shewe your faces before your enemyes in this matter, beinge so raithe an example and spectacle in Christe's Churche as in this realme onelie to be found, and in none other. Thus humblie besechinge your good honors to take in good parte this rude and playne speache that I have heare used of muche good zeale and will I shall nowe leave to trouble your honors anye longer.

13. Cf. Geoffrey of Monmouth, *History of the Kings of Britain*, IV.19, where the monks are named Duvianus and Faganus. Tanner 302 is as MS.

14. Tanner 302 has 'renew'.
15. *Sic.*
16. I Cor.14.34.
17. 'Approve' repeated in MS.

3. [*House of* Lords] B*ishop* S*cot's speech on the uniformity bill,* 27/28 A*pril* (?)

Text from BL Cott.Vespasian DXVIII, copy.
Other MSS. London: BL Harl.2185, later copy, and incomplete.
Oxford: Bodley, Tanner 302.
Printed. J. Strype, *Annals of the Reformation* (1824 edn) I, ii.438-50.

Cott.Vespasian DXVIII, fos.112-23

The oration of Doctor Scotte, busshop of Chester, made in the parliamente house, *anno* 1559.

This bill that hath beene here reade nowe the thirde tyme dothe appeare unto me suche a[1] one as yt is muche to be lamented that it should be suffered, eyther to be reade or any eare to be given unto yt of Christian menn so honorably assembled as this ys; for yt dothe not only call into question and doubte those thinges which we ought to reverence withoute any doubte moving, but maketh further ernest request for alteracione, ye, rather for the cleare abolyshinge of the same. And if that our religione (as it was here of late) discretly, godlye and learnedlye declared doth consiste partly in inward thinges in feythe, hope and charitie, and partly to outwarde thinges, as in common prayer and the holly sacramentes universally ministred, nowe as concerning those outwarde thinges, this bill dothe clerely in verie deade extinguishe them, setting in theire places I can not tell what; and the inward yt doth also shake that it leaveth theim verie bare and feble. For first, by this bill Christiane charitie ys taken away in that the unitie of Christe's Church is broken, for it is said that *nunquam relinquent*[2] *unitatem qui non prius omittunt charitatem*: men doe never forsake the unitie which do not first lose charitie. And Sainte Paul[3] sayethe that charitie is
f.112v *vinculum perfectionis*, / the bonde or chayne of perfection, wherwith we be knyte and joyned together in one, which bonde being losed we must nedes fall one from another into diverse partes and sectes as we for wo[e][4] do at this present tyme.

And as towchinge feythe, yt is evident that diverse of the articles and misteries thereof be also not only called into doute, but partly openly, and partly obscurlye; and yet in verie deade as the other flatly denyde. Nowe theis two – I meane feythe and charitie – being in this case, hope is eyther lefte alone or ells presumption set in higher place, whereupon for the most parte desperacion dothe followe, from the which I praye God preserve all men. Wherafore theis matters motioned yn this bill wherin our holle religione consisteth we ought, I saye, to reverence and not to call into question, for as a lerned man writythe, '*Que patefacta sunt querere, que perfecta sunt retractare, et que definita sunt convellere, quid aliud est quin de adeptis gratiam non referre,*' that is to saye, 'To seake after thinges which be manifestly opened, to call bake or to retracte thinges made perfecte and to pull up againe matters defined, what other

thing is it then not to give thankes for benefittes received'. Likewise sayeth holly
Athanasius, '*Que nunc a tot et*[5] *a talibus episcopis probata sunt, ac decreta clareque
demonstrata supervacaneum est / denuo revocare in judicium*'. 'It is a superfluouse thing',   f.113
sayth Athanasius, 'to call in [judgment] againe matters which hath byn tryed,
decried and manifestly declared by so many such bushopes' – he meaneth as wer at
the Counsell of Nicene.[6] For no man will denie, sayth he, but if they be now
examined againe and of newe judged, after that examined ageyne and againe, this
curiositie will never come to an ende. And, as it is saied in *Ecclesiastica Historia*, '*Si
quotidie licebit fidem in questionem vocare, de fide nunquam constabit*: yff it shal be lawfull
every daye to call our feythe into questione we shall never be certaine of our feythe'.[7]
Nowe if Athanasius did thinke that a man ought not to doubt of matters determined
in the Councell of Nicene, wher were present but iij[c] and eyght busshopps,[8] howe
muche lesse ought we to doubte of matters determined and practysed in the holle[9]
Catholique Churche of Christe by iij hundred thowsand bushoppes, and how
many more I can not tell. And as for the certentye of our feythe, wherof the storrie of
the Churche dothe speake, [it is] a thing of all other most necessarie: yf it shall hange
upon an acte of Parliament we have but a weake staffe to leane unto. And yet I shall
desire yow to take[10] me here / as to speake yn derogation of the auctoritie of the   f.113v
parliament, which I acknowledge[11] to be of greate strengthe in matters whereto yt
extendythe, but for matters of religion I doo not thinke yt ought to meddell withall,
partelye for the certaintie which ought to be in our feythe and religione and the
uncertenty of the statutes and actes of Parliament. For we se that oftentimes that
which is established by Parliament one yere is abrogated the next yere folowing, and
the contrarie allowed; and we se also that one kinge disaloweth the statutes made
under another. But our faithe and religione ought to be most certen and one in all
tymes, and in no condicion wavering,[12] for as St James saith, 'He that doubtes or
staggareth in his feythe is like the waves of the seae and shall obteine nothing at the
handes of God'.[13] And partly for that the parliamente consisteth for the most parte
of the noble men of the realme and certaine of the commons, beinge lay and
temporall men, which although they be of good wisdome and lerning, yet not so
studied nor exercised in the scriptures, the holy doctors and practyse of the Church
as to be accounted judges in suche matters, neyther dothe it appertaine to theire
vocation. Yea, / that by your owne judgement[14] as may wel be gathered of one facte   f.114

1. 'A' supplied from Harl.2185.
2. MS reads '*relinquunt*'; this reading from Harl.2185.
3. Col.3.14.
4. MS appears to read 'for woo'; Harl.2185 appears to read 'for wo', and Tanner 302 omits the two words. J. Strype, *Annals of the Reformation* (1824 edn), I, ii, has 'see we'.
5. '*Et*' supplied from Harl.2185.
6. Cf. *Thomus ad Antiochenos*, 5 and 9; *Ad Afros Epistola Synodica*, 1–2.
7. Cf. comment of Sophronius in Socrates,

Ecclesiastical History, ii.xl.
8. Sic, and in Harl.2185 and Tanner 302; cf. A. Neander, *General History of the Christian Religion and Church* (1851), iv.18.
9. Harl.2185 has 'holy'.
10. Tanner 302 has 'not to take'.
11. MS reads 'knowledge'; this reading from Harl.2185.
12. MS reads 'wafering'; this reading from Harl.2185.
13. James 1.6–7.
14. Tanner 302 has 'confession'.

which I remember was done this present parliament, which was this. Ther was a noble man's sonn arrested[15] and committed unto warde, which matter, being oppened here unto your lordships, was thought to be an iniury to this House. Thereupon, so well the young gentleman as th'officer that did arrest him and the partie by whose meanes he was arrested, were all sente for and commaunded to appere here before your lordships, which was done accordinglye; and yet before the parties were suffered to come into the House it was thought expedient to have the holle matter considered, lest the House shuld intermedle with matters not appertaining unto it: in treating wherof ther wer found iij poinctes. First, was a debte, and that your lordships did remitt to the common lawe; the seconde was a fraude which was offered to the Chauncerie, bicause neyther of both did appertaine to this courte; and the third was the arrest and committeing to warde the saied gentleman, wherein this House toke order. Nowe, if that by your lordships' owne judgement the parliament hath no auctoritie to medle with matters of the common lawe, which is grounded upon common reason, neather with the Chauncery,

f.114v   which / ys groundyde upon conscience, which ij thinges be geven naturallye to man, then muche less maye it intermedle with matters of feythe and religion farr passing reason and the judgement of men suche as the contents of this byll be, wherin ther be iij specially to be considered; that ys, the weghtynes of the matter, the darknes of the case and difficultie in trieng out[16] the trewthe, and thirdly the danger and parell if we do take the wronge waye. As concerninge the first, that is the weightynes of the matter conteyned in this bill, yt is verie greate; for yt is no money matter, but a matter of inheritaunce, yea, a matter touching[17] life and deathe, for our helthe and salvacion, our deathe and damnacion dependeth upon yt. Here is sete before us (as the scripture saieth) life and deathe, fier and water: if we put our hand into the one we shall live, if we take hould of the other we shall die. Nowe, to judge in theis matters here propounded, to[18] decerne which is life, which is death, which is fier that will burne us, which is water that will refreshe and comforte us, is a great matter and not easlie perswaded of every mann. Moreover, ther is an other greater

f.115   matter here to be considered, and that is that / we do not unadvisedlie condeme our fathers and [their] doinges, and justifie ourselves and our doinges, which both the scripture forbiddeth. This we knowe, that this doctrine and forme of religion which this bill propoundeth to be abolished and taken awaye ys that which our fathers were borne, brought up and lived in, and have professed here in this realme without anye alteracion or chaunge by the space of ten hundred yers and more, and hath ben also professed and[19] practised in the universall Church of Christ sence the Apostles' time. And that which we goe aboute to establishe and place for it is latelie brought in, alowed no where, nor put in practise, but in one realme onlie, and that but a smale time and against[20] the mindes of all Catholique men. Nowe if we do consider but the antiquitie of the one and the newenesse of th'other, we have just cause to have the one in estimacion for the long continuance thereof unto such time as we see evidente cause whi we should reiecte it, and to suspecte the other as never heard of

f.115v   here before unto such time as we see suche cause whi we should receave[21] / yt, seing that our forfathers never hearde tell of it.

　　But now I do call into remembraunce that I did heare yeasterdaye a noble mann in this House saie,[22] making an answere unto this, as it were bie procurance, that our forefathers lived in blindnesse, and that we have iust occasion to lamente theire ignorance; wherunto me thincke it maye be answered that if our forefathers wer here and heard us lament their doinges it is verie like they wold saie unto us as our Saviour Christ saied to the woman which followed him when he went to his deathe and weepte after him, '*Nolite flere super nos, sed super vos*'[23]: wepe not on us for our blindnesse, but weape over yourselves for your owne presumption in taking upon you so arrogantlie to justifie yourselves and your owne doinges and so rashelye condeme us and our doinges. Moreover, David[24] doth teache us a lesson clere contrarie to this noble man's saing, for he biddeth us in doubtfull matters go to our fathers and lerne the truthe of them yn theis wordes, '*Interroga patrem tuum, et annunciabit, etc*: Aske of the father, and he shall declare the truthe unto the[e], and thy auncestors and they will / tell yow.' And after, in the sayde[25] psalme, '*Filii qui nascuntur, etc*: the children which shall rise up shall tell unto theire children that it may be knowen from one generacion to another'.[26] David here willeth us to learne of our fathers and not to condemne theire doinges. Wherefore, I conclude (as concerning this pointe) that this byll, conteyning in it matters of so great weaght and importaunce, it is to be deliberatyd on with great diligence and circumspection, and examined, tryed and determined by men of great lerning, vertue and experience.

    And as this matter is weghtie, and therfore not to be passed over hastely, but diligentlie to be examynyde, so yt is derke and of greate difficultie to be so plainley discussed as that the truthe maye manifestly appere, for here be, as I have saied, ij bookes of religion propounded, the one to be abolished as erronius[27] and wicked, and th'other to be establised[28] as godly and consonante to scripture. And they be bothe concerning one matter, that is the true administracion of the sacramentes according to the institution of our Saviour Christ, in the which adminstracion ther be iij thinges / to be considered. First is the institution of our Saviour Christ for the matter and substeaunce of the sacramentes; the seconde is the ordinaunces of the Apostles for the forme of the sacrementes; the thirde is the addicions of the holly fathers for adorning and perfitinge of the administracion of the said sacramentes: which three be all dewlie, as we saie, observede and that of necessitie in this booke of the Masse and ould service, as all men do knowe which understande it. The other booke which is so muche extolled dothe take awaie two of theis thinges, and in verie

f.116

f.116v

15. MS reads 'arrest'; this reading from Harl.2185.
16. MS reads 'ought'; this reading from Harl.2185.
17. MS reads 'twouching'.
18. 'To' supplied from Harl.2185.
19. 'And' supplied from Harl.2185.
20. MS reads 'againe'; this reading from Harl.2185.
21. MS and Harl.2185 have 'referme'; this reading from Tanner 302.
22. MS reads 'saied'; this reading from Harl.2185.
23. Luke 23.28.
24. *Sic*, and in Harl.2185: Moses in Deut.32. 7. Tanner 302 includes the correct citation.
25. *Sic*. Tanner 302 has 'And David in the 77 Psalme . . .'
26. Psalm 78.6-7.
27. *Sic*.
28. *Sic*.

deade, maketh the third a thing of nought. For first, as concerninge tradicions of the fathers as in the Masse, *confiteatur, misereatur, kirieleyson, sequences preces,*[29] *sanctus, agnus dei*, with suche other thinges, and the ordinances of th'Appostylls, a[s] blessings, crossinges, and in the administracion of diverse of the sacramentes, exufflations, exorcismes, invucacions, praing towardes the est, invocaciones to saintes, prayers for the deade with suche other, this booke taketh away either in parte, or els clerelie, as thinges not allowed. And yet dothe the fathers thereof contende that it is moste perfecte according to Christe's institutione and th'order of the primitive Churche. But to let th'ordinaunces of th'Appostles and two tradicions of theim[30] passe, which

f.117   notwithstanding / we ought greatlie to esteme and reverence, lett us come to the institucion[31] of our Saviour Christ, wherof they talke so much, and examine whether of those ij bookes cometh nereare unto it.

And to make thinges plaine, we will tacke for example the Masse, or as they call it, the Supper of the Lorde, wherin our Saviour Christ (as all th'ollie fathers do gether of the scripture) did institute iij things which he commaunded to be done in remembraunce of his deathe and passion untill his comming againe, saieng, '*Hoc facitis, etc*: Do ye this.' Wherof the first ys the consecracione of the[32] blessed body and bloud of our Saviuor Christ; the seconde, the offering upe of the same [to][33] the Father; the thirde, the communicatinge, that is, the eating and drinking of the saied blessed body and bloude under the formes of brede and wine. And as concerning the first two, St Chrisostom saythe thus: '*Volo quiddam edicere plane mirabile et nolite mirare,*[34] *neque turbamini, etc*.' 'I woll',[35] saythe St Chrisostom, 'declare unto you a marvillous thing, but marvell not at yt, nor be not troubled. What is this? It ys the hollye oblacione, whether Peter, or Paul,[36] or a prest of any deserte do offer it is the

f.117v   verie same which Christ gave unto his disciples, and / which prestes do make and consecrate at this time. This hath nothing lesse than that. Why so? Bycause men do not sanctyfie this, but Christe which did sanctifie that before, for like as the wordes which Christ did speake be the verie same which the prest doth now pronounce, so it is the verie same oblacion.' Theis be the wordes of St Chrisostome wherein he testyfieth so well the oblacion and sacrifice of the bodie and blod of our Saviour Christ, offered unto God the Father in the Masse, as also the consecrating of the same by the prest. Which two be bothe taken away by this booke as the auctors therof do willingly acknowledge, crieng out of the offering of Christe after then [?],[37] notwithstanding that all th'olly fathers teache it, manifestlye affirming Christ to be offered after a blodie manere. But if theis men did consider and understande what doth ensue and followe of this their affirmacion, I thinke thei wold leave theire rashenes and returne to the truthe againe; for if it be true that they saie, that ther is noe externall sacrifice in the Newe Testament, then doth it followe that ther is no

f.118   presthood under the same, whose office is, / saieth Sainte Paule, to offer up giftes and sacrifices for sinne.[38] And if ther be no presthood, then is there no religion under the Newe Testament: and if we have no religion, then be we *sine deo hoc mundo*, that is, we be without God in this worlde. For one of theis do necessarilie depende and followe upon another, so that if we graunte one of theis, we graunte all; and if we take awaye one, we take awaye all. Note, I beseche your Lordships, th'ende of theis men's doctrine, that is, to set us without God. And the like opinion they hould touching the consecration, having nothing in theire mouthe but th'ollye Communion, which after th'order of this booke is holly in wordes and not in deade, for the thinges is not there which should make it hollye, I meane the bodie and bloud of Christ, as may thus appere. It may justlie in verie deade be called th'olie Communion if it be ministerd trulie and according as it ought to be, ffor then wee res[eave][39] Christe's holly bodye and bloude into our bodies and be ioyned one with him, like two peces of weax which being moltoun / and put together be made   f.118v one, which similitude St Cirill and Chrisostom doo use in this matter; and St Paull saythe that we be made bone of his bonys and fleshe of his fleshe.[40] But by th'order of this booke, this is not done; for Christe's bodye is not there in verye deade to be receyved, for the onely way wherby it is present ys by consecracion, which this booke hath not at all, neither dothe it observe the forme prescribed by Christ nor followe the manner of the Churche. The Evangelist doth declare that our Saviour toke bread into his handes and did blesse it, and gave it to his disciples, saing, 'Take ye, eate. This is my body which is geven for yow; do this yn remembraunce.' By theis wordes ('Do this') we be commaunded to take bread in our[41] handes, to blesse yt, breake yt, and having a respect to the letter, to peruse the wordes spoken by our Saviour, that is: '*Hoc est corpus meum*', by which wordes, sayeth St Chrisostom, the bread is consecrated.[42] Nor[43] by th'order of this booke neyther dothe the prest take the bread in his handes, blesse it, nor breke it, neither hath he any regarde or respecte to the bread when he reherseth the wordes of Christ, but dothe passe theim over as / he wer telling a tale or rehersinge a storie. Moreover, whereas by the mindes of all   f.119 good writers her is[44] required, yea, and that of necessyte, a full mynde, intente to do that which Christ did, that ys, to consecrate his body and bloud with other thinges following; wherefore the Churche hath appointed in the Masse certain prayers to be said by the prest before the consecration, in which theis wordes be: '*Ut fiat nobis corpus et sanguis domini nostri Jesu Christi*', that is, your prayer is to this ende, that the createures maye be made unto us the body and bloude of our Lorde Jesus Christ.[45] Here is declared the intente so well of the Churche, as also of the prest which saithe

29. MS reads '*preses*'; this reading from Harl.2185.

30. Tanner 302 has 'the traditions of the ould fathers' instead of 'two tradicions of theim.'

31. Harl.2185 has 'justificacion'.

32. MS reads 'his'; this reading from Harl.2185.

33. Edge of MS worn.

34. *Sic*; Tanner 302 has '*mirari*', and Harl.2185 does not give the Latin here.

35. *Sic*, and frequently hereafter.

36. MS reads 'Powell'; this reading from Harl.2185.

37. MS unclear here: Harl.2185 omits the dubious word, and renders the previous word as 'they' rather than 'then'. Tanner 302 has 'once', makes the previous two words 'oftener than', and the offering *un*bloody.

38. Heb.5.1. J. Strype, *Annals of the Reformation* (1824 edn), I. ii, comments: 'This is expressly spoken of the high priestes of the Old Testament.'

39. Harl.2185 has 'reserve'.

40. Cyril, *Commentarius in Joannem*, bk.19 on John 15.1; cf. Chrysostom, *In Matthaeum Homilia, lxxxii alias lxxxiii*, 5; cf. Ephesians 5.30.

41. This reading from Tanner 302; MS and Harl.2185 have 'your'.

42. Chrysostom, *De Proditione Judae Homilia*, 1.6.

43. *Sic*, and in Harl.2185; Tanner 302 has 'but'.

44. MS reads 'his'; this reading from Harl.2185.

45. Harl.2185 omits '*nobis corpus . . . unto us*'.

Masse. But as for this newe boke, ther is nothing mencyoned yn it that it dothe ether declare eny suche entente or[46] make such request to God, but rather to the contrarie, as doth appere by the request therin made in these wordes: 'That we receive in[47] theis thy creatures of bred and wine maye' and so furthe, which wordes declare that they entende no consecration at all. And then lett them glorie so muche as they wille in their Communion: it is to no purpose, seing the bodie of Christ is not there, which, as I have said, is the thinge which should be communicated. |

f.119v   Ther did yesterdaye a noble man in this House saye that he did beleve that Christ is there receyved[48] in the Communione sett out in this boke, and being asked if he did worship him there, he said 'No', nor never wold so long as he liveth; which is a strange opinion that Christ shulde be enywhere and not to be worshipped. They saye they woll worship him in heven but not in the sacrament, which ys muche like as a man wolde saye that when the Emperour sytteth under the clothe of his estate princly appareled he is to be honorede, but if he come abrode in a frise cote he is not to be honored, and yet is all one Emperoure in clothe of goulde under his clothe of estate and in a frese cote abrode in the strete, as yt ys one Christ in heven in the forme of man and in the sacrament under the formes of bread and wine. The scripture, as St Augustine doth interpretate[49] it, doth commaunde us to worshippe the body of our Savioure, yea, and that in the sacrament in theis wordes, '*Adorate scabellum etc.*: worship his footestole, for it is hollye'. Upon the which place St Augustine writeth

f.120   thus: 'Christe toke fleshe off the fleshe of the blessed Virgine his mother | and in the same fleshe he did walke, and the same fleshe he gave us to eate unto helthe; but no man woll eate that fleshe except he worshipp it before. So it is founde oute howe we shuld worship his foote-stole. And we shall not onelie sinne in worshipping, but we shall sinne in not worshipping'.[50] Thus saith St Augustine; but as concerning this matter, yff we woll consider all thinges well we shall see the provision of God marvelous in it, for he provideth so that the very heritykes and enemies of the truthe be compelled to confesse the truthe in that behalfe: for the Lutherans, writing against the Swynglians, do prove that the true naturall bodie of our Saviour Christ is in the sacrament; and the Swinglians against the Lutherans do prove that then it must needes be worshipped there. And thus in their contentions dothe the truthe burst out, whether they woll or no. Wherfore in mine opinion of errores the fonder ys to saie that Christ is in the sacrament and yet not to be worshipped, then to saie that he is not ther at all, for eyther they do thinke he is but there in imaginacion or

f.120v   fansye, and so not in verie deade, or els they be Nestorians and thinke[51] | that it is a body onlye, and not his divinitie: which be bothe devylishe and wycked.

Now, my lordes,[52] consider I beseche yow the matter here in variaunce, whether your lordships be able to discuse them according to lerning so as the truthe may appere or not: that is, whether the bodye of Christ be by this newe boke consecrated, offered, adored, [and] truelie communicated or no; and whether theis thinges be regarded[53] necessarilie by th'institutione of our Saviour Christ or no; and whether the booke goeth nere the truthe. Theis matters, my lordes, be as I have said weightie and dearke, and not easie to be discussed; and likewise your lordships maye thinke of the rest of the sacramentes which be either clerelie taken awaie or ells mangled after the same sort by this newe booke.

The thirde there to be considered is the greate daunger and parell that doth hange over your heds if yow do take upon yow to be judges in theis matters and judge wronge, bringing bothe yourselves and other from the truthe / unto untruthe, from   f.121 the high waye to bye pathes. It is dangerous enough, our Lord knoweth, for a man himselfe to erre, but it is muche more dangerous not onlie to erre himselfe, but also to lead all other men in to erroure. It is said in scripture of the king Jeroboam to aggravat his offences, that *peccavit et peccare fecit Israell*: he did sinne himselfe and caused Israell to sinne.[54] My lordes, take heade that the like be not saied by yow. If yow passe this bill yow shall not onelie, in my judgemente, erre yourselves, but yow shall also be the auctors and causers that the holle realme shall erre after yow; for the which yow shall make an[55] accompte before God. Those that have read stories and knowe the discourse and order of the Churche in discussing matter[s] of controversie in matters of religion canne testifie that they have ben discussed and determined at all times by the clergie onelie, and never by the temporalitie. The heresy of Arrius, which trobled the Church in the time of Constantine the / Great   f.121v which was Emperour, was condemned in the Counsell of Nice; the heresie of Eutiches in the Councell of Calcedoney under Martine; the heresie of Macedonus in the first Counsell of Constantinople in the time of Theodosius; the heresy of Nestorius in [the] Ephesyn Councell in the tyme of Theodosius the Younger. And yet did none of theis good emperours assemble theire nobilitie and commons for the discussing and determining of theis controversies, neither asked their mindes in theim, or went by nombre of voices or polls to determen the truthe, as is done here in this realme at this time.

We may comme louwer to the third Counsell [of] Toletane in Spaine in time of King Reccared,[56] and to the Counsell in Fraunce aboute 800 yeres agoo in the time of Carolus Magnus; which bothe following th'order of the Churche by licence of the Pope did pronounce[57] the clergie of theire realme to be gathered and assembled together for reforming of certaine errors and enormities with / in theyr said realmes,   f.122 whereunto thei neyther called theire nobilite nor commons, neyther did eny of theim take apon themselves either to reason or despute in discussing of the controversies, neither to determine theim, being discussed, but lefte the hole to the discussing and determinacion of the clergie. And no marvell, if theis, with all other Catholique princes, used this trade. For the emperours that were heretickes did never reserve any suche matter to the judgement of temporall men as may appere to theim that reade the stories of[58] Constantius and Valens[59] which procured diverse assemblies, but

46. MS reads 'either'; this reading from Harl.2185.
47. *Sic*, and in Harl.2185: 'receiving'? Tanner 302 omits 'in', and has a fuller version of the request.
48. MS and Harl.2185 read 'res'; this reading from Tanner 302.
49. *Sic*.
50. Augustine on Psalm 98.5 in *Enarrationes in Psalmos* (99.5 in Authorised Version.)
51. 'And thinke' repeated on f.120v.
52. Harl.2185 breaks off here.
53. Tanner 302 has 'requyred'.
54. 1 Kings 14.16.
55. 'An' repeated in MS.
56. MS appears to read 'Herred'; blank in Tanner 302, which continues 'about the yeare of our Lord 574'. The reference must be to Toledo III, 589.
57. Tanner 302 has 'procure'.
58. MS reads 'by'.
59. MS reads 'Constantius Valensi and'. Tanner 302 has 'Constans Valens and Ursatius'.

allwaye of the cleargie for the establishing of Arrius' doctrine, and Zeno th'emperour which did the like for Eutyches' doctrine, with many other of that sorte.

f.122v   Yea, it dothe appere in th'Actes of the'Apostales that an infidell / wold take no suche matter apon him. The storie is, St Poule, havinge continued at Corinthe one yeare and a half in preaching of the Gospell, certaine wicked persons did arise against him and brought him before theyr vice-counsell called Gallio, lainge unto his charge that he taught the people[60] to worshipp God, contrarie to theyr lawes; unto whom the vice-counsell answered this: '*Si quidem esset iniquum aliquid aut facinus pessimum, o viri judei, recte vos sustinerem. Si vero questiones sunt in verbo et nominibus legis vestrae, vosipsi viderites.[61] Judex horum ego nolo esse.*' 'If that man', saith Gallio, 'had committed eny wicked acte or cursed crime, ye Jewes, I might justly have herde yow; but and yt be concerning questiones and doubtes of the wordes and names of your lawe, that is to saie if it be touching your religione, I will not be judge in those matters'.[62] Marke, my lordes, this shorte discourse, I beseche your lordships, and ye shall prove that all the Catholique princes, heretike princes, yea, and infideles,

f.123   hath from time to time refused to take apon / theim that your lordships gothe aboute to chalenge to do.

But now, bycause I have been longe, I will make an ende of this matter with the sayinges of two noble men in the like affares. The first is Theodosius, which saied thus: '*Illicitus est enim(?) qui non sit ex ordine sanctorum episcoporum ecclesiasticis se ministere tractatibus*'. 'It is not lawful', sayth he, 'for him that is not of th'order of th'ollie busshoppes to entermedle with their treating of ecclesiasticall matters.[63] Likewise said Valentinianus th'Emperour, being desired to assemble certain busshoppes for th'examining of a matter of doctrine, in this wise: '*Mihi qui sum in sorte plebis, fas non est talia curiosius scrutari. Sacerdotes, quibus ista curae sunt inter seipsos quocunque; loco voluerint conveniant.*' 'It is not lawful for me', said the Emperour, 'being one of the laie people, to serche oute suche curious matters, but lett the prestes, unto whom the charge of theis thinges do belonge, meate together in what place soever they wolle' – he meaneth for the discussing therof.[64] But and if theis emperours hade nothing to do with such matters, howe should your lordshippes have to doo withall?

60. MS reads 'pople'.
61. *Sic.*
62. Acts 18.14-15.

63. Cited from the acts of the Council of Ephesus in Neander, *op.cit.*, iii.190.
64. Sozomon, *Historia Ecclesiastica*, vi.7.

4. [House of Lords] Abbot Feckenham's speech on the uniformity bill, 27/28 April(?)

Text from Corpus Christi College, Cambridge, 121, copy.
Other MSS. London: BL Cott. Vespasian DXVIII, Harl. 2185.
Oxford: Bodley, Tanner 302.
Printed. J. Strype, *Annals of the Reformation* (1824 edn), I, ii.431⁄8.
Somers Tracts, I.58⁄62.

Corpus Christi College 121, pp.129⁄37

The oration of Doctor Fecnam, Abbott of Westminster, made in parliament house, anno 1559[1]

Honorable and my verye good lordes, havynge at this present two sundrye kyndes of religion here proponed and sett furthe before yow, and your honors being alredye in possession of the one of them – and your fathers before yow – for the space of xiiij[c] yeres past here in this realme like as I shall hereafter prove unto yow, th'other religion is here set forthe in a boke to be receyved and established by th'auctoritie of this High Court of Parliament and to take his effect here in this realme at midsomer[2] next commynge; and your honors being (as I know right well) desyrous to have perfect and sure knowlege which of bothe theis religions is the better and most worthy to be established here in this realme and to be preferred before the other, I shall for my part and for the discharge of my dutie first unto God, seconde unto our soveraigne ladie the Quene's Highnes, thirdlye unto your honors and to the holl commons of this realme here set forthe and expresse unto yow three breiffe rules and lessons wherbye your honors shall be able to put difference betwixt the true religion of God and the counterfett, and therin never to be disceaved.

The ffirst of theis iiij rules and lessons is that in this your serche and tryall⁄makyng your honors must observe which of them both hathe byne of moost antiquitie and[3] most observed in the Churche of Christe of all menn and at all tymes and seasons and in all placys. The[4] second, which of them bothe is of it selfe the more stedfast[5]

---

1. This title is from the Cott. Vespasian DXVIII copy, f.86. The copy in Corpus Christi College, Cambridge, 121 is not attributed to Feckenham, but it (and the subsequent copy of Heath's speech) is preceded on p.127 by this description: 'A discourse of certaine Romanistes exhibited to the Quene's Counsell immediatly uppon Quene Elizabethe's comming in, amongest which was thought Dr Hethe to be the penner of the said discourse'.

2. Cf. *SR*, IV.355.

3. 'Of moost antiquitie and' supplied from Cott. Vespasian DXVIII.

4. 'The' supplied from Cott. Vespasian DXVIII.

5. MS reads 'staied'; this reading supplied from Cott. Vespasian DXVIII.

p.130 religion and alwaies one and[6] agreable with yt selfe. / The thirde and last rule to be considered of your wisdomes is which of thes religions dothe breede more humble and obedient subiectes, first unto God, and[7] second to our sovereigne ladie the Quene's Highnes and all superiour powers.

Touching the first rule and lesson, it can not be trulye affirmed or yet thought of anye mann that this newe religion here now to be set forthe in this boke hath[8] bene observyd in Christe's Churche of all Christen menn at all times and in all placys, when the religion expressed in this boke hath bene observed onlye here in this realme, and that for a short tyme, as not moche passyng the space of ij yeres, and that in Kynge Edward the Syxte dayes; wheras the religion and the very same manner of serving and honoryng of God, of the which ye are at this present in possession of,[9] did begynne here in this realme xiiij[c] yeres past in Kyng Lucius' dayes, the first Christian kynge here in this realme, by whose humble lettere sent unto the Pope Eleutherius he did send in to this realme ij holye monckes, th'one called Damianus and th'other Faganus. And thei as embassadors sent from the sea apostolique of Rome did bryng into this realme so many yeres passed the verye same religion wherof we are now in possession, and that in the Latten tongue like as Gildas the auncient historiographer of the Bryttan Storyes dothe wytnesse in the begynnyng and prologue of his boke.[10] The same religion so longe ago begone hath bene observed ever synst here in this realme, not only of the inhabitantes[11] theirof, but also generallie of all Christen menn and in all places of Christendom, untyll the late daies of Kyng

p.131 Edward the / vj[th] as is aforesaid: wherebie it appearethe unto all menn that listethe to see how that by this first rule and lesson the auncient religion and manner of servyng of God where of we are alredie in possession is the verye true and perfect religion and of God.

Touchyng the second rule and lesson of triall and probacion, whether of bothe theis religions is the better and most worthie of[12] observacion here in this realme, is this, that your honours must observe which of them bothe is the more stedfast[13] religion and alwaies one and[14] agreable with yt selfe, and that this new religion here nowe to be set forthe in this boke is no stedfast[15] religion, nor alwaies one nor[16] agreable with yt selfe. Who seethe it[17] not when in the late practise theirof in Kyng Edward the vj[th] dayes how chaungeable and variable was it unto yt selfe, every other yere havyng a newe boke devised theirof, and everye boke being sett forthe as thei professed according to the syncere worde of God? Never a one of them did in all poyntes agree with the other, the first boke affirmying the vij sacramentes and the reall presence of Christe's bodie in the holye Euchariste, the other deniing the same; the one boke did admitt the reall presence of Christe's bodie in the sacrament to be receyved in one kynde with knelyng downe and great reverence, and that in unleaven bredde, the other boke would have the Communion received in bothe the kindes, and that in leaven[18] bredd settyng, without any reverence but onlye to the bodie of Christ which is in heaven: and the thyng most worthye to be observed of your honors is how that either[19] boke made a shewe to be sett forthe according to the

p.132 syncere worde of God and not / one of them did agree with an other. And what great marvell, I praye yow, when the authors and devisors of the said bokes coulde not agree emonge themselfes, nor yet any one mann of them might their be fownde that did longue agre with hymselfe.

And for proofe theirof I shall first begynne with the Germayne wryters, the cheiffe scholemaisters and instructors of our cowntre menn in all theis novelties. I do rede in an epistle which Philippe Melancthon did wryte unto one Frederico Miconio how that one Carolastadius was the first mover and begynner of this late sedicion in Germanye touchyng the sacrament of the altare and the deniall of Christe's reall presence in the same;[20] and when he shuld come to interpretate[21] theis wordes of our Saviour Christe: '*accepit panem benedixit, fregit,*[22] *dedit pro discipulis suis, dicens, "Accipite et commedite. Hoc est corpus meum quod pro vobis tradetur" digito (inquit ille) monstrabat visibile suum corpus*', by the whiche interpretation of Carolstadius Christe shuld with the one hande geve unto his disciples bredd for to eate, and with the other hande poynte unto his visible bodie that was their present and saye, 'This is my body which shall be betrayed for yow' Martyn Luther, moche offended with this folishe exposition made by Corolastadius of theis wordes of Christe (*Hoc est corpus meum*), he gevethe an other sence and saieth that *Germanus sensus verborum Christi* was this: *per hunc panem vel cum isto pane, en do vobis corpus meum.*[23] Swinglius, fyndyng moche fault with this interpretacion of Martyn Luther, wryteth that Luther therin was / disceived, and how that in theis wordes of Christ (*Hoc est corpus meum*) this verbe substantyve, *est,* must be taken for *significat,* and this worde *corpus*[24] must be taken *pro figura corporis,* so that the true sence of theis wordes of Christe (*Hoc est corpus meum*) by Zwinglius' supposall is: *Hoc significat corpus meum, vel est figura corporis mei.*[25] Peter Martyr, being of late here in this realme, in his boke by hym sett forthe of the disputacion whiche he hadde in Oxforthe with the lerned studentes their of this matter, he geveth an other sence of theis wordes of Christe contrarie to all the rest and

p.133

---

6. MS reads 'alwaies forthe one and'; this reading supplied from Cott. Vespasian DXVIII. This use of 'forth' recurs in this copy and probably depends on the ellipsis of 'goes'.

7. 'And' supplied from Cott. Vespasian DXVIII.

8. MS reads 'have not'; this reading supplied from Cott. Vespasian DXVIII.

9. *Sic.*

10. The reference must be to Geoffrey of Monmouth, *History of the Kings of Britain*, iv.19, where the monks are named Duvianus and Faganus.

11. MS has 'inhabitaunces', as does Cott. Vespasian DXVIII; this reading supplied from Harl.2185.

12. 'Of' supplied from Cott. Vespasian DXVIII.

13. MS reads 'staied'; this reading supplied from Cott. Vespasian DXVIII.

14. MS reads 'alwaies forthe one and'; this reading supplied from Cott. Vespasian DXVIII.

15. MS reads 'staied'; this reading supplied

16. MS reads 'alwaies forthe one nor'; this reading supplied from Cott. Vespasian DXVIII.

17. 'It' supplied from Cott. Vespasian DXVIII.

18. Other MSS refer to 'loaf bread.'

19. MS reads 'everye'; this reading supplied from Cott. Vespasian DXVIII.

20. *Corpus Reformatorum*, ed. C.G. Bretschneider (Halis Saxonum, 1834), Band ii, Spalte 31.

21. *Sic.*

22. 'Fregit' supplied from Cott. Vespasian DXVIII.

23. Letter of 4 January, 1526 to Reutlingen, in *Luthers Werke: Kritische Gesamtausgabe* (Weimar, 1883'), band 19, 121; *Sermon von dem Sacrament . . .* in *ibid.*, band 19, 498; and cf. *De Captivitate Babylonica . . .* in *ibid.*, band 6, 511.

24. MS reads '*corpus quod pro vobis tradetur*'.

25. Letter to Matthew Alber, 16 November 1524, cited in G.R. Potter, *Huldrych Zwingli* (1978), 98'9.

their saiethe, '*Quod Christus accipiens panem dixit, "Hoc est corpus meum", quasi diceret, "Corpus meum fide perceptum erit vobis pro pane, vel instar panis"*'; of whose sence th'Englishe is this: that Christe's bodie receyved by faithe shulde be unto the receyvers as bred or in the steade of bredd.[26].

But here to ceasse any further to speke of theis Germayne wryters I shall drawe now nere home,[27] as unto Doctor Cranmere, late Archebisshop of Canterburie here in this realme. How contrarie was he unto hymselfe in this matter, when in one yere he did set forthe a cathechisme in th'Englishe tongue and dedicated the same boke to Kynge Edward the vj[th], wherin he dothe most constantlye affirme and defende the reall presens of Christe's bodie in the holie Euchariste; and verie shortlye after he did set forthe an othe boke wherin he did most shamefullie denye the same, falsefying bothe the scriptures and doctors to no small admiracion of all the lerned readers.[28] Doctor Ridleye, the notablest lerned of that opinion within / this realme, did set forthe at Paule's Crosse the reall presence of Christe's bodie in the sacrament with theis wordes which I herde, being their present, how that the Devyll did beleve that the Sonne of God was able to make of stoones bred. And we Englishe people, which do confesse that Jesus Christ was the very Sonne of God and yet will not beleve that he did make of bred his verye bodie flesshe and bludde, therfore we are worse then the Devyll, seing that our Saviour Christe by expresse wordes he dothe most playnlye affirme the same, when at his last supper he toke the bredde and said unto his disciples, 'Take, eate: this is my bodie which shall be geven for yow.' And shortlye after, the said Doctor Rydleye, notwithstandyng this most playne and open speache at Paule's Crosse, did denye the same.[29] And in the last boke that Doctor Cranmer and his complises did set forthe of the Communion in Kyng Edwarde's dayes, theis playne wordes of Christe (*Hoc est corpus meum*) did so incomber them and trobled their wyttes, that thei did, in the same last boke, leave out this verbe substantyve (*est*) and made the sence of Christe's wordes to be their Englished: 'Take, eate this my bodie', and left out their 'This is my bodie'; which thing being espied by others, and great fault fownd withall, then thei were fayne to patche up the matter with a little peace of paper clapt over the forsaid wordes, wherin was wrytten this verbe substantyve (*est*). The dealyng therof bothe by the Germayne and Englishe wryters being this uncerten, and one of them ageinst another, your honors may be well assured that / this religion which by them is set forthe can be no constant and stayed religion, and therfore of your honors not to be receyved; but great wisdom it were for your honors to refuce the same untyll yow shall perceive more better[30] agrement emonge the authors and setters forthe therof.

Touchyng the thirde and last rule of tryall-makyng and puttyng of difference betwixt religions, it is to be considered of your honors which of them bothe dothe brede the more obedient, humble and better subiectes, first and cheiflye unto God, seconde unto our soveraigne ladie the Quene's Highnes and to all other superiour powers. And for some triall and probacion hereof, I shall desire your honors to considre the soden mutacion of the subiectes of this realme synce the deathe of good Quene Marye, onlye caused in them by the prechers of this new religion, when in Quene Marye's dayes your honors do know right well how the people of this realme did lyve in an order and would not runne before lawes, nor openlye disobeye the

p.134

p.135

Quene's Highnes' proclamacions. Their was no spoylyng of churches, pluckyng downe of aulters, and most blasphemouselye tredynge the sacrament under their ffeete, and hangyng up of the knave of clubbes in the place theirof; their was no scotchynne[31] or cuttynge of the facys, legges and armes of the crucifixe and the imagies of Christe; their was no open fleashe eatyng nor shambles kepyng in Lent and dayes prohibited. The subiectes of this realme, and in speciall the nobilitie and suche as were of / her honorable Cownsell, did in Quene Marye's dayes knowe the   p.136 waye unto the churches and chappels, their to begynne their daye's worke with caulyng for helpe and grace by humble prayers and serving of God. And now, synce the commyng and raigne of our most soveraigne and deare ladie Quene Elizabethe, by the onlye preachers and scaffold players of this new religion, all thinges are chaunged and turned upsidowne, notwithstandyng the Quene's Highnes' most godlye proclamacions made to the contrarie, and her most vertuouse example of lyvinge sufficient to move the hartes of all obedient subiectes unto the due service and honor of God: but obedience is gone, humilitie and mekenes cleane abolished, vertuouse, chast[32] and straight lyvyng abandoned[33] as thoughe thei had never bene harde of here in this realme; all degrees and kyndes of menn being desyrous of flesshelye and carnall libertie, whereby the yong springoldes and childerne[34] are degenerate from their naturall fathers, the servauntes contemptors of their maisters' commaundement, the subiectes disobedient unto God and all superior powers. And therfore, honorable and my very good lordes, of my part to minister some occasion unto your honors to avoyde and expell out of this realme this new religion, whose frutes are alredie to manifestlye knowen to be as I have repeted, and to persuade your honors, as moche as in me liethe, to persever and contynue the same religion / whereof ye are in possession and have alredie made profession of the   p.137

26. *Disputatio in Eucharistiae Sacramento Habita in Celeberrima Universitate Oxoniensi* (1549), f.79v; 'Peter Martyr's Disputations holden at Oxford about the Sacrament of the Lord's Supper' in J. Foxe, *Acts and Monuments* (1877 ed), VI.297-305.

27. MS reads 'whom'; this reading supplied from Cott. Vespasian DXVIII.

28. I.e. the Lutheran Catechism: Justus Jonas, *A short instruction into Christian religion, being a Catechism set forth by Archbishop Cranmer in 1548, together with the same in Latin, translated from the German by Justus Jonas in 1539*, ed. E. Burton (1829), 176-7, 207-8, cited in Peter Brooks, *Thomas Cranmer's Doctrine of the Eucharist* (1965), 44-5; *An Answer to a Crafty and Sophistical Cavillation devised by Stephen Gardiner* (1551) in *Writings and Disputations of Thomas Cranmer*, ed. J.E. Cox (Parker Soc., 1844).

29. Cf. M. Maclure, *The Paul's Cross Sermons,*

1534-1642 (Toronto, 1958), 43; 'Peter Martyr's Disputations holden at Oxford: the Determination of Dr Nicholas Ridley' in Foxe, *op.cit.*, VI.332-5; *A Brief Declaration of the Lord's Supper* (1555) in *The Works of Nicholas Ridley*, ed. H. Christmas (Parker Soc., 1841).

30. *Sic.* Cott. Vespasian DXVIII omits 'more', and Tanner 302 has 'farther probacion and better tryall'.

31. *Sic*; Cott. Vespasian DXVIII has 'skurching', and Harl.2185 has 'scurching'. Tanner 302 abbreviates the whole to 'ther was no hewinge and cutting donne of the crucifixe and images . . .'

32. MS reads 'chastitie'; this reading supplied from Cott. Vespasian DXVIII.

33. 'Abandoned' supplied from Harl.2185; Cott. Vespasian DXVIII has 'aboundane', and Tanner 302 has 'vanquished amongest youth'.

34. *Sic.*

same unto God, I shalle reherse unto yow iiij thinges wherbie the holy doctor St Augustine was continued in the Catholique faithe and religion of Christ which he had receyved and would by no meanes chaunge nor alter from the same.

The first of theis iiij thinges was *ipsa authoritas ecclesie Christi miraculis inchoata spe nutrita, caritate aucta, vetustata firmata*; the second thing was *populi Christiani consensus et unitas*; the third was *perpetua sacerdotum successio in sede Petri*; the fourthe and last thing was *ipsum Catholice nomen*.[35] Yff theis iiij thinges did cause so noble[36] and lerned a clerke as St Augustine was to continue in his professed religion of Christ without all chaunge and alteracion, how moche then owte theis iiij poyntes to worke the lyke effect in your honors and not to forsake your professed religion: first, because it hathe authoritie of Christe's Churche; second, it hathe the consent and agrement of all Christen people; third, it hathe confirmacion of all Peter's successors in the see apostolique; fourth, it hathe *ipsum Catholice nomen*, an in all tymes and seasons called the Catholique religion of Christ.

Thus[37] bolde I have bene to troble your honors with so tediouse and longe an oration for the discharge (as I said before) of my dutie, first unto God, second unto our soveraigne ladie the Quene's Highnes, third and last unto your honors and all other subiectes of this realme, most humblye besychyng your honors to take it in good part and to be spoken of me for the onlye causes aforesaid and for none other.

35. See G.G. Willis, *St Augustine and the Donatist Controversy* (1950), 113-20 and works cited there.

36. Tanner has 'wittie'.

37. MS reads 'this'; this reading supplied from Cott. Vespasian DXVIII.

1. Lord Keeper's opening speech, 25 January

Text from BL Harl.5176. Earlier copies in Harl.398 and Add.48065 (Yelverton 71), from which some alternative readings have been taken, are not on the whole as reliable.
Other MSS. London: BL Cott.Titus F1 (and its copies, Harl.2185 and Stowe 358), Lansd.211; University Library 300. Oxford: Bodley, Eng.Hist.d.144; Exeter College 127. Cambridge: University Library Dd.iii.20, Ii.v.8; Gonville and Caius College 64 (copy of Cott.Titus F1). Herts. CRO: Gorhamby xii.B.2. Dublin: TCD E.1.34. California: Huntington Library, Ellesmere 2573, 2579. Washington: Folger Library 89.2, 1276.10, 7036.
Printed. D'Ewes, 11-14.

Harl.5176, fos.105v-8v

An oration made the three and twentith day[1] of Januarye *anno primo Elizabethae Reginae* to the nobles and commons in the presence of her Majestie, in the beginninge of the parliament holden then, *et in anno Domini* 1558.

My lordes and maisters all: the Queene's most excellent Majestie our naturall and most gratious soveraigne Lady, having as you knowe summoned hether her high courte of Parliament, hath commaunded me to open and declare unto you the chiefe causes and consideracions that moved her Highnes thereunto. And here my Lordes I wishe, not without great cause, there were in me abilitie to doe it in such order and sorte as is beseeminge for the majestie, honor and understanding of this presence, and as the great weightines and worthines of the matter doth require it to be done; the remembrance whereof and the number of mine imperfections to the well performing of it, doth in very deede, playnely to speake, breede in me such feare and dreade that as from a man abasshed and astonied you are to heare all that I shall say therein. True it is that some comforte and encouraging I take throughe the hope I have conceived by that I have seene and hearde of your gentle sufferance with others, whereof I looke upon equall cause equallye with others to be a partaker, and the rather for that I am sure good will shall not wante in me to do the[2] uttermost, and also because I meane to occupye as small a tyme as the greatnes of such a cause will suffer, thinking that to be meetest medicine to cure your tedious hearinge and mine imperfect and disordered speaking. Sommarilye to say, the immediate causes of this sommons and assembly be[3] consultacion, advise and contentacion, for although divers thinges that

1. *Sic*; see p. 3; Sir Nicholas Bacon was appointed Lord Keeper on 22 December 1558 in place of Lord Chancellor Heath.
2. MS reads 'his'; this reading from Harl.398.
3. MS reads 'bene'; this reading from Harl.398.

are to be done here in Parliamente might by meanes be reformed without Parliamente, yet the Queene's Majestie, seeking in her consultacions of importaunce contentacion by assente and suertie by advise, and therewith reposinge her selfe not a little in your fidelities, wisedomes and discretions, meaneth not at this tyme to make any resolucion in any matter of weight before it shalbe by you sufficiently and fully debated, examined and considered.

Now the matters and causes whereupon you are to consulte doe chieflye and principally consist in three[4] poyntes. Of theis the first is the well making of lawes for the accordinge and unitinge of the people of this realme into an uniforme order of religion, to the honour and glorie of God, the establishment of his Church and tranquilitie of the realme. The seconde for the reforming and removing of all f.106 enormities and mischeifes that doe, or might, hurte or hinder / the civill orders or pollices of this realme. The thirde and last is advisedly and deepely to wey and consider the state and condicion of the realme, and the losses and decayes that have of late happened to the imperiall crowne thereof, and thereuppon to devise the best remedyes to supplie and relieve the same.

For the first, the Queene's Majestie, having God before her eyes and being neither unmindfull nor uncarefull of his devine preceptes and counsells, meaneth and intendeth in this conference first and chieflie there should be soughte the advauncemente of Gode's honor and glory as the suer and infallible foundacion whereupon the pollicie of every good publique weale is to be erected and builte, and as the straite lyne whereby it is wholly to be directed and governed, and as the chiefe pillar and buttreuxe wherewith it is[5] continually to be sustayned and maynteyned. And like as the well and perfect doing of this cannot but make good successe in all the rest, so the remisse and loose dealinge in this cannot but make the rest full of imperfeccions and doubtfullnes, which must needes bring with them continuall chaunge and alteracion, thinges much to be eschewed in all good governaunces, and most of all in matters of faithe and religion, which of their natures be, and ought to be, most certaine and stable. Wherefore her Highnes willeth and most earnestly requireth you all, ffirst and principallye for the dutie you beare to God whose cause this is, and then for the service you owe to her Majestie and your countrie, whose weale it concerneth universallye, and for the love you ought to beare to yourselves whom it toucheth one by one particularly, that in this consultacion you will with all humblenes, singlenes and purenes of minde conforme your selves together, usinge your whole indeavor and diligence by lawe and ordinaunce to establish that which by your learning and wisdomes shalbe thought most meete for the well perfourminge of this godlie purpose; and this without respect of honour, rule or soveraignetie, profitt, pleasure or ease, or of any thinge that might touche any parson in estimacion or opinion of witt, learninge or knowledge, and without regarde of all other manner of private affection. And therewith that you will also in this your assemblye and conference clearely forbeare and, as a greate enemye to good councell, flee from all manner of contentious reasoninges and disputacions and all sophisticall, captious and frivolous argumentes and quiddities, meeter for ostentation of witt then consultacion in weightie matters, comelyer for schollers then for counsellors, more f.106v beseeminge for schooles then for parliament / howses; besides that commonly they

be greate cause of much expence of tyme and breed few good resolucions. And like
as in councell all contention would be eschewed, even so by councell provision
would be made that all[6] contentious, contumelious or opprobrious wordes, as
'heretike', 'schismatike', 'papist', and such like names and nurces of seditious
faccions and sectes may be banished out of men's mouthes, as the causers, continuers
and increasers of displeasure, hate and malice, and as utter enemyes to all concorde
and unitie, the very marke that you are now to shoote at. Agayne, as in proceeding
heerein greate, and warye consideracion is to be had that nothing be devised or done
which any way in continuance of tyme were likely to breede or nourishe any kinde of
idolatrye or superstition; soe on the other side great heede is to be taken that, by noe
licencious or loose handelinge, any manner of occasion be given whereby any
contempte or irreverent behaviour towards God, or godlye thinges, or any spice of
irreligion might creepe in or be received. The examples of fearefull punishmentes
and plagues that have followed these fower extreamityes – I meane idolatrye,
superstition, contempte and irreligion – in all ages and tymes are more in number
than I can declare, and better knowen then I neede make recitall to you of. And yet
are they not so many or better knowen then be the continuall budding benefittes and
blessinges of God to those that have forsaken those extreamityes and imbraced their
contraryes. And for your better encouraginge to runne this right and straite course
(although that which is said ought to suffice thereto) I thinke I may affirme that the
good king Ezechias had noe greater desire to amende that was amisse in his tyme,
nor the noble queene Hester a better harte to overthrowe the mightie enemye to
Gode's elect, then our soveraigne Ladye and Mistris hath to doe that that may be iust
and acceptable in Gode's sight. Thus forced to this by your duties to God, feared
thereto by his punishmentes, provoked by his benefittes, drawen by your love to your
countrye and your selves, incouraged by so princely a patronesse, let us in Gode's
name goe about this worke, endevoring our selves with all diligence as I have before
saide, to make such lawes as may tende to the honor and glorye of God, to the
establishment of his Churche, and to the tranquilitie of the realme. And thus much
for the first parte shall suffice.

For the seconde, there is to be considered what thinges by private wealthe's devise
have[7] bene practized and put in ure within this realme, contrary or hurtefull to the
common wealthe of the same, for which noe lawes be yet provided; and whether the
lawes before this tyme made be / sufficient to redresse the enormityes they were mente   f.107
to remove; and whether any lawes made but for a tyme be meete to be continued for
ever, or any made to be perpetuall and yet meete to be continued but for a tyme or
presently to cease; besides, whether any lawes be to severe and to sharpe or to softe
and to gentle. To be short, you are to consider all other imperfeccions of lawes made
and all the wantes of lawes to be made, and thereupon to provide their meetest
remedyes respecting the nature and qualitie of the disorder and offence, the
inclination and disposition of the people, and the manner of the tyme.

4. MS reads 'theis three'; Harl.398 omits   6. MS reads 'noe'; this reading from
   'theis'.   Harl.398.

5. MS reads 'is to be'; Harl.398 omits 'to be'.   7. 'Have' supplied from Harl.398.

For the thirde and last (a marvailous matter), I cannot see how a good true English man can enter into the consideracion of it but it must breede in his breast two contrary effectes: comfort, I meane, and discomforte, joy and sadnes. For on the one part, how can a man, calling to his remembraunce that God of his devine power and ordynance hath brought the imperiall crowne of this realme to a princesse that soe noblie, diligentlie, willinglie and carefully doth by the advises of all the states of the realme seeke all the wayes and meanes that may be to reforme all disorders and thinges that be amisse, to continue and make firme that that is good, to assist and encourage those that be honest and iust, to correct and amend those that be dishonest and evill, to execute iustice in all poyntes to all parsons and at all tymes without rigor and extremitie, and to use clemency without indulgence and fonde pittie; a princesse, I say, that is not, nor never meaneth to be, so wedded to hir owne will and fantasie that for the satisfaction thereof she will doe any thinge that were likely to bring any bondage or servitude to her people, or give any iust occasion to them of any inwarde grudge, whereby any tumultes or sturres might rise as hath done of late dayes, thinges most pernicious and pestilent to the common wealth; a princesse that never meaneth nor intendeth for any private affection to advaunce the cause or quarrell of any forreigne power or potentate to the destruccion of her subiectes, to the losse of any her domynions, or to the impoverishing of her realmes; a princesse to whom nothing – what, nothing? – noe, noe worldly thinge under the sunne is so deare as the hartie love and good will of her nobles and subiectes, and to whom nothing is so odible as that that might cause or by any meanes procure the contrary: how can, I say, a man remember this wonderfull benefitt but of necessitie must needes hartely reioyce and give God thankes for the same? But, my Lordes, the handling of the princely vertues of this noble princesse, the causes of our reioycing, of purpose I pretermitte, partely because I have ever supposed it not altogether meete for this presence, but chiefly for that it requireth a perfect and excellent orator in whom both arte and nature concurre, and not to[8] me, a man in whom both fayles. Marye! I wish in my harte an apt parson might ofte have meete presence and iust occasion to handle this matter as the worthines of it requireth.

But as the causes of our reioysing for such respectes be (thankes be to God) both many and great, so for other respectes the causes of our sadnes and discomfort be f.107v   neither few nor little. / But here, upon great cause as a man perplexed and much amased, I stande not knowing what is best to be done. Very lothe I am to utter that which is most unpleasant for me to speake and as uncomfortable for you to heare. But because sores and woundes be hardly cured except they be opened and searched, therefore constrayned of necessitie I see I must trouble you with these sad matters. What man that either loveth his soveraigne, his countrie, or hymselfe thinketh of and weyeth the great decayes and losses in honnor, strength, and treasure, yea and the perill otherwise that hath happened to this imperiall crowne of late tyme, but must needes inwardly and earnestly lament and bewayle the same? Could there have happened to this imperiall crowne a greater losse in honour, strength and treasure then to loose that peece, Callice I meane, which was in the beginning so nobly wonne and hath of longe tyme so honorably and pollitikely in all ages and tymes and against all attemptes both of force and treason bene defended and kept? Did not the keeping of this breed feare to our mightiest enemyes and made our faynte freindes the more assured and the lother to breake? Yea, hath not the wynninge and keeping of this bred throughout Europe honorable opinion and reporte of the English nation? Agayne, what one thinge so much as this hath preserved and guarded your[9] marchantes in all their traffiques and entercourses, or hath bin so great an helpe for the well uttering of our chiefe commodities, or what so much as this hath kept a great part of our sea coastes from spoyling and robbing? To be short, the losses of this is much greater then I am well able to utter, and as yet, as I suppose, is able to be understanded of any.

And yet, my lordes, if this were the whole losse, then might men have some hope in tyme to come to recover that that in tyme hath bin thus sodainely and strangely lost. But when a man looketh furder and considereth the marvailous decaye and waste of the revenewe of the Crowne, the inestimable consumption of the treasure levied both of the Crowne and of the subiect, the exceeding losse of municion and artillerie, the great losse of divers valiant gentlemen, men of very good service, the incredible sommes of money owing at this presente and in honour due to be payde, and the biting interest that is to be answered for the forbearing of this debt; and therewith remembring the strength and mightines of the enemy and his confederates, and how ready he is upon every occasion upon every side and in every tyme to anoye you, and how the tyme most meete[10] for that purpose draweth on at hand; agayne, if a man consider the huge and wonderfull charge newlie growne to the Crowne, more then ever before hath bin wonte, and now of necessitie to be continued – as first the mayntenance of garrison in certaine places on the sea coastes, as Portesmouthe and others, with new munition and artillerie, besides the new increased charge for the continuall mayntenance of the English navy to be ever in readines against all evill happes, the strongest wall and defence that can be against the enemyes of this iland; and further also the new augmentacion of charge for the mayntenance of garrison at Barwick and the ffrontiers northwarde – / indeed, I must confesse that in thease matters mine understanding is but small and mine experience and tyme to learne lesse, but, in mine opinion, this doth exceed the auncient yearely revenues of the crowne, besides that double so much is of necessitie to be presentlye spent about the fortefyinge of theis places in buildinges. When, I say, a man remembreth and well considereth these thinges, it maketh hym so farre from hope of recovery of that that is lost without some ayde or contribucion of the subiect, that he will iudge all to little to make and prepare good defence for that that is lefte. Heere perchaunce a question would be asked, and yet I would mervaile to heare a question made of so playne a matter: what should be the cause of all this? If it were asked, thus I meane to aunswere: that I thinke no man so blinde but seeth it, no man so deafe but hath heard it, nor no man so ignorant but understandeth it. Marry! withall, I thinke there is no man so hard harted, thinking of it, but must with a moiste eye pittie it, nor no man so unnaturall but for the restoring of it would adventure lande, lymme, yea, and lyfe.

f.108

8. *Sic* in MS and in Harl.398; Add.48065 reads 'in'.

9. *Sic* in MS and in Harl.398; Add.48065 reads 'her'.

10. 'Most meete' supplied from Harl.398.

But now to the remedyes, wherein onlye this I have to say: that as the well looking to the whole both loste and lefte universallie is the onely suer preservacion of everie one particularlie, so seemeth it of all congruence and reason meete that every one particularlie should, by all wayes and meanes readily and gladly according to his power, concurre and ioyne to relieve and assiste the whole universallie; neither can I see (thinges standing as they doe) how any that loveth his countrye or hath witt to forsee his owne suertie, can withdrawe from this. Is there any, trowe yee, so madde that having a raunge of howses in perrill of fyer, would not gladly plucke downe parte to have the rest preserved and saved? Doth not the wise merchant in every adventure of daunger give parte to have the rest assured? These cases well compared, small difference shalbe found. And for all this (a straunge matter and scarse credible) with how deafe an eare and how hardly the Queene's Majestie may endure to heare of any devise that should be burdenous to her subiectes I partly doe understand and divers other[s] perfectlye perceive. Is not the case marveilous pittifull that the necessitie and neede of this ragged and torne state by misgovernaunce should, by force, so bridle and restrayne the noble nature of such a princesse that she is not able to shew such liberalitie and bountifulnes to her servantes and subiectes as her harte and inclination disposeth her Highnes to? What a griefe and torment is this to a noble minde? What a griefe? Suerlie such a griefe as but by[11] a noble minde who feeles it cannot be sufficientlie understande. But for the more playne declaration of her Highnes' disposition in this matter, her Highnes hath commaunded me to say unto you, even from her owne mouthe, that were it not for the preservacion of yourselves and the suertie of the state, her Highnes would have sooner adventured her lyfe (which our Lord long preserve) then she would have adventured to trouble her loving subiectes with any offensive matter, or that should be burdenous or

f.108v   displeasante unto them. And for the further notefying of her / Highenes' minde heerin, she hath commaunded me for to say unto you, that albeit you yourselves see that this is noe matter of will, noe matter of displeasure, noe private cause of her owne, which in tymes past have bene sufficient for princes' pretences (the more pittie!), but a matter for the universall weale of this realme, the defence of our countrie, the preservacion of every man, his howse and familie particulerlie; yet her Majestie's will and pleasure is that nothing shalbe demaunded or required of her loving subiectes but that which they of their owne free will and liberallitie be well contented readily, gladly, franckly and freely to offer; so greate is the trust and confidence that she reposeth in them and the love and affection that her Highnes beareth towardes them, nothing at all doubting but that they will soe lovingly, carefully and prudentlie wey and consider this great and weightie matter that such provision shall out of hande be taken therein as her Highnes shalbe preserved in all honor and royall dignitie, and you and the rest of her loving subiectes in common quiette and suertie.

Now to make an end, the Queene's Majestie's pleasure is that you, her trustie and welbeloved knightes of her shieres and burgesses, according to your laudable custome shall repayre to your common howse, and there deliberately and advisedlie electe, or rather, amonge so many alreadie elect persons, selecte one both grave and discreete, who after he be by you presented and that presentacion by her Highnes admitted, shall then occupie the office and roome of your common mouth and speaker. And for[12] your day of presentacion the Queene's Majestie givethe you *etc.*[13]

11. MS reads 'to', as does Harl.398; this reading from Add.48065.

12. MS 'of'; this reading from Harl.398.

13. '*etc.*' supplied from Harl.398.

2. Lord Keeper's speech enabling the Speaker, 25 January

Text from BL Harl.5176. In three earlier copies, in Harl.398, Harl.1877 and Add.48065 (Yelverton 71), the speech is incorporated in another made by the Lord Keeper in the Star Chamber in 1568. *Other* MSS. London: BL Cott.Titus FI (and its copies, Harl.2185 and Stowe 358), Lansdowne 211 (which, although distinguishing this speech from that in the Star Chamber, retains the concluding paragraph from the inflated Star Chamber speech); University Library 300. Oxford: Bodley, Eng.Hist.d.144; Exeter College 127. Cambridge: University Library Ii.v.8 (as Lansd.211); Gonville and Caius College 64 (copy of Cott.Titus FI). California: Huntington Library, Ellesmere 2573, 2579. Washington: Folger Library 89.2, 7036.
Printed. D'Ewes, 15⁄16.

Harl.5176, fos.108v⁄9

An aunsweare to the oration of Sir Thomas Gargrave, chosen to be Speaker of the parliamente, disablinge himselfe thereunto, but yet admitted.

Sir Thomas Gargrave, the Queene's Majestie doth right well perceive and understande your comely and modest manner in the disablinge of your selfe to this office and rome whereunto her trustie and welbeloved knightes and burgesses have enabled and elected you, and doe now presently presente you. And therewith also hath heard your peticion and suite made with all humbleness and reverence for your dischardge in this matter. For answeare whereof, her Majestie hath commaunded me to say unto you that she thinketh yourselfe right well to understande that, by the orders and rules of good governaunce and pollicie, power and authoritie to receive or refuse any office of service in any common wealth should not be permitted to be in th' arbitramente of hym who is thereunto orderly called or appoynted; nor that the iudgement and decerninge of abilitie and disabilitie in service perteyneth to the person called, but to the caller, as doth right well appeare by a similitude that is olde and common, but / neithre unapte nor untrue. That is, like as to the heade of a naturall bodye perteyneth the appoyntmente and as it were the marshallinge of the same bodye to the particular service and office; so to the head of every bodye pollitique, be it empire, kingdome, or lesse state, belongeth immediatelye or mediatly derived, the assignement and admitting of every member of the bodye to his ministrye and dutie. And as the contrarye doinge in the former weare monstrous in nature, soe surely the contrary doing in the seconde were monsterous in reason. Now her Majestie having this authoritie in her as head of the pollitique bodye of this

f.109

realme, and therewith being crediblie informed of your approved fidelitie, wisdome and discretion, of the long experience that you have had in parliament matters, thinketh that if her Highnes should assente to your desire it should be preiudiciall both to the service of her Majestie and the common wealth of her realme. Besides also, for somuche as you have bene chosen and enabled to this office and place according to an auncient and laudable order by so many wise, sage and discreete knightes and burgesses, to whose iudgement and opinion her Highnes thinketh it meete and conveniente for her to have great regarde and to give much creditt and fayth, that for that respect also her Majestie may not conveniently graunt your peticion. Agayne, your selfe in seeking in humble and reverent manner your owne discharge by disablemente have in very deed by the well, comely, modest and orderly doing thereof given noe small cause whereby you are to be enabled.

And therefore her Majestie upon these respectes and divers other doth now presently admitte and approve this eleccion and presentacion made of you, nothing at all doubting but that you will with such diligence, faithfulness and circumspection use and exercise your office as thereby the good hope and expectacion that her Majestie hath conceived of you by that she hath heard of others already, shalbe, by that her selfe shall see and heare, not only confirmed but also increased and augmented; and so as her Highnes' loving subiectes of her common howse shall have neither iust cause to repente their election, her Majestie her admission, nor you your selfe th'assumpcion and taking upon you this chardge.

3. Lord Keeper's speech in reply to the Speaker's petitions, 25 January

Text from BL Harl.5176, copy.
Other MSS. London: BL Cott.Titus F1 (and its copies, Harl.2185 and Stowe 358). Oxford: Exeter College 127. Cambridge: Gonville and Caius College, 64 (copy of Cott.Titus F1). California: Huntington Library, Ellesmere 2579. Washington: Folger Library 89.2, 7036.
Printed. D'Ewes, 16-17.

An aunsweare to the Speaker's oration made after his admittance.

Maister Speaker, the Queene's Majestie hath hearde and doth well understande your wise and discreete oration full of good meaning, good will, and good matter, the effecte whereof as I take it may be devided into three partes: of those the first conteyneth the commendacion of the Queene's Highnes; the seconde certaine good wishes and desires of yours, honorable, profitable and commodious for the realme to be followed and put in execucion; the thirde divers peticions concerning the exercise of your office and the libertyes and priviledges of the common howse. For the first, the Queene's Majestie giveth you most hartie thankes as for a good exhortacion made to her Highnes to become such a one as yee have commended her for, but not acknowledging those vertues to be in her Highnes, marye, confessing that such as she hath be Gode's giftes and graces; and therewithall her Highnes wisheth (as she trusteth you all doe) that for Englande's sake there were as manye vertues in her as would serve for the good govermente of this her realme committed to her royall chardge, and desireth you all with her to give God daylie thankes for those that she hath, and to make humble peticion to graunte such increase of the rest as to his devine providence shalbe thought for his honour most meete. For the seconde, her Majestie trusteth and ver[il]y beleeveth that those good desires and wishes of yours are so deepely graven and perfectlie imprinted in the hartes of the hearers that the good successe and sequell that shall come thereof will evidentlie declare that you have not in vayne spoken them, nor they necligentlie hearde them. For the thirde and last, you have devided into theis fower peticions. The first, for your accesse to the Queene's Highnes and her nobles for your reportes and conference. The seconde, that you may be borne with if any thinge by you in your reportes be mistaken or overslipt, and that without preiudice of the Howse it might be better declared. The thirde, libertye of speeche for the well debating of matters propounded. The fourthe and last, that all the members of the Howse and their servantes may have the same freedome from all manner of suites as before tyme they used to have. To theis peticions the Queene's Majestie hath commaunded me to say unto you that her Highnes is right well contented to graunt them unto you as lardgely, as amplye and as liberallie as ever they weare graunted by any her noble progenitors, and to confirme the same with as great an authoritie, marye, with thease admonitions and cautions. First, that your accesse be voyde of importunitie, and for matters needefull, and in tymes convenient. For the second, that your diligence and / carefullness,   f.110 Maister Speaker, be such that the defaultes in that parte be as rare as may be, whereof her Majestie doubteth little. For the thirde, which is for libertie of speach, wherewith her Highnes is right well contented, but so as they be neither unmindfull nor uncarefull of their dutyes, reverence and obedience to their soveraigne. For the fourth and last, great heede would be taken that noe evill disposed person seeke of purpose that priviledge for the only defrauding of his creditors, and for the mayntenance of iniuryes and wronges. Theis admonicions being well remembered, her Majestie thinketh all the sayde libertyes and priviledges well graunted. To make an ende, only this I have to put you in minde, that in the sorteinge of your thinges you observe such order that matters of the greatest momente and most materiall to the state be chieflye and first sett forthe soe as they be not hindered by perticuler and private billes, to this purpose, that when theis matters be paste this assemblie may sooner take ende and men be licensed to take their ease. I have sayde.

4. Queen's reply to petition to marry, 10 February

Text from BL Lansd.94, copy.
Other MSS. London: BL Harl.6021 (Hayward's *Annals*: an independent version), Loans 29/240 (Duke of Portland MSS, Miscellaneous letters and papers: an independent version not far removed from Lansd.94); PRO SP Dom.Eliz.2/22 (as Duke of Portland, but incomplete), 41/4 (later copy of 2/22, misdated in Calendar). Oxford: Bodley, Rawlinson D723 (as Lansd.94). Cambridge: University Library Gg.iii.34 (as Duke of Portland). *Printed*. R. Grafton, *An Abridgement of the Chronicles of England* (1563), 179v-80 (as Duke of Portland); Holinshed, IV.178-9 (from Grafton, *op. cit.*); J. Hayward, *Annals*, ed. J. Bruce (Camden Society, 1840), 31-3 (from Harl.6021); D'Ewes, 46-7 (as Lansd.94, but taken from another MS, written by Alexander Evesham in 1590 from an untraced printed text); J. Stow, *Annales* (1631), 636-7 (from the Evesham MS); W. Camden, *Elizabeth* (1866 edn), 26-7 (an independent version from an unknown source).

Lansd.94, f.29 and v

Fryday the xth of Februarye. The answere of the Quene's Highnes to the peticion proponed unto hir by the lower howse concerning hir mariage.

As I have good cause, so do I give yow all my hartie thankes for the good zeale and loving care yow seme to have, as well towardes me as to the whole state of your countrie. Your peticion I perceyve consisteth of 3 partes, and myne answere to the same shall depend of twoe.

And to the first parte I may saye unto yow that from my yeares of understanding, syth I first had consideracion of my self to be borne a servitor of almightie God, I happelie chose this kynde of life in which I yet lyve, which I assure yow for myne owne parte hath hitherto best contented my self and I truste hath bene moost acceptable to God. From the which, if either ambition of high estate offered to me in mariage by the plesure and appoyntment of my prynce, wherof I have some recordes in this presence (as yow our Lord Threasorer well knowe); or if the eschuinge of the danger of myne ennemys or the avoyding of the perill of deathe, whose messenger or rather contynuall wacheman, the prince's indignation, was not litle tyme dailie before myne[1] eyes (by whose meanes, al[tho]ugh [I kno]we or iustlie may suspect, yet I[2] will not now[3] utter, or if the whole cause were in my sister hir self, I will not nowe burthen hir therewith, because I will not chardge the deade): if any of these, I saie, could have drawne or dissuaded me from this kynd of life, I had not now remayned in this estate wherin yowe see me. But so[4] constant have I[5] allwayes contynued in this determynacion, although my youth and woordes may seme to some hardlie to agree together, yet is it mooste true that at this daie I stand free from anie other meaninge that either I have had in tymes paste or have at this present; with which trade of life I am so throughlie acquainted that I truste God, who hath hitherto therin preserved and led me by the hand, will not nowe of his goodnes suffer me to goe alone.

For the other parte, the manner of your peticion I do well like of and take in good parte, because that it is simple and conteineth no limytacion of place or person. If it had bene otherwise, I muste nedes have myslyked it verie muche and thought it in yow a verie greate presumption, being unfitting and altogether unmete for yow to require them that may commande, or those to appoynte whose partes are to desire, or suche to bynd and lymite whose duties are to obaye, or to take upon yow to drawe my love to your lykinges or frame my will to your fantasies; for a guerdon constreined and a gifte frelie geven can never agree together. Nevertheles, if any of yow be in suspect, that whensoever it may please God to enclyne my harte to an other kynd of life, ye may well assure your selves my meaninge is not to do / or determyne   f.29v
anie thinge wherwith the realme may or shall have iuste cause to be discontented. And therefor put that cleane out of your heades. For I assure you — what creditt my assurance may have with yow I can not tell, but what creditt it shall desarve to have the sequel shall declare — I will never in that matter conclud any thing that shalbe preiudiciall to the realme, ffor the weale, good and safetie wherof I will never shune to spend my life. And whomsoever my chaunce shalbe to light apon, I truste he shalbe as carefull for the realme and yow — I will not saie as my self, because I can not so certenlie determyne of any other; but at the least wayes, by my good will and desire he shalbe such as shalbe as carefull for the preservacion of the realme and yow as my self. And albeit it might please almightie God to contynew me still in this mynde to lyve out of the state of mariage, yet it is not to be feared but he will so woorke in my harte and in your wisdomes as good provision by his healpe may be made in convenient tyme, wherby the realme shall not remayne destitute of an heire that may be a fitt governor, and peraventure more beneficiall to the realme then suche ofspring as may come of me. For although I be never so carefull of your well doinges and mynd ever so to be, yet may my issue growe out of kynde and become perhappes ungracious. And in the end, this shalbe for me sufficient, that a marble stone shall de[clare that a Queene, having raigned such a tyme, lived and][6] dyed a virgin.

And here I end, and take your cominge unto me in good parte, and give unto yow all eftsones my hartie thankes, more yet for your zeale and good meaning then for your peticion.

---

1. MS torn; missing words shown in square
   brackets supplied from Rawlinson D723.
2. 'I' supplied from Rawlinson D723.
3. MS torn; 'now' supplied from Rawlinson
   D723.
4. 'So' supplied from Rawlinson D723.
5. 'I' supplied from J. Stow, *Annales* (1631).
6. MS torn; missing words supplied from
   Rawlinson D723.

5. Lord Keeper's speech at close of Parliament, 8 May

Text from BL Harl.5176. Earlier copies in Harl.398 and Add.48065 (Yelverton 71), from which some alternative readings have been taken, are not on the whole as reliable (both are misdated).
Other MSS. London: BL Cott.Titus F1 (and its copy, Harl.2185), Lansd.211 (misdated), Harl.1877 (misdated and contains only the section on the execution of laws); University Library 300 (two copies, both misdated). Oxford: Bodley, Eng.Hist.d.144 (misdated); Exeter College 127. Cambridge: University Library Dd.iii.20, Ii.v.8; Gonville and Caius College 64 (copy of Cott.Titus F1). Herts.CRO: Gorhambury xii.B.2. Dublin: TCD E.1.34 (misdated). California: Huntington Library, Ellesmere 2573 (misdated), 2579. Washington: Folger Library 89.2, 1276.10 (misdated), 7036.
Printed. D'Ewes, 32-5.

Harl.5176, fos.110-14

An oration made the eight of May in the parliament howse before the Queene's Maiestye the parliament then ending being in *anno Domini 1559*.

Maister Speaker, the Queene's Majestie hath heard how discreetely and wisely you have declared the proceedinges of this session in the common howse. For aunswere whereunto and for the better significacion to be made to my lordes heere of the upper howse of her iudgement of the parliament men and thease parliament matters, her Majestie's pleasure and commaundement is that I shall open and utter unto you three thinges. The one is what her Highnes understandeth by your doinges in this parliament of your wisdome and diligence. The seconde of your liberalitie and benevolence and therewith how comfortable the former is and how thankefull the seconde is. The thirde what her Highnes would have you doe for the good execucion of the lawes now devised by you, and of the rest heretofore devised by others. And here, my lordes and maisters all, albeit / in labouring to beare this burden I am much more like to fall then but[1] to fainte under it, because neither I am able to performe it as the Queene's Highenes hath commaunded it, nor as your desertes iustly crave it, nor as my will wisheth and desireth it; neverthles my trust is that ye will pardon my weakenes and wante so as no note of arrogancie or follye be ascribed to me for it, seing as you knowe by dutie driven I doe it. I had rather, and I knowe it were much better for me to be silent, and soe to have noe neede of your pardon, then by speache to all your paynes in hearinge, and to mine owne also in speaking, to deserve to pray it, if mine office would so suffer. But now to the matter.

f.110v

For the first parte, when her Majestie considereth how in the debatinge of the great and weightie causes of this parliament ye have banished all sodaine, rash and swifte proceedinges, daungerous enemyes to all good councells, and in place thereof have taken such conveniente tyme and leysure as the weightines of the matters for their better consideracion hath required; and againe what freedome of speeche hath bene used and permitted for the playne declaracion of every man's knowledge and conscience, yea, how men in some cases and some places have bin rather by gentle perswasion provoked thereto then by any sharpe manner of speeche of men of councell disswaded therefro; and therewith also how learnedly and cunningly the disputable matters being of momente have bene argued and reasoned, how gravely and deepely weyed and considered, how advisedly and considerately resolved and concluded; and lastly with what well nighe an universall consent and agremente they have bene by you enacted and established, besides remembring also your great studyes, endeavors and diligences for the opening and declaringe what might be saide *pro et contra* in all cases of doubte to the ende (as it seemeth to her Highnes) that when all was sayde and hearde on both partes that by any of you could be inferred or produced, then that which thereupon should for all respectes appeare to stand most with the honor and glory of God and the common wealth of the realme might be the better and safelyer agreed upon and determyned: when her Majestie (I saye) /   f.111 remembreth and considereth thease thinges, she saithe she cannot but muche commende and allowe your wisdomes and diligences herein greatly to her comforte and consolacion, and much to all your prayses and commendacion. For now her Highenes verely trusteth that like as noe manner of determinacion in Parliament neyther can ne ought by any private man be infringed or undone, soe thease determinacions of yours in this fourme begonne, proceeded and concluded cannot hearafter iustly, no,[2] not by wordes be impugned or gaynesaide: ffor seing all men have thus at leisure and with libertie upon the making of theis lawes franckly declared their opinions and knowledge like wise and learned men, soe the lawes being made and past her Highenes doubteth nothing but that they will like good, humble and obedient subiectes willingly and humbly yeelde and submitte themselves to the lawe as to the thinge whereby eache man inioyeth his livinge, libertie and lyfe, and the rather also because that no man in obeyinge the lawes made at this session being of the greatest moment should thereby be forced any otherwise to doe then either hymselfe hath by lawe alreadie done, or els others have before this tyme done, whom both for wisdome, vertue and learning it shall not be unseeming any man here (without offence be'it spoken) to followe and take example of. And thus muche for the first parte.

For the seconde – which concerneth your liberalitye and benevolence – her Majestie hath commaunded me to saye unto you that your wise and grave consideracion had and used in the grauntinge of a present ayde and reliefe towardes the relieving and dischardging of the presente chardge, wherewith the realme at this tyme of her comming to the crowne was and yet is charged, is by her Highenes taken in

---

1. 'But' supplied from Harl.398.   2. 'No' supplied from Harl.398.

thankefull parte. And soe is the restitucion of the continuall revenue[3] as some supplymente towardes the mayntenaunce of the continuall chardge of late tyme growen to the crowne, as you have heard, and of necessitie to be continued aswell for the suertie of you all as for the conservacion of the whole estate. And here my lordes

f.111v and maisters all, I take it to be my dutie to doe you to understande of certaine noble / and princely observacions and consideracions had by her Highenes of thease your doinges, much suerlie to all your comfortes, whereof one is in that she forgetteth not that thease grauntes be made not by subiectes that have of longe tyme bene free from all manner of taxes, lones and subsedyes, and so well able to beare this burden, but by subiectes – much to her griefe when she thinketh of it – that have bene well nigh continually charged and burdened with theis thinges to the universall impoverishing of the whole realme and (that worse is) noe wayes to the strengtheninge, amendinge or honouring of the same, but rather to the weakeninge, decayinge and dishonouring thereof: playnely to speake, shrewed effectes to followe soe contrary causes, and bitter fruites to be brought forthe by soe plentifull plantes, whereby it is evidente, yea, and to evidente (if it pleased God otherwise) that thease supplymentes are to be borne not of your superfluityes but rather of your necessities, marye, of necessitie also so to be, to withstande a greater necessitie which otherwise might touche you and all others in suertie. The seconde observacion is your readynes and willingnes in graunting, whereof her Majestie maketh a very great accoumpte, perceyvinge thereby that neither sharpe nor warme wordes, nor yet earnest or longe perswasions, used amongst you have drawen you to this, but that the same hath rather bene by you willinglie, readilye and franckly offered then by any of the meanes above remembred at your handes craved, a playne and a manifest argumente that theis your grauntes have altogether proceeded from the benevolent mindes and heartie affections that you beare to your soveraigne ladye and countrie, which benevolence and affection her Majestie accepteth and taketh for the greatest benefitte and most pretious jewell that a subiect can present to his soveraigne. And to be shorte in this matter if '*Bis dat qui cito dat*'[4] be a true sayinge you deserve great commendacion for your small staying. Hereunto also her Highenes addeth a thirde, that is the generalitie of the consente to thease grauntes, knowing with what difficultie and diversitie of opinions in some tymes past thease thinges have been brought to passe. It is a certaine and infallible grounde that every good thinge the greater it is the better it is; nowe this unanimitye in consentinge being (as

f.112 undoubtedly it is) a good thinge, hath not her Majestie / (trowe yee) to reioyce in the universallitie thereof? Yes, surely, and thinkes and thankes you therefore accordinglye. To make an ende of this parte her Highnes hath speciallye commaunded me to saye unto you that when she calleth to remembraunce what you have graunted, who hath graunted, and the fourme of grauntinge, she findeth herselfe earnestly disposed, if your suertyes and the states would soe suffer, as freely to remitte thease grauntes as you did gladly graunt them. And where in tymes past long and vehement perswasions have bene in thease cases used to such as occupyed your places, for the greate diligence and carefull circumspeccion to be had for the true leveyinge of that which hath bene graunted, for the common numbers respecte altogether themselves as private men, and not themselves as members of the whole bodye, whereby against all reason and righte the realme hath bin often defrauded of the greatest parte of the benevolence graunted: this notwithstanding, her Highenes hath willed me heerein to use fewe woordes and onely for theis respectes, least else those which have shewed such liberalitie and benevolence in grauntinge might seeme to be suspected by her either of fidelitie or diligence in levyeinge, whereof she thinketh her selfe assured, and thereupon reposinge her truste she doubteth nothing but by your good service theis thinges shalbe as truly aunswered as they have bene gladly graunted, and that this faythfull trust thus reposed by her Highenes in your true service shall serve her to better purpose then any wordes that could be spoken by me on her Majestie's behalfe. And besides she thinketh (which is to be noted much, surely) that it were better to adventure the losse of a great parte of that which is graunted (which she hopeth shall not happen) by speaking to little then to adventure the diminishing of any parte of that she taketh her selfe assured of (your benevolente myndes I meane) by speaking one worde to much.

Nowe to the thirde and last which conteyneth the Queene's Majestie's pleasure for the well executinge of lawes. Here, my lordes and maisters all, remembring your wisdomes and fidelityes, albeit that it be not much needefull to put you in minde to how small purpose good lawes doe serve being not daylie and diligently executed, yet because the aunciente order hath bene that somewhat should be sayde for your remembraunce in theis matters, therefore it is thought meete that I should trouble you with a few wordes. I am suer you all iudge if a man / would be very diligente to   f.112v provide a fayre sorte of torches to guide hym in his goeing by nighte, and yet would be as necligente in lightinge any of them when he goeth in the darke, should shewe a notable poynte of follye, much like to a man that seeking to clense his garden and grounde from weedes and bryers carefully provideth many sharpe and meete tooles and instrumentes for that purpose and when he hath so done, layeth them all fayre up in a howse without occupyinge any of them. And is it not as great a fondenes (trowe yee) for men to use their indeavors to make good lawes to governe men's doinges and to weede out those that be evill in the common wealth and thereupon to binde them fayre in bookes and so lay them up without seing to the execucion of those lawes? Yes, surely, wherefore yee see that as there hath bene used by you great wisdome and discretion in devisinge of some, soe is it very necessary that like diligence and payne be taken by you and others in seeinge to the good execucion of all, the effecte of which chardge consisteth principally in three poyntes: the first in conservacion of the Queene's peace; the seconde in the administracion of iustice betweene subiect and subiecte; the thirde in the observacion of one uniforme order in religion accordinge to the lawes now established. For the first, yee are to forsee the avoyding of all manner of frayes, forces, ryottes and rowtes, and the discoveringe and revealinge in tyme of all manner of conspiracyes, confederacyes and conventicles; and in this parte also you are to provide for the swifte and speedie appeasing of all manner of tumultes, sturres and uprores if any happen, and for the diligent and

---

3. The clerical first fruits and tenths.

4. Though the maxim has been attributed to Seneca, its origin probably rests with

Publius Syrus (*Sententiae*, li.235), who, however, has '*celeriter*' rather than '*cito*'.

severe punishment of all manner of fellonyes, burglaries, and such other like enormyties, matters as you knowe against the Queene's Majestie's peace, crowne and dignitie: ffor the well doinge whereof two thinges are chiefly to be eschewed. The one is slothfulnes, the other is uncarefulnes; for how can iustice banish thease enormityes where her ministers be so slouthfull that they will never creepe out of their dores to any courte, sessions or assises for the due administracion thereof, excepte they be drawne thereto by some matters of their owne, nor cannot endure to have their eares troubled with hearinge of controversies of their neighbours for the good appeasinge of the same, or how can the uncarefull man that maketh noe accoumpt of

f.113   any of the common causes of his countrie / but respecteth onely his private matters and commoditie become a diligent searcher out, follower and corrector of felons, murderers, and such like common enemyes to the common wealthe? And yet true it is that such careles and slouthful men doe dayly courten[5] and cloke these their faultes with the title of quietnes, coveting to be counted good and quiet men where in very deed they seeke only ease, profitt and pleasure to them selves, and that to be sustayned and borne by other men's cares and labours as drones doe among bees; but if every man should doe soe who seeth not but that thinges would runne shortely to ruine in defaulte of order, for they may easilye iudge that it is a madnes to seeke the conservacion of any perticular member, and to suffer the whole bodye to decaye? But being well served by some men's opinions, as they care for none, so should none care for them, or els (that better were in mine opynion) they would be used by men as drones be used by bees. And thus much for this parte. For the seconde, yee are to provide that all embraceryes, mayntenaunces and champerties, the utter enemyes to the due execucion of iustice betweene subiecte and subiecte, be neither committed by any of you, nor yet, as neere as you can, be suffered to be committed by any others – a very behoovefull matter to be both carefully and earnestly looked unto as unto the roote and feede of all iniustice – and specially if any of thease faultes light upon any person that hath authoritie and rule in the countrie or hath an office of iustice to execute amongste the people. Is it not (trowe you) a monsterous disguisinge to have a iusticer a maynteyner, to have hym that should by his othe and dutie set forthe iustice and righte, against his othe and dutie offer iniurye and wronge, to have him that is specially chosen amongste a number by the prince to appease all brablings and controversies, to be a sower and maynteyner of strife and sedition amongst them, seeking his reputacion and opynion by leading and sweyinge of iuryes accordinge to his will, acquiteinge some for gayne, inditeinge other for mallice, bearing with him as his servante, overthrowinge the other as his enemye, procuringe all questmongers to be of his liverye or otherwise in his daunger, that his winkes, frowninges and countenances may direct all inquestes? Surely, surelye, it is true that thease be they that be subverters and perverters of all lawes and orders, yea, that make dayly the lawes that of thier owne nature be good to become instrumentes of all iniurye and

f.113v   mischiefe; / thease indeede be they of whom such examples would be made as of the founders and maynteyners of all enormities, and theas be those whom, if yee cannot reforme for their greatnes, yee ought heere to complayne of for their evillnes. And thus much for the due administracion of justice. And as to the thirde, which is the observacion of one uniforme order in religion, you are to[6] indeavor yourselves to the best of your powers and understandinge, draweinge together by one lyne in all poyntes, to further, sett forthe and maynteyne the same, which by greate and deliberate advise heere in Parliamente hath ben established: and here great observacion and watche would be had of the withdrawers and hinderers thereof and speciallie of those that subtillye by indirecte meanes seeke or procure the contrarye. Amongst thease I meane to comprehende aswell those that be to swifte as those that be to slowe, those, I say, that goe before the lawe or beyond the lawe, as those that will not followe. For good governaunce cannot be where obedience fayleth and both theise alike breaketh the rules of obedience, and these be those which by all likelyhode should be beginners, maynteyners and uphoulders of all faccions and sectes, the very mothers and nurces to all sedicions and tumultes, which necessarilye bringe forthe destruccion and depopulacion: of thease therefore greate heede woulde be taken, and upon thease being founde, sharpe and severe correccion accordinge to the order of lawes would be imposed and that in the beginninge, and without respecte of persons, as upon the greatest adversaryes that can be to unitie and concorde, without which noe common wealth can longe endure and stande, whereupon you knowe all our standinge and falling whollie consisteth and the suertye of our Soveraigne alsoe. A matter most marvellous, that the lawe whereby men possesse all that they have, and their lives alsoe, should not be able to directe men's accions so as thereby all faccions and sectes, founded for the more parte eyther upon will or upon the glory of men's wittes and invencions, should not sufficiently be repressed and brideled. Now for the handesome bridelinge of the ffaccions of men, I see not that a better way can be taken then is used by the horsemaister, whoe provideth for the good governance of his horse bittes or brakes accordinge to the tendernes or hardenes of his mouthe, whereunto he addeth a certaine and well taught hande. And like as it is very well to be allowed that none other bitte or brake should be provided for thease faccious folkes then by lawe may be forged, soe where it not meete that any of that kinde, be it never so sharpe, should be omitted if the case soe requireth, and this woulde be executed by a certaine and well taught hande: ffor it cannot be but the winkeinge or withdrawing / from medlinge in this matter, or the   f.114 remisse and loose handelinge thereof, must of necessitie overthrowe in tyme the whole that is done, and soe shall you loose the whole fruites of all your labours, and putt your selves, your countrye and the Queene's Maiestye also (whom our Lord preserve) in perill, which nowe being warned you may easilye see and provide for. And this is all that at this tyme I have to saye. And therefore here to make an ende, her Majestie is contented according to your peticion to graunte her royall assente to such ordinaunces and lawes as be[7] devised and agreed upon by you in such order and forme as by the clarke of the parliament according to that auncient order shalbe redde and declared. I have sayde. Reade, Clerke.[8]

---

5. I.e. curtain.
6. 'To' supplied from Harl.398.
7. MS has 'bene'; this reading from Harl.398.

8. 'Reade, Clerke' supplied from Gorhambury xii.B.2.

THE SECOND PARLIAMENT
FIRST SESSION
11 JANUARY ⁄ 10 APRIL 1563

Documents

SEPARATES: HOUSE OF LORDS[1]
1. Lords' petition, 1 February
2. Lord Keeper's speech to the Queen in her gallery at Westminster, (?) March

SEPARATES: HOUSE OF COMMONS
1. The order of proceeding to the Parliament and opening proceedings, 12 January
2. Lord Keeper's opening speech, fuller version
3. Sir Ralph Sadler's speech on the succession
4. Common's petition, 28 January
5. Queen's answer to the Commons' petition, 28 January
6. Robert Atkinson's speech on the oath of supremacy, (?) March
7. Sir William Cecil's speech on fish days
8. Closing proceedings and speeches, 10 April
9. Separate texts of the Queen's speech at the close of session, 10 April

---

1. Montague's speech against stiffer penalties for recusancy is not included: though Strype (*Annals of the Reformation*, 1824 edn, I.i, 442⁄6) cited a Foxe MS as his source no MS version of the speech has come to light (see n.7, p.5).

Although it had been summoned for Monday 11 January this session was not opened until the following day. As in 1559 'fowle weather' was in part responsible for the delay.[1] Documents 1 and 8 are important guides to the impressive procedure involved in assembling and dispersing Parliament: elaborate ritual of procession; summoning the estates to learn of the sovereign's intentions; the instruction to the Commons to elect a Speaker and the subsequent ceremony securing his election and presentation; and finally, his customary requests to the Queen at the end of the session and her response to them, are all here, and with material from 1559 and 1566 in particular, reveal much of the framework for parliamentary business.

Cecil expected that the session would be short and would occupy itself with granting a subsidy and the process of legislative reform: indeed Lord Keeper Bacon once again unfolded the Queen's view of the assembly along these lines, stressing that the Commons use their privileges with discretion and urging that business should be dealt with 'so speedilie as can be, whereby this assembly may be again at their liberties'.[2] But the problem of 1559 which had produced the petition to Elizabeth for her marriage remained, and it had been stressed by the smallpox attack of 1562. It was in these circumstances that Bacon spoke of propounding matters of God's honour and glory and providing for the safety of the commonwealth.[3] As the session went on the depth of feeling on such matters became clear. For many, the safety of the commonwealth could only be guaranteed if Elizabeth married and secured the succession. The alternatives were only too clear: civil strife and the possible triumph of a foreign and Catholic candidate. We may never know exactly when Sir Ralph Sadler drafted his speech on the succession or whether it was delivered, but it is included here as an introduction to the many subsequent parliamentary statements on the matter.[4] It shows how powerful nationalist feeling could become on either side of the Border and how a considerable body of English opinion revolted against the thought of a 'strange prynce over us'. Fears of that kind emerged in a Commons petition [Doc.4] drawn up on 17 January by a committee including Privy Councillors in its membership, and presented to Elizabeth at Whitehall on 28 January.[5] It is worth noting that the petitioners perhaps took Bacon

1. *EP*, I.41; BL Cott.Titus F1, f.59; *CJ*, I.62.

2. BL Cott.Titus F1, f.75v.

3. *EP*, I.86-7; T. Wright, *Queen Elizabeth and her Times* (1838), I.121; BL Cott. Titus F1, f.66; Harl.5176, f.89.

4. Doc.3; *EP*, I.104; Sadler had been engaged in negotiations with the Scots on border problems and, more recently, with the Protestants there. He was to become a Privy Councillor in 1566.

5. *CJ*, I.62-3.

at more than his word when they justified themselves by referring to his injunction to consider first matters of major importance for the preservation of the realm: they saw the early settlement of both the marriage and the succession as essential to that task.[6] The document is interesting too in that it dealt with Elizabeth's repeatedly expressed opinion that a known order of succession would increase rather than decrease the possibility of destructive factional disputes. The Queen's answer was short, but not as much to the point as the Commons wished [Doc.5]. She may indeed have virtually promised to marry when the time was right, but she also made great play of the Commons' declared total dependence on the 'feeble thread' of her life, and reminded them harshly that she, and she alone, had saved them from disaster. But however Elizabeth reacted in this reply to the activities of these supplicants, she none the less gave apparent sanction once more to the petition when she approved 'the matter and some thereof.'

The Lords presented their own petition four days later on 1 February [Lords Doc.1].[7] It fully supported the Commons, stressed the practical constitutional difficulties following the death of a sovereign with no known successor, and insisted that the two issues of marriage and succession should not be separated and should be solved before the end of the session. This positive attempt to constrain the Queen to act along well-defined lines produced little more than anger, though we have unconfirmed reports that consideration was given to a bill which would have limited the succession to a number of named candidates.[8] Certainly in a second petition drawn up by the Lords [Lords Doc.2] no mention was made of the succession issue. But on the question of marriage there was no relaxation of pressure: indeed the text bears a strong resemblance to their first petition. Though we cannot be sure that Bacon uttered this oration, or if he did when he did so, the draft speech is evidence of the persistent anxiety, even desperation, of the Queen's principal subjects.[9]

The end result of this concerted parliamentary pressure was the well-known, though not so well understood, speech which Bacon himself had to read for Elizabeth to the assembled Lords and Commons at the end of the session. Several versions are printed here, including Elizabeth's own heavily amended draft [Docs.8, 9]. Much attention was lavished on a text whose prose remained baffling: well might Bacon doubt his 'owne opening thereof and therefore desyre her Majestie that her meaninge might be written.'[10] After her earlier speech she can have done nothing here to quieten the anxiety of her audience.

Preoccupied though the Commons may have been by marriage and succession their attention could not be monopolized by these issues. A closely connected, though distinct, matter was the survival of the Anglican settlement and many, including the government it seems, considered that the time had come to stiffen the penalties for those refusing to take the oath of supremacy. Members in committee surpassed the government in the severity of their proposals and carried wide, though not unanimous, support with them. Robert Atkinson, member for Appleby and lawyer of the Inner Temple, voiced a number of objections. Taking offence against the notion of the penalties of treason being applied to religious offenders, he argued that the maximum penalty permitted by preachers was excommunication; and he appealed to the proposition that religious conviction must be felt from within and not imposed from without by force. Finally, he attempted to demonstrate that the bill, if it were passed, could not succeed in its stated purpose of guaranteeing the Queen's power [Doc.6]. The same notion – that the bill before the House could not succeed in its stated purpose – emerged, curiously enough, in Cecil's speech for the maintenance of the Navy [Doc.7]. It is the fullest surviving record of any of his parliamentary speeches, and the only real glimpse of the debate behind the social and economic legislation of the session beyond the official *Commons Journals* entries. In this remarkable instance Cecil argued with fastidious logic (and contrary to the spirit of the title at the head of his text) that making Wednesday a fish day could have no substantial effect on the strength of the Navy. The bill passed however, and Wednesday became Cecil's fast.[11]

On the afternoon of Saturday 10 April the session came to an end. Speaker Williams reminded the Queen yet again of the Commons' hope that she would marry, asked her to give her assent to the bills they had passed and to accept their humble gift of the subsidy. In his turn the Lord Keeper expressed Elizabeth's thanks for supply, regretting that it had been necessary to ask for it, and stressed the need for thorough execution of any laws which might receive the royal assent. He then read Elizabeth's speech on marriage and succession. The bills which had passed both Houses were dealt with by the Queen, and Bacon announced the first prorogation of the parliament until October of that year: subsequent prorogations meant that it did not meet again until 30 September 1566.

6. BL Harl.5176, f.89, or Cott.Titus FI, f.75v, for this possible interpretation of Bacon's speech.
7. *EP*, I.109 thus dates the document.
8. *EP*, I.111-12.
9. *EP*, I.112.
10. BL Cott.Titus FI, f.80v.
11. *EP*, I.114-16.

1. [House of Lords] Lords' petition, 1 February

Text from PRO SP Dom.Eliz.27/35, a clerk's copy with marginal notes by Cecil, but containing a number of misreadings, corrected here from BL Add.32379.

Other MSS. London: BL Cott.Titus F1 (and its copies, Harl.2185 and Stowe 358, which is incomplete), Harl.1877, Harl.5176 (misdated), Lansd.211, Sloane 105, Stowe 354, Add.35838, Add.48065 (Yelverton 71); PRO SP Dom.Eliz.27/37 (late copy of 35); University Library 300 (2 copies). Oxford: Bodley, Eng.Hist.d.144, Carte 105, Tanner 79 (misdated in catalogue); Exeter College 127 (preceded by a description of the delivery of the petition on 1 Feb. 1563). Cambridge: University Library Dd.iii.20, Gg.iii.34, Ii.v.8; Corpus Christi College 543 (misdated); Gonville and Caius College 64 (copy of Cott.Titus F1). Herts. CRO: Gorhambury xii.B.2. Northants. CRO: Fitzwilliam of Milton Political 95. Longleat, Wilts.: Bath, Dudley iii.39. Dublin: TCD E.1.34
Printed. D'Ewes, 105–7 (misplaced under 1566).

SP Dom.Eliz.27/35

[Endorsement in Cecil's hand on SP Dom.Eliz.27/36, applying to 35 also: '*anno v° Elizabethae*

The orations made in the parlement by the Lordes and Commons with the Queene's Majestie's answer therto.']

1563 An humble sute and peticion made by all the lordes spirituall and temporall unto the Quene's most excellent Majestie our most gratious soveraigne Lady.

Most humbly besecheth your excellent Majestie your faithfull, loving and obedient subiectes all your lordes, both spirituall and temporall assembled in Parliament in your upper howse, to be so much their good lady and sovereigne as according to your accustomed benignity to graunte a gracious and favorable hearing to their peticions and sutes which with all humblenes and obeysance they are come hither to present to your Majestie, by my mouth, in matters nearely[1] and dearly towching your most royall person, the'imperiall crowne of this your realme, and th'universall weale of the same. Which sutes, for that they do tend to the suerty and preservation of these three[2] thinges, your person, crowne and realme, the dearest iewelles that my lordes have in the earth, therfore they think them selves for diverse respectes greatly bound to make these peticions: as[3] first by their dutie towardes God, then by their allegiaunce to your Highnes, and lastly by the[4] faith they ought to beare to their naturall contry. And like as, most gratious soveraigne Lady, by these bondes they shuld have ben bounde[5] to have made the like peticions upon like occasion to any prince that it shuld have pleased God to have appointed to reigne over them: so they think them selves doble bounden to make the same to your Majestie, considering that besides the bondes before remembred they stand also bound so to do by the great and manifold benefittes that they have and dayly do receave at your Highnes' handes, which (shortly to speke) be as great as the fruites of peace and commen quiett, mercy and iustice can give, and this with great care and charge[6] to you self. And thus my lordes diverslye[7] bound, as your Majestic hath hard, are nowe to open to your Majestie their humble peticions and suites, consisting in two poyntes, which not sonderly nor th'one without the other, but both ioyntly they humbly desire your Highnes to assent unto. The former is that it wold please your Majestie to dispose your self to mary, where it shall please you, with whom it shall please yow, and assone as it shall please you. The second, that some suche[9] certen limitacion might be made how th'imperiall crowne of this realme shuld remain if God call your Highnes without any heire of your body (which our Lord defend) as these your lordes and nobles and other your subiectes then living might sufficiently understand to whom they shuld owe their allegiances and duties due to be don by subiectes, and that they might by your Majestie's license and by your favour commune, treate and conferre together this parliament time for the well doing of this.

1 A petition to marry wher, with whom, and as soone as shall pleas
2 For the succession[8]

The former of these two, which is your mariage, they do in their hartes most ernestly wish and pray for, as a thing that must nedes brede and bring great and singuler comforte to your self and unspeakeable ioy and gladness to all true English hartes. But the second carieth with it such necessity that without it they can not see how the safety of your royall person, the preservation of your imperiall crowne and realme shall, or can be, sufficiently provided for.

1 Marriage

2 Succession

Most gratious soveraigne Lady, the lamentable and pitifull state and condition wherin all your nobles and counsellors of late were when it pleased God to lay his heavy hand over you, and the amazednes that most men of understandinge were, by the bruite that grewe by that sicknes, broughte unto,[10] is one cause of this peticion.

The Queene's Majestie's sicknes

The second, the aptnes and oportunity of the time, by reason of this parliament, wherby both such advise, consideration and consent as is requisite in so great and weighty a cause, may be better had and used now then at any other time when no parliament is.

The third, for that th'assenting to, and performing of these peticions can not (as

3

1. MS reads 'merely'; this reading from Add.32379.
2. MS reads 'two'; this reading from Add.32379.
3. MS reads 'and'; this reading from Add.32379.
4. MS reads 'their'; this reading from Add.32379.
5. MS reads 'bold'; this reading from Add.32379.
6. 'And charge' supplied from Add.32379.
7. 'Diverslye' supplied from Add.32379.
8. Marginal notes are in Cecil's hand.
9. 'Suche' supplied from Add.32379.
10. MS reads 'and the amasednes by the brute that grew of that sicknes, that brought most men of understanding unto'; this reading from Add.32379.

they think) but brede terror to your enemyes, and therfore must of necessity bring great suerty to your person, and specially by addicion of such lawes as may be ioyned to this limitacion for the certen and sure observing of it, and preserving of your Majestie against all practises and chances.

4   The fourth cause, for that the like (as is supposed) hath ben don by diverse of your noble progenitors both of old time and late dayes, and also by other princes your neighbours of the gretest state of Europe, and for that experience hath tought that good[11] hath come of it.

5   The vth, for that it appeareth by histories how in times past persons inheritable to crownes, being votaries and relligious, to avoyde such dangers as might have happened for want of succession to kingdomes, have left their vowes and *Constantia 50* monasteries and taken them selves to mariage: as[12] Constantia, a nonne, and heire to *annorum* the kingdome of[13] Cisell, maried after fifty yeres of age to Henry the vj[th] Emperor of that name,[14] and had issue Friderike the Second; and likewise Peter of Aragon being a monk, maried the better to establish and pacify that kingdome.[15] Againe, Antoni[n]us Pius is asmuch commended for that, not two dayes before his death, he saied to his counsaile, '*Laeto animo morior, quia filium vobis relinquo*', as Pyrrhus is of all godly men detested for sayeng he wold leave his realme to him that had the sharpest sword. What but want of a successor knowen made so short an end of so great an empire as Alexander the Great did leave at his death?

6   The sixt cause is for that my lordes doo iudge[16] the performing of this will brede such an universall and inward contentacion, satisfaction, ioy and gladnes in the hartes of all your true and loving subiectes that is likely and probable[17] yow shall find them in all your[18] commandementes redy and glad to adventure their goodes, landes and lives in your Highnes' service according to their bounden duties, which of necessity must brede greate suerty also to your Majestie.

7   The seventh, because the not doeing of this, if God shuld call your Highnes without heire of your body – which God grante be never seen, if it be his will, and yet your Majestie right well knoweth that princes and their ofspring, be they never so great, never so strong, never so like to live, be yet mortall and subiect every day, yea, every hower to Godde's call; my lordes think this happening and no limitacion made, can not by their iudgement but be the occasion of very[19] evident and great danger and perill to all states and sortes of men of this realme by the factious, sedicious and intestine warre that will grow through want of understanding to whom they shuld yeld their allegiances and duties, wherby much innocent blood is like to be shedd and many of those to lose their lifes that wold now gladly bestowe them for your sake in your Majestie's service.

[8]   The viij[th], for that the not performinge of this, the other happeninge, dothe leave the realme without governaunce,[20] which is the gretest danger that can happe to any kingdome. For every prince is *anima legis*, and so reputed in lawe, and therfore upon the death of the prince the lawe dieth: all the offices[21] of iustice wherby lawes are to be executed do cease, all writtes and commandementes to all parties for the execution of iustice do hang in suspence, all commissions for keping of commen peace and for the punishment of offendrs do determin and loose their force. Wherby it followeth consequently that strength and will must rule and nether lawe nor reason during

such vacation and interreigne, which in such an uncertenty of succession is like to last so long as it is to be feared (if Godde's mercy be not the greter) that the realme may therby become a praye to strangers (which our Lord defend) or at the least lose the great honor and estimation that long time have apperteyned unto it.

And like as, most gratious Soveraigne, my lordes have ben moved for the worldly respectes aforesaid to make these their humble peticions to your Majestie, so by the examples, counsailes and commandementes that they have hard out of the sacred scriptures, and for conscience' sake, they feele them selves constreyned and forced to do the like. God (your Highnes knoweth) by the course of the scriptures hath declared succession and having of children to be one of his principall benedictions in this life, and of the contrary he hath pronounced otherwise. And therfore Abraham prayed to God for issue, fearing that Eleazar his steward shuld have ben his heire, and had promisse that kinges shuld procede of his body; Anna the mother of Samuell prayed to God with teares for issue; and Elizabeth (whose name your Majestie beareth), mother to John Baptist, was ioyfull when God had blessed her with fruite, accompting her self delivered therby of a reproche. And as[22] this is a b[l]essing of private howses, so it is much more in kingdomes, as it playnly appeareth by the[23] two kingdomes of Israell and Juda. Unto the kingdome of Juda, conteyning but ij tribes or theraboutes, God gave lineall succession by descent of kinges, and therfore it continued a long time; the kingdome of Israell, conteyning x tribes or therabout, often destitute of laufull heires, the one half of the people following one, and the other half an other, by warres and sedicions weakened, came sone to ruyne, as playnly appeareth by the third and fourth booke of Kinges. Againe, in the time of the Judges, because there was no ordinary succession, the people were often times overrunne and caried to captivity. Besides, it is playne by the scriptures that godly governaunces and princes, as fathers of their countreys, have alwayes ben carefull to avoyde the great evill that might ensue through want of a certen limitacion of succession. And therfore Moises did assigne Josua to be his successor, and David his son Solomon, wherby a great sedicion was appeased, begon by Adonias. Of these there be many examples.

Further, seing it may easely be gathered by experiences of all ages past that civile warres, effusion of Christian blood, and consequently ruyne of kingdomes, do followe where realmes be left without a certentie of succession, and that your Majestie is also informed of the same and sued unto here for redresse, if therfore no

11. MS reads 'goodnes'; this reading from Add.32379.
12. 'As' supplied from Add.32379.
13. 'Of' supplied from Add.32379.
14. There is a heavily abbreviated, illegible marginal addition at this point in the text, ending with 'H[enry] 6'.
15. Constance was about 40 at this point and had been married to Henry for about nine years; Peter is probably Pedro II.
16. MS reads 'doeng'; 'doe iudge' supplied from Add.32379.

17. MS reads 'probably'; this reading supplied from Add.32379.
18. 'Your' supplied from Add.32379.
19. MS reads 'Our'; this reading from Add.32379.
20. 'For that . . . governaunce' supplied from Add.32379.
21. MS reads 'officers'; this reading from Add.32379.
22. 'As' supplied from Add.32379.
23. 'The' supplied from Add.32379.

sufficient remedy shuld be by your Highnes provided, that then it shuld be a dangerous burthen before God to your Majestie, and you were to yeld a streight accompt to God for the same, considering you are placed, as the prophet Ezechiell sayeth, *in altissima specula* of this commen wealth, and seeth the sword coming and provideth no remedy for it.

Lastly, the spirit of God pronouncethe[24] by the mouth of St. Paule to Tymothe, that whosoever maketh not due provision for his family is in danger to Godward; and also by the mouth of St. John, that whosoever seeth but one brother in necessity, and doth shutt upp the bowelles of pity and compassion from him, hath not the love of God remayning in him. Wherby it is playne and manifest how fearefull a thing it were if[25] this whole[26] realme, conteyning so many families, were not in this[27] perillous case upon their sute provided for, or if the bowelles of mercy shuld be shutt up from so many thowsandes which every way were like to fall into extreme miseries if God shuld call your Highnes without certenty of succession – which we pray to God may never happen. Most excellent Princes, the places of the scriptures conteyning the said threatenings be sett furth with much more sharp wordes then be here expressed.

Thus, most gratious Soveraigne, your lordes and nobles both spirituall and temporall have as breffely as they can first shewed to your Majestie how diversly they take them selves bound to make these their humble peticions unto you, and then what their peticions be, and after that what reason for worldly respectes and what by the scriptures and for conscience' sake have moved them thus to do: which here upon ther knees according to their bounden duties they most humbly and ernestly pray your Majestie to have good consideration of, in time, most gratious Soveraigne, in time, in time,[28] and to geve them such favorable and comfortable answer to the same as some good effect and conclusion may growe therof the end of the cession of this parliament, the uttermost daye of their[29] gretest hope, wherby this commen weale, which your Highnes found to be *lateritia*, as Augustus did his, and by your great providence is now become *marmorea*, shall not for want of reforming thus, if God shall call your Highnes without heire of your body, be in more dangerous state and condition then ever it was, that any man can remember.[30] True it is that sute is made by my lordes not without great hope of good successe by reason of experience that they have had of your bountifull goodness shewed to them and the rest of your loving subiectes divers and sundry wayes sence the begining of your reigne, which they praye to God long to continue to his honour with all felicity.

God blesse and save your Majesty.

---

24. MS reads 'promiseth'; this reading from Add.32379.
25. MS reads 'of'; this reading from Add.32379.
26. 'Whole' supplied from Add.32379.
27. MS reads 'thus'; this reading from Add.32379.
28. *Sic.*
29. MS reads 'the'; this reading from Add.32379.
30. See Suetonius, *Divi Augusti Vita*, ch.28.

2. [House of Lords] Lord Keeper's speech to the Queen in her gallery at Westminster, (?) March

Text from BL Harl.5176, copy.
Other MSS. London: BL Harl.398, Harl.1877, Sloane 105,
Add.48065 (Yelverton 71), and University Library 300; all earlier
copies than Harl.5176, but on the whole less reliable. BL Lansd.211,
Add.35838. Oxford: Bodley, Eng.Hist.d.144. Cambridge:
University Library Ii.v.8 (misdated in catalogue). Herts. CRO:
Gorhambury xii.B.2. Northants. CRO: Fitzwilliam of Milton
Political 95. Dublin: TCD E.1.34. Washington: Folger Library 89.2,
1276.10.

Harl.5176, fos.93-4

An oration made in the tyme of the saide parliamente in the name of the nobles and the lordes of the spiritualtie unto the Queene's Highenes in her gallerye at Westminster moveinge her Maiestie to marriage.

May it like your Maiestye to understande that all my lordes here presente and all the rest bothe spirituall and temporall, beinge the whole bodye of your Higheness' upper howse, have agreed and assented that I (albeit much unmeete, and unworthie) for them and in all their names shoulde make unto your Majestie their most humble sute and peticion, to be so much their good Ladye and Soveraigne as, according to your accustomed benignitie, to graunte them a favorable and gratious hearinge of their opinions, counselles, desires and wishes in a matter very neerelye and dearelye touchinge your most royall person, the imperiall crowne of this realme, and the universall weale of the same, and therein themselves alsoe, and all others your Highenes lovinge subietes every one from the highest to the lowest, and theire whole posterityes and sequeles; nevertheles alwayes and altogether humblinge and submitteinge the whole that I shall saye and every parte thereof with all dutie and obedience (as reason is) to your Majestie's consideracion and correction. And here I have thoughte meete because your Higheness shoulde the better understande the whole discourse of this matter, first to open the occasion of this sute, then how diversly my lordes all thinke themselves bounde to make it, and lastly what theire opinions, counselles and desires be concerning the matter conteyned in it. For the first, the occasion grewe upon the readinge of a bill exhibited on Wenesday last[1]

---

1. *EP*, I.112: perhaps 24 March. See Spanish ambassador's report of 28 March for reference to moves in the Lords, including talk of an Act for the continuation of authority in the event of Elizabeth's death (*Cal. SP Spanish, 1558-67*, 317).

before my lordes conteyninge matter concerninge the succession of the crowne of this realme. Uppon the well weyinge and consideringe whereof it evidentlye appeared unto them that neyther by that byll, nor by any other acte alreadye made, any certaine and open declaracion or limitation is made to whom the crowne should remayne if God should call your Highnes without heire of your bodye, which our Lord forbid. And here callinge to theire remembrance that the onelye meane to have an heyre to the greate, yea, and unspeakeable comforte and ioye of all your subiectes, is the honorable state of matrimonye, first instituted as your Highenes knoweth by God in most pure place, then commended, yea, and honored by his sonne here on earthe with the first frutes of his miracles knowen, and ever since the beginninge by his providence continued as the chiefe and most necessarie cause of our beinge nowe, and of all those that have bin or hereafter shalbe: my lordes (I say) remembringe this, and therewith alsoe that all princes, be they never soe greate, never soe younge and like to live, be yet mortall, and subiecte every daye, yea, every hower to Godde's call, and lastly consideringe in what miserable state and condicion (if God should soe call) this realme and the members thereof should stande, and to what a marveilous number of greate and imminente daungers, perilles and mischiefes it shoulde be subiecte; they all thoughte they had most iust occasion to become humble peticioners to your Maiestye for the helpe thereof. For the seconde parte, they thinke themselves so bounden to make this peticion that without offence to God, to your

f.93v   Maiestie, and to their countrye it might / not be pretermitted. First to God, for that it cannot be that a man can keepe his othe and homage made to your Higheness and crowne, and in so greate and weightie a cause as this is be forgetfull or neglecte the contents thereof: and what an offence that is to God, is easie to iudge. For the offence to your Maiestye, surelye every subiecte and liege man, without exception, knowinge any daunger or perill to the Crowne or state, or any parte thereof, and not revealinge and counsellinge his liege ladye or soveraigne therein, or some such of her Highnes' ministers to whome he may have accesse, without doubte offendeth your Maiestye in the dutye of his allegiaunce, as it is evidente in perticular offences touchinge the Crowne, and if so, then howe much more in this universall matter. Againe, for the offence of their countrye, how can a man knoweinge his countrye to be towardes perill and daunger, and not seekinge all the wayes and meanes he may by foresighte to prevente and withstande them but must be thoughte greately to offende his countrye? And thus I trust it appeareth to your Maiestye that upon iust occasion and greate dutie and bonde I am now to open to your Highnes the wishes, desires and councelles of all my lordes here presente. The effecte whereof briefelye and summarilye to speake consisteth in this, that it please your Maiestie to dispose your selfe to marrye, where you will, with whom you will, and as shortlye as you will, as the most honorable presente and sure meane and waye to increase comforte to yourselfe, and to avoyde all manner of daunger and perill that might happen either to your crowne or to the common weale of the realme. For your selfe, how can it be possible but that such an honorable coniunction, makinge your choyce as we doubte not but you will, must needes breede and bringe to your Highenes' person of comforte, quietnes and delight, three of the chiefe worldely jewells pertayninge to lyfe? Nowe to bringe in causes of proofe heereof I leave as vayne matter, beinge so evidente and apparaunte of it selfe. Onelye one comforte I would put your Maiestye in minde of and that is if your Highnes coulde conceive or imagine the comforte, suertie and delighte that should happen to your selfe, by behouldeinge an impe of your owne that shoulde in tyme to come by Godde's grace inheritte and enioye the imperiall crowne of this realme to the great reioyceinge of all your lovinge subiectes, it would (I am assured) sufficiently satisfie to amove all manner of lettes, impedimentes and scruples (if there be anye) that might hinder this their desire. Now for the state and universall weale of the realme can any waye be devised soe sure and certaine for th' avoydinge of all daunger concerninge the same, as to devise that which every member therof doth hartely wishe and continuallie pray for? Very certaine and true it is that well nighe all daungers and troubles that in tymes past have risen upon chaunges of states, have ever taken their foundacions upon non certainetyes and doubtes of tytles that either have bin / in deede, or els have bin imagined to be. And therefore I may most assuredlye conclude that that which is the most certaine and presente remedye to remove the occasion of such non certeinetyes and doubtes must of necessitye be allowed in reason to be the greatest defence againste all such daungers and perilles, and the most sure stay that can be devised for the common weale. And is there any thinge that can bringe that soe perfectlye, soe safely, and so shortely to passe as this? The fearefull slaughters, the pittifull effusion of bloude, the miserable spoyles that have so ofte happened by sufferance of non certenties of titles to crownes be more lamentablye to be thoughte of then needefull to be by me talked of, consideringe they be, as they be in deede, so notoriously knowen. But and it like your Highenes, if the examples be both manye and true that for the increase of amitye onelye, diverse marriages of princes have bene made within the degrees prohibited to all other persons, and sometyme to religious, yea, sometyme contrarye to solempne vowes otherwise before made, what then oughte the avoydeinge of the daungers before remembred imminente to a realme moove a princesse of the same realme to doe in a cause noe waye prohibited, but every way honourable, commendable and profitable, and where all the giftes of nature and of grace alsoe concurre to the furtherance thereof. But here forgettinge my selfe, and fearinge that I shoulde be troublesome to your Maiestye in a matter that I trust God hath alreadye, or nowe presentelye or shortelye will soe incline your Highenes' harte unto, that fewe wordes might serve, I leave any further on my lordes' behalfe to moove your Highenes therin, submitteinge and committeinge the whole that I have sayde to your Highenes' consideracion and correccion. And here for my parte I most humbly beseech your Maiestye that if any thinge in this my declaracion have past me undiscreetely, or uncomelye done, that your Highenes woulde be so much my gratious Ladye as not to impute it unto me otherwise then for wante of understandeinge in soe weightie a cause. And againe I desire my lordes all that if any thinge have beene pretermitted by me agreed to be sayde, or any thinge helpe me with their declaracions. And on the other side if I have perfourmed my commission that they will soe affirme it.

f. 94

1. The order of proceeding to the Parliament and opening proceedings, 12 January

Text from BL Cott.Titus F1, copy.
Other MSS. London: BL Add.37526 contains the order of proceeding, and an account of the opening proceedings which omits the text of the speeches; it is in the hand of Robert Glover, later Somerset Herald, and may be the basis of Cott.Titus F1, which clearly derives from an heraldic source. Stowe 358 has a full copy of Cott.Titus F1, Harl.2185 a copy of the speeches only. Harl.158 has the order of proceeding, with a very brief account of the opening proceedings, and a list of peers in their order. Cambridge: Gonville and Caius College 64 (copy of Cott.Titus F1).
Printed. D'Ewes, 58–66.

Cott.Titus F1, fos.59–60v, 65–75v

Parliamento Anno 5° Elizabethae.
Th'order in proceedinge to the parliament on Tuesdaie the 12 of January 1562, *anno 5 Elizabethae Regine,* from the Pallace of Westminster at the White Hall unto the churche and soe to the parliament howse, for that the day before beinge Monday – which day it was appointed on – the Queene's Majestie came not abroad for the fowle wether, but certen of the lordes went and proroged the same till this day by commission for the Queene, as th' Erle of Arundell, Lord Steward, and others.

5to Elizabethae 1562. This sessions ended Saterday the 10 of Aprill next, being Easter even.

Item. About eleven of the clocke the Queene's Majestie tooke her horse at the Hall dore and proceeded in manner as followeth:

Percullyce ⎱ First, all gentlemen 2 and 2. Then esquires, knights and banneretts and lords beinge no barons or under age.
Then the trumpetters soundinge.
Then the Queene's Sergeant, Mr Carus, in his syrcote, hood and mantle unlyned of scarlett.
Then Mr Gerard, the Queene's Attorney, and Mr Ruswell, Sollicitor.
Then Anthony Browne, Justice of the Common Pleas, and Mr Weston of the King's Benche.[1]
Then the Barons of the Exchequer.

Roudgdragon
f.59v ⎱ Then Mr Corbett and Mr Whydon of the King's Benche, two Justices.
Then Sir Thomas Sanders, cheif Baron of the Exchequer, and Sir James Dyer, chiefe Justice of the Common Pleas.
Then Sir William Cordall, Master of the Rolls, in his gowne and Sir Robert Catlyn, cheif Justice of the Common Place: all theis Justices and Barons of

th'Exchequer in their scarlett mantles, hood and syrcote edged with myniver, the mantle shorter then the syrcote by a foote.

Then Knightes Counsellers in their gownes, as Sir Anthonie Cooke, Sir Richard Sackvil, Sir William Petre, and Sir Ambrose Cave.   *Rougcrosse*

Then Sir William Cecill, cheif Secretary, and Sir Edward Rogers, Controller.

Then William Howard bearinge the Queen's cloke and hatt.

Then in all barons 40,[2] but there in number present 30,[3] as px. St. John of Bletshoe[4], px. Hundsdon, px. Hastings of Lowghborough, px. Chandoys, p. Northe, px. Ethingham,[5] but nowe as Lord Chamberlayne, px. Darcy of Chiche, Pagett, p. Sheffeld, p. Willughbie, p. Riche, sick Wharton, p. Evers, p. Cromwell, px. St. John, px. Mordant, px. Borough, px. Wentford;[6]   *Chestre*

pr. Windsor, p. Vaux, yong Sands, px. Mountegle, px. Darcy of Menell, Ogle, px. Mountioy, px. Lumley, px. Latimer, Dudley,[7] px. Scrope, n. pr. Grey of Wilton,[8] Stafford, pr. Cobham, n. pr. Dacres of the North, p. Dacres of the South, pr. Morley, pr. Barkley, pr. Strange, Zouch, Audley, pr. Clinton, but nowe Lord Admirall, pr. Burgavenny:[9] their mantles, hoods and syrcotes of scarlet furred and two rowes of myniver on their right shoulder.   *Lancastre*

Then proceeded the bishops, all that were there present were but 22,[10] as Glocester, and St. Asseph, Chester, Carlyll, and Peterborough, Norwich, and Exeter, Lichfeild and Coventrie, and Bath and Welles, Rochester, and St. David's, Salisbury, and Lincolne, Bangor, and Worcester, Ely, and Herford, Landaff, Chichester, and Winchester, Durham, and London: their robes of scarlet lyned and / a hood downe their backs of myniver.   *Richmond*   *f.60*

Then the viscounts, their robes as the barons but that they had two rowes demi of miniver, as the Viscont of Byndon, the Viscountes px. Mountague and px. Her[e]ford.[11]   *Somersett*

Then th'erles, but ix present: th'Erle of Hertford, present Pembrooke, and px. Bedford, yonge Southampton, Warwick, yong Bath, pr. Huntington, Ireland Sussex,   *Norrey*

Cumberland, pr. Rutland, px. Worcestre, px. Derby, px. Shrewsbury, Westmerland, px. Northumberland, yong Oxford, and pr. Arundell;[12] their robes of scarlett with iij rowes of mynyver.

Then the pr. Marquis of Winchester, but nowe as Lord Treasurer, and the

---

1. *Sic*; Weston too was Justice of Common Pleas.
2. 41 with the addition of Dudley from Add.37526.
3. *Sic*; although only 15 barons are actually marked 'p' or 'pr' for present, Add.37526 marks 31 barons as present.
4. I.e. 'proxy'. In this document words and abbreviations printed as superiors indicate interlinear glosses in the original.
5. *Sic*, i.e. Effingham.
6. *Sic*, i.e. Wentworth.
7. Supplied from Add.37526.
8. I.e. 'not present'.

9. Add.37526 gives no 'proxies', but has 'p' against the name of each baron except Ethingham (thus spelt in this manuscript also), Paget, Wharton, Sandys, Ogle, Dudley, Stafford, Zouch, Audley and Clinton.
10. Add.37526: 'All the xxij bishops were present except Landaff and Carlyle'.
11. Each viscount marked present in Add.37526.
12. Add.37526 marks as present the earls of Pembroke, Bedford, Huntingdon, Rutland, Worcester, Derby, Shrewsbury, Northumberland and Arundel.

Clarencieulx | px· Marquis of Northampton; the Duke of Norffolk went as Erle Marshall.

Then the Lord Keeper's Serieant and the Seale, and after Sir Nicholas Bacon, Lord Keeper of the Great Seale, in his gowne.

Then the two Archbishops of Yorke and of Canterbury[13] in their robes as th'other bishops afore.

Here Clarencieulx and Norrey.

Then the Queene's Serieant at Armes, and after Garter.

Then the px· Duke of Norfolk with the gilt rod as Erle Marshall, the Lord Treasurer with the capp of estate, and the Erle of Worcester with the sworde.

Then the Queene's Majestie on horseback, a litle behinde [her] the Lord Chamberlaine and Vicechamberlaine,[14] her Grace apparrelled in her mantle open before, furred with ermyns, and her kyrtle of crymson velvett close before and close

f.60v   sleeves, but the hands turned up with ermins, / and a hood hanginge lowe round about her necke of ermins; over all a rich coller sett with stones and other jewells, and on her head a riche calle. And next after her the Lord Robert Dudley, Master of the Horse, leadinge the spare horse. And after all other, ladies two and two in their ordinary apparell. Beside the Queene went her footmen, and alonge of either side of her went the Pencyoners with their axes. After the ladies followed the Captaine of the Gard, Sir William St. Loe, and after him the Guard.[15]

In which order her Majestie proceeded to the north dore of the church of Westminster where the Deane there and the Deane of the chappell mett her, and the whole chappell in copes; and St. Edward's staffe with the martlett in the topp was delivered unto her, her arme for the bearinge therof assisted by the Baron of Hunsdon, the canapie borne over her by Charles Howard, armiger, Sir George Howard, Sir Richard Blunt, Sir Edward Warner, Sir John Perrott and Sir William Fitzwilliams, knights, her Grace's trayne borne upp by the Duchesse of Norffolk, assisted by the Lord Chamberleyn and Master of the Jewelhowse,[16] her Maieste's robe or mantell borne up[17] and assisted for the weight therof from her armes by the Lord Robert Dudley, Master of the Horse, and Sir Francis Knolles, Vicechamberlaine; and so orderly proceeded to the traverse beside the table of administracion (although other princes have used to be placed in the quire till the offeringe, but not now, for that there was neither Communion nor offeringe). And soe, she placed, all the lords sate downe on formes beside the traverse, the spiritualtie on the north side and the temporaltie on the south side, the sworde and capp of estate laid downe on the table.

Then the quire sange the English procession; which ended, Mr Noell, Deane of Paule's, began his sermon, and first made his prayer orderlie for the Queene's Majestie and the universall Churche, and especiallie for that honourable assemblie of the iij estates there present, that they might make such lawes as should be to God's glorie and the welth of the realme, and then began his sermon, which was the first Psalme,[18] to this effect followinge.

[fos.61-4v: the sermon][19]

f.65   In the meane time that the Queene was at the church the Earle of Arundell (Lord Steward) went to the parliament house to see the returne of the writtes, and then came to church agayne.

The sermon ended and a psalme sunge, her Majestie and the rest orderly on foote proceeded out of the south doore, where she delivered the Deane the scepter, and so proceeded into the parliament chamber where the Queene staied a while in her privy chamber till all the lords and other were placed. And then her Highness came forth and went and sate her downe in her royall place and chaier of estate, (the sword and cap of maintenance borne before her), and when she stood up her mantle was assisted and borne up from her armes by the Lord Robert Dudley, Master of the Horse, and Sir Frances Knolles, Vicechamberlen.

The Lord Keeper sate alone on the uppermost sack untill the Queene was sett, and then went and stood without the rayle on the right hand the cloth of estate, and the Lord Threasurer holding the cap of estate on the right hande afore the Queene, Garter standing by him, and on the left hand standing the Earle of Worcester with the sword, by him the Lord Chamberlayne.

The Duke of Norfolk began the first forme, and the Vicount Mountague ended it ffor that the Vicount Bindon was not there.[20] The Lord Clinton, Lord Admirall, began the forme behind that, of barons, and / the Lord Seint John of Bletsoe ended it.   f.65v

The Archbishop of Canterbury began the bishop's forme, and the Bishop of Gloucester ended the same.

On the wooll sack of the right hand and north side sate Sir Robert Catlyn and Sir James Dier, chief Justices, Sir William Petre, Anthony Browne, Corbett and Weston, Justices, and Mr Gerrard, the Queene's Attorney.

On the sack on the left hand and south side sate Sir William Cordall, Master of the Rolles, Sir Edward Sanders, chief Baron, Justice Whiddon, Serieant Carus, and Mr Ruswell, the Queene's Sollicitor. And at their backes sate Sir Richard Rede, Doctor Yale and Doctor Vaughan.

On the neither[21] sack sate Doctor Huick, Spilman, clerk of the parliament, and Mr Marten, clerk of the Crowne. And behinde them kneeled Mr Smith, Allen, Dyster, Nicasius, Cliffe and Permitter. At the side hand[22] of the Queene sate on the ground three or ffower ladyes and noe more. And at the back of the rayle behind the cloth of estate kneeled the Erles of Oxford and Rutland, under age, the Erle of Desmond, the Lord Roos, the Lord Herbert of Cardiff and divers other noblemen's sonnes and heires.

The Queene beeing sett, the lower howse was lett in. Then the Queene's Majestie commaunded the Lord Keeper to open the cause of calling and assembling of this parliament, who beganne in this manner: /

f.66

The Lord
Chancelor
Spech.[23]

'My lordes and other of this honourable assemblie, you shall understaund that my

13. The Marquis of Northampton and the two archbishops are marked present in Add.37526.

14. Sir Francis Knollys.

15. Punctuation of this paragraph is based on T. Milles, *Catalogue of Honor . . .* (1610), 66, describing the procession of 1584. See also *HC*, 349, and D'Ewes, 58–9.

16. John Astley.

17. 'By the duchesse . . . borne up' supplied from Add.37526.

18. Add.37526 reads: 'and tooke his theme out of the 4 Psalme'.

19. Printed in *Nowell's Catechism*, ed. G. E. Gorrie (Parker Society, 1853), 223–9.

20. I.e. Bindon was lower in precedence than the other two viscounts.

21. *Sic.*

22. *Sic.*

23. *Sic.*

most dread and soveraigne ladie the Queene's Majestie here present hath commaunded me to declare the occasion of this assemblie, which I am not able (but unmeete) to doe as it ought to be done amonge such a noble, wise and discrete companye. Howbeit, knowing th'experience of her Majestie's bearing with such as do their good willes, and your honours' patience in bearing with me in the like afore this tyme, it encourageth me the better herein, not doubting of the like at this present. Therefore my lordes, the occasion is that necessarie matters to be provided for might be here propounded, skanned, and after agreed upon and ended, which afterwardes shold remayne and contynue. Which matters in my judgment maye well be devyded into two partes: one, touching religion, for the setting forth of God's honour and glorye; and the other concerning pollicie for the common wealth, aswell for provision at home as to provide for the forreine enemye abroade.

'Which said matters of religion maie againe be devyded into two partes, ffor Gode's cause being sincerely weyed, considered and followed bringeth good successe in all affayres, and being not followed but neglected or made light of, how can anie thing prosper or take good effect? And the greater the personages be which so abuse the same, the greater the fawlt is to the damage of the whole common wealth, ffor all men's eyes be fixed on those who be in aucthoritie: ffor as the head is,

f.66v even so is the / foote and after the superior followeth the inferiour. For as Gode's lawe of it self is perfect, soe that there is no imperfection therein but that which cometh of our selves, wherein I cannot excuse neither the spiritualty nor laitye, ffor as the preachers be not soe diligent in their vocation of preaching as they ought to be, even soe we of the laitye be neither so diligent in hearing nor yet in doing as we should be, and thirdlie some of the laitye in not giving creditt unto it, as it ought for to be:[24] ffor as all in aucthoritye ought to be credited, and their doinges taken in the best parte, yet I would wishe the same shold contynue no longer then they do well. And where att this present there is great wante of ministers, and yet some of them that be, be much insufficient, which considering the tyme are to be borne withall, not doubting the circumspeccion of the bishops in well looking to the placing of such which shall be appointed hereafter, and those which be and will not be reformed to have sharpe punishment. For as heretofore the discipline of the church hath not bene good, and againe that the ministers thereof have bene slouthfull, even so for want of the same hath sprunge two enormities: the first is that for lack thereof everye man liveth as he will, without feare; and secondlie, manie ceremonies agreed upon, but the right

f.67 ornamentes thereof are either lefte / undone or forgotten. As in one pointe for wante of discipline it is that so fewe come to service and the Church soe unreplenished, notwithstanding that at the last parliament a lawe was made for good order to be observed in the same, but yet, as appeareth, not executed. Therefore if it be too easie, lett it be made sharper, and if allready well, then see it executed. For the wante of discipline causeth obstinacie, contempt and growing of heresies: therefore better to be winked at and unspoken, then bruited abroad and unperformed. Therefore, in my opinion, the devise is good, that in every diocesse there is officers appointed and devyded as hath bene thought good to sitt for redresse of these and such like errors twise or thrise a yeare, till the faultes be amended; in which well doing the head officers are to be borne withall and mainteyned, and lawes to be made for the purpose. The cheif care of which said former matters perteyneth to you, my lordes of the spiritualty, wherein you must take paines to travell, whereunto are lawes to be ioyned not onelie for the more perfecting of the same, but for the maintenance aswell of the heades as the ministers thereof.

'Nowe to the second parte, of policy for the common wealth. For as there be faultes for want of discipline, so are there faultes in the imperfection and want of executing, which imperfection must be looked into, and want of lawes, which needeth to be provided for and made; and to consider if there be not too manie lawes for one thing, and those so large and busie that neither the commons / can   f.67v understand the same, nor yet well the lawyer, which would be brought into some breifer and better order and then executed. For which purpose it is necessarie to take care to have good ministers thereof, and secondly to banish all fearefullnes for executing of the same, and over and besides that, to appointe proved men to inquire of those ministers, whereby they maie have the better regard to their dutie. For even as the visitacion of the Church is and was well appointed for the Church, soe nowe is the like to be appointed for the temporaltye: ffor if the lawes be not well executed, my parte is not the least thereof, which yearelie I would be glad to heare of. The third for the enemie aswell here bredd amonge us as abroade. For, whereas the Quene's Maiesty att her entraunce founde this realme in warre with forreine power, att which tyme lacke of treasure, artillery, force, and other thinges caused her to agree to a peace, allthough not to the best, howbeit for our suertye she spared no cost to bring it to passe; which notwithstanding, of later tyme certeine old cancred enemyes to this realme attempted to putt in execution to bring the Scottes to the governaunce of Fraunce and so being a firme land to ours to have bene our utter enemye, which daunger the Queene foreseeing sought by all meanes, aswell by her ambassadors as others, to stay the enterprise, but could not; and therefore holpe her neighbours in Scotland, and so disappoynted that attempt, or elles / afore this tyme I doubt the   f.68 Scottish territorie would have been too litle to have holden them, but that they would have troubled us not onelie att Barwick but at the walles of Yorke. Which said attempt being by the meanes of her Majestye staied and letted, the said bent enemye hath attempted the like in Fraunce to the whole disturbaunce of all Christendome, and all done for the mischeife of this realme (joyned with a divelish conspiracy within our selves tending to the aydinge of the forreyne enemye, and by their owne confession to have raysed a rebellion within this realme).[25] And for that by none of her Grace's travelles or meanes she could there staie there enterprise or make them agree, she was forced the rather to stay the same, to take a holde being offered unto her for our surety till further good order were taken, or a good stay for the same for the suretie of this realme, to the no litle charge of her Majestye. For in these proceedinges and in repayringe of these and other like faultes I dare be bold to say (for that I am thereof assured) it hath cost her Majestie as much as two the best subsidies which att anie tyme hath bene within this realme, and all att her owne proper

24. *Sic.*
25. The abortive conspiracy of Arthur Pole and others: Pole was caught in October 1562 and found guilty of treason on 26

February 1563. (*DNB sub* Pole, Arthur; C. Read, *Mr Secretary Cecil and Queen Elizabeth* (1955), 253.

charges without either strayning of her subiectes or havinge ayde of them towardes the same. Howbeit she yet thinketh it well spent. For often it chaunceth that money is better spent then spared, as the common saying is: that penny is well spent which afterwardes saveth a pounde. And so in this, if that money had not bene soe spent /

f.68v   in staying in tyme their attempted enterprises, it would afterward have turned to the noe litle preiudice nor yet small charge of this realme. And where afore this tyme commonly princes have had some veyne or delight to spend treasure upon for their pleasure, which the Queene hath none, but onelie for the common wealth and surety thereof, so that we maie iustly and most fortunatelie say to her great praise that the relieving of the realme's necessity is our prince's whole delight. And notwithstanding all the disbursementes of these her great charges, yet she was (as I right well knowe) very hardlie brought to and perswaded to call this parliament, in which she should be driven to require any aide or by anie meanes to charge her subiectes, if by anie other meanes it might have bene holpen; and so her Maiesty her selfe commaunded to be declared, and I for my part and so do others very well knowe. For the commons litle thinke or consider what a trouble want is to her, wherby shee is forced to aske of them (which surelie is against her nature) but that she is thereunto forced for the surety of this realme.

'And for that the nether howse cannot, beinge so manie together, but of necessitye must have one to be as a mouthe, ayder or instructor unto them for the opening of matters, which is called the Speaker, therefore go and assemble your selves together

f.69   and elect one, a discreete, / wise and learned man to be your Speaker. And on Fridaie next the Quene's Majestie appointeth to repayre hither againe for to receyve the presentment of him accordinglie.'

Then the clerke of the parliament read the names of such as should heare and trye the peticions for England, Fraunce, Scotland, Ireland, Gascoigne and Guyen[26] *etc.*

Then the Lord Keeper adiourned the parliament till Fridaie next. And then the Quene returned to her chamber and shifted her, and so did all the lordes, and then waited on her to the water side, where she tooke her boate and departed to the Whitehall, from whence she came, and they till Fridaie att their pleasures.

Fridaie the xv[th] of Januarie 1562. The Queen's Majestie at her privie stayres tooke boate and went by water to the parliament howse about 2 of the clock, the lordes and heraldes waiting on her to the landing place on the backside of the parliament and so brought her to her privye chamber, where she shifted her and putt on her roabes and the lordes theirs as the first daie. And then she repaired to her seate and the lordes to theirs, with the sergeantes and gentlemen ushers before her, the Lord Marquesse of Northampton bearing the cap of estate, the Duke of Norfolk the rodde of the Marshalsey, and the Earle of Northumberland the sword. The Lord Robert

f.69v   Dudley, / Master of the Horse, and the Baron of Hunsdon susteyned her mantle from her armes, and her trayne was borne by the Lord Chamberleine, Vicechamberlayne and Mr Astley, Master of the Jewell House; and the Lord Keeper standing att the back of the rayle on the right hande, and the Lord Treasurer on the left. And so all beinge in order, the doore was opened to lett in the nether howse, who had chosen Mr Williams of the [Inner][27] Temple for their Speaker, who was then brought in unto the barre betwene Sir Edward Rogers, Comptroller of the Queene's Howse, and Sir William Cecill, chief Secretarie, making in theyr comming three obeysaunces, coming downe first to the nether doore, right afore the Queene, and then proceeded up to the barre. And so being placed att the barre, the said Speaker alone made againe three obeysaunces, and then began, as followeth:

'Right excellent and most vertuous Prince, our renowmed dread soveraigne Lady, on Tuesday last it pleased your Highnes, by the mouthe of the right honourable the Lord Keeper of the Greate Seale, for the more ease of the nether howse of this parliament to commaund them to go and assemble themselves together and to elect one being wise, discrete and learned to be their Speaker. After which consultacion had (with one voyce) they did elect / me, being indeed insufficient, as by and for dyverse causes I did then to them declare. Howbeit, whether it were that they being so manye wise men together at the electing of me and therefore would not seeme to speake againe against their owne elections, or for[28] what other cause I knowe not, but they refused my denyall and stood to their said choise and nowe present me here to be att your Grace's appointment. I therefore knowing my owne imbecillity and yet not arrogantlie refusing the same, as one among the Romanes chosen from the ploughe to a place of estimacion and after went to the plough againe, even soe I a countryman fitt for the same, and not for this place, most humblie desire your Majestie to discharge me hereof, and to appoint some other more abler; and I, as I am bounden, will not onelie praye for your Highnes, but also serve your Majestie and my country to my power in the place of a cittizen, whereunto first I was elected and appointed.'

Then the Queene called the Lord Keeper to her, declaring to him her opinion for the answering of him, whereupon he returned to his place and answered as followeth:

'Mr Williams, the Queene's Majestie hath well heard and pondered your speach and doth well perceyve your modest and humble manner in the disabling your self to that place whereunto her welbeloved subiectes have elect and chosen you and nowe accordinglie present you, and also hath heard your suite for discharge of the same roome. And for answer she hath comaunded me to declare unto you that she commendeth well / your modest and humble manner in so disablinge your self, knowing that judgment apperteyneth to the caller and not to the partye called. And forasmuch as her Majestie is credibly informed aswell of your knowledge and experience in other parliamentes as in other greate and waighty matters, she thinketh now therefore she cannot disable you without some perill to the realme, and the rather for that the wise knightes, cittisens and burgesses have nominated and chosen you, she cannot graunt your peticion; and besides that, your modest order in disabling your self doth right well declare your ability to furnish the place: ffor

Speaker's speach when he was presented to the Queene.

f.70

The Lord Keeper's answere to the Speaker.

f.70v

26. MS reads 'Groyen'; this reading from Add.37526. For trying the petitions, see D. Pasquet, *The Origins of the House of Commons* (1964 edn), 198-9.

27. Blank in MS. Thomas Williams was to die on 1 July 1566 at the age of 52, the first Speaker to die in office. (*DNB sub* Williams, Thomas.)

28. 'For' repeated in MS.

which causes she doth allow this election and presentacion made of you, not doubting your care to be such but that the good opinion her Maiestye and the burgesses have of yow be augmented and increased and the burgesses have of yow shall be augmented and increased and the burgesses not to repent their election. Therefore your office is to take it upon yow.'

Whereunto the Speaker answered as followeth:

'Most honourable, although afore this tyme the place hath bene furnished with orators, and therfore their matter intreated of worthilie called an oration, yet I nowe, voyde of anie such knowledge, require that name to be left, and that it maie beare the name of an epistle with a request. And for the better understanding thereof I will

f.71

devide the matter into three partes, one for tyme past, and the second tyme present, / and the third tyme to come.

'But fearing to fall betwene two mounteynes as to be counted either ungrate or dissembling, I know not what to say. But yet, seeing savage beastes forget not them who do well unto them, as appeareth by the storie of a lion out of whose foote a certen man tooke a thorne, which said person being afterwardes cast to the same lyon to be devoured, the lyon not forgetting but remembring the former kyndnes shewed unto him would not devoure him, but gentlie ever after followed the said man, even soe, without too much ingratitude cannot I cleare let passe your Majestie's manifold benefittes extended upon us, which although worthilie to be declared they passe my capacity now to expresse, yet thinke it blasphemie to suffer it cleane to be untouched; and therefore in some part will put in remembraunce the same, which I will devide into twoo partes, the one spirituall, the other temporall. For the first, when God planted your Highnes in this place you found it not soe furnished with treasure as other your predecessor have, althoughe if you had, yet occasions enough to occupye it; which notwithstanding you did not take the extremity of penall statutes and other forfeites due to you but pardoned all such as in a tyme convenient requyred it.[30] Also your Majestie did vouchsafe to take upon you the charge of both the states, aswell spirituall as temporall, and soe purged this Churche of all ill service and / placed therein service to Gode's honour. Further, what great plague and dearth happened by ill money this 20 yeares last past, which within one yeare is brought to good againe with little losse of your subiectes; your Majestie preventing

f.71v

also aswell the attempt in Scotland (made by your common enemye there) as nowe of late againe in Fraunce which otherwise, if it had not bene forseene, would have turned to the no litle perill and losse of this your crowne and subiectes thereof. Also your Highnes hath bene author of good lawes as appeareth by those made both at the last parliament and by your other proclamacions since. Further, finding this realme at your entrance in warres, brought it in peace. All the which former proceedinges hathe bene a great charge unto your Majestie, which although the revenues of your crowne be small, yet hath it hitherto onelie bene done of your owne charge, as the last daie by the Lord Keeper it was declared. And for the last part and principall point of all other, your Highnes hath brought and restored againe Gode's doctrine into this realme, for which your humble subiectes most heartily give thankes to God and you, by the mouth of me their appointed Speaker.

'For the second poinct (beeing time present), your Majestie is the head, and the bodie the spiritualtie and temporaltie; which bodie is to be devided into three estates, the lordes spirituall, the lordes temporall, and the Commons whose mouth I am, which by noe meanes can prosper one without the other. For as any estate devided cannot well continue, so in this, and therefore say *nosce teipsum*, not minding to speak theis wordes only to your Highnes but to the whole body. For although the head may lack a member of the bodie and / yet continue, yet so cannot the member   f.72 want the head, nor yet the head want the whole bodie, but the want of the one of theis last twoo shalbe the ruine of th'other. And therefore, of necessity for the sure preservation of the whole it behoveth them firmely to ioyne together. For though your Majesty be the head, and therefore the chief care perteyneth unto your, yet your Majestie cannot throughlie redresse the same without knowledge of the faultes, nor yet well understand the whole state, except the other partes of the bodie ioyne with you and putt to their helping handes. I finde in divers histories great commodities growe to princes by serching out diversly not only the wantes of their subiectes but knowledge of theire talke, whereby the better they both understand their owne faultes and the flatterers which they had about them. Which order the wise and prudent Marcus Aurelius used and long time reigned honourably; the noble conquerour Alexander in the beginning of his raigne used the same, but leaving that order[31] and having noe regard to his living was destroyed, which like example was seene by that notable and valiant warriour Julius Caesar. And beeing encouraged by theis worthie examples, and other, to enter into some abuses used in this realme, I will only speake of three, beeing all three notable monsters, necessity, ignorance, and error.

'Necessitie is growen amongest our selfes so that noe man is contented with his degree though he hath never so much. But where she is, as the proverbe saieth, she hath noe lawe. For howe nowe be all schooles, benefices and other like roomes furnished? And yet those for schooles so fewe that I dare say a hundred schooles wantes in England, which afore this time hath beene; and if in every schoole there had beene but a hundred schollers, yet that had beene ten thousand. So that nowe I doubt whether there be so many learned men in England as the nomber of want of theis schollers. /

'The second monster is her daughter, ignorance. For, for want of ten thousand   f.72v schollers which those schooles were the bringers up of, and for want of good schoolemaisters, bringeth ignorance. But the occasion of theis twoo monsters is for want of livinges and prefermentes. For covetousnes hath gotten the livinges, as by impropriacions, which is a decay of learning, ffor by it the tree of knowledge groweth downeward and not upward as it was first meant and made for, and groweth thereby daylie to the great dishonour both of God and this common wealth. The universities are decaied and great market townes and others without either schoole or preacher,

---

29. *Sic.*
30. See *Cal. Patent Rolls, 1558–60*, 149⁄ 246, for an extensive pardon roll.
31. Williams is probably recalling Alexander's rejection of advice to marry and produce an heir before setting off for the Persian invasion, a decision which resulted in considerable confusion after his death.

ffor the poore vicar hath but only xx^{li} and the rest beeing noe small somme is impropriate and so thereby noe preacher there, but the people beeing traded up and led in blindnes, for want of instruction become obstinate. And therefore to see to it, and that impropriacions may be redressed, notwithstanding the lawes already made.

'The third monster is error, a serpent with many heades, many evill opinions and evill life, as Pelagians, Libertines, Papists and such other, leaving Gode's comandementes to followe their owne traditions, affections and mindes. But if the Papists be, as indeed it is, an error and as wee allowe it, let us seeke the redresse thereof ffor that the poore and ignorant be thereby abused; untill which redresse be had, you nor your realme neither at home nor abrode shall ever be well served of such people which be so devided, and therefore speedily looke to it and weede out this wickednes and error which in theis our daies is too much knowen. For yf your godly proclamacions were not so soone forgotten, they would be amended. In the countrey

f.73   I heard tell, but since hether walking in the streetes oftentimes more oathes / then wordes. A pitifull hearing! – ffor if the Ægiptians by whose lawes the people lost their handes, and amongest the Barbarians lost their lives for swearing, and specially if it were a lie, alack, if it were so punished amongest them, beeing infidells, what, shall there be no punishment amonge us, beeing Christians? Is truth further from us professing the name of Christ and beeing Christians, then from them beeing infidels? But even as Tantalus was plagued, so are we: ffor although he had apples even hanging at his mouth, yet could not eat any of them, and having a river of water as it were running by his lippes, yet could not drinck, but was, as he died for hunger and thirst, even so are we plagued, ffor having Gode's word and his name even in our mouthes, yet we live as infidells or as them furthest from the same. And so having ynough yet there is scarcity. And that we avoyd this blasphemy and th'other monsters, your humble subiectes desire your Highnes to see to the lamentable estate of this common wealth and to the redresse of the same.

'Having perused times past and times present let us goe to, and well remember the time to come. For Cato sayeth a thing well begonne shalbe well ended.[32] Againe, as the end of that thing is good which was well looked to and foreseene in the begining, so then followeth of a good begining, a good ending. For that noble capten Haniball environed with his enemies in a strange country sounded his trumpet to councell and thereby prospered. So your Majestie hath nowe called the prelates, nobles, and commons to councell for suretie of the realme. We nowe so therefore assembled, as diligent in our calling have thought good to move your Majestie with the assent of

f.73v   this assemblie to build a strong forte for the suretie of this realme, to the repulsing / of your enemies abrode, which must be sett uppon firme ground and stedfast, having twoo gates, one commonly open, th'other as a posterne, with two watchmen at either of them, one governor, one lievetenant, ffower soldiers and noe good thing there wanting: the same to be named the feare of God. The governor thereof to be God, your Majestie the lievetenant, the stones the heartes of faithfull people, the two watchmen at the open gate to be called knowledge and vertue, the other twoo at the posterne called mercy and truth; all beeing spirituall ministers.

'This fforte is invincible if every man will feare God, ffor all governors reigneth and governeth by the twoo watchmen, knowledge and vertue. And you beeing the lievetenant see justice with prudencie their sister executed, shall then rightly use the office of a lievetenant. And for such as depart out of this forte, let them be lett out at the posterne by the twoo watchmen, mercy and truth, and then you shalbe well at home and abrode. The charge of this fort is yours, beeing lievetenant; by justice your place is setled, whereunto obedience ought to be taught and done, which your Majestie ought to looke to. And so nowe the feare of God to be a sure forte, the subiectes' heartes the stones, knowledge, vertue, mercy and truth the ffower watchmen, God the governor, and your Majestie his lieuetenant, is well proved. Therefore to build uppon this forte, the feare of God, is nothing lacking to a happie life. For by God are all / princes appointed, who put downe Saul and made David king, who sought only Gode's glory and so prospered, as did likewise Josaphat, Josias and Exechias. And also Ahas and others, as long as they sought Gode's glory prospered, but forgetting God were overthrowen. Therefore first of all and continually vouchsafe to seek Gode's glory and his true honour, and then you shall have this ffort well built and by you well governed. f.74

'Further I have to be a sutor to your Majestie, that when matters of ymportance shall arise whereuppon it shalbe necessary to have your Highnes' opinion, that then I may have free accesse unto you for the same, and the like to the Lordes of the upper house.

'Secondly, that in repayring from the neather house to your Majestie or lordes of the upper house to declare their meaning, and I mistaking or uttering the same contrary to their meaning, that then my fault or imbecility in declaring thereof be not preiudiciall to the House, but that I may againe repaier unto them the better to understand their meaning, and so they to reforme the same.

'Thirdly, that the assembly of the said lower house may have franck and free liberty of speech to speak their mindes without any controllment, blame, grudge, menaces or displeasures according to the old ancient order.

'Finally, that the old privilege of the House might be observed, which is that they and theirs might be at libertie, franck and free, without arrest, molestacion, trouble or other domage, to their bodies, landes, goodes, and servantes with all other their liberties during the time of the said parliament, whereby they may the better attend and doe their dutie. All which priviledges I desire to be inrolled as at other times it hath beene accustomed. /

'And thus having beene tedious unto you with my speach voyd of eloquence, I crave your pardon and desire your Majestie to accept my heart and good will as well as this time as after. And I will pray as I am bounden for your honour long to raigne over us.' f.74v

Then the Queene called the Lord Keeper, declaring her opinion for answering him, which he did as followeth:

'Mr Speaker, the Queene's Majestie hath heard and very well weighed your eloquent

Lord Keeper's speech

---

32. The saying is proverbial. Cf. Plato, *Republic*, ii.377B.

oracion (which you in the begining required might not so be called, but that it might beare the name of an epistle, with a request) full of good meaning and good matter well gathered, devided and sett, which you devided (as I gather) into ffower partes, three by you applied into three times, past, present and to come, and the 4th for your peticions.

'For times past, beeing the first, you opened the benefites receaved by us all from the Queene's Majestie since her entrance to the Crowne, which you devided into twoo, th'one spirituall, th'other temporall; and so in some parte related the same, and thus passed with times past.

'The second part, for time present, after you had therein declared many notable examples of princes which serched privily to understand the commons' talk and opinion and the benefit thereof arising, you declared to be in this common wealth three notable monsters, *viz* necessity, ignorance and errour, which to redresse you desired the prince's aide. |

f.75   'And in the third parte, for time to come, you declared howe the Queene's majestie and this parliament, in your opinion by building a forte named the feare of God, might take order and live surelie in time to come.

'And in the ffowerth parte made fower peticions, the first for free accesse to her person and upper house, the second for well taking your meaning, the third and fowerth for free libertie of speach and persons.

'Nowe for the answering of them her Majestie hath commaunded me to say that for the first parte she commendeth much those godly vertues that you opened to be in her, and also those beautifull budding benefites which you declared to come from her, and doubteth not the rather by this your remembring of them but they shalbe hereafter on her parte performed; ffor which she thanketh you, thinking all thinges well bestowed when they are well remembered.

'In the second parte you declared certen monsters which trouble this religion and would be redressed, the remedy whereof you declared in your third parte, wherein she desireth you to travell for the bringing of it to passe.

'And for the ffowerth parte, beeing your peticions, which be also fower: ffor the first, beeing for free accesse to her person, she granteth it, not doubting your discrecion to use it as rathe as may be, not out of time, nor yet without it be in matters of great ymportance; ffor the second, that if you mistake their meaninges that they may notwithstanding redresse the same without preiudice to them, this also she granteth, although as she thinketh unneedfull ffor that she trusteth you will not offend therein.

'And for the third, to have free speach, she granteth also, so that it be reverently used. And to the last poinct, for them and theirs to be free without disturbance, she is
f.75v   pleased therewith, howbeit great regard would / be therein had, not thereby to avoyde or delay their creditors, but to be well used according to the meaning of the first grant thereof.

'Nowe a worde or twoo more. I would advise you to make your lawes as playne and as fewe as may be, ffor many be burdenous and doubtfull to understand. And secondarily, to make them as brief as the matter will suffer. And thirdly, that you proceed to the great and weightie matters first and th'other of smaller ymportance after, and that so speedilie as can be, whereby this assemblie may be againe at their libertie'. And so ended.

Then the Speaker and neather house did their reverence and departed. And the Queene returned into her privy chamber, and shifted her, and the Lordes likewise. And then she repayred to her barge, and so to Whitehall untill which place the sword was borne to and fro and officers of armes wayted on her Highnes.[33]

Which sessions of Parliament continued till Easter even the tenth of Aprill after, and then adiourned or proroged till the second of October following.

33. 'On her Highnes' supplied from
    Add.37526.

2. Lord Keeper's opening speech, fuller version

Text from BL Harl.5176, copy.
Other MSS. BL Cott.Titus F1 (misdated 1576).
Printed. D'Ewes, 192⁄5 (misplaced under 1572).

Harl.5176, fos. 89⁄92

An oration made in the beginninge of the seconde parliamente being in *anno quinto* of her Majestie's raigne, and *anno Domini* 1562 by the Lord Keeper Sir Nicholas Bacon.

The Queene's most excellent Maiestye, our most deare and gratious soveraigne Ladye, hath given me in commaundement to declare unto you the causes of the summons of this assemblye for a parliamente to be houlden here at this tyme, wherein albeit I meane to imploye my whole indeavoure to the uttermost of my power and understandeinge; yet must I needes confesse that neither you shall have it done as the maiestye of this presence, neither as the gravitye of the cause requireth it to be done. And yet, the ofte experience that I have divers and sundrye tymes had of the Queene's Majestie's greate benignitie and gentlenes in bearinge with and well accepteinge the doeinges of those that to her services putt theire good willes and diligence, and besides alsoe the proofe of your patiences heretofore in a like case, hath so muche incouraged me that (I truste) it shalbe done, although not cunninglye nor eloquentlye, yet plainely and trulye, and soe as it may be well understande and easily borne awaye, and therewith alsoe as briefelye as the greatenes of such a matter will suffer. Truthe it is th'originall and principall cause of this assemblye is that thinges here proponed may be orderlie and diligentlye debated, deepelie considered, and thereupon wiselye concluded. And to the ende alsoe that those conclusions soe made maye the rather by such an universall consente as in Parliamente is used to remayne firme and stable.

Now the matters that are in this parliamente to be proponed consiste altogether in two partes: the former in matters of religion for the better mayntenaunce and settinge forthe of Gode's honour and glorye; the seconde in matters of pollicie for the more perfitt uphouldeinge and establishinge of the Queene's Majestie's honor and royall estate, and the preservacion of the common weale committed to her chardge. The causes of religion are againe to be devided into two, that is, into matters of doctrine and doeinges of discipline. The thinges of pollicie I meane alsoe to parte into other two, that is, into matters concerninge the good governaunce of subiectes at home, and into causes of defence againste the enemye abroade. And thus by this processe you see you are, as in deede you oughte, firste to consider in this your assemblye of

Gode's cause, which faithefullie, sincearelie, and diligentlie done, like as it can not
but bringe good successe to all the reste; soe, doubteles, colde, luke-warme,
doubtefull or doubledealinge therein cannot but breede, nourishe and bringe forthe
faccions, divisions, dissentions, seditions, *etc.*, to the greate daunger and perill of all
the rest. And the greater that the personages be in authoritie and dignitie that thus
deale, the greater of necessitie must the daunger be of the common weale. And
because Gode's lawe and doctrine beinge the first braunche, is of it selfe every way
perfitt and absolute, therefore the whole faulte and lacke toucheinge that braunche
must lighte altogethers upon our selves that oughte to take the benefitte of it: as first
and chiefely upon ministers of this doctrine, eyther for not preachinge and teachinge
it by worde and example of lyfe soe purelie and reverentelye as they mighte, or els not
soe diligentlie as they were bounde; and secondarilie upon us, eyther for not
heareinge it soe desireouslye, or els heareinge it by forgettinge and not followinge it
soe effectuallie as we shoulde; thirdelye for that many of us of the laytie doe not / yeelde
and give that estimacion, countenaunce and creditte to the ministers of this doctrine
which of right they oughte to have, and that may greately hurte the settinge forthe of
it. For this (me thinkethe) may be houlden for firme by the rules of good
governaunce, that all officers both spirituall and temporall that have governaunce,
duringe the tyme of theire offices oughte to be conserved in creditte and estimacion.
For howe can any thinge be well sett forthe and governed by them that wante
creditte? Marye, for my parte let the tyme of their office last as theire doeinges doe
deserve. Fourthely, because of the wante of the number of ministers that oughte to be,
and be not, and for the insufficiencye of those that be for divers respectes: but therein
the Queene's Highenes doubteth nothinge but all that which the difficultie of tyme
in soe greate a scarsitie of men meete to be ministers will suffer to be done, shalbe by
my lordes the bishoppes done in this behalfe, and that as speedilye, diligentlye and
carefullye as can be. And therewith if any person admitted or to be admitted to this
ministerye shall hereafter, eyther of arrogancye or of ignoraunce, sowe any strange
doctrine contrarie or varyeinge from that which by common consente of the realme is
published, to the breache of unitie, that he shall by those to whom it apperteyneth
sharpelye and speedilye be refourmed, all feare and favoure sett a parte. Thus much
for doctrine.

    Ye are alsoe earnestlie to thinke and consider of the discipline of the Churche, as
of one of the stronge pillers of religion, which doubteles at this tyme hath two greate
lackes. The first, the imperfection of lawes for the continuaunce of it, which hath
growen eyther by reason that sundrye of the olde ordinaunces made for that purpose,
by disuse or otherwise have not their force, or els for that most of the lawes that
remayne be such as for their softenes fewe men can make any accoumpte of. The
seconde imperfeccion is the slouthefullnes, corrupcion and fearefullnes of the
ecclesiasticall ministers and officers in the due execucion of such of thease lawes as be
good and yet continue. To true it is that hereby at this present two greate enormityes
doe daylye growe. The former that men of wealthe and power, given to be evill,
maye in their contryes live what dissolute and licencious lyfe they luste, and bothe
temporall and spirituall offende daylie in all the braunches of symonye, the very
canker of the Churche, without feelinge of the rodde of this discipline. The seconde

f.89v

that manye of the laudable rightes and ceremonyes of the Churche or [1]perteyninge to the ministers of the same, agreed upon by common consente, the very ornamente of our religion, are eyther very evill kepte, or els at the lest have loste a greate parte of theire estimacion. And here amongste many faultes throughe the wante of discipline to remember you of one perticular, a matter of greate momente. Howe commeth it to passe that the common people in the countrye universallie come so seldome to common prayer and devine service, and when they doe come be there manye tymes

f.90   soe vainely occupied or at the least doe not / there as they shoulde doe, but for wante of this discipline? And yet to the helpe of this there was at the last parliamente a lawe made, but hitherto noe man, no, noe man — or verye fewe — hath seene it executed. And playnely to speake, lawes for the furtheraunce of this discipline unexecuted be as roddes for correccion without handes. It cannot be denied but as superstition is everye waye to be abhorred for feare of idolatrie, soe certainelye the losse of this discipline is alwayes to be avoyded, least els contempte, contempte that necessarilie must followe, may cause irreligion to creepe faster in then a man would thinke: for of all other the most pestilent and pernicious thinge, never suffered or allowed in any common wealthe, noe, not amongste the Ethinques,[2] that were most barbarous. But here it may be saide, the mischiefe appeareth; what is the remedye? And that it were better not opened in such a presence, then opened without remedye bothe devised and declared. In mine opinion the remedyes may easilye be devised; all the difficultie is in the well executeinge of them. As first, if the chiefe personages of this realme bothe in towne and countrye would give good example, it cannot be but it woulde doe verye muche to the remedieinge of a greate parte of this mischiefe. Secondarilie, the devideinge of everye of the diocesses accordeinge to their greatenes into deaneryes (as I knowe commonlye they be) and the committeinge of thease deaneryes to men well chosen (as I thinke commonly they be not); and then the keepinge of certen ordinarye courtes at theire prescript tymes for the well executeinge of thease lawes of discipline, as they ought to be, with a severe controllemente of thease inferiour ministers by the bishoppe or his chauncellor, not byenuallie or tryenuallie, but every yeare twice or thrice, must of necessitie without great difficultie doe much in shorte tyme to the reformacion of this, the chiefe officers ecclesiasticall beinge well backed and the lawes of them selves beinge first made sufficient and perfecte, which in this parliamente may be easilye brought to passe. And because the proceedinge in matter of discipline and doctrine doe chiefelye concerne my lordes the bishopps both for theire understandeinge and ecclesiasticall function: therefore the Queene's Highenes looketh that they beinge called together heere in Parliamente should take the chiefe care to conferre and consulte of thease matters, and if in theire conference they shall finde it behoovefull to have any temporall acte made for the amendemente or reformeinge of any of thease lackes, that then they will exhibite it heere in Parliamente to be considered of; and soe *gladius gladium iuvabit*, as before tyme hath bin used, foreseeinge alwayes that all lawes and ordinaunces for thease matters of doctrine and discipline be uniforme and of one sorte throughoute all the whole realme. And thus much concerning matters of religion, beinge the first parte.

Nowe to the seconde, that is matters of pollicie. And therein first for the good governaunce of the subiecte at home, the lackes and defaultes whereof, as in discipline soe in this, standes altogether eyther in the imperfeccion of lawes or els in the fearefullnes, slouthfullnes or corrupcion of temporall officers that ought to see to the due execucion of them. / For the helpe of the former yee are to examine whether any lawes alreadye made are to sharpe or to sore, and so overburdenous for the subiecte, or whether any of them be to loose or to soft, and soe overdaungerous to the state, ffor like as the former may put in daunger manye an innocente perticulerlie, soe the seconde may putt in perill both the nocente and innocente, and the whole state universallie. It is written: *Acriores sunt morsus intermissae libertatis quam retentae.* Yee are also further to examine the wante and superfluitie of lawes, as whether crafte, mallice or covetousnes hath devised any wayes or meanes to defraude lawes already made, or howe to doe any iniurye, outerage or mischiefe for which there is noe lawe that hath his beinge to reforme it, or whether the common wealth or state of this realme by reason of any imperfeccion or cause is like to fall to any daunger or perill. For herein the greater the daunger is, the greater would your care and consideracion be for the removeinge of it. Ye are also to examine whether there be to many lawes for any one thinge, which breedeth soe many doubtes that the subiecte is sometyme to seeke howe to observe them, and the councellor how to give advise concerninge them. And as to the seconde imperfection, which is the wante of the due execucion of the lawes, because I can not perceive but all the rest and all lawes made, and to be made, without this is but vayne matter, therefore I have thought ofte with my selfe what might be the best remedye, if not to make all lawes perfectly executed (for that I can hardely hope of), yet to make them in much better case then nowe they be. And when I had all thoughte, I coulde finde noe more helpes but this. The first, by having greate care in the choyce of thease officers that have the execucion of lawes committed unto them. The seconde, by makeinge sharpe lawes to doe as much as may be for the banisheinge of slothe, corrupcion and feare from them. A thirde waye there is which I meane to open to you, and nevertheles to leave it to your iudgementes. This it is: there woulde be throughoute the realme a trienniall or byenniall visitacion in his nature made of all the temporall officers and ministers that by vertue of theire office have in chardge to see to th'execucion of lawes. By this I meane that the Queene should make choise every seconde or thirde yeare of certaine experte and proved persons, to whom commission should be graunted to trye out and examine by all meanes and wayes the offences of all such as have not seene to the due execucion of lawes accordeinge to the offices and chardges committed to them by the prince, and the offences soe founde and certified to be sharpelye punished without remission or redemption. Of effecte much like this, and to like ende, was the visitacion of the Churche first devised, whereof came in the beginninge great good, doubteless; and reason I see none but that the like oughte to followe uppon a like visitacion made amongst temporall officers. And whether the olde commissions of *oyer* tended somewhat to this ende I doubte. Certainelye if the lawes and statutes / of this realme shall not be indifferently, uprightly and diligently put in execucion (as my truste is they shalbe) speciallie in the great and open courtes of the realme, then my burden (I must confesse) is equall with the greatest; and yet for my parte I

f.90v

f.91

---

1. 'Or' supplied from Cott. Titus F1.   2. I.e. heathens.

woulde gladly every yeare heere and feele of such a comptroler.

Nowe to the last and greatest, which is the defence against the forreyne enemye abroade and his confederates bred and broughte up here amongst our selves. And because thease matters be by occasion now chiefely in hande, and that the dealinges of the outwarde enemye be matters that goe to the whole lande and that this presence representeth (ye knowe) the whole, therefore of all congruence it seemeth reason that all we for and in the name of the whole consider carefullie of this cause, and give presente assistaunce for the helpe of it. And to the ende yee may be the more able to give good counsell and advise herein, it hath bene thoughte meete I should summarilye and shortely make you priveye of thease proceedinges, which shalbe the better understande if I begin at the roote as I intende. This it is. The Queene's Maiestye at her cominge to her crowne findeinge this her realme in a ragged and torne state, and yet in warre with a mightie enemye, the chiefe ffortresse of the same lost to the realme's greate dishonor and weakeninge, her ffrontier townes not sufficientlie fortified, the revenewe of the Crowne greatelie spoyled, the treasure of the realme not onlye wasted but the realme besides alsoe greatelie indebted, the staple and store of all manner of municion for the realme's defence marveilouslye consumed, the navye and sea matters nothinge in the state they nowe be — was forced to give eare to a peace with some other condicions then els it is like her Highenes would have come to, to the end that most of thease daungerous defaultes might be in tyme of peace sufficientlie for the suretie of the realme be[3] provided for. Whereupon indeede her Highnes (peace beinge concluded) entred into the refourmeinge and supplyeinge of most of all thease greate lackes, and for the well doinge of them hath not forborne to take any care or payne, neither hath she slacked for the compasseinge of this to spende her owne treasure, to sell her owne lande, and to prove her creditte at home and abroade to the uttermoste: and all this for your suertie and quietnes. Here wantes the causes why the Queene's Highenes sente her forces to Lyethe in assisteinge the Scottes, and to Newhaven in assisteinge the Admirall and others against the Guysians, and a declaracion of the great chardges that grewe thereby; the particularityes be not yet written because the lawes be missinge, and to gesse at them were not meete lesse a man mighte misse in parte, which were a greate matter, beinge spoken in such a presence as they were. For the mayntenaunce of this matter noe chardges would be winssed at, noe payne pinched at, noe care untaken, noe labour forsaken. Thus have you hearde the somme of all thease proceedinges, whereby it is playne and evidente that like as our most deere and gratious soveraigne Ladye hathe for the preservacion of common quiett and for our suertie against the forreyne enemye forborne noe care nor travaile in deviseinge, noe more hath she noe chardge nor expense in perfourmeinge. I may safelie affirme, because I am well able to / prove it, that the chardges of the maynteyninge of thease affayres and that that hath bene done since the Queene's Majestie came to her crowne in the supplieinge of the daungers before remembred amounte to asmuche as two of the greatest subsedyes that I can remember: a matter not possible to be borne for that that[4] is past, nor to be continued for that that is to come, by the ordinarye revenewe of the Crowne, and yet of necessitie to be done, excepte all (which God forbid) should come to ruine. If when any parte of the naturall bodye happe to be in daunger, the heade and every parte

f.91v

hasteth to releeve, what would then be done (trowe yee) when perill is offered to the whole and every parte? Agayne, howe inconveniente and unnaturall it is when daunger is offered to the whole, that the head should take the whole care, and beare the whole burden, and all the members remayne uncarefull or unchardged; and therewith howe light the burden is when it is borne of manye is well understande of us all. But hereof I make a staye because there is noe doubte but that your good willes and towardenes upon thease consideracions be such as this last speeche of myne needethe not. And soe doubteles the Queene's Highenes takethe it. And yet, your wisdomes well knowe that the office and duetie of this place which I occupye craveth thus muche to be saide at my hande, and for that purpose chiefelie tolde (I truste) ye take it, and not for any necessitie to drawe them by perswasion that otherwise of theire owne disposicion be forwarde enoughe. The declaracion of the proceedinges being uttered, I doe assure my selfe to suffice men of your understandeinge and inclinacion: ffor howe can a man thinke that any is soe voide of reason that he would not gladlye offer anye ayde against the forreyne enemye that he were able to make for the safetie of his countrye, his soveraigne, himself, his wife and children, especiallie when by proofe it is playne that the Queene's Majestie hath alreadie and daylie doth employe her owne treasure, yea, and her landes and creditte, not in any glorious tryumphes, superfluous and sumptuous buildeinges of delighte, vayne and chardgeable embassages, neither in any other matters of will and pleasure (I meane noe expence to be noted in a prynce of fower[5] yeares raigne), but, as farre as men can iudge, in the service of her realme, in necessarie defence of her people, and for the anoyaunce of her enemye. Yet hath it bene seene or this, that princes' willes, pleasures and delightes have bene followed in expences as necessities: and nowe (God be thanked) the doeinges have bene such since the Queene's Highenes' raigne that to the indifferente man it will appeare probable and playne that the releevinge of the realme's necessitie is become the prince's delighte; a good chaunge, God continewe it. A[6] marvellous meete example for us to followe. And yet it is scante credible howe longe it was, and in the ende with what difficultie the Queene's Highenes came to agree that this example shoulde be followed by us, in beinge contente that / this parliamente should be summoned that is mighte be moved that the realme shoulde contribute to the realme's defence; with such difficultie indeede, that if any other way coulde have bene devised (her honor and realme's suretie saved) this had never bene attempted, soe lothe she is any offensive matter by burden or chardge shoulde be proponed to her lovinge subiectes, whose goode willes, love and favoure accordeinge to theire duetyes she maketh more accoumpte of then eyther of treasure or lande, yea, asmuche as of her owne lyfe, which our Lorde longe preserve; and soe from her owne mouthe she hath commaunded to say to you. Ohe, what a griefe it is (trowe yee) to a prince when he findeth such wante that he is not able soe to consider of the services of his servantes and subiectes in this daungerous and necessarie service as theire desertes doe crave, knoweinge that most commonlye the very lyfe and harte of the servante and soldier, which soe often offereth himself to the

f.92

---

3. *Sic.*
4. 'That' supplied from Cott.Titus F1.

5. Cott.Titus F1 reads 'seaventeene'.
6. 'A' repeated in MS.

cannon, the pique, the fyre and water, is either overthrowne or sett up as regarde is
had of his perilles, excepte there be some odde men (as they call them) of that
perfeccion that make vertue and well doeinge theire marke, and not rewarde, who
houlde for firme that *recti facti merces est fecisse tantum*. But *rara avis in terris*[7] *etc*; yea,
these are so rare as counsell cannot be given that princes' services should hange on
the helpe of such hope. And yet those be the perfectest and best. But the worlde is not
served by suche. To give good wordes is a good thinge, but ofte used, be it never soe
cunningelye, without deedes (where power serves) is reputed but as wynde, and is in
deede verelye *dare verba*. Marye, power servinge not, then it deserveth greate
commendacion: for it is asmuche as can be done, ffor *ultra posse non est esse*. But
thereof thinkethe little the greatest number. But to a prince who knoweth thus
muche, and daylie thinkethe and feeleth of it, what a tormentinge trouble is suche a
wante thinke you? Thease wantes when they happen woulde be holpe, and must be
holpen: but here I have gone somewhat further then eyther I meante or perchaunce I
needed. If I have so done, I pray you applye it to the best as I mente it: and soe there
must needes come good of it. And thus no further to trouble you, but to make an
ende.

Ye have hearde first the causes of this assemblie; secondarilie, what I thinke meete
to be remembred for matters of doctryne and disciplyne; thirdely, what for the
governaunce of the subiecte at home and what hath bene done for defence of the
enemye abroade. Your offices and duetyes be carefullie to consider of thease matters,
which I have rather summarilie remembred then effectuallie discoursed. The former
perteyneth to myne office as a remembrauncer, the seconde to you as executors of
those remembraunces. And because you of the nether howse cannot without an
head thus doe, therefore it resteth that you accordeinge to the auncient order of your
selves choose some wise and discreete man, who after he be by you chosen and
presented, and that presentacion by the Queene's Majestie allowed shall then be your
Speaker. And daye for your presentacion is given by her Highenes untill Fridaye
nexte.

---

7. Two very commonly employed tags. For
the first see Seneca, *Epistolae ad Lucilium*, 81,
sect.20; for the second Juvenal, *Satires*, vi,
line 165.

3. Sir Ralph Sadler's speech on the succession

Text from BL Add.33593, original in Sadler's hand.
Printed. Sadler's State Papers, ed. A. Clifford and T. Park (1809, 2 vols.), II. 556-61.

Add.33,593, fos. 3-4v

I am not fitte to speke in so grete a matier as this is, wantyng wisedom, lerning and experyence required to be in him that should iudge of the same, but because I have harde some speche uttered here touching the tytle of the Quene of Scottes to th'imperiall crowne of this realme, wherein it semeth that she hathe som fautours[1] and favourers [in this House],[2] I am the rather moved to utter myn affection in that parte. In dede I am not so well lerned in the lawes of the realme that I can or will presume or take upon me to iudge or discusse of titles. I can not say who hathe the best and most iust title to succede the Quene's Majeste in her imperiall crowne (God preserve her Highnes in helth long to enioye it with moche felicite), but being a mere naturall English man I do fynde in meself a gret mislyking to be subiect to a foreyn prynce, a prynce of a straunge nacion; and me thinkes we shulde not be so unnaturall as to seke or desire a straungier to reigne over us rather then a prynce of our owne nacyon. And for the Quene of Scottes, though she were in dede next heire in bloodde to the Quene's Majeste, yet being a straungier, by the lawes of the realme, as I understande, she can not inherite in Englonde,[3] which is a good argument to me that the nature of English men hath alwaies so moche detested the regiment of straungiers that they have made lawes to barre all tytles which any straungier may clayme of inheritaunce within the realme.

We have had good experience of the Scottes, how moche they have disdayned to have a prynce of our nacyon to reigne over them and that they have rather chosen to abyde all extremyte of the warres and force of Englonde then / they wolde consent to f.3v
have an English man to be theyr kyng and governor, whereof I can shew you a good and trew example; and also I can tell you what affection and disposicion I have founde in the Scottes themselffes by their owne confession and sayeinges unto me in this case. Not long after the deth of the last King of Scottes I was sent into Scotland by the King then our sovereign lorde King Henry viij[th] to move a maryage bytwen Prynce Edward that then was and the Quene of Scottes that now is.[4] And I had to do therein with the Quene then Douagier of Scotland, mother to the Quene that now is, and also with him that was then governor of Scotland, who semed to lyke very well of the matier, although in dede they did but dissemble as it did playnely

1. I.e. supporters.
2. Crossed out.
3. See M. Levine, *Tudor Dynastic Problems* (1973), 110-11 for discussion of 25 Ed.III, st.1(1351) in *SR*, I.310, and *EP*, I.133 for

students' debate in 1566 at Lincoln's Inn on foreigners and the succession.
4. In 1543, after Solway Moss and the death of James V.

appere afterwardes. But yet they semed to lyke so well of it that they were content to sende theyr ambassadors hither to treate of the matier here with the King himself; whereupon the Kyng appoynted certen of his counsaile by commission to treate with them, whereof insued a long treatie from Easter till it was almost Mighelmas, for the Scottes used many delayes only to wynne tyme, and yet at the last they agreed uppon the mariage and the treatie was made and sealed by the commissioners on both sides and also afterwardes ratefied both by the Kyng here and also by the governor in Scotland. And amongst other thinges it was pacted and couvenanted in the treatie that the yong quene shoulde be delyvered into Englonde when she shoulde accomplisshe the age of x yeres, and in the meane season a gentilman and a gentilwoman of Englond with a convenyent nomber of English men and women, not above the nomber of xl as I remember, shoulde remayne in Scotland aboutes the yong prynces for her better educacion after th'Inglish maner; and also that vj noblemen of Scotland or their next heires shoulde remayne in Englond as hostages and pleges for the delyverie of the yong quene into England at her age of x yeres, and as any of the hostages either shuld dye or / or retorne into Scotland, others shulde be sent to supplie their places of like degree so as alwaies vj shulde remayn in Englonde as pledges untill the yong quene were delyvered into Englonde. This was fully agreed and no soner agreed then it was fourthwith violated and broken on their parte, for when it cam to the poynt that the hostages shoulde repaire into Englonde, not one noble man of Scotland wolde either com himself or suffer his next heire to lye in Englonde as hostage and pledge for the delyverie of the yong quene according to the treatie. So as the hole treatie was violated and broken and no parte of it performed on their parte.

f.4

Now whilles this matier was in treatie, and after it was agreed on and before it was ratefied, I had sondry conferences with dyvers Scottish men to understande their affections and amongst others with one Otterborn, Sir Adam Otterborn, a knight, reputed to be a wise man as any was in Scotland; he was sundry tymes ambassador here with King Kenry the viij[th] from the last King of Scottes. And with him I discoursed of the grete benefite and quyetnes lyke to insue of that maryage bytwen those ij prynces whereby the ij° realmes should be unyted and conioyned under one regyment.[5] And in our talke it semed to me that he coulde not chose but breke out in these wordes, 'Whie think you', quod he, 'that this treatie wilbe performed?' 'Whie not?' quod I. 'I assure you', quod he, 'it is not possible, for our people', quod he, 'do not lyke of it; and though the governor and som of the nobylite for certen respectes have consented to it, yet', quod he, 'I know that few or none of them do lyke of it and our comen people', sayeth he, 'do utterly mislyke of it.' I tolde him agayn that it was verye straunge to me to understonde their affections to be suche, considering the greate weale and benefite that must nedes insue of it, th'oportunyte and occasion thereof being offered as it were by Godde's divine providence, having lefte unto them a yong prynces and to us a yong prynce, by the mariage of which ij° prynces thes ij° realmes, being knytte and conioyned in one, the subiectes of the same which have ben alwaies infested with the warres might lyve in welth and perpetuel peax. 'I pray you', quod he, 'give me leave to aske you a question'; and this was his question in these wordes and termes which I will reherse unto you. 'If', quod he, 'your lad were

a las and our las were a lad, wolde you then', quod he, 'be so ernest in this matier and coulde you be content that our lad shoulde mary your las and so be King of Englonde?' I answered that considering the grete good that might insue of it I shoulde not shew myself zelous to my countrey if I shoulde not / consent unto it.   f.4v
'Well', quod he, 'if you had the las and we the lad we coulde be well content with it; but', sayeth he, 'I can not beleve that your nacyon coulde agree to have a Scotte to be King of Englonde, and lykewise I assure you', quod he, 'that our nacyon, being a stoute nacyon, will never agree to have an English man to be King of Scotlande. And though the hole nobilite of the realme wolde consent unto it yet our comen people and the stones in the strete wolde ryse and rebelle ayenst it'. This was his sayeng unto me, and others also sayed asmoche to lyke effect, whereby you may the better understonde the affection and disposicion of thes Scottes in this case. And even as they sayed it folowed, for by and by after the treatie was ratefied the governor and nobilite of Scotland revolted from it; contrary to their othe, lyke false forsworn Scottes, wher[upon] the warres insued whereof they worthely fele the smarte at this daye.

Now if thes proude beggerly Scottes did so moch disdayn to yelde to the superioryte of England, that they chose rather to be periured and to abyde the extremytee of the warres and force of Englonde then they wolde consent to have an English man to be their kyng by such laufull meanes of maryage, whie shulde we for any respect yelde to their Scottisshe superioryte, or consent to establisshe a Scotte in succession to the crowne of this realme, contrary to the lawes of the realme, and therby to do so grete an iniurye as to disinherite the next heire of our owne nacyon? Surely for my parte I can not consent unto it. And I feare leest I may say with the Scotte that though we do all agree unto it yet our comen people and the stones in the strete wolde rebelle ayenst it. So that where it is thought to be for a perpetual concorde, it wolde rather turne to a perpetuell discorde, both amongst our selffes and with the Scottes for ever. Thus have I declared myn affection concerning the regiment of a straunge prynce over us, wherein whatsoever may be gathered of my wordes I meane aswell to my countrey as becometh a naturall and good English man, and no lesse honour and suretie to my prynce then apertyneth to th'office and duetie of a trew subiect.

5. Note Sadler's claim that the notion of Anglo-Scottish union was evident in the 1540s, and see the 1546 edition of Vergil's *Urbinatis Anglicae Historiae Libri Vigintisex*, which tells the story of Henry VII dealing with fears of political union arising from marriage (Levine, *op.cit.*, 40, 143.)

4. Commons' petition, 28 January

Text from PRO SP Dom.Eliz.27/35, a clerk's copy with marginal notes by Cecil; some preferable readings from another contemporary copy, Northants. CRO: Fitzwilliam of Milton Political 169, and from BL Cott.Titus FI.
Other MSS. London: BL Harl.2185 and Stowe 358 (copies of Cott.Titus FI), Stowe 354, Add.33271, Harl.6842 (f.83, incomplete); PRO SP Dom.Eliz.27/37 (later copy of 35). Oxford: Bodley, Carte 105. Cambridge: Gonville and Caius College 64 (copy of Cott.Titus FI). Longleat, Wilts.: Bath, Dudley iii.33.
Printed. D'Ewes, 81-3; *Nugae Antiquae*, ed. H. Harington and T. Park (1804), I.69-79.

SP Dom.Eliz.27/35

1563

Your commons in this your Majestie's present parliament assembled, most high and mighty Princesse and our most drede sovereigne Lady, as they do dayly to their commodity and comforte fele and receave the inestimable benefittes of your most gratious government of this your realme in peace and suerty, so do also most thankfully acknowledg the same, beseching almighty God long to blesse and continue your most prosperous reigne over them. And among all those benefittes which they dayly receve of your Highnes, they have willed me at this tyme in their names to recognise unto your Highnes that they accompt it not the least, but rather emong the gretest of them all, that your Majestie hath at this time assembled your parliament for supplieng and redressing the gretest wantes and defaultes in this your commen weale, and for th'establishing the suerty of the same; which your Majestie's most gratious meaning hath ben at your commandement signified unto us by the ryght honourable the Lord Keper, namely in this, that he willed first to have consideration of the gretest matters that nerest towched the estate of our realme and the preservation therof, seming therin to expresse unto us the conformity of your Majestie's mind in having principall respect to the matters of the gretest weight, for that respect assembling[1] this our parliament. And forasmuch as your said subiectes see nothing in this wholl estate of so great importance to your Majestie and the wholl realme, nor so necessary at this time to be reduced into a certenty, as the sure continuaunce of the governaunce and th'imperiall crowne therof in your Majestie's person and the most honorable issue of your body, which almighty God send us to our highest comforte, and, for want therof, in some certen limitacion to guide the obedience of our posterity. And where almighty God to our great terror and dreadfull warning lately towched your Highnes with some danger of your most noble person by sicknes, from which so sone as your Grace was by Godde's favour and

Issew[2]

The Queen's late sycknes

mercy to us recovered, your Highnes sent out your writtes of Parliament, by force wherof your subiectes are at this present assembled,[1] your said subiectes are both by the necessity and importance of the matter and by the convenience of the time, calling them immediately upon the recovery, enforced together and confesse your Majestie of your most gratious and motherly care for them and their posterity have summoned this parliament principally for stablisheng some certen limitacion of th'imperiall crowne of your realme, for preservation of your subiectes from certen and utter distruction if the same shuld not be provided for in your life, which God long continue. They can not (I saye) but acknowledg how your Majestie hath most gratiously considered the great daungers, the unspeakeable miseries of civill warres, the perillous intermedlinges of forreyne princes with seditious, ambicious and factious subiectes at home, the wast of noble howses, the slawghter of people, subvercion of townes, intermission of all thinges perteyning to the maintenance of the realme, unsurety of all men's possessions, lives and estates, dayly interchang of atteindors and treasons: all these mischeives and infinite other most like and evident, if your Majestie shuld be taken away from us without knowen heire, which God forbidd, to fall upon your subiectes to the utter subvercion of the wholl realme, wherof you have charge under God, if good provision shall not be had in this behalf. Your Majestie hath weighed the examples of forein nations, as what ensewed the death of great Alexander, when for want of certeyne heires by him begotten or apointed, the varieties of titles, the diversity of disposicions in them that had titles, the ambicion of them that under[3] colour of dowtfulnes of titles forsoke all obedience of titles, destroyed the dividers of his dominions, and wasted ther posterity with mutuall warres and slawghters. In what miserable case also was this your realme it self when the title of the Crowne was tossed in question betwene two royall howses of Lancaster and York, till your most noble progenitors King Henry the vij[th] and the Lady Elizabeth his wife restored it to setled unity and left the crowne in certein course of succession. These thinges, as your Majestie hath upon your owne danger most gratiously considered for our comforte and safety, so we your most humble subiectes, knoweng the preservation of our selves and all our posterity to depend upon the safety of your Majestie's most royall person, have most carefully and diligently considered how the want of heires of your body and of certein limitacion of succession after you is most perillous to your Highnes, whom God long preserve emong us. We have ben admonished of the great mallice of your forein enemies, which even in your life time have sought to transferre the right and dignity of your crowne to a stranger; we have noted their dayly most dangerous practises against your life and your reigne. We have hard of some subiectes of this land most unnaturally confederate with your enimies to attempt the destruction of your Majestie and us all that live by you. We feare a faccion of heretickes in your realme, contentious and malicious papistes, least they moste unnaturally[4] against their contry, most madly against ther owne safety, and most trayterously against your

[margin] Alexander dyed without childre

[margin] Lancaster York

1. MS reads 'assembled'; this reading from Fitzwilliam of Milton 169.
2. Marginal notes are in Cecil's hand.
3. MS reads 'had', as does Fitzwilliam of

Milton; this reading from Cott. Titus F1.
4. 'Confederate . . . unnaturally' supplied from Fitzwilliam of Milton 169.

Highnes not only hope of the wofull daye of your death but also laye in wayte to advaunce some title under which they may renue their late unspeakeable cruelty, to the destruction of goodes, possessions and bodies, and thrawldome of the sowles and consciences of your faithfull and Christian subiectes. We see nothing to withstand their desire, but only your life. Their unkindness and cruelty we have tasted; we feare much to what attempt the hope of such oportunity, nothing withstanding them but your life, will move them. We find how necessary it is for our preservation that there may be more sett and knowen betwene your Majestie's life and their desire. We see, on the other side, how there can be no such danger to your Majestie by ambicion of any apparaunt heire established by your benefitt and advauncement, for want of issue of your Majestie's royall body, as you are now subiect unto by reason of the desire and hope, we know not of how many, that pretend titles and trust to succede you, whose secret desire we so much more feare because nether their nomber, force nor likelyhoode of disposicion is knowen unto us, and so we can the lesse beware of them for your preservacion. We find also by good proofe that the certein limitacion of the crowne[5] of Fraunce hath in that realme procured so great quiett as neither the person of the prince in possession hath ben endangered by secrete or open practise nor the commen wealth molested by civill discencion through any quarrell attempted for the title of that crowne. And, somewhat nerer home, we have also remembred the miserable estate of Scotland after the death of King Alexander[6] without any certein heire or limitacion to whom the crowne of Scotland shuld remain, by reason wherof the wholl estate of that realme was left open to the ambicion of many competitors[7] and most grevous desolation and spoyle, that grew upon such division; which afterward gave occasion to King James the vth to limitt the crowne of Scotland to certen noble families of that realme, wherby they at this present enioye that quiett suerty which we do want. And all your Majestie's progenitors, kinges of the realme, hath in this behalf ben so carefull that from the Conquest to this present daye the realme was never left, as now it is, without a certein heire living and knowen to whome the crowne after the death of the prince shuld appertein, so as your Majestie of your singuler care for us and our posterity hath at this time assembled us for establishment of this great and only staye of our safeties. We again (o most gracious soveraigne Lady) acknowledg our selves and all that we have to depend upon your preservation, being according to our bounden duty most carefull for the same, are in most humble manner come to your Majestie's presence. And I, the mouth appointed for them, together with and in the name of all your most loving, naturall and obedient subiectes do present unto yow our most lowly sute and peticion: that, forasmuch as your Majestie's person shuld come to most undowted and best heires of your crowne, such as in time to come we wold most comfortably see and our posterity shall most ioyfully obey, it may please your most excellent Majestie for our sakes, for our preservation and comfortes, and at our most humble sute to take your self some honorable husband whom it shall please yow to ioyne to you in mariag; whomesoever it be that your Majestie shall choose, we protest and promisse with all humility and reverence to honour, love and serve as to our most bounden duty shall appertein. And where by the statute[8] which your most noble father assented unto of his most princely and fatherly zeale to his most loving subiectes for limitacion of succession of the imperiall crowne of this realme, your Majestie is last expressly named within the body of the same act, and for that your subiectes can not iudg nor knowe any thing of the forme or validity of any further limitacions sett in certentie for want of heires of your body, wherby some great dangerous dowbt remayneth in their hartes to their great greif, perill and unquietnes, it may please your Majestie by publication of certeinty alredy provided, if any such be, or elles by limitacion of certeinty, if none be, to provide most gratious remedy in this great necessity which, by your most honorable and motherly carefulnes for them, hath occasioned this assembly, that in this convenient tyme of Parliament upon your late daunger most gratiously called by yow for that cause, your Grace may now extend to us the gretest benefitt which otherwise or at other times perhappes shall never be able to be don againe, so not only we, but also all ours hereafter and forever, shall owe no lesse but as to your Majestie's propagation[9] of succession that we do alredy owe to your most noble grandfather King Henry the vij[th] his uniting of division. And your subiectes in their behalfes for your Majestie's further assurance, wherupon their owne preservation wholly dependeth, shall employe their wholl endevors, wittes and powers to revive, devise and establish the most strong and beneficiall actes and lawes for the preservation and suerty of your Majestie and your issue in the imperiall crowne of this realme, and the most penall, sharp and terrible statutes to all that shall but once practise, attempt or convey against your safety, that by any possible meanes they may invent and stablish, with such limitacions of condicions and restreintes to all in remaynders, such grevous paynes and narrowe animadversions to all that shall enterprice or imagin any thing in preiudice of your Highnes and your issue, as your Majestie shall not have any iust cause of suspicion but most assured confidence in all your faithfull subiectes, continually watching and warding for your preservation, which God long continue that you see your children's children to his honor and comforte, and encline your gratious harte to our most humble peticion.

---

5. MS reads 'ruine', as does Fitzwilliam of Milton; this reading from Cott. Titus F1.

6. Alexander III.

7. MS reads 'competites', as does Fitzwilliam of Milton; this reading from Cott. Titus F1.

8. 35 Hen. VIII, c.1 (1543‑4) in *SR*, III.955.

9. MS reads 'propagyon'; this reading from Fitzwilliam of Milton.

5. Queen's answer to the Commons' petition, 28 January

Text from PRO SP Dom.Eliz.27/36, a clerk's copy with a marginal note by Cecil; some readings from BL Add.33271.
Other MSS. London: PRO SP Dom.Eliz.27/37 (late copy of 36).
Oxford: Bodley, Rawlinson D.723 (misdated in catalogue).
Northants. CRO: Fitzwilliam of Milton Political 170. Longleat, Wilts.: Bath, Dudley iii.37.
Printed. Nugae Antiquae, ed. H. Harington and T. Park (1804), I.80⁄3.

SP Dom.Eliz.27/36

The spekar of the parliament[1]

Williams. I have hard by yow the commen request of my commons, which I may well terme (me thinketh) the wholl realme because, they geve, as I have hard, in all these matters of Parliament their commen consent to such as be here assembled. The weight and greatenes of this matter might cause in me, being a woman wanting both witt and memory, some feare to speake, and bashfulnes besides, a thing appropriat to my sex. But yet the princely seate and kingly throne wherin God, (though unworthy) hath constituted me, maketh these two causes to seme litle in myne eyes, though grevous perhaps to your eares, and boldeneth me to saye somewhat in this matter, which I meane only to towche, but not presently to answer: for this so great a demaund nedeth both great and grave advise. I reade of a philosopher, whose dedes upon this occasion I remember better then his name, who always when he was required to give answer in any hard question of schole poyntes, wold reherse over his alphabett before he wold procede to any further answer therin, not for that he could not presently have answered, but to[2] have his witt the riper and better sharpened to answer the matter withall. If he, a commen man, but in matters of schole tooke such delaye the better to shew his eloquent tale, great cause may iustly move me in this so great a matter towching the benefitt of this realme and the safety of yow all to differ myne answer till some other time, wherin I assure yow the consideration of my owne safety (although I thank you for the great care that yow seme to have therof) shalbe litle in comparison of that great regard, that I meane to have of the safety and suerty of yow all.

And though God of late semed to touche me, rather like one that he chastised then one that he punished, and though death possessed almost every ioynt of me, so as I wished then that the feble threed of life, which lasted (me thought) all to long, might by Clotho's[3] hand have quietly ben cutt of, yet desired I not then life (as I have some witnesses here) so much for myne owne safety, as for yours. For I knew that in exchanging of this reigne, I shuld have enioyed a better reigne, where residence is perpetuall. There nedes no boding of my bane. I know now aswell as I did before that I am mortall; I know also that I must seke to discharg my self of that great burthen that God hath layed upon me. For of them to whome much is committed, much is required. Think not that I, that in other matters have had convenient care of you all, will in this matter towching the safety of my self and you all be careles. For I knowe that this matter towcheth me much nerer then it doth you all, who, if the wortst happen, can loose but your bodies; but if I take not that convenient care that it behoveth me to have therin, I hasserd to loose both body and sowle.

And though I am determined in this so great and weighty a matter to differ myne answer till some other time, because I will not in so depe a matter wade with so shallowe a witt; yet have I thought good to use these few wordes, aswell to show you that I am nether careles nor unmindfull of your safety in this case, as I trust yow likewise do not forgett that by me yow were delivered whilest yow were hanging on the bowgh redy to fall into the mudde, yea, to be drowned in the donge, nether yet the promise which yow have here made concerning your duties and due obedience, wherwith I assure yow I meane to charg yow, as further to lett you understand that I neither mislike any of your requestes herin, nor the great care that you seme to have of the suerty and safety of your selves in this matter. Lastly, because I will discharg some restles heades, in whose braines the neadeles hammers beate with vaine iudgment that I shuld mislike this their peticion, I saye that of the matter and some therof I like and allowe very well; as to the circumstances, if any be, I meane upon further advise further to answer. And so I assure yow all that though after my death yow may have many stepdames, yet shall yow never have any a more naturall[4] mother then I meane to be unto you all.

---

1. Marginal note in Cecil's hand.
2. 'To' supplied from Add.33271.
3. MS reads 'Clois'; this reading from Add.33271. Elizabeth is talking of the 'feeble thread' of her life, and it is likely that she would have invoked Clotho, one of the Greek *moirae*, as the spinner fate who represents life.
4. 'Naturall' supplied from Add.33271.

6. Robert Atkinson's speech on the oath of supremacy, (?) March

Text from Gonville and Caius College, Cambridge, 392, copy.[1]
Printed. J. Strype, *Annals of the Reformation* (1824 edn), I.i.446⁄55
(probably from a Foxe MS, in possession of Strype, purchased after
his death by Harley – see *DNB sub* Foxe, John).

Gonville and Caius College 392, pp. 185⁄201

An oration made in the parlement house by Mr Robert Atkinson, student in the Inner Temple, the [blank] of Marche in the vth yeare of the raigne of Queene Elizabeth, against the bill of the othe.

Right honourable, yee have heard the effect of this bill contayninge in it selfe that all those that shall by any open acte mainetaine foraine iurisdiction or shall refuse the othe which is likewise for the abolishinge of all foraine power, that such offenders shall for their first offence incurre the daunger of *praemunire*; and if they eftsones offend [again], then to be adiudged in case of high treason. Whether any foraine power be lawfully to be received within this realme or whether in conscience a man ought to take this othe, that matter I purpose not as now to dispute, for that is already put out of question by consent of the whole realme in high court of Parlement in the first yeare of the raigne of our soveraigne Lady that now is, against which it shall not become me [to] reason. But whether an offence committed against that statute be so sharpely to be punished as this bill here requireth, that is the question that we have in
p.186 hand; wherein I thinke that the punishment limited in this bill is too rigorowse, / and though this acte went forward yet no benefite could therof grow to the common wealth.

If the offence were treason, as it was said this other day in the Howse that it was, and that the offenders therein were traytors even by the common lawes of this realme as men [who] thought to take the crowne from the king and give it to the pope, then would I thinke no punishment to little[2] for it, and pitty it were that even for the first offence it were not made death. Howbeit if it may be proved unto you that the maintenance of foraine iurisdiction was not by the lawes ever accounted treason, then I trust their will no good man thinke but that the offence not beinge so great the punishment ought not to be so great neither. I well agree that the ancient writers of the law, as both Bracton and Bryton, have in their writinges called the king God's vicare in earth,[3] and I well assent to that that Skipwithe sayeth, that their is the deanry of Pikeringe in Ireland belonginge to the archebishoppricke of Dublinge and that is of this court[4], that if an English man bee made archebishopp then he shall
p.187 have the deanery as / his free chappell, and if an Ireyshe man, then the kinge: his

reason is *quia reges sacro oleo uncti spiritualis jurisdictionis sunt capaces*, because the sacred majestie of a prince anoyneted with holie oyle hath capacitie of spirituall jurisdiction. I likeqwise agree to the saying of Bryan where he saith that a great doctor of law once told him that a preist by prescription might be impleaded in the kinge's temporall court *quia rex est persona unita ex sacerdotibus et laicis*, because the person of a kinge is mixte of preisthood and laitie.[5] Of all which wee may gather that by the comon lawes the kinge may have the temporall profits of a spirituall promotion and also implead a spiritual person in his temporall court. All which notwithstandinge I am sure noe auctoritie can be shewed to prove that the affirmeing the pope ought to have jurisdiction in those or other like matters or that the iurisdiction of them ought not to appartaine to the kinge was ever yet accounted treason.

And therefore suppose that the kinge had brought a *quare impedit* against a spirituall person, which is a plea meere temporall, determinable / in his temporall   p.188 courte, and that the spirituall person had thought to appeale to Rome in stay of the iudgement; had this beene treason? Nay surely, though, without some open acte shewinge the same [it] was never taken to be treason, not it was yet never seene that a man in such case was bound to discover his conscience upon his othe. But goe further. Suppose he had expresly said before witnesse he would appeale to Rome; nay, suppose he had appealed to Rome indeed: had this beene treason? Nay it was never yet but *praemunire*, and not *praemunire* nother tyll the statute of 2 Ez.[6] made it so. And yet was this an offence against the kinge's crowne and dignitie. But so are many offences that are not treason nor are not, as he said, *crimina laesae maiestatis* but *crimina minutae maiestatis*.

If then to affirme that the pope ought to have iurisdiction in a temporall matter were not treason, much lesse were it treason to affirme the same in a spirituall matter, as to say that the consecration of archebishoppes belonged unto him or that the order of service and sacraments ought to be directed by the see apostolicke. What the judges have said in / our lawe in the behalfe of the pope, that spare I here for my   p.189 dutie's sake to speake of: I am sure it was much more then I have hitherto said, and yet were they as skilfull, I beleive, in knowinge what treason was, as lothe to offende therein as was that gentleman that went about with so many reasons to prove it treason. Nor I doubt not but even at those times when princes suffered this offence to remaine unpunished and when the subiects offended in it, that yet they had as great a care to mainetayne the royall dignitie of the crowne and were otherwise as voyde of trayterouse hearts as those that now thinke themselves best subiects.

1. Volume 2 of the 'Miscellaneous Collections' of Robert Hare, member in this Parliament, but given by William Moore. (See *DNB sub* Hare, Robert and Moore, William.)
2. *Sic.*
3. Bracton, e.g. fos.IV, 5v; J. Britton, *An English Translation and Notes*, ed. F. M. Nichols (Washington, 1901), 2.

4. *Sic.*
5. YB 10 Hen.VII, Hil, pl.17 (cited by S. B. Chrimes, *English Constitutional Ideas in the Fifteenth Century* (1936), 387.
6. MS originally read '27 Ez.', the 7 being later crossed out; the reference is presumably intended to be to the statute of I Elizabeth.

And therefore we read that in time of Edward the First the pope willed the kinge to take[7] peace with Scotland, and he made him answer that towchinge his temporalties he knewe noe pere in his realme.[8] And the like lettres were sent in time of Henry the Sixt and Humfrey that was Duke of Glocestre hurled them in the fire.[9] And whosoever readeth the statute of *praemunire* made in 16 Richard 2[10] shall find that all the lordes, both spirituall and temporall, said that they would sticke with the

p.190   kinge in the mainetenance of his crowne and dignitie / to the death, and they were thereof severally examined to the intent that their opinions might be knowne. If then it have beene proved that the offence hath not beene treason nor that the offenders theirin have not otherwise borne trayterous heartes I trust that the offence not beinge soe great yow will not without cause goe about to encrease the punishment.

Let us therefore never goe about to aggreive the matter or make it worse then it is, but let us consider it but such as it is indeed, that is an offence in this religion and an offence against the statute made in the first yeare of the Queen's Majestie. And then whether such an offence be to be punished by death either for the preservation of the common peace or els by the expresse lawes of God, that matter falleth further in consultacion.

As for the scriptures I must confesse my selfe ignorant in them as the thinge that is not my profession nor in which I have beene exercised; yet thus much have I heard the preachers say that are now, that though in the olde law idolatry have beene punished by death, yet since the comminge of Christ – who came to winne the

p.191   world by peace / and bad 'Put up thy sword' – the greatest punishment that hath beene taught by the apostles for offendors in case of religion hath beene by excommunication. For religion, say they, must sinke in by perswasion; it cannot be pressed in by violence. And therefore they called the acte of the six articles that was made in xxxj° of Henry the Eight 'the whip with the sixe lashes'; and as for the dealinges in Queene Marie's dayes they much disliked them, callinge the bishops 'blood suckers' and bid fie on those tormentors that delighted in nothinge else but in the death of innocents, that threatened the whole realme with their fire and their fagottes, murtherers, that they were worse then Caiphas, worse then Judas, worse then the traytors that put Christ to death, and that with such vehemencie and stomacke as I assure you I marvaile me how it can possibly come to passe that they should now desire to establish that as a law which they thought then so farr unlawfull.

And indeed many a solemne clerck and holie father hath theire beene in the Church that have much misliked that cruell handling and have wished rather the

p.192   opinions of the men to be taken away then the menn / themselves and would have them convinced *magis verbo quam vi*, or rather by the word then by the sword. Howbeit what was the cause why in all Christian realmes offendors in religion have been punished by death; and, farther, how farr the punishment that is here devised exceedeth that in rigour and crueltie; and lastly, how offendors in this case of religion ought not to be punished by the one nor the other, that matter shall I make so plaine and so evident unto you that I trust no charitable man will consent to the passing of this bill.

First as for excommunicacion: that was thought so easie a punishment that it was the thinge that they gladliest would have wished, ffor what could please them better that had already forsaken the true faith then to be banished from the company of all such as beleeved otherwise then themselves? Therefore was fyninge and ransominge devised against the Manicheys; but that would not serve, for either had they nothinge to loose or els were willinge to loose that that they had. Then was it farther devised that they should be emprisoned, but imprisonment would not helpe neither, for the / number of them was such as prisons could not hold them and the keepers   p.193 many times were corrupted. Then was banishment devised, but that was worst of all other, for then would they by there lettres openly defame those by whome they for their nawtinesse had received any domage, and further, not keeping their consciences to themselves, ceased not by preaching in woodes and cellars, by dealing in hucker mucker seditious bookes of their owne makinges, keeping of midnight lectures, making of enterludes and balades, to allure other selie[11] soules to their naughtinesse: so farr forth that if better remedie had not beene provided this canker would have crept over the whole body of Christendome. Nor they were not so contented neither, but fell to open violence, as robbing and spoilinge of churches and takinge of other menn's goodes from them; in so much that the stories of the Church make mention that when the Macedonyans and the Catholiques should come before the deputie of Philippus they fell upon them and slew them to the number of three thousand. / For which violence of theires it was ordained by consent   p.194 through Christendome that violence should be offred them againe and their offence for common quiet's sake and for the peace of the Church punished in this sort, that is to say, that if it were by open witnesse proved that he had offended that yet he might for the first offence abiure if he would and upon penance and repentance made be received [in]to the Church againe; but if he eftsones fell in relaps then he should be left to the secular hands. Which punishement as it was, was yet much more easy then that which is here devised – ffor there you see unlesse he had beene convinced by witnesse for some open acte done he was without daunger of the law, but here, though he intend to live under a law and keepe his conscience to himselfe, yet will we grope him and se what secretly lyeth in his breast, and to the intent he shall not dally with us we offer him an othe which many a man shall take that understandeth not what it meaneth – there you see the first offence was not punished but he should have leisure to bethinke him and mend. But here the very first offence is punished, and by what punishment, forsooth, by the iudgement / of *praemunire*, which is losse   p.195 of lands and goods, his body in prison at the Queene's will and pleasure; and yet he in noe great surety of his life neither, ffor if any man upon displeasure should kill him, his freinds might well lament his death but they could not punish it, ffor a man attainted in *praemunire* is, pardye,[12] out of the protection of the kinge and of the law.

7. *Sic.*

8. See T. Rymer, *Foedera* (1739–45), I pt lv. 5–6, 9–11.

9. These incidents were recalled in 1486, though the details are imprecise. See Chrimes, *op.cit.*, 51–3, 379–80 and n.7;

J. Ferguson, *English Diplomacy, 1422–61* (1972), 126–8.

10. 16 Rich.II, c.5 (1392–3) in *SR*, II.84–6.

11. Defenceless.

12. By God; indeed.

Yea and besides all this not a man dare give him his almes least he should be an aider and maintayner within the compasse of this statute.

Therefore me thinke the law was a great deale better and surely much more profitable for the common wealth that was made in the first yeare of the Queen's Maiestie, ffor there we see the first offence is not so greevously punished; and if every ecclesiasticall person, every iudge and other officer, every one that is of the Queene's ffe, every man that shall sue livery, all schollars in the universities be sworne as they

p.196   must be by the same statute, what mischiefe can there be wrought but it shalbe espied and quenched? Is it not, thinke you, an easier way to wyn menn (for winn them we must if we should do well) to leave a gapp for him open to promotion if he / embrace theise proceedinges then if he refuse yt to take that that he hath from him? Ys it not a sufficient punishment that noe man shall by his witt or learnening,[13] soe longe as he continueth that opinion, beare any office or have any countenance in his common wealth? What better proofe can you have of the goodnes of the law then that you see since that time noe great breach of the law, no seditious congregations, no tumultes, but the common peace well kepte, and every man lived under a law without disturbance of the Queen's proceedinges? So that that punishment beinge sufficient it is in vaine to desire a greater to keepe them under. Let us follow the example of the Queen's Maiestie, whose gratious highnesse hath with such clemencie ruled over us and so tempred her iustice with mercy as I wene never prince since the Conquest (I speake it without flatery) hath for the time raigned over us in quieter peace with more love and with lesse exaction: the honour be to her gratious Maiestie and those good counsellors that have had the state in hand.

But goe to: suppose it were passed for a law, what great good could we reckon

p.197   should grow to the common wealth by it? You will say a sort of stubborne papists / should be rid out of the way who if they lived would be put causers of sedition; and sedition must needs be the cause of desolation. Surely if the whole number that thinke against the oathe in their conscience should refuse the oathe and for their offence be executed, the realme could not choose but be much weakened and a great deale the lesse able to defend it selfe. We may partly see it by the universities that what with the one side and the other have beene so shaken for religion that learneing is almost quite decayed in them and if provision be not made all like to come to a barbarous ignorance.

But suppose you that the greater part will refuse the oathe? Thinke you that all that take it will upon the takinge of it change their consciences? Nay, a false shrew is there that will lay his hand to the booke when his heart shalbe farre of. Of this hath this House full experience, for in the bill of conveyinge over of horses there was a clause that whosoever should convey over any horse and would sweare that it was for his necessarie travaile, it was lawfull; and because that men sticked not at such a

p.198   trifle to forsweare themselves that clause was / repealed, and upon like consideracion by the grave advise of this House was the oathe left out of the subsedie book.[14] If men for such trifles will forsweare themselves it can not choose but be perilous when their goodes, landes, libertie and life shall depend upon it, and namely in a matter whereof for the most part they have noe knowledge but all one to them whether it be soe or otherwise, and so protesting that to be in their consciences whereof they are in doubt they should wilfully forsweare themselves. And if theise men were seditious before, now will they become tenn times more seditious, neither shall the Queen's Maiesty be ever a whit the surer – which is the title and (as it should seeme) the onelie meaninge of this bill[15] – for if he were rebellious before, now will his heart become more rebell for that he is inforced to periurie, and that mischeife will he secretly keepe in his minde and shew it then when he thinketh it will doe most harme. Or els if he be not thus wickedly disposed then he will linger on in dispayre and with violence at the last seeke to destroy himselfe, which were to lamentable to heare of, and we the cause of all / this mischeife.   p.199

Let us therfore for the honour of God leave all malice and notwithstandinge religion let us love together, for it is no pointe of religion one to hate another. Let us make an end of division for feare least our enemies who are mightie and now in the feild might peradventure, finding us at dissention amongest our selves, the easilyer vanquish us; wheras if we cann agree and love together ther shalbe none doubt but we shall put them now to the worse whome we have so ofte vanquished before. Let us doe as the good mother did before Salomon, who when she had contention before the wise kinge for her owne child with the common harlot and when the matter went so hard that he could not tell to whom to give it but thought to devide it, the tender love of the mother consideringe that the childe's division should be the childe's distruction could not suffer that but was content to yeild up and give away her interest. So let us for the love of God forget and forgive all greves for the common wealthe's sake and let us love one an other, for so shall noe division / worke the   p.200 desolation of our kingedome. And when we have all done, to this we must come at last. We see in Germany where after so longe contention and so great distruction and wast of their country at the last they are come to this pointe that the papist and protestant can now quietly talke together and never fall out about the matter.

I beseech you therefore, right honorable, that you will well remember the trust that your country hath put you in, and since you have the sword in your hand to strike, be well ware whom you strike:[16] for some shall you strike that are your neere freindes, some your kinesmenn, but all your countrymenn and your even Christian. And though you may like these doinges yet may it be that your heyres after you shall mislike them, and then farwell your name and worshipp. Remember that men that offend this way, they offend not as murtherers and theeves doe, that is of malice and wicked intent, but through conscience and zeale, at the least wise through opinion of religion; and if it shall happ them to dye in a wronge opinion then shall wee not onelie / destroy the[ir] bodies, of which theire is smalle force, but their soules, which   p.201 is a losse that will never be recovered. And if they should against there conscience take the oathe to save their lives, and some peradventure in doubt of the matter, then should they fall into periurie and we the causers of it. And since they keepe their consciences to themselves and live under a law why are they to be punished by so

13. *Sic.*
14. See *SR*, IV. 448, 464/78 (cf. 304); *CJ*, I. 63, 65; D'Ewes, 80, 84.
15. 'For the assurance of the Queen's

Majesty's royall power', *SR*, IV. 402.
16. 'Be . . . strike' supplied from J. Strype, *Annals of the Reformation* (1824 edn).

sharpe a law? And though some peradventure have offended you yet doe not for their sakes punish the rest who never offended you, but rather for the other's sakes, who are the greater number, forgive all. Follow the example of the good mother in Salomon or rather the example of the Queene's Maiestie, whome I pray God may long raigne over us and her issue after her.

7. Sir William Cecil's speech on fish days

Text from PRO SP Dom.Eliz.27/71, a draft in a clerk's hand, much amended by Cecil (final draft printed, alterations being footnoted).
Printed. R. Tawney and E. Power, *Tudor Economic Documents* (1924, 3 vols.), II. 104‒10, noting most of Cecil's amendments.

SP Dom.Eliz.27/71

[Endorsed 'Argumentes for increase of the navye.']

Argumentes to prove that it is necessary for the restoring of the navye of England to have more fish eaten and therfor[1] one daye more in the weke ordeyned to be a fissh daye, and that to be Wednesdaye rather than any other.

First, it cannot be denied but that the navye is knowen to be decayed, wherof there is more cause to make a lamentacion then to yeld a demonstration. The decaye is in twoo partes. The one in lack of shippes and vesselles in the subiectes' handes. The other, which is the greatest, in lack of marinors.

As to the lack of shippes there be many causes, wherof some be remediles, and some maye be remedyed, wherof some very hardly, and some more easely. The causes remediles are these. The ancient navigation into to[2] the Levant is diminished by reason of the haunte of the Turkes and Mores that now haunt those seas, and dayly increass there navy there, and by reason also that the spicery that was in the Venetians' handes is come to the Portigales and Spaniardes by ther[3] meanes of there Indias. An other cause is by an order made in Spayne that no wares of that contry shalbe caried from thence in any stranger's bottom, if there be any Spanish to be had, so as [by] experience it hath bene lately proved that a nombre of English shippes fraughted thyther have bene constrayned to retorn empty. So as westward the navigation is deminished in this manner by these causees which are remedyless thrugh our power. Lykewise estward and northward the navigation is empeched by causees ether remedyless or at the lest hard to be remedyed: the recovery of the Iles of Island into the possession of the Kyng of Denmark and his augmentation of his toole at the belt; the possession also of the townes of Rigar, Revell and Nerva, wherof the Moscovit hath gotten on, the King of Sweden the other, and therby warrs mayntened betwixt them.

The causes of lack of shippes that may be hardely remedyed ar sundry: decaye of tymber to buyld shippes; decaye of harborowes and havens, Dover, Rye, Sandwych, in the north.

The causees of hyndrance of English navigation that may be by lawes remedyed with tolleration or some tyme ar these:
1.the trade of a commoditees comming to this realme is most used by strangers, as the wynes, the oade out of France;

2. the hearinges and other sea fissh taken upon our coast and brought and sold by strangers into the portes of the realme to the very inhabitantes of the portes that wer wont to be fishermen;

3. the prohibition of carieng of sea fissh and sellyng of it out of the realme by English men.

1. Remedies for these iij latter must nede be these iij provisions. first that wynes and oade shall not be brought into this realme but in English bottoms, as hertofor by

2. lawes hath bene provyded. Next that no Englishman shall buy any fressh hearing that

3. is taken by a stranger. Thirdly, that it shalbe lefull to cary and sell sea fissh out of the realme.

Now it is to be considered whither these iij remedies, being authorised by law, are able to restore both shippes and marinors, for if they be, than wer it convenient to seke no furder. But although they must doo some good, yet shall it be proved that they can

[1.] nothyng tend to the recovery of that which the realme hath very nede of. First note that the statute made for restraint for bringing in of French wynes, which is the first remedy, which was continued from 4 Henry 7 untill 5 Edward 6,[4] at which time a tolleration [was made] for strangers to bring in wynes *a primo Februarii ad primum Octobris,* and yet before 5 of Edward 6 the navy of England both in shippes and marynors was manifestly decayed and in dede hath somewhat more decayed sence that

2. estatut. And concerning byeng of fissh of strangers, which is the second remedy, that order contynued from 33 Henry 8[vi] untill *primo Mariae,* and yet the navy also in that

3. tyme manifestly decayed. As to the third remedy it is sene also that non was prohibited to cary and sell hering out of the realme untill *anno 2 Marie,* and yet it is certaine and manifest that befor that tyme the nombre of fisshermen were decayed in this realme. And because it will be sayd that speche is used of decaye but no prooffe, thus it is proved. The nombre of shippes decayed from 36 Henry 8 untill the last of King Edward ar 59 and all of 100 above, and from *primo Marie* untill 1560 45, being all above 100 tonnes. So that it followeth that although these iij remedies be provided, yet the same cannot make such a restitucion of the navye but that it shall decaye as it did whylest these remedies were in use; adding to it also that before these lettes were devised, and whylest the remedyes were in use, there was a more universall eating of fissh by observation of fish dayes in the realme than is now. Wherfore it must nedes be concluded that some other thing must be provided to increass the navy and to multyply marinors, and in the meane tyme, after marrinors shalbe multiplied, though shippes shall not be so plentifully builded, yet the royal navy shall be furnished with English marinors and therby by Godde's grace be hable to defend the realme against all foreyn power. For otherwise to multiply shippes and to lack marynors is to sett armur uppon stakes on the sea cost and to provyde no people to wear it, or to buyld castells and put no soldiors in them.

The very ground that naturally serveth to brede marinors is the trade and conversation upon the sea, which is divided into ij sortes: the one is to cary and recary marchandizes, the other is to take fish; for the thyrd, which is exercise of pyracy, is detestable and can not last. For the first, so that the trade may be reduced into English men's handes as nere as may be, the realme is in as good case for multitude of merchandize both caried out and brough[t] in as in any age it hath ben, and to saye the truthe, the realme abundeth with both, and overmuch with the forrayn in so much as ye make lawes ageynst it, and therfor this trade is not to be augmented. For the other, that is the trade of fisshing, how it is decayed manifestly appeareth upon all the sea coastes by decaye of the port townes, the peres and harborowes: which if they be not shortly remedied will grow remediles.

The causes of the decaye of fisshing must be the lack of the use of fisshing, which must be divided into ij partes, small eating of fissh in the realme and no selling of it abroade. As to the latter part, which is for selling of fyssh by English men out of the realme, [it] was prohibited in *anno primo Mariae* and not before, but yet if it [is] now sett at lardg how long it wilbe or any trade can be gotten to utter any quantytie shall sone appeare by this playne demonstracion. No sellyng can be wher no byeng will be, and that ther will be ether none or small byeng abrod shall apperer[5] by this reason. First for Scotland, Norwaye, Denmark, Freeseland, Zeeland, Holland and Flanders: it is sene there plenty is such that they do not only yerly take sufficient for them selves, but also doo serve other contreys with the same, as England and in some parte Fraunce, and than now resteth only Fraunce to receave that commoditie from us, for as for Spayne, they serve them selves with the fishyng in Irland uppon the south cost. And how France of late yeres aboundeth with fisshermen lett the navigation to the new found land testifye, where there be occupied above v^c sayle yerely, which, accounting but xxx^{tie} to a vessell, wher in dede they usually occupy xl,[6] maketh the nombre of xv[7] thousand men. They also send to fissh for hearing upon the coast of England yerely above v^{c8} sayle, which, having but x in a vessell, maketh v[9] thowsand. So as France being thus provided for by them selves of fish, ether sufficient or very nere, it may be very dowtfull that no great sale can be made of fish to be taken by English men out of the realme, and so consequently no great good can insue of the devise to license Englishmen to sell fyssh out of the realme of a long tyme, at the least untill the French shalbe forced to leave the trade of fisshing . . .[10] and yet this liberty is to be allowed to help some part . . .[11]

Wherfore all these thinges considered, that the trades which have bene of marchandise into Levant and Spayne is decayed, the trades of navigation into Island and Estland is impeched, the buyldyng of shippes is costly and difficult for lack of timber, the experience of the statutes prohibiting strangers to bring in fissh and wynes proveth that notwithstanding those prohibitions the navy and marinors have decayed, and on the other side selling of fissh out of the realme hath no present great vent: it must nedes followe that the remedyes must be sought to increase marrynors by fishyng as a cause most naturall, easy and perpetuall to brede and mayntene marynors.

And then are we to compare whither more fish shalbe eaten then presently is or

1. Words printed in light type are insertions and amendments.
2. *Sic.*
3. *Sic.*
4. 4 Hen. VII, c.10 (1488⁄9), continued 23 Hen.VIII, c.7 (1531⁄2), modified 5 & 6 Ed.VI, c.18 (1551⁄2) in *SR*, II.534⁄5; III.374; IV.154.
5. *Sic.*

6. 'xxx^{tie}' altered from 'xx^{tie}', and 'wher in dede they usually occupy xl' inserted by Cecil.
7. Altered from 'ten'.
8. Altered from 'iij^c'.
9. Altered from 'iiij' (*sic*).
10. MS cut away.
11. MS cut away.

hath lately or in former tymes bene. And here we must speke to them whose fathers within these 27 yeres lived when more fish was eaten within the realme then ever this statute, makyng no more but Wednesday a fish day, will or can procure. And how than shall this be called such an innovation which shall not be hable to restore the realme, for necessary defence of the same, to the state it was in xxvij yeres past, which is about the xxvij[th] yere of King Henry the Eight? In which very yere was there a law made, made[12] in favor of tillage, which was not than in such decaye, by which estatute was given to the King the moytie of the rentes of all landes converted from tillage into pasture sence the first yere of King Henry the vij[th],[13] which was the iust space of l yeres. And yet I think no argument of innovacion stayed men to accord to that lawe for the necessitie, but well I knowe it passed and was made a lawe, as I wish this to be.

And to prove that making of Wednesdaye a fissh daye will not cause so much fissh to be eaten in the realme as was eaten abowt *anno xxvij°* Henry 8, which is but xxvij[tie] yeres past, thus by collecion I prove it. The Wednesdaies that by this acte shalbe fissh dayes, shall be in nombre but xxxij or xxiij[14] at the most. Which is thus proved. Of lij Wednesdayes in the whole [year], vj are in Lent, iiij Imbring[15] Wednesdaies; then commonly, as by example of this yere it happeneth, iij or iiij[16] other Wednesdayes are the fasting evens of the Ascension, Midsomer, and Saints Simon and Jude; and now to be excepted ij[17] in Christmas and Easter weke [and Whitson weke][18]: all which make xv,[19] so there remayneth but xxxvij[20] for[21] the which ye may take awaye certen fastes relinquished, as St Lawrence even, Assumption, Nativitie and Conception of our Lady, being iiij, so there remaineth but xxxiij.[22] Here is the grete burden, to eate fissh uppon xxxiij[23] daies distributed a sondre in every weke, which is not after the rate for every hundreth daye in the yere x daies.

And now it is to be seene whither this burden will ether encrease so many fissher men as men may be afraied that they will overgrow other states of men and percase be daungerouse, as some hath gessed, though without great pondering or forsight of speache; or whyther it will cause as much fissh to be eaten as was about the xxvij yer of the reigne of King Henry the viij[th]. About that time were in this realme v[c] howses of relligion that paied tenthes to the King, as by the booke of xth may appeare, besides fryeries, which may be estemed to ij or iij[c], but I will leave them to serve for a surplus of my accompt. Colledges also and all commandrees I will leave and the iiij houses of observantes which I will forbeare that did eat fish all weyse. These v[c], accompting but I to a howse — though many had no less than a hundred, some ij[c] — maketh xxv[m] persons, all which nombre did eate fissh lxxvj daies in the yere which be not now observed for fissh, that is xx in Advent, xx in Septuagesima, the Wednesday through the yeres, being in nombre, besides Lent, Advent, Imbring and Septuagesima, xxxvj, which made lxxvj, besides certen dayes of peculier vowes. What quantitie of fissh these spent may be also gessed by this reckoning of fflessh: xxv[m] men are allowed in bief for one daye ij[c] oxen, that is for lxxvj daies xv[m] oxen, which may be estemed was spared by their fast, and now is spent, and so much the less fish. Adde to this the expences of fissh thrugh the whole realme the xl daies in Lent without eating of whitmeate, which may be accompted well a third part, that is at the least xiij daies more fissh then is now spent. Add to this also the forbearing utterly to eat flessh upon any fissh daye, so as sence I can remember not so much as the King had license and Sir Brian Tuke was noted as an owle[24] only for having a license; which was occasion of eating so much fissh as now is eaten in flessh apon fish dayes. Add also the unyversall observation of the Wednesdaies by a great multitude of people in the realm for superstition, I think exceding the relligiouse persons that observed Wednesdaye, wherof they be not many left; and if they be I think the more parte eateth whit meat and not fissh, because it is not to be had on the Wednesdays commenly. Beside this, though Wednesday shuld be ordained a fissh daye, yet consider how many shall not eate fish by this ordenaunce, that I think the nombre is more then the one half of the realme, being thus collected: of those that will eate no fish on Wednesdaye may be collected a third parte of the people, beyng husbandmen, laborers and poore howsholders with there children and servantes; and of those that before the making of this estatute did eate and will hereafter be the most nombre of people dwelling on the sea coast or nere therto, being poore. So as to conclude, a small nombre of welthy, delicate people shall observe this daye and yet of them no small nombre will by license or without licenss breake it, which may be gessed by the humors of men in this Howse that ar so ernest ageynst it. Now therfore it will follow that comparing the quantytie of fissh that is lykely to be eaten on this Wednesdaye being so few dayes in nombre, and so many not intending to eate ether by license or by povertie and custome, or so many as before did eate, the burden to eate fish will not be great to many nor the quantitie comparable to that which may be gathered was eaten before xxvij[tie] yeres. And therfore it must of reason be allowed in so great a necessytie for the realme, being also not the full help of the nede, and yet the best, surest and easiest to be found. As for the reasons of commoditie, many may be devised: the saving of flessh, the frugalitie in men's howshouldes.

12. *Sic.*
13. Cecil's correction from 'viij[th]'.
14. Altered from 'xxxv or xxxvj'.
15. I.e. Ember.
16. Cecil's alteration from 'iij'.
17. Altered from 'iij'.
18. Deleted.
19. Altered from 'xvj'.
20. Altered from 'xxxvj'.
21. I.e. 'from'?

22. Altered from 'xxxij'.
23. MS reads 'xxxij' uncorrected.
24. Tuke was secretary to Henry VIII and Treasurer of the Household from 1528. The reference to an owl is mysterious. Was he called this simply because he ate meat, or because he was astute enough to get a licence to do so, or because owls were an old symbol of hatred?

8. Closing proceedings and speeches, 10 April

Text from BL Cott. Titus FI, copy.
Other MSS. Copies of Cott. Titus FI: London: Stowe 358,
Harl. 2185 (speeches only). Cambridge: Gonville and Caius
College 64.
Printed. D'Ewes, 73-6.

Cott. Titus FI, fos. 77-81v

Satterday the tenth of Aprill, Easter even, about 3 of the clocke the Queene's
Majestie came by water from the Whitehall and landed on the backside of the
parliament chamber, and so, th'Erle of Northumberland bearing the sword afore
her, the Dutchesse of Norffolk the trayne, she proceeded up into her privy chamber
and there apparrelled her self in her parliament robes; duringe which tyme the lords
likewise put on their robes and tooke their places.

On the upper sacke sate the Lord Keeper till the Queene came and then he went
to his place at the raile on the right hand to the cloth of estate. On the woolsacke on
the north side sate Sir Robert Catlyn and Sir James Dyer, the 2 cheif Justices, Sir
John Mason, Serieant Carus, and Mr Ruswell, the Queene's Sollicitor, and Doctor
Yale.

On the sacke on the south side sate Sir William Cecyll, Secretary, Sir William
Cordall, Master of the Rolls, Justice Weston, Serieant Southcote, Mr Gerard, the
Queene's Attorney, and Doctor Hewes.

On the nether sacke sate Mr Spilman, clerke of the Parliament, Mr Powle,
deputie and joint patentee with Mr Martin, clerke of the Crowne, Mr Honing, and
some clerks of the signet, Dister and Permitter. Before which nether sacke stood a
litle table.

Then the Queene's Majestie, beinge apparelled in her parliament robes with a
calle on her head, came forthe and proceeded upp, and tooke her seate, the Duke of
Norffolk as Erle Marshall with his gilt rod before her, with the Marques of
Northampton bearing the capp of mayntenance, and stood on her right hand, and
the Erle of Northumberland [bearing] the sword on her left hand, the Queene's
mantle borne up over her armes by the Lord Admirall and Lord of Hunsdon, her
trayne borne by the Dutchesse of Norffolke assisted by the Lord Chamberlaine and
Mr Astley, Master of the Jewel Howse. And so her Majestie beinge placed the Duke
of Norffolk, the Lord Admiral and Lord of Hunsdon tooke their places. And from
f.77v   tyme to tyme as her Majestie stood up her mantle / over her armes was assisted up
with the Lord Robert, Master of the Horse, and Sir Francis Knowles,
Vicechamberlaine.

Then all beinge placed Mr Williams, the Speaker, was brought in betweene Sir
Edward Rogers, Controller, and Sir Ambrose Cave, Chancelor of the Dutchy,

and after one obeysance made proceeded downe to the wall and from thence came up to the rayle, in the way makinge 3 obeysances. And after he was at the rayle he made other 3 obeysances, and then began his oration as followeth.

'Thus it is, most excellent and vertuous Princesse *etc.*, as nature giveth to everie reasonable creature to speak, soe is it a grace to be well learned. And I representing the mouth of such a bodie as cannot speake for yt self and in the presence of your Majestie's person and nobles must most humblie desire and crave of your Highnes to beare with my ymperfeccion, *etc.*

'This commonwealth hath bin by God's provydence first instituted, and since by man's policy contynued, wherin justice and good counsell is most to be preferred, for Cave wrytinge to the Kinge of Cipres saith that the ancient lawe-makers and authors of good lawes be worthie to be praysed and had in perpetuall memorie. And such are the lawes that we have made and as be and have bin in thys common-wealth as in my opinion doe excell and passe all other humane lawes.

'Amongst divers authors of good lawes wee have sett forth unto us, to th'ende they should not be forgotten, 3 queenes, th'one named Palestina, the queene raigninge before the Deluge, who made lawes aswell concerninge peace as warre.

'The second was Cerus, the queene which made lawes concerninge punnishment of evill doers.

'And the third was Marc:[1], wife to Bathelacus, mother to Stillicus, the kinge who erected lawes for the maintenance and preservacion of the good and well-doers. /

'And since that time Etheldred,[2] a kinge in this realme, established lawes, and set in most beaten, crosse, and high wayes, a crosse, theron a hand with a ringe of gold pointinge to the most usuall way, which allsoe stood untaken away or diminished during his lief.

'And soe yow are the 4th queene establisher of good lawes, our most dread soveraigne Lady, for your time as happie as anie of the three, which happiness at this present I lett slipp, and desire, as all our harts doe, that some happie marriage to your contentacion might shortlie be brought to passe. Your Majestie, findinge this realme out of order and full of abuses, have continuallie had a specialle care to reforme the said abuses. And for the more expelling thereof have congregated together this assembly, wherby partlie to your contentacion for restoring of the same to his old pristinate estate, and for money and peace, is all that cheiflie we have done; for which purposes we have agreed upon and have made certen lawes, which, untill your Majestie have granted your royall assent unto and soe geven lief thereunto, cannot be called lawes.

'And herein requiringe of your Majesty three peticions, two for the Commons and one for my self. The first for such lawes as they have made, beinge as yet without lief and so no lawes, that yt would please your Majestie to grante your royall assent unto them. Secondlie that your Highnes would accept their doinges in good parte,

f.78

---

1. *Sic*; the reference seems to be to Marcia, and 'Bathelacus' and 'Stillicus' may be corruptions (Geoffrey of Monmouth, *The Kings of Britain*, III.13).

2. I.e. Edwin? See Bede, *History of the English Church*, II.16.

and that the imperfeccion of their labors by your acceptance may be supplied. For as appeareth in sondrie histories the persons of those prynces and subiectes have longe contynued which have well used themselves one towardes th'other, which without neglectinge of my dutie I cannott in your presence so lett slipp. For as in divers histories the noble Alexander, havinge presented unto him by one of his poore soldiers the head of one of his enemies, he not forgettinge the service of his soldyer, although therin he had done but his dutie, he gave unto him a cupp of gold, which first the soldier refused, but after that Alexander had commaunded yt to be filled with wyne / he receaved yt; wherby appeared the noble and liberall harte of the sayd Alexander.

'Allso Zenophon writinge of the lief of Cyrus who, beinge liberall of gifts, havinge vanquished Croesus, and he marvelled at his liberality and said yt were better to keepe it by him then so liberally to depart from yt; unto whome Cyrus answered that his treasure was innumerable, and appointed Croesus a day to see the same. And therupon tooke order that his subiectes should afore that tyme bringe in their treasure, which beinge innumerable and more then Cyrus could by anie other meanes could[3] have gotten, Croesus much wonderinge therat, Cyrus sayd, "Thou causedst me to take of my subiectes and retaine the same, but what neede I to take when they soe frankly will bringe in unto me, and so as occasion serveth readie contynually to supplie my want, therfor how can I be but rich havinge such subiectes? But yf they be by my meanes or anie other were poore, then were I poore allsoe."[4]

'Which two worthie examples of Alexander and Cyrus your Majestie hath not forgotten to ensue, but with the like zeale have hitherto allwayes used us, and now especially at this present, at your most gracious and free pardon, for the which and all other they by me their mouth doe most humbly thanke yow, knowledginge such and soe much love and zeale of their partes towardes your Majestie as ever any subiects did beare towardes their prince and governor. And in token therof with one assent doe offer to your Highnes one subsidie and two ffifteenes, humbly beseechinge your Majestie to accept yt, not in recompence of your benefittes, but as a token of their dutie, as the poore wydowe's ffarthinge was accepted, as appeareth in the Scripture. /

'Thirdlie, that yt may allso like your Majestie to accept my humble thankes in allowinge and admitting me, being unworthie, to this place and bearing with my unworthie service and last of all my unfittinge wordes, uplandish and rude speech; beseechinge God to encline your Majestie's hart to marriage, and that he will so blesse and send such good successe therunto that we may see the fruit and children that may come therof, so that yow and they may prosperously and as longe tyme raigne over us as ever did anie kings or princes, which God for his mercie's sake grant unto us'. And soe he ended, makinge his obeysance.

Then the Queene called the Lord Keeper unto her, commaundinge him in her name to answer him as she then declared unto him, which followeth.

'Mr Speaker, the Queene's Majestie hath heard howe humblie and discreetly yow have declared the proceedinges of your nether house, and for answere hath commaunded me that I should utter 3 or 4 thinges; the first for her royall assent to the actes made at this parliament, secondly how comfortably and allso thankfully her Majesty accepteth your liberalitie, thirdly for th'executinge of the lawes.

'Here, my lords and masters, although I cannot declare nor open yt unto yow as her Majestie hath commaunded me, and therfore willinglie wold hold my tonge yf I might, which for that I cannot be so excused, say unto you as followeth, not doubtinge of her Highnes' clemency in bearing with me herein. /

'First, her Majestie considereth how wisely yow have done for the abolishinge of　f.79v the Romish power, the common enemie of this realme, remembringe your care for the defence of the same realme, your respect for the maintenance of victell, the banishment of vagabonds and releif of the poore, with other; and therfore alloweth your worthie proceedinges herein.

'Secondlie, your liberalitie and benevolence, wherin your wise consideracions towards her charges ys by her Majestie taken in thankfull parte. And I take yt to be my dutie to putt yow in remembrance that although this subsidy and ffifteens ys made and to be borne by subiectes not daily accustomed therunto, but that at her first entrance she had the like, and that the grant therof ys more liberall then afore hath bin accustomed, and that yt is of your necessitie, yet it is to withstand a greater necessitie that for fault therof would ells have ensued; therfore that peny ys well spent that saveth a groat. Which also hath bin granted neither with persuasions, threats, nor sharpe wordes, which afore this tyme hath bin accustomed, but by one generall consent of yow all, wherin appeareth your good wills and benevolent mindes yow beare to her Majestie, which zeale she most accepteth and as she hath cause thanketh yow.

'Againe by her Majestie's commaundment, she remembringe by whome, who, and to whome this was granted, doth thinke as freely as yow have granted the most parte wherof hath bin accepted,[5] and lest those that so freely have offred should not be as readie towards the gatheringe, thinketh it much better to loose the some granted then to leese your benevolent mindes. /

'Thirdlie, to th'execucion of lawes I have little to say, although the wholle　f.80 substance consisteth therin, because I did in the beginninge of this parliament declare my opinion in that matter; and therefore, as nowe yow have to your charges taken paynes in makinge good lawes, soe put to your helpes to see this and all other executed. For as yt is infallible that a thinge don unconstrayned ys much better then when they be constrayned thereunto, even so her Majestie willeth yow to looke well without more words to th'execucion, lest her Grace should be driven to doe as she doth in her ecclesiasticall lawes, make commissions to enquire whether they be done or no; wherby she shall knowe those justices and officers who have done their dutie and are to be used in service of justice, wherof her Majestie desyreth to have manie; and againe she shall understand who are to be barred from the like romes, and the penall statutes to be on them executed after this gentle warninge, which enquirie I knowe ys like to fall on me aswell as on other. Howbeit, yf justice be not executed I shalbe glad to see this order taken. Notwithstandinge her Majestie hopeth that this

3. *Sic.*
4. Xenophon, *Cyropaedia*, VIII, ii. 15-23.

5. MS reads 'excepted'; this reading from Harl.2185.

her admonicion shall not neede, for that yow see lawes without execucion be as a torche unlighted or body without a soule. Therfore looke well to th'executinge. Here endeth the iij thinges her Majestie commaunded me to say unto yow.

'Besides theis her Maiestie hath to answer your peticions; and as to the first in which yow desyre her royall assent to such matters as yow have agreed upon, to that she saith howe at this present she is come for that purpose. /

f.80v   'And for th'other peticions, to accept in good part aswell your service as the travells and doings of the nether house this parliament. And to that she answereth howe she doth not only accept them in good parte, but allsoe thanketh both yow and them for the same. And touchinge your request before this made unto her for her marriage and succession, because yt is of such ymportance, wherby I doubted my owne opening therof and therfore desyre her Majestie that her meaninge might be written, which she hath done and delivered to me to be read, as followeth:

'"Since there can be no dewer debt then princes' words, which I would observe, therfore I answer to the same, thus it is. The two peticions which yow made unto me doe containe two thinges, my marriage, and succession after me. For the first, in effect to lett slipp wherin yf my fruite had bin decayed yow might the better have spoken therein, or yf anie thinke I never meant to trade that lief, they be deceaved; but yf I may hereafter bende my minde thereunto the rather for fullfillinge your request I shalbe therwith very well content, *etc*.

'"For the second, the greatnes thereof causeth me to say and pray that whiles I lyve I may linger here in this vale of miserie for your comfort, wherin I have witnes of my studie and travell both for your suretie and mine; and soe nowe with *nunc dimittis* I ende, which cannot be without I see some glance of your suretie after my gravestone, *etc*."'

Then the Lord Keeper commaunded the clerke of the Crowne to read the actes, wherupon Mr Thomas Powle as joynt patent[ee] / and in the absence of Mr Marten,

f.81   clerke of the Crowne, stood up before the litle table sett betweene the woollsackes and, after obeysance made, began to read the title of the same as followeth.

'An act for assurance of her Highnes' tytle.'[6] Then Mr Spilman, clerke of the parliament, standinge upp answered, '*La Royne le veult*'; and then both of them together made obeysance. And then so forward was read the tytle of all the rest of the statutes, and unto all those to which her Majestie granted her royall assente Spilman said '*La Royne le veult*', and to private statutes he answered '*Soit fait come les desirent*'; both the which were in number 51 statutes. And vj more wherunto she granted not her assent, and therunto Spilman answered '*La Royne se advisera*'. And after the reading of every answer they did their reverence.

And to the act of subsidie Spilman answered in French howe the Queene gave thankes to her Lords and Commons.

And to the pardon he answered howe the Lords and Commons gave her Majestie their most humble thankes; and soe altogether made their obeysance.[7]

Then the Lord Keeper declared howe the Queene's Majestie had commaunded him to proroge that session of Parlament untill the second of October then next comminge, untill which time every man might depart at his pleasure and take their ease. And then the Queene rose and proceeded into her privy chamber and shifted and then to her barge and soe to the Court, which was about vj of the clocke.

At everie tyme her Majestie stood up, her / mantle over both her armes was   f.81v
assisted and borne up by the Lord Robert Dudley, Master of the Horse, and Sir
Francis Knowles, Vice-chamberleyne.

This daie this parlament was proroged till the second of October then next. And
then because of the plague in London yt was againe proroged, I thinke till October
or November 1564, *anno 6 Elizabethae Reginae*. And then proroged till the last of
April 1565, *anno 7 Elizabethae Reginae*. And then proroged till the 4ᵗʰ of October
1565, *anno 7 Elizabethae Reginae*, and then till February 1565, *anno 8*, and then till 30
September 1566.

6. Cf. *SR*, IV, i.402-5.

7. See *LJ*, II.225 for the correct forms of answers to bills, and for thanks for the subsidy and the pardon.

9. *Separate texts of the Queen's speech at close of session, 10 April*

i. Text from BL Lansd.94, the Queen's draft, all in her own hand.
ii. Text from BL Harl.5176, the copy nearest to the Queen's own draft, with some preferable readings from Add.32379.
Other MSS. London: BL Cott.Titus FI (and its copy, Harl.2185), Add.33271. Cambridge: Gonville and Caius College 64 (copy of Cotton). Hatfield, Herts.: Hatfield 153/138, noticed in HMC *Salisbury*, I.272 (fair copy of Lansd.94).
Printed. D'Ewes, 107-8 (misplaced under 1566).

Lansd.94, f.30

[Endorsed 'x Aprill 1563. The Queen's speche in the parlement uttred by the Lord Kepar'.]

[A duar d A duer] Sins ther can be[1] [never] no dewar det than princes' word [ougth no man crave wiche for to], to kipe that unspotted for my part, [I w] as one that wold be lothe that [that wiche] the selfe thing that kipes the marchant's credit from crase shulde be the cause that princes' [saings] speche shulde merite blame and so ther honor quaile, [and since] an answer therfor I wil make [as tied to my behest] [unto the . . .[2]]: and this it is. [The gret] The two [huge scroles that] peticions that [bothe Hous] you [. . . gave] presented me in many wordes exprest, conteined thes two thinges in some as of your cares the gretest, my mariage and my successar; of wiche two the last I thinke is best be toched, and of the other a silent thoght may serve, for I had thoght it had bine so desired as [not] none other [fruict] tree's blossomes shuld have [mached] bine [mencioned] minded or[3] [that] hope of my fruict had bine denied you. [And by the way] And by the way, if any here dowte that [am] I am as it wer by vowe or determination bent never to trade that life, put oute that heresie, your belefe is awry: for as I thinke it best for a privat woman, so do I strive with my selfe to thinke it not mete for a prince; and if I can bend my wyl to your nide I wyl not resist [it] suche a mynde.[4] But to the last thinke not that you had nided this desier if I had seen a time so fit and it so [mete] ripe to be [p] denounced. The gretenes of the cause, therfor, and nide of your retournes, dothe make me say that wiche I think the wise may easely ges: that as a short tyme for so longe a continuance ought not passe by rote, as many telleth tales, even so, as cause by conference with the lerned shal shewe me matter worthy utterance for your beholfes, so shal I [as . . . more] more gladly pursue your good after my dayes [than with] than with my prayers [. . . while I live than] be a meane to lingar my living threde. And this moche more than I had thogth wil I adde for your comfort: I have good record in this place that other [wais] menes than you mencioned have bine thoght of, perchanche for your good as muche and for my surty no les, wiche, if presently coulde conveniently have bine [finished] executed, had not bine differed. But I hope I shal die in quiet with *nunc dimittis*, wiche can not be without I se some climpes of your folowing surty after my grave[d][5] bones.

Harl.5176, f.97 and v

A speach used by her Majestie unto my Lord Keeper in the parliament howse in the ende of a session.

Since there can be no duear debt then princes' worde, to keepe that unspotted for my parte, as one that would be lothe that the self thinge which keepeth marchantes' creditt from crase should be the cause that princes' speeche should meritte blame and soe their honour quaile, therefore I will an aunswere give. And this it is: the two peticions that youe[6] presented me, expressed in many wordes, conteyned in somme these two thinges as of your cares the greatest: my marriage, and my successor.[7] Of which two I thinke best the last be touched, and of the other a silente thought may serve: ffor I had thought it had bene so desired as none other tree's blossome should have bene mynded or ever hope of my fruite had bene denyed you. And yet, by the way, if any here doubt that I am as it were by vowe or determinacion bente never to trade that kinde of lyfe, putt out that heresie, ffor your beliefe is therein awrye: ffor thoughe I can thinke it best for a private woeman, yet doe I strive with my selfe to thinke it not meete for a prince. And if I can bende my liking to your neede I will not resiste such a minde. But to the last thinke not that you had needed this desire if I had seene a tyme soe fitt and it soe ripe to be denounced. The greatenes of the cause, therefore, and neede of your returnes, doth make me say that which I thinke the wise may easily guesse: that as a shorte tyme for so longe / continuaunce ought not to passe by roate, as many tell their tales, even soe, as cause by conference with the learned shall shewe me matter worthy utteraunce for your behoofes, soe shall I more gladly pursue your good after my dayes then with my prayers whilest I live be meane to lingar my livinge thredd. And thus much more then I had thought will I adde for your comforte: I have good recorde in this place that other meanes than[8] youe[9] mencioned have bene thought of, perchaunce for your good as muche, and for my suertie noe lesse, which, if presently and conveniently could have bene executed, it had not nowe bene differred or overslipt. But I hope I shall die in quiett with *nunc dimittis*, which cannot be without I see some glimpse of your followinge suertie after my graved bones.

f.97v

1. Words printed in light type are insertions; words in square brackets are deletions.
2. '. . .' represents an illegible word.
3. I.e. ere.
4. 'And by the way . . . suche a mynde' is a marginal insertion.
5. MS torn.
6. MS reads 'yee'; this reading from Add.32379.
7. MS reads 'succession'; this reading from Add.32379.
8. MS reads 'that'; this reading from Add.32379.
9. MS reads 'ye'; this reading from Add.32379.

THE SECOND PARLIAMENT
SECOND SESSION
30 SEPTEMBER 1566,
2 JANUARY 1567

Documents

Since the first session in 1563, Elizabeth had suffered further illness and Mary of Scotland had given birth to James, circumstances which strengthened the fears of those pressing for a solution of the succession problem. Most of the documents here are connected with the development of the major political struggle between the Queen and the Commons in which Elizabeth's political isolation became apparent, and whatever she claimed about the rebellious nature of the House, the members' complaint about her inactivity over her marriage and the succession was broadly supported in the Lords and the Privy Council itself.

The death of Speaker Williams on 1 July 1566 necessitated the election and presentation of a successor in Richard Onslow, only recently appointed Queen's Solicitor, and demonstrating in the traditional disabling speech [Doc.1] that he was capable of new heights of sophisticated pedantry. There is no doubt that Onslow was a Queen's man: it emerged both in this speech and again at the end of the session [Doc.14], and his intervention in the Dalton affair [Doc.9] and the addition to one of the versions of the Queen's message of 24 November [Doc.10.i] reveal how he might be expected to manage debate. At the same time, he was no apostle of absolute monarchy. He took the opportunity in his final speech to deliver himself of a minor homily on the law, in which he made it clear that though the common law allowed the prince prerogatives, it did not give him liberty to act arbitrarily [Doc.14].

There are among the Petyt papers in the Public Record Office two draft speeches intended for the Commons, both of them copies and neither of them dated or attributed to a named author. Their contents are inherently interesting, though their dating is problematic and they are included in the session for 1566 with some hesitation. The first of them is a short speech consisting of a recommended strategy for dealing with a 'bill' on the succession; but since we have no knowledge of a bill as such coming before the House, we cannot say if this speech was ever delivered [Doc.3]. It may be connected with the other copy, which is a lengthy, repetititve essay on the elementary necessity for providing for a known order of succession, and which despite its tedious and sometimes naive development, makes some telling, fundamentally sensible points in refutation of Elizabeth's arguments for silence on the matter of the succession, and in favour of free speech [Doc.2]. Mention of the subjects' enthusiastic grant of a subsidy 'the last parliament', and the comments it prompted, may be a reference to the first session of the reign and would place the speech itself either in 1563 or 1566.[1] The speaker had frequent recourse to Biblical texts, and the tone and sentiments are in places strikingly reminiscent of Peter

Wentworth's 1576 speech: perhaps we have an early unrecorded and possibly undelivered draft of his, though not belonging to 1566. Alternatively, brother Paul may have been responsible originally for this document, which could therefore be seen as part of the moves of 11 November, when he posed his three questions to the House and sparked off a lengthy debate.[2] Or is it perhaps 'Mr Lambert's' speech from 8 November, when he made moves to limit the succession?[3] However, one sentence may be more revealing than anything else in the document. Towards the end of his long discourse the author says: 'I have prepared a bill that the House may be possessed of the matter, wherin I have thought good to offer unto her Majestie a subsidie. . .'.[4] There is a fair chance, that is to say, that we are dealing with Molyneux's speech of 18 October, together with another member's prepared speech in support should Molyneux's suggestion and bill be adopted.[5]

Sadler's speech [Doc.4] – also undated – was considered by the editor of *Sadler's State Papers* to have been delivered in the first parliament.[6] There are good reasons, however, for placing it in 1566, and particularly to 18 October, when the Clerk notes that Sadler had spoken.[7] Molyneux's action came the day after the Comptroller had suggested the subsidy be debated, a suggestion which may not have been well received at the time; and Sadler's speech is most obviously a response to this particular challenge, as he stressed, perhaps more heavily than usual, the justification for more taxation and then attacked uncompromisingly the notion of 'myxing or mingling' the subsidy with other matters.

But despite Sadler's speech and other attempts by Councillors to persuade the Commons to keep off the succession question, a committee of the House succeeded at last in agreeing with the Lords that both Houses should petition Elizabeth to settle the matter. That was on 4 November; but before they had a chance to do much more, the Queen addressed 30 of each House in her palace on the afternoon of 5 November. We have her own corrected draft of the first few sentences of the speech [Doc.5.i], otherwise we rely on the full report of a member of the delegation [Doc.5.ii]. Cecil was instructed to deliver this message to the Commons: an attempt at a fairly full summary seems to have been abandoned, and he chose not to rely on his brief notes of the speech [Docs.6.i & ii]. The version which was presented to the House the following day – and, according to Cecil's endorsement of it, the one to which the whole delegation had agreed – differed considerably in tone from the original as we know it, and from his incomplete summary [Doc.6.iii]. While conveying the essence of the Queen's message, it had little of her sneering indignation: there was no mention, for example, of 'unbrydelyd persons', of the 'errors' she 'took offensive to hir self', or of her famous refusal to be by 'vyolence constreyned to doo anye thynge'.

Only five days after Cecil's report, Paul Wentworth posed his questions, seemingly probing the nature of the Commons privilege of free speech [Doc.7]. They were provoked by the activities of Councillors, who yet again attempted to stifle further debate on the succession which had arisen despite the Queen's message.[8] At this point the services of Speaker Onslow were invoked to relay once more the instruction that there should be no discussion of Elizabeth's marriage and succession. We have a document [Doc.12], drawn up by Cecil, though not too precisely dated by him, which may have been a memorandum to the Council on the matter, or as Froude thought, a 'rough sketch' for the Commons' proposed address to the Queen on 16 November.[9] It certainly reflects the tone of the earlier part of that address, and we should remember that Cecil was on the committee drawing up the document; but it contains the additional notion that Parliament should be temporarily prorogued in order to allow Elizabeth to marry – negotiations with the Archduke Charles had been in hand since 1565 – after which it might be reassembled to deal with the succession.

In any event, the proposed petition dated 16 November [Doc.8] formed the Commons' response to the Speaker's message and was one of the three draft petitions drawn up by a committee of the House, all amended by Cecil apparently acting on the committee's behalf. A strong note of loyalty served as a framework for the recollection of the Queen's earlier promise to marry, together with prayers that God might induce her to carry out this resolve quickly and to determine the succession. The final section crystallized the issue into one of the Commons' liberty of free speech, the main amendment indicating the committee's strength of feeling. Though the petition was not officially presented, Elizabeth could not remain ignorant of the situation,[10] but before her next statement to the Commons Robert Melville, the Queen of Scots' London representative, complained that a member of the Commons had spoken of the succession. James Dalton had allegedly declared himself against the accession of any 'Scot or stranger' [Doc.9.i], but while confessing that a poem about Mary's son James, then five months old, 'had moved him', Dalton produced his own version of the story [Doc.9.ii].[11] This was almost the end of the matter. The Council drew up a document in the Queen's name [Doc.11] calling on the Commons to affirm or deny Melville's charge, though it is not clear if Elizabeth knew of this move in the first place; but she evidently thought it better not to pursue the matter in the House, and the document therefore lapsed.

In this case Elizabeth may have thought that discretion was the better part of valour, for on the day before the Dalton question was to be raised she had conveyed her own message to the House on the subject of the Commons' liberty of free speech. The drafting of this speech was, not surprisingly, a difficult task, and we have three versions which probably reflect part of the problem [Docs.10.i-iii]. It was the third text which was conveyed to the House on 25 November: it revoked the commands given previously to prohibit discussion of the succession, but the reasoning behind this change of attitude is significant.[12] Elizabeth claimed that, despite the speeches of

1. PRO SP 46/166, f.6; BL Harl.5176, f.111v. Comments were also made on the subsidy grant of 1563, though not apparently with the same degree of enthusiasm: BL Cott.Titus F1, f.79v.
2. *CJ*, I.76.
3. *Ibid.*
4. PRO SP 46/166, f.9v.
5. *CJ*, I.74.
6. *Sadler's State Papers*, ed. A. Clifford (1809, 2 vols.), II.547.
7. *CJ*, I.74.
8. The MS is not dated, and the speaker not named; its contents, however, place it unmistakably. See *CJ*, I. 76; D'Ewes, 128; BL Add.5123, fos.10v-11.
9. *EP*, I.144; J. A. Froude, *History of England* (1856-70), VII.450n.
10. *EP*, I.156.
11. *EP*, I.158.
12. *EP*, I.156-7.

one or two members, there had been no general inclination to 'reiterate that suyte' (succession), so that her orders were not necessary. She also hoped that she would not be troubled any more in the matter for the moment. Moves for a discussion of the liberties of the House [Doc.10.i] were too dangerous to accept and here, as in the other two drafts, they were ignored completely.

The session ran for more than another month, and it was not a happy time for Elizabeth. One third of the subsidy had to be surrendered in order to induce the Commons to revive the bill granting it; and its preamble was then transformed to include a declaration to the effect that Elizabeth had promised to settle the succession when she and her Council thought the time right. The Queen was also confronted with a whole collection of bills on religion, 'Bill A' carrying wide support in both Houses. It was in an effort to push this bill through that the Commons refused to pass an important government bill which would have continued the life of a number of statutes.[13] It was in these circumstances that Cecil drew up his 'memorial to the Queen' [Doc.13]. He dated it 'November', yet the inclusion of the bill for religion – which must refer to Bill A – means that it was not composed before 14 December.[14] The first two items convey some of his frustration over the progress of the major issues of the session, and if Elizabeth saw the memorandum she may have taken offence at them; but thereafter we see the thorough minister at work again, surveying the current state of the commonwealth, and finally turning his attention to probable developments on a number of fronts.

The Queen dissolved Parliament on 2 January 1567 [Doc.14]. Speaker Onslow indulged himself with a long speech in which he not only asked Elizabeth to accept the subsidy and assent to legislation, but delivered his thoughts on the nature of government and the limitation of the sovereign power. He also revealed his strongly Protestant outlook and took the opportunity of repeating yet again the request that Elizabeth should marry. Lord Keeper Bacon's reply showed her disquiet over the main points of conflict in the session, and in her own speech she pressed home her attitude to parliamentary privilege and the succession [Docs.14 & 15]. Her evident anger at some members was coupled with a careful insistence that she had no intention of infringing the liberties of the Commons. We cannot know if her own draft [Doc.15] accorded more closely with what was said than did the report in the account of the closing proceedings, but her amendments show an appreciation of the wisdom of mixing reproof with reassurance. At one point she became 'zealous', and her subjects ceased to be 'rangling'; and later we can see how the insertion of the undertaking about liberties moderated the prevailing tone of her message.

13. *EP*, I.160–9.   14. *EP*, I.169–71.

1. Proceedings and speeches on presentation of the Speaker, 30 September and 2 October

Text from BL Cott. Titus F1, copy.
Other MSS. London: BL Stowe 358, copy of Cott. Titus F1.
Cambridge: Gonville and Caius College, 64, copy of Cott. Titus F1.
Printed. D'Ewes, 96-9 (2 October only).

Cott. Titus F1, fos.100-5

Parliamento anno 8ᵛᵒ Elizabethae.
Mundaie, 30 September 1566 *anno 8° Elizabethae Regine*, began the second sessions of the Quene's second parliament, as followeth:

The nether howse that daie being assembled, Sir Edward Rogers, the Queen's Majestie's Comptroller of her howse, declared unto them how that since the last sessions of parliament God had taken to his mercye Mr Williams their Speaker, advising them to repaire to the upper howse, desyring the lordes to be suitors for them to the Queen's Majestie that shee wold graunte them free election for a newe Speaker. Whereupon that afternoone the Lord Keeper, the Lord Threasurer,[1] the Duke of Norffolke and the Marquesse of Northampton with fower knightes Counsellors of the nether howse repaired to her Highnes, whose request by her lettres patentes she graunted. And soe the next daie being Tuesday they chose for their said Speaker Mr [blank][2] Onslowe, the Quene's Sollicitor, who the next daie was presented to her Majestie and allowed as followeth.

Wednesdaie, 2 October 1566

About three of the clock the Quene's Majestie tooke her barge and landed on the backside of the parliament chamber, and so the Earle of Northumberland bearing the sworde, the Lady Strange the trayne, with the lordes in their dailie apparrell and the heraldes attending on her she proceeded up into her privy chamber to prepare her self, during which tyme the lordes and justices putt on their parliament roabes and tooke their places, saving those absent marked with this lettre A, or otherwise noted.[3]

First on the forme of the north side together with the upper forme att the nether ende / sate the bishops as followeth:
Dr Matthew Parker Archbishop of Canterbury,^sick[4]

f.100v

---

1. Winchester.
2. Richard.
3. Compare this list of attendances with that
of *LJ*, I.626.
4. Words in superior position indicate interlinear glosses in MS.

Dr Yong Archbishop of Yorke,
and Edmund Grindall Bishop of London.

Pilkington Bishop of Durham
Sands Bishop of Winchester[5]
Berkley Bishop of Bath and Wells
John Best Bishop of Carlile
Barloe Bishop of Chichester
Jewell Bishop of Salisbury[sick]
Allee Bishop of Excester
Davies Bishop of St Asse
Gest Bishop of Rochester
Skamler Bishop of Peterborough

Horne Bishop of Winchester
Bullingham Bishop of Lincolne
Bentam Bishop of Lichfield and
Coventry
William Donham Bishop of Chester
Scorie Bishop of Herford
Davies Bishop of St Davids
Parkhurst Bishop of Norwich
Cheiny Bishop of Glocester
Jones][6] Bishop of Landaffe
quaere, whether Bangor be made and his
name.[7]

Att the formost forme on the southside sate these peeres as followeth:
William Paulett, Marquesse of Winchester, Lord Threasurer. Thomas Howard,
Duke of Norffolk and Earle Marshall. William Parre Marquesse of Northampton,
Henry Fitzallen Earle of Arundell[In Italie], [Edward] Veere Earle of Oxford[warde],
Thomas Percy Earle of Northumberland, [Charles] Nevill Earle of Westmerland,
George Talbott Earle of Shrewesburie, Edward Stanley Erle of Derbye, [William]
Somerset Earle of Worcester, [Edward] Manners Earle of Rutland[ward], Henry
Clifford Erle of Cumberland, Thomas Ratcliffe Earle of Sussex, Henrie Hastinges
Earle of Huntington, [William] Bourchier Erle of Bathe[ward], Ambrose Sutton Erle
of Warwick, [Henry] Wriothesley Erle of Southampton[ward], Francis Russell Earle
of Bedford, Deputie of Barwick, William Herbert Earle of Pembrooke, Edward
Seymer Earle of Hertford, Robert Sutton Earle of Leicester and Master of the Horse,
Walter Devoreux Viscount Hereford, Anthonie Browne Viscount Montague, and
Thomas Howard Viscount Byndon. /

f.101   Att the forme at their backes and the nether forme att the nether end sate these
peeres:
Edward Fynes lord Clinton, Lord Admirall. William Howard Baron of
Effingham, as Lord Chamberleyne. Henrie Nevill Lord of Aburgaveny, [George]
Tuchet lord Awdley[ward], [George] Zouche lord Zouch, Henrie Stanley lord
Strange, [Henry] Berkley lord Berkley, [Henry] Parker lord Morley, [Gregory]
Fynes lord Dacres of the Sowth, [George] Dacres lord Dacres[ward], William Broke
lord Cobham, [Edward] Stafford lord Stafford, Antonie Grey lord Grey of
Wilton, Henry Scroope lord Scroope of Bolton, Lord Warden of the West
Marches towards Scotland. Edward Sutton lord Dudley, John Lumley lord
Lumley, [James] Blount lord Montague;[8] [Cuthbert] Ogle lord Ogle, [John]
Darcye lord Darcie of Menell, William Stanley lord Mountegle, [William] Sandes
lord Sandes, [William] Vaux lord Vaux, [Edward] Wyndsor lord Wyndsor,
Thomas Wentford lord Wentford,[9] [William] Boroughe lord Borough, John
Mordant lord Mordant, John Pawlett lord St John[A.] [Henry] Cromwell lord
Cromwell, [William] Evers lord Evers, Thomas Wharton lord Warton[A],
Richard Rich lord Rich, William Willoughby lord Willoughby, John Sheffeild

lord Sheffeild, Henry Pagett lord Pagett, Roger North Baron of Carthelage, Edmund Bridges lord Chandois, Edward Hastinges Baron of Loughburrough, Henry Carey Baron of Hunsdon, and John St. John Baron of Bletsoe.

All the peeres abovesaid, their mantles, hoodes and surcotes furred with mynyver, (their armes put out on the right side, and over the sholder, the duke [blank] barres of mynyver, the marquesse three, the earle three, / the viscount two and the barons two.   f.101v

Item; on the upper sack of wooll sate the Lord Keeper till the Queene came, and then went to his place att the raile. On the woollsacke on the northside sate Sir Robert Catlyn and Sir James Dyer, the Quene's two Cheif Justices, Mr Corbett, Weston and Southcott, Justices of both Benches. On the woollsack on the sowthside sate Sir William Cecill, the Quene's principall Secretarie, Sir William Cordall, Master of the Rolles, Sir Thomas Saunders, cheife Baron, Baron Whyddon, [Thomas] Carowes, the Queene's Serieant, [Gilbert] Gerrard, the Queene's Atturney. And on the nether sacke sate Mr Vaughan and Yale, Masters of the Chancery, Mr Spilman, clerke of the parliament, Mr Martyn, clerk of the Crowne, and Mr Pole his ioynt pattentee, and behinde them kneeled Smyth, clerk of the counsell and Jones, clerk of the signett, Permitter and Dister.

Then the Quene's Majestie being apparelled in her parliament roabes with a call on her heade came forth and proceeded forth and tooke her seate, the Marquesse of Northampton carying the cap of maintenance and after stood on her right hand, the Duke of Norffolk his Marshalle's rodd and the Earle of Northumberland the sword and stood on her lefte hand, with the heraldes and serieantes of armes before her, her Majestie's mantle borne upp on either side from her sholders by the Lorde Chamberleyne and Lord of Hunsdon, who / allwaies stood still by her for the   f.102 assistinge thereof when she stood up, her trayne borne by the lady Strange assisted by Sir Francis Knolles, Vicechamberleyne. Att the left hand of the Queene and sowthside kneeled the ladies, and at the rayle att the Quene's back on the right hand stood the Lord Keeper and on the lefte hand the Lord Threasurer.

Then the Quene as afore being placed, att the sowth doore came in the nether howse bringing in betwene Sir Edward Rogers, Comptroller of the Quene's howse, and Sir Francis Knolles, her Vicechamberleyne, Mr Onslowe, the Quene's Sollicitor, whom they had chosen for their Speaker. And after a reverence done proceeded downe to the wall and from thence came up to the raile, in the waie doinge three reverences, and then began to say as followeth:

'If it please your royall Maiesty, most excellent and vertuous Princesse, att the humble suite of the knightes, citizens and burgesses of your nether howse of Parliament nowe assembled was signified from your Majestie by the mouthe of the Lord Keeper by force of your Highnes' lettres of commission your pleasure and graunt of free election to the said knightes, cittizens and burgesses to choose a fitt and learned man for their Speaker in stead of Thomas Williams esquier their late

---

5. *Sic*; Worcester.

6. In this description of the procession names in square brackets have been supplied: in each case the manuscript has a blank space.

7. Rowland Meyrick had died in January

1566, and Nicholas Robinson was elected to succeed him at the end of July 1566. He was present according to *LJ*, I.626.

8. *Sic*; Mountjoy.

9. *Sic*; Wentworth.

Speaker, whome it hath pleased God to call to his mercie; ffor which they have commaunded me in their names to render to your Majestie their most humble

f.102v   thankes, and also further have commaunded and forced me to / my great greife to signifie to your Majestie how accordinglie they have proceeded to an election and chosen and assigned me (as I maie saie, being most unworthy) to speake in this place for this parliament. And for that I wold not be obstinate I am forced to wound myself with their sworde, which wounde yet being grene and newe your Majestie being the perfect phisition maie cure in disallowing that which they have allowed, for that without your consent it is nothing; and although I, beinge very loath to trouble your Highnes, have made suite and used all the waies and meanes to avoid it, but cold finde no remedye, and therefore am driven to seeke remedie att your handes. For though I have the experience of theire uprighteousnes, wisdome and knowledge which chose me, who if they wold have found anie fault in me I wold lightlie have beleived them (notwithstanding that we are for the most part naturallye given to thinke too much of our selfe), but in this that they seeme to enable me to this calling whereof I know my self unable, I can not creditt them, no more then the simple patient greivouslye tormented with sicknes will not beleive the phisition, nay, the whole Colledge of them, if they saie he have no greife, paine or sicknes. I therefore do not attempt this releasing of me for anie ease of my self but wold be glad to serve your Majestie to the uttermost of my power in the office of Sollicitourship whereunto I am appointed, and not in this, being unfitt for the same, and that for dyvers causes. For

f.103   first, I consider, I have / to deale with many well learned, the fflower and choice of your realme, whose deepe understandinges my witt cannot atteyne to reache unto, no, if they for great carefulnes wold often inculcate it into my dull head to signifie the same to your Highnes yet my memorie is so slipper by nature and sicknes that I shold likely loose it by the waie; but if perhap I kept parte thereof yet I have no other knowledge to help myself withall but a litle in the lawe, farre inferior to dyverse of this Howse, and so shold want learning and utterance to declare their meaning as it requireth, speciallie when I consider your royall Majestie, a princesse endowed with so many vertues, learning and flowing eloquence, it will abash and astonne me. And therefore fynding these infirmities and others in me thinke my self most unworthy of this place. I trust therefore onelie in your Highnes that you will disallowe this eleccion and the rather for that by the true intent of your said lettres it maie not be gathered that they should elect any of your Majestie's officers. For although the wordes be to have their free election, yet the lawes for the reverence thereof setteth it at libertie. As for example we fynde in the lawe that if it wold please your Majestie to graunt licence to a deane and chapter to purchase to them and their successors a C^{li} yearlie, which wordes be generall, yet if the purchased landes be holden *in capite*, this graunte is voyde. And againe if you grant the fynes and

f.103v   amerciamentes of all your tenantes to / one who often chaunceth to be shreive of a shire, yet being shreive he cannot have them. So this me seemeth (if it please your Highnes) serveth my case. Another cause there is for lack of substance to mainteyne this my countenance. But yet your Majestie's goodnes in this pointe stoppeth my mouthe, for that I have none other living but in manner by you. So for all these consideracions and dyvers others, as it shall please your Majestye to consider, I humblie desire your Highnes to disallow this eleccion, commaunding them to repaire againe together and to choose another more fitt to serve the same.' And so ended, and did his reverence.

Then the Quene called the Keeper, declaring her opinion in answering him, who returning to his place said as followeth:

'Mr Onslowe, the Quene's Majestie hath heard and well understanded this disabling your self to this office and doth well perceyve your earnest suite to be discharged of the same; and for answer hath comaunded me to saie that she doubteth not but you verie well understand that when one is chosen to serve the common wealth, it is not in him which is called to appoint or disable himself, but the caller who hath appointed him thereunto. Also there is an old similitude that like as it apperteyneth unto the head to dispose every inferiour member in his place, so it perteyneth to the Quene's Majestie being the heade to appoynte every one in her common wealth. This being true and her Maiestie withall remembring your fidelity and longe experience in parliament matters, and againe chosen by so learned and expert men, thinketh therefore your fitnes needeth not to be disputed here, and therefore, they giving unto you such faith and creditt, / according to an auncient   f.104 custome she cannot but do the like. And also you in disabling your self have abled your self, and therefore she doth allowe and approve this their election, nothing doubting her opinion in your ability to serve this turne.' And so ended.

Mr Onslowe's answer.

'Seing it hath pleased your Majestie to ratifye this election, I to the uttermost of my power shall serve your Highnes and this common wealth. But first my humble suite is that it wold please your Majestie to accept my good will, and the better to discharge my dutye towardes them which have chosen me, that in great matters sent fro them I maie have accesse to your Maiestye at tymes convenient as the waight shall require. Secondlie, if by weakenes I shall mistake the effect and meaninge of the matters committed to me by the knightes, cittizens and burgesses, and thereby against my will shall misreport them, that then thereby this commonwealth may take no detriment, but that I maie conferre againe with them the better to understand their meaning, and soe with more wordes to utter the same unto you. And I shall pray, as I am bounde, to God for your long and prosperous raigne over us.'[10]

Then her Majestie called the Lord Keeper and commaunded him to answer him, which he did as followeth:

'Mr Speaker, the Quene's Majestie hath heard your humble petitions and request made unto her, th'effect whereof she gathereth to stand in two pointes; first, for accesse to her person, and secondlie, for good interpretacion of your meaninge, and also larger declaracion thereof, if need be. For the former, her Highnes / as her   f.104v noble progenitors have done is well contented that in convenient tyme and for convenient causes, in convenient place and without importunity, for that these

10. J. A. Manning, *Lives of the Speakers of the House of Commons* (1851), 231, and *EP*, I.135, both comment that since this was merely another session of the parliament of 1563, there was no need for Onslow to request the full set of privileges.

partes now touched have not bene afore this so well handled as she trusteth now it shall be, which considered, as free accesse she graunteth you as any other hath had. For the second pointe, because no man att all tymes maie do so well but sometimes thinges maie be uttered which maie be mispoken, for which cause in that tyme also you shall have her entreatable. But she thinketh your circumspection to be such as she shall not therein need. And so an end.

'Nowe a word or two to remember you here present of both the Howses. First, this it is that I wold advise you in this your proceedinge to preferre the most weightie matters first, and not trouble your selves with small matters and of no weight, and therein also that all be done to understand the truth and to avoyde all superfluous matters and loosing and driving awaye of tyme. Secondlie, it is profitable that all my lordes and you others that be here consider that longe tyme requyreth great expences, and therefore wishe you to make expedicion the rather to avoyd the same, and yet not meaninge such expedicion that anie thinge needfull to be done shold be lightlie passed over and not substantiallie done and seene unto, but onelie I meane that ye

f.105   should settle your selves whollie to waighty matters and / those which be necessarie, and to spare superfluous thinges and which needeth not. And this is the some I have to saie.'

Then the Speaker and nether howse made their reverence and departed, and the Queene returned into her privy chamber and there shifted her, and then repaired to her barge and so to the Courte.

2. *Speech on nominating an heir and a bill of succession*

Text from PRO SP Dom.Eliz.46/166, copy.

SP Dom.Eliz.46/166, fos.3-11v

A speech touching the nominacion of a successor to the Crowne at the putting in of a bill for the same.

Mr Speaker, the heathen man Tully said that man is not borne for himself only, but partlie for his parentes, partlie for his children, and partlie for his cuntrie. And surely, Mr Speaker, I doe condemne him as very unnaturall that regardeth neither parentes not[1] children, and him most unnaturall and unworthie to live in any common wealth that regardeth not his cuntrie, for the which I intend to deale, by Gode's sufference and your patience, sithence great necessitie urgeth it; hoping that I shall not neede to use any preamble to move you to be attentive, for that the matter itself is of most weightie importance and concerneth the whole realm universallie and every one therin particulerlie. And therefore I will proceede to what I have to say.

The providence and care of God by the government of the princes and most chieflie towardes this realm of England for the quiet, profitable and sure government of the same, I doe thinke (considering the nature of the people) to be soe great and loving that we ought continually to meditate therof and to be thankfull therfore, especiallie in this place and assemblie. And to declare some part of his great goodnes therin is my purpose, for that I doe iudge the time and place most convenient therfore. And first will I declare what the word 'king' doth signifie; then will I shew the office of a king.

The word or name of a king doth signifie a ruler or governour, an high officer, and of great care if he doe carefully looke unto it, and may well be termed an head. Now, what is the office of an head? The office of the head consisteth in these two pointes: first, carefullie to devise and put in execucion all / things most commodious for the whole bodie and every member therof; then, wisely to foresee and prevent the evills that may come to any part therof, and to that end God hath placed therin the brayne to devise, and every member giveth place therunto, and patientlie performe their duties. He hath also (for helpes) placed therin the eye to looke about and the eare to hearken for all things, either beneficiall or discommodious. And lastlie, to his great glorie he hath created the tongue to utter the same, where the good may be received and the evill prevented. This king, this head, with the consent of the whole

f.3v

---

1. *Sic.*

bodie and through the providence of God, weying that his eye and eare cannot be in every corner of his kingdome and dominions at one instant to view and hearken out the benefittes or inconveniences that might growe to the head, bodie, or any member therof, hath established this honorable counsell of everie part of the same absent from the king's eye and eare, the which is termed a parliament, that is, a speech uttered from the heart, from the mynd, yea a free speech wherfore this counsell was ordeined to be absent from the king's eye and eare. The reason is that as th'office of a king is an high thinge, even soe he most commonly listeth himself on high and can hardlie endure plaine speech, being inured to pleasing things. Therfore, to prevent the evills of trayterous flattery and divellish dissimulacion and many other inconveniences, the providence of God, I say, hath ordeined by lawe that in this House every one hath free speech and consent, and that he doth iniury to the whole realme that makes any thing knowne to the prince that is here in hand without consent of the House, or that bringeth any message from her Majestie into this House to draw us from free speech and consent.

Mee thinkes I heare one obiect that I goe too farr, for so there may be a law made
f.4   to endanger the present state of the prince. / I answere that true it is (if God forsake us) we may give our consentes in this place, as in any other, to indanger the present state of the prince; yet it is noe lawe. Wherin marke the providence of God, for that he would have free speech and free doings in this place; and to withdraw her Majestie's mynd from misliking therof, he hath removed all daungers from her Majestie, for he hath taken all power out of our handes, soe that we cannot in this place doe her Majestie any harme if we were therin never soe willing. The reason is he hath ordeined by lawe that all things agreed upon by the Parliament are dead and noe lawes, untill she hath quickened them and given them life by her royall assent. Thus you see that God hath, of his great mercy and favour, providentlie provided both for the prince and people in this place. These great benefittes of God towardes us are not here to be neglected, but to be used with thankesgiving to his glorie and the common commoditie of this noble realme. And I doe hope that it wilbe thankfullie taken, both of the prince and state, if every one of this House will discharge his dutie and conscience according to the confidence that of the whole realme is reposed in him: for the whole realm hath chosen us to sitt here diligentlie to enquire what is beneficiall or hurtfull for the same, and to provide accordinglie. Wee sitt not here to take care for ourselves only and so to hearken out what the prince or such a magistrate that is in greatest favour with her doth affect, and to feede their humors to attaine such a suite: that were meere impietie. Let love be without dissimulacion, sayth St Paul, for if our doings heere proceede not of love unto the prince and state, but be seasoned with dissimulacion, they are malicious unto them both. For this principle cannot be gaynsayd: that which is good or evill for the head is good or evill for the whole bodie and for everie member therof; and that which is good or evill for the bodie or any member therof, is good or evill for the head. Surely he that feedeth the prince's affection to the hurt of the common wealth hurteth and
f.4v   hateth aswell her Majestie as the commonwealth. / And he that hurteth the prince to benefit the common wealth hurteth and hateth aswell the common wealth as the prince; for the prince and commonwealth ioyned together make a perfect man

consisting of head, bodie and members, and cannot be separated. Then to conclude this point. Doest thou love the one? Thou loveth both. Doest thou hate the one? Thou hatest both. For in truth the prince cannot love or hate her self, but she must love or hate the common wealth, and the common wealth can neither love or hate itself but it must love or hate the prince in like manner. Then seeing this knot is so indissoluble, the greatest love that any man can shew unto them both is to provide for the greatest mischiefe towardes them both, the which is my speciall and dutifull intencion.

Now methinkes, I have the wise and politique men of this world saying in my eare: 'Thou foole, beware for offending the Queene's Majestie.' To them I answere: yee foolish flattering politiques, would yee avoide the prince's displeasure? Do well then, and soe shall yee be praised of the same. But if yee doe evill, then feare, for shee is the minister of God, to the benefitt of him that doth well and to take vengance of him that doth evill. These sentences of the Holy Ghost, and the reasons above recited, may sufficiently prick forward any that feareth God or loveth the prince and state to seeke out the inconveniences that may any way offend or indanger either of them, to the end that they may be here presented. In such causes we ought all to sett aside feare and to be bould. And although I be one of the meanest and simplest of this House, yet out of very love to my prince and cuntrie I will open unto you one of the greatest woundes and soares that is unto our prince and this noble nation, and such as one as doth most touch both the prince and her counsell in honor and conscience (God's holy religion only excepted), yea and doth also declare so much the want of love and dutifull consideracion of this House to the safetie of this most noble ile of England as none can more. /

This greivous wound is that want of the establishment of the succession of the   f.5
Crowne of England; and for that the right therof is not universallie knowne, this wound, I say, if it be not healed in time will make infinite woundes, yea, and the same soe incurable as are like to make this noble realm a prey unto those that ambitiouslie gape for and devise the confusion and utter ruyne of the same. What English heart can, without teares, dulie weigh these intolerable miseries in his mynde? An hard heart hath he that hath either read or heard of the dissention for the crowne from King Henry the 4th untill King Henry the 7th and will not endeavour himself, to the utmost, to prevent the like. Every kingdome devided within itself, sayth Christ, shalbe desolated. If two titles did hazard the crowne heretofore, what then are many like to doe hereafter? I remember that I sayde a little before that the neglecting to foresee and provide for this mischiefe did touch the prince and the counsell in honour and conscience, and this House in that they shewed want of love and dutifull consideracion to the safetie of this noble realme. Now I doe thinke it requisite first to shew how it toucheth her Majestie in honour, and then to proceede to the rest in order. But before I enter into this discourse, I will shew my coniectures what might move her Majestie to be soe unwilling that a successor should be knowne, and answere them according to my simple discretion.

The only cause is her Majestie thinketh it to be dangerous or hazardfull unto her place or person. The reasons that may move her Majestie so to thinke are these: the first is the great and seacret seeking and depending of the nobilitie and gentrie upon her Majestie when she was princesse; the second is that for the few things could be spoken, either in the privie counsell or privie chamber of the Queene her sister but they were revealed unto her Majestie; the third is the attempt of Wyatt and a great

f.5v   part of the nobilitie ioyned with him to depose her sister and to sett up her Majestie; / the fourth is the continuall practises for the deposing of Queen Mary; the fift, and last, the generall mislike that the subiectes had conceived of Queen Mary. But before I answere these, I will protest unto the living God that if I thought it dangerous to our gratious Queene I would not deale in it; but of a truth I am fullie perswaded that it wilbe a great safetie unto her Majestie, and I doubt not to prove it by good reason.

Now to the obiections. All these five before rehearsed are answered in the first and last; that is to say, the nobilitie and people did seeke unto and depend upon the Queene's Majestie in her sister's time, but this was only through a generall misliking that they had conceived of her sister, which is proved by this one reason. It is not the nature of such as seeke for advancement to tarry or gape for dead men's shoes, espetially when the prince is so bountifull as was Queen Mary. Then is neither the espetiall consideracion of their duties, nor of her Grace's bounty, could keepe them within the limittes of their allegiance. It must needes follow that the generall causes moved that generall misliking that brought so many perills to her sister, and not for that the successor was knowne.

Now I thinke it good to shew those generall causes. First the Protestantes, which wanted the libertie of their consciences, attempted things dangerous to her Grace. Then, universallie, both the Protestantes and Papistes, seeing her unnaturall marriage with a prince of a strange cuntrie and the many dangerous attemptes practised by the strangers unto the Crowne of England, withdrew their heartes whollie from her insomuch as none more desired the removing of the crowne from her head then the Papistes themselves. And therof I had good experience in her Grace's time, for, I assure you, I was then attempted to give my consent therunto by as arrogant Papistes as any were in England. And when I refused it and asked what they meant, one answered 'Doest thou not see that she goeth about to overthrowe the Crowne of England?' Soe that I doe prove by these reasons that is was the love that the nobilitie and subiectes of the realme did beare to the Crowne and the perill that they saw it in through her government that withdrew their heartes from her, and not the knowledge of the successor. Now the Queene's Majestie hath not matched with

f.6   a stranger; neither doth she / communicate with them to the danger of the Crowne; neither doth she maynteine Papistrie, but openlie pronounceth herself an enemy therunto: therfore, noe reason why a successor knowne should be any danger unto her Majestie. And considering the quiet government that we live in under her, noe reason can move us to desire a change. And I would he were hanged that would wish any other change than this, that her Majestie may be stirred up to set forth the glory of God most ferventlie and to love the state most heartilie.

Now I will returne from my digression unto the matter and shew how it toucheth the prince in honour to provide that a successor be knowne. First, the etimologie of this word 'king' in the Greeke doth signifie, as I have heard, the foundation or holder up of the people. Then since God hath placed her Majestie to be the upholder of the people of England, and that, if for want of a knowne successor after her decease, this people committed to her charge should, through unnaturall dissention, for the maynteyning of sundry titles that might now be easily discussed in her Majestie's life time, shedd infinite quantity of innocent bloud and therby the state be utterly overthrowne, what great dishonor would this be to her Majestie? And presently, what greater dishonor can there be to her Majestie then that the enemies to our state and religion – the French and Scots, the auntient enemies of this realm – which doe dailie expect a time of revenge of their old cankered and malitious heartes, should determine and say within themselves, 'There wil be no time like to that when the Queene's Majestie is dead, for she is so unnaturall that she will not suffer a successor to be knowne. Then will all the realme be together by the eares, and there be many pretended title to tyre them withall, soe that then we shall revenge our quarrells at the full, and have of them our wills': as there is no doubt but this is both their thought and seacret speech. Lastlie, the nobilitie and commons of this realme have at all times yealded subsedies and levies most willinglie unto her Majestie without any repining, as for example the last parliament a subsedie was graunted unto her Majestie, and not one that did denie it, or that would seeme to deminish one penny of her Majestie's demaund. It was there openly sayd that the like full consent was never seene before that time. I graunt that in soe doing they did but their duties, for Christ sayth, 'Give unto Caesar that which / is due unto Caesar'. Even so, it is Caesar's dutie to yeald protection and defence unto his people. Now what greater dishonour can there be unto her Majestie than to denie th'establishing of a successor, for want wherof is like to ensue much unnaturall dissention and bloudshed, especially of her Majestie's most deare and loving subiectes?   f.6v

Now I will shew you how it toucheth the Queene's Majestie in conscience to make the successor knowne. First, the king is a ruler, yea, such a ruler as is by God made the head, and the people the body. And what the office of the head is, I shewed you in the begining, that is to say, carefully to devise and put in execucion all things most commodious for the body and every member therof; then, wisely to foresee and prevent the evills that may come unto any part therof. Therfore, hearken now what the spirit of God sayth of a king. 'Behold', sayth Esay,[2] *caput* 32; 'a king shall reigne in justice, and princes shall rule in judgment'. The prophett Ezechell calleth kings by the name of 'shepherds' (34.23) saying, 'I will sett a shepheard over them, and he shall feede them, even my servant David. He shall feede them and be their shepheard'. And 1 Timothy, 2.1[3] are these wordes: 'I exhort therfore that first of all supplicacions, praiers, intercessions, and giving of thankes be made for all; for kings, and for all that are in authoritie, that we may leade a quiet and peaceable life in all godliness and honestie'. Now let us examine the contentes of these three sentences of the Holie Ghost what kings ought to be, how they ought to governe.

First, Esay sayth they ought to rule and reigne in justice and judgment, by which wordes are meant an upright government both in religion and policie. And wheras Ezechiell doth compare the king to a shepheard, saying 'even my servant David shall feede them and be their shepheard', by these wordes are to be considered what the dutie and office of a shepheard is. The dutie of a shepheard consisteth in three

2. I.e. Isaiah (Esayas), 32.1.   3. I.e. 1 Timothy, 2.1-2.

pointes: first, to see his sheepe fedd, yea, and with such meate as is good and wholsome for their preservacion, and not with such meate as will rott and destroy them; the second is to keepe and defend them from the wolfe, or any other thing that may or will destroy or annoy them; the third is to cure them of their greifes and diseases. And the words of St Paul are that we should make prayers for kings and magistrates. I pray you, Mr Speaker, marke to what end: that, sayth he, we may leade a quiet and peaceable life in all godliness and honesty. The which is as much to say as pray for the Queene's Majestie and her magistrates that they may governe in such sort / that the people committed to their charge may leade a quiet, not a quarrelous, and peaceable, not a bloudy, life; for soe it beseemeth godliness and honestie.

f.7

Now I will make my collection. The summe of that which concerned the Queene's Majestie in honour to establish the succession consisteth in these 4 pointes. First, her Majestie ought to be an upholder, and not an overthrower, of the people. Secondly, she ought carefully, naturally, and religiously to end all titles and contentions that may hazard the state or shedd innocent bloud. Thirdly, she ought to remove the eyes of all forreyne enemies from espying or taking any advantage wherby they may revenge their malice and ease their malicious heartes to the perill or preiudice of the Crowne of England. Fourthlie, she ought not to denie th'establishment of a successor, for want wherof is like much unnaturall dissention and bloudshedd, espetiallie of her Majestie's most deare and loving subiectes, wherby the realm may be in hazard to become a prey to the enemy; but rather that she would suffer the same quietlie in this place to discusse the title of succession, to keepe us in naturall love, dutifull obedience and safetie. These things, I say, if they be not in time prevented, wil be the greatest dishonour to her Majestie that can be. And to conclude this matter, I doe affirme that they wil be the greatest danger unto her Majestie's present estate that may be. The reason is the chiefest and readiest meane presentlie to robb her Majestie of the heartes of her subiectes is to let them knowe that she loveth them not, and that she careth not what become of them after her decease: and the leaving of such a title undiscussed, as will sett them all together by the eares after her decease, is a manifest token therof, and so it is the readiest way presentlie to withdraw their heartes from her Majestie unto the great perill and danger of the present estate.

Now I will give you the summe of those reasons that are to move her Majestie in conscience to establish the succession. First, her Majestie is the head of this noble nation and we, the English people, her bodie. And Esay sayth a king shall rule and reigne in justice and judgment; Ezechiell compareth a king to a shepheard; and Paul exhorteth to pray for kings and magistrates, that we may live quiet and peaceablie in all godliness and honestie. All this is as much to say that the Queene's Majestie ought, yea, it is her / bounden duty to bring up us her people in the feare of God and true religion, politiquely to governe us that we may be defended from all perills, and to binde up and heale woundes that we may live quietlie and peaceablie in all godliness and honestie; the which cannot be without the succession be established and all inconveniences – I meane so many as may by Godlie policie – be prevented. Soe that to conclude, both these I doe affirme: that the Queene's Majestie

f.7v

is bound, both in honour and in conscience, to establish the succession; and it is the best and surest way for her Majestie's present safetie, for she cannot stand without the heartes of her people. And as to that sayd, that it toucheth the Counsell in honour and conscience to move her Majestie to provide a knowne successor, forasmuch as by the scriptures kings and magistrates ought all to runne one course and be guided by one rule. The reasons before rehearsed concerne them as nearlie as the prince; howbeit much more are they to be blamed then the prince for that this great and universall inconvenience hath not been prevented before this time. For if God had not prevented[4] her Majestie's life thus long – as I beseech God she may live many yeares to his glorie – had we not all felt the smart of it ere this time? Yes, no doubt; and it would have proved noe sporting game for the best of them.

Therfore, I doe most humblie and heartily beseech their honours faithfullie to discharge that trust that the prince reposeth in them, and the charge that they tooke upon them when she made them counsellors; and also to consider what a great burthen of conscience is now laid upon them, for God did not put into the princes's heart to chuse them into that place too much to beare with any thing, either to the offence of God, to her Majestie's danger, or to the danger of the state. Howbeit I doe greatlie feare that they are all too slack and fearfull in stirring up her Majestie to pittie the lamentable desolation that may ensue to her people for want of a knowne successor. To / prove it, let this serve for a president. Sure I am that their honours doe   f.8 perfectlie see that if God should take the Queene's Majestie to his mercie the succession being not established, that the whole realme would be in an hurlie burlie, and that they doe cast this in their myndes: 'if such a title take place, I am utterlie undone', sayth one; 'if such a title take place, I am utterly undone' sayth another. And thus, this mischeife not prevented, they see an utter confusion, both of themselves and of the state alsoe. Now forsomuch as their honours have suffered this universall mischeife to be thus long unprevented, to the great slaunder of the regiment and perill of the prince's honour, conscience, and safetie, and their own also: I say and speake it dutifully that they doe all yeald too much unto her Majestie, either of feare, or of want of dutifull regard to this weightie cause. To this one answereth, 'her Majestie sheweth us great reasons to prove it to her present perill'. To that I answere that their wisdomes are such, if love did overcome feare, that they are able to yeald unto her Majestie great reasons to prove that the contrary is to her perill of soule, bodie and honour. If their honours doe thinke that the people of the realme doe not finde the want of their fidelities in this behalf to the prince and state, they are deceived and greatlie deceive themselves. And soe to this I conclude that I doe greatlie feare that some of them have not that great care which God requireth at their handes in this weighty matter. But I pray God to forgett and forgive their wantes past, and presentlie to stirr up their heartes faithfullie and effectuallie to deale therin, for Moses, that good and godlie magistrate, is to be had in perpetuall memory as a patterne to be followed, who desired God to wipe him out of the booke of life for the people's sake. And I would gladlie have their honours to revolve in their myndes what good opinion or estimacion they deserve of the people, and whether that

4. *Sic.*

f.8v
through their neglect and not continuall calling upon her Majestie for the preventing of this mischeife, they are not hereafter / (if God in mercie doo not prevent it) in great perill to be reputed and used rather as enemies unto the state then as lovers and faithfull counsellors, if it be not prevented in her Majestie's life. And if their honours thinke that they can stay and overrule the people by having the treasure of the realme and the munition in their handes, they are much deceived. Let the late president of Queen Mary suffice them therin for a warning, and us for a dailie terror to affright us from trusting them too much and from being carried into treason with them; for they will, in all likelyhood, goe 3 or 4 waies. Therfore let it serve us for a lesson to enquire and learne where the right is that we may give place therunto, that soe God may blesse our doings and withold this his heavie curse from us, pronounced in these wordes: 'for your iniuries and iniustices your kingdome shal be transferred from one people to another people.'

Now to the last point, wherin I did charge this House with want of love and dutifill consideracion to the safetie of this noble ile of England. Certaine it is that the law hath made this counsell the eyes, the eares, and the tongue of the prince and realme; even soe certaine it is that that which is good or evill for the prince is good or evill for the whole state, *et econtra*;[5] for the prince and state, ioyned in one (as I sayd before) make a perfect man of head, bodie and members, and cannot be separated. Now to the dutie and office of these three. First, the eye ought to be vigilant and watchfull that noe perill come to the head or bodie. Then, the eare ought carefullie to hearken out all things either hurtfull or beneficiall for the head or body. And the

f.9
tongue is the messenger to utter them in that place where they are to be received or reiected according to their qualities, whether they be good or evill, the which / is this counsell. Now since we be chosen of prince and realme of a speciall trust and confidence by them reposed in us, to be their eyes, eares, and tongues to see, hearken out and utter in this House all that is beneficiall or dangerous, if we, I say, shall hereafter neglect and deceive this great trust and omitt to prevent this lingring and universall mischeife, to meete, the not establishing of the succession, what are our eyes, eares and tongues but trayterous eyes, eares and tongues, and soe good for nothing?

Well, since we have heretofore sinned against heaven in this case and against this noble realme of England, God, for his great mercie's sake, graunt that we may now rise againe with Peter by weeping repentance, and make recompence, for now is the time. If we doe protract it and feigne this or that excuse, it will help us noe more then when Evah, when she had eaten of the forbidden fruite, to say the serpent had deceived her, or, as Adam sayd, 'the woman whom thou gavest me gave it unto me.' Noe, noe, this excuse did not serve them, but we doe feele the smart of their disobedience and so shall all our posteritie doe unto the worlde's end. Now since noe excuse will availe, but that we must either, in this counsell, serve God or Beliall, shew ourselves true Englishmen, or traytors. Whensoever any conceipt or terror shall, in this place, draw us back from speaking to the glorie of God, or the commoditie of this honourable state, let us learne of Christ and say, 'Away, Divell, with thy hellish conceipts'; for if, when Herod had caused all the male children in Jury to be slaine from two yeares olld downwardes, then was heard in Rome a voyce of great mourning, lamentacion and weeping, Rachell weeping for her children, and would not be comforted, what voices of great mourning, lamentacion and weeping will there be heard in England, where every Rachell shall weepe for father, brother and children and cannot be comforted, because they / are not able to prevent these inconveniences. I doe therfore advise you all to crie out as lowde as you can and not to leave of untill her Majestie hath looked upon us with her eyes of mercy, pittying this our intolerable misery, for the spirit of God sayth in Zacharie:[6] 'the Lord is with you while yee be with him, and if yee seeke him he wil be found of you; but if yee forsake him, he will forsake you.' Thus I humblie and heartily beseech you all to discharge you fidelities to God, your prince and cuntrie, wherby the Queene's Majestie and the magistrates' honours and consciences may be unblemished in their carefull and dutifull providing that this worthy realme may long continue English and be preserved. To this end, I say, crie out and lift up your voices like trumptetts and leave not of, that the sound of this lamentable voice of Rachell's may not be heard in England; for (to our comfort) God hath promised that if we seeke him he wil be found of us. But I advise you to shunne his threate, for he sayth further, if we forsake him he will forsake us. And as I wished you all to be earnest and carefull, even of the great love that in dutie you ought to beare unto our England, speedily to prevent and hinder this great and universall mischeife, even soe I doe most heartily beseech you to be careful for the present state of the Queene's Majestie.

And that our earnest desires and carefull heartes may appeare unto her Majestie for the preventing of this great and universall daunger, I have prepared a bill that the House may be possessed of the matter; wherin I have thought it good to offer unto her Majestie a subsidie and two fifteens and tenths to obteine her Majestie's loving, willing and favourable consent unto this weightie cause that importeth both her Majestie and the whole estate above all earthlie things; beseeching you of this House with all cheritie to have consideracion therof. And my humble suite is alsoe that every one unto whom this speech is directed will beare with the homelines / and playnesse of the stile, imputing it to the weightines of the matter; for I tell you, Mr Speaker, that I speake for all England, yea, and for the noble English nation, who in times past (with noe small honour) have daunted and made the proudest nations agast, for the preservacion wherof God graunt us all to be heartie and wise in him. And so I humblie and earnestlie beseech the Queene's Majestie to have in her gratious remembrance the naturall wordes spoken by her most noble father unto his people, the which are these:[7] 'But when we remember our mortalitie, and that we must die, then doe we thinke that all our doings in our life time are clearly defaced and worthie of noe memory if we leave you in trouble at the time of our death; for if our true heire be not knowne at the time of our death, see what mischeife and trouble shall succeede to you and your children, th'experience wherof some of you have

f.9v

f.10

---

5. *Sic.*
6. See 2 Chron., 15.2. 'Zacherie' is 'Azariah'.
7. There is at this point a marginal reference to 'Grafton, fol.1176', that is to p.1176 of R. Grafton's *A Chronicle at Large...* (1569). This does not of itself destroy the possibility of placing the speech in 1566 since the citation may be a later addition; and in any event, Henry's speech to the 1529 parliament had already been printed by Edward Hall some 20 years earlier.

heard, what mischeife and manslaughter continued in this realm betweene the two Houses of Yorke and Lancaster, by the which dissention this realm was like to have been clearlie destroyed.' If her Majestie doe print these wordes in her heart and prevent this perill to her people, then doth she declare herself to be a deare mother and tender nource over them, and shal be sure to make herself strong with their Christian and heartie good wills, even the surest fortresse that her Majestie can possiblie build. Sure I am – in dutifull love be it spoken – that there is nothing at this present, Mr Speaker, that doth so much weaken her Majestie and draw away the heartes of the rude and ignorant people from her Majestie, as the not preventing of this mischeife, for they are more commonly ledd and caried away with this prophane reason of the heathen, 'We will love them that love us'. And let him that most dearlie loveth, or hath most cause to love, the Queene's Majestie revolve this in his mynd. If God should take her Majestie, the succession / being not established, I know not what shall become of my self, my wife, children, landes, goodes, friendes or cuntrie; for in truth, noe man doth know what. And therfore every man hath great cause to meditate hereof, for it concerneth everyone. I say that this meditacion being gravely, maturely, and wisely pondered to remember that her Majestie will not settle the succession, will (without the assistance of God's grace) coole the heate of love in any, how fervent so ever it be. And let him speake the truth herein from his heart and lie not.

Therfore, God for his great mercie's sake, grant that the Queene's Majestie's loving eyes may be opened and her noble heart mollified, wherby those great mischeifes, both to herself and the whole state, may be her loving and favourable consent be speedily prevented. And so to conclude I heartilie beseech you all, with Jesus the sonne of Sirach, to doe your duties betimes and the Lord will give you a reward at this time.[8] Follow his counsaile, Mr Speaker, I advise you, least if we neglect this time, God's vengeance doe light iustly upon us all; for I tell you, Mr Speaker, that the queene's Majestie, the Counsell and this House shall answere for all the innocent bloud that shal be spilt in this cause. Wherfore I take you to record this day with me, a poore member of this House and commonwealth, that I am pure from the bloud of all these men, even as St Paul did when he had discharged his dutie in all good conscience. Therfore, Mr Speaker, let every one of this House follow the matter presently and earnestlie, for they that doe not shall wash their handes in innocency with the two innocentes Judas and Pilate, who betrayed and condemned the innocent lamb Jesus Christ. For unanswerablie should our faultes before God the the world, and too, too lamentable were the case, Mr Speaker, if noble England should die with our Queene through our slacknes, rechlesnes and fearfullnes, since / we doe palpablie see the perill and dare not use good, lawfull and godly meanes to prevent it.

Therfore noble England, being now in great distresse (as is before sayd) it crieth out in most dolefull wise by me, the poore and simple advocate therof, sayinge: 'Helpe, o yee my noble, faithfull counsellors and subiectes inheritors, help this my feeble and weake estate that I may long live and be preserved to your use' – Mr Speaker, oh that noble England should intreate us here to performe it to our owne uses – 'for I have noe meane to help me but you, and to that you were especially borne; and there is no time and place to heale my sicknes but this.' Therfore, let each degree imprint in his heart these wise and naturall wordes of John, Duke of Albanie, a Scott: 'To defend his cuntrie', sayd he, 'is the office of a king, the honour of noblemen, the very service of chivalrie, and the dutie naturall of the commonaltie'. And whereas it is thought of many of this assemblie that her Majestie wil be greatly greived and offended with me for attempting this weightie cause, I cannot perswade myself that it will soe fall out; nay, I doe verily looke for the contrary, for how can it be that her Majestie will mislike with him that doth most dearlie honour and love her, and in faithfull and true love to her Majestie seeketh that which will procure unto her the great favour of God and wonderfull love of all her nobilitie and subiectes, and so mightilie strengthen her as the setling of the succession must of necessitie doe? For therby shall her Majestie's whole people and state be preserved. But if great displeasure should grow unto me therby, thinke not that it should be greivous, but ioyous unto me, for I doe acknowledg unto you all that I was borne to honour God and in him to serve my prince and commonwealth truly, faithfullie   f.11v and heartilie. And therfore, soe long as I have the testimony of a true heart and a good conscience and am sure that my speech tendeth only to the honour of God, to her Majestie's safetie and to the preservacion / of the whole realme, I doe as little accompt of my head in respect of the preserving of this, or any of these causes, as I doe of the least hayre therof. And soe eftsoones I doe most heartily and earnestlie beseech you all to give this bill a reading, and cause all England to laugh, for it hath wept too, too long through our faultes, unanswerable to God and the whole realme, who have put their only trust in us the prevent the perills therof. Therfore God, for his great mercie's sake, graunt us now faithfull heartes to stick heartily to this bill, wherby it may have a prosperous proceeding and happie successe; for it may abide noe longer delayes without looking for the utter subversion of the whole realme, which God forbidd, for all hope of issue of her Majestie's bodie for the stay of these mischeifes is in reason clearlie extinct.

8. Ecclesiasticus, 2.8?

3 . Speech on bill of succession

Text from PRO SP Dom.Eliz.46/166, copy.

SP Dom.Eliz.46/166, fos.1 and v.

A speech touching the receiving of a bill for establishing the succession of the Crowne, with direction how to proceede therin etc.

Mr Speaker, I heartily reioyce that it hath pleased God to stirr up the heartes of this House soe willinglie to accept and receive this bill. And for the speedie and prosperous successe therof, I doe thinke it good to move you, Mr Speaker, to move the House to take order that you and they doe whollie goe (this afternoone) to the Queene's Majestie, giving her to understand that we have received a bill into the House for th'establishment of the succession of the imperiall Crowne of England. The order of our humble suite unto her Majestie I have drawne such sort as (in my simple witt) I do thinke it most convenient to be done unto her Majestie, considering the great perill that the Crowne of England hath of long time and doth yet abide by protractinge th'establishment of the succession therof: humblie praying you, Mr Speaker, that the Clerke may give it a reading, and that the House may presentlie consider of it. And that immediatlie after that the House hath considered of it, some of this House may be presentlie sent unto the Lordes in the name of the whole House, giving them to understand that it hath pleased God (of his singuler and mercifull favor unto noble England) to stirr us up to receive a bill into the House for th'establishment of the succession of th'imperiall Crowne of England, then the which we doe verily perswade ourselves that noe earthlie thing can be more ioyfull unto their honours; and to shew them alsoe that we are determined to goe unto the Queene's Majestie this afternoone with that message and humble suite, the which we have in writing sent unto their honors, humblie beseeching them to ioyne with us therin, giving them to meete that we doe assure ourselves that the faithfull love and true heartes that they doe beare unto the Queene of England — ioyned with their godlie and naturall compassions by weying and pittying / also the undoubted and helplesse miseries that will befall upon themselves, their posteritie, and the infinite nombers of each degree of the people of England if this mischeife be not now presentlie foreseene and prevented — will make them all ioyfull travellers and earnest suiters with us unto her Majestie for th'establishment of the imperiall Crowne of this her Majestie's and our noble countrie of England, without the which nothing can be looked for but an utter subvercion of the whole realme and people of the same, a case most highlie to be regarded, pittied and carefully prevented of noblemen; for it is the honour and dutie of noblemen to doe their hearty endeavours to preserve their countrie, and to that end as on especially they were borne and made noble.

4. *Sir Ralph Sadler's speech on the subsidy and succession*

Text from BL Add.33591, original in Sadler's hand.
Printed. Sadler's State Papers, ed. A. Clifford and T. Park (1809, 2 vols.), II.548-52, but placed in the first parliament.

Add.33,591, fos.8-11

Touching these matiers which now be com in question amongst us I will with your favour in few woordes say my poure mynde and opynyon; ffirst I will speke to the matier of the subsidie which was first moved, and then to the others.

Touching the subsidie: trewly no man lyving wolde be more loth then I to set fourth or to speke in the furtherunce of any thing in this place whiche might seme to be chargeable or burdenous to my countrey, but when I do consider of the grete and weightie causes which at this tyme do in dede urge and require a subsidie I can not pretermitte ne passe the same over with sylence, but rather have thought it my duetie to commende the same to your wisedomes and good consideracions. And if any man shall conceyve of my speche or percase not loking into the depth and botom of the matier shall thinke or iudge of me that I speke for the profite and commodytee of the Queen's Majeste rather then for the benefite and common weale of my countrey; if any man here shall so thinke of me, to him I answer that if I speke for the Queen's Majeste, in so doing I speke not ayenst the common weale of my countrey, for her Majestie is the hed / of our commen weale, and being the hed of our comen weale   f.8v that which is good for the one can not be evill for th'other. And therfore I may the more boldely speke in that which I thinke is profitabl, commodious and good for both. Surely in my poure opynyon there was never greter cause whie we shulde graunte a subsidie: the necessitee of the tyme did never more require it. For we see that the whole worlde, our neighbours rounde aboute us of long tyme have ben and yet be in armes, in hostilite and in grete garboyle.[1] Onelie we rest here in peax and quyetnes, thankes be to God therfore and the good governement of the Queen's Majeste. Mary it is a poynte of wisdom in the tyme of peax to provide for the warre; when we see our neighbours' houses on fyer it is wisdom to provide and forsee how to kepe the smoke and sparkes of the same as farre from our owne as we can. The principall and chief cause of this hostilite and garboyle abrode is for the matier and cause of religion. The malice of the enemyes and adversaries of Godde's ghospell doth increase and waxeth very hotte. The late accidentes in Fraunce, the grete tyrannye, the horrible and cruell murders and slaughters whiche have ben commytted and executed there upon those of the religion, the lyke whereof hathe

---

1. I.e. tumult.

never ben harde nor redde of, doth playnely shew and declare the dedely hatred and malice of the papistes ayenst the professours of Godde's ghospell and trew religion. How gredy, how thirstie they are of innocent bloode doth playnely appere; what faith, what trust is to be given to their woordes and promyses all men may see. In

f.9   dede, they do but watche their tyme / and therfore we had nede to beware of them and to provyde for their malice in tyme. We have harde and we here daylie of secret conspiracies and grete confederacies betwen the Pope, the French King and other prynces of the popish confederacie ayenst all princes protestauntes and professors of the ghospell, of the which the Queen's Majeste is the chief patronesse and protectrix at this day. It is not unlyke, nay it is not to be doubted but that those prynces of that popish confederacie assone as they can settle and establish the Romishe religion within their owne territories and domynyons, will forthwith converte and employ all their forces to restore the same also in Englonde where they may be sure to fynde a grete ayde of our owne nacyon, of our English papistes here at home besides those which be abrode to helpe and further the same. In dede Englonde, the Queen's Majeste is the onelie and greatest marke which the adversaries of Godde's gospell do shote at, and therfore her Majeste had never greater cause, never more nede to arme herself, to make herself strong and to furnish her coffres with treasure, whereby she may be the more able to defende her realme and subiectes and to incounter and mete with the malice of her enemyes. This I doubte not all wise men do evydently and playnely see; and if there were none other cause then this, surely it were sufficyent to persuade us willingly to condiscende to the graunte of a subsidye, as I doubt not but such as be zelous to advaunce the glorie of God and his gospell, such as do love the Queen's Majeste and their countrey, will in these daungerous days shew themselfes

f.9v   liberall and willing / to departe with a small porcion of their goodes such as they may well forbere, for to resiste and impugne the malice of the enemyes of Christe's ghospell which do daylie ymagyn and seke the utter ruyn and distruction of all the trew professors of the same. If there were no other cause I say but this it were sufficient to require a subsidie. And yet is there another cause of gret moment, of grete importaunce, and that is the matier of Irelande which hathe ben well remembred here. In dede the Queen's Majeste and her noble progenitors of long tyme have ben at gret charges in Irelande whereof hitherto they have had small profite or commodytee; and yet of force her Majeste must contynew, yea rather increase the charge if she will reape any frute or commodytee thereof, the onelie way whereunto is to subdue and bring that lande to civilite and obedience. And [who] will not gladly contribute and bere a burden to so good an ende and purpose? If that lande may be made civile and obedient, if the people there which now be barbarous, wilde and savage, lawles without law or iustice, if they may be brought to the knowledge of God and of his worde and of their dueties to their prince and sovereigne, and so to lyve civilie and obedientlie under law and iustice, no doubt but as they must nedes increase and growe therby into welth and quyetnes, so then in stede of the gret charges which the princes of this realme have alwaies susteyned for the stay of the lande in obedience, gret profite and a good yerelie revenue will arrise and grow to the crowne of Englonde. So that all men of reason must nedes confesse that the cost and charge employed thereaboutes shalbe well bestowed, and every man ought, and I

thinke will gladlie and willingly contribute towardes the charge. The charge in dede
hath ben and wilbe grete for the tyme, yea so grete that her Majeste shall not be able to
bere it ne to susteyne it / without the helpe and contribucion of her good and lovyng   f.10
subiectes. The charge is an extraordynary charge, and we be taught by experience
that when princes be charged with such extraordynary charges they ar inforced to
seke extraordynarye wayes and meanes of ayde and relief. In such cases comenly they
have recourse to the benevolence, good will and ayde of their good and lovyng
subiectes, for their owne ordynarye revenues will do no more then bere their
ordynary charges. The princes' ordynary revenue will not suffice nor extende to
mayntene such extraordynarie charges. And therfor as of force her Majeste must be
constreyned to seke som other way of relief either by way of subsidie, lone or other
contribucyon at th'andes of her good and lovyng subiectes, as all prynces in such
cases ar inforced to do, so we of duetie ought to have care and good consideracion of
the same and gladlee and willingly to contribute and bere with her Majeste
according to our porcions, according to our habilitees lyke good and loving
subiectes. I shall not nede to use any persuasions to move or persuade you thereunto:
in dede, I will not go about to persuade you, the causes of themselfes ar sufficient to
persuade you, being men of wisedom and iudgement, men selected and chosen of
the best and wisest sorte of the hole realme, such as can decerne and iudge moche
better then I can what is fitte for good subiectes to do in this case. And therfore
having by this my shorte speche uttered and declared myn owne affection to further
this matier of subsidie I leave it to your wisedomes and good consideracions, trusting
that every man here will shew himself aswell affected as I am to further the same and
to do therein that which is fitte for good subiectes to do according to our duties.

   Now to th'other matier touching the succession. Surely I can not but moche
commende the zelous and good mynde of him that hathe brought it here in question,
and for myn owne / parte I wisshe and desire from the bottome of my herte that som   f.10v
good successe and effecte might folowe of it. And yet I am not of opynyon that it is
fitte for us to deale with it at this tyme, specyally not to myxe or myngle it with the
matier of the subsidie whereby we might seme as it were to condicyon and
couvenante with her Majeste, as who wolde say, if her Majeste will graunte us the
one we will the more willingly graunte the other; this kynde and maner of
condicyonyng with the prynce is not, I thinke, fitte for us to use, for thereby we
shulde not onely extenuate and moche disgrace the frankenes and liberalitee of our
graunte of the subsidie, but also I feare we shulde rather hinder then further the other
matier which we so greatly wisshe for and desire. Th'other matier, the matier of
succession, is a thing which I thinke we do all hunger and thirst for, but yet I see not
how we can deale with it onles it cam from the Queen's Majeste. It is a matier farre
out of our reche and compase and it were in vayne, yea, mere folie in us to deale with
suche matiers as we can not arreche. We ought to thinke that the Queen's Majeste
and her nobilitee (whom it doth most chiefely concerne and belong unto) be not
unmyndefull nor lesse carefull of it then we be. And yet if any gret cause hidden and
unknowen to us do move her Majeste to stay and forbere to deale in it untill a better
tyme and oportunyte may serve for the purpose, we ought to satisfie and content our
selffes with it and to referre it hollie to her Majeste. Wherfore myn advise shalbe that

we do procede in the matier of the subsidie simplie, without condycyon, without myxing or mingling any other matier with it and that we do shew our selffes good and lovyng subiectes in the good expedicion of the same. And for the other matier concerning the succession, let us pray to God in whose handes the hartes of prynces

f.11   are that it will please him of his infinite goodnes to dispose the harte / and mynde of her Majeste so to consider of it and so to deale in it and in such convenyent and due tyme as may be not onely for her owne suretie but also for the suretie and quyetnes of her realme and subiectes. This is my pour advise: and if all men here knew asmoche as I do, I thinke they wolde the soner and the more easely be persuaded to be of myn opynyon.

5. Queen's speech to delegation from both Houses, 5 November

i. Text from PRO SP Dom.Eliz.41/5, fragment of the Queen's own draft.
ii. Text from Cambridge University Library Gg.iii.34, copy.
Other MS. BL Stowe 354 (as Cambridge, omitting introduction.)
Printed. EHR, XXXVI (1921), 514-17 (from Stowe 354).

SP Dom.Eliz.41/5

[Endorsed by Cecil 'A part of the begynning of the Queen's Majestie's speche to the 30 lordes and 30 commons on Tewsday the vth of November 1566 *anno regni* 8.[1] The Queen's own hand.']

If the order of your cause had mached the waight of your matter the one might well have[2] craved reward and the other muche the soner satisfied; but whan I call to mynd how [far of from a princely hart] far from dutiful care [and], yea rather how ny a traiterous trik, this tumblin cast [b] did springe, I muse how [muche] men of wit can so hardly use that gift the hold. [To b] I marvel not [at] muche that brideles colts do not knowe ther ridar's hand, whome bit of kingely reine did never snafle yet. Whither it was fit that so great a cause as this shuld have had his beginning in suche a publik place [as wher] as that, let it be well waighed. [If all If] Must all ivel bodings that might be recited [war] be founde litel inough to hap to my share? [Let] Was it wel ment, think you, that those that knewe not how fit this matter was to be graunted by the Prince wold preiudicat ther Prince in agravating the matter, so all ther arguments tended to my careles care of this my dere realme?

Cambridge University Library Gg.iii.34, pp.208-12(ii)

The speche of the Queen's Majestie had the next parlyament followynge the Tewsdaye after Alhalloun daye to the Duke of Norfolke, the Archebusshope of Yowrke, and xxviij mo of marquesys, erles, busshopes, vicontes and barrons, and to xxx^ti knyghtes and esquiers of the lowere howse as ffollowythe, as I could carrye away by remembrans. /

Sir Edward Rogers, knyght, and Controlor of her Majestie's howse	Sir Thomas Gargrave, knyght Sir Thomas Gerrard, knyght Sir Wylliam Chestere, knyght	p.209

1. Altered from '9°'.

2. Words printed in light type are insertions; words in square brackets are deletions.

Sir Fraunces Knoles, knyght, Vicechamberleyn to here Majestie
Sir Wylliam Cycyll, knyght, princypall Secretorye
Sir Ambrose Cave, knyght, Chauncelor of the Duchye
Sir Wylliam Petere, knyght, one of here Majestie's Prevye Counceyle
Sir Raphe Sadlere, knyght
Sir Waltere Myldmaye, knight
Sir Rychad[3] Cordall, knyght
Sir Nycholas Throgmerton,[4] knyght
Sir Thomas Wrothe, knyght
Sir Nycholas Arnolde, knyght
Sir Peter Carowe, knyght

Sir John Chichestere, knyght
Sir John Sellenger, knyght
Sir John More, knyght
Sir George Turpen, knyght
Sir John Parret, knyght
Sir Morrice Berkleye, knyght
Sir Harye Asheleye, knyght
Sir John Thynne, knyght
Sir Robert Wyngfeld, knyght
Walter Haddon, esquire
Thomas Fleetwood, esquiere
Wylliam More, esquiere
Hary Knoles, esquiere
Blener Hasset, esquiere
[Anthony][5] Colleye, esquiere

'Yf that ordere had byn observyde in the begynnynge of the mattere and suche consyderacion had in the prosecutynge of the same as the gravetye of the cause had requyred, the successe thereof myght have bynne otherwyse then nowe yt ys. But those unbrydelyd parsons whose hedes were nevere snaffled by the rydere dyd rashelye entere into yt in the comon howse, a publyke place; where Mr Bell[6] with his complyses alegyd that theye were naturall Englyshe men and were bound to theyre countreye, whiche theye sawe muste needs peryshe and cum to confucion onles sum ordere were taken for the lymytacion of the succession of the crowne. And ferthere to helpe the mattere, muste needes preferre / theyre speches to the uppere howse, to have yow, my Lordes, consente with theyme; whereby yow were sedusede and of symplysytye dyd assente unto hyt, which yow wold not have donne yf yow had forseene before consyderatlye the ymportaunce of the mattere. So that there was no mallyce in yow, and so I doo ascrybe yt. For wee thynke and knowe yow have iuste cause to love us, consyderynge owr mercyfulnes shewed to all owr subiectes syns owr reygne. But there, two busshops with theyre longe oracions sowght to persuade yow also with solome mattere, as thowghe yow, my Lordes, had not known that when my brethe dyd fayle me I had bynne ded unto yow, and that then, dyynge withowt yssue, what a dangere hyt were to the whole state; which yow had not known before theye told yt yow. And so yt was easelye to be seene *quo oratio tendit*. For those that sholde be stopps and stayes of this great good, and advoydynge of so manye dangers and peryls, howe evyll myght they seme to be. And so to agrevate the cause ageynste me. Was I not borne in the realme? Were my parentes borne in anye forreyne contreye? Ys there anye cause I shold alyenatte my self from beynge carefull over this contreye? Ys not my kyngdome here? Whom have I opressede? Whom have I enrychede to other's harme? What turmoyle have I made in this common welthe that I shold be suspected to have no regarde to the same? Howe have I governyde syns my reygne? I wylbe tryede by envye hyt self. I need not to use manye wordes, for my deeds doo trye me.

'Well, the mattere whereof they wold have made theyre petycion (as I am informed) consystythe in too poyntes: in my marryage, and in the lymytacion of the

p.210

succession of the crowne, wherein my mariage was fyrste plasede, as for manere sake. I dyd send theym aunswere by my counseyle I wolde marrye (althowghe of myne own dysposycion I was not enclyned thereunto), but that was not accepted nor credyted, althowghe spoken by theyre Prynce. And yet I usede so manye wordes that I coulde saye no more. And were yt not nowe I had spoken those / wordes, I wold never speke theyme ageyne. I wyll never breke the worde of a prynce spoken in publyke place, for my honour sake. And therefore I saye ageyn, I wyll marrye assone as I can convenyentlye, yf God take not hym awaye with whom I mynde to marrye, or my self, or els sum othere great lette happen. I can saye no more exept the partie were presente. And I hope to have chylderne, otherwyse I wolde never marrie. A strange ordere of petycyoners that wyll make a request and cannot be otherwyse asserteynyde but by the prince's worde, and yet wyll not beleve yt when yt ys spoken. But theye (I thynke) that movythe the same wylbe as redy to myslyke hym with whom I shall marrie as theye are nowe to move yt, and then yt wyll apere they nothynge mente yt. I thowght theye wold have byn rathere redye to have geven me thankes then to have made anye newe requeste for the same. There hathe byn some that have or[8] thys sayde unto me theye never requyred more then that theye myght ones here me saye I wold marrie. Well, there was never so great a treason but myght be coveryde undere as fayre a pretence.

'The seconde poynte was the lymytacion of the succession of the crown, wherein was nothynge sayde for my saftye, but onelye for theym selves. A straunge thynge that the foote sholde dyrecte the hede in so weyghtye a cause, which cause hathe bynne so dyllingentlye weyede by us, for that hyt tochythe us more then theyme. I am sure there was not one of theym that evere was a seconde parson as I have byn, and have tastede of the practyses ageynst my systere, who I wolde to God were alyve ageyne. I had great occacions to harken to theyre mocyons, of whom sum of theym are of the comon howse. But when frends faule owt, truthe dothe apere, accordynge to the olde proverbe; and were yt not for my honour theyre knaverye sholde be known. There were occacions in me at that tyme. I stode in dangere of my lyffe, my systere was so ensenst ageynst me: I dyd dyffere from here in relygeon, / and I was sowght for dyverse wayes. And so shall never be my successore. I have conferred before this tyme with those that are well learnede, and have askede theyre opynyons tochynge the lymytacion of succession, who have bynne sylent; not that by theyre sylence after lawlyke maner theye have seemyde to assent to hyt, but that in deede theye cowlde not tell what to saye consyderynge the great peryll to the realme, and most dangere to myeself. But nowe the mattere muste needs goo trymlye and pleysauntlye when the bowle runnythe all on the one syde. And, alas, not one amongste theyme all wold aunswere for us, but all theyre speches was for the suretye of theyre countreye. They wold have xij or xiiij lymyted in successyon, and the mo the bettere. And those shalbe of suche upryghtnes and so devyne as in theyme shalbe

p.211

Aliquando intentio[7]

p.212

3. *Sic.*
4. *Sic.*
5. Blank in MS; name supplied.
6. *CJ*, I.75 shows the prominence of Bell and his friends in the Commons committee's negotiations with the Lords.
7. Marginal comments in a later hand.
8. I.e. ere.

devynytye hyt self. Kynges were wonte to honour phylosophers; but yf I had suche I wold honour theym as angels that shoulde have suche pietie in theym that theye wolde not seeke where theye are the seconde to be the fyrste, and where the thyrde to be the seconde, and so forthe. Yt is sayde, I am no devyne. In deed I studyed

Her devocion nothynge els but devynytye tyll I came to the crowne; and then I gave mye self to the studye of that which was meete for government, and am not ygnorant of storyes wherein aperythe what hathe faulen owte for ambycion of kyngdomes – as in Spayne, Naples, Portyngall, and at home; and what cockynge hathe bynne betwene the fathere and the sonne for the same. Yow wold have a lymytacion of succession. Trulye, yf reason dyd not subdewe wyll in me, I wold cause yow to deale in hyt, so pleysunt a thynge yt sholde be unto me. But I steye yt for your benefytte. For yf yow shold have lybertie to treate of yt, there be so manye competytors – sum kynsfolkes, sum servantes, and sum tenantes; sum wold speke for theyre mastere, and sum for

p.211(ii) theyre mistris, and / everye man for his frende – that yt wolde be an occacion of a greatere charge then a subsydye. And yf my wyll dyd not yelde to reason, yt shold be that thynge I wold gladlyeste desyre to see yow deale in yt.

'Well, there hathe bynne errore; I saye not errors, for there were too manye in the prosedynge in thys mattere. But wee wyll not judge that theyse attemptes were donne of anye hatred to owr person, but even for lacke of good forsyght. I doo not marveyle thowghe *Domini Doctores* with yow, my lordes, dyd so use theym selves therein, syns aftere my brother's dethe theye openlye preched and sette forthe that my systere and I

Her mercy were bastardes.[9] Well, I wyshe not the deathe of anye man, but onelye this I desyre: that theye which have byne the practyzers herein may before theyre deathes repent the same, and showe sum open confession of theyre faulte, wherebye the scabbede sheepe may be knowne from the hole. As for my owne parte I care not for deathe, for all men are mortall; and thowghe I be a woman yet I have as good a corage

Her magnanimity awnswerable to mye place as evere my fathere hade. I am your anoynted Queene. I wyll never be by vyolence constreyned to doo anye thynge. I thanke God I am in deed indued with suche qualytyes that yf I were turned owte of the realme in my pettycote I were hable to lyve in anye place of Chrystendom.

'Your petycion is to deale in the lymytacion of the succession. At this present yt ys not convenyent, nor never shalbe withowt sum peryll unto yow, and certeyn dangere unto me. But were yt not for your peryll, at this tyme I wolde gyve place, notwithstandynge my dangere. Your perylls are sondrye wayes: for sum maye be tocht who restythe nowe in suche terms with us as ys not meete to be disclosed,

p.212(ii) eythere in the comon howse or in the uppere howse. / But assone as there maye be a convenyent tyme and that yt maye be doone with leaste peryll unto yow, althowghe never withowt great dangere unto me, I wyll deale therein for your saftye and offre it unto yow as your prynce and hed, withowt request. For yt ys monstruous that the ffeete sholde dyrecte the hed. And therefore this ys my mynde and aunswere, which I

---

9. Presumably a reference to the proclamation of Jane Grey as Queen. See G. Burnet, *History of the Reformation* (1865), V.357-61; F. A. Youngs, *The Proclamations of the Tudor Queens* (1976), 61 & n.

wold have to be shewede in the twoo howses. And for the doynge thereof, yow, my Lorde Chyef Justice[10] are meetyst to doo yt in the uppere howse, and yow Cicyll in the neythere howse.' And therewith spekynge of the Spekere, that the lowre howse wold have had theyre Spekere there, wherein theye dyd not consydere that he was not there to speke; she sayde she[11] was a spekere in deede, and there endid.

10. Sir Robert Catlyn or Sir James Dyer.   11. MS reads 'he'; this reading from Stowe 354.

6. Queen's speech of 5 November reported to the Commons, 6 November

Three drafts in Cecil's hand:
  i. PRO SP Dom.Eliz.41/7.
  ii. SP Dom.Eliz.41/8.
  iii. SP Dom.Eliz.41/9.

SP Dom.Eliz.41/7

[Endorsed by Cecil 'v November 1566 *anno* 8. A breeff of the substance of the Queen's Majestie's answer to the lordes and commons being in nombre lx. This was not reported.']

First hir Majesty tooke uppon hir the knolledg of a petition intended to be made by both the Howsees, consistyng of ij partes, the on for mariadg, the other for lymitation of succession; wherin she allowed not of the manner of the begynning nor of the procedyng, iudgyng the same not answerable to the gravite of the matters, for therin she thought such regard was not had of hir self as she had deserved. And so, usyng the common proverb that they which had evill neighbors must saye somewhat for them selves, she made mention of hir government from the begynning with what care she had used the same, without sekyng any particular benefitt by iniuryeng of others, without brekyng of law or justice, without sekyng of the blood of any person and such lyke. And for that which she tooke offensyve to hir self she noted ij thynges which she termed errors: the on that before this matter was begun in the nether houss she was not made prive; the other that by the assentyng therto of the nobilite, and by publication abrode of the necessite of the matter, of the imminent perill if it wer not graunted, she found it to touch hir self so directly as the whole perrill was throwen uppon hir self, if ether she refused it, or did but delaye it. Nevertheless, she sayd that although she might herof conceave great unkyndnes, yet she cold not thynk the error to come of any evill will, but of lack of forsight towardes hir.

Afterward she entred to show hir opinion of both the matters in order.

For hir mariadg she thought she had so answered therin that she looked rather for thankes than for any new petytion, addyng that she knew some persons that wer wont to saye they wold desyre no other reward but to be hir messynger to denounce the assurance of hir contentation to mariadg. But now for furder satisfaction of such as have taken hir former spechees that she wold marry to be but a phrase of spekyng, she remembred of what weight the word of a prince was, spoken in a publick place; and that though she had hertofor declared hir mynd to be repugnant to marriadg, yet that ought not to make men doutfull now, seyng she now sayth that she is determyned to marry, which she wold prove by dedes as soone as tyme and occasion might serve, if almighty God shuld not take awey ether hir own person or the person of hym with whom she ment to marry. And furder assurance she cold not make but by speeche, for except the person were ther presently she cold doo no more. And she semed to take it unkyndly that any boddy shuld use any such spechees as might brede a mistrust of hir havyng of children or of the liff of hir children, for in such casees she sayd the best wold be hoped for and trusted; and she did certenly trust in Gode's goodnes to have children, for otherwise than for the hope she had therof she wold never marry. And so in this matter she concluded that she cold not use any furder meanes to satisfy them which desyred hir mariage but by speche, and therfore required to be beleved.

The other matter, for lymitation of the succession, she sayd as she cold not deny but that it was necessary and proffittable, so had it also great perrills therin to enter at this tyme into the decision therof, aswell in respect of hir self as of hir people. And for the perrill of hir owne person, she sayd she had considered aswell of the storyes of this realme as of forreyn, as Naples, Portyngale and Spayne, and such lyke, and she thought it not nedefull to report how daungerooss it had proved to the state wher second persons wer appoynted; and for hir self she had experience of the gret daungers whan she was a second person and yet a sistar to the late Quene, sufficient to move hir to fynd the state perilloss. Nevertheless, consideryng the weight of the matter, if she wer not also fully perswaded of the great perrills that presently might follow towardes hir people if she shuld enter presently into [MS breaks off here]

SP Dom.Eliz.41/8

v Novemb[e]r 1566. A breeff note of sondry thynges contened in the Queen's Majestie's answer made.

Orderly and quiet government
No lack of care: no iniury to any
        no enrychyng by any man's harme
        no man's blood sought.
For hir mariadg, she thought it shuld have bene better accepted for she knew some that was wont to saye they wold never desyre other reward but to be the reportor of hir mariadg with creditt.
The succession doutfull to trye.
Perilloss to: the Queen hir self
       the people: for the nombre of competitors having so many frendes;
             some kyn, some allyed, some frendes to frendes.
Decision wold make devision for respect of some personages with whom she
             standeth in such termes, as presently to enter into the
             matter might bryng more perill than is seene, and
             percase more costly to remedy than a subsidy wold
             serve.
Errors without mallyce or evill will. And if any wer, she ment no avendg but that they might or they dyed acknolledg ther fault.

A second person perilloss as by storyes of Naples, Portyngale, Spayn.
Unkyndnes that the matter was so handeled as the whole daunger of denyeng must come from hir:
for the commens desyred it and thought it necessary not to be delayed so as the delaye of an howre bred perill; the nobilite lyked it; and therfor the Queen only to beare the burden, though not of denyeng, yet of delayeng.

SP Dom.Eliz.41/9

[Endorsed by Cecil 'v Novemb[e]r 1566. The report made to the common hows of the Queen's Majestie's answer by the mouth of me the Secretary, William Cecill, with the consent of 30 lordes and 29 commoners.']

v November. The some of the Queen's Majestie's speche to the lordes and commens assembled to the nombre of lx.

She tooke knolledg of the petition that was to be made to hir consistyng of twoo partes, the one for hir mariadg, the other for the lymitation of the succession of the crown. Wherin she allowed not the manner of the procedyng in respect of the weight of the matters, but imputed that which she thought therin amiss to lack of forsight than any evill meaning in any person.

And as to hir mariadg, she sayd she thought she had so satisfyed by hir answer therto that she looked rather for thankes than for request. But for furder satisfaction of any person that might therof dout because she had in hir former spechees expressed hir contrary disposition of mynd, she sayd that ought not to move any person consideryng she hath certenly declared hir mynd to be now otherwise, and that she is fully determyned to marry and that shuld be proved by hir dedes as soone as tyme and occasion wold serve, if almighty God shuld not take awey ether hir own person or the person of hym with whom she ment to marry. And at this present she cold use no other meane to satisfy the doubtfull but with the word of a prince, which being in so publick a place ought not to be mistrusted; and except the person were present she cold not now otherwise procede, nor in this matter cold use any other wordes for the purpooss than she had, and so in the end required to be beleved. In the matter of mariadg, she trusted in God['s] goodnes to have children, for otherwise she protested that she wold never marry.

The other matter, for lymitacion of the succession, she sayd as it was necessary, which she wold not deny, so did she know therin such perrills to enter into the decision therof at this present tyme as she was fully perswaded in hir mynd, consideryng the competitors on all sydes, and for other causees to hir knowen not mete for this present to be dyvulged abrode, that it was nother for hir self nor for hir people voyde of great perill. For she sayd she knew many causees and some of hir own experience, having bene a second person to a sistar, the late Quene, how perilloss it was for hir own person; but yet if she did not also see how perilloss it was for hir subiectes at this tyme she wold not forbeare for hir own perill to deale therin. And yet ment she not so to neglect it, nor to be careless therof, but whan so ever she shuld fynd it less perilloss for hir realm than it is now she wold shew hir self to have regard therof befor they shuld require it, and wold be therof the begynnar as was convenient for a prynce to be towardes hir people, for she wold be loth to lyve to be forced to doo that which by justice and reson she ought to doo. And concluded with a request not to missinterpret hir wordes but to report hir meaning to both the Howsees.

7. Paul Wentworth's questions on privilege, 11 November

Text from PRO SP Dom.Eliz.41/16.

SP Dom.Eliz.41/16

[Endorsed in a later hand 'Questions about the liberty of the Hows in freedom of speech for succession']

Whether hyr Hyghnes' commawndment, forbyddyng the lower howse to speake or treate any more of the successyon and of any theyre excuesses in that behalffe, be a breache of the lybertie of the free speache of the Howse or not?

Whether Mr Controller,[1] the Vicechamberlaine[2] and Mr Secretarye, pronowncyng in the Howse the sayd commawndment in hyr Hyghnes' name, are of awthorytye suffycyent to bynde the Howse to scylence in that behalffe, or to bynde the Howse to acknoledge the same to be a direct and sufficient commawndment or not?

Yf hyr Hyghnes' sayd commawndment be no breache of the lybertie of the Howse, or yf the commawndment pronownced as afore is sayde be a suffycyent commawndment to bynd the Howse to take knoledge theroff, then what offence is it for anye of the Howse to err in declaryng his opynyon to be otherwyse?

---

1. Sir Edward Rogers.   2. Sir Francis Knollys.

8. Proposed petition of the Commons to the Queen, 16 November

Text from PRO SP Dom.Eliz.41/22, third draft, as amended by Cecil.
Other MSS. SP Dom.Eliz.41/20,21, earlier drafts, both amended by Cecil.

SP Dom.Eliz.41/22

[Endorsed by Cecil '16 November 1566. A forme of a petition to the Queen's Majesty by the Commens.']

We your Majestie's most humble, faithfull and obedient subiectes, being limitted by almighty God['s] order to resort to your Majesty only for succor in all our commen distresses, could find no quietnes nor rest in our mindes untill we had obteyned this access to your Majestie's presence; to whom we come in most lowly manner to declare our inward generall sorrowe, conceaved of some dowte of your Majestie's favorable meaning towards us upon certen conferences lately had in our commen howse. And knowing by good experience the abundance, not only of your mercy but also of your dexterity and justice in giving gratious eare to all partyes before yow will make any determination, we do here in the presence of almighty God (whose vicegerent we know yow to be) on our knees, and with our hartes full of all humility, manifest and make assured to your Majesty that we all your Majestie's humble subiectes, representing to your Majesty your obedient wholl comminalty of your realme, have no wise intended or prosequuted anything in our late conference but the renewing of a former sute made in the last session to your Majesty; which we were fully persuaded, being obteyned,[1] shuld tend to the glory of God, to your Majestie's honor and suerty, and to the tranquillity and perpetuall quietnes of all your realme. And though your Majesty might for some other respectes unknowen to us for a tyme conceave, ether in the whole, or in some part, otherwise of our meaning, yet we, best knowing the very truth and certenty of our owne hartes and intentions, do most humbly with all manner of lowlynes here present our selves to your Majesty, most humbly requiring yow in the name of him by whom yow do reigne over us, to accept this our most faithfull and true declaration of our wholl intentions, and interprete our doinges with the gratious contenance of your accustomed favour; regarding rather our owne testimonyes in the simplicity of truth than any other coniectures, which in such cases by misreporting or mistaking of speches may in your Majestie's mind stirr upp and nourish dowtefulnes of our

1. Insertions in Cecil's hand are printed in light type.

meaninges, who without all dowte do and will remayne perpetually addicted and devoted principally to the preservation of the honor, weale and suerty of your most royal person and the succession of the same, which God give us life to see.

And thus having for avoyding of troble to your Majesty, in a matter of gretest moment for us, used but few wordes and yet with truth, we are by assured hope of your [good and mercifull][2] graciooss good nature raised up as subiectes not abiected from your princely favor, and so consequently boldened to render with all ioy and thankfulnes our most humble and abundant thankes for the ioyfull signification made to us from your Majesty, of your most happy resolute determination to marry. In which we do behold, as in a glass, by God's grace the success of most certein comforte and surety to your Majestie's owne royall parson, and of felicity perpetuall, by hope of Godd's blessing of your Majesty with children, to us your poore subiectes now living, and all our posterity after us. And so we all, and every of us, do undowtedly esteme therof as of a principall treasure and fortress, both for your Majestie's owne person and all our lyves.

And therfore we do here in your Majestie's presence most humbly call upon the name of almighty God, beseching hym to produce this your most happy determination to a spedy, honorable good end, to the furderance wherof your Majesty shall have our continuall prayers to God and our dayly service to your self.

Next to this, most gratious soveraigne Lady, considering it appeareth by your Majestie's answer that your Majesty hath not found it mete at this present tyme for divers respectes to procede now at this tyme in such sorte concerning the consideration of the succession of this your crowne, as it might seme we had very great and ernest desyre, and yet your Majesty doth not meane, whensoever yow shall find better oportunity in respect not so much of your person as of the state of your realme, to neglect [the] or pretermitt the due consideracion therof, but therin to do that which justice and reason shall move yow to: we your Majestie's most humble subiectes do receave this your Majestie's answer according as we are bound by our obedience, being most sory that any manner of impediment hath appeared to your Majesty so great as to staye yow from proceding in the same. And therfore at this present tyme we can but desyre that it may please almighty God to grant yow such oportunity of tyme with removing the impedimentes which at this tyme hath stayed your Majesty, so as that which your Majesty shall herafter do and intend therin may be to the satisfaction of your self, and your subiectes in comeforte and surety.

And because we your most loving subiectes have (sence your Majestie's answer herin given to us) receaved some messages and commandementes importing some dowtes not only that your Majesty might conceave of us some lack of duty in receaving of this your answer, but also by the manner of the wordes expressed in the same that we deserved as it were to be deprived or at the least sequestred, much to our discomfort and infamy, from an ancient, laudable custome allways from the beginning necessarely annexed to our assembly, and by your Majesty allways confirmed, that is, a lefull suffrance and dutifull liberty to treate and devise of matters honorable for your Majesty and profitable for your realme; we being not only in some sort informed that your Majesty ment not by any your commandement to diminish [y]our [gracious former grants in this behalf] accustomed lawfull libertyes, but also being perswaded that if your Majesty shuld find in us no lack of duty in receaving your answers obediently, yow wold withdrawe from us all signification of misliking, and wold rather augment, or at the least confirme, your grantes tending to our laudable liberties, than to diminish or abridg the same: and therfore, most gracious soveraigne Lady, we are of necessity as people stricken with a dutifull feare of your Majestie's displeasure, moved to make declaration to your Majesty that before your message sent to us to stey furder proceding in our former sute we had made no determination to deale therin any wise to your discontentacion. And therfore we beseche your Majesty of your princely care and motherly love towardes us your servantes and children, that we may continue in this course of our humble duty, as your faithfull, lowly subiectes, honoring, serving and obeying yow like children for duty, reverence and love, without the burden of any unnecessary, unaccustomed or undeserved yoke of commandement, that it may be herby confirmed to the world to your immortal prayse how your Majesty doth excell all your progenitors in quiett governing and ruling, and we also [the] all our forfathers' subiectes of this realme in universall, harty, free and unconstrayned obedience.

2. Words in square brackets are deletions.

9. *Reports of James Dalton's speech, 22 November*

i. Text from PRO SP Dom.Eliz.41/28, late copy, endorsement of original noted as having been in Cecil's hand.
ii. Text from SP Dom.Eliz.41/29, late copy, original noted as having been in Dalton's hand, endorsed by Cecil.

SP Dom.Eliz.41/28

[Endorsed '24 November. Mr Melvyn's[1] informaction against Mr Dalton for speche in the commons houss. 1566, *anno 9 Elizabethae.*']

The wordes that Daltenn spak in the parliament hous:
'The booke conteinthe great reasons againste the Quene and her.'
'God forbede and I never truste to see the daye that ever any Scott or stranger shall have any intreste in the crowne of this realme, for it is againste the law thatt any person other then such as be borne the prenci's subjects holde merette in this lande'.

SP Dom.Eliz.41/29

[Endorsed '22 November 1566.[2] James Dalton's speeche according to his report.']

A motion being made against corrupt and wicked bookes that came from beyond the sea,[3] and I happening to behold a slanderous libell in the House – in whose handes I remember not – touching the Prince of Scotland, titling him 'Prince of Scotland, England and Ireland', and being very much moved therewith, commending the former motion wished provision against slanderous libells. And said: 'How say you to a libell lately set forth in print, calling the Infant of Scotland "Prince of Scotland, England and Ireland"? "Prince of Scotland, England and Ireland"?' quoth I. 'What enemy to the peace and quietness of the realm of England, what traitor to the crown of this realm hath devised, set forth, and published this dishonour against the Queen's most excellent Majesty and the crown of England? "Prince of England", and Queen Elizabeth as yet having no child? "Prince of England", and the Scottish Queen's child? "Prince of Scotland, and England"? And Scotland before England? Who ever heard or read that before this time? What true English heart may sustain to heare of this villany and reproach against the Queen's Highnes and this her realm? It is so that it hath pleased her Highnes at this time in part to barr our speech, but if our mouthes shall be stopped, and in the mean time such despite shall happen, and pass without revenge, it will make the heart of a true Englishman break within his breast'. With the indignity of this matter being as it were sett a fire, I was carried with the flame thereof, well I know not whither, but I suspect some thing escaped me unwares that made some doubt that I would have entred into some title of the crown, in so much that Mr Speaker said to me, 'It were not well you entre into any title.' But what I said I do not remember, but sure I am that I did not speake these wordes, that no person might inherit the crown of this realm except he were a subject of the realm of England. For I answered Mr Speaker that I did not mind to deale with any title of the crown, and thereupon making my conclusion, that it were good there were provision against such spreading of infamous libells, I did leave to speake any further. And this is all that I can remember that I spoke in this matter.

James Dalton.

---

1. Sic.
2. MS reads '1560'.
3. *CJ*, I.78: no mention of a motion, but a first reading of a bill against seditious books on Thursday 21 November.

10. Queen's message to the Commons, delivered 25 November

Three drafts:
i. PRO SP Dom.Eliz.41/30, in Cecil's hand, amended by the Queen.
ii. SP Dom.Eliz.41/31, in the same contemporary hand as 22 (the proposed petition of the Commons to the Queen).
iii. SP Dom.Eliz.27/45 (misplaced under 1563), contemporary hand.
Other MS. SP Dom.Eliz.41/15, late copy of 31.

SP Dom.Eliz.41/30

[Endorsed by Cecil '24 November 1566 *anno* 9. The report of the Queen's Majestie's messadg to the common howss for delyveryng of the same from a command'.]

24 November. To be declared to the commen howss by the Spekar.

The Queen's Majesty hath commanded me to lett yow understand that wheras shortly after she had gyven hir answer to certen of the lords and certen of this Howse, in the matters intended to have bene required of hir Majesty, as the necessite of the tyme and other weighty considerations presently moved hir, uppon [information gyven to hir that] the sight of certain [notes] matters wiche[1] some persons intended, under pretence of dealyng in the former sute, to propound [certain speciall matters] in this Howss touchyng the crowne of this realme, very unmete for the tyme and place, and certenly daungerooss to the commen quietnes of hir subiectes now assembled, did by hir Majestie's commandment will yow all to stey your procedyng any furder in the sayd matter at this tyme; and now being informed by such of this Howss as she hath cawse to creditt, that ther [nether was nor] is not now any determination of this Howse to receave or allow any such daungerooss matter as she befor did dout, is therfor pleased to delyver yow at this time[2] hir formar commandmentes, not dowtyng but yow will be answerable in your whole doynges to the good opinion which hir Majesty is induced to conceave of yow in this behalf, and thynketh it good that yow have regard to the expedition of the matters of most moment remaynyng amongst yow, consideryng the expence of the tyme past, and the shortnes of that which is now to come, the terme endyng also so shortly as it shall.

An addition[3]

If any person after this messadg shall ether presently or at any tyme after, duryng this session in the commen howse, begyn any speche tendyng directly or indirectly to make any declaration of any particular title to the succession of the crowne of this realme, the Spekar shall furthwith in hir Majestie's name command the party to cess of from any such furder spekyng and shall declare to the whole Howse that so is her Majestie's express commandement.

This manner of answer hir Majesty hath thought best, without any furder answer to the request that hath bene made to have leave to conferr uppon the libertyes of the Howse, for as much as therof must nedes have insued more inconvenience than wer mete.

Lord Kepar
Duke of Norfolk
Marquis of Northampton
Comes Lecester
Lord Admyrall
Lord Chamberlen

Mr Knolls	Sir Robert Catlyn
William Cecill	Sir James Dyar
	Sir Edward [illegible]
	Mr . . . [illegible]

SP Dom.Eliz.41/31

A some of that which were convenient to be declared to the Speker by the Queen's Majesty.

Wheras we had understanding of certen motions made in the commen howse for the reiterating of a peticion after our answer given therto in the presence of a nombre of the lordes and commens, and therupon dowting that the commens in the said Howse (notwithstanding our answer) wold renew their said intended sute to us — wherin we had alredy shewed our resolute determination not to have the same matter treated upon in this present tyme for sundry weighty respectes to us knowen — and therfore, also meaning to have them to procede to treate of other matters, we did send them word by waye of commandement to forbeare for that tyme to treate any more upon the said matter. Considering now that we have ben sence that tyme fully informed that there was no determination of our said commens to molest us at this time with reiteration of the said suite, and that they have of them selves forborne to treate theron, and are much perplexed to have a commandement with so streight wordes sent to the wholl Howse, where no nede was, we be pleased to deliver them of that burden of our commandement, and do content our selves with their obedient behaviour, not meaning to preiudice any part of the laudable liberties hertofore

1. Amendments (deletions in square brackets, insertions printed in light type) are in the Queen's hand.
2. Originally, the MS was amended (not by Elizabeth) from 'to remove hir formar' etc., and both Cecil and the Queen have evidently overlooked the necessity of inserting 'from'.
3. Probably occasioned by Melville's protest against Dalton's speech.

granted to them frely comming without commandement or constraynt. And so we will yow the Speker to declare to our commons, and in our name putt them also in remembrance of the great charges aswell of them selves as of our nobility growing by prolongation of this parliament, and therfore advise them to use expedition in the concluding of such matters as shall seme necessary.

SP Dom.Eliz.27/45

The Queen's Majeste, being informed that notwithstanding hir late aunswere made to a chosen number of the uppre and lower housses in the matier of succession, the same nevertheles by some speches in the neither housse semed to be revived; and dowbting lest it might further procede than were convenient, hir Majeste in that respect sent twoo commaundmentes for silence therin, th'one by certain of hir Privie Councell, th'other by the Speaker. Nevertheles hir Majeste understandeth now, by good information, that albeit the speaches of some particler men semed to inclyne to reiterate that suyte, yet there followed no generall consent nor resolution of the hole Hous, wherby she fyndeth that thoes commaundmentes were not necessary, as being sent before such hole resolution. And therfore, both for that cause, and for that no scruple or dowbte shold remayne in the myndes of hir loving subiectes, either of hir Majestie's displeasure towardes them, or of any other thing that might preiudice them, contrary to hir good meanynge, is pleased to revoke and cancell thoes commaundmentes as nedeles to be sent, assuring hir self that all hir good and loving subiectes will stay them selfes uppon hir said answere, without pressing hir Majeste any further therin at this tyme.

11. *Queen's message about Dalton,*
26 November

Text from Hatfield 155/38 (HMC *Salisbury*, I.341), original in
Cecil's hand.
Printed. Haynes' State Papers (1740), 449.

Hatfield 155/38

[Endorsed by Cecil '*pro* James Dalton. 26 November 1566 *anno 9° Elizabethae*']

The Queen's Majesty hearyng by some commen report that on of this Howse, named James Dalton, shuld on Frydaye last, in declaryng his mislykyng of a certen infamoss booke lately printed in Pariss (being in dede very deragatory to the Crowne and dignite royall of hir Majesty), enter into certen speechees and assertions concerning the right and title of succession of this Crowne, and therin to taxe and abass the estate of the Queen of Scottes, with whom hir Majesty is in amyty.

Forasmuch as hir Majesty perceaveth it far unmete and dangerooss, for any person of his owne heade, to sett furth or abass any particular title of this Crowne, the consideration wherof belongeth properly to hir Majesty and the three estates of the realme; and that the sayd James Dalton hath bene demanded, whyther he did in his sayd speche utter any such assertion; and hath answered, that he did not ether speke, or had any meaning to speke, to sett out or abass any particular title to the succession of this Crowne; but did, being inflamed with a naturall offence ageynst the falss entitlyng of the booke, largely speke ageynst the same, and therby did make sondry tymes mention of the Queen of Scottes, and specially of the Prince of Scotland, wherby he suspected that some might mistake his speche: wherfor hir Majesty meaning herin, consideryng the case toucheth a prince with whom hir Majesty is in good amyty, to have the question demanded of the House, whether he did use any such assertion as is above mentioned or no.

12. Notes on Parliament matters, October, November

Text from PRO SP Dom.Eliz.40/102, in Cecil's hand.
Printed. Froude, VII.450-1, in footnote (except Latin notes at end, omitted).

SP Dom.Eliz.40/102

[Endorsed by Cecil 'Parlement matters October/November 1566']

That the mariadg may procede effectually.

That it may be declared how necessary also it is to have the succession stablished, for sondry causees:

suerty and quietnes of the Queen's Majesty, that no person may attempt any thyng to the furderance of any supposed title whan it shall be manifest how the right is satled. Wherunto may be also added sondry devisees to staye every person in his duety, so as hir Majesty may reign assuredly;

for the comfort of all good subiectes that may remayn assured how and whom to obey lawfully, and how to avoyde all errors in disobedyence. Wherby cyvill warrs shall be avoyded.

And because presently it semeth very uncomfortable to the Queen's Majesty to here of this at this tyme, and that it is hoped that God will direct hir hart to thynk more comfortably herof, it may be required that hir mariadg might procede with all honorable and convenient spede; and that if hir Majesty can not condiscend to enter into the disquisition and stablishyng of the succession in this session, that yet for the satisfaction of hir people she will proroge this parlement untill an other short tyme within which it may be sene what God will dispose of hir mariadg, and than to begyn hir parlement ageyn, and to procede in such sort as shall seme metest then for the matter of succession. Which may with more satisfaction be done to hir Majesty if she shall than be marryed.

anno 2 Henry 2   *Inter Henrie 2 et Robertum fratem pactum est ut alter uter eret alterius heres sed postea bellum fuit suscitatum et Robertus fit captivus.*[1]

anno 32 Henry 2   *Ordinatum est quod Matildis filia Henrici 2ⁱ eret heres. Stephanus invasit regnum, et auxilio magnatum contra juramentum prestitum Matildae fit rex.*[2]

---

1. This reference, and the next, is of course to Henry I: see *Anglo-Saxon Chronicle*, *sub* 1101, and A. L. Poole, *From Domesday Book to Magna Carta* (1955), 120-1.

2. *Chronice Rogeri de Hovedene*, ed. W. Stubbs (Rolls Society, 1868), I.187-8; Poole, *op.cit.*, 131-3.

Post varia bella pactum est inter Stephanum et Matildem quod Stephanus maneret rex pro vita et post eum Henricus filius Matildis.[3]   9 Stephen

Henricus 2ᵘˢ filium suum Henricum in regni societatem accerserit; unde [. . .][4] *bella civilia discordiam inter Ricardum Regem et Joannem fratrem consequuntur.*[5]   15 Henry 2

3. The year seems to be 1153, when Stephen and Henry, rather than Matilda, made a compact: Poole, *op.cit.,* 165; T. Rymer, *Foedera* (Hagae Comitis, 1739-45), I.5.

4. One word illegible in MS.

5. The reference is to the decision to crown Henry the Young King: the coronation took place in 1170.

13. Memorial to the Queen at the end of the Parliament

Text from PRO SP Dom.Eliz.41/36, in Cecil's hand.
Printed. See C. Read, *Mr Secretary Cecil and Queen Elizabeth* (1955), 370, for a version of it.

SP Dom.Eliz.41/36

[Endorsed by Cecil 'Memoryall to the Quene at the end of the parliment 1566 *Mense Novembris anno 8° Elizabethae.*]

The succession not answered.
The mariage not followed.
A subsydye to be levyed.
The oppression of the informors not amended.

Cloth.[2]

The commission of inquisitors to unmete persons.[1] Lether.[3]
The bill of relligion stayed to the comfort of the adversaryes.
The abridgment of such parcell of the pardon as though it be no proffitt gretly to the
    Queen's Majesty, yet was it most plausible to the Commens.[4]
Daungers insuing: generall discontentations;
    the slender execution of the subsydy;
    daunger of sedition in sommer by persons discontented;
    the uncerteny of the success of the motions in Flaunders.[5] If they end in force for
    relligion, then *etc.*
Irland. Men. Victell. chargeable last yer's disordre.
Callis. Ap[ri]ll.[6]

---

1. *CJ*, I.81.
2. *SR*, IV.489.
3. *SR*, IV.497.
4. Cecil's precise meaning is not clear. He seems to be saying that Elizabeth had appeared to be more generous than was the case in fact. It is worth noting that all fines, amerciaments and issues up to the value of £6 were included in the general pardon of 1563, while the Act of 1566 specifically exempted *all* fines from the pardon (*SR*, IV.463,520).
5. Negotiations for the resumption of normal commercial relations were as yet incomplete.
6. The reference is to the fact that Calais was due to be returned to Elizabeth on 2 April 1567. Read has 'apparel' for Aprill' and relates it to the question of clerical apparel on which the Houses were unable to agree (C. Read, *Mr Secretary Cecil and Queen Elizabeth* (1955), I.358-9, 370.

14. *Proceedings and speeches at close of Parliament, 2 January 1567*

Text from BL Cott.Titus F1, copy.
Other MSS. Copies of Cott.Titus F1: London: BL Cott.Titus F1
(another copy), Cott.Titus CVII (Queen's speech only), Stowe 358.
Cambridge: Gonville and Caius College, 64.
Printed. D'Ewes, 113-17.

Cott.Titus F1, fos.117-22

A relation of suche speeches as passed at the breakinge upp of the parleament *anno* 9 Elizabethe.

Thursdaye, the 2 of Januarye 1566 *anno* 9 of Elizabethe *Regine*, betweene 2 and 3 of the clocke the Queene's Majestie came by watere from the White Hall and landed one the backe side of the parleamente chamber and so, the Earle of Westemerland bearinge the swoard before her, the Ladie Strange the traine, with the lordes in their daylie apparrell and herraldes attendinge on her, she proceeded up into her privie chamber to prepare her selfe in her parleament roabes, duringe which tyme the lordes and justices put one their parleamente robes and tooke their places.

And one the upper woolsacke sate the Lord Keeper till the Queene came, and then wente to his place at the raile on the right hand the cloth of estate.

On the woolsacke of the north-sid sate Sir Robarte Catline and Sir James Diere, the 2 cheife Justices, Sir Richard Rede and Mr Gerrarde, the Queene's Atturney.

On the sacke one the south side sate Sir William Cordall, Master of the Roles, Justice Browne, Justice Welche and Serieante Carus.

One the weste sacke sate Vaughan and Yall, Masters of the Chancery, Mr Spilman, clerke of the parleamente, Mr Powle, deputie and joynte pattente with Mr Martyne, Clerke of the Crowne: affore which sacke stood a litle table.

Then the Queene's Majestie being appareled in her parleamente robes with a call on her head came forth and proceeded up and tooke her place, the Marquese of Northampton carrienge the cap of maintenance and stood on her right hande and the Earle of Westemerland the sword on her lefte hande with the herroldes and sergeantes of armes before her; the Queene's mantle borne / upp one either side from her armes by the Earle of Leicestere and the Lord Hunsdon, who alway stoode still by her for the assistynge when she stood upp, her traine borne by the Ladie Strange, assisted by the Lord Chamberlene and Vicechamberlen. At the left hand of the Queene and on the south sid kneeled the ladies, and behind them at the raile stood the Lord Keeper one the right hand and the Lord Treasuror one the left hand with diveres yonge lordes and peers' eldeste sonnes.

f.117v

Then all beinge placed Mr Onslowe the Speakere was brought in betweene Sir Francis Knowles, Vicechamberlen, and Sir Ambrose Cave, Chancelor of the Duchey; and after reverence done proceeded downe to the wall, and from thence cam upp to the raile, in the waye makinge 3 reverences, and standinge there made other 3 like reverences and then begane his orratione as followeth:

'Moste exelente and vertuous Princes, *etc*: where I have bene elected by the knightes, cittizenes and burgeses of this your nether house of Parleament to be their mouth or speaker and therunto appointed and allowed by your Majestie to supplie the said rome to the bewrainge of my wantes, specially that herby I shalbe forced utterly to discover the barrennes of my learninge before this moste noble assemblie, which not a litle greeveth mee and would gladlie be excused, consideringe the trewe sayinge howe ther is no difference between a wisman and a foole yf they maye keepe silence, which I require; but againe consideringe your Majestie's clemency, takinge in good parte the good will of the partie for wante of abillitie, which putteth me in remembrance and good hope, perswadinge me that you will not take your said clemencie from me contrarie to your noble nature.

'Againe, when I considere my office as Speaker which is noe great matter beinge f.118 but a mouth / to uttere thinges appoynted me to speake unto you and not otherwise, which consistethe only in speakynge and not in any other knowledge, wherby I gather howe it is necessarye that I speake simply and plainlie accordinge to the trueth and truste reposed in me; and thus consideringe whose mouth I am which chose me to speake for them, beinge the knightes, cittizenes and burgeses, who were not also by the comones chosen for theire elloquence, but for theire wisdome and discresione, by this meanes beinge fitte men to whome the commones have comitted the care and charge of them selves, wives and children, landes and goodes, and soe in their behalfe to forsee and take ordere in and for all thinges necessarye: thus they beinge chosen by the plaine commones it is necessary they ellecte a plaine Speaker fitt for the plaine matter, and therefore well provided at the firste to have such a one as shall use plaine wordes, and not either so fine that they cannot be understood or else so elloquente that nowe and then they mise the cushen.

'So nowe when by occasione of beholdinge your Grace and this noble assemblie I considere the maniefould and great bennefites which God sondrelye hath sente unto this country − for although God hath graunted the benefite of creation and conservation with many other comodities to all nationes of the world, yet this our native country he hath blessed, not onelie with the like, but also with much more fruitefulnes then any other, of which greate inestimable bennefite of Gode's prefermente, which appeareth the bettere by the wantes that otheres have of the same, I am occasioned to speake of, the rather to move and stirre upp our heartes to give moste hartie thankes to God for the same.

'Nowe to speake of governemente by successyon, election, religeon or pollecye. Fyrste, as the bodie yf it should wante a head were a greate monster, soe is it lykewise f.118v yf it have many heades, as yf upon / every severall member were a heade; and to speake of one heade, although in the body be diveres memberes which be made of fleshe, bones, sinowes and joyntes, yet the one heade therof governeth wisely the same, which yf it should wante wee should be worse then wild beastes without a head and so worthelie caled a mo[n]sterous beaste. Againe, yf the bodie should be governed by many heades, then the same would soone come to distructione by reasone of the contraversie amonge them, who wold never agree but be destroyed without any forren invasion. Therfore God saieth it is needfull that the people have a kinge, and therfor a kinge is graunted them; and soe therfor the beste governmente is to be ruled by one kinge, and not many, who maye maintaine and cherish the good and godlie and punish the ungodlie and offenderes.

'As for governement by ellection, in that is greate varience, parciallitie, strifes and partakinges, as for the example amongeste the reste, take out one which is caled the moste holieste election, as is that of the Pope, and see and wey howe holily and quietly it is done, called indeed holy and quiete, but utterlie unhollie and unquiete, with greate partes takinges and strifes.

'Nowe touchinge religeone, to see the providence of God, howe that many nationes be governed by one prince, which is unpossible but that God ordereth it soe, by whom the order of regimente is appointed and that in his scriptures, wherfor the subiectes ought to obaye the same, yea, although they were evell, and much more those that be good; so God hath here appointed us, not a heathen or unbeleevinge prince as he might, but a faithfull and one of his owne children to governe us his children. In which governemente the prince serveth God 2 waies, as a man and as a kinge: in that as he is a man he ought to live and serve / God as one of his good creatures; and in that he is king,[1] and so Gode's speciall creature, he ought to make lawes wherby God maye be truly worshipped and that his subiectes doe noe iniury one to an other, and specially to make quietnes amonge the minesteres of the Churche, to extinguish and put away all hurtefull or unprofitable cirimonies in any wise contrary to Gode's worde, in which pointe wee have in your Majestie's behalfe greate thankes to give unto God in settinge foreth unto us the libertie of Gode's word, wherof affore wee were bereaved, and that you have reformed the stat of the corrupte Churche, nowe drawinge sowles out of dangerous errores which before, by that corrupted, they were ledd and brought unto.

'And concerninge pollecye, God hath comitted unto your Highnes 2 swoardes, the one which may be caled the swoard of warre to punish owtwad ennemyes withall, and the other the swoard of justice to correcte offendinge subiectes; in which pointe of pollecie your Majestie is not behind your noble progenetores, ffor allthough at your enterance you found this realme in warre and ungarnished with munition, you have to your greate charge not onely made perfect peace but furnished the same with weapones, armore and munition – and that with such store as nevere was before – but also dislodged those oure auntiente ennemies which were planted and placed, yea, even upon the walles of this realme.

'And concerninge pollecie in lawes, as boanes, sinowes and jointes be the foarce of a naturalle body so is good lawes the strength of a common wealth. And your lawes be consysted in ij poinettes: the common lawes and the statute lawes. For the comone lawes, they be so grounded one Gode's lawes and nature that 3 severall nationes governinge heare have all allowed the same, which is not inferiore but rather

f.119

---

1. MS reads 'god'.

f.119v   superior and more / indifferente then any other lawes, for by our commone lawes, although therby for the prince is provided manie princely prerogatives[2] and royalties, yet is it not such as the prince cane take money or other thinges or doe as he will at his owne pleasure without ordere, but quietly to suffer their subiectes to enioy their owne without wrongfull suppressione, wherin other princes be at their libertie and doe take as pleaseth them.

'Aristotle saith the lyfe of the prince is the maintenance of the lawes, and that it is better to be governed by a good prince then by good lawes, and soe your Majestie as a good prince is not givene to tiranye contrarie to your lawes, but have and do pardone diveres offenderes of your lawe, as nowe, for example, of your speciall grace you have granted your moste generall and free pardon either without or seekinge or lookinge for, wherby it is the bettere welcom. Againe, your Majestie hath not attempted to make lawes contrary to ordere, but orderly have caled this parleamente for that purpose, who have perceaved certen wantes and therunto have put their helpinge hand (for often of evell manneres good lawes are brought foreth), of the which we beseech your moste excelent Majestie so many as you shall allowe to inspire the breath of your Majestie's powre, wherby they maye be quickened which nowe wante life and so made lawes.

'Furthermore, concerninge paymentes[3] to be made to the prince, is as to delivere the same to Gode's minesteres who are appointed alwaies for our defence, wherfore your humble subiectes doe offer a subsedie and [blank] to be paid in to your Majestie's treasure, which although it be but as a mite or farthinge yet the good will is to be reputed as the pore widowe's was in the gospell. Wherin I muste [not] omitte

f.120   to doe that which never Speaker did / before, *viz*: to dissire your Majestie not to regard this simple offers of oures but therin to accepte our good willes – wherin your Highnes hath prevented me in takinge in the beste parte our good willes, and required us to retaine in our owne handes parte of our guifte; and so rather your selfe and your revenewes [suffer] then us – and compting it in our purses to be as in your owne. And so is our dutie besides the pollecie therof, it beinge for our owne defence and also honestie, for that wee have receaved so manie benefites by your Majestie: for he which doth a good turne deserveth the prayes, and not he which goeth aboute after to reward, or doth reward the same.

'Also givinge our most humble thankes to God for that your Highnes hath signefyed your pleasure for your inclinatione to marriage, which affore you[4] were not givene unto; which is done for our safegarde that when God shall call you, you maye leave of your owne bodie to succede you, which was the greate promis that God made to David, and the greate requeste that Abraham desired of God when God promised him exceedinge greate reward, who said, "Lord, what wilte thowe give me when I goe childlese and a ladd [b]einge the child of the stuardshipe of my house is myne heire?" Therfore God grante as your Majestie hath defended the faith of Abraham you maye have the lyke desire of issue with him, and for that purpose that you would moste shortely embrace the holly state of matrimony, to have one, wher and with whom God shall appointe and beste lyke your Majestie and so the issue of your owne bodie, by your example, rule our posterities; and that we maye obtayne this lett us give our moste humble thankes to God for his manifold benefites bestowed upon us, and praye for the raigne of your Majestie's issue, after your Majestie's long desired raigne and governemente'. And so ended and did his obaysance. /

The Lord Keeper's answere to Mr Speaker the 2 of January 1566 *anno* 9   f.120v
Elizabeth, aftere the Queene had caled him and told him her minde.

'Mr Speaker, the Queene hath herd and understood your wise and elloquente orration, wherby princepallie I gather 4 thinges: firste disablinge your selfe, second concerninge governement, therdly touchinge the subsedy, and lastelie in givinge of thankes, which also was intermingled verie wisly in all partes of your orratione.

'And for the firste pointe, in disablinge your selfe, you have therin contrarelie bewraied your owne ablenes.

'For the second, concerninge governance aswell by successyone as ellectione, for religion and pollecy, in which discourse you have[5] delte verie well and[6] therfore I leave it and meane to speake onlie a fewe wordes in your laste word, pollecie. Polleticke orderes be rules of all good actes, and touching those that you have made to the overthrowinge of good lawes,[7] they deserve reproofe aswell as the othere deserve praies; in which like case you erre in bringinge her Majestie's prerogative in questyon,[8] and for that thinge wherin she mente not to hurte any of your liberties, and againe the graunte of her letteres pattentes to be in questyon[9] is not a litle marvell, for that therin you find faulte, which is nowe no newe devised thinge, such as affor this hath bene both used and put in practice: howebeit, as her Majestie accordinge to her nature is mild and full of clemencie, so is she loth herin to be too awster, and therfore although at this time she suffer you all to departe quietly into your countryes for your amendmente, yet as it is needfull, so she hopeth that the offenders will hereafter use them selves well. Againe, touching the good lawes, wherin you have taken greate paines in makinge, yf they be not executed / they be not onely as roddes   f.121 without handes to execut them or as thes torches without light, but also breedeth greate contempte: therfore looke well to the executione, for yf it be not done the faulte is in some of us which she putteth orderlie in trust[10] to see don accordingly.

'For the 3 pointe, concerninge the presentement of the subsedie, her Majestie biddeth me saye that when the lordes sperituall and temperall and you her commones have graunted it, soe she trusteth you wilbe as carefull in gatheringe it, which to have I and others be witeneces howe verie unwillinge and loath she was to

---

2. MS reads 'prerogavives'.

3. Although the meaning of the passage from 'Furthermore, concerning payments...' to '...doth reward the same' is clear, the syntax presents difficulties. Neale (*EP,* I.172) supplied 'not' after 'Wherin I muste...', and 'suffer' after '...your revenewes...' in order to clarify matters. I have re- punctuated the passage in an attempt at further clarification.

4. MS reads 'your'.

5. 'You have' repeated in MS.

6. 'And' repeated in MS.

7. The reference is probably to the Commons' treatment of the government bill for the continuation of certain statutes (*EP,* I.168-9; *CJ,* I.74,81; *LJ,* I.664; *Cal.SP Spanish, 1558-67,* I.606).

8. Bill A of the so-called alphabetical bills on religion.

9. See the criticism in the Commons of the commission of inquisitors, *CJ,* I.81.

10. MS reads 'in us'; this reading from Cott.Titus F1.

take, but to avoid further inconveniences. And lastely concerning knowledge of benefites and givinge of thankes, which as you have well declared be many, yet one in comparrisone above alle, yea a fruite above all other and wherby you maye enioye all the other, which is her marriage, wherof she hath put you in good hope.

'Further, I have to put you in remembrance of three thinges. And for the firste pointe is that wher now you acknowledge benefites and as you have cause givene thankes, so secondlie that you be not unmindfull therof herafter to doe the like, and thirdlie that in all your doinges herafter you shewe your selves that all these benefites be had in remembrance and not forgotten, for that should be a thinge againste reasone in humaine creatures specially, therfore now it behooveth you, as you have knowledged[11] benefites and for them givene thankes in the firste pointe, so that you see the other two observed, and then her Majestie will not faile thankefully to accepte the same.' And soe ended.

The Queene caled the Lord Keeper and then he returned to his place and bade the clarke reade the actes and then Mr Powle stook upp and after reverence don said, f.121v 'An acte for the confirmacion of archbishopes / and bishopes', wherunto Mr Spilman answered, '*La Roine le Veult*', which said, both together did their obaisance; and so did the like after the readinge of all the reste. But after those wherunto her Majestie graunted not her assente the clerke said, '*La Roine se advisera*', and after the three joynteres, as of the Countice of Warwicke, the Ladie Cobham and the Ladie Stafforde's, with other like privat statutes, he said, '*Soit fact comme les desirent*', and afte[r] the act of the graunte of the subsedie hee said, in French, 'The Queen thanked her lordes and comones', and to the generall pardon he said, 'The lordes spirituall and temperall with the comones gave her Majestie their moste humble thankes'; all which tyme the Queene stood upp havinge in her handes the breefe of the said actes being in number [blank].[12]

Then the Queene standinge said, 'My lordes and others the comones of this assemblie, although the Lorde Keeper hath accordinge to ordere verie well answered in my name, yet as a peraphrases I have a fewe wordes forther to speake unto you, which notwithstandinge that I have not bene used nor love to doe it in such open assemblies, yet nowe, not to the ende to amend his talk but remembringe that commonlie princes' owne wordes be better printed in the heareres' memorie then those spoken by her comaundement, I meane to saye thus much unto you.

'I have in this assemblie founde so much dissimulacion, havinge alwayes professed plaines[13] that I marvell therat; yea 2 faces under one hoode (and the bodie rotten) beinge covered with 2 viseres, successyon and libertie, which they determined muste be either presently granted, denyed, or referde, in grantinge wherof they had their desires, and in deniinge or defferringe theirof (those thinges beinge so plawdabl as in deed to all men they are) they thought to worke me that mischeefe which never forraine ennemye could bringe to passe, which is the hatred of my commones. But alacke they begane to perce the v[e]ssell before the wine was fined, f.122 and begane a thinge / not foreseeinge the end, howe by this meanes I have seene my wellwilleres from my ennemyes and cane as me seemeth verie well devid the Howse into fowre: firste the broacheres and workeres therof who are in the greateste faulte; secondly the speakeres who by elloquente tales perswaded otheres are in the nexte degree; thirdlie the agreeres who beinge so light of credite that the elloquence of the talles so overcame them that they gave more credite therunto then to their owne wittes; and lastlye are those which sate still muite and medled not therewith but rather wondred, disallowinge the mattere, who in my oppinione are moste to be excused. But do you thinke that either I am unmyndfull of your suretie by successyon, wherin is all my care, consideringe I knowe my selfe to be mortall? No I warrante you. Or that I went aboute to breake your liberties? No, it was never my meaninge, but to staye you before you fall into the dich, for all thinges hath his tyme; for although perhappe you may have after me on bettere learned or wiser, yet I assure you non more carefull over you. And therfore henceforth whethere I live to see the like assemblie or no, or whosoevere it be, yet beware howe ever you prove your prince's patience as you have nowe done myne. And nowe to conclud, all this notwithstandinge (not meaninge to make a Lente of Christemas), the most parte maye assure you to departe in your prince's grace.'

Then she said openly to the Lord Keeper saing, 'My Lord you will doe as I bade you,' who then said alowde: 'The Queene's Majestie hath agreed to dissolve this parleamente, therfore every man[14] may take his ease and departe at his pleasure.' And the Queene rose and shifted her and tooke her barge and repaired to the Courte beinge paste 6 of the clocke, and ther after her risinge she made Anthonye Browne, one of the Justyces of the Common Pleas, a knight.[15]

11. Here follows the passage 'that in all your doinges . . . againste reasone', repeated in MS.
12. 36 bills passed both Houses; Elizabeth allowed 34 (*EP*, I.171; *LJ*, I.666).
13. *Sic*.
14. 'Man' repeated in MS.
15. He died in May 1567.

15. *Separate version of Queen's speech at close of Parliament*

Text from BL Cott.Charter IV.38(2), draft in the Queen's hand, amended by her.
Other MSS. London: BL Harl.2185 (copy of Cott.Charter IV.38(2), misdated), Harl.1877, Harl.5176. Cambridge: Gonville and Caius College 64 (copy of Cott.Charter IV.38(2), misdated). Hatfield, Herts.: Hatfield 138/163 (printed in HMC *Salisbury* XIII.214-15).

Cott.Charter IV.38(2)

I love so ivell counterfaitting and hate so muche dissemulati[on][1] that I may not suffer you depart without that my admonitions may shewe your harmes and cause you[2] shun unseen perill. Two [clokes][3] vissars have blinded the yees of the lokers one in this present session so farfurthe as under pretence of safing all the have done none good. And thes the be: succession and liberties. As to the first, the prince's opinion and good wyll ought in good ordar have bine felt in other sort than in so publik a place [ons to] be uttered. It had bine convenient that so waighty a cause had had his originall from a zelous prince's consideration, not [of a] from so lippe labored orations out of suche [rangling] subiects' mouthes; wiche, what the be, time may teache you knowe, and ther demerites wyl make them acknowelege how the have done ther lewde indevour to make all my realme suppose that ther care was muche when myne was none at all. Ther handeling of this dothe well shewe, the being holy ignorant, how fit my graunt [was] at this time shuld be to suche a demaund. In this one thinge [the] ther imperfaict dealings ar to be excused, for I think this be the first time that so waighty a cause passed from so simple men's mouthes as began this cause. As to liberties, who is so simple that doutes whither a prince that [h] is hed of all the body may not commaund the fete not to stray whan the wold slip? God forbid that your liberty shuld make my bondage, or that your lawful liberties shuld anywais have bine infringed. No, no, my commandement [brake] tended no whit [therof] to that ende, [as] the lawfullnis of whiche commandement, if I had not more pitied you than blamed you, might easely by good right be shewed you, perchanse to ther shame that brede you that colored dout. You wer sore seduced [and]: you have met with a gentil prince, els your nideles scruple [had] might perchaunce have brede your caused[4] blame. And albeit the southing[5] of suche be reprovable in all, yet I wold not you shuld thinke my simplicitie suche as I can not make distinctions amonge you: as of some that broched the vessel not wel fined and began thes attemps not forseeinge wel the ende; others that respected the necessary faches[6] of the matters and no whit understode circumstanssis expedient not to have bine forgotted therin; others whos eares wer deluded by pleasing perswations of comen good whan the very yelding to their owne inventions might have bred all your woes; others whos capacities, I suppose, yelded ther iugement to ther frindes' wit; some other that served an eechoe's place. Well, amonge all thes sondry affects[7] I assure you ther be none, the beginnars only except, whom I ether condemne for ivell mynded to me or do suspect not to be my most loyall subiects. Therfor I conclud with this oppinion whiche I wyll you to think unfainedly tru: that as I have tried[8] that you may be deceav[ed][9], so am I perswaded you will not begile[10] the assured ioy that ever I toke to se my subiects' love to me more staunche than ever I felt the care in my self for my selfe to be great; wiche alone hathe made my hevy burden light and a kingedome['s][11] care but easy cariagge for me [wiche if I hopt not more for conscience than for glory I could willingly wische a wisar my rome]. Let this my displing stand you in stede of sorar strokes never to tempt to far a prince's [pow] paciens, and let my comfort pluk up your dismayed spirite and cause you think that, in hope that your folowing behaviors shall make amends for past actions,[12] you retorne with your Prince's grace[s]: [and w of] whose care for you doubt you not to be suche as she shall not nide a remembrancer for your wele.

1. MS torn; '̣on' supplied.
2. Words printed in light type are insertions in the MS.
3. Words, or letters, in square brackets are deletions in the MS, unless otherwise indicated.
4. *Sic.*
5. I.e. maintaining.
6. I.e. faces, as in Harl.1877 and 5176;
Harl.2185 has 'fetchers'.
7. I.e. dispositions.
8. I.e. proved.
9. Binding obscures; '̣ed' supplied.
10. I.e. deprive me of.
11. '̣'s' supplied.
12. MS illegible; 'past actions' supplied from Harl.2185.

THE THIRD PARLIAMENT
2 APRIL ⁄ 29 MAY 1571

Documents

Lord Keeper Bacon's opening speech was a strong and straightforward explanation of the Queen's need for financial assistance and the requirements of general law reform; he also reinforced what Bishop Sandys had already preached about the dangers facing the Church.[1] The use of the same Latin tags which appeared in 1563 emphasizes the formalized framework within which particular appeals were being made, and when he closed the session, Bacon's fulsome thanks for the subsidy grant were also couched in well-tried terms. As Lord Keeper, his personal concern with the problem of local execution of parliamentary enactments appeared again in a noteworthy passage. [Docs. 1, 2.] Attention then shifted to those few men whom the Queen said had led the House on to religious matters: they had called the Queen's 'grantes and prerogatives also into question, contrary to their dutie and place that they be called unto . . .'. They were audacious, arrogant and presumptuous and they had earned Elizabeth's utter condemnation.[2] Bacon may have departed from this text in delivery, but there is not much doubt that the strength of the attack was maintained, or even increased, by giving closer definition to the nature of the offence.[3]

Hooker's journal, covering the whole session, and that of an anonymous member (2-21 April) are the first surviving unofficial accounts of parliamentary proceedings under Elizabeth. Hooker's shortcomings were outlined a century ago.[4] Much of the document simply lists bills before the House, and Hooker frequently misses bills noted in the *Commons Journals*, though damaged pages make exact correlation impossible. But his description of bills is sometimes fuller, for example on the afternoon of 11 May, even though he apparently missed the last three bills at the same time. He may, of course, have left early; he may have arrived late the following morning when he seems to have missed the first three bills. For 15 May there is no entry at all. This may be evidence of Hooker's being 'no marvel of diligence or accuracy', but his committee work presumably contributed to his difficulty in compiling a full record, if indeed that was his intention.[5] It is less than fair to dismiss him as a chronicler of 'trivialities and matters of form', for his perception is sometimes sharper than the anonymous journalist's. His account of the Lord Keeper's reply to the Speaker's petitions on 4 April bears close examination, and he has noted the Queen's parting shot at the same time. He alone recorded an order on 9 April preventing two readings of bills within three days, though it appears to have

1. *EP*, I.185-6.
2. Corpus Christi College, Cambridge, 543, f.21.
3. Devonshire RO, Bk.60h, f.9.
4. By J. B. Davidson in *Trans. Devons. Assoc.*, XI (1879), 442-4, 464-72.
5. Devonshire RO, Bk.60h, fos.3v, 6v.

been disregarded almost immediately; but whether it had a more pronounced and enduring effect on private bills in particular needs to be tested, because it looks as though many afternoon readings were being staggered in this way.[6] In his account of the last day of the session, which he places at 30 May, Hooker has made valuable additions to our knowledge, for there is his brief indication of Bacon's delivered, rather than drafted, speech and Elizabeth's own intervention.[7]

The anonymous journal is more thorough than Hooker as a record of bills before the House, generally corresponding very closely with readings registered in the *Commons Journals*. But it differs most obviously from Hooker in its extensive reporting of debate, in attempts to divine the motives behind royal and privy council action, and in its comments about response to that action, and to the speeches of the individual members. Though Bacon had defined the privilege of free speech with more care than in previous sessions, the Speaker had soon to deliver a message, on Tuesday 10 April, reinforcing that definition.[8] The author of the anonymous journal comments that this was the result of Bell's speech against licences on Saturday 7 April: but there had been two days of tough debate on a number of topics, and the journal depicts vividly the tension and urgency of those days. Strickland moved Norton's presentation of the religious bills; then came Bell's speech (supported by Popham) and Lovelace added the abuse of purveyance. Hooker records the outcome which Neale described as 'the first committee for grievances'. On Monday 9 April the government's treasons bill attracted Norton's famous addition, and the vigorous debate which this produced was followed by another, on church attendance, in which Fleetwood directly attacked the Prayer Book.

If freely elected voices were to be freely exercised in the House certain obstacles had to be removed. On 10 May, Thomas Long of Westbury, Wiltshire, was accused of having bribed his way into the Commons, and when Goodere opposed Norton's stratagem on 12 April, he accused him of being 'doubly disposed and with a favorable affeccion bent for some body and some espetial party'.[9] There were apparently other suspicions of this sort, and when a committee investigated complaints that some members had 'sold' their voices, Norton succeeded in clearing himself as Hooker says, 'namely for the Cambridge matter', presumably the bill for exempting Cambridge and Oxford from the purveyors' grasp.[10] For the moment however, Norton denied Goodere's claim and enunciated the doctrine that speech should be free, though within bounds of 'loyalty', and free of unjust slanders.[11] This view was common: on 14 April the journalist reports extensive ill-feeling about Gilbert's describing Bell as an 'open enemy' because of his speech against licences, though at the moment no-one seems to have been prepared to vindicate Bell's showing of 'common greefes in due sort unto her Majestie.'[12] By 20 April however, Peter Wentworth, having apparently brooded on the matter during the Easter recess, attacked Gilbert's unfair and inaccurate reporting of Bell's speech because it bred fear into members 'which should be free'.[13] At this point Hooker notes that Gilbert was three times denied the freedom to speak in his own defence.[14] It was in this atmosphere that Strickland's absence from the House provided vigorous discussion that same day.

A striking characteristic of the anonymous journal is that it highlights the contribution to debate made by the lawyers in the House. Recorder Fleetwood seems to have been the most loquacious of them, taking evident care over his speeches by preparing notes beforehand and basing his arguments on the solid bedrock of precedent. He spoke on an extensive range of topics during the three weeks covered by the journal, including church attendance, treason, Bristol merchants, usury and irregular land transfers; and his intriguing readiness to veer between discretion and audacity as far as the Queen was concerned and still emerge as a guardian of the royal prerogative is an important and illuminating picture of what one imagines to be a complex, though far from unusual, political animal. In revealing this the anonymous journal performs perhaps its most important service, which is to emphasize the perspective in which parliamentary proceedings should be seen. Though the House did not limit its discussion on the succession, treason and religion as Elizabeth had wanted, and though its progress on commonwealth matters was slow in the early weeks, business was soon after approached in a mature and energetic manner.[15] The short report on the first reading debate on the vagabonds bill, lost this session but to re-emerge in 1572, is enough to show a lively approach and a variety of offered solutions.[16]

It is perhaps an indication of the journalist's legal background that he gave extensive coverage to the affair of the Bristol merchants and the bills for borough representation and usury. The second reading debate on the Bristol merchants bill was soon dominated by lawyers involved in an important discussion of the royal prerogative, its limits and the commonwealth.[17] Eight days later, on 19 April, the form and workings of society came under fairly extensive scrutiny again when members debated the nature of borough representation in parliament.[18] The usury bill provides one of the best examples of members' readiness to debate in a considered, even formalized manner, though as Fleetwood said, all the arguments had been aired in the House on previous occasions. Members had obviously come to the chamber with well-prepared speeches, so the Treasurer's early attempt to halt debate failed. There is a striking contribution from Dr Thomas Wilson, who rose and warned the assembly of a long speech to follow.[19] And when all this was done, and despite what he had said earlier, Fleetwood rehearsed the legalities of the matter,

6. *Ibid.*, f.3 and v; *CJ*, I.84, 86 *et passim*; H. Elsynge, 'The method of passing bills in Parliament', *Harleian Miscellany*, V.226ff, makes no mention of staggered readings; (W. Lambarde), 'The order, proceedings . . .', *Harleian Miscellany*, V.260, says 'one bill may be twice read in one day'; and see Hooker, 'The order and usage . . .', in V. F. Snow, *Parliament in Elizabethan England: John Hooker's Order and Usage* (Yale, 1977), 189 and n.126.

7. Devonshire RO Bk.60h, fos.8v and 9; *EP*, I.236-40.

8. TCD MS 535, fos.10v and 11.

9. *CJ*, I.88, and note Hooker's account and marginal addition, f.6v; TCD MS 535, fos.14v and 15.

10. *CJ*, I.93; Devonshire RO Bk.60h, f.8v.

11. TCD MS 535, f.15v.

12. *Ibid.*, f.24 and v.

13. *Ibid.*, f.33v.

14. Devonshire RO Bk.60h, f.4v.

15. *EP*, I.235.

16. TCD MS 535, f.20 and v.

17. *Ibid.*, fos.12v-14.

18. *Ibid.*, fos.24v-29.

19. He had completed his *Discourse on Usurye* which was to be published in 1572.

apparently confusing at least one member, and concluding, though to what end is not clear, that 'the wordes of an act of Parliament are not ever to be followed, for that sometyme the construccion is meere contrarye to what is written'.[20]

20. TCD MS 535, fos.29-33v.

1. Lord Keeper's opening speech, 2 April

Text from BL Cott.Titus F1, copy, with corrected and variant
readings from PRO SP Dom.Eliz.46/166, copy.
Other MS. Cambridge: Gonville and Caius College, 64 (copy of
Cott.Titus F1).
Printed. D'Ewes, 137-9.

Cott.Titus F1, fos.123-6v

Parliament *anno 13° Elizabethae*

A speache delivered by the Lord Keeper Sir Nicholas Bacon in the begininge of the
parliament held at Westminster *anno 13° Elizabethae* 1571.

The Queene's most excellent Majestie our most dread and gracious soveraigne Lady
haveinge comaunded me to declare unto yow the causes of your callinge and
assembly at this tyme, which I meane to doe as briefely as I can, leade thereto as one
very loath to be tedeous to her Majestie, and alsoe because to wise men and well
disposed (as I iudge yow be) a fewe wordes doe suffice. The causes be cheifely two:
th'one to establishe or dissolve lawes as best shall serve for the good governance of the
realme, th'other soe to consider for the Crowne and state as it may be best preserved in
the time of peace and best defended in the time of warre, accordinge to the honour
due to it. And because in all counselles and conferences first and cheifely there should
be sought the advancement of God's honour and glory as the sure and infallible
foundacion whereupon the pollicy of every good publique weale is to be erected and
builte, and as the straight line whereby it is principally to be directed and governed
and as the cheife piller and buttres wherewith it is continually to be sustained and
maintained, therefore, for the well performeinge of the former touchinge lawes yow
are to consider first whether the ecclesiasticall lawes concerninge the discipline of the
Church be sufficient or noe, and yf any wante shalbe founde to supply the same; and
thereof the greatest care ought to depende of my Lordes the Bishops to whom the
execution thereof especially pertaines and to whom the imperfections of / the same
be best knowne: this is the tyme *gladius gladium iuvaret*. And as to the temporall lawes,
yow are to examine whether any of them already made be too sharpe or too sore
overburthenous to the subiectes or whether any of them be to loose or too softe and
soe over perillous to the state, for like as the former may put in danger many an
innocent without cause particulerly, soe the seconde may putt in perill both nocent
and innocent, and the wholl state universally, *acriores enim sunt morsus remissae quam
retentæ libertatis*. Yow are alsoe to examine the wante and superfluity of lawes; yow
are to looke whether there by too many lawes for any thinge, which breedeth soe
many doubtes that the subiect somtime is to seeke howe to observe them and the
counsellor howe to give advise concerninge them. And heare an ende of the first
cause of your callinge, concerninge lawes.

f.123v

Nowe to the seconde, which concerns a sufficient provision for the Crowne and state. Herein yow are to call to remembrance howe the Crowne of this realme hath bin many ways chardged extraordinarily of late, not possibly to be borne by the ordinary revenues of the same and therefore of necessity to be relieved[1] otherwise, as heretofore it hath comonly and necessarily bin, for like as the ordinary chardge hath always bin borne by ordinary revenues soe the extraordinary chardges have always bin sustained by an extraordinary reliefe. This to those that be of understandeinge is knowne to be not only proper to kingdomes and empires, but alsoe is, hath bin and ever wilbe a necessary peculier pertaineinge to all comon wea[l]th[s] and privat states of men from the highest to the lowest; the rules of reason hath ordained it soe to be.

But here I rest greatly perplexed whether I ought to open and remember unto yow such reasons as may be iustly produced to move yow thankefully and readily to grante this extraordinary reliefe or noe. I knowe the Queen's Majestie conceaveth soe great hope of your prudent foreseeing what is to be don, and of your good willes and readines to performe that which by prudency yee forsee, that fewe or noe perswasions at all are needefull for the bringinge this to passe. Nevertheles, because by the auncient / order heretofore used it is my office and duty somwhat to say in this case, and because alsoe all men that be present neither understand alike or remember alike, therefore I meane with your favour and patience to trouble yow with a fewe wordes touchinge this pointe. True it is that there be two thinges that ought vehemently to move us franckly, bountifully and readily to deale in this matter; the former is the greate benefittes that we have received, the seconde is the necessity of the cause. Yf we should forgette the former we are to be chardged as most ungrate and unthankefull, and the forgettefullnes of the seconde doth chardge us as uncarefull of our owne liveinges and libertyes, and of [our] lives: the former moveth by reason and the seconde urgeth by necessity.

And here to beginne with the former, albeit that the benefittes that the realme hath received by God's grace and the Queene's Majestie's goodness both for their nomber and greatenes be such as[2] may more easily be marveiled at then worthily waighed and considered, yet meane I to remember yow breifely but of three of them, whereof the first and cheifeest[3] is restoreinge and settinge at liberty God's holy worde amongest us, the greatest and most precious treasure that can be in this worlde, for that either doth or should benefitte the best degree, our myndes and soules: and looke howe much our soules excell our bodyes, soe much must needes the benefittes of our soules excell the benefittes of our bodyes, whereby alsoe as by a necessary consequent we are deliverd and made free from the bondage of the Romaine tyranny. The[re]fore this is to be thought of as[4] the most principall benefitte both for the soule and body that can any way happen unto us. And thus much for the firste benefitte.

The seconde is the inestimable benefitte of peace dureinge the time of tenn wholl yeares raigne togeither and more. And what is peace? Is it not the richest and most wished for ornamente / that pertaines to any publique weale? Is not peace the marke and ende that all good govermentes directes their actions unto? Nay, is there any benefitte, be it never soe great, that a man may take the full commodytie of without the benefitte of peace, or is there any soe litle commodytie but thoroughe peace a man may have the whoall fruition of it? By this we generally and ioyfully possesse all, and without this generally and ioyfully possesse nothinge. A man that would sufficiently consider of all the commodityes of peace ought to call to remembrance all the miseries of warre, for in reason it seemes as great a benefitte in beinge deliverd of th'one as the possesseinge of th'other; yet if there were nothinge, yet the comon and lamentable calamity and miseries of our neighbours round about us, for wante of peace, may give us to understand in what blessednes we be in that possesse it. Well, [some] there be that never acknowledgeth benefittes to their value whilest they possesse them but when they be taken from them, and soe finde their wante, *bonam nostram dum possidemus fore sperumne.* Mary, such be not worthy of them. Nowe is it possible, trowe yow, that this blessed benefit of peace could have bin from tyme to tyme thus longe conserved, conferred upon us, had not the inwarde affection and love that our soveraigne beares towardes us, her subiectes, bred[5] such care over us in her breaste as for the well bringinge this to passe she hath forborne noe care of minde, noe travaile of body, noe expence of her treasure, noe sale of her landes, noe adventureinge of her creditte either at home or abroade? A plaine and manifeste argumente howe deare and precious the safety and quiet of us her subiectes be to her Majestie. And can there be a greater perswasion to move us to our power to tender the like? Well, here is an ende of the benefittes of peace.

The thirde is the greate benefitte of clemency and mercy. / I pray yow hath it bin seene or read that any prince of this realme dureinge wholl tenn yeares raigne and mor hath had his handes soe cleane from blood? If noe offence were, it was her Majestie's wisedome in governinge the more to be wondred at, and if offences were, then was her Highnes' clemency and mercy the more to be comended, *miserecordia eius, supra omnia opera eius.* Besides, like as it hath pleased God tenn yeares and more by the ministery of our said soveraigne to blesse this realme with these two inestimable benefittes of peace and clemency, soe is there noe cause but the same might by God's grace have continued twenty yeares longer without intermission had not the rageinge Romaniste rebelles intertained the matter. And here it is to be noted that this mercyfull and peacefull raigne of tenn yeares time and more hath happened in the tyme of Christe's religion nowe established; I cannot thinke that any man can followe me in this in tyme of the Romishe religion rule, since the Conqueste. Nay, a man might affirme that this is an example for times to come without any like in times paste; compareinge *singula singulis,* what should I say? These be the true fruites of true religion. I could further remember yow of the benefittes of justice, the benefitte of restoreinge your money to fines, yea, I could put yow in minde, but I thinke it needes not it happened soe late, of a subsedy granted, whereof the Queene's Majestie of her owne bountifullnes remitted th'one half;[6] was the like here in Englande ever seene or read of? But beinge out of doubt that these benefittes already remembred be sufficient of themselves to move yow to be thankfull to your power, I leave any

f.125

---

1. MS reads 'relived'; this reading from SP Dom.Eliz.46/166.
2. MS reads 'greatenes such and'; this reading from SP Dom.Eliz.46/166.
3. *Sic.*
4. MS reads 'us'.
5. MS reads 'breed'.
6. Cf. Anonymous Journal (TCD MS 535, f.3).

f.125v longer to detaine yow in this pointe. And albeit a subiecte cannot yeald any benefitte to his soveraigne in the same nature / that he receiveth it, because every benefitte is more then duty and more then duty [a] subiecte cannot yeald to his soveraigne, yet it cannot be denied but [a] subiecte['s] acknowledginge of benefittes received, ioyned with goodwill to yeald as farre as ability will reach, doth sufficiently satisfie for the subiecte, for *ultra posse non est esse*. To your best therefore addresse yee. And thus much concerninge benefittes.

Nowe to the seconde parte concerninge urgeinge by necessity. True it is that the extraordinary matters of chardge happened since the laste assembly here, urgeinge to have by necessity a reliefe granted, amongst many others, be these. First, the great chardge in suppresseinge [the] late northen rebellion, with chardges alsoe in reformeinge those the Queene's Majestie's enemyes in Scotland that assisted[7] the rebelles and made roades into England, the continuall groeinge expences by reason of Irelande, as in subdueinge the rebelles within the realme and in withstandeinge the Scottes northwarde, and other forraigne forces intendeinge invasion southwarde; to theis three chardges by lande yow may add a fourth by sea, as the preparacion and setteinge foorth of shipps partly for the defence against all chaunces of forraigne forces suspected and intended, partly for the safe conducteinge of the wares and merchandizes of the realme in greater strength and longer cutte then heretofore hath bin used. Theis and such like extraordinary chardges whereof there be sundry, with the remaines and lagges of ould chardges not possibly to be borne by the ordinary revenue, and yet of necessity to be expended, doe greatly exceede any extraordinary aide heretofore comonly granted. Againe, the greate decay of the Queene's Majestie's customes by reason of stay and alteracion of trafique (albeit upon iust occation) hath bredd noe small wante, for althoughe in time it is not to be

f.126 doubted / but that will growe againe to his ould course and continue with greate surety, yet in the meane time this wante must some way be supplyed; ffor yow knowe the horse must be provided for whilest the grasse is in groweinge – at the leaste, lett us doe soe much for our selves as we doe for our horse, for our selves it is that is to be relieved in this case. This I must needes say, that if the Queene's Majestie did use in matters of experience to doe as comonly princes heretofore have used to doe, then with the more difficulty might such extraordinary aide be assented unto, and yet of necessity to be had to withstande a greater[8] necessity. It hath bin in tymes paste that prince's pleasures and delightes have been comonly followed in matters of chardge as thinges of necessity, and nowe (God be praised) the relieveinge of the realme's necessity is become the prince's pleasure and delight: a noble co[n]version, God continue it, and make us, as we ought to be, earnestly thankefull for it, a princely example shewed by a soveraigne for subiectes to followe. To discend in some perticulers, what neede I to remember to yow howe the gorgeous, sumptuous, superfluous buildinges of times past be for the realme's good by her Majestie in this time turned into necessary buildinges and uphouldinges; the chardgeable, glitteringe, glorious triumphes into delectable pastimes and shewes, the pompes and solempe[9] ambassadores of chardge into such as be voide of excesse and yet honorable and comely. This and such like were draweinge dames[10] able to dry upp the floweinge fountaines of any treasurye, these were quilles of such quantity as would soone make the many pipe[s] to serve in tyme of necessity such an expendit is[11] hardly satisfied by any collector; and yet those imperfections have bin comonly princes' peculiers, especially younge. [One] free from these, *rara avis, etc.* And yet / (God be thanked) a phenixe, a blessed birde of this brood[12] God hath blessed us with. I thinke it may be affirmed, and that truely, that there hath not bin any matter of greate chardge taken in hande by her Majestie in this happie raigne of xij yeares and more, that hath not bin thought before meete and convenient to be done for the weale and profitte of the realme, soe farr her Highnes is from the spendinge of treasure in vaine matters. And therefore the rather howe can a man make any difficulty to contribute accordeinge to his power specially in the maintaininge of his soveraigne, his countrey, his self, his wife, his children, and what note, haveinge soe longe a proofe by experience of such an imployment? Here I would put yow in mynde of extraordinary chardges to come which in reason seemes evident, but soe I shalbe over tedeous unto yow and *frustra*[13] *fit per plura quod fieri potest per pauciora*[14]. And therefore here I make an ende doubtinge that I have tarried yow longer then I promised or meante or perchance needed (your wisedomes and good inclinacions considered), but yow knowe thinges are to be don both in forme and matter; and my trust is, yf that I have stayd, [I] may be warranted by either or by both, and that yow will take it in good parte.

f.126v

7. MS reads 'resisted'; this reading from SP Dom.Eliz.46/166.
8. MS reads 'greated'.
9. SP Dom.Eliz.46/166 reads 'pompous and solemne'.
10. I.e. dams (?): MS unclear at this point. SP Dom.Eliz.46/166 has 'draines', and

Anonymous Journal, f.2, has 'camelles'.
11. MS reads 'in'; this reading from SP Dom.Eliz.46/166.
12. MS reads 'birde'.
13. MS reads '*frastra*'.
14. MS reads '*poaviora*'.

2. Lord Keeper's speech at the close of Parliament, 29 May

Text from Corpus Christi College, Cambridge, 543, copy.
Other MS. BL Cott. Titus F1.
Printed. D'Ewes, 151⁄4.

Corpus Christi College, Cambridge, 543, fos.21⁄5

A speeche used in the end of the parliament *anno terciodecimo Elizabethae Reginae et anno domini* 157[1].

Master Speaker, the Queene's Majestie hath heard and doth verie well understand how discreetlie and wisely you have declared the proceedinges of this session in the nether howse, for answere wherof and for the better significacion what her Majestie's opinion is both of parliament men and of parliament matteres, this is to lett yow understand her Majestie hath commanded mee to say unto yow that, like as the greate number of them of the lower howse have in the proceedinges in this session shewed themselves modest, discreet and dutifull as becomes good and dutifull subjectes and meete for the places they bee called unto, so ther bee certeine of them, although not many in number, which in the proceedinges of this session have shewed themselves audacious, arrogant and presumptuous, calling her Majestie's grantes and prerogatives also into question contrary to their dutie and place that they bee called unto and contrarie to the express admonicion given in her Majestie's name in the begining of this parliament, which yt might very well have become them to have had more regard unto. But her Majestie saith seeing they will thus wilfully forgett themselves they are otherwise to bee remembred. And like as her Majestie allowes and much commendes the former sorte for the resp[ec]tes aforesaide, so doth her Highnes utterlie disallowe and condeme the second sorte for their audacious, arrogant and presumptuous follie, thus by frivlous and superfluous speech spending the time and medling with matters neither perteining unto them nor within the capacitie of their understanding. And thus much concerneing Parliament men of the nether howse.

f.21v And as to my lordes heer of the upper howse, her Majesty / hath commanded mee to lett them know that her Highnes taketh their dilligence, discretion and orderly proceedinges to bee such as redoundeth much to their honour and comendacions, and much to her comfort and consolacion. And heare and end touching Parliament men.

Now as touching Parliament matteres: her Majesty hath commanded mee to open and declare unto yow her opinion conceived therin touching two thinges; th'one is concerneing the subsidie and benevolence, the other concerneing th'execucion of lawes. As to the former which concerneth the subsidie and benevolence her pleasure is that I shall say unto you that in your dealeinges in that matter shee hath noted three thinges principally, everie of them tending much to the setting forth of your benevolence and good willes: the first who yt was that granted, the seconde the manner of the granting, the third what yt was that was granted. As to the first, her Majestie forgetteth not that it is a grant made proceeding from the earnest affeccions and heartie good wills of her good, dutifull and obedient subjectes for the greatest parte, and therfore hath commanded mee to say unto yow that shee maketh a greater accompt of the good willes and benevolent mindes of her good and loveing subjectes than shee doth of tenn subsidies, which as yt ought to move us (I doubt not but yt doth) to bee and continew such as bee worthie such an estimacion and acceptacion. Againe, her Majesty forgetteth not that besides this is a grante not by subjectes that never made the like grant heertofore but by such as have granted and contributed from time to time as the necessarie chardge of the realme and their owne suerties hath required, which doth also much commend and sett forth this benevolence of yours. And thus much concerneing the persons that have granted.

As to the second, which is the manner of the granting, her Highness knoweth very well that before her time theise manner of grantes have sundrie times passed not without greate difficulties, with long perswasions and sometimes / sharpe speeches.   f.22 But this contrariwise without any such speech or other difficultie hath bynn freely and frankelie offerred and presented; and like as the former did much extenuate their benevolence, so is this of yours therby greatly extended. Yt is written, and very truly, concerneing benevolences that *qui diu distulit diu noluit*; and therfore iustlie concluded, *bis dat qui cito dat*, which sayeinge shee cannot but applie to you in the proceedinges of your grantes. Againe, the universalitie of consent doth greattly commend also your dealeinges in this matter, for a more universall consent then was in this will hardly bee heard of in any, and therfore much the more comendable. And thus much touching the manner of the gift.

And as to the third, which concerneth the thing given, her Majesty saith that shee thinketh yt to bee as greate as any heertofore hath bynn granted, and therfore yow are to receive condigne thankes for yt. And hath further willed mee to say that if the service of the realme and your suerties would so permitt and suffer yt her Majesty would as gladly, as readily and as frankly remitt this grant as yow have freely and liberrally granted[1] yt. Thus I have commended unto yow the three princely observacions that her Majesty hath conceived of this benevolence of yours, much to your comfort and greately to her Majestie's honor and comendacion to yow for granting to her Highnes for this honorable acceptance. For her Majesty shall by this grant receive no commoditie or benefitt but rather a continewall care in despending and employeinge of it about the necessarie affaires and service of the realme and your suerties. And yet it is a greate comfort to her[2] Majesty to see you thus frankly and freely to ioyne with her selfe the realme and yow.

Now to the second and last part which concerneth th'execucion of lawes which I

---

1. 'Granted' repeated in MS.

2. MS reads 'your'; this reading from Cott. Titus F1.

f.22v   meane to divide into two partes: the former is the execucion of your grant, the second
is the / execucion of lawes now made by you and of the rest made before by otheres.
As to the former I am to remember yow that, like as yt hath pleased the Queene's
Majesty thus princely, honorably and thankefully to thinke of and accept this free
and liberrall grante of yours, so certainly if the like diligences and endevours bee not
used by such of yow as choise[3] shalbee made of by her Majesty for the due putting in
execucion of this grante, then suerlie those that shalbee remisse or negligent, as by
that meanes her Majesty and the realme shalbee defrauded of any part of that hath
bynn thus freely granted, shall therby minister iust occasion to her Highnes to have
their fidelitie and truth towardes her Majesty much to bee suspected and charged,
which would touch them very neer. Neither is yt an offence that would be
pretermitted,[4] but surely punished. Why, and the cause were betweene common
persons, cann ther bee a greater untruth and unthankefulnes than for a man to make
a grant in apparence willinglie and readily and then in existence to seeke wililie and
craftily to defraude[5] the same grant? This amongst honest persons is utterly detested.
And if so, how then ought it to bee thought of betweene the prince and his subject
wher for diverse respectes the bond is there as greate, for the subject is bound by the
dutie of his alleagiance to serve his prince truly and so is by his oath and so is hee by
the great trust that by the prince's choice is comitted unto him (as a comissioner in
this matter above otheres). Plainelie to speake, yt may bee affirmed, and that iustly,
that such as shalbee in comission for th'execucion of this grant and shall deale
partially for favor, or for feare, or for love to their freindes or to themselves, or
negligentlie or remissly of purpose wherby her Majestie shall not bee answered of that

f.23   that is due unto her, such I say may iustly bee charged as men forgetting / their dutie
to God, to their soveraigne and to their country. It cannot bee denied but that the
numberes respect only theire private profittes and not the universall profitt of the
realme which is their suerties and defence; they respect themselves as private persons
and not as members of the universall bodie: but their imperfeccion would bee
supplied by the wisdome and perswasion of such as the Queene's Majesty shall
committ trust unto by her commission to see this subsidie well and truly leavied.
And thus much for the execucion of your grante.

Now as to the execucion of lawes made by yow and of the rest made heertofore by
otheres, I am to remember yow that all theise labours, travailes and paines taken
aboute the lawes now made and before time taken about the rest heertofore made and
all the charge susteined by the realme about the makeing of them is all in vaine and
labor lost without the due execucion of them; ffor it hath bynn saide, a law without
execucion it is but a bodie without life, cause without an effect, a countenance of a
thinge and in deed nothinge, penn, inke and paper serveing asmuch towardes good
governance of the common weale as the rudder or healme of a shipp serveth to the
governance of yt without a governor and as roddes serve for correccion without
handes. Weare yt not a meer maddnes for a man to provide faire torches to guide his
goeing by night and when hee should use them in the night to carry them unlight; or
for one to provide faire and handsome tooles to pruine and reforme his orchard or
garden and lay them upp without use? And what a thing else is yt to make
wholesome and provident lawes to guide our goeing in the common wealth and to

pruine and reforme our manners and then to close those lawes in faire bookes or
rowles and to lay them upp safe without seeing them executed? Surelie in reason ther
is noe difference in theise examples saveing that theis makeing of lawes without
execucion bee in much worse case then theis vaine provisions before remembred, for
those, albeit they doe noe good yet they doe noe harme, but the makeing of lawes
without execucion doe verie much harme for yt breedes and bringes forth contempt
of lawes and lawe-makeres and all magistrates, which is the verie foundacion of all
misgovernance; and therfore the offence must needes bee great / and haienous in
those that are the causeres of this — indeed they bee the very occasioners of all iniuries and
iniustice and of all disorders and unquietnes in the common-wealth.

f.23v

    Now lett us consider who these bee, the better to provide a remedie against this
mischeife; for certeine and evident yt is that the Queene's Majesty who is heade of the
law doth all thinges meete for her Majestie to doe for the due execucion of them.
First, shee giveth her royall assent to the makeing of them; then the most materiall of
them shee commandeth to bee proclaimed and published and yet ceaseth not ther
but shee graunteth out her commission into everie of her sheires to men which are, or
should bee, of the greatest consideracion within the limittes of their charge, which
for the better executeing of them are sworne to see th'execucion of her lawes to them
committed within the limittes of their commission. And yet besides all this, by her
Majestie's[6] comandement a number of theis justices are yearelie once att the least
called into her Highnes' Starr Chamber and ther in her Highness' name exhorted,
admonished and commanded to see to the due execucion of their chardges. And
thus yow see her Majestie enacteth, proclaimeth, committeth, exhorteth,
admonisheth and comandeth from time to time. Yea what cann bee devised meete
for her Majesty to doe for the help of this that is left undone? Surelie nothing, greatly
to her Majestie's honor and renowne. Wheruppon yt followeth necessarily and
consequently that the whole burthen of this offence and great enormitie must light
uppon us that are putt in trust by her Majesty to see theis lawes executed, and
certeinely this offence groweth greate or little as the trust committed for the execucion
of lawes is greate or little; and therfore it standeth us greatly uppon to use our whole
cares[7] and endeavores to the helpe of this heerafter. Were it possible, trowe[8] yow that,
if the justices (being disperced through the whole realme as they bee) did carefullie
and diligently endeavor them selves according to the trust committed to them by
their soveraigne duely and truly to execute their charge, as they bee bound by their
oath to God and by their alleagiance to their soveraigne, and by their dutie to their
natureall country, / yea, and rightly considered by the love they should beare to
themselves and their posteritie — for if their country doe not well they shall speed but
illfavoredly — weare it possible, I say, if this weare thus donne, that lawes should be[9]

f.24

---

3. MS reads 'cheifly'; this reading from
    Cott. Titus F1.
4. MS reads 'permitted'; this reading from
   Cott. Titus F1.
5. MS 'reads 'defend'; this reading from
   Cott. Titus F1.
6. MS reads 'Majestie'; this reading from

Cott. Titus F.1.
7. MS reads 'eares'; this reading from
   Cott. Titus F1.
8. MS reads 'throw'; this reading from
   Cott. Titus F1.
9. 'Be' supplied from Cott. Titus F1.

thus remissely and negligently executed? Noe, doubtless. Is it not trowe[10] yow a monsterous disguising to have a justicer a mainteiner, to have him that should by his oath and dutie sett forth iustice and right, against his oath offer iniurie and wronge; to have him that is spetially chosen amongst a number by the prince to appease all brabling and controversies to bee a sower and mainteiner of strife and sedicion amongst them, seekeing his reputacion and opinion by leadeing and swayeing of juries according to his will, acquitting some for gaine, inditeing otheres for malice, beareing with him as his serveant or freind, overthrowing the other as his enemie, procureing all questmongeres to bee of his liverie or otherwise[11] in his daunger, that his winkes, frowneinges and countenances may direct all enquestes? Surelie, surely, these bee they that are subverters of all good lawes and orders, yea make daylie the lawes which of their nature bee good to become instrumentes of all iniuries and mischeife. Theis indeed bee they of whom such examples would bee made as of the founders and mainteineres of all enormities; and theise be those that if yow cannot reforme for their greatnes yee ought heere to complaine of for their illnes. And like as this is not saide to those that bee good, so is this and much more to bee saide and donne against those that bee ill.

But heer yt maie bee saide, the mischeife appeares, what is the remedie? If not to make all lawes perfectlie executed (for I cann hardlie hope of that), yet to make them in much better case then now they bee. And when I had all thought I could find no more helpes but theise. The first, by haveing greate care in the choise of these officers; the second, by sharp correccions imposed uppon such offenderes. For the banishing of sloth ther would bee through out the realme a tryenuall or byenuall visitacion in his nature made of all temporall officers and ministeres that by virtue of their office have in chardge to see to th'execucion of lawes: by this I meane / that the Queene's Majesty should make choyse[12] everie second and third yeare of certeine expert and proved persons to whom commission should bee granted to try out and examine by all good meanes and waies the offences of all such as have not seen to the due execucion of the lawes, accordinge to the offences so founde and certified to bee sharpelie punished without remission and redemption. Of effect much like this, and to like end, was the visitacion of the Church first devised wherof came in the begining great good doubtles: and reason I see none but that the like good ought to follow uppon a like visitacion made amongst temporall officers. Now to find out theise faultes seemeth no hard thing, for amongst many other waies ther is one verie plaine, evident and easie, and that is wher offences doe abounde in any country contrarie to the lawes which the justices should see reformed and ther nothing donne by them for the reformeing of those offences, I doe not see but makes a full charge of their uncarefulnesse and negligence, wherby they are well worthie uppon certificate made as is aforesaid to bee removed from all governeance to their perpetuall ignorance and to the comendacion of all those that remaine as good officeres; and besides to sett such other paines uppon them as by law might bee iustified. If this were once or twice donne I doubt not but the examples followeing of the doeing of yt would cause greater dilligence to bee used in the execucion of lawes then now ther is. And the better to understand which bee those justices that doe offend and which not, ther might bee order taken that the name of everie iustice that hath prosecuted

f.24v

any offender for any offence committed contrary to any lawe which by the comission
that hee is in hee is authorized to see punished might bee entred into some role, and
also how oft, and how many, of those kinde of offences hee hath so prosecuted for a
declaracion of his dilligence, wherby yt might appeare when such a visitacion
should come who hath bynn carefull and who hath bynn negligent, to the end that
the slothfull, drowsie droanes might bee severed from the diligent and carefull bees.
And like as I could wish this to bee donne concerneing offices of meane degree, so
doe I desire that the same course might bee taken with the greater and greatest for so
jus should bee *equabile*. And if ther bee nothing donne heerin but thinges left as they
have bynn then must yow looke to have your lawes executed as they have binn, if not
worse, for wordes / will not reforme this matter as I have seen by proofe. And this is   f.25
the summe that I have to say att this time concerneing the execucion of lawes.

10. MS reads 'throw'; this reading from
    Cott.Titus F1.

11. 'Or otherwise' repeated in MS.
12. 'Choyse' supplied from Cott.Titus F1.

1. Anonymous journal, 2-21 April

Text from TCD MS 535, copy.

Other MSS. London: BL Cott.Titus F1, Stowe 358 (copy of Cott.Titus F1); PRO SP Dom.Eliz.46/166. Oxford: Bodley, Rawlinson C 680. Cambridge: Gonville and Caius College 64 (copy of Cott.Titus F1, stopping short in the middle of entries for 6 April).

Remembrances of the parliament holden at Westminster the second day of Aprill in the xiij^th yeare of the raigne of our soveraigne lady Queene Elizabeth *anno* 1571.

Her Majestie about eleven of the clocke came towardes Westminster in the auncient, accustomed, most honorable passage, havinge first ridinge before her the gentlemen sworne to attend her person, then Batchlor Knightes, after them the Knightes of the Bathe, then the Barons of the Exchequer, and Judges of either Bench, with the Master of the Rolles, her Majestie's Atturney Generall, and Solicitor Generall, whome followed in order, then the bushopps, and afterward the earles, then the Archbushoppe of Canterbury.

The hatt of mayntenance was carried by the Marquesse of Northampton and the sword by the Earle of Sussex. The place of the Lord Steward for that day was supplyed by the Lord Clinton, Lord Admirall of England. The Lord Greate Chamberlaine was the Earle of Oxenford, and the Earle Marshall by deputacion from the Duke of Norfolke was the Earle of Worcester.

Her Majestie sitting in her coach in her imperiall robes and a wreath or coronett of gold sett with rich pearle and stone on her head, her coach drawne by two palfreies covered over with crimson velvett, drawne out, imbossed and imbroidered verie ritchly; next after the chariott followed the Earle of Leicester in respect of his office of the Master of the Horse, leadinge her Majestie's spare horse. And then forty-seaven ladies and women of honour. The guard in their riche coates goinge on every side of them, the trumpetors before the first soundinge, and the herolds ridinge and keeping their roomes and places orderly.

In Westminster Church the Bushoppe of Lincolne[1] preached, duringe which tyme of the sermon the knightes, cittizens and burgesses were particulerlie in the House (comonlie called the lower house) sworne to the supremacie before the Lord Steward, Sir Francis Knolls, Sir James Crofts,[2] Sir Walter Mildmaye, Sir Raphe Sadler and Sir Thomas Smyth, which beinge donne and her Majestie come from the sermon, the lordes all on foote in order as afore, and over her head a rich canopie was caried all the way from Westminster Church; shee beinge entred into the over house of the parliament and there sittinge in princely and seemely sort under a highe

f.1v

and rich cloth of estate, the robe supported by the Earle of Oxenford, the Earle of Sussex kneelinge holdinge the sword on the left hand, and the Earle of Huntington standinge houldinge the hatt of estate, and the lordes all in their roomes on eich side of the chamber, that is to say, the lordes spirituall on the right hand, and the lordes temporall on the left side, the judges and her learned councell beinge at the woollsackes in the middest of the chamber, and at her Highnes' feete on eich side of her kneelinge one of the groomes or gentlemen of the Chamber, their faces towardes her, the knightes, cittizens and burgesses all standing belowe the barrs.

Her Majestie then stood upp in her regall seate and with a princlie grace and singuler good countenance (not to bee expressed but by the very shewe, or to bee conceaved but by him that can in minde imagine such a prince), after a long stay shee spake a fewe wordes to this effect, or thus: 'My right lovinge lordes, and you all our right faythfull and obedient subiectes, wee in the name of God, for his service, and for the safety of this state, are here nowe assembled (to his glorie I hope), and pray that it may bee to your comfort, and the comon quiett of us,[3] you,[4] and all ours for ever'. And then lookinge on the right side of her towardes Sir Nicholas Bacon, Lord Keeper of the Greate Seale of England, standinge a little besides the clothe of estate and somwhat backe, and lower from the same, she willed him to shewe the cause of the parliament.

Hee keeping his place sayd to this effect, that it had pleased her Majestie to call that assembly for two causes; the first for supplying all imperfeccions which are in this her realme and our comon weale, either for lacke of lawes, where there is want, or otherwise for redresse / if ought bee amisse. The second cause hee sayd was for defence of the state. For the first part hee wished that they would bend the force of their wisdomes to finde and trye out if there be ought which in tyme to fore, or by our forefathers, hath not bene seene or sufficiently attayned to, either for honour, securitie, comoditie or ease of her Majestie or of her subiectes; then, to consider if the lawes already made bee to the offences fitt and rightly apportioned, as nether more sharpe and severe then there is due cause, nor more myld or remisse then is right and fitt; thirdly, that where as the varietie of laws have in some certaine poyntes occasioned to the learned cause of doubtes, that by the discretion and wisdomes of the states assembled they might bee reduced to a plaine certainety.

On the second cause, which was for defence, hee first shewed that in every body, both naturall and pollitique, the first and most principall care must bee for the head, which not beinge served and supplyed with all convenient necessaries, the bodie with the head and all should runne to ruine and the members havinge from the head their helpe and onely stay, should of everie weaknes of the same first rewe and feele the smart. Hee shewed that her Majestie of the revenues of the Crowne and ordinarie advauncementes, by customes and such like, could not defray the excessive chardges which doe import the state. And first hee sayd the comon and knowne continuall

f.2

---

1. *Sic*, here and in Cott.Titus F1, Rawlinson C 680 and SP Dom.Eliz. 46/166. Cf. Hooker, who has the Bishop of London.

2. *Sic*.

3. MS reads 'our'; this reading from Cott.Titus F1.

4. MS reads 'yours'; this reading from Cott.Titus F1.

chardg of her Majestie[5] is greate; the suppressinge of the northerne rebelles hath beene very greate; the chardge of the frontiers, and dauntinge the forces of the Scottes, sworne and knowne to have bent themselves and confederated to the annoyaunce and greater hurt of this realme and her subiectes, hath bene excessive greate; and the maintenance of the navy was, is, and still must bee greate: soe greate as if the fountaine of her revenues were farre greater, yet by soe many, such, and soe greate camelles[6] would the same too spedely bee drawne dry. Hee shewed alsoe that by breach of the entertrade with Flaunders her customes are diminished, and her chardge for defence of her subbiectes' passage beinge nowe more further and more f.2v   perrilous then to fore, is thereby increased. And, albeit it / will ensue that in tyme there shall bee greater and better increase both to the Crowne and to the realme by this latter trade, yet for the meane tyme there must regard bee had least the proverbe should bee verefied, that while the grasse groweth the steede starveth. And as wee thinke not much to imploy chardge on that which we breede even while it is yonge and is not yet in plight or able to serve us, but to count the expence well bestowed, lookinge to the effect and end which will ensue, even soe must wee for the tyme make our accompt, rekoninge and assuring ourselves of a comodious sequell both profittable and honorable, not to bee bound to the devotion or direccion of the Flemishe prince.

   Hee shewed for causes why wee should be willinge to give ayd to her Majestie these two: ffirst the benefittes of her receaved; the second necessitie,[7] importinge us deeply, and inforcinge us narrowly, to depart with some little, to save, protect, and thereby the rather to enioy the whole rest. Of her Majestie's benefittes hee shewed three principally: first the greate and inestimable benefitt which by Gode's grace, and shee the meane, hath bene powred uppon us, the quiett of conscience, the purity of religion, the deliverie from the tyranny and oppression of the Pope and popelings, wherein hee could say that the sumes of moneyes yearely levied and delivered to the Romaine see did farr surmount the revennewes of the Crowne, of all which the realme was robbed of this poynt of benefitt; and for the extollinge of the same hee stood somewhat longe, addinge that howe much heavenly thinges are better then earthly, soe much this guift and blessinge is better then any other. The second of her Majestie's benefittes (hee sayd) was peace, such and soe rare as for soe longe tyme noe histories doe record, or example bee to bee shewed of the like, a president from perfect government to all posteritie, without spott or interruption if the insolency and desire of Romishe rule (for soe hee tearmed it) had not disturbed it. What peace was, and the benefittes thereof he shewed learnedly and at lardge; the misery and calamitie f.3   of our neighbours on every side he did / well explaine and lively sett forth. The third of the happie blessinges which wee have enioyed by her Highnes and her gratious naturall disposition is (hee sayd) clemency, soe greate and rare as the like is not to bee remembred, whereof all sortes and all states, from tyme to tyme, at all tymes have bene partakers: offenders to her owne person pardoned, the extremitie of the lawes not used, by wayes of benevolences, contribucions and such like nothinge wrested, the nobilitie soe tendered, the gentry soe comforted and encouraged, and the comons soe to their wishe and likinge protected, that not to bee remembred it were the unnaturall and most detestable argument of ingratitude. And to conclude hee sayd that hee was perplexed when hee should speake or thinke of this benefitt of her clemencie, which if hee might soe apply the text, hee woulde pronounce it *miserecordia eius super omnia opera eius*. Other benefitts he sayd there were many to bee remembred, as the benefitt of justice, and due administracion of the lawes, which soe sincerely by her Majestie's meanes hath bene (duringe her whole raigne) ministred, that the good may reioyce and noe man of right may complaine. The alteracion of the coyne from drosse to pure silver is (he sayd) somwhat greate and good, and here hee remembred (which is seldome seene of a prince) that shee hath not spared to remitt of a subsedie graunted her of late well neere the one haulfe, a third part and more. It can never bee obiected (sayth hee) that shee hath spent or wasted the treasure of the state, what other princes in gay and gorgeous buildings wastfully, in banquettes, tryumphes, or such like expensivelie, in overchardgeable and sumptuous embassies superfluously, shee hath not; and yet shee hath not omitted any thinge which might bee to the honour of the realme to sett it forth honorably. And when other princess hardly may bee enduced to omitt such pleasures, shee hath settled her selfe to make that most pleasant to her which is for your, and our preservacions, and for our safety: this (sayd hee) in her progenitors hath bene seldome seene, in forraine govermentes is never found. It is in a prince *rara avis in terris*; but wee yet (God bee praysed) have a bird of that broode. | f.3v

This is the sum of the whole which in many wordes and longe tyme hee uttered, intermixinge many things worthy the remembringe tendinge to the shewe of our blessed state under her goverment, but surely noe wordes might suffice or skill serve to containe the tennour of that speech, if it shoulde or coulde bee toulde with due report, even as I thinke the hearers wholy in conscience did acknowledge right well. Therefore his Lordship did conclude, that rather of forme and order to say somwhat then for declaracion of any newe or unknowne matter he had sayd what hee had, leavinge the more deepe consideracion thereof to the hearers themselves.

This his speech ended and the proxies of the Earles of Shrewsburie, Darby and [blank][8] beinge read with others of sundry of the barons absent (in French as is accustomed), the Lord Keeper spake againe sayinge:

'There rested nothinge but that you of the lower house should goe together and of your selves to make choyce of some fitt man to be your Speaker'.

Wee then cominge to the House and being there sett, Sir Francis Knowlls in a fewe plaine wordes tould a tale to the purpose as afore, and then sayd for his owne part hee liked of Mr Seriant Wray to bee Speaker. The question asked, some sayd 'Yea', but noe man denied, whereuppon Mr Treasurer, Sir Francis Knolls, and Mr Comptroller, Sir James Croftes, risinge, requested him to take his place, which without further intreatie hee did. Thus then placed, standing upp at his seate hee made a short and honest excuse why hee should not bee chosen. This endinge, and tyme beinge agreed uppon for presentinge of him to her Majestie on Wednesday (*viz*) the iiij[TH] of Aprill, the sittinge of this the first day was dissolved.

---

5. 'Majestie' supplied from Cott.Titus F1.
6. *Sic*, here and in Cott.Titus F1.
7. MS reads 'very necessarilie'; this reading from Cott.Titus F1.

8. Blank in all MSS. *LJ*, I.667, also records a proxy for Warwick, though not clearly for this day.

Aprill iij^d　The iij^d of Aprill nothinge was done.

Aprill iiijth　In the afternoone the Speaker, Mr Wray, was by the whole House brought to the presence of her Majestie sitting in her Highnes' seate of estate, in manner as before, in the second day, is described, where first hee made suite that albeit hee could not obtaine of the lower house to bee disburdened of that place and some other fitter to

f.4　bee chosen, that her Highnes would vouchsafe to have consideracion / of the greatenes of the service, and therefore to require them eftsoones to returne to the House and to make a newe choyce; which his peticion beinge by the Lord Keeper at the assignacion of her Majestie aunsweared it was sayed, that aswell for that her Highnes had understood of him, as for that the Commons had chosen him, his request could not bee graunted. And therefore hee beinge by her royall assent approved, was accepted as Speaker.

Hee then desired to bee heared to say somwhat concerning the orderly goverment of a comon weale, which to bee duly done (he sayd) there were three thinges requisite: religion, authoritie, and lawes. By religion, hee sayd, wee doe not onely knowe God aright, but alsow howe to obay the kinge or queene whom God shall assigne to raigne over us, and that not in temporall causes, but in spirituall or ecclesiasticall, in which wholly her Majestie's power is absolute; and leavinge all proofes of divinity to the bushopps and ffathers (as hee sayd hee would) hee proved the same by the practice of princes within this realme, and first made remembraunce of Lucius, the first Christian kinge, who havinge written to Elutherius the Pope, *anno* 1300⁹ yeares past, for the Romans lawes, hee was answered that hee had the holly scriptures, out of the which hee might drawe to himselfe, and for his subiectes, lawes by his owne good discretion, for that hee was the viccar of Christ over the people of Brittaine. The Conquerour (hee sayd) in the ereccion of Battaile Abby graunted that the Church should bee free from all episcopall jurisdiccion. Henry the Third gave unto Ranulphe, Bushoppe of London,¹⁰ the Archbushoppricke of Canterburie by these wordes: *Rex etc. Sciatis quod dedimus dilecto nostro Ranulpho Archipiscopatum Cantuariensem quem instituimus anulo et bacculo.* The ringe, hee sayd, was the signe of perfeccion, the staffe the signe of pastorall rule, which hee could not doe if these kings had not had and used an ecclesiasticall power. In the reportes of the lawe wee finde that an excommunicacion of a certaine person came from the Pope under his leaden bull, and was shewed in abatement of an accion brought at the commen lawe, which beside that it was of noe force, the kinge and judges were of

f.4v　minde that hee who brought it had deserved / death, soe to presume on any forraine authority; which authority being nowe by Gode's grace and her highnes' meanes abolished, and the freedome of consciences and the truth of Gode's word established, wee therefore had greately to thanke God and her.¹¹

For authoritie, or the sword whereby the comon wealth is stayd, three things (hee sayd) are requisite, men, armour and money. For men, their good willes (hee sayd) was most, being of it selfe a stronge fortresse. For armour the necessitie hee shewed in part, and howe requisite treasure was hee a little declared. And hee concluded that all three must bee conioyned, men, armour and money.

Lastly, for lawes, the third stay of the comon wealth, (hee sayd) there must bee consideracion in makinge of them, and care in executinge: in makinge such as by the providing for one part of the comon wealth the rest should not bee hindered, which were in deede a matter most pernitious, and this hee vouched out of Plato, *De Legibus*;[12] ffor execucion (hee sayd) that since the lawe of it selfe is but mute, sett in paper, not able to doe ought, the magistrate, except hee alsoe will bee mute, must bee the doer, and then is it to bee sayd a good lawe well made, when it is well executed, for *anima legis est executio*. Whereuppon hee sayd somwhat in comendacion of her Majestie, who had given free course to her lawes, not sendinge or requiringe the stay of justice by her letters or privie seales, as heretofore sometyme hath bene by her progenitors used, nether hath shee pardoned any without the advise of such before whome for offendors have bene arraigned and the cause heard.

His oration ended, hee then made four peticions: the first that the persons, servants and goodes of all cominge to that assembly might bee free from all arrestes; then that for cause of conference they might have accesse to her Majestie; thirdly, if any sent should not truly report or in part mistake the meaninge of the House, that the same should bee by her Highnes favorably heard; / lastly that in the House all f.5 men might have free speech.

This oration ended, by direccion from her Majestie and instruccions given what shoulde bee sayd, the Lord Keeper answeared thus, devidinge his oration into three partes: the first where hee had some times incerted comendacions of her Majestie, hee sayd her Highnes woulde not acknowledge soe great perfeccions to bee in her, but sayde they should bee instruccions for her better proceedings in tyme to come; the second part of his oration hee sayd concerninge the rule for orderinge of the comon wealth shee well liked of, and wished that as hee had well conceaved it, and well uttered the same, soe hee and others would endeavour the execucion thereof. For his peticions hee sayd her Majestie's pleasure was the first to bee graunted, with this caution, that noe man should under their shaddowes untruly protect any others; for the second hee sayd at tyme convenient her pleasure was they should come freelie; the third part hee sayd shee could not imagine amonge soe many wise men could happen, but if it should, her Grace could bee content to remitt it; the fourth was such that her Majestie, havinge experience of late of some disorder and certaine offences, which thoughe they were not punished, yet were they offences still, and soe must be accompted: he therefore saied they shoulde doe well to meddle with noe matters of state but such as should be propounded unto them, and to occupy themselves in other matters concerninge the commen wealth.[13]

The bill for cominge to service and receavinge the communion was read[14] but not Aprill v[th] spoken unto for that the House was called, whereabout the whole tyme was spent by the callinge whereof, forasmuch as it did appeare that there were nyne burroughes which had sent upp burgesses more and other then at the last parliament had done; it was therefore agreed that they which were returned shoulde forbeare their cominge

9. *Sic*; see Bede, I.4; *DNB sub* Lucius.
10. I.e. Chichester?
11. Mr J. Barton of Merton College, Oxford, suggests that the reference should be to an excommunication *of* his Treasurer, and identifies the case

    involved here to 30 *Ass.*, pl.19 (30 Ed.111).
12. See especially Book iv, 715b.
13. See *EP*, I.188-90.
14. This bill was in fact read on 4 April (*CJ*, I.82; Hooker).

untill such tyme as their titles might be approved before some to bee assigned by the House and the Queene's learned councell. The townes were: in Cornwell Foy and f.5v   [East Looe];[15] in Gloucestershire / Cirencester; in Oxenfordshire Woodstocke; in Kent Quinborghe; [East Retford in Nottinghamshire; Christchurch in Hampshire; and Aldeburgh and Eye in Suffolk].[16]

[April vi[th]]   Certain things beinge first moved and agreed uppon for orders of the House, and punishment of two yonge gentlemen[17] which not beinge of the House the day before had entered, being concluded of, one Mr Strickland, a grave and auncient man of greate zeale, and not perhapps (as hee himself thought) unlearned, hee first stood upp, and in a longe discourse, tendinge to the remembraunce of Gode's goodness in giveinge to us the light of his word, together with gratious disposition of her Majestie, by whom as by his instrument God had wrought soe greate things, and our slacknes and carelesnes in not esteeminge, and not followinge the tyme and blessinge offered, but yet still as men either not sufficiently instructed what is truth, or soe that wee thinke it not convenient to publishe and protest it openly, and that all reprochfull speeches of the slaunderers might bee stopped, the drawbackes brought forwardes, and the overruners, such as rune and exceede the rule of the lawe, to be reduced to a certainetie, hee thought it was *operis pretium* to be occupied therein. For which purpose, hee sayd, the professors of the gospell in other nations had written and published to the world the confession of their fayth, as did those of Strasburghe and of Franckford, and for which purpose alsoe greate learned men in this realme had travailed, as Peter Martir, Paulus Fagius, and other whose workes hereuppon (hee sayd) weere extant.[18] And before this tyme thereof an offer was made in parliament that it might bee approved,[19] but either the slacknes or somewhat els of some men in that tyme was the lett thereof – or what els (hee sayd) hee would not say. This booke, hee sayd, rested in the custody of Mr Norton as hee guessed, a man nether ill-disposed to religionn or a negligent keeper of such matters of chardge, and thereuppon requested Mr Norton might bee required to produce the same. Hee f.6   added alsoe that after soe many yeares as nowe by / Gode's providence wee have bene learninge the puritie of Gode's truth, that we should not permitt for any cause of policy of other pretence any errors in matters of doctrine to continue amonge us. And therefore, sayd hee, the Booke of Commen Prayer, althoughe (God bee praised) it is drawne very neere to the sinceritie of the truth, yet are there somthinges inserted more superstitious or erronious then in soe highe matters bee tollerable, as namely, in the ministracion of the sacrament of baptisme, the signe of the crosse to bee made with some ceremonies, and the ministracion of the sacrament by women in tyme of extremitie, and some such other errors, all which, hee sayd, might[20] well bee without note of choppinge or changinge of our religion chaunged or whereby the enemies might slaunder us, beinge a reformacion not contrariant but directly personant[21] to our profession, that is to have all thinges brought to the puritie of the primitive church and institucion of Christ. Hee spake at lardge of the abuses in the Church of England or in the churchmen, as first that papistes knowne are permitted to have ecclesiasticall goverment and great livings; that honest, godlie and learned protestantes have little or nothinge; that boyes are dispenced with to have spirituall promotions; that by frendshipp with the masters of the faculties, either unable men are qualified, or some one man allowed to have too many severall livinges. Finally hee concluded with peticion that by authority of that House some of them, to some convenient number, might bee assigned to have conference with the lordes of the spiritualty for consideracion and reformacion of the matters by him remembred.

Mr Norton, a man wise, bolde and eloquent,[22] standinge upp sayd hee was not ignorant (but had longe tyme since learned) what it[23] was to speake on a suddaine, or first before the rest of men in Parliament; yet, beinge occasioned by Mr Strickland, hee was to say that truth it is hee had a booke tendinge to that effect, but (quoth he) the booke was not drawne by those learned men whom hee named, but by vertue of the act of xxxij[24] at the assignacion or by the devise of seaven bushopps,[25] eight deanes, eight / civilians and eight temporall lawyers, who havinge in chardge to make ecclesiasticall constitucions, tooke in hand the same, which was drawne by that learned man Mr Doctor Haddon, and penned by that excellent learned man Mr Cheeke, whereuppon hee sayd that consideracion had bene, and some travell bestowed by Mr Foxe of late, and that there was a booke newly imprinted to bee offered to that House, which he did then and there presently shewe forth. And for the rest of Mr Strickland's motions hee sayd hee was of his mynd cheefely for the avoydinge and suppressinge of symoniacall engrosmentes.

f.6v

It was concluded by the House that xxj should be espetially assigned to have care of that booke, and to have conference with the bushopps therein.

The bill for cominge to devine service was againe reade; the effect whereof was that every subiect not sicke and in plight able to come should once every quarter come to his parrishe church to the service there, and every yeare once at the least to receave the comunion. To this bill and for the mayntenance thereof Sir Thomas Smyth argued and in part wished the bushoppes to have consideracion thereof. After whom Mr Fleetewood moved that the penallty of that statute should not goe to promoters. Hee sayd it was but a devise of late brought in, in the tyme of Kinge Henry 8, the first yeare of his raigne;[26] and shewed the evilles and inconveniencies which did growe by these men's doinges, wherein noe reformacion was sought but private gaine to the worst sort of men. Hee sayd alsoe that matter of goinge to the church, or for the service of God, did directly apertaine to that court, sayinge that wee all have aswell learned this lesson – that there is a God who is to bee served – as

15. Blank in all MSS.
16. Line blank in MS and in Rawlinson C 680; Cott.Titus F1 and SP Dom.Eliz.46/166 read 'etc'. See *CJ*, I.83.
17. Thomas Clarke and Antony Bull (*CJ*, I.83).
18. Strickland is speaking of the newly edited *Reformatio Legum*.
19. The bill of 27 February 1559 'for making of ecclesiastical laws by thirty two persons'.
20. 'Might' supplied from Cott.Titus F1.
21. Cott.Titus F1 reads 'preservant', as does SP Dom.Eliz.46/166; Rawlinson C 680 has 'consonaunt'.
22. 'A man . . . eloquent' supplied from Cott.Titus F1 (not in Rawlinson C 680).
23. MS reads 'is'; this reading from Cott.Titus F1.
24. 32 Hen.VIII, c.26 (1540) in *SR*, III.783-4, and cf. 27 Hen.VIII, c.15 (1553-6) in *SR*, III.548-9.
25. Cott.Titus F1 reads '8 bishopps', Rawlinson C 680 'vij bishopps'.
26. Cf.1 Hen.VIII, c.4 (1509-10) in *SR*, III.2.

have the bushopps. Hee proved by the old lawes vouched from Kinge Edgar that the princes in their parliamentes have made ecclesiasticall lawes and constitucions, as these: that if any servant should worke on the Sabboth day by the comaundement of his master, hee should bee free, if of himselfe, hee should bee whipped; if a free

f.7   man should worke hee should bee bound,[27] / or greevously to bee amerced. Hee concluded with request that it might bee committed to some of the House and not to expect the bushopps, who perhappes would bee slowe.

Sir Owen Hopton of Suffolke moved very orderly that the presentacion of such defaultes should not depend uppon the relacion of the church wardens, who beinge simple men and fearinge to offend, would rather incurre the daunger of periurie then displease some of their neighbours. Hee shewed for proofe experience.

Then was there an act read for preservacion of woodes; the tenour of which bill was, to save from spoyle and bringinge to sale yonge poles, and cuttinge of boughes, within twenty miles of London. This bill gave occasion to speake of a generall regard to bee hadd of woodes throughe the realme, whereof sundry devises were, as by Mr Bell to stay and prohibite the evill practises of purveiors, who takeinge under pretence of her Majestie's service what they woulde at what price they themselves liked, it enforced the owners, not alone not to regard the keepinge of woodes, but withall to make spoyle. Hee advised therefore to make suite, thereby to prevent such oppression. This was prosequuted and soe farr by others reasoned unto, and finally by Mr Seriant Jeffereis, that the bill exhibited for London was dashed, and a bill with generall purveiance ordered to bee drawne.

Aprill vij   Mr Strickland first moved that Mr Norton might be required to deliver such bookes as hee had.

Mr Nudigate hee moved that where on of the causes for calling of the parliament (and perhapps the cheefest) was for a subsedie, hee thought it not amisse to make offer of a subsedie before it should bee required; which speech was not liked of by the House, *etc.*

Sir Frauncis Knolls made a longe needeles discourse concerninge the subsedy.

Mr Bell sayd that a subsedie was by every subiect to bee yeilded, but for that the people were robbed (by two meanes) it would hardly bee levied: namely by lycenses and the abuse of promooters, for which if remedie were provided, then would the subsedie bee payd willingly, which hee proved, for that by lycenses a fewe were

f.7v   enriched and the multitude impoverished. / Addinge that if a newe burden should bee layd on the backes of the comons, and noe redresse of the comon evilles, then there might[28] happely ensue that they woulde lay downe the burden in the middest of the way, and turne to the contrary of their duties.

Mr Popham affirmed Mr Bell's speech and added this more: the abuse of treasurers of the Crowne, as manie havinge in their handes great masses of money, with the which either they themselves or some others their ffrendes doe purchase landes to their owne use and after become backruptes, and soe cause or practise an enstallment of their debtes, as of late some one hath stalled a debt of thirtie thousand powndes, which occasioned the lacke in the prince's coffers.

Mr Seriant Lovelace argued that every loyall subiect ought to yeild to the releife of the prince and what without any condicion or lymitacion; notwithstandinge, hee did well like of the former motion and thought it very requisite that those evilles might bee provided for to the end aforesayd, unto the which hee added three more. First, the abuse of purveiors, wherein hee had to desire the Councell and the masters of the Houshould to consider of it, and to be willing to yeild to reformacion; and in his opinion it should not bee amisse to take away the purveiors and to limitt everie county to a proportionable rate, soe should her Majestie bee better served and the comons eased. The second, the reformacion of the Exchequer for the chardge that groweth by respite of homage, which hee wished might bee payd in some other sort in a sume certaine. The third, another reformacion, which is uppon a greate abuse in the Exchequer by sendinge out uppon every fyne levied the writt *ad ostendendum qualiter et quo titulo etc.*

Mr Comptroller of the Queene's Houshould sayd in fewe wordes that hee, beinge one of the masters of the Houshould, would doe his endeavour for reformacion of all things rising by the purveiors.

Mr Sanpole,[29] sometyme of Lincolne's Inne, liked well of the motion for the subsedie and commended the motions of the gentlemen before, affirminge that they were verie necessarie to be thought of, unto which hee was to adde one more (*viz*) the / abuse of collectors, sheweinge for cause that they doe retaine their chardge   f.8 sometimes a yeare, sometime more, in their owne handes, and for that they are but meane men appoynted to that office, they offtentimes convert it to their owne use, perhapps never able to satisfy the same, whereby the people are unwillinge to pay, for if they should understand her Majestie should have it presently, they would more willingly pay it, and therefore wished the better sort of every county should bee assigned to that chardge.

Mr Goodyere spake to this effect, that every man ought to yeild to the subsedie, and rather to offer it then to stay untill it should bee demaunded; desiringe that the subsedie might presently and onely goe forwardes without the hearinge of any more complaintes for that they might be infinite, and already more were remembred then in one parliament coulde bee reformed; wherein sure hee shewed a greate desire to winne favour, *etc.*

A bill was exhibited intituled 'For the preservation of the Queene's Majestie in the   Aprill 9 royall estate and crowne of this realme', the effect whereof was that to goe about within the realme or without, by speech or act to depose or remove her, by any person *etc.*, or to say shee is not lawfull Queene, or to say shee is an infidell, or hereticke, or schismaticke, or such like, to bee treason.

This bill beinge read, Mr Norton in a longe discourse made declaracion howe that her Majestie was and is the onelie piller and stay of all safetie, aswell for our pollitique quiett as for the state of religion, and for religion the very base and piller throughout Christendome; and therefore since wee maie see howe happie wee are with her,[30] and by her lacke what mischeefe may growe wee doe not knowe, hee

27. Cott.Titus F1 reads 'bond', SP Dom.Eliz.46/166 'bonde', and Rawlinson C 680 'bande'.
28. 'Might' supplied from Cott.Titus F1.
29. Cott.Titus F1 and SP Dom.Eliz.46/166

have 'Sampole', as does this journal on f.12; Rawlinson C 680 has 'Sanpoole'.
30. MS reads 'and therefore with her howe happy wee are, since wee may see'; this reading from Cott.Titus F1.

sayd therefore that for preservacion of her estate, our care, praier, and cheefe endevour must bee. And as hee right well liked of the bill, soe did hee thinke there were further some things to be added worthy, yea and necessarie to bee conioyned. First, that whosoever in her life hath done, or shall make claime to the imperiall crowne of this realme, that hee, or they, or their heires, to bee forbarred of any claime, challenge, or title to bee made to that crowne at any tyme hereafter; and that everie person who

f.8v   shall maynetaine that tytle to bee accompted a / traytor. And further that whosoever shall say the court of Parliament hath not authoritie to enact and binde the title of the crowne, to be adiudged a traytor. Of all which hee shewed a draught of an act for the Parliament, drawne and devised by himselfe, whereof hee prayed convenient consideracion might bee, and that the same (if it should soe seeme good to the House) might be conioyned to the former and other bill, *etc.*

Mr Cleere of Norfolke, a gentleman of greate possessions, made hereuppon a staggeringe speech: his conclusion I did not conceave.

Sir Frauncis Knolls thought it convenient that what was in the first bill might stand by it selfe, and the rest to bee added in another bill by it selfe; which beinge hee could yeild his consent, and this hee opened with many wordes.

Sir Nychollas Arnold liked of the whole tenor of both billes, but to have soe slanderous wordes imprinted of her Majestie, as that it might bee intended that there may bee soe wicked a man as to call soe good a princesse by soe vile and hatefull tearmes, hee woulde not have it to bee left to posteritie, but that in generall wordes the same might bee reached. Hee alsoe wished consideracion might bee hadd whether in former lawes the same or such like speeches bee not provided for, to save thereby confusion.

Sir Henry Norris, late ambassador in Fraunce, thought the bill good, reasonable, and necessary in all poyntes; whereunto, in a short, myld, and plaine speech, hee wished might bee added that to give ayde to any nowe beinge for the cause of religion beyond the seas, and to convay any comoditie from hence to their releife, should bee as treason. Hee shewed for proofe his owne experience duringe the tyme of his service in Fraunce, constantly affirminge for truth that they, fostered with our aydes, are wholly bent, given, and imployed to devisinge, practisinge and raysinge of some mischeefe, quarrell or hurt to her Majestie or the state, soe that of infinite evilles thereby risinge, or which may rise, wee are to our selves the verie nurses

f.9   and / principall aydes. Their desires to doe it, their abilities to execute it, the tyme howe well to serve them for it: howe farr these consideracions might stretch, the wise (hee sayd) might see.

Mr Yelverton of Graye's Inne argued to this effect. First to prove that the matters of practise to the disturbaunce of her Majestie's title in the crowne to bee contayned in the statute 25 Edward 3,[31] and therefore not needefull to bee here eftsoones renued; and for the wordes of slaunder, hee thought it not amisse to bee within the letter of the statute. Withall hee craved to knowe whether it were meant that by the bill aswell the heire as the partie should bee forbarred, which if it were soe, then, sayd hee, it was as it should bee. Lastly, hee concluded that hee was of mynd that all, aswell what was preferred by Mr Norton as the rest, should bee contayned in one bill.

Mr Fleetewood learnedly shewed the due makinge of lawes to bee for the one of these three endes, the glory of God, the profitt of the prince and realme, or safetie of our selves; and since the tenor of this bill did soe directly tend to the satisfyinge of them all hee could not but thinke it a matter most worthy the consideracion. But, sayd hee, in matters of such wayght wee may not proceede but slowly and with good advise. Hee shewed howe that he himselfe hath for hasty speech, as on the first motion, before the Councell sustayned reproch.[32] Againe, hee sayd, the suddaine comittment of billes doth often occasion the lacke of convenient qualificacion, and very often is the cause that the billes bee never heard of againe, and in steede of committinge for consideracion bee committed to the chest of forgettfullnes, or quite cast out of doores. He therefore craved and advised that the bill might bee the second tyme read some other day and that accordinge to the waight of the matter men woulde in the meane tyme throughly thinke thereof.

Mr Alford was of that mynd, and somwhat sayd to that effect, whereuppon for this cause by the House day was assigned till the twelveth day of this moneth for the second readinge.

The bill then for cominge to comon prayer over and above the former lawe *etc.* and receavinge of the comunion every man: every man to come to his parrishe church once in the quarter on the payne of xij^{li}[33] and to receave the comunion once in the yeare on the payne of one hundred markes *etc.*; / that inquisition should bee   f.9v made, that churchwardens should present, that ordinaries should certifie on paynes *etc.*; provision for gentlemen's chapells, for ambassadors, strangers, sicke men, and persons imprisoned, and a proviso for the tyme of plague.

Mr Thomas Snagge shewed at lardge the inconvenience of the old lawe for cominge to service, and of this if they both bee conioyned: for, sayd hee, by the former lawe it is enacted that the service shall not bee sayd, or sacramentes ministred, in other sortes then is in the Booke of Comon Prayer prescribed. Hee shewed howe different the same was in many places used from the prescribed rule, as noe part of those prayers observed, but a sermon and some such other prayers as the minister should thinke good in place thereof, whereuppon hath greate divisions, discordes and dislikes growne amonge and betweene greate numbers. And since it is lawe that in this sort service shall bee, and that whosoever shalbee at any other forme of service shall incurre the penalties prescribed, and that the ministers they will not nor doe not as they should, hee thought the proceedings in this sort should occasion a dilemma in mischeefe, for if hee come not hee shall loose xij^{li}, if hee doe come and bee present and the service not sayd to the prescribed tittle of the booke, hee should loose one hundred markes.

Mr Aglyonby, burges for the towne of Warwicke, moved that the lawe might bee without exception or priviledge for any gentleman in their private oratories. This did hee prove out of Plato his lawes and Cicero, both prescribing for the observacion of the lawe an equalitie betweene the prince and the poore man, not givinge scope to the one above the other. Hee remembred the authoritie of Lactantius Firmianus

---

31. 25 Ed.III, st.v,c.2 (1351–2) in *SR*, I.319–20.

32. Cf. fos.6v, 7.

33. So Rawlinson C 680, and SP Dom.Eliz.46/166; but Cott.Titus F1 has 'xiid', and Hooker gives 30*s*.

makinge this onely difference betweene man and beast, that all men doe acknowledge and knowe there is a God,[34] and in this respect there should bee noe difference betweene man and man: withall hee sayd the more noble the man the more good his example may doe. Hee therefore concluded that for soe much of the

f.10   lawe, soe that the same / might bee generall, hee was of good likinge. But for the other matter concerninge the receavinge of the sacrament, he argued that it was not convenient to enforce consciences. He shewed the authoritie of doctors (which hee vouched without notinge the place or the sentence); hee sayd it was the opinions of the fathers and learned men of this land, and therefore wished they might bee consulted with; finally hee concluded that *bonae leges e malis moribus proveniunt*, but noe lawes may make a good man fitt to receave that greate misterie but God above. This whole speeche hee tempered with such discretion as in such case was seemely, and whatsoever hee spake hee spake it under correccion *etc.*

Mr Stricland standinge upp first prayed hee might bee excused for that hee was to speake on a suddaine and unprovided. For the first part hee approved what Mr Aglionby had sayd. For the second hee sayd hee could not bee of that mynd, for as hee vouched out of Esderas the Church, yea the consciences of men were by the prophett restrayned. Withall hee sayd consciences may bee free, but not to disturbe the comon quiett. Hee shewed the practice and doings of the Pope, the banishment of the Arians; that the sword of the prince for lacke of lawe must not bee tyed; the Isralites hee sayd were constrayned to receave the Passover; and finally hee concluded it was noe straitninge of their consciences, but a chardge or losse of their goodes, if they could not vouchsafe to bee as they should bee, good men and Christians.

Mr Dalton reasoned to this effect, that there could ensue noe inconvenience by those two lawes, which were intended to bee contrary. His reason was, except the service bee accordinge to the lawe, noe man is to stay there noe more then if hee bee bound to come to heare service, if there bee noe service, hee is not to forfeite. For answeare of Mr Aglionby hee sayd, the matter of conscience did not concerne the lawe makers, nether were they to regard the error, curiositie or stiffneckednes of the evill, ignorant or froward persons, for bee it they did proceede orderly to the dischardge of their owne consciences, let them care whom it behooveth. Hee was of mynd gentlemen shoulde not bee excepted, for the causes aforesayd; but hee wished provision might bee made for such which bee imprisoned, or could not come for

f.10v   feare of / arrestes. Hee wished alsoe this lawe might have continuance but to the end of the next parliament.

Mr Fleetwood shewed the great consideracion to bee had of the old Booke of Comon Prayer wherein some hidd things were caried as matters of noe accompt, and yet are indeede lawes. 'For', sayd hee, 'cominge to the Bushopp of London and desirous to learne the warrant of deprivacion of such who refused to fullfill some of the prescribed orders, I was willed to looke on the Booke of Comon Prayer. Of all things under heaven I never loked'[35] quoth hee, 'for a lawe in the rub[r]ickes of a mattins booke; but since soe it is, let it bee better seene unto, and let further or other order bee taken for such hidden matter wrapped upp in cloudes.' Hee further wished that noe authoritie should be given to others in hidden sort to ordaine any thinge havinge the force of lawe, as hath bene experienced in the bill of Barwicke to give authoritie to the Captaine *etc.*, and for the Phisitions of London to have oversight of victualles, both which lawes have bene repealed;[36] and that statute required by Henry 8 to authorise him to make by his proclamacion lawes could not be allowed but with this caution, that it should not extend to touch the life, landes or goodes of any man. Hee incerted somwhat concerninge the voyces of burgesses of the parliament, which hee concluded to bee of every burroughe which is incorporate as *liber burgus*. Hee sheweth alsoe that absence for service of the Queene or matters of necessity neede not to bee provided for by statute since by the lawe they are to be dischardged.

Mr Robert Snagge wished greate care for the avoydinge of the double lashe accordinge to the argument of his brother. Hee motioned the reformacion of the universitie, of the private schoolemasters in gentlemen's houses, and of the Inns of Court.

Mr Speaker signified that by the mouth of Master Atturney hee was advertised her Majestie's pleasure to bee that wee should speake of matters propounded onely, / and not to make newe motions every man at his owne pleasure, as of late her Majestie was informed wee had done. Aprill x f.11

This advertisement grewe of somwhat spoken by Master Bell the eight[37] day of this moneth concerninge lycenses graunted by her Majestie to doe certaine matters contrary to the statutes, wherein hee seemed (as was sayd) to speake against her prerogative: but surely soe orderly did hee utter what hee spake as such who were touched might be angry, but iustly to blame him it might not bee.

A bill was the first tyme read, bindinge all men to weare capps (made in England) on the Sundayes, other then such as might dispend twenty markes yearely *etc.*

A bill for comission of sewers,[38] warrantinge all such lawes as shall be made by sixe, whereof three to bee of the quorum, to bee as effectuall as if the same were certified *etc.* and the Queene's royall assent were given, with some provisoes and circumstances not greatly materiall. This bill was the nynth[39] day read, and a warrant given for the ingrossinge thereof, and not spoken of further.

A bill that all sheriffes should in Hillary tearme returne the names of ffree houlders into the Kinge's Bench, Commen Pleas, and Exchequer, and to autherise the puny[40] justice in every of theis benches to returne all *venire facias*: the justice to have for every *venire facias* xij^d, *etc.*

A bill for reversinge of the act of Parliament made for the incorporacions of the Marchantes of Bristoll was read.[41] This bill was the eleaventh day read and argued

---

34. See for instance *De Opificio Dei*, ch.2; *Divinae Institutiones*, vii, ch.4.
35. 'I never loked' supplied from Cott. Titus F1.
36. 32 Hen. VIII, c.27 reversed grants, not an Act, concerning Berwick, but cf. *Rot.Parl.*, vi.394 and 11 Hen. VII, c.61 (1495) in *SR*, II.626–7.
37. *Sic*: 7 April.
38. MS reads 'shewers'; this reading from Cott. Titus F1.
39. *Sic*: Cott. Titus F1, SP Dom.Eliz.46/166 and Rawlinson C 680 have 'xj^th' (cf. *CJ*, I.84).
40. I.e. 'puisne'.
41. 8 Eliz. (1566), noted in *SR*, IV.483.

unto, as after shall appeare in the remembrance of that day.

A bill priveledginge all persons indebted to goe to church, to tarry safe, and to returne without arest, and to punishe the sheriffe for any attachment in this behaulfe.

A bill to meete with subtill practices of such corporacions of cathedrall churches as shall surrender their houses into her Majestie's handes and to take the same againe thereby to defeate leases by them made within a yeare, which statute did imply an explicacion of part of a statute made *anno* 31 Henry 8 *etc.*[42]

The committees of the subsedie made returne of their resolution (*viz*) that iiij^s should bee payd for landes, and ij^s viij^d of / goodes, at two paymentes (*viz*) October next and October 1572, and two fifteenes, in September next, and September 1572.

An act to give lycence to burgesses to bee chosen freelie, contrary to the statute of first of Henry 5.[43]

A bill for the inkeepers within three miles of London to bee bound to their ordinances of London, and for search to bee made by the wardens of the Company of Inkeepers was read.

A bill for the removinge of a schoole, nowe beinge in Lawnsdon in the County of Kent, unto Gainsborroughe in the same county was read.[44]

A bill for the benefitt of clothworkers in the citty of London to have the old lawe enlardged, and a greater paine.

A bill for avoydinge of fraudulent feofmentes, fines and guiftes, thereby to deceave the true creditors, makeinge the covin averable.

A bill to provide for the good service of churches by fitt ministers:[45] and therefore first to bee enacted that noe man should bee instituted which should not first subscribe the articles agreed in the synode 1562, and to make publicacion of the same in his parrishe church, on payne to bee deprived *ipso facto*; who soe shall mayntaine the contrary to bee deposed *and libitum episcopi*; noe man to bee instituted not of the age of two and twenty yeares; noe man to have cure except he can render an accompt of his beleefe in Latine, or hath the guift of preachinge. All qualificacion contrary to this act to bee voyd. Noe man to have a benefice of xxx^{li} except hee be a preacher.

A bill for the towne of Lostewhethell in Cornewall to have knowledge of statutes accordinge to the statute of Acton Burnell.[46]

A bill for malmesies and sweete wines to bee landed at Southampton onely.

A bill that the Queene's ordinarie servantes in the cheque rolle should not bee returned on juries.

A motion was made by Mr Comptroller to knowe the pleasure of the House whether the comittees for the cause of religion should conferre with the bushopps and lordes / assigned from the higher house, or to stand at the direccion of the bushopps. It was spoken unto of many, but Mr Norton was of mynd it should bee called a suite, neverthelesse to conferre, and not to stand at the direccion of the bushopps further then their consciences should bee satisfied. Whereunto Mr Elverton[47] agreed, perswadinge that the authoritie might bee continued in that House *etc.*

A bill for avoydinge of disorderly presentacions, wherein was contayned first that all grauntes of advousons for lives or yeares to bee voyd, and the patrons to bee brought to their old estates; then that all grauntes made duringe such tyme as the church is full to bee voyd; thirdly that whosoever shall take any thinge for to present, or on a presentacion shall save or reserve to himselfe any thinge, shall loose his patronage duringe his life.[48]

Hereuppon Mr Sampole orderly argued to the first poynt, persuadinge that to resigne what before hath bene given is iniurious and unreasonable, to take away a right (provided by any man) or given to a schoolemaster for his service, or to the mayntenance of a scholler in the universitie, were not convenient.

Sir Frauncis Knowles in a longe speech endevored to persuade that to reverse what was done amise was noe evill; shewinge further that such a man to whom an advouson hath bene graunted at the tyme of the graunt was a fitt man,[49] but the same man after (as wee are all subiect to evill) may fall, and nowe is not fitt to have any such chardge, and therefore hee concluded it were well to bringe it to the first founder to deale from henceforth sincerely.

Mr Ellverton eloquentlie[50] persuaded it to bee noe reason for a man to reverse his owne act, and moved further that hee could not conceave any reason why there should not bee aswell an estate for life or yeares for an advowson as an estate of inheritance; and since an advowson is assettes to / the heire in judgment by lawe,   f.12v why might hee not sell the same for life or yeares? And albeit a presentacion is of noe value, for nothinge is to bee given for it, yet the *jus presentandi* is somwhat, since that to pleasure a frend is noe lesse to bee reckoned of then to profitt our selves. Hee alsoe moved that in reason the presentee who shall come in by symony is aswell to bee punished as the presentor, and since it is ordayned that the patron shall loose the patronage duringe his life uppon every such compact, that the preist should for the like bee made unable to take any benefice duringe his life.

Mr Strickland endevored the answearinge of Mr Sampole, sayinge that in presentacions to spirituall benefices nether service nor frend are to bee respected, but the guift to bee to[51] a fitt man free without affeccion.

Mr Cleere made motion that even as there was provision for the avoydance of presentmentes, soe sayd hee alsoe that the like in reason should bee for bandes, but such was my ill happe I coulde not understand what reason hee made.

The bill for Bristoll's corporacion for Marchantes to bee dissolved was then read the second tyme.

Mr Comptroller moved that before some committees both parties might bee heard and the controversie appeased.

Mr Fleetwood argued that there might appeare rashnes or want of discretion in

42. 31 Hen.VIII, c.6 (1539) in *SR*, III.724-5: the reference here seems to be to Section 2.
43. 1 Hen.V, c.1 (1413) in *SR*, II.170.
44. *Sic*; cf. Hooker and *CJ*, I.84.
45. Bill B (*CJ*, I.84).
46. I.e. statute of merchants, 11 Ed.1 (1283) in *SR*, I.53-4.
47. I.e. Yelverton.
48. Bill D (*CJ*, I.84).
49. MS reads 'footeman' as do Cott.Titus F1 and SP Dom.Eliz.46/166; this reading from Rawlinson C 680.
50. MS reads 'elegantly'; this reading from Cott.Titus F1.
51. 'To' supplied from Cott.Titus F1.

them who should now reverse what of late they did; but leavinge to speake hereof hee entred into a good discourse of the prerogative which might hereby bee touched if they should enter to overthroughe her letters patentes, to whom by lawe there is power given to encorporat any towne,[52] and she is sworne to preserve her prerogative, and noe man but with reverence and submission may speake thereof. Hee shewed the statute[s] of Edward 1, Edward 3 and Henry 4 with a savinge of the prerogative;[53] hee vouched the clarke of the parliamentes' booke to bee that noe man might take of the statute for wills *etc.* but that the kinge first gave lycence, for that his prerogative in the wardes was thereby touched. In Kinge Edward 6 tyme lycence was sued for to the Lord Protector to talke of matters of prerogative. Hee remembred the booke of 20 of Henry 6 for the parliament of Ireland called by the Cheefe Judge (as is for him / lawfull), where it was questioned what by Parliament might bee done, whether they might depart with any one of the kinge's townes, fortes or peeces: it was agreed they might not. And soe did hee conclude that to talke hereof, forasmuch as her letters patentes and prerogative was touched, *Rege non consulto*, was perrilous. Hee made also mencion of the statute which authoriseth all merchantes to traffique by sea *nisi publice prohibentur*: hee sayth the others were prohibited *etc.*

Mr Yonge of Bristoll in the behaulfe of the comoners reasoned to this effect: first, shewinge the losse which hath growne to the Queene in her customes; then the private monopoly wrought and occasioned by the Marchantes, the controversies which have ensued by this meanes amonge them; then the subtill meanes whereby the statute was procured without the consent of the Maior and comons by such which were put in trust.

Mr Alford sayd hee might not speake of the prerogative aptly for that hee was not learned in the lawe, but made some remembrance of what hee had there seene concerning the act of Parliament for Southampton,[54] whereby it appeared that without an act of Parliament her Majestie's letters patentes were not sufficient, and therefore would the act to passe by petition. Hee shewed howe unreasonable it was to forbidd men to traffique noe whither. Hee shewed the perticuler prohibitions in London, as noe man not of the guild or house to traffique to Flaunders, or not of the Company to the Northeast in Muscovia; but generally to forbidd all trafique had noe reason. Withall hee sayd to straiten their owne cittizens and to leave all forrainers at libertie was more unreasonable; and soe did hee understand their cause to bee.

Mr Popham, Recorder of the cittie of Bristoll, spake to this effect, that hee therefore stayd untill by direccion of wiser men speakinge first hee might thereby the rather bee induced to leane to the right, and what is for truth the most reasonable and fitt in this behaulfe. For being / moved (as hee sayd) with regard of double duty, which way to encline or howe to bee drawne, hee stood very doubtfull untill such tyme as by the deepe consideracion with himselfe and perfect direccion of others hee was now growne to a resolucion what in that case for the comon comoditie of the citty should bee the best; his chardge and oathe to the citty moved him, and as his dutie to the place present did enforce him to speake plainely his conscience. And therefore first to[55] the matter moved by Mr Fleetwood concerninge the prerogative hee sayd it was most cleere her Majestie might thereby create at her pleasure

f.13

f.13v

corporacions of bodies polletique; yet that the prince by her owne graunt might establishe any such trade privatelie or peculiarly to appertaine to any one company, it could not bee, as the case of Southampton did assure and the comon opinion of the learned is on that part of the Greate Charter of England which ever is construed to the[56] publicke comoditie and is not meant to the avayle of any private company or bodie, which he ment uppon these wordes of the statute, *nisi Rex publice etc.* And it cannot bee sayd to bee a publique prohibition what is done by private letters patentes, but it is requisite the significacion of the prince's pleasure to bee by proclamacion made openly, and that must (sayd hee) bee generall for all the subiectes and not for some of any one private limite, place, or company. All which hee concluded with this rule, that the perticuler cause of the subiect is not passed by the generall words of the prince, but *quere* thereof, for that surely hee ment not as his wordes were in this poynt. For cause in reason why the act of Parliament at the last session made should bee reversed, hee shewed the covin used in the last parliament in penninge of the act, for (quoth hee) in the letters patentes there is a proviso that the guild[57] should not have continuance except it were to the comoditie of the cittie, which proviso in the statute is utterly omitted. Whereuppon, not to deale with the matter of prerogative at all, hee desired the act of Parliament to bee reversed, and to leave the letters patentes in force, to have their validitie accordinge to the lawe. / For further proofe that in respect of the publique state of the cittie it ought to bee otherwise, hee made a longe discourse of the decay of the navy, of the hinderance of the marriners, the private monopolie wrought by the Marchants, and of the comon complaint of the countrey. Hee sayd alsoe that the chardge for mayntenance of the state of the citty stood not on the Marchantes onely, but of the other comons, whose burden groweth very greate when they are to beare the office of mairallty or sheriffalty, as the chardge of the maior is 1000 markes, and the sheriffe's chardge 500 markes: hee sayd it could not bee lesse.

f.14

The House hereuppon was moved to allowe of this latter act for reversinge of the former and ordered it might be engrossed.

The House beeinge eftsoones moved by Mr Comptroller for the cause of Bristoll they were pleased to comitt the hearinge of the matter on both sides to fifteene of the House and for that purpose appoynted the comittees *etc.*

Aprill xij

A bill was read then for the ease of the inconveniences which doe growe out of the Exchequer by the processe for homage and *quo titulo ingressus est,* the effect of which was that the certainety of every man's title should bee conteyned[58] in an estreate and delivered to the sheriffe to yeeld accompt thereof uppon his accompt as hee doth for the rest; and, for knowledge of all tenures and alienacions, that from the Comon

52. Blank in MS; 'any towne' supplied from Cott.Titus FI.

53. 28 Ed.I, *artic. sup. cart.* c.20 (1300) in *SR,* I.141; 14 Ed.III, stat. 4, c.5 (1340), or 18 Ed.III, stat. 3, c.7 (1344) in *SR,* I.294, 303; 9 Hen.IV, c.8-9 (1407) in *SR,* II.161.

54. 5 Eliz. (1562-3), noted in *SR,* IV.402.

55. MS reads 'by'; this reading from Cott.Titus FI.

56. MS reads 'bee'; this reading from Cott.Titus FI.

57. MS reads 'gould'; this reading from Cott.Titus FI.

58. MS reads 'mayntayned'; this reading from Cott.Titus FI.

Pleas there should bee certificate of all fynes, and from the Chauncery of all lycences of alienacion.

A bill intituled 'For declaracion of certain treasons' was then the second tyme read, yea even as espetially for that purpose that day was assigned. The tenour whereof was that whatsoever person *etc.* within the realme of England or without should imagine, practice or goe about *etc.*[59] any deadly hurt to her Majestie, or[60] shall practice *etc.* any thinge against[61] the Crowne ether of England or Ireland, or shall say, write or signify that shee is not lawfull Queene, or shall publishe, speake, write or declare in any sort that shee is an heretique, infidell, schismaticke, tyrant, or usurper, to bee highe treason *etc.* There were in this bill cer[t]aine provisions for the

f.14v   triall of treasons / comitted beyond the seas.

To this bill were annexed by adicion (of Mr Norton's devise as was before sayd) these poyntes. First, that whosoever have or hath or hereafter shall make claime to the crowne of England duringe her Majestie's life, or shall say shee hath not lawfull right, or shall refuse to acknowledge her to bee the undowted Queene *etc.*, that everie such person or persons to bee sayd traytors; and that they and their issue shalbee forbarred of all right or title to bee made to the crowne of this realme at any tyme hereafter, and that the ayde and mayntenance of every such person or persons to bee sayd treason.[62] And further to say or hould opinion that the Queene's Majestie with the court of Parliament had noe authoritie to limitt and appoynt the crowne of this realme and all the right thereof to bee treason.

The bill beinge read and speech expected, Mr Goodyeare, with some shewe of former care for that cause, entered to the utteraunce of a longe speech, and with wrested eloquence spake to this effect. First hee made a sollemne protestacion of his sincere fayth, truth and loyalty to her Majestie, to the state, and to the House. Hee shewed many of the singuler and true blessings which wee have by her Highenes' meanes, and religiouslie prayed for her preservacion; settinge out amplie *verborum phaleras et picte tentoria lingues.* But to the matter, his whole discouse stood uppon these three poyntes: what hee thought of the persons there assembled, what hee disliked in the matters of the bill propounded, and why hee did soe. Of the persons hee sayd hee verely beleeved the whole company in truth and true meaninge to have a care and harty well wishinge for her Majestie's safetie, acknowledginge and reposinge in her the verie anchor of our safety; but whether all were with a sincere meaninge to the state of the Crowne hee knewe not, but rather thought the contrary. But yet of the most and most honorable hee thought (hee sayd) nothing amisse; but some surely, hee sayd, were doubly disposed and with a favorable affecion bent for some body,

f.15   and some / espetiall party.

For the substance of the first bill, hee sayd hee was of cleere mynd, well likinge and approvinge the whole thereof except (quoth hee) that the same bee not already by former lawes provided for; and hereunto hee further added that if any man should say that the papistes doe not erre in sayinge or speakinge soe slaunderously of her Majestie, the same to bee alsoe taken for treason. For addicions concerninge the first which did respect cleerely the tyme past, and to make treason of a fault already committed, which at the tyme of the perpetratinge of the same offence was not in that degree, it was a president most perilous which might occasion such and soe great evilles as easily might not be conceaved: of the present tyme man's wisdome might iudge, of future tyme man's pollicie may reach to, but to call againe the tyme past, or to raise what is dead in any kind, man may not, nor in reason is to bee presumed. Hee sayd the like hath not bene seene, and where hee hath read thousandes of lawes, yet did hee never finde such a president, an extreamety rare and never practised, noe not in these the most greatest matters of fayth and religion that wee doe nowe soe earnestly intreate of. The enemy to God, the papist, (hee sayd) is most hatefull, yet is noe man so hardly bent as to have them punished, much lesse to suffer death, for what is past; whether her Majestie hath pardoned what is past wee doe not knowe, and whether her Highnes' pleasure bee that it should bee talked of, noe man hath yet made report. Withall it may happely occasion (sayd hee) dislike betweene her Majestie and the House, which were hatefull; but doubtles, hee prophesied,[63] it woulde occasion perill such and soe great that the greatest speaker therein, yea those who should give them most or best wordes, coulde give noe warrantize, nether is it that the sequell hereof may bee warranted for the right of a crowne, which wordes may not bee straytned. Thus much considered, and the pleasure of the prince beinge herein not determined, hee therefore advised (and more then soe, by wordes of vehemency) urged stay. Hee further sayd that the / penninge of the first article of the additions was clouded, involved with secret understandings, not to be understood but of such who more curiously would and more cuningly coulde looke therein then hee. For matters of title to the crowne hee sayd hee nether knewe any, nether durst to entermeedle or cause to take knowledge of any. And concludinge, againe hee sayd that for the obscuritie of the sence hee must needes condemne the same, since that *veritas est nuda, simplex et plana.*

f.15v

Sir Thomas Smyth, her Majestie's Principall Secretarie, nether condemning[64] or approvinge what before had bene spoken by Mr Goodyeare, made motion that the billes might bee devided, least the one might bee the hinderance of the other.

Mr Norton in his accustomed manner of naturall eloquence first shewed that that assembly should bee of speech free, soe that the same did not exceede the boundes of loyalty; and as in speech free, soe ought it alsoe to bee free of uniust slaunders and undeserved reproches. For soe much as might concerne him, hee protested that hee nether thought nor ment any other tytle then the sole preservacion of her Majestie, and to that end was he and the whole House (as hee supposed) setled and bent, she being of this realme,[65] not alone in respect of our goodes and landes the singuler stay, but of truth and religion, yea of all Christendome, not *magna* but in this world *spes sola*. And since that consultacion is noe other then *consultare in commune*, hee was aswell to remove the surmise of ambiguitie as the slaunder raised of any doublenes[66] in him. The wordes (quoth hee) are plaine these and noe other, that whatsoever

---

59. MS reads 'or'; this reading from Cott.Titus FI.

60. 'Or' supplied from Cott.Titus FI.

61. 'Against' repeated in MS.

62. MS reads 'traytors'; this reading from Cott.Titus FI.

63. MS reads 'promised'; this reading from Cott.Titus FI.

64. MS reads 'commendinge'; this reading from Cott.Titus FI.

65. MS reads 'religion'; this reading from Cott.Titus FI.

66. MS reads 'doubtes'; this reading from Cott.Titus FI.

person duringe the life of her Majestie have or shall imagine, intend or goe about the deposinge *etc.*, them and their heires to bee barred of any title. And (sayth hee) where ambition hath once entred such is the nature of the same that it never will bee satisfyed, and the thirst for a kingdome is unquenchable: withall in comon experience wee see that betweene two for a small matter in suite, when it shall f.16   passe / against the one, thoughe by perfect triall, yet will hee who looseth never acknowledge that hee hath either offered or defended an iniurie. Hee sayd, for workinge of greate matters greate tyme is required, and such[67] a mischeefe as to overthrow a crowne is not in a day compassed, and therefore what hereafter is thought or ment to bee executed is already begone, compassed and devised. Tyme must therefore bee taken, and therefore in tyme and at all tymes it is to bee prevented. Where it is sayd the like hath not beene seene, and a miracle made of this nowe as if there were noe former president never seene of the like, or ever heard of, it is noe longer since then Queene Marie's tyme, when to the parliament it was suggested that the congregations in the Citty of London assembled did use this kind of prayer to God, either to convert her or to confound her, it was enacted that every person who soe and in such sort had prayed, or who soe after should, should bee taken for a traytor.[68] The cause of Bennet Smyth is not soe strange nor soe longe since but it may bee remembred: his transgression was not such nor soe to bee adiudged of att the tyme of the offence perpetrated as it was afterwardes,[69] yet by authoritie of Parliament the offence precedent was from the old nature altered and hee, who before at the tyme of the offence untill the makinge of the lawe was not to have dyed, but to bee priviledged by his clergie, was nowe by an act made after executed by judgment.[70] And surely if in the case of a private man, as was this Bennet Smythe's, such consideracion and soe good discretion was, who can imagine it to bee odious? Noe, who is it that woulde not the like or greater care should bee had for a prince, and of soe good a prince as shee[71] for whom our conference now is? But yet wee are chardged with affeccions partiall, setled myndes, doublenes. Whether this speech bee an offence to the House hee earnestly craveth the judgment of the House, for that it might seeme by the gentleman's earnestnes who spake that someon his frend[72] f.16v   whom hee was bent to serve should bee touched: whereuppon for his owne / part hee eftsoones protested hee had noe certaine resolucion with himselfe of any tytle, but was to bee satisfied by the consent of that assembly howsoever, addinge further, if his motions might not soe in soart as they were like, he offered this proviso to bee added: that if any person who hath made any such claime shall disclaime and renounce all tytle duringe her Highnes' life, the same person *etc.* to bee then restored to the old state. *Quere*, for that Mr Norton in private speech with mee hereof sayth hee ment not soe.

Mr Comptroller, after some declaracion of greife, perceived the matter grewe to heate, as verely the greatest number of the House were more then moved with the vehemency of Mr Goodyeare's speech, and that men were disposed to talke at large of matters contrary or repugnant unto the bill. Hee therefore wished that the addicions from the principle bill might bee severed, for that the first came in and was exhibited to that House by her Majestie's learned councell, the other part was but the devise of a private man, which devise, thoughe it iustly deserved comendacions, yet was it not in his fancy to bee conioyned with that which came in otherwise.

Mr Snage argued to this effect: hee would in makinge of lawes playnes of speech to bee used, all entrapmentes to bee shunned and avoyded; and here hee moved why in the statute of Edward 3, whereby it is enacted that all such who shall endeavour, compasse or imagine the death of the kinge *etc.* should bee traytors *etc.*, should not that bee sayd sufficient, reachinge as farr and comprehendinge as much as this latter devise. For the regard of the tyme past hee could have noe likinge; and what was in Queene Marie's tyme practised (under correccion) hee tooke to be noe charitable president. Concerninge the authority of the parliament hee did conclude nothinge, but sayd it was a prevencion. |

Sir Frauncis Knolles shewed that hee could not utterly dislike of the conioyninge   f.17 of the addicions sith that they rise all of one grownd, and that they both are good and charitable. Whereof hee acknowledged her Highnes to have intelligence, and the cause already to have bene in conference by her councell. And for the word *hath* hee sayd it was noe such obsurditie, but with good zeale it might be mayntayned, and therefore such vehemency and sharpnes of speech was more then requisite, yea, more then convenient, and for the obscuritie[73] (hee sayd), of men that would meane well it could not bee misconstrued; and to stay and prevent devises past hee thought it but honest pollecy, which beinge noe otherwise used in a prince's case is not to be disliked. Hee made remembrance of her Highnes' unwillingnes to punishe such offences, and therefore, thoughe the lawe bee sharpe, yet such is her mildnes that if any have offended, for soe much as may concerne her person, surely hee thought it would not bee executed, and soe her clemency, tempered with authoritie, could never growe to crewelty. Wherein what his conscience was hee thought not fitt to make further shewe thereof, but simply and playnly hee would deale therein, not meaninge to treate in such sort as if to seeke to deserve any thinge or thanks of her Majestie for what hee did, yet hee did it alsoe as mindfull of his owne safety.

One other then spake, shewinge the wayght of the matter which then was in hand to rest aswell on[74] the generall safety of the subiectes as on the preservation of her Majestie's person, and therefore hee could not but approve the effect of the whole both in bill and addicion, albeit for the paynes in the bill expressed hee was somwhat variant from that which was there offered, and in the understanding of some wordes hee was doubtfull, as for the worde *compassinge* hee made some question, and of this *bodily hurt* hee had noe perfect intelligence, since | that hurt of   f.17v body may growe by greife of mynd, and greefe of mynd perhapps by small cause. He

---

67. MS reads 'musters'; this reading from Cott. Titus F1.
68. 1 & 2 Ph. & Mary, c.9 (1554-5) in *SR*, IV.254.
69. 'Afterwardes' supplied from Cott. Titus F1.
70. 2 & 3 Ph. & Mary, c.17 (1555) in *SR*, IV.292-3 removed Benet Smith's benefit should he be found guilty. But see 28 Hen. VIII, c.1 (1536), and 32

Hen. VIII, c.3 (1540) on benefit of clergy (*SR*, III.651-2, 749).
71. 'Shee' supplied from Cott. Titus F1.
72. MS reads 'frendes'; this reading from Cott. Titus F1.
73. MS reads 'obsurditie'; this reading from Cott. Titus F1.
74. MS reads 'one'; this reading from Cott. Titus F1.

also sayd that savinge in the statute of 27 Henry 8, hee hath not read it.[75] But further hee sayd that hee who would not allowe her for lawfull Queene, in his conceipt should also bee a traytor; but for the speakinge of these most slaunderous wordes of heretique, infidell, schismatique, *etc.*, hee would not any man to bee for the first offence taken as a traytor, for that the not acknowledginge of the supremacy, beinge a farr greater offence, is but the payne of *premunire*. And therefore, except the same offence might alsoe bee made treason, hee could not like thereof; but if it should soe seeme to them good that it should bee, as hee indeede wished, then was hee well pleased to put them both to one predicament. And for the word *heretique* hee sayd that the papistes all of force must bee enforced to say her Majestie is one, or that they themselves must bee content to carry the name and to bee noted *nomine*, as they are *re et veritate*, heretiques: which name they willingly will not beare. Hee further sayd that with the rest of those wordes of slaunder hee thought it might doe well to insert the name papist ('that if any should say her Majestie to be an infidell, papist, or heretique, *etc.*, to bee a traytor'), for that some say in these dayes there are who doe not spare to say her Majestie is of an other religion then is published, and that it is the sole doinge of her councellors whereby the doctrine (in sort as it is) is[76] thus published, and not hers. Hee alsoe addeth that his wishe was noe man might bee attainted of these wordes except the speech or publicacion might bee testified by two wittnesses. For the addicions hee sayd assuredly they might not bee severed from the first bill, not

f.18   alone as matters material dependinge on the / first bill, but stretchinge soe farr to the maintenaunce of the first that without them the first may seeme to bee nothinge. For, sayd hee, there can bee noe remedy provided except the cause of the greefe bee knowne and the same cause removed, whereof the rebells of the north gave cleere experience: for doubtles when they pretended the reformance of religion, they sought to rent upp the grownd and subverte the stay thereof, which was her Majestie's person, and by them hee wished us to learne at last and weighe wiser. Hee sayd the court of Chauncerie will straitly decree for savinge and quiet keepinge of a quiet possession, oft lookinge to and orderinge thinges[77] before past; and shall not the court of Parliament doe the like for the tytle of the crowne? And the auncient lawes of the realme, hee sayd, doth mayntaine the same, as longe before the 35 Henry 8 the statute of 5 Edward 3 in such like cases hath ordayned that the heire for the father's offence shalbe punished. *Consule locum citatum.*[78]

This man's speech by Mr Munson in the whole was mayntayned, and by reason doubtles by good force warranted, which for some causes I cannot write. This I remember in the end he concluded further, that it were horrible treason in his conscience to say that the parliament hath not authoritie to determine of the crowne, for then woulde ensue not alone the annihilatinge of the statute of 35 Henry 8 but that the statute made in the first yeare of her Majestie's raigne of recognicion should alsoe bee made voyd, a matter contayninge greater consequent then convenient is to bee uttered.

Mr Hennage moved the House to this effect that ether the bill from the addicions should bee severed, or both to bee referred to the Queene's learned councell to

f.18v   consider of the conveniencie thereof and then / by them to bee exhibited *etc.* But of his opinion he yeilded noe further proofe.

Mr Longe, a yonge gentleman, woulde have proved the word *have* and a regard of the tyme past not to bee amisse, for that at the tyme of the offence the malice of the offender was as greate as it is nowe at this present.

Mr Fleetwood endeavoured to prove the overchardginge of a bill with larger wordes then was convenient, and more provisoes then to the purpose, to have bene oft the overthrow of that which was truly ment, wherein the cunninge adversary when hee knoweth not howe to subvert directly hee will by this meanes easily and subtilly insert more, pretendinge a face of more forwardnes then the rest, when indeede his hart is bent to the hinderance of the whole, and to speake directly his shame should bee to greate. For proofe and experience hereof hee remembred the conning of the prelates in Henry 4['s]tyme, and after in Edward 4 his tyme, when Kinge Edward required the suppressinge of all such abbies as Kinge Henry 6 had erected: to hinder this, contrary to the king's meaninge, some woulde needes add the colledges in Cambridge which by him were alsoe founded, to the which when by noe[79] meanes the House may bee induced, as well the intent of the first as of the last was subverted. The like alsoe hee remembred of the 2 yeare of King Henry 7 in the matter of treasons which all men would have yeilded to, the counterfeite frendes heaped in to give the kinge free libertie of restitucion to whome hee woulde of all, both goodes and possessions, whereof the inconvenience beinge seene, stay was made of the whole: soe that what men may not directly without face of further frendshippe, they doe covertly. Hee concluded therefore it were well and most safety to make two bills *etc*. And to bee referred to the Queene's learned counsell as Mr Hennage had devised.

Mr Seriant Manwood, first answearinge the meaning[80] of the word *bodely hurt*, hee sayd it must be intended when violence or force is done or offered to the bodie and not otherwise nor els where; and whether the wordes / of slaunder should bee   f.19 treason hee thought that thereof there was greate reason it should bee, for (quoth hee) who soe shall affirme her Highnes to bee an heretique dothe doubtles wishe her the[81] paines of an heretique (that is) to be burnt *etc*. Hee further would have to bee added to these wordes of the bill, 'that who soe shall imagine, goe about, clayme *etc*.', this much more: 'that who soe shall affirme himselfe to have tytle, to bee a traytor'. Hee was of further opinion that it could bee noe clowding[82] of the bill to have a matter of the same nature added, beinge alsoe provided for the same purpose, a good consequence and necessarily concurringe with the effect of the bill. And for the authoritie of the parliament hee sayd that it coulde not in reasonable construccion

75. Presumably the reference is to 28 Hen. VIII, c.7 (1536) in *SR*, III.655-62, though the term 'bodily hurt' is not used as such. 26 Hen. VIII, c.13 (1534) in *SR*, III.508-9, talks of 'bodily harm', and 25 Hen. VIII, c.22 (1533-4) in *SR*, III.473 mentions 'peril to the person', as does 28 Hen. VIII, c.7.

76. 'Is' supplied from Cott. Titus F1.

77. 'Thinges' supplied from Cott. Titus F1.

78. 'Shalbe . . . *citatum*' supplied from

Cott. Titus F1. 35 Hen. VIII, c.3 (1543-4) in *SR*, III.959; even if 25 Ed. III is here intended, the claim (as here expressed) is odd.

79. MS reads 'more'; this reading from Cott. Titus F1.

80. Blank in MS, supplied from Cott. Titus F1.

81. 'The' supplied from Cott. Titus F1.

82. Cott. Titus F1 and SP Dom. Eliz.46/166 have 'clogging'.

bee otherwise, for who soe shall deny that authority, doth in truth deny the Queene to bee Queene or the realme to bee a realme. *Quere dum allogorye yey*[83] *enduce de un neelde trayant lee threede.*

There were hereof other speeches, as by Mr Alford of the[84] obscuritie, and Mr Dalton in answeare and defence of the written wordes, but nothinge more then before in effect was sayd.

This day Doctor Lewes and Doctor Yale were sent from the lordes of the over house unto us with a bill amonge them agreed uppon to this effect, that treasurors, receavers, collectors, *etc.* should not convert her Majestie's money to their owne private use, nor wilfully to consume the same, which if they shoulde doe then that offence to bee fellony, provided that the debt must bee above 300[li]. *Enter auters le cause de ceo est le faite de le S[or] Treasurer per 30000[li] enstall et ceo fait discovert per Brinigam de Ireland per grand parte.*[85]

Aprill xiij
f.19v

A bill for the Haberdashers of London *etc.*, whereby it was prayed to bee ordayned that the former lawes for the true makinge of hatts[86] might be revived and / for the limitacion of the penalties, the moytie whereof they prayed might bee to the Company of the Haberdashers *etc.* And further that it might bee enacted that the government and oversight of the artificers usinge this trade might bee to the master and wardens of the company within the citty of London.

The bill of the former day sent from the Lordes concerninge collectors was read, to the which Master Henry Smyth spake, commendinge the bill with many wordes, and thought convenient that thereunto might thus much more bee added: that if any debtor of the Queene's whose debt is already enstalled should have by any meanes any landes accrewed unto him, that the same might bee extended, any conclusion or agreement to the contrary notwithstandinge.

A bill for repeale[87] of the statute made 2 Edward 6 concerninge usury, and revivinge of the statute made *anno* 3 Henry 8, was the first tyme read and nothing sayd thereunto.[88]

A private bill for the makinge of cloathes within the towne of Shrouesbury, and for repealinge of the former lawe, was then the first tyme read.[89]

A bill against all[90] symonicall dealings, wherein it is prohibited for the patron to have any profitt for him or for any other out of the benefice *etc.* and noe lease to bee made by the parson but to his curate, and the parson to make[91] his residence at the parsonage by the space of 60 dayes every yeare at the least, what cause of dispensation whatsoever *etc.*[92]

Thomas Snagge treated hereuppon, shewinge that the cause of the slaunder which the papistes have against the Church of England, in that they say coblers, tinkers, taylors, millers, *etc.* are of the ministery, groweth hereby, that the livings are detayned by the patrons / from the spiritualty in their owne handes to theire owne private uses, whereas the first originalles of the reasons of patronages beinge considered it appeareth that nothinge is left to the patron of right. The manner of their originall hee shewed ar lardge, and that the same was in graunt *Deo et ecclesie,* and concluded that the patron hath nothinge but a bare nominacion, in deed (if it bee truly used) worth or to bee valued at, since that dealinge sincerely hee is nether to respect comoditie, blood, affection or frendshippe *etc.*

f.20

A bill against vagaboundes was first read: the contentes I writt not.

Mr St Johns moved that an old bill before thys tyme exhibited into the House concerninge this matter might bee perused *etc.*

Mr Saunders[93] endeavoured to prove this lawe for beggars to bee oversharpe and bloody, standinge much on the care which is to bee hadd for the poore, sayinge that possible it might bee with[94] some travill had by the justices to releive every man at his owne house and to stay them from wandringe. His experience hee shewed, and what was done in the county of Worcester.

Mr Treasurer talked to this effect, that hee would have a Bridewell in every towne, and every tipler in the countrey to yeild twelve pence yearely to the mayntenance thereof.

Doctor Willson, the Master of the Requestes, argued thus, that poore of necessity wee must have, for soe Christ hath given untill his latter cominge; and as that is true, soe sayd hee alsoe that beggers by Gode's word might not be amongst his people, *ne sit mendicus inter vos.* His experience hee shewed throughe the greatest part of Christendome, concludinge that such loosnes and[95] lewdnes was noe where as here. Hee sayd it was noe charity to give to such a one as wee knowe not, beinge a straunger unto us. Thus, sayd hee, did the Locreses constitute by their lawes; even as of theeves did the Gretians iudge of them. To the / paine of the constable for their remisse dealings hee wished might bee enioyned imprisonment.

f.20v

Thus much beinge hereof in effect spoken, it was resolved and concluded that certaine to the number of fifteene should by the House have in comaundement to peruse all old devises and to consider of a newe bill to be drawne by a day assigned, which was the 17 of Aprill.

A private bill for one Mr Skevington[96] was read whereby was supposed a deceite practised by one Sacheverill for conveyinge of landes contrary to the true meaninge, by subtill forginge of a false deede in place of the true deede, which was read. It

[April xiv]

83. MS reads '*peye*'; this reading from Cott. Titus F1.
84. 'The' supplied from Cott. Titus F1.
85. The specific reference appears to be to Sir Henry Sidney (see HMC *De L'Isle and Dudley*, I.378, 423-4, 440.) Part of the complicated process of keeping track of royal revenue collectors' debts may been seen in the shrieval accounts ('states and views' sections of the memoranda rolls, PRO E368), and two of Sir Henry Sidney's debts appear on sheriff John Smith's shrieval account for Kent for the year 1600-1 (PRO E368/514).
86. Probably 7 Ed.VI, c.8 (1552-3) in *SR*, IV.172, reviving 22 Ed.IV, c.5 (1482-3) in *SR*, II.473-4.
87. MS reads 'report'; this reading supplied from Cott. Titus F1.
88. The Acts are 5 & 6 Ed.VI, c.20 (1551-

2) in *SR*, IV.155, and 37 Hen.VIII, c.9 (1545) in *SR*, III. 996-7.
89. 8 Eliz., c.7 (1566) in *SR*, IV.489-90.
90. MS reads 'the'; this reading from Cott. Titus F1.
91. MS reads 'made'; this reading from Cott. Titus F1.
92. Bill E (*CJ*, I.84).
93. Cott. Titus F1 reads 'Mr Sandes'; neither name appears in the (incomplete) list of members for this parliament in the Cheshire RO, DLT (formerly de Tabley additional MSS, no. 6.
94. MS reads 'without'; this reading from Cott. Titus F1.
95. MS reads 'of'; this reading from Cott. Titus F1.
96. Thus, and also in SP Dom.Eliz.46/166; Cott. Titus F1 has 'Sherington', Rawlinson C 680 has 'Skennington'.

shewed the confession of Sacheverell and thereuppon prayeth restitucion with dischardge of all mayne incumbrances duringe such tyme as it was in the possession of Sacheverell.

Mr Fleetewood endeavoured to prove that all such sinister, faulse, fraudulent, or covenous dealings being opened in that place, albeit that the party pray not redresse, yet beinge made apparant, by that highe court ought not to bee pretermitted without due consideracion and convenient punishment to bee by the House assigned, and the party to bee brought to the barr of that House. For proofe thereof hee shewed in the tyme of Kinge Henry 4 that the abusinge of one of that House cominge home into his countrey for what hee had done or spoken in the House, was after adiudged of there in that place, and a lawe presently made for what before was not thought on.[97] The like hee shewed to bee done in Henry 8 tyme concerninge an examinacion had at Seriantes Inne *etc.*[98] Hee remembred a president of one John Rue, for that hee meaninge to have cousoned a merchant of London in sale of a certaine sume of money unto him due to bee payd out of the Exchequer as hee pretended, whereas of truth the money was before receaved by him who soulde the debt: judgment was given for that subtiltie, of the losse of his goodes, the profittes of his landes, and of imprisonment perpetuall.[99] For every conspiracie the judgment is by lawe (sayd hee)

f.21   *vulnus,*[100] even as in the case of attaint, to have the house turned upp, the / meadowe eared *etc.* Hee shewed alsoe that in the tyme of Edward 3 one meaninge to have the price of woolls to fall gave out that there was likelyhood of warres to bee bettweene the Kinge of England and the Kinge of Denmarke, by which meanes the traffique of the Staple was like to be stayed: whereuppon it was presently ordayned that hee should bee banished, thoughe that for that purpose there were noe lawe before.[101]

A private bill was read for the ereccion of a free schoole in Southwarke.

Mr Strickland exhibited a bill for reformacion of the Booke of Comon Prayer to this effect: first, for takinge away of copes, surplesses, *etc.*; then for the needeles confirmacion of children (as hee tearemed it), the childishe askinge of questions of the children at baptisme, the kneelinge at the communion, the ministracion of the sacramentes in private houses, the givinge of a ringe at marriage, and such like, that without these matters the booke might bee established.

Mr Treasurer reasoned to this effect, that if the matters motioned to bee reformed were hereticall, then verely it is presently to bee reformed; but if they are but matters of ceremony then it behooveth to referre the same to her Majestie who hath authoritie as cheefe of the Church to deale therein. And for us to meddle with matters of her prerogative (quoth hee) it were not expedient. Withall hee sayd what cause there might bee to make her Majestie not to rone[102] and ioyne[103] with those who seeme to bee earnest, wee are not to search: whether it bee for that orderly and in tyme shee hopeth to bring them all with her, or what secrett cause or other scrupelositie there may bee in princes, it is not for all sortes to knowe.

Mr Comptroller argued to this effect as afore, commendinge the zeale, but the place and tyme (hee sayd) was not fitt, and since wee have acknowledged her to bee supreme head, wee are not in these petty matters to rune before the rule, which to doe

f.21v   and wherein to offend were folly. Howe forwardly wee were hee did referre to / our owne consideracions, insinuatinge in some sort that our headie or hasty proceedings contrary and before lawe, did rather hinder then helpe.

Hereuppon one Mr Pistor,[104] a gentleman betwixt the age of l and lx yeares, desired to bee heard, and with a grave and seemely countenance and a good naturall eloquence shewed howe conscience enforced him to speake and rather to hazard his creditt then to the offence of his conscience to bee silent, albeit hee would willingly acknowledge that many hundredes of that honorable and worshippfull assembly were well able to teach him, and hee indeede willinge to learne of them. All the matters of his greife was that in matters of most importance, standinge us uppon for our soules, stretchinge further and higher to every of us then the monarchy of the whole world, was either not treated of, or soe slenderly that after nowe tenne dayes continuall consultacion nothinge was concluded. Those causes hee shewed to bee Gode's, the rest all are terrene, yea trifles in comparison, call ye them never soe greate, or pretend ye that they import never soe much: subsedies, crownes, kingdomes, he knewe not, hee sayd, what they were in comparison. This hee sayd hee knewe, whereof hee most thanked God, that *primum querite regnum Dei et hec omnia adijcientur vobis.* This rule is the direccion, and this desire shall bringe us to the light whereupoon wee may stay, and then to proceede for the rest, for in his word and by him wee learne, as sayth St Paul, to correct, reforme, *etc.* Our very home truly is not here, for *non habemus hic permanentem,* and the justice of God, hee sayde, moved terror unto all. Which hee seemed to meane concerninge the bill before mencioned, not makinge any mencion of Mr Stricklande's propositions; and soe did hee sett it forth with vehemency that there lacked noe modesty and with such eloquence that it nether seemed studied or over much affected, gravely and learnedly throughe the whole, and noe / whitt too longe but with good likinge.

f.22

After him Mr Robert Snagge did speake, and farre after indeede for order, proofe, or matter. Hee entered into the discourse of Mr Stricklande's articles and seemed to mayntaine them [except] this,[105] namely not to kneele at the receavinge of the communion,[106] but rather if a lawe thereof should bee made to ly prostrate, to shunne the old superstition, or otherwise to sett every man at libertie in this behaulfe according to his devotion; hee iudged it to bee nothinge contrary to the prerogative,

97. The reference is probably to Haxey's case, though it is not impossible that Fleetwood, or the diarist, has confused Henry IV and Henry VI and that Thomas Young is intended: C. Wittke, *The History of English Parliamentary Privilege* (Ohio, 1921), 23-5.

98. Strode's case? (See *SR*, III.53-4.)

99. I cannot trace this case, though Mr J. Barton tells me that the procedure by complaint to Parliament and reference to the King's Bench was usual enough. No year-book for 19 Ed.III was available in 1571, and there seems to be no summary in Fitzherbert's *Abridgement*: it may be that the reference here is wrong.

100. MS reads '*vialuns*'; this reading from Cott.Titus F1.

101. This seems to be based upon one of the charges brought against a Lombard in a case of concealment of the king's customs (43 *Ass.*, pl.38). I owe this reference to Mr J. Barton.

102. I.e. run.

103. 'Ioyne' supplied from Cott.Titus F1.

104. MS reads 'Pistory'; this reading from Cott.Titus F1, which agrees with the contemporary list of members for this parliament.

105. Cott. Titus F1 reads 'them, thus'.

106. 'At the . . . communion' supplied from Cott.Titus F1.

and these direccions hee thought good to bee left out of the booke which shoulde bee a lawe *etc.*

In fine it was ordered the Queene's Majestie first to bee made privie before wee shoulde any further proceede therein.

The bill for the commission of shewers[107] *etc.* was the third tyme read, agreed uppon, and sent by xij of the House to the Lordes.

One Mr Carleton exhibited a bill into the House against lycenses, dispensations, faculties, and rescriptes to bee by the Archbushoppe of Canterbury graunted contrary to the word of God, and for the reversinge of the statute made in the 25 Henry 8,[108] by which statute the Bushoppe of Canterbury is made as it were a pope, procured by the bushopps of that tyme, and a liberty to fill upp full an authoritie, as by readinge of the statute may bee noted (as hee sayd).

Mr Alford, learned in the civill lawes, argued to this effect, that of necessitie it must bee that those dispensations for mariage and for non residencie must depend uppon the discretion of some body, and not soe presisely, or with soe possitive a lawe to bee ruled that there should never bee varience from the written word. Absence of a preacher imployed in ambassies or otherwise for greater matters may fall out to bee more convenient for the service of a good Christian profession then to bee ever tyed at home to the stake. The like hee sayd of marriages to bee stayed at tymes. Withall hee sayd the office of / faculties is aswell to the prince's profitt as the archbushopp's, which by this bill is not medled with, and soe the mischeefe cheefely ment to be redressed nothinge looked into.

Mr Elverton argued to this effect: first, hee sayd he thought noe Christian woulde reason to the contrary of that bill since that it was onely provided that lycences shuld not bee graunted against the word of God. As for discretion talked of, hee knewe not what hee ment, but discretion (hee sayd) it was not to talke of any thinge out of the bill, and for discretion to make diversitie of tymes hee knewe none. But this statute hee thought did not reach to helpe that which is indeede the sore, that is the provicion or constitucion which yet resteth in force this notwithstandinge; and for the liberty of any Christian bushoppe which may bee a tender point[109] to search contrary to the expresse word of God, hee thought it needles.[110]

Mr Dalton hereuppon sayd that hee was of mynd that the bill was made nothinge, nor nothinge therein contayned: for the bushoppe, hee sayd, can doe nothing contrary to the word of God.

Mr Biddle to the contrary provinge, if these lawes of Parliament (quoth hee) are to bee performed uppon certaine payne, and albeit the lawes be pursuaunt the word of God, yet the penallty may bee dispensed, which for the matter of discretion motioned to rest in some body; and for diversity of tymes hee sayd somwhat, but not much materiall.

Mr Seriant Manwood shewed the cause of the bill to bee the pretence of greefes which first are to bee shewed and then to bee considered. The meaninge of the lawe hee approved, but how farr the same might stretch hee knewe not, and therefore hee thought requisite that there should bee a perticuler declaracion of the greifes and what the abuses were which are intended to growe by these lycenses, for to conclude without knowledge and in a generality it were overmuch obsurd. /

f.22v

Mr Fleetewood learnedly and withall pleasantly argued of this word *discretion*.   f.23
Hee sayd hee had read it oft, and that hee had beene troubled with it, as in this: 'the
Queene is sworne to minister justice with mercy and discretion.' What mercy is (hee
sayd) hee knewe, but what discretion was hee would gladly learne. Hee sayth it
cometh of the word *discerno*,[111] to see, but that is uncertaine. Hee sayd that a good
corner of England was governed by wisdome and discretion: hee sayd the lawe is it
should bee soe, but when the execucion[er]s of this statute are to deale to their
likings, if a poore man have lawe on his side then they say their discretions will not
serve them, and when conscience doth give it him then they say the lawe is against
them. And here did hee directly discipher and in a proper sort gird one who had
sayd in open unto [him], 'Mr Fleetewood, you are a lawyer but I am a judge'. This
man, sayd hee, might have witt, but hee nether had lawe, wisdome or discretion,
other than in his owne judgment: whom hee ment many did guesse. Hee alsoe sayd
that her Majestie had authority to execute lawes, but not to make lawes; and for
rescriptes or faculties what they[112] bee in all the world hee sayd for his life hee knewe
not. Hee sayd hee had read of *facultas loquendi* in Terence: the rest hee knewe
nothinge of. And for the dispensations of non residentes hee had not further regard
but, let the incumbent bee where hee list, in iudgment of the lawe hee is ever
inhabitinge on his benefice sayth the lawe. Hee further sayth that by the statute of
Carlill[113] it appeareth and it was enacted that churchmen should have the landes of
the Church to teach and instruct the kinge and his people, and for the keepinge of
house and other deedes of charity, which if they should not doe hee sayd they did
then breake the lawe, and howe farr the archbushopp's lycence to bee from his
church in such a case might serve hee would bee advised. In fine hee concluded as
Mr Manwood had done *etc*.

Seriant Lovelace shewed howe in the makinge of lawes two things are to bee
considered, the greife and the remedy. The greife wee see, which is that
such / dispensations and lycences have passed to the greate hinderance of God's due   f.23v
service. Howe nowe it may bee remedied is the question. If those who indeede have
or should have the chest of knowledge and will not orderly as they ought distribute
and give out the same, hee knewe not the helpe. For bee it (quoth hee) that such
lycences are utterly against the word of God, and the same cometh before the
temporall judge to bee tryed, yet cannot hee soe pronounce of it for that in such case
by the auncient lawes of the realme and by other the certificate of the bushoppe is to
bee expected, who whether hee will against himselfe[114] or his owne doings certifie, it
is not to bee doubted that hee will not, and soe the whole travell in makinge of the
lawe nothinge.

---

107. *Sic*, as in Cott.Titus F1, SP
      Dom.Eliz.46/166 and Rawlinson
      C 680.
108. 25 Hen.VIII, c.21 (1533-4) in *SR*,
      III.464-71.
109. 'Point' supplied from Cott.Titus F1.
110. Punctuation is clearly a problem here:
      SP Dom.Eliz.46/166 brackets

'which . . . search'.
111. MS reads 'biscerno'; this reading from
      Cott.Titus F1.
112. MS reads 'there'; this reading from
      Cott.Titus F1.
113. 35 Ed.I, c.1-4 (1306-07) in *SR*, I.150-2.
114. 'Who . . . himselfe' repeated in MS.

By rule of the House the bill was committed.[115]

Mr Norton made motion by warranty of this court, by the wisdome and godly care which in matters of waight was to bee imployed, that to avoyd the shamefull and most hatefull usage amonge the ecclesiasticall judges for deliveringe of clerkes convict uppon their oathes, and the manifest periury there[116] by their lawe against all lawe comitted, some order might bee taken. Hee proved it might not bee sayd a liberty of the Church except they will claime a liberty to sinne, wherein indeede their principall liberty hath stood, and for the which they have not spared to hazard, nay give theire[117] bodyes and soules to become traytors to God and man. Thus did that rebell Bushopp Beckett whose principall quarell and cause of all his stirre was that the kinge would have punished one of his marke, a preest, for an abhominable incest comitted by him, which triflinge fault forsooth, this holly saint could not brooke to bee rebuked by a temporall judge, *hinc illae irae.* Hee shewed it could not bee sayd a priviledge or encouragement to learninge, since it was noe other but a cloake for their naughtines, and for such as might bee of the Pope's suite, as well appeared in that it was allowed to none but to such as might enter their hollie orders, and not to one

f.24   who had two wives *etc.* He shewed / at lardge the circumstaunce of the practised order uppon the purgations of such clarkes, declaringe of truth soe disordered and hatefull doings that the whole House resolved to have care for redresse.

There was then next after by the pollicy of Sir Humpfrey Gilbert a motion made by one whom I knowe not, to have in talke the greifes which before had bene uttered in the House concerninge the deceiptfull dealings of treasurors and receavors, the reformacion of the Exchequer for homage *etc.*, the foule dealinges of promooters, purveiors *etc.*, and for the grauntinge of lycences by the Queene contrary to the forme of sundry statutes. Hereuppon Sir Humphrey Gilbert standinge uppe, and some introduction made in fyne speech to crave patience and tolleracion of the House, hee endevoured to prove the motion of Mr Bell made some dayes before[118] to bee a vayne devise to bee thought of and perrilous to bee treated, since that it tended to the derogacion of the prerogatives imperiall, which who soe should attempt, in his fancy could not otherwise bee accompted then for an open enemy: for what difference is it to say the Queene is not to use the priviledge of the Crowne, and to say shee is not Queene, since they are soe linked together that the one without the other possible may not bee. Wee are (sayd hee) to give to a comon constable the right and regard of his office, which if wee shall deny her, what is it els then to make her worse then the very meanest? And albeit experience hath proved such and soe great clemencie in her Majestie as might make us perhapps to forgett our selves, yet it is not to sport or venture much with princes; yea, let bee that our meaninges bee good and right honest, yet if it bee not soe thought of, howe *etc.* Then hee remembred the fable of the hare which fledd (uppon the proclamacion that all horned beastes should depart the Court) lest his eares might bee sayd to bee hornes. This did he further inculate with the significacion that if wee should in any sort meddle with these matters, her Majestie might looke to her owne power and thereby finding her validitie to suppresse the strength of the chalenged liberty, and to challenge and to use the same her own power any way, and to doe as did Lewis of Fraunce who delivered the crowne there[119] out of wardshippe (as hee tearmed it), which the sayd French

kinge / did upon the like occasion. He alsoe sayd other kings had absolute power,   f.24v
as Denmarke and Portugall, where, as the Crowne became more free, soe are all the
subiectes thereby rather made slaves. This speech of his was many wayes disliked as
implyinge many occasions of mischeefe, but for the tyme hee was not further
answeared then that it seemed hee did mistake the meaninge of the House and of the
gentleman the motioner, who woulde noe otherwise to bee taken nor otherwise for
the House to deale in the matter then to shewe their common greefes in due sort unto
her Majestie.

The parliament by the consent of the House was then, for that it was Easter eve,
adiurned untill the Thursday ensuing (*viz*) the 19 day of Aprill.

The Fryday in the forenoone, Mr Nowell preached at the Court; in the afternoone
Mr Doctor Cole preached at Paule's Crosse, the briefe of whose sermon was in[120]
the reportes of the doings of the xxij^th day of Aprill.

On Easter day in Paule's preached the Bushopp of London, the Munday at
the Spittle, Mr Nowell, the Tuesday in the same place Doctor Pearce, on the
Wednesday in the place aforesayd Mr Elmer: these two last sermons are in the
remembraunce of the parliament of the xxij^th day of Aprill. Duringe which tyme of
Easter Mr Strickland, soe often before mencioned, for the exhibitinge of the bill for
reformacion of ceremonies, and his speech thereuppon, was called before the lordes
of the Privy Councell and required to attend uppon them, and to make stay from
cominge to the House in the meane season.

First was read a bill intituled 'For the true making of Kentishe cloathes'. The   Aprill xix
substance of the bill was that noe cloathes should bee sould but in Blackwell Hall, at
the faires of Maydstone,[121] *etc*. This bill was not liked of many,[122] but not effectually
argued unto of any man for that it was the first readinge.

The bill for the reversinge of the statute of 1 Henry 5 and 34 Henry 6[123]
concerninge the warrantes given unto burroughes to choose their burgesses was read,   f.25
to the which noe man spake effectually untill Mr Warmcombe / of Hereford
standinge upp sayd to this effect, that it behooved all those which were burgesses to
see to that bill, for (quoth hee) this may touch and over-reach their whole liberties, as
not havinge whereunto to stay, but that lordes' letters shall from henceforth beare all
the sway; and to this effect was the whole that hee sayd.

Mr Norton first made explanacion of the meaninge of the bill to bee (as hee sayd)
to shame the imperfeccion of choyce, which is too oft seene, by sendinge of unfitt
men, and lest happely any thinge might bee obiected to the imperfeccion of the
parliamentes, which may seeme to bee scant sufficient by reason of the choyce made

115. 'By rule . . . committed' supplied from
Cott.Titus F1.

116. MS reads 'whereby'; this reading from
Cott. Titus F1.

117. MS reads 'the'; this reading from
Cott.Titus F1.

118. I.e. 7 April, f.7 & v.

119. MS reads 'then'; this reading from
Cott.Titus F1.

120. MS reads 'on'; this reading from
Cott.Titus F1.

121. MS reads 'Mardeston'; this reading from
Rawlinson C 680.

122. MS reads 'may'; this reading from
Cott.Titus F1.

123. 1 Hen.V, c.1 (1413), in *SR*, II.170; '34
Henry 6' is 23 Hen.VI, c.14 in *SR*,
II.340-2.

by burroughes, for the most part, of strangers, not burgesses, whereas by the possitive lawe noe man ought to bee chosen for burgesses but very resientes and inhabitantes. Hee sayd further that the choyce shoulde bee of such which were able and fitt for soe greate a place, without respect or priviledge of place, for that by reason of his beinge a burgesse it might not bee intended hee was any thinge the wiser. Withall hee argued that the whole body of the realme and good service of the same was rather to bee respected then the private regard of place or priviledge of any person.

　　Then sayd the Speaker, and prayed the opinion of the House whether they could like the bill should bee engrossed; and cominge to the question, some some sayd noe, the greater number seemed to say yea, whereuppon one standinge upp sayd thus, as farr as my memory may serve to report:

　　'I runne wholly with the pretence of the bill that burroughes decayed may bee eased and releived, knowinge assuredlie the same honorable for the realme, and in many respectes profitable and comodious for those who doe inhabitt the countreyes adioyninge to such decayed townes: that it is soe I will not stand to persuade. Howe farr this lawe may helpe them I knowe not; if they be decayed then it is most fitt for them that of their owne company there may bee some whoe feelinge their smart can best make relacion of their state, and knowinge their countrey may devise / of such helpes as without the hurt of other places may restore the old ruines. All things are in change, and nothinge soe suppressed downe but by grace may in tyme and by good pollicie bee againe raised upp.

f.25v

　　'But to open my meaninge shortly, the whole question is what sortes of men are to come to this court and publique consultation in Parliament, whether from every quarter, countrey, and towne there should come (as I might say) home dwellers, or otherwise men chosen by discretion, it forceth not whome, ne forceth it whence. I am surely of mynd that nether for the good service of her Majestie, safety of our countrey, or[124] standinge with that libertie which of right wee may challenge, beinge borne subiectes within the realme, this scope is to bee given or such loosenes of choyce to bee permitted. That the whole land of this realme wee knowe is to bee for three purposes imployed, and thereby three sortes of men as it were created, the one part given in ffrancke allmaine or[125] for devine service, to be used for the glory of God and ministracion of his word; the second part to bee houlden for defence against our enemies by the sword; the third for the mayntenance of our livelihoodes at home, and for necessary imploymentes here. Of these three growndes in the first division, there groweth to our knowledge three sortes of men: the ministers and teachers of the gospell, of whome wee must have care, and with whom in makinge of lawes wee must conferr if wee will bee Christians; the second are the nobility, knightes, and souldiers, the defendors and fortresses against our enemies; the third sort bee the providors, devisors, and executors of all things necessary, comodious or seemely for a settled estate which hath the happines to live where there is *pax et justitia*, for encrease of our wealthes, sustenance of our lives, the covering of our bodies, or what els soever is necessary for us. Such are the councellors, such bee the judges and ministers / of the lawes, such bee the tillers of the earth, such bee marchantes, such bee victuallers, and in this degree bee those who doe use manuary or mechanicall artes. Of [126] these all in like sort as the others regard, care, and respect must bee

f.26

hadd, they throughly consulted with, the generall and particuler estate is by them to bee knowne if wee meane to proceede for the publique weale or endeavour for the same a true perfeccion, these last sortes makinge one kinde, or are most ample and therefore most effectuall to bee dealt with as yeildinge to the rest supplement, *consilium et auxilium*. The second are most necessarily to bee thought of. The first are best and first to bee followed. But those all are to bee in one knott conioyned and as members of one body in one to bee used: we may in regard of religion lye in the dike, as the fable is, long enough,[127] without any our owne aydes, and if wee[128] doe nothinge but pray for the helpe of Hercules; wee may not trust alone to the sword least the comon knowne sayinge of Cicero shoulde turne to our shame, *parvi sunt foris arma nisi consilium domi*,[129] nether on preachinge or prayinge to God alone, since for drivinge away of a dogge there is, the countrey man sayth, some vertue in a stone if it bee conioyned with St John's Gospell. I meane that every part of the body should doe his owne part to the ayde of the other, the hand to helpe the hand, the foote the foote, *etc*. This hath moved our forefathers and on this grownd hath it growne that in this court where wee are to consider of all and, as occasion may serve, to alter, constitute or reforme all thinges as cause shall bee, that wee doe knowe all, and by the aydes of all sortes of men soe farre as may bee to helpe all. Howe may her Majestie or howe may this court knowe the state of her frontiers, or who shall make report of the portes, or howe every quarter, shiere, or countrey is in state? Wee who nether have seene Barwicke or St Michaelle's Mount can but blindlie guesse at them, albeit wee looke on the mapps that / come from thence, or letters of instruccions sent from thence: f.26v some one whom observacion, experience and due consideracion of that countrey hath taught can more perfectly open what shall in question thereof growe, and more effectually reason thereuppon, then the skillfullest otherwise whatsoever. And that they shoulde bee the very inhabitors of the severall counties of this kingdome who should bee here in tymes certaine imployed, doubtles it was the true meaninge of the auncient kings and our forfathers who first began and established this court might bee founde.

'But leavinge what I cannot reach unto – the first constitution and freedome of this court – I meane thus much of auncienty, the old president of Parliament writtes doe teach us that of every countrey their owne countreymen, and burroughe their owne burgesses, shoulde bee. The writt to the sheriffe of the shire and burroughe is directed soe; and the writts to the citties beinge counties is (quoth hee) "*vobis ipsis elegatur*[130] *duos cives etc.*" doth prove soe. The statute in *anno 1°* Henry 5 for confirmacion of the old lawe was therefore made, and not to create a newe unknowne lawe; and that other in the 34[131] of Henry 6 was therefore made to

---

124. MS reads 'of'; this reading from Cott. Titus F1.
125. MS reads 'of'; this reading from Cott. Titus F1.
126. MS reads 'if'; this reading from Cott. Titus F1.
127. 'Long enough' supplied from Cott. Titus F1.

128. 'If wee' supplied from Cott. Titus F1.
129. *De Officiis*, i.76.
130. *Sic*; '*elegate*' in Rawlinson C 680.
131. Omitted here and in Cott. Titus F1 and SP Dom. Eliz.46/166, supplied from Rawlinson C 680; but the statute is 23 Hen. VI, c.14 (see f.24v).

redresse the mischeefe which by breach of that old lawe did growe, doe conclude it
soe without contradiccion, soe that tyme it was thought fitt to continue the auncient
use, liberty, priviledge and conveniency of service. Wee knowe that such who have
spent their whole tyme in study or have seene alone the manner of goverment of other
nations, and can tell you howe the crowne of Fraunce is delivered out of
wardshippe, or otherwise to tell a tale of the Kinge of Castile and Portugall howe
they in makeinge of lawes use theire owne absolute discretions, the Kinge of
Denmarke useth the advise of his nobles alone, and nothinge of his comons, or paynt
you out the monstrous goverments of the comon people in some part of Germany, or
the mangled commonwealthes of the apes, or shadowes of the greate citties which
f.27   nowe are to bee seene in Italy: surelie / these men all, except they knowe alsoe our
owne homes, are not to bee trusted to conclude for our home affaires. Doubtlesse the
best learned for matters of comodity to bee raysed or to bee wrought in his owne
countrey may happely give place to his owne neighbour, even as wisely and
learnedly a gentleman sayd of late, in every continent according to the matter there
must bee discretion of men, as for merchandize the merchant, and soe forth *unicuique*
suo arte perito credendum: wee allowe it for a maxime. And I meane this wholly to noe
other end but since wee deale universally for all sortes and all places, that there bee
here of all sortes and all countreyes, and not (seing you list soe to tearme it) thus to
ease them of townes and burroughes that they may choose at liberty whom[132] they
list. Yet can I hardly call that a liberty which is contrary to that which the kinge or
queene comonlie graunteth as a free guift, and by these wordes, *et de maiori et uberiori*
gratia nostra etc. dedimus potestatem etc. quod de seipsis eligant[133] *duos burgenses*, or *duos cives*.
Wee take it to bee more for a man to have of his owne[134] then to have by any man's
discretion for another. It hath bene of late oft and well sayd that to nominate another
to a benefice is nothinge in value worth, but if it bee that a man may take the benefice
himselfe it is both valuable and estimable. It cannot hurt that is ever good for mee
if it bee ever tyed in most neerest sort unto mee; and on this reason yee say in lawe that
the estate tayle, which must continue in our onely bloode, is better then the estate in
ffee simple, which may goe further from us and to bee given to a straunger at
pleasure. Mischeefes and inconveniences there bee which may growe by this libertie,
but a mischeefe it might bee to mee and inconvenient alsoe perhapps to utter the
same.

'I will not speake thereof but dutifully, nether doe I see any thinge that is amisse at
this present. What was done an hundred yeares since I may tell safely, and even thus
it was: a duke of this realme wrote his letters to a cittie which I knowe, to this effect,
f.27v   whereby hee did signifie / that a parliament was to bee summoned in short tyme for
greate causes, hee was to crave the ayde of all his frendes and, reckoninge them
amonge the rest, hee wished them[135] of four undernamed to choose two. The letters
under the duke's seale are yet preserved. But heare you the answeare: hee was written
to with due humblenes that they were prohibited by lawe, they might choose none of
them. I will venture a little neerer. In Queene Marie's tyme a councell of this realme
(not the Queene's Privy Councell) did write to a towne to choose a bushopp's
brother (and a great bushop's brother it was in deede) whom they assured to bee a
good Catholique man, and willed them to choose to the like of him some other fitt

man. The councell was answeared with lawe; and if all townes of England had done the like in their choyce the Crowne hadd not beene soe wronged and the realme soe robbed with such ease at that parliament and truth banished as it was. What hath bene may bee, there is noe impossibilitie. It will bee sayd I mistake, it is not meant but that townes shall bee at liberty to choose whom they list. I say that that abilitie is the losse of libertie, for when by lawe they may doe what they will, they may not well deny what shalbee required. It is too truly sayd, *rogando cogit qui rogat potentior etc.* And I have knowne one, to avoyd a gentleman beinge neere him his offence, who was as hee knewe desirous to buy his land, did on small cause bynd himselfe to others not to alien his landes from his heire: this knowne, (I meane that hee was bound), the gentleman was contented to suffer him to keepe his owne quietly which otherwise hee woulde not have done. Surely lawe is the onely fortresse of the inferior, to the contrary of which lawe the greatest will not crave. Thoughe nowe at this present as there is cause (God bee praysed) wee neede to feare nothinge, yet hereafter what heretofore hath bene wee may feare, either for maintenance of factions, or mayntenance of mischeefe. Againe I say it may bee: what heretofore was possible againe may bee. Wee stand and have stood of late uppon the notorious manifestacion of the authoritie of the parliament; except withall you keepe the auncient / usage of the same, and withall endeavour the freedome thereof, in effect you doe nothinge (if I guesse aright).

f.28

'It is further sayd in some townes there are not men of discretion fitt: they bee not the wiser, sayd the gentleman which before spake, for that they are burgesses. I can never bee persuaded but that either the lord whose the towne is, bee the towne never soe little, or the steward (if that it bee the Queene's), or some good gentleman of the countrey adioynant will either assigne them one who knoweth the towne and can bee content to bee free amonge them and to serve by their appoyntment for their countrey and for them, or els for some reasonable ffee such as bee of their learned councell and who knowe them and their countrey will deale for them. I meane it not soe strictly that those who should bee chosen should bee dwellers in the towne, but to be either of the towne or towardes the towne, borderers and neere neighbours at the least, and to this effect I would the bill were framed.

'I stand too longe hereon and aboundance of matter occasioneth confusion. This is all: it was meant at the first, and first institucion of parliamentes, that men of every quarter and of all sortes should come to this court; that they should bee freely chosen, this in every age hitherto hath seemed best. To alter without cause is not convenient; to give every towne libertie may offer in tyme inconveniency; none soe fitt for every countrey as those who knowe the same; to choose of their owne it is a liberty, noe burthen; to loose then their liberty I thinke it a badd commodity, call it as you list, an ease[136] or howe els, by such kinde of release in easinge men of their wealthes or of some good part of their livinge beeshrewe too oft our charity. And in like sort and with like reason it seemeth to mee this lawe is inferred out of the preface of the same,

---

132. MS reads 'when'; this reading supplied from Cott.Titus F1.
133. Rawlinson C 680 reads '*eligatur*'.
134. MS reads 'more to have for a man in his owne'; this reading from Cott.Titus F1.
135. 'Them' supplied from Cott.Titus F1.
136. MS reads 'easy'; this reading from Cott.Titus F1.

for thus it is penned: "for as much as some townes are decayed and have not of their owne, lett every towne doe what they list". Of particuler propposition to make a generall conclusion it is against our rules, and nothinge, sayd the philosopher, more absurd[137] then *non causam pro causa*. Some townes cannot send fitt, therefore noe towne can sent fitt: it soundeth very strangely. If you seeke to helpe let the plaster bee

f.28v
fitt for the sore, and let not the salve bee stretched / too farre lest the whole and sound fleshe by the broade spreadinge of the salve doe either smart, frett, or fester. The medecine which healeth the sicke man may bee poyson for the sound and whole man. All citties and borroughs should not bee thought of alike; and yet all provided for as there is due cause. Let there bee therefore due consideracion howe to heale not to hurt. And I woulde wishe that according to the wayght of the matter it might be rather stared on then thus abruptly ruled over, and while wee flee Silla wee fall not into Caribdis: while wee say that burroughes cannot send to this highe court soe fitt men as bee convenient, that wee in alteringe the auncient usage, which is the onely warrant and sole stay of all freedome in Parliament, it may happely bee sayd wee have noe Parliament nowe within this realme, nor liberty at all for any such to bee houlden.'

Mr Bell in answeare of this did collect the substance of the whole which had bene sayd, and in lovinge discourse shewed that it was necessary all places should be provided for, and not burroughes onely, beinge but one member of the whole comon wealth; and for that some of them have nether wealth to provide fitt men, nor of themselves any in any sort convenient, hee thought not amisse if in respect of those manifest wantes convenient supply shoulde bee. But if without the venture of the warrant of Parliament such alteracion might not bee, hee then thought it not amisse to stay to bee advised. And for the obiection of the danger which may ensue by reason of the letters of noble men, hee coulde not (he sayd) but thinke convenient to prevent the same, and therefore wished that there might the penalty of 40[li] bee imposed uppon everie burroughe which shoulde make such eleccion at the nominacion of any noble man.

Mr Alford reasoned to this effect, that above all things necessary care ought to bee for the choosinge and havinge of fitt men to supply the place, that there bee noe imperfeccion, and therefore noted one great disorder, that very yonge men not experienced for learninge sake were oft chosen, throughe whose default hee knewe not, whether letters of noble men or affeccion in the countrey, their owne ambitions

f.29
or the careles account of the eleccion, or what els was the cause he knewe / not; but it was not as it shoulde bee, hee sayd it was to bee seene. Whereuppon hee woulde that none should bee of that House not of xxx yeares at the least. And for the choyce of townes men hee sayd hee was of this mynd, that Moyses and Aaron should bee conioyned together and that there should bee one of their owne, or some gentlemen neere them who had knowledg of the state of the countrey, and the other a man learned and able to utter the mynd of his opinion, since that the knowledg locked upp in the breast not beinge orderly opened, all is to noe purpose, and this part is requisite for consultacion as the other. Soe that hee seemed to conclude the lawe should bee in force for the one burgesse and at liberty for th'other.

There was noe man spake or offered to speake more hereof, but the opinion of the

House beinge asked, they thought it convenient to comitt it, and not bee engrossed.

The bill for the reversinge of the statute made in the first[138] yeare of Kinge Edward 6 concerninge usury and approvinge of the statute of Henry 8 was read the second tyme, to the which much was spoken.

First one Mr Clarke spake to this effect, that the referringe of punishment mencioned in the bill, beinge put to the ecclesiasticall judges for soe much was nothinge, for that they are ether to punishe by the civill lawe, comon lawe, or temporall lawe. The civill lawe would not ayde them, for that by the lawe there is allowance of usury *ad*[139] *centesimam usuram*,[140] the comon[141] lawe is abolished, and the temporall in that respect sayth nothinge: soe that the pretence may seeme to bee somewhat, but the effect thereby wrought is nothinge. Yet that it was ill, nether Christian nor pagan never denied. Aristotle beinge asked what usury was, hee sayd it was *preter naturam*, and therefore coulde not be defined.[142] And Plato beinge demaunded the same question, hee sayd it was *idem ut hominem occidere.*[143] St Augustine confirmeth the same.[144] And the very word of the Psalmes answeareth to the question, '*Domine, quis habitabit in tabernaculo tuo?*' he sayd, '*qui iuvat proximo suo et non decepit et qui pecuniam suam non dedit ad usuram.*'[145]

Mr Treasurer argued[146] to this effect, that the execucion of the lawe appertayneth to the Queene, the penalties and forfetures / of all which appertaine to her Highness[147] by her power to despence with the same. Whereby it ensueth that bee it ill, yet whether it shall as an ill bee punished it resteth in her[148] to judge of, and since the sore of the comon wealth is to bee taken away, yet thoughe the lawe bee tollerable, givinge some little liberty, and not allowing any thinge, whereas covertly to take usury away hee thought it impossible.   f.29v

Mr Wolley, hee first learnedly and artificially makinge an introduction to the matter, shewed what it might bee thought of for any man to endeavour the defence of that which everie preacher at all tymes, followinge the letter of the booke, doth preach against. Yet, sayd hee, it is convenient, and beinge in some sort used is not repugnant to the word of God. Experience hath proved the greate mischeefe which doth growe by reason of excessive takeinge to the destruccion of yonge gentlemen, and otherwise infinitely; but the mischeife is of the excesse and not otherwise, since to take reasonable or soe that both parties might doe good was not[149] hatefull, for to have any man to lend his money without comodity, hardly shoulde you bringe that to passe. And since every man is not an occupier that hath money, and some such indeede who hath not money yet may have skill to use money, except you should

---

137. MS reads 'obscured'; this reading from Cott. Titus F1.
138. *Sic*; see f.19v & n.
139. MS reads 'as'; this reading from Cott. Titus F1.
140. Justinian's *Codex*, iv.xxxii, 26, sect.2.
141. *Sic* in all MSS, except SP Dom.Eliz.46/166, which has 'canon'.
142. *Politics*, I, iii.23.
143. *Laws*, ix.870 and *Republic*, viii.555 deal with the social consequences of excessive

money-making.
144. Letter to Macedonius in *Fathers of the Church*, XX (New York, 1953), 301.
145. Psalm 15.
146. MS reads 'agreed'; this reading from Cott. Titus F1.
147. 'To her Highness' supplied from Cott. Titus F1.
148. 'In her' supplied from Cott. Titus F1.
149. 'Not' supplied from Cott. Titus F1.

take away or hinder good trades, bargaining and contractinge it cannot bee. God did not soe hate it that hee did utterly forbidd it, but to the Jewes amonge themselves onely, for that hee willed that they should live as breethren together, for unto all others they were at lardge, and therefore to this day they are the greatest usurers in the worlde. But bee it as it is indeede evill, and that men are men and noe saintes to doe all things perfectlie, uprightly or brotherly, yet *ex duobus malis minus malum eligendum est*; and better may it bee borne to permitt a little then to take away and prohibite utterly all traffique, which hardly may bee mayntayned generally without this. But it will bee sayd it is contrary to the expresse word of God, and therefore an ill lawe. If it were to appoynt men to take usury it were to bee disliked, but the difference is greate
f.30   betweene that and[150] permitting or allowinge, / and suffer a matter to passe unpunished. It may bee sayd that *nudum mundum pactum*[151] *non parit obligationem*, but there must bee somwhat given in consideracion; let bee that there is nothinge given[152] of the lenders, yet there is somwhat *simile, et omne bonum exemplum et omnis lex in se aliquam habet mali*, for that some body shall wringe thereby. Wee are not (quoth hee) soe straitned to the word of God that every transgression should bee severely punished here: every vayne word is forbidden by God, yet the temporall lawe doth not soe utterly condemne it. As for the wordes of the scripture, hee sayth the Hebrewe soundeth this in answeare of this, '*quis habitabit in tabernaculo tuo?*' it is sayd, '*qui not dat pecuniam suam ad morsum*':[153] soe that it is the bytinge and oversharpe dealinge which is disliked and nothinge els. And this hee sayd was the mynd and interpretacion of the most famous learned man Beza in these dayes and of one Bellarmine[154] who sayd that the true interpretacion of the Hebrewe word is not *usura* but *morsus*.

Mr Doctor Willson, Master of the Requestes, first shewinge that in a matter of such waight hee could not shortlie speake, and acknowledginge hee had throughly studied the matter, desired therefore the patience of the House. First endeavouringe to prove that the comon state may bee without usury, then shewed howe even the ignorant of God or his lawes, findinge the evilles thereof, by their lawes redressed it and utterly prohibited the use thereof: as the Athenians who caused all the writings taken for interest money to bee burnt; the like did Lycurgus[155] by a lawe made by him, and seinge the fyre (sayd hee) hee did never see soe fayre a flame as those bookes yeilded. Hee then made a definition of usury, sheweinge that it was the takinge of any reward or sume over and above the due debt. To take any thinge for that which is not myne is roberie: forthwith uppon the delivery of lone money it is not myne, and the lawe is that *mutuum*[156] must bee free. And here shewed the difference betweene locacion and *mutuum*,[157] the one implyinge a contract, the other none.[158] Hee remembred out of Ezechiell and other the prophettes sundry places of scripture, and
f.30v   vouched St Augustine his saying that to take but a cupp of wyne is / usury and damnable. This hee seemed to say in aunsweare of that which before had bene pronounced, that it was noe usury except it were *morsus*. Hee shewed losse may growe by usury: first to the Queene, then to the common[159] wealth. To the Queene in this, that men not usinge their owne money, but findinge greater gaine in usury, doe imploy the same that way, soe that her custome must decrease. To the comonwealth, for that who soe shall give hire for money is to raise the same in the

sale of his comodity: all trades shall bee taken away, all occupacions lost, for eich man seekinge most ease and greatest gaine without hazard or venture will further imploy his money to such use. Hee shewed it to bee soe hatefull in the judgment of the comon lawe that an usurer was not admitted to bee a wittnes, nay after his death to the comon sepulture of Christians. And for that this discourse had bene longe, hee inserted this tale with meaninge for recreation of the hearers. In Italie (quoth hee) a greate knowne usurer beinge dead, the curate denied him the comon place of buriall. His ffrendes made suite: the preist would not heare. In fine the suitors sought then of a pollcie to bringe to passe that hee might bee buried in the church, which was this. The parson of the church accustomably did use to have his bookes carried from his house to the church on his asse, and the asse by oft goinge was not to bee driven, but knowinge his joyrney, as soone as hee was laden woulde of himselfe goe to the church doore. They desired the parson his asse might carry the dead body and where hee should stay, the carcasse to bee layd; to which request the preist agreed. The body was layd on the asse who feelinge a greater burthen then hee was used to beare did runne towardes the towne, never stayinge untill hee came to the comon place of execucion. This tale merily tould, hee then againe entred to his matter and proved the condemnacion of usurie and userers by th'authoritie of the Nicen and divers other Councells.[160] Hee shewed how the devines doe call usury a spyder, an aspis, a serpent, and a devill, *etc.* Hee shewed howe in nature the offence[161] of homicide and of usury are to bee compared, and by examples proved them to bee the ruines of the / comonwealth when such practises for gaine should bee, as that of the   f.31 comonwealth of Rome *etc.* The manner of exchange nowe used in London and howe much abused hee shewed, a thinge in old tyme not practised but by the kinge, as it was in Edward 3['s] tyme, when thereby the kinge obtained such treasure and soe excessive wealth that it was first wondered at, then guessed that it grewe by the science of alchimistry. Hee heere shewed the practise of the Lowe Countreys, of Germany, and namely the doinge of the Fulkers to the verie beggeringe of greate and mighty princes. Hee vouched the authoritie of Sir John Cheeke in that place concerninge the same matter, and the mynd of the auncient Englishe lawe writer [blank][162] who sayth that the offence of usury in life the bushoppe is to punishe, but after his death his executors shall not have his goodes, but they appertaine *ad*

150. 'That and' supplied from Cott. Titus F1.
151. MS reads '*partem*'; this reading from Cott. Titus F1.
152. 'Given' supplied from Cott. Titus F1.
153. MS reads '*morsam*'; this reading from Cott. Titus F1.
154. Blank in MS; supplied from Cott. Titus F1.
155. Blank in MS; supplied from Cott. Titus F1.
156. MS reads '*mutum*'; this reading from Cott. Titus F1.
157. MS reads '*comituum*'; this reading from Cott. Titus F1.

158. MS reads '*nomen*'; this reading from Cott. Titus F1.
159. MS reads 'comomon'.
160. MS reads 'and proved by the authority of the Councell Niceen, Agathensis and others there condempned of usury and usurers'; this reading from Cott. Titus F1.
161. MS reads 'office'; this reading from Cott. Titus F1.
162. In all MSS: see Ranulphus de Glanville, *De Legibus et Consuetudinibus Angliae*, VII.16.

fiscum.[163] Hee concluded that the offence in his conscience should be adiudged felonie.

Mr Bell sayd this matter beinge soe ample had enforced greate speech, and was for cuninge men a fitt theame to shewe their wittes and skills, yet (sayd hee) it standeth doubtfull what usury is: wee have noe true definition, and in our lawes wee have little written thereon but this, *usura non currat super infantem,* and not much more.[164] But to answeare the obiections: where it is intended that this not punishinge of it by the temporall judge may seeme to bee an approbacion of it, or to leave it to the Church may seeme as if we had noe care, for that hee thinketh to put over an offence to an other judge may not bee soe sayd, if[165] to the Church it may appertaine and they may well correct it. Hee further shewed that the priviledge of the Church is by statute uppon this poynt expressed, namely *de articulis cleri.*[166] Hee sayd wee must not curiously sift Cicero his paradoxes and pronounce that *peccata sunt equalia, hoc est quod omne peccatum est peccatum,* and noe further but to every man accordinge to his transgression to make a reasonable payne.[167] Thoughe he who stealeth two pence doth aswell steale as hee who stealeth an hundreth powndes, yet wee have degrees: wee have *petite* larcenie and that which is greater, both faultes, both to bee punished, both to bee hated, but difference there is in ministringe the paine, yeoven[168] accordinge to the / greatnes or smallnes of the offence. For the one there is death, for the other not soe. In the statute for punishinge of periury, 5 Elizabeth,[169] there are sundry degrees of periurie, not for that there is lesse periurie in the one then in the other, but that there is greater hurt occasioned in the one then in the other. In answeare of the scriptures alledged, hee sayd the lawe of God is if wee bee striken on one cheeke to turne the other, or if thy coate bee taken away to give alsoe thy gowne; the litterall sence is not to bee taken, or as there is cause a[170] reasonable construccion must bee. Soe hee concluded thoughe it were a sinne, yet it was to bee punished here in earth accordinge to the good or badd, or rather greater hurt and lesse hurt which doth growe thereby.

One after endeavoured the answeare of Mr Willson but with a protestacion of his insufficiency *etc.* and then shewed how the devines have not yet agreed what is usury; but for his owne part hee was to encline to the opinion of the learned of these dayes whose interpretacion of the litterall sence and skill[171] of the tongues [blank][172] doe appeare, which tooke[173] that for noe usury which is without greevance. Hee made a difference of the lawe of God concerninge the devine majestie, and what is concerninge man or contayned in the second table, sayinge that nothing is to bee sayd in that degree sinne in it selfe, but by the circumstance soe is it knowne whether it bee good or badd. To kill is prohibited, yet sometime not to kill is evill: Phinees killed, and was therefore comended. And thefts at tymes have bene in scripture approved. But that it might bee used to strangers, albeit those the chosen children of God amonge themselves might not use it. But let bee whether it bee utterly unlawfull or in some sort to bee tollerated it is a question, and untill it bee determined for the comon comoditie and mayntenance let it bee as hetherto it hath beene[174] used. And for the comon sort of contractes, barteringes,[175] bargaines of corne for clothe, silke for land, chevaunces, what they bee, whether usury or noe, wee knowe not. That all should bee well / it is to bee wished, but that all may bee well done amonge men it is

f.31v

f.32

more then to bee hoped for. Wee are noe saintes; wee are not of perfeccion to followe the letter of the gospell. Who soe striketh thee one the cheeke *etc.* and this text, *dato nihil inde sperant,* these are noe expresse comaundementes, for the first the lawe of nature doth direct, and for the other alsoe the same lawe in effect maketh defence. Surely there can bee noe sinne where there is noe breach of charitie. To doe that therefore to another which wee woulde to our selves (the state, circumstance and case to our selves counted) is comendable and not to bee improoved. If wee our selves bee to borrowe, who is it that would not in extremetie give a little to save much money? It is sayd the usurer may (or doth) growe rich: who hath dislike in a comonwealth that there should bee *homines boni frugi?*[176] They are to bee considered and may bee good more then for one purpose. Hee further stood on this, that God did not absolutely forbid usurie, which surely if it had bene utterly ill, hee would have done. And hee added that the cannon lawes were cruell in their censures, and wished they shoulde bee noe more remembred then they are followed.

Seriant Lovelace to this effect argued, that usury was of money onely; protested that hee hated all kind of usury, but yet the greater the ill was, the more and greater hee did hate the same, but to prohibitt it with soe sharpe and extreame a lawe as to loose all, hee thought it would bee the grownde of greater coveteousnes. Withall hee added that to prohibite the ill of coveteosnes in generalitie were vayne, voyd and frivolous, since that the speech and the act it selfe is indefinite, comprehendinge all kind of our accions and doings, and therefore as utterly vaine it were to prohibite it in vayne wordes of a generallity. To prohibit drunkennes, pride, envy, surfettinge *etc.* were somwhat in some particuler sort: to doe it generally, albeit that wee knowe that it is every way damnable, and damned by the direct and written word of God, it were but follies, of these great evills to the which man of his nature is borne and made / prone and too apt. When wee may not reach to the best, farthest and   f.32v uttermost, wee must as wee may stay by degrees, as to say there shalbee noe sleight or deceite in makinge of this kind or that kinde of wares, that the husbandman shall till his arrable land, hee shall not keepe above such a number of sheepe, that there shall bee noe forestallinge, regrating[177] *etc.*, and this in particularity, whereas otherwise generally amonge sinfull men to prohibite this sinne or that sinne utterly on a[178]

163. MS reads '*fistum*'; this reading from Cott.Titus F1.

164. 20 Hen. III, c.5 (1235/6) in *SR,* I.3.

165. Thus Rawlinson C 680; MS reads 'of'. Cott.Titus F1 has 'laid off' rather than 'said of', SP Dom.Eliz.46/166 has 'layd of'.

166. 9 Ed.II (1315/16) in *SR,* I.171/4; but 15 Ed.III, c.5 (1341) deals specifically with usury in *SR,* I.296.

167. *Paradoxa Stoicorum,* III.

168. Cott.Titus F1 reads 'even', as does SP Dom.Eliz.46/166.

169. 5 Eliz., c.9 (1562/3) in *SR,* IV.436/8.

170. MS reads 'or'; this reading from Cott.Titus F1.

171. MS reads 'kill'; this reading from Cott.Titus F1.

172. And in Rawlinson C 680.

173. MS reads 'looke'; this reading from Cott.Titus F1.

174. MS reads 'alsoe may bee'; 'hetherto . . . beene' supplied from Cott.Titus F1.

175. MS reads 'batteringe'; this reading from Cott.Titus F1.

176. MS reads '*fringi*'; this reading from Cott.Titus F1.

177. MS reads 'regradinge'; this reading from Cott.Titus F1.

178. 'On a' supplied from Cott.Titus F1.

payne, it may not bee, but thus rather, hee that shall soe sinne shall suffer or loose soe much. Whereuppon he concluded[179] that there shoulde bee degrees in the punishment of usury, as hee that should take soe much to loose or be punished thus, hee that should take more, more deeply.

Mr Fleetewood shewed that all these argumentes longe since with greate skill and very oft have beene opened in this place. Hee sayd it was *ingenui pudoris fateri per quem profeceris.* Mr Cheeke, he said,[180] argued and soe farr forth explained this matter as the learner was thereby sufficiently informed and the learned were fully satisfied: his papers of his speech hee sayd hee had not lost, and therefore coulde shewe as much cuninge as the cuningest which had bent and endeavored himselfe thereunto. Hee sayd hee had read the civill lawe, and of the cannon lawe somethinge, but howe well hee did understand it hee woulde not promise ought. What usury was, hee sayd hee was not to learne: call it if wee list *proxima homicidio,*[181] or howe els by a description he forced not much, for if there were not civill lawe it were not much to bee accounted of for any certainety in this case thereby to bee hadd. And the most auncient lawes of this realme have taught us hereof somewhat, as the lawes of [blank][182] doe make to us mencion of usurie, soe doe the lawes made in Lucius' tyme, and those of Athelred whereby it was ordayned that witches and usurers should bee banished; Kinge Edward the Saint hee referreth and appoynteth the offendor herein to suffer ordalin.[183] Then was there a greate kind of usury knowne, which was called / toras, and a lesser knowne by the name of [blank].[184] Glanvile in the booke *De Legibus Antiquis*[185] maketh mencion of an inquiry of Christian usurers. In the Tower hee sayd hee had seene a comission awarded to the Master of the Courtes (hee named not what court) to enquire of usurers, and the punishment of them hee sayd was whippinge. Hee sayd further by scripture hee knewe it was damnable, and therefore whether it were good or not good, it was noe good question. For the matter of implicacion whether by the pretence of the lawe it might bee intended that it was in any sort allowed, hee sayd it might bee soe construed, and compared therewith the statute of tythes where it is sayd that untill after seaven yeares for heath grownd broken upp noe tythe shall bee payd: the construction hereuppon is cleere.[186] Hee shewed alsoe that usury was *malum in se,* for that of some other transgressions her Majestie may dispence before with, but for usurie, or to graunt that usury may bee used, shee possibly cannot. Hee further sayd that the wordes of an act of Parliament are not ever to bee followed, for that sometyme the construccion is meere contrary to what is written, as in the statute of *Magna Carta, nisi prius homagium fecerit;* and some statutes are wincked at by non observacion or otherwise, soe that they seeme to bee noe lawes, even in those things which wee practise most, as in the statute of Glosester for the oath to be taken in debt and domage *etc.*[187]

Mr Dalton hee endeavoured to prove that Mr Fleetwood mistooke the bill, but in fancy hee mistooke his argument.

Mr Norton shewed that all usury is bitinge; as in the word *steale* is contayned all what iniurious takinge away of men's goodes, and as slaunderinge is sayde murtheringe or homicide, soe is usury iustly ever to bee sayd bytinge, they both beinge soe corelated or knitt together that the one may not bee without the other. Hee concluded that since it is doubtfull what is good, that wee shoulde be mindfull of the

f.33

true old saying *quod dubitas ne feceris,* and for that *quod non ex | fide est, peccatum est,*   f.33v
therefore hee wished noe allowance should bee of it; hee was somewhat longe. These
argumentes ended, the House rose and nothinge concluded.

A bill for the assises to be kept at Worcester in somer was the first tyme read.   Aprill xx

The bill for cappers was the second tyme read; and ruled that the same should
bee engrossed.

The bill that the returne for *venire facias* should bee made by the justices was the
second tyme read, whereby Mr Sampole argued to prove that the inconvenience or
evill which groweth by the sheriffs is not soe great but the doings of the justices may
be aswell doubted of, soe that *dum vitamus Caribdim incidimus in Sillam.* In fine the bill
was quashed.

The bill for such who bee fledd beyond the seas without lycence or shall not
returne within a certaine number of dayes after their licences expired to loose their
landes and goodes, and to avoyd convenous guiftes, was the second tyme read and
not then effectually spoken unto by any man.

Mr Wentworth very orderly in many wordes stirred the remembrance of the
speech of Sir Humphrey Gilbert which had bene some dayes before. Hee proved his
speech (without naminge him) to bee an iniurious speech to the House. Hee noted
his disposition to flatter and fawne on the prince, comparinge the nature of the
camelion unto him, which can change himselfe unto all coulours save white; even
soe, sayd hee, this reporter can change himselfe to all fashions saveinge to honesty.
Hee shewed then the greate wronge done to one of the House by a misreport made to
the Queene (meaninge Mr Bell). Hee shewed his speech to tend to noe other end
then to inculcate feare into those which should bee free. Hee requested care for the
creditt of the House and for the maynetenaunce of free speech. Two meanes hee sayd
there were of orderlie proceedinges and to preserve the liberties of the House to
reprove lyers, inveighing greately out of the scriptures and otherwise against lyers, as
this of David, 'Thou o Lord shall destroy lyers', the saying / of Salomon *etc.*   f.34

Mr Treasurer signified his desire to have all things well, sayinge hee would not
enter into judgment of any; but, hee sayd, it was convenient that ill speeches should
bee avoyded and the good meaninge of all men to bee taken without wrestinge or
misreportinge, and the meaninge of all men to bee shewed in good sort without
unseemely wordes.

---

179. MS reads 'included'; this reading from
     Cott. Titus F1.
180. 'He said' supplied from Cott. Titus F1.
181. MS reads '*homisidio*'.
182. As in Cott. Titus F1, SP
     Dom.Eliz.46/166 and Rawlinson
     C 680.
183. *Sic,* and in Cott. Titus F1, SP
     Dom.Eliz.46/166 and Rawlinson
     C 680. Cf. W. J. Ashley, *An Introduction
     to English Economic History and Theory*
     (1925), I pt 1, 195, 220n; R. Schmid,

Die Gesetze der Angelsachsen (Leipzig,
1858), 518; Wilson's *Discourse . . . ,* ed.
R. H. Tawney (1925), 257, 375.
184. As in Cott. Titus F1, SP
     Dom.Eliz.46/166 and Rawlinson
     C 680.
185. VII.16.
186. 2 & 3 Ed. VI, c.13, sect. 5(1548) in
     SR, IV.56.
187. 6 Ed.1 in *SR,* I. 45-50.
188. Not noted in *CJ.*

Mr Speaker endeavoured and moved an unitie in the House, makinge significacion that the Queene's Majestie had in plaine wordes declared unto him that she had good intelligence of the orderly proceedings amongst us, whereof shee hadd as good likinge as ever shee had of any parliament since shee came unto the crowne, and wished wee should give her noe other cause but to continue the same; and added further her Majestie's pleasure to bee to take order for lycenses, wherein shee had bene carefull, and more carefull woulde bee.

Mr Carleton with a very good zeale and orderly shewe of obedience made significacion howe that a member of the House was detayned from them (meaninge Master Strickland), by whose comaundement or for what cause hee sayd hee knewe not. But forasmuch as hee nowe was not a private man but to supply the roome, person and place of a multitude especially chosen and therefore sent, hee thought nether in regard of the countrey, which was not to bee wronged, nor for the liberty of the House, which was not to bee infringed, that wee should permitt him to bee detayned from us, but, whatsoever the intendment of his offence might bee, that he should bee sent for to the barre of that House, there to be heard and there to answeare.

Mr Treasurer in some sort gave advertisement to bee wary in our proceedings and nether to venture further than our assured warrant might stretch, nor to hazard our good opinions with her Majestie on any doubtfull cause. Withall hee wished us not to thinke worse then there was cause, for the man (quoth hee) that is meant is nether
f.34v   detained nor misused, but on consideracions is required / to expect the Queene's pleasure uppon certaine especiall poyntes, wherein hee sayd hee durst to assure that the man shoulde nether have cause to dislike nor complaine since soe much favour was meant unto him as hee reasonably coulde wishe. Hee further sayd that hee was in noe sort stayd for any wordes or speech of him in that place uttered but for exhibitinge of the bill into the House against the prerogative of the Queene, which was not to bee tollerated. Nevertheles the construccion was of him rather to have erred in his zeale and bill offered then malitiously to have ment any thing contrary to the dignitie royall. Lastly hee concluded that oft it hath bene seene that speeches have bene examined and considered of *etc.*

Sir Nicholas Arnould with some vehemancie moved care to bee had for the libertie of the House, which hee was inforced, hee sayd, rather to utter, and soe to runne into any danger of offence of others, then to bee offended with himselfe.

Mr Bedell[189] desired the liberties of the House to be learned.

Mr Comptroller replyed to the effect as Mr Treasurer before had spoken.

Mr Clare[190] tould a longe tale howe the prerogative is not disputable, and that the safetie of the Queene is the safety of her subiectes. Hee added howe that for matters of divinitie every man was for his instrucion to repaire to his ordinary, beinge a private man; where hee utterly did forget the place hee spake in, and the person was meant, for that place required and permitted free speech with authoritie, and the person himselfe was not as a private man, but publique, by whom even the ordinary himself was to bee directed. Hee concluded that forasmuch as the cause was not knowne hee therefore would the House should stay *etc.*

Mr Elverton sayd hee was to bee sent for, arguinge to this effect. First hee sayd the
f.35   president was perrilous, and thoughe in this happy time of lenety / amonge soe good

and honorable personages, under soe gratious a prince, nothinge of extremitie or iniurie was to bee feared, yet the tymes might bee altered, and what nowe is permitted, hereafter may bee construed as of dutie and enforced even on this grownd of the present permission. Hee further sayd that all matters not treason or too much to the derogacion of the imperiall crowne was tollerable there, where all things came to bee considered of, and where[191] there was such fullnes of power as even the right of the crowne was to bee determined, and by warrant whereof wee have soe resolved that to say the parliament had noe power to determine of the crowne was highe treason. Hee remembred that men were not there for themselves but for their countreys, and shewed it was fitt princes to have their prerogative but yet the same to bee straytned within reasonable limittes. The prince, hee shewed, could not of her selfe make lawes, nether might shee by the like reason breake lawes. Hee further sayd that the speech uttered in that place and the offer made of the bill was not to be condemned as ill, for that if there were any thinge in the Booke of Comon Prayer ether Jewishe, Turkishe or popishe, the same was to bee reformed. Hee alsoe sayd that amonge the papistes it was bruted that by the judgment of the Councell Strickland was taken for an heretique: it behooveth therefore to thinke thereof.

Mr Fleetwood shewed first in some wordes the order of civill argument which hee vouched out of [blank][192] to this effect, that tyme must bee knowne and place observed. Hee then sayd that of experience he could report *anno 5°* of this Queene a man was called to accompt of his speech;[193] but hee woulde not, he sayd, meddle with such late matters, but what he had learned in the parliament rolles hee thought convenient the knowledge and consideracion. In the tyme of / Kinge Henry 4 a   f.35v bushoppe of the parliament was comitted by comaundement of the Kinge to prison: the parliament resolved to be suitors for him.[194] And in Henry 5[195] his tyme the Speaker himselfe was comitted and with him one other: the House hereuppon stayed, but reamedy they had none, then to bee suitors to the Kinge for them.[196] Whereuppon hee resolved the onely and whole helpe of the House for ease of their greife in this case to bee humble suitors to her Majestie, and nether to send for him, nor demaund him of right.

Duringe this speech the Councell whispered together, and thereuppon the Speaker made this motion, that the House should make stay of any further consultacion hereuppon. The next day, by what warrant or consultacion I knowe not, hee[197] came to the House somwhat after the House was sett and a bill had

189. As in Cott.Titus F1, SP Dom.Eliz.46/166; Rawlinson C 680 has 'Mr Beadle'.

190. Cott.Titus F1 and Rawlinson C 680 have 'Cleere', SP Dom.Eliz.46/166 has 'Clere'.

191. MS reads 'when'; this reading from Cott.Titus F1.

192. As in Cott.Titus F1, SP Dom.Eliz.46/166, and Rawlinson C 680.

193. Probably a reference to James Dalton speaking on the succession in 1566

(9 Elizabeth).

194. Fleetwood is possibly referring, confusedly, to Haxey's case (Wittke, *op. cit.*, 23-4).

195. *Sic*; Henry VI.

196. See J. S. Roskell, *The Commons and their Speakers in English Parliaments* (1965), 252-4, and the references cited there, and cf. Fleetwood in 1576 (Cromwell's diary for 1576, f.120 and v).

197. I.e. Strickland.

bene read and then was to bee comitted; whereuppon many of the House even uppon the first sight of him in gratefull sort cryed that hee might bee one of the comittees in that bill.

This day a bill for reversinge of a statute made *anno 8ᵛᵒ* of this Queene concerninge drapinge within the towne of Shrouesbury was read the second tyme, and ordered to bee ingrossed.

The act for cominge to comon prayer and for receavinge of the comunion was the second tyme read, the effect of the bill is before, *etc.*

Aglionby argued that there should be no humane, positive lawe to inforce conscience, which is not discernable in this world. To come to the churche, for that it is publique and tendeth but to prove a man a Christian, is tollerable and convenient, and not to come to churche maie make a man seeme irreligious and soe no man, for that by religion onely a man is knowne and discerned from brute beastes, and this is to be iudged by the outward shewe; but the conscience of man is internall, invisible, and not in the power of the greatest monarch in the worlde, in no lymittes to be streightened, in no bondes to be conteyned, nor with anie pollicie of man (if once decaied) to be againe raised. Hee shewed that neither Jew nor Turke doe require more then the submission to the outward observaunce and a convenient silence, as not to dislike with what is publiquely professed. But to inforce anie to doe the acte which maie tende to the discovery of his conscience, it is never founde. Hee shewed the difference betwene the coming to church, and receiving of the communion; the one hee allowed to be comprehensible in lawe, the other hee could not allowe. And in aunswere of that which before had beene said, that the conscience was not streightened, but a penaltie of the losse of their goodes onely adiuged, whereof (no doubt) the lawe of God and the lawe of nations had given to the prince an absolute power, hee said to this, out of Cicero *De Legibus*, that man of his owne nature is to care for the safetie of man as being reasonable creatures, and not the one to seeke to bereave the other of his necessary livelyhood, adding out of the same booke this saying of Tully, *qui Deum non curat, hunc Deus ipse iudicabit.*[198] Hee shewed out of St Paule that wee must not doe ill that thereby good maie growe. Wee must not take from him that is his, to the ende therby to make him doe what is not in his power. To be fitt for soe great a mysterie, God above of his free guifte maie make a man. To come unworthilie, the penaltie is appointed: St Paule hath pronounced it to be death and damnacion, as guiltie of the bloode and death of Christe. Not to come, our compulsary lawe shall nowe condemne. Soe that this is our favour heerein to be extended, either to begg or to be exiled from our native countrie. Hee said ther was noe example in the primitive Church to prove a commaundement of coming to the communion, but an exhortacion. Hee said St Ambrose did excomunicate Theodosius, and forbidd him to come to the communion, because hee was an ill man. And for us to will and commaund men to come bicause they are wicked men, it is too straunge an inforcement, and without president.

Agmondesham, without regard of anie thinge spoken before, maketh mencion of a decree in the Starr Chamber, made by nyne of the Privie Councell, signed with their handes and the handes of the chiefe justices, concerning the receiving of the communion by gentlemen of the Temple. This decree, made by soe grave and learned men, hee thought for himselfe and to his owne conscience was a staie what to iudge, and a direction or president for others what to followe. The tenor of the decree for soe much as it did concerne the reformacion of the howses of courte and principall places, to be thought and considered of, which hee wished might be inserted in the lawe. The mocion was well liked and he required to bring the same the next daie, which was doone.

Norton shewed that where manie men be, there must be manie myndes, and in consultacions convenient it is to have contrary opinions, contrary reasoninges and contradiccions, thereby the rather to wrest out the best; but this by the rule of reason, and reasoning must be *sine iurgiis.* Hee then said that not onely the externall and outward shewe is to be sought, but the very secrettes of the harte in God's cause, who is *scrutator cordium,* must come to a reckening, and the good seede so sifted from the cockle that the one maie be knowne from the other. A man baptized is not to be permitted amonge us for a Jewe. And heere somwhat slipping from the matter in speeche, hee moved that all suspected of papistrie might make this oath, that they did acknowledge the Queen to be Queen for anie thinge the Pope in anie respecte might doe, noting some imperfection in the former oath. To this ende (quoth hee) are theis bulles now sente to discharge men of their allegeaunce, and to give free pardon of synnes, soe that hee who thus shoulde be pardoned should from henceforth in no sorte communicate with the professors of the ghospell. And nowe (quoth hee) the very touchstone of triall, who be those rebellious calves whom the bull hath begotten, must be the receiving of the communion, which who soe shall refuse wee maie iustly saie he favoreth *etc.* And men are not otherwise to be knowne but by the externall signe. To aunswere and satisfie the obiection of dilemma before in the daie of the first reading made concerning the disorder of certaine ministers in saying of the service contrary to the iniunction of the booke, hee wished this proviso might be added, that mistaking of chapters, misreading, *etc.* should be reckened for no offence, soe that there be no Masse sounge or popish service used in Latyn, *etc.* And thus the bill rested to be further considered of.[199]

Henry Sackeverell was brought to the barr of the House there to bee heard concerninge the cautell practised and wrought against Mr Skevington, which hee confessed.

The bill of cominge to service and receavinge of the comunion was againe read. Aprill xxj

Mr Warnecombe moved that the certificate of the bushopps should bee noe conviction. Whereunto Mr Saundes answeared that the certificate groweth onely / uppon a confession, and soe noe wronge can be wrought. f.36

Sir Thomas Smyth after some speech concerninge the bill and the approbacion of every part generally allowed of the whole, savinge the proviso annexed by Mr Norton, which hee sayd was opposite in obiect.

---

198. Cf. *De Legibus*, I, vii.22–3, xii.33; II, viii.19.

199. These three speeches of Aglionby, Agmondesham and Norton are omitted in the MS, which has only one sentence:

'The bill was noe further spoken off at this tyme, but rested to bee considered of hereafter'; they are supplied from Cott.Titus F1.

The bill of the subsedie was then read, the which being ended:

Mr John Yonge offered the House some speech and, lycense beinge obtayned, hee sayd to this effect, that the burthen of the subsedie and chardge by lones oft imposed by the prince uppon us, and the chardge of the richest and most noblest prince being considered, it were not amisse if it[200]

200. All MSS break off here, though SP
    Dom.Eliz.46/166 adds, in another hand,
    'were granted'.

2. Hooker's journal, 2 April-30 (sic) May

Text from Devonshire RO, Bk 60h, original?
Printed. Trans. Devons. Assoc., XI (1879).

Devonshire RO, Bk 60h, fos.1-9v[1]

[2 April]
On M[on]ed[a]y . . . the ij of A[pril, the first da]y of the parla[ment], the Quene's Majestie about xij of the clock . . . fro[m] Whytha[ll] unto Westminster beinge attended and accompanyed with all the bishop[ps] and lords of the realme yn theire parlament robes, her Highnes rydyng in a wagon rychely apparelled and adorned. The same day Doctore Sandes, Bishop of London, preached before her; his theme was '*Tim[et]e Deum et servit[e] ei in veritate*' (Samuel 12), upon which text his dyscourse was how that religion is cheffe[ly] to be sought in virtue and trewth, and that princes without it coud not well rule nor govern, and that princes ought to directe theire doings yn trew religion and to governe th[eir] people yn trewth, equitie and justice. This sermon ended, her Majestie went to the higher howse where the Lord Keper made an oracion, the same toochinge specially three poynts – trew religio[n], the goverment of the prynce, and the dutefullness of the subgects – concluding yn the ende that the necessitie of the prynce was greate which by the subgects was to be consydered: for as the synowes do conioyne and knytt the members of the bodye together and without theyme the body cannot be, even so, money beinge as the synowes to conioyne and meanteane the necessytie and state of the common welth, the prynce cannot be without it. This oration ended, the lower howse was willed to assemble theyme selffs together and to chose unto theyme selffs a Speker, and to present him the Thurseday folowinge; but the Quene shortned the tyme and apoynted the Wenesdaye. Then the lower howse assembled theym selffs, and emonge others made choyse of Sergeaunt Wraye to be the Speker. And then the court was adiourned untyll the Wenesday folowinge at one of the clock at afternone, but before this tyme whyles the sermon was at Westmynster, the lower howse was assembled and everie man there beinge was sworne to the Quene, as also order taken that [n]one shoulde enter yn to that Howse being of that companye oneles he were sworne upon payne *etc.* The Lord Ademyrall, Sir Francys Knolls, Sir Ralff Sadler and Sir Walter Myldemay takyn every mane's othe / . . .
[4 April]
[Quen]e's Majestie . . . ynge yn . . . the lordes came and [pre]sented u[nto] . . .   f.1v

---

1. Attempts to repair the MS in the 1870s consisted mainly in sticking paper of limited opacity over the decayed sections of the folios, and in some cases this has made the MS more difficult to decipher, even with ultra-violet light. I have generally adopted the printed version's means of representing decay and illegibility.

Speker havinge donne his dutefull obeysance and made [hi]s [o]racion declaringe how that, accordinge to the comandement geven on Moneday past the lower howse had made chose of a Speker and [ha]d apoynted him, but, forasmiche as he wanted the lernying, gravitie, know[ledge] and experience as ought to be yn suche a rome and pl[ace] and that there was good ch[o]yse of othere miche more meete and fytt c[hoys]e yn that Howse then was he, that the[r]for it wold playse her H[ig]hnes to commande the saide Howse to assemble theym selffs and to m[ake] choyse of some better and more meter man. To this the Lord Chauncelor[2] awnswered that the Quene's Majestie had had good tryall of his knoledge, wysedome and lernying, and therefor wold not dyscredytt him of that which she knew to be yn him and further, forasmiche as so many wyse expert and greate men had upon good consideracions made choyse of him, she wold not so frustrate and dyscredytt their doings, and therefor willed him to go forthwards and not to refuse to take that charge upon him. Then begynneth the Speker his oracion, proving that lawe was the mayntenance of all realmes, kingedomes and comon welthes: the lawe was doble, th'one of religion, and th'other of comon welthe. Of religion the prynce was the cheffe protector and governore yn his owne realme and no foreyn potentate, as by sundry examples and histories of the lande was to be proved. First, of Lucius the first Christian Kinge of this lande, who of his owne authoritie brought yn and established Christian religion within this lande, lyke the Conqueror buyld the abbey of Battel, placed monks yn it and gave great pryvelegs unto it, never asking leave or seeking to the Pope for the same. Kinge Henry the iij[d] made a lawe that who so ever dyd seeke for sentence of excommunicacion at the see of Rome shold dye for it. By which examples it appereth that the kings of this realme were th'onely and sole governors of the same yn causes of religion; the lawes of comon welthe stode either yn armmes or yn peax: which too poynts when he had at full dyscoursed he made an

f.2   ende. Then the Lord Keper made / [a]wns[er] . . . [pryve]legs, custo[ms] and lyberties . . . yn times past they . . . yed: nam[ely] first that everie of that Howse might h[ave fre]e access for selff and his men to the saide parlament, and that none of they[m] might be molested, vexed or sorried. Secondarily, that every man myght have free speeche and without interr[up]tion or troble to speke his mynde freely. Thirdly, that if he careiyng yn any messag[e] to her Highnes shold be mystaken and speke any thing otherwyse than yn his comyssion that it might [n]ot b[e] taken to the worst nor any advantage to be had thereof. To the first, the Lord Chauncelor awnswereth that everie m[an] there came to the makinge and devysinge of good lawes and theref[or] none there coulde or ought to make breache of any lawes wheref[or] if any man beinge yn debt dyd procure him selff to be of that Howse to th'ende to dyffer his credytors it were unreasonable that any suche pryveleg shold be graunted. To the ij[d], that her Highnes thinketh it not meet that any sholde have further lybertie to speke or talke yn that Howse of any matter other then that which is there to be proponed, and that they sholde leave to talk *rhetorice* and speke *logice*, to leave longe tales which is rather an ostentacion of wytt then to any effecte, and to deale with these things as there were to be proponed: that goinge effectually to the matter they might dyspatche that they were sent for and that they might the souner returne home. To the third, the Quene understode well of his wysedome, gravitie, and lernyinge and that she mystrust not of any suche symplicitie to be yn him but if it sholde so come to passe she wolde beare therwith. This donne the Quene arose, wishinge they wolde be more quiet then they were at the last tyme. Then the lower howse repayred agayn to the Howse where there was redd a byll that every man borne and resyding within this realme sholde on every festywall day repaire to the church to the dyvine service, upon payne of xxx^{sh}, and that on / . . . parish churche   f.2v and once . . . pon . . . forfeyte of . . . ecepts . . . [pr] offyts . . . his lyff: . . . half[e t]hereof . . . to the . . . so the Howse arose and departed takinge order that who soever came after the mornyng praier should for everie tyme pay iiii^d.

[5 April]
On Thurseday, the Howse beinge assembled, it was th[ou]g[ht] good that everie burgesse sholde be called by [nam]e because it semed that the Howse, beinge very full, ther [we]re more there then ought to be. And yn serch [mad]e, Thomas Clerk and his felowe of the Ynner Temple were founde to be yn Howse, being none of that company, whereupon they were comytted to the Sergeaunt's warde, and upon Saterday folowenge were dyschardged.

On Fryday there was mocion made that the bookes dvised for the ecclesyaticall lawe and for religion, as well yn the tymes of Kinge Henry the viijth and of King Edward, sholde be brought yn to the Howse, and for examyninge of which books certeyne comitties were apoynted. Also the byll for comynge to the churche was redd, and the same also being yn certeyn poynts impugned, was comytted. Also a byll for preservacion of woods about London was redd, which beinge enlarged and made generall, was also comitted.

[7 April]
On Saterday the books for religion which were yn the custodie of Mr Norton were brought yn to the Howse and there beinge redd were lyked of; namely the bill that no man sholde be priest before he were xxiiij yeres of age, that none sholde have a benefyce of xxx^{li} by the yere onles he were a preacher, that none shold have ij benefycs oneles they were both within xx^{ti} myles together, that none sholde be absent from his benyfyce above iiii^{xx} daies yn the yere, that he shall not sett his benyfice to ferme to any man other then to his curat, that no patron shall sell his advowsion nor take any guyft or pencion *etc.* with many other lyke. Thes bills were comitted to certeyn of the / Howse to cause . . . theym . . . to the byshops for a tyme by theym to . . .   f.3 sholde meete them to . . . [s]holde consi[der] and thincke of the subsidie for which . . . was the . . . called whose tale was mich myslyked, nevertheles . . . Thresurer, Mr Bell, Mr Norton, Mr Comptroller, Mr Popham and other . . . dyd affirme that mocion to be necessarye, nevertheles that a peticion might be made to the Quene for the comons for theire helpe agaynst promotors, for despensacions, for perveyors, for collectors spendinge the Quene's money, and dyverse other lyke abuses; and for these poynts there were comytties apoynted for bothe for draweng the booke of the subsidie, as also for su[ch] artycles as wherewith the comon welthe was greved.

[9 April]
   On Moneday the ixth of Aprill order was taken that too of the Howse shold[e] be

2. *Sic.*

there apoynted to go to the byshop of London for a precher, who on everie mornynge at vii of the clocke sholde rede a lecture of iii quarters of an howre yn the parlament howse. Also a byll that it sholde be highe treason who so ever mayntyned, dyvysed, spake or wrote any evell agaynst the Quene, her state, honor or dignytie. And who so ever dyd[3] pretend any tytle [to] the Crowne now after her dethe to be dishabled, he and his heires for ever *etc.* with many other artycls. And upon readinge of this byll order taken that no byll shold be redd twyse together within the dystuance of three daies because everye man sholde be advysed, and that warning shold before hand be geven for the reedyng of it. Also the byll comytted for comying to the church was redd and the provyso that gentlemen sholde be excepted was myslyked.
[10 April]
On Tweseday the xth of Aprill was redd a byll that everie man not dyspendynge xx[ti] marks by the yere and above xiiij yeres of age shoulde have and were everie holy daye a knytt wollen capp vpon payne of — .

Also a byll for the comyssion of sewers to contynewe.

Also that the justices of the Benche and Comon Pleax shall returne impaneles and juries, and everie shiriff to send up a booke of the hundred[er]s and freeholders.

Also a byll for the repeale for the corporacion of the Marchants Adventurers of Brystowe.

A byll for the construynge and[4] a braunche of a statute for leases of monasteres. /

f.3v   . . . subsydie of iiij[s] the . . . pounde yn lands and ii[s] viii[d] . . .

[A byll] . . . the sheri[ff] . . . [bur]gesses for pl[ ] . . . her no persons . . . a[   ]ude to h[bu]rgesses.[5]

[A byll for] th'assisse of weights, measures and emong innedholders within iiij myles of London.

A byll for the removinge of the schole from Loug[hton[6] to] Gaynsbury yn Lyncolneshere.

An act for clothe workers of London.

An acte for conveyghuances made by accomptaunts for . . . lands frawdulently and decetfully.

An act that everie prest shall openly reede the publyque confession and also not to preach any false doctryne upon payne of deprivacion oneles he do recant *etc.*

Also this day there were xxxv[e] of the lower howse apoynted to meete with xx[ti] lords of the higher howse to consulte of religion.
[11 April]
On Weneseday the xi[th] of April an byll for the contynuance of the acte of Acton Burnell for Lustythiall.

A byll agaynst the fynes and conveighaunces made by accoumptuntes fraudulentlye.

An acte for Southampton for the custome of malemeseys.

An acte that the Quene's ordynary servaunts yn checke roll shall not be returned by any shiriff.

An acte that no advowsons shalbe geven for terme of yeres nor to be solde or geven for rewards.
[12 April]

On Thurseday an acte for respect of homage *et titulo guo ingressus est.*

An act for treasons yn depryvinge or speaking agaynst the Quene's Majestie *etc.*

[13 April]

On Fryday the xiij^{th 7} of Aprill a byll passed the lords of the higher howse was redd agaynst the thresurers, recevers, collecters, and gatheres of the Quene's moneys, to pay theire whole recepts after and within iii monethes warnynge: upon [payne (?)] of felonie oneles theire recept be under iii^{cli}, which felonye not to extende to th'attente of his children or debarringe of the wyve's dowry.

An acte agaynst usurye.

An act for the repeale of an acte made for Shrewesburye.

An act agaynst vagabonds to be felons.

An order for the comyttinge of the corporacion of the Brystowe Marechaunts to xij^c of the Howse, of which I am one. /

[14 April]   f.4

On Saterday a byll for the false convey . . .

A byll for a schole to be m[   ] at.⁸

A byll for ref[   ] . . . [cer]emonyes⁹ . . . as knellyng t[o] the [   ]on baysinge and . . . howses cop[es], . . . surpls, albs etc.

A byll for sewers sent to the Lords.

An act agaynst the dyspensacions, lycenses, faculties, and composacions *etc.* of the Bishop of Canterburie.

A mocion for clercks convicte.

[16 April]

On Moned[a]y yn Easter weke the comitties for the corporacion of the Merch[ant]s of Brystowe, viz. Mr Comptroller, Sir Nicholaus Poyns, Sir John Thynne, Sir Nicholaus Arnolde, Sir John White, Mr William Fleetewode, Mr Norton, Mr Alford, Mr Hall of Yorke, Mr Hoker, Mr Popham, mett at Starre Chimber at iii of the clocke at afternon, and after longe dyscoursing of the matter it was agreed and concluded that the councell lerned which the Merchaunts had brought with them, and all others savinge the comytties, sholde go out of the dores; and then thought good to amende the bill yn certeyn words which were somewhat sharp and to advertyse the Howse for the repeale of it.

Memorandum that one Mr. Strykelande was commanded to his howse for puttinge of a byll agaynst certeyne ceremonyes of the Churche, about which there was some busynes yn the Howse for his delyverie.

[19 April]

On Thurseday the xixth of Aprill a byll put yn by the Londoners that all Kentishe and Sussex clothes to be brought to Blackwell Hall.

A bill for the burgesses redd the ij^d tyme and comitted, the same beinge apoynted to be dyscoursed at the Temple the Saterday folowinge.

A byll agaynst usury the ij^d reedinge.

3. 'Dyd' repeated in MS.

4. *Sic:* 'of'?

5. For free election of burgesses.

6. Cf Anonymous Journal above, f.11v.

7. MS has 'xiith'.

8. Southwark (Anonymous Journal, f.21).

9. I.e. Strickland's bill.

[20 April]

On Fryday the bill for cappers redd the ij^d tyme.

A byll for makinge of clothes at Shrewesbury, the ij reedinge.

A byll agaynst fugitives: upon this byll one Wentworth toke occasion to speke, and toochinge the lyberties and pryveleges of the Howse inveighed agaynst[10] [certeyne members / of] the Howse that had enformed the Quene untrewly of a . . . mo[c]ion mad[e] in this Howse by Mr Bell, chardgeth the . . . to be . . . trewthe to have[e d]ysclosed the secrets . . . and to have falsely enformed the Quene, namyng . . . flatterer, a lyer and a naughtie man. This yn th'end . . . out to be Sir Humfrey Gylbert for he fyndinge him selff . . . wolde have spoken, but he had the de[nia]l three tymes by the Howse.　　　　　　　　　　　　　　　　　　　　　　　　　f.4v

Also the byll for comynge to the Churche red[d] the ij^d.

Also this day mocion was made for one Mr Stryke[l]an[de], who puttinge yn of a byll to the Howse concernynge the rubryks and . . . ceremonyes of the communyon booke without consent of the councell, was commanded to kepe his howse from Saterday last u[nti]ll this daye, but yn the'ende upon this communi-cacion[11] it was so ordred that the day folowing he came agayne to the Howse.

[21 April]

On Saterday the byll for comynge to the churche was agayne talked of and the same comytted.

Also the byll of subsydies was redd.

Also the Lords sent . . . to the lower howse for a company of theyme to come to theyme which was done and they then were willed to perswade the Howse to deale yn matters of avayle and to proceede to some ende.[12]

Also a byll of devyse intytuled 'The comon releff for every person at his deth to give his best garment to the bancke apoynted.'

Also the Lords sent a byll for dyspensacions, bulls and other instruments come from Rome.

Also mocion was by them then sent that the Quene consydering the hote, dry and contagiose tyme thought good that the Howse shold leave pryvat matters and proceede to such as wer of avayle *etc.*

[23 April]

f.5　On Moneday the 23 of Aprill a byll was redd agaynst promoters, but the same beinge devised by th'Eschequer men, and seemynge yn effect rather to geve a more scope to theym then to restrayne theyme, the same was reiected and certeyn of the Howse apoynted to drawe a newe booke *etc.* In this byll Mr Bell spake mich of the Quene's prerogatyve, alledginge that the same might and ought to be spoken yn that Howse: and how / that yn the tyme of Kinge Henry the . . . him to the citie of Yorke f[　　] to . . . f[　　]ers the same . . . being . . . comon welthe . . . he knew . . . ever repealed.

Also an acte from the higher howse for bulls come and sent from Rome [which], beinge imperfect, was comitted to be amended.

Also a byll agaynst collectors of the Quene's monies, which bill being [founde] n[o]t to be so full and perfect as it ought to be, was comitted to be amended.

Also the byll for repeale of the corporacion of the Merchaunts of Brystowe was comytted to be engrossed.

[24 April]

On Twesday the 24 daye a byll for shiriffs' allowances for the justices [of] the assysses' dyetts to be made by the Lord Thresurer, chamberleyn of th'Eschequer, *etc.*

A byll agaynst usury.

A byll agaynst fugityves.

[25 April]

On Wenesday the bill for respecte of homage. 2.

The bill for subsidie. 2.

[26 April]

On Thursday a byll agaynst massyng prests goinge yn dysguysed apparell and conveighinge of money and boks beyond the seas.

The bill agaynst treasons. About this bill was mich adoo, beinge a question made whether the bill and the addycions annexed to the same sholde be as one byll; the Howse was devyded, and the negatyve parte was vi^{xx} xviij^{n}, and th'affirmative viij^{xx} x^{n}:[13] and so the bylls were conioyned.

This daye a recytall was made of all the bylls put yn to the Howse, which were yn nomber lx^{ti}, and then order taken that the bylls of religion and then the bylls twyse redd sholde be first dyspatched, and for the residue to be examyned and perused by such as were apoynted comytties, and such as they sholde [hold?] good to be redd to be allowed, th'others to be reiected.[14]

[27 April]

On Fryday the 27 daye the byll for usurie redd and engrossed.

A byll for conservacion of an unyformitie emonge the clergie, sent to the Lordes.

A byll for Skevington sent to the Lordes.

A byll against popish prests dysguysinge them selffs, sent to the Lordes.

A byll for treason, sent to the Lordes.

A byll for respect of homage, comytted.[15] /

[28 April]

[On Saterday the] 28 daye a byll agaynst ecclesiastycall persons *etc.* not to have . . . benefyces . . . of Brystow[e pa]st and sent to the Lordes.

[A byll for S]hrewsbury sent to the Lordes.

[A byll agaynst] fugityves sent to the Lordes.[16]

[A by]ll agaynst usury sent to the Lordes.

[30 April]

On Moneday the 30 daie a byll for the justyces' dietts.

A byll for comynge to the churche. This was agayne comitted to be [mad]e perfect.[17]

A byll for churches to be served with meete and convenyent mynesters.

f.5v

---

10. 'Sir Humfrey Gylbert because' apparently crossed out here.

11. MS appears to read 'coicacon'.

12. *CJ*, I.85.

13. Cf. *CJ*, I.86, where the difference is 36.

14. Cf. *CJ*, I.86.

15. *CJ*, I.86: 3rd reading, though see following day.

16. Cf. *CJ*, I.87, where bill passed Commons, 1 May. 'A byll ageynst fugytyves' crossed through under 1 May.

17. Cf. *CJ*, I.86, where ingrossed.

[1 May]

On Tweseday the first of May a byll for fynes and recoveries.

An act for the justyces' dyetts, sent to the Lordes.

An acte for the attendure of the Erles of Westmerland, Nortumberlande and others the northern gentlemen, the nomber of the which 57, came from the Lordes.

An act for lettres patents to have a constat.

This day an awnswere came from the Quene that concerninge rytes and ceremonyes she, beinge supreme hedd of the Church, wolde consider thereof as the case sholde require.

[2 May]

On Wenesday a byll for ioyfels and myspleadinge.

An act that benefyced men shall not apoynte their benefycs to any evell or symonyacall uses.

An [act] agaynst promoters. 1.

An acte agaynst vagabonds. 1.

An act for respect of homage apoynted to be brought yn the next mornynge.

[3 May]

On Thurseday the 3 daye a byll of a braunche of a statute made for fyshynge *anno quinto domine* Elisabeth renewed and enlarged, and that all heweys for fishers shalbe reduced to crosse sayles.

An act for assuraunces of landes which by secret devyses ar conveighed.

An act that parishe churches may be provyded of good pasters and mynesters. About this byll there was mich a do concerninge the worde 'mynester' and 'prest', as also very sharpe talk toochinge pryvat men.

A byll of usury brought from the Lords with a priviso by theym made and the same beinge threse redd was confyrmed.

A byll from the Lordes for the legitymacion of Peregrynn, the sone of Mr Bartewe and the Duches of Suffolke. This was redd threse and passed.

A byll for makynge good of patents exemplyefied or constats sythens the 27 of Henry the viij^th to be good yn lawe, onles the said patents were lawffully surrendred and cancelled. /

f.6   [4 May]

On Fryday the 4 of May a byll for . . . Stawnton.

A byll agaynst lycenses and dyspe[nsa]cions of the . . .

A byll for fynes and [recove]ries.

A byll for comynge to the church, sent to . . .

A byll for respect of homage, engrossed.

A byll for [en]crease of tyllage *etc.* 2.

A byll for Southampton, engrossed.

[5 May]

On Saterday v^th of May a bill for the watercourse of Stamford.

A byll agaynst the Bishop of Canterbury's dispensacions.

A byll agaynst vagabonds, amended.

A byll for the atteynture of the rebells yn the northe.

A byll for respect of homages past.

[7 May]

On Moneday the viith of May a byll agaynst the Bishop of Canterbury's dyspensacions redd the ij^d tyme.

A byll for cappers, past.

A byll for symonyacall practyses, past.

A byll against vagabond, engrossed.[18]

A byll for meantenance of tyllage, past.

A byll for fynes vouchers and recovriyes.

A byll for Southampton: this was mich reasoned and dyffererde tyll the next day.[19]

[8 May]

On Twesday the viijth of May a byll for meanetenaunce the navye.

A byll for the subsidy, past.

A byll for Southampton, past.

[9 May]

On Wenesday the ixth of May a bill agaynst promoters.

A bill for avoydinge of corrupt presentacions and none to be made for yeres but for lyff.

A byll agaynst bulls.

A byll for fynes and recoverys, past.

A byll agaynst despensacions of the Bishop of Canterbury.

A byll agaynst tellers.

[10 May]

On Thurday the xth of May a byll for the watercourse called Weyland at Stamford, past.

A byll for th'increase of the navigacion.[20]

A byll for woods, comitted.

A byll for Norffolk and Suffolk to have serveral shereffs.

A byll for Acton Burnell at Lustuthyell. /

[11 May]

[On Fryday the] xith a bill for collectors of the xth . . . for periury of c[ler]ks convicte, . . . severall sh . . . severall sheres . . . asors amended by the Lordes and sent downe.

[A by]ll agaynst fraudulent guyfts, feoffements, and conveighaunces of goods or lands.

[A] byll for one Rodberie yn Somerset.[21]

A byll agaynst promoters, past.

A byll against corrupt pres[ent]acons, past.

Memorandum that on yeresterday and this day there was mich adoo about Thomas Longe, one of the burgesses for Westburye-under-the-Playne, and wher order was taken that the maior of the same towne and on[e] ot[her], having received iiij^l of the saide Longe, sholde repaye the same and xx^l to the Quene, and th'oblegacion made

f.6v

18. Cf. *CJ*, I.88: provisos, rather than bills.
19. Cf. *CJ*, I.88.

20. Cf. *CJ*, I.89: provisos rather than bills.
21. I.e. Maurice Rodney: *CJ*, I.88-9.

to theym for theire indemnytie by L[on]ge to be cancelled. It was this day ordered that the saide maior and his felowe to be sent for by a sergeant at armes and they to be comitted to warde.[22] At afternone the Howse sat also, and according to an order taken that on Monedayes, Wenesedayes and Frydayes the Howse sholde sytt as well at afternones as at the forenones for the hyring and allowinge of pryvat bylls,[23] and then wer redd as folowethe:

A byll for pavinge the wayes without Aldersgate.

A byll for weyghinge [a]t Dorchester.

A byll for xij sheres yn Wales to trye felonyes.

A byll for the havens yn D[evo]n and Cornewall: this byll was comitted, of which nomber I am one.

A byll for cognysaunces of pleas yn the Stannery.

A byll for cordewayners.

A byll for pavinge of Ipswyche.

[12 May]

On Saturday the xij[th] of May of byll for ioyfoyls comitted.

A byll for collection of the tenth.

A byll for orderinge of tythes, which byll was reiected.

[14 May]

On Moneday the 14 of May a byll that noo person to have ij benefycs but a precher.

A byll for false conveighaunces of goodds and lands.

A byll for collectors of the xth, past.

A byll for periurie of clerks convicte to be pardoned by course, past.

A byll for Acton Burnell at Lustuthiall, past.

A byll agaynst leases of hospytalls.

A byll agaynst great hossen.

A byll for settinge of hopps.

A byll for wyndynge of wolls.

A byll for Coggeshall clothes.

A byll for legittymacion of Watson.

A byll for erectyage of a parish church at Lyverpole. /

f.7   [16 May]

On Weneseday the 16 of May a byll for taking . . .

A byll agayn[st] makinge and we[ari]age of great . . .

A byll agaynst fraudulent guyffts of g . . .

A byll agaynst fraudulent guyffts and conveigh . . .

A byll agaynst vowchers yn reall actions.

A byll for servinge of curs with good pastors, past.

A byll for severall sheriffs yn Norffolk and Suffolk.

A byll that the maior of London shall have the serche of clothes solde in fayres kept yn Kent and Sussex *etc.*

A byll for lewd[e] person fleeinge out of Great Yermouthe to be fethered[24] and punyshed.

A byll for makinge of Tawnton clothes.

A byll agaynst exactions yn Wales called comothe.

A byll for preservacion of havens yn Devon and Cornewalle.

A byll for relesynge of freholders yn Mydlesex.

A byll for preservacion of wills and testaments.

A byll for the contynuaunce of releff to the hospitalls of London.

[17 May]

On Thurseday the 17 of M[ay] a byll that of all Kentyshe and Suffolke clothes to be caried out of the realme, everye tenthe cloth to be wrought within the realme.

A byll for repeale of clotheworkers within the realme put yn by the Londoners, but reiected.

An act for sewers, come from the Lordes.

An act for treasons, come from the Lordes and past.

A byll for repealinge of fyshe Wenesdayes, past.

A byll that no ordynary shall make commutacion of penuance without th'advyse of too justyces, upon payne of xx^l, past.

A byll for avoydinge of delayes yn reall causes, past.

A byll for banckeruptes.

A byll for great hosses.

A byll for severall shireffs yn the counties of Cambridge and Huntyngdon.

[18 May]

On Fryday the 18 of May a byll agaynst great hosses, past; the Lordes denye it.

A byll for preservacion of woodes, past.

[19 May]

On Saterday the 19 of May a byll for bringnyng of foreyn wares prohibited.

A byll for tryall of felonyes yn Wales.

A byll for vagabonds past: the Lordes have overthrowen it.

Also x bylls from the Lordes, whereof v were such as were before sent unto theyme and by them yn certeyn poynts amended.

An act for Rodney yn Somerset shere, past. /

[21 May]   f.7v

[On Moned]ay the 21 of May an act for the subsidie of v^s the pounde [the cler]gie, past. . . . [for] revyvynge [of] certeyn statutes. . . . [co]mynge to churche comitted to certeyn comitties of[f the] Lordes. . . . for banckerupts.

[An] act for a freeschole yn Southwarke, past.

An act for severall sheriffs yn Beddford and Bucks, past.

An act for the restytucion yn blood of Watson, past.

A byll that no howey shall crosse the seas.

This day order was taken that the Howse sholde dayly sytt at th'afternone as the Lordes do the lyk.

---

22. *CJ*, I.89. Marginal note at this point: 'T[homa]s Longe was lyce[nse]d to departe home, but immediately after, he was sent to Brydwell and on Wytsone Eve, the ij of May, he sett upon the pyllorie yn Chipsyde for his sedyciouse words, viz. that the Quene sholde be

dedd, which he affirmed that beinge at the Duke of Norffolk's howse one of the servaunts of the saide Duke shode so say unto him and willed him to tell the same to others.'

23. *CJ*, I.88 (9 May).

24. *Sic*: fettered?

A byll for jurors to be eased yn Shropshere.

A byll that none of the Quene's check roll servaunts to be returned by sheriffs.

A bill for the preservacion of havens yn Devon.

A byll for the Erle of Lecestre to buylde an hospitall at Warwyk towne.

A byll for the restytucion yn blood of the heires of Henry Brewerton.

A byll agaynst fraudulent guyfts, whereby to defeate delapidacions, and that no lesse to be made above xxi yeres or iij lyves.

A byll for the restytucion yn blood of the children of Sir Thomas Wyett.

[22 May]

On Tweseday the 22 of May an act for Porter and Grevell; which Porter stole and married the daughter of Tyrell, and they bothe made a false conveighaunce of the lands.

A byll for archerey.

An act from the Lordes for symony, to be amended.[25]

A byll for the water of Welland to be made navigable.[26]

A byll for comynge to the churche, which came from the Lordes to be amended, was muche dyscoursed but not concluded.

The bylls for tellers and treasons sent from the Lordes to be amended.

A byll for purveyors at Oxford and Cambridge.

A byll from the Lordes against promoters, with addicions.

A byll agaynst fraudulent guyfts to avoyde dylapidacions.

An act for the Erle of Lecester's hospitall, past.

An act for the comission of sewers to be amended.

An act that the Quene's servaunts of check roll shall not be returned, past.

[23 May]

On Weneseday the 23 daye a byll for paving the streetes at St Botulphe's without Algate, past.

An act for pavinge of Ipswyche, past.

A byll agaynst fraudulent guyfts of deedes of any leasor thereby to avoyde the awnsweringe for lapidacions.

An act for bryngnynge yn to the realme wares prohibited, past.

An act that churches may be served with good pastors brough[t] and amended by the Lordes, past.

A byll for removing a schole from Lawton to Gaynsbury, overthrowen. /

f.8   An act . . .

A byll for co[mynge] . . .

An act for archer[ie].

An act for restytucion yn blood of Sir Thomas Wy[ett] . . .

An act for tryall of jurors yn Shropshere and He[refordshire].

An act for tryall of felonyes yn severall sheres of Wales.

An act [agaynst] promoters sent from the Lordes with addicions.

A byll that no purveyors shall [i]ntermedle at Oxford or [C]a[mbridge] within fyve myles, past.[27]

A bill for tellers and recevers came from the Lordes.

[24 May]

On Thursday the 24 of May a byll agaynst banckerupts, past.

An act that no howies or plate shall crosse beyond the seas.

An act for r[evi]vinge of certeyn statuts, *viz*: tyllage, regratynge, woods, atteynts, mylche kyn, to contynewe for ever; rotherbeasts, weanelings, butter, tyllage, the releff of the poore, for fyshinge, gaoles, foreyn wares, bowes and bowstaves, graynes, to contynewe to th'end of the next parlament, past. [28]

An act for comynge to the church, sent, amended by the Lordes and agayne amended and returned. [29]

A byll for bringnynge the river of Lee to London.

An act for restytucion yn blood the heires of Sir Henry Brewerton, past.

An act for restytucion of the lands to Tyrell which was by false devyse of Lodewyke Grevell and Porter was conveighed, and the daughter of the saide Tyrell stollen away and maried to the saide Porter, past.

[25 May]

On Fryday the 25 an act that no purveor of the Quene's shall take any grayne within fyve myles of Cambrydge, past.

An act for the havens yn Devon and Cornewall, past.

A byll for the incorporating of Weymouth and Mylcomb. 2.

An act for severall shereffs yn the severall counties of Buckyngham and Bedford, past. [30] This bill came from the Lordes.

A byll for the encrease of tyllage.

[26 May]

On Saterday the 26 of May an act for tellers, past.

An act for the ryver of Lee to be brought to London.

A byll for the incorporating of the unyversities of Oxford and Cambrydge, past.

An act for Southampton amended by the Lordes with a proviso, and allowed.

An act for the incorporatinge of the townes of Weymouth and Mylcombe, past.

A byll for lymitacion of lawers' excessyve ffees.

An act for meantenaunce of tyllag, past. /

[28 May]   f.8v

[On Moneday the 28] of May a bill for the La[dy Berk]eley to make a [ioy]nter, past.

. . . the ryver of [Lee] to be brought to London, past. [31]

. . . of the lawers' fees.

. . . Hugh Osborne of the rates of rents . . . which(?) everye . . . pay for respect of homage.

[This d]ay there was mich ado about suche men of the Howse as were []ected and bourdened to have received fees [yn] the Howse for the preferringe or speking to any byll, of which Norton, [one of] the burgesses for London, was chardged

25. Sent up to the Lords, according to *CJ*, I.91.

26. Sent up to the Lords, according to *CJ*, I.91.

27. *CJ*, I.92: 2nd reading, and passed on 25 May, as Hooker also says.

28. Cf. *SR*, IV.560-2.

29. CF. *CJ*, I.92.

30. Still being considered on 28 May (*CJ*, I.93).

31. Provisos (*CJ*, I.93).

32. See *CJ*, I.93 (29 May).

namely for the [Cambr]idge matter. This matter was comytted to certeyn of the
Howse and by them the same salved.[32]
[29 May]
On Twesday the 29 of May a byll for lawers' excessyve fees, past.
    An act for shotynge yn hand gonnes, past.
[30 May]
On Weneseday the 30 of May the generall pardon was redd.

    These bylls past, Sir Walter Myldemay made motion that as all they there mett
together yn peax and love, so dyd wyshe they sholde so depart and that no advantage
sholde be taken of any words there past, but all to be best. After him Grymstone dyd
the lyke, makynge mocion also that a collection sholde be made for the releff of the
Frenche Churche, which was donne and amounted about xxx[1]; and that the Quene
might be moved for the recoverye of Ireland yn to good order, whereby a gayne wolde
growe to her and an ease to all her subgects: towards which her subgects gladly wolde
contrybut of the[ir]e goods a nother subsidie *etc.* This his was contynewed by Norton,
Gylbert and the Lord Deputie and well lyked of all the whole Howse. At lengthe the
Speker stode up, and he made the lyke requests of love and amytie as also craved the
good will of every person there, and that if he hadd slypped yn any thinge they shold
impute it to his ignoraunce and not to any wyllfullnes, and that he was and wolde be
prest, not onely to do his best for that Howse, but also for every one of theyme to his
uttermost if he might staunde theym in steed.

    At after none, about v[e] of the clock, the Quene's Majestie came to the higher
howse, and going yn to a severall rome apoynted for the purpose, she apparelled her
selff yn her royall robes of Parlament and a coronet on her hedd, and then came yn to
the hygher howse and satt yn the seate of estat; and then all things being settled the
Speker came, and beinge without the lowest barre at the mydle, after he had made
his three obeysaunce, made his oracion declaringe how that the comon howse of
Parlament, beinge assembled by her commandement, had condyscended upon
sundrye and dyverse lawes, as well for and concernynge religion, as also for her
salfytie and for the comon estate of the realme, which nevertheles were no lawes
untyll that she had allowed and geven her consent there unto, which donne, then were
they lawes and to be obeyed, observed and kept as lawes. In observacion of which,
and of all other lawes, was required justyce, obedyence, and exequution. Then he
declared of the good will and hartie love the lower howse bare unto her, and how
that freely, without the denyeinge of any one person or of any demaunde or mocion
made, they have geven her a subsidie and to x[th] and xv[th], which thoughe it were
according to her Majestie's deserts, yet seinge / theire good . . . her high[ness] . . .
dys[   ]ge that . . . the lower howse had [   ]sh . . . which he knewe was rather
of ignorance hop[ed] . . . remitt it. Wh[en] he had thus ended, the Lord Keper . . .
particular poynte . . . particular aw[nsw]ere, and as for . . . awnswered. The
subsidie the Quene thanck . . . the guyft thereof not to her, but to that(?) chefly
app[   ] . . . she hathe to employ and bestowe it. And as for the . . . awnswereth
that they the [   ] were of too sorts, th'one . . . lyketh . . . the other arrogant,
audaceous and presumptu[ous] . . . for arrogantly and presumptuosly they have
there reasoned . . . her prerogative, contrarie to her will and pleasure for all . . . they

f.9

sholde first have beenne debated yn the Convocacon, and by the bish[op]s and not by theym. Lykewyse the prerogatyve toochethe her Majestie and her authoritie, which w[ithou]t her favor ought not to be had yn question. These therefor that so audacyosly and arogantly have dealed yn such matters may not lok[e] to rece[ve] further favor then by the statuts of this realme is ordayned. This donne, the bylls begann[e] to be redd wh[er]eof too were brought unto her and havinge perused them called the Lord of Burley unto her, who after they had talked awhile the bylls were delyver[ed] to the clerck of the parlament named Mr Spyllman and then he returned to his place; and there one of the saide bylls was redd which was the byll of treasons. Then the Quene stoode up and spake her selff as foloweth: 'In this parlament it was shewed us of a byll devysed of for our savitie agaynst treasons, whereof when we had the sight it lyked us not; nevertheles beinge perswaded by our counsell of the necessytie thereof, and that it was for our salffitie, we were contended the same sholde proceede. This byll beinge brought yn to the lower howse, some one lerned man dyd put to the same one other byll additionall, which stretched so farre that others might unwares be yntrapped full miche agayst our good will and pleasure. And this beinge brought ynto us, we myslyked it verie miche beinge[33] not of the mynde to offer xtremitie or iniurie to any person; for as we mynde no harme to others so we hope none will mynde unto us. And therefor reservinge to everie his right, we thought it not good to deale so hardely with any bodie as by that byll was ment.' And so when she had saide her mynde, the byll (which yn deede was amended before) was allowed.

As for the byll of respyte of homage whereof the comons fynde them selffs so miche greved, as also the excessive ffees of the lawers, her Majestie wyll yn tyme see the reformacion and take order therein.

This parlament beganne on Monedaye beinge the ij[de] of Aprill[34] 1571 and ended the Weneseday beinge the xxx[th] of May folowinge, which are yn the whole lix dayes. Also there is to be allowed unto me for my travells towards and from the parlament viij dayes, so th[e]n yn the whole amount to lxvij daies which at iij[s] the daye amount to xiij[l] viij[s]. /

The actes . . . *xiij° domine* Elizabeth.   f.9v

[An act] whereby certeyn offensis be made [trea]son.

[An act agayn]st bryngin[g] yn of bulls from the sea of Rome.

. . . fugytyves over the seas.

. . . the lands, tenements, goodds *etc.* of recevers and tellers by lyable to there debts.

. . . agaynst fraudulent guyfts and alyenacion.

. . . that constathes of patents to be avelable and good.

[An act] for banckerupts.

[An] act agaynst usury.

[An] act for the comyssyon of sewers.

An act against frawdes, defeatynge remedyes for dilapidacions.

An act for meantenenaunce of navigacion.

33. 'Miche beinge' seems to be repeated in MS.   34. Hooker wrote 'July' first.

An act to reform dysorders touchinge mynesters of the Churche.
An act for the encrease of tyllage.
An act for bryngynge yn of bowestaves.
An act that no howye nor platt shall crosse the seas.
An act for cappes.
An [act] for leases of benyfyces with cure.
An act that none of the Quene's purveiors shall deale within fyve myles of Oxford or Cambridge.
An [act] for dyvisyon of shereffs yn sundry sheres.
An act for pavinge without Algate.
An act for pavinge of Ipswyche.
An act for revivinge of certeyn statutes.
An act for th'atteyndre of the rebeles yn the northe.
An act to make the reyver of Weyland navygable.
An act to make Peregryn Barton a free denyson.
An act for the towne of Southampton.
An act for the towne of Brystowe.
An act for the towne of Lustuthiall.
An act for Skevington.
An act for Morys Rodney.
An act for the Erle of Lecester to founde an hospitall.
An act for restytucon yn blood of Sir Thomas Wyatt's children.
An act for incorporatinge of Weymouthe and Mylcombe.
An act for restytucion yn bloodd of Henry Brewton.
An act for incorporating of bothe the unyversities.
An act for th'assuruance of the Lord Barkeley's lands.
An act for Tyrrell.
An act for bryngeyng the ryver of Lee to London.
An act [for] a subsydie of the clergie.
An act for a subsydie of the temporaltie.
An act for the Quene's pardon.

THE FOURTH PARLIAMENT
FIRST SESSION
8 MAY-30 JUNE 1572

Documents

SEPARATES: HOUSE OF LORDS
1. Sir Nicholas Bacon's speech on Lord Cromwell's case

SEPARATES: HOUSE OF COMMONS
1. Herald's account of opening proceedings, 8 and 10 May
2. Causes against Mary Queen of Scots shewn to a committee of both Houses, 13 May
3. Points from Arthur Hall's speech, 15 May
4. Arguments against Mary Queen of Scots presented to Elizabeth by some of both Houses, 26 May (?)
5. Committee's settlement between Francis Alford and others, 27 May
6. Reasons for executing the Duke of Norfolk provided by Thomas Digges and Thomas Dannet, 31 May
7. A form of a petition for executing the Duke of Norfolk provided by Thomas Norton, 31 May
8. The bill which passed both Houses against the Queen of Scots, 25 June

JOURNALS
1. Fulk Onslow's journal, 24-31 May, 25 June
2. Anonymous journal, 8 May-25 June
3. Thomas Cromwell's journal, 8 May-30 June

The decision to call a new parliament came later in the year and reflected Elizabeth's reluctance to meet an assembly, but the need to deal with the aftermath of the Ridolfi Plot was clear. The documents for this session naturally reveal the importance of providing for the Queen's safety, and after the opening ceremonial procedures on 8 and 10 May [Doc.1], the Crown lost little time in presenting a carefully marshalled list of charges against Mary Stuart, the main ones ranging from her claim to the throne of England and her request for recognition as heir apparent, to her alleged involvement with Elizabeth's enemies at home and abroad [Doc.2]. The mood of the House was predictably hostile, and when Arthur Hall spoke for the second time on 15 May in opposition to Thomas Norton and in favour of leniency, he could scarcely make himself heard: on 19 May he was called to the bar to explain his views. The second point in Document 3 is particularly interesting in view of Hall's eventual dismissal from the Commons in 1581, but at this stage Sir Francis Knollys' intervention seems to have prevented his being punished severely.[1]

In the meantime the Lords and Commons met in joint committee and decided to petition Elizabeth for the Scottish queen's execution. The petition – 'this laborious document,' as Neale rightly called it – may have been presented on Whit Monday, 26 May [Doc.4], and at the Court of St James on 28 May Elizabeth told the committees' deputation that she could not, for the moment at least, act upon the suggestion made in the petition and supported by a majority of the Council and Parliament.[2] She also forbade further discussion of her cousin's fate while a new bill excluding her from the English succession was being drafted. Parliament's attention shifted to the Duke of Norfolk, convicted of treason in January for his part in the Ridolfi Plot, and by Saturday 31 May there was a strong feeling in the House that the Speaker should present Elizabeth with convincing reasons why she should delay no further over Norfolk's execution.[3] At least three members had been busy before the debate preparing written arguments, and while there is no positive evidence that the papers of Digges and Dannet were formally introduced, one of our diarists tells us that Norton presented 'a paper in writing'.[4] His own contribution, the work of an experienced parliamentary draftsman, was carefully organized almost in the form of a bill; Digges' and Dannet's arguments, though no less forceful, were more loosely constructed. The assumptions common to all three papers were that

1. *EP*, I.253-7, 260-61; Oxford, Bodley: Tanner 393, f.58.
2. *EP*, I.268-74.
3. *EP*, I.273-4,278-80; *CJ*, I.98.
4. MS 3186 (Braye MS), f.3.

Elizabeth was bound by duty to execute Norfolk to make herself and the nation safe, that Parliament's voice was the expression of this moral and political duty, and that in this instance at least that voice should be heard and acted upon lest 'her Majestie be recorded for the onely prince of this land with whome the subiectes therof could never prevaile in any one sute' [Docs.6 & 7].[5] The bill excluding Mary from the English succession was finally drafted on Elizabeth's orders, but ran up against considerable debate in the House on 6 June, Yelverton in particular being critical of a number of points. Some of the alternative readings noted in the version printed here [Doc.8] reflect part of his argument as reported by Thomas Cromwell.[6] The amended bill, together with the proviso suggested by Norton, was ready for Elizabeth by 26 June, though she allowed no further progress and it was never revived.[7]

The two remaining separates for this session are a mundane, though for the individuals concerned no less important, contrast to the business of Mary Stuart. We have two instances of Parliament's intervention in judicial affairs demonstrating the ability of each House to act as a court and influence activities of other courts of the realm. During the second reading debate on the bill against fraudulent conveyances Francis Alford claimed to be a victim of fraudulent deals, and requested remedy. In response a committee was appointed and reported to the House on 24 May upholding Alford's complaint, his adversaries apparently being persuaded by the Commons' authority to return to Chancery for a final settlement [Doc.5].[8] Bacon's argument [Lords Doc.1], developed on 30 June 1572, was probably part of the determination of Lord Cromwell's case in the Lords on that day. Cromwell, seeking parliamentary privilege against threatened attachment by Chancery, found the Lord Keeper protecting Chancery jurisdiction and, incidentally, defining the royal prerogative on which it was based. Even so, the Lords upheld Cromwell's claim to privilege, though only as long as no better cause were shown by the Queen's prerogative, common or statute law, or any other precedents.[9]

Three surviving diaries of varying length and quality add greatly to our understanding of this session. Onslow's account is largely a catalogue of bills before the House in the week 24-31 May, but fortunately he did record some of the debate on Mary, and his is the only account we have of St Leger's move on 30 May for the execution of Norfolk, one day when Thomas Cromwell himself was away from the House.[10] Onslow also left a summary of the bill which eventually came before the Commons for its third reading on 25 June, including the famous proviso regarding Mary's claim to the succession. Outside the formal journals, his 'diary' is the only example of a Clerk's notes to have survived for the period 1559-81, though it is not clear if the document represents a preliminary stage of Onslow's note-taking, later to be polished and reduced into part of the finished official journal, or whether its existence was completely independent of his professional activities and composed, as it were, at his leisure. The bills noted here occur in the order seen in the printed *Journals*, though several items included in this document will not be found there, for example, a decision about the Speaker, and details of the bill concerning Mary Stuart; a 'torn' bill is also better described here.[11] And Onslow's commenting on the quality of speeches ran counter to contemporary 'professional' practice.

The two other diaries are more extensive, though distinct in character. The anonymous journal is almost entirely preoccupied with Mary Stuart and Norfolk, covering the opening weeks (8-25 May) and then referring to stages of the main debate after that time: in the midst of this is an unexpected and graphic eyewitness account of the scene at Norfolk's execution on 2 June. This selective approach produced a record of variable quality, even within its own terms of reference. There is, for example, no specific mention of the significant roles played by Wentworth, Snagge and Norton on 31 May in the agitation against Norfolk; or of Norton's as the author of the proviso to the bill against Mary – at this point the diarist had distilled the speeches of at least 16 members into a few lines.[12] Thomas Cromwell's is the only one of these three journals with pretensions to being a comprehensive account of proceedings throughout the session, taking in both opening and closing procedure, though his involvement in the committee work of the House was already removing him on occasion from the main arena of debate. But even when he was present it is unfortunate from our point of view that his interest does not seem to have been roused in quite the way we should want. Cromwell leaves no record of the House's reaction to Elizabeth's ban on the reception of religious bills, though the anonymous commentator thought that a threat to the liberty of the Commons was recognized at the time.[13] Again, it was the unknown diarist, not Cromwell, who seemed more perceptive of pressure being exerted on the Speaker for the second reading of the bill against Mary on 6 June.[14] The finer significance of this kind of omission cannot be discussed here, and it should not detract from the value of Cromwell's work. Although he failed occasionally to note a reading, his record of bills tallies almost exactly with that of the Commons Journal, and in at least two instances (19 May, 4 June) he mentions a bill of which the official journal takes no cognisance.[15] Elizabeth wanted Parliament to deal quickly with the limited official programme only, but the amount of time spent on other bills (many of them apparently private) is impressive: a sustained use of committees and afternoon sittings allowed some 70 bills to be considered in only 32 working days. Mary Stuart and Norfolk remain of prime importance for Cromwell, easily occupying more than half the bulk of the journal, yet there are full accounts of other matters exciting the concern of members. There is, for example, coverage of the extensive debate on the bill which sought to prevent fraudulent land conveyances; of the move to revive the proposed poor law reform of 1571; and of the bill to regulate weapons, partly so that 'one only kind of bullet should be used [so] that one souldier in tyme of neede

5. BL Add.48023, f.162.
6. TCD MS 1045, fos.52v-3.
7. *EP*, I.281-90, 309-10.
8. TCD MS 1045, fos.19-20, 43v.
9. D'Ewes, pp.203-4; BL Harl.249, fos.119-20.
10. HL MS 3186 (Braye MS), f.IV; TCD MS 1045, f.46v.
11. Cf. *CJ*, I.95, 99; and see *EP*, I.379.
12. Oxford, Bodley: Tanner 393, fos.60v-62.
13. *Ibid.*, f.59.

14. *Ibid.*, fos.59,62.
15. The bill for the sale of fish, TCD MS 1045, f.24v. Cromwell also mentions a bill for brewing, which though not appearing in the Commons Journal for 1572, is noted for the session of 1576. Cromwell's memory and notes have probably become confused, and the episode may indicate that the journals were written up at some time well after the event (f.49v; *CJ*, I.106).

might supply the wante of another'.[16] Other bills concerned fewer people, yet aroused considerable interest. Cromwell gives a good account of the complex proceedings, involving the participation of legal counsel from outside the Commons' membership, in the dispute over the Earl of Kent's lands; while the parliamentary activities of local interest groups emerge on more than one occasion. There is, for instance, the stark statement about the bill for free fishing (unnoticed in the *Commons Journals*.[17] And in his account of the debates on the waxchandlers' bill, London's wood supplies and the plan to bring more water to Worcester, Cromwell reveals some of the ways in which Parliament functioned as a testing ground for private interest, and records an apparently widespread antipathy to any suggestion of monopoly. The armoury bill as first drawn up appeared to have been conceived in the interests of a small group of men and was criticized in that light.[18] But the constitutional difficulties raised in the debate on the bill prohibiting leather exports were, in a sense, the most significant, though they have gone unnoticed in the discussion of monopolies at the end of the reign.[19]

Another important matter to occur in the journals is what must, for the sake of convenience, be called 'freedom of speech'. Speaker Bell's request for the privilege was apparently more extensively developed than had previously been the case, and it bears careful examination, as does the Lord Keeper's response, for that too is reported as containing an extra ingredient.[20] As the session developed and Elizabeth's reluctance to act against Mary became more evident, members were from time to time overtaken by a sense of inhibition, and the Speaker grew less willing to act as the Commons' spokesman, transforming himself explicitly into their mere messenger by his insistence that they commit to paper any statement they wished to be conveyed to the Queen.[21] At the end of the session, on 30 June, he made a special point of assuring Elizabeth of the Commons' loyalty to her, the Queen in reply professing surprise and all but claiming that Bell was being over-sensitive in his belief that malicious elements were bent on tale-telling and discrediting members.[22] It may well have been this sense of unease in the House which seemed to add a degree of urgency to the desirability of unanimity and so encouraged members to be intolerant of dissident voices and sweep aside the qualms of the one or two individuals who were not happy about suppressing Arthur Hall's minority view.[23]

16. TCD MS 1045, f.50v.
17. *Ibid.*, fos.24v–25.
18. *Ibid.*, fos.34v–5, 50v–1, see also fos.47, 60v; 32v–3; 23v,51 and v for reactions to monopoly.
19. *Ibid.*, f.48.
20. *Ibid.*, fos.4v–5v; and see Neale's comment,

EP, I.246.
21. TCD MS 1045, fos.4, 39v, 58 and v; Oxford, Bodley: Tanner 393, fos.60 & v, 61v–3; *EP*, I.305–07, and see 278 for Neale's explanation of Bell's reticence.
22. TCD MS 1045, fos.71 and v.
23. *Ibid.*, fos.15v–16v, 24v, 26.

1. [*House of Lords*] *Sir Nicholas Bacon's speech on Lord Cromwell's case*

Text from BL Hargrave 249, copy.
Other MSS. London: BL Hargrave 227, Hargrave 281, Harl.39.
Lambeth Palace 250. Oxford: Bodley, Tanner 91. Norfolk: formerly
at Keswick Hall, Norwich: Gurney MSS (HMC, 12.ix.155), dispersed
in sale room. Northants. CRO: Finch-Hatton 84/14.
Printed. Sir Nicholas Bacon, *Arguments Exhibited in Parliament* (1641).

Hargrave 249, fos.206-7

The argumentes exhibited by the Lord Keeper Sir Nicholas Bacon in Parliament
proveinge that noblemen's persons bee attachable for contemptes committed by
them in the Queene's Majestie's Courtes of Chancerie disobeyinge the decrees in the
Courte; which came in question upon an attachment awarded out of the same
Courte to the shirieffe of Norffolke to attach the bodie of the Lord Cromwell for
disobeyinge a decree made in the said court betweene one Taverne[r], plaintiffe, and
the said[1] Lord Cromwell defendant; which attachment so executed by the said
shirieffe, and the bodie of the said Lord Cromwell broughte prisoner in the said
Courte of Chancery.

Firste, he saithe that for a contempte committed by a noble man againste his prince
his person is attachable by the lawe. But if a nobleman disobey a decree made in the
Chauncerie in a matter examinable there hee comitteth a contempte against his
prince, and therefore by the common lawe his bodie (for his contempte) is
attachable.[2] And this the rather because the decrees given there be given *coram
nobis in cancellar[ia]*.

Secondarilie, he saithe that if a noble man committ a contempte againste the
Queene's Majestie's prerogative in one of the highest degrees his bodie for that is
attachable by lawe; but if a noble man disobey a decree made in the Chauncerie and
warranted to be made by her Highnes' prerogative in one of the highest degrees, hee
comitteth a contempte againste that prerogative / and therefore his bodie for the same   f.206v
is attachable by lawe. And the cause whie hee thinketh thus: a prerogative in one of
the highest degrees is for that the prince by his prerogative hath power to order causes
otherwise then the lawe is, and to helpe the subiectes in a cause wherein hee hath noe
other helpe in lawe, which seemes in reason as great a prerogative as may bee.

Thirdly, it hath bene alwaies used that[3] noble men have bine and yett bee called

---

1. 'Of the Lord . . . and the said' supplied
from Hargrave 281.
2. Marginal note at this point: 'Noblemen

may bee attached for contempte.'
3. MS reads 'the'.

into the Chauncerie for matter examinable in the same Courte, and the same proceeded in and ordered. And if use and custome have allowed of this, then of all congruence it must allow this necessarie dependences of the same, which is the execucion of these orderes, for otherwise that use should have bene altogether in vaine. And other meanes in the Chauncerie for execucion in these orderes is there none but by attachment, and therefore of necessarie dependances upon such orderes thus used they are to be allowed. And as to that which hath bene said – that there hath bene noe use of that execucion by attachment – it maie bee answered that noble men were of that consideracion that they never disobeyed anie of those orderes, and therefore no cause of that use.

Fourthlie, to grante a courte power to heare and order and not to execute the same is a plaine absurditie; and againe, to leave all coppieholders of noble men without remedie if they be removed from theire coppieholdes by their lordes, and all other menn without remedie againste a noble man in matters of equitie, seemes a great inconvenience and much preiudiciall to the comon weale consideringe how great the number of these maie bee, besides what an inconveneint thinge it is to have a noble man bring a matter into the Chancerie and the Courte shall have power to doe iustice for him, but not against him. This is not *ius aequabile* and all these things are to followe in his opinion, excepte these attachmentes in the causes before remembred be allowed.

Fiftlie, forasmuch as the Chauncerie is warranted to heare and order causes by vertue of the Queene's Majestie's prerogative where otherwise by lawe the subiecte hath noe helpe, and alsoe to quallifie the extremitie of the lawe, therefore if all causes examinable in Chancerie for the respectes aforsaid betwene a noble man and another man should be taken from the heareinge and ordering of the Courte, that must needes be in derogacion of the said prerogative, which hee thinketh ought not to bee f.207   without the Queen's Majestie's privicie. And therefore praieth / as he hath often done that her Highnes may be made acquainted with this cause before anie order bee takenn therein.

Finis.

1. *Herald's account of opening proceedings, 8 and 10 May*

Text from BL. Add.5758, copy.

Add.5758, fos.73·4

The order of her Majeste's procedinge to the Parliament Howse the 8 of Maye 1572 the 14th yeare of her reigne, beinge then at St James.[1]

The Quene's Majeste did take her coche at the garden dore of St James and was conveyed thoroughe the parke by her nobles, prelates and gentlemen and ladies *etc.* to White Hall where her Majeste stayed the space of one hower and there put on her robes and a diadeame of gowld with riche stones and jewelles on her hed. This done, she came from her pryve chamber in White Hall with her nobilite thorough the chambers to the hall and so to the common brydge called the Water Gate where her Highenes toke her barge and was rowed to the Kinge's Bridge at Westminster, wheras her coche was reddy with all her nobles and bushops in theyre robes on horsback, all men in order placed. And her Majeste beinge sett in her coche the gentlemen pensioners with theyre axes, the sargentes and [officers of arms][2] set were[3] on horsback and the esquiries with others on foote on eache side of her Highnes' coche in good order. Next to her Majeste rod th'Erle of Kent with the cape of mayntenance and th'Erle of Rutland bearinge the sword next before. Then th'Erle of Oxeford, Lord Great Chamberlen of England, and with him th'Erle of Worcester, being for that tyme appoynted to be Erle Marshall, caryed the rodd next before. Then the Lord Admyrall[4] beinge appoynted to be Lord Steward for that parliament. Then Mr Garter Kinge of Arms with ij gentlemen hushiers, he ryding in the myddest betwene them. Then the ij Archebushoppes, of Canterbury and York. And so every noble man and the bushoppes and barons ij and 2 *etc.* in theyre degrees and places in order, with the herauldes on eache syde. And so cam her Majeste thorough the pallays into the Kinge's Street and from thence to the north dore of the cathederall churche of St Peter in Westminster where there was made redy a place with carpettes, stole and cushions for her Majeste wher her Majeste allighted. And beinge placed therin the Deane of Westminster with divers other of the chanons, prestes and queresters beinge redy at the said dore to receyve her Majeste, the Deane kneled downe and sed a chapter with certen prayers; which don he delivered unto her Highnes the rod of sylver and gylt with a dove in the tope of it which her Majeste toke and caryed in her hand. And then ther cam six knightes

1. Rather than Whitehall because of plague: 3. *Sic.*
    EP, I.242.   4. Earl of Lincoln.
2. Crossed out.

with a canapie under the which her Majeste was conveyed from the same litell north dore with the hole quyer of chanons and queresters singinge unto the west dore of the quyer, and so to the upper end of the same where was prepared a travers into the which her Highnes was conveyed, where she continewed duringe the sermon that was made by the Bishop of Lincolne. The sermon being done her Majeste was conveyed under the canapie agayne and so with her nobles, prelates, barons and ladyes *etc.*, every man in order as before, brought her to the est dore of the churche and so to the west dore of the parliament howse where at the stayer foote the cannapie was taken away and delivered to the footemen which were reddy there to receyve the same as a fee dewe unto them. Then her Majeste was conveyed up to the parliament howse wher ther is a place made redy to withdrawe her selfe; stayed there a litell space untill the lords and bushopes had taken theyre places. And then her / Majeste cam forthe, the hatt of mayntenance, sword, the Lord Marshall and Lord Chamberlen, and Garter King of Heraldes and gentlemen hushers goinge before to make place, she was brought to the royall seatte preparred on degrees with carpettes, cheyre, stole, cushions, under a riche clothe of estate. The Lady Leneux caryd the trayne all this tyme. Thus her Majeste beinge sett in her chayre of estate th'Erle of Kent with the hatt standinge on the right hand and the Lord Chamberlen with him, th'Erle of Ruttland and th'Erle of Worcester with the sword and rodd on the left hand, *viz* all placed, the lower howse cam into the same place. The Lord Keeper stode up on the right hand of her Majeste['s] clothe of estate, havinge a place there made for him, began an oration declaringe the cause of her Majeste's sommoninge of this highe court of Parliament: which done the knightes and burgesses beinge appoynted to repayre to the lower howse to chose theyre Speker. Then her Majeste cam downe from her seat to her withdrawinge chamber where she put of her robes and in the meane tyme the lords shiffted them. Which don, her Majeste cam forthe and the lordes and gentlemen went on before with the sword and rod caryed and the heraldes on the sydes of the noble men. And so cam downe the pryve stayres on the est syd of the parliament howse to the Queen's Brydge where she tooke her barge, the sword and Marshalle's rodd delivered to the gentlemen ushers. Other lordes departed and her Majeste was rowed to Whitehall stayres whereas she before had taken barge and so went thoroughe the howse to the parke where her coche was reddy, and with dyvers noblemen and ladyes retorned to St James agayne. And this was the end of the fyrst daye of her Majeste's goinge to the parliament howse *viz* viij[th] of Maye 1572 *anno* xiiij[th] of the Quen's Majeste's reigne.

10th of Maye 1572.

The Satterdaye followinge beinge the xth of Maye 1572 her Majeste went agayne from St James to Whitehall in her coche to the hall dore where she alighted and with her nobles, ladyes *etc.* was conveyed to the common brige called the Watergate where she entred her barge rowed by he[r] watermen to the Quene's Bridge at Westminster where her nobles, ladyes and gentlemen, her gentlemen pensioners there with theyre axes, redy to receve her. And the sword and Marshalle's rodd borne before her from the water syd with the Lord Chamberlen, gentlemen hushers, sargantes of arms and heraldes before, her Grace cam to her withdrawinge Chamber there made redy. Then the lords and bushoppes went into the utter chamber to make them reddy, to put on theyre robes, and cam and sat in theyre places in the parliament howse, savinge suche noble men as were appoynted for the hatt, sword and rood of the Marshall, Chamberlen and such other, the huishers and Garter, which all stayed for her Majeste who cam forthe with a dyadem on her hed and in her roobes proceded in such order with the said lordes before her unto her seat royall. And there being sett and the lower howse called in, Mr Bell, the Speaker, beinge chosen by the assent of the knightes and burgesses of the same Howse, who cam in betwene Mr Threasurer[5] on the right hand and Mr Comptroler[6] on the left hand, after his dewtie obeysance made to her Majeste he began an oration in / the disabling   f.74 of himselfe and prayed to be sent back agayne and that ther might be a better choyse made of a more fite man then he, or to this effect. Then her Majeste called to the Lord Keper and willed him to deliver her pleasure of the good opinion and her allowance of him; which don he began a new oration touching divers poyntes and of allowance or[7] as I take hit from her Majeste in his accesse to her Majeste and of free speche to be had in the Howse. This ended her Majeste called the Lord Keper and deliver[ed] to him her answere, which when he had done the Speaker and other were lycensed to depart; and her Majeste cam downe and withdrewe her selfe to her chamber as before where she put of her robes and was conveyed by the back stayers to the said Quene's Brige and there toke her barge and cam to the foresaid comon stayres at the Whithall and so to the dore. There in the court she mounted into her coche and manye of the noble men, gentlemen and pensioners with theyre axes waighted on her thoroughe the parke to St James: which was the 2nd daye of the same parliament, 1572. Which parliament continewed long by sundery prorogations.

---

5. Francis Knollys.
6. James Croft.

7. 'Or' inserted in the same hand.

2. Causes against Mary Queen of Scots shewn to a committee of both Houses, 13 May

Text from BL Add.48049 (Yelverton 54), copy.

Add.48049 (Yelverton 54), fos.249·50

xiij° Maii 1572

Principall causes shewed agaynst the Queen of Scottes by the Queen's Majestie's learned cownsell

To the lordes of the upper howse	] in nomber xxj[1]	] bushoppes vij erles vij barons vij
To certayne of the nether howse	] in nomber xliiij	] of knightes and burgesses.

The causes as they opened them may be reduced into fyve heads.

The fyrst ⎤ Clayme to the crowne of England in possession, with refusall and delay to renownce the same. ⎦

Givyng of the armes of England withowt difference in scutcheons, cote armes, plate, aulter clothes, ripper clothes whiche weare openly seen at triumphes *etc.*

Writynge of the style of Queen of England, Scotland, Fraunce and Ireland, in lettres patents: durynge hir coverture and after. The renuntiation of the style *etc.*, agreed on in the treatie at Edenburghe, fyrst delayed in Fraunce, after in Scotland: in the end refused except the Queen would declare hir by Parlament heire apparent, and leave the succession in the Ladie Lenox.

A pedigree conveighynge hir three wayes to the crowne, one as descendyng from the oldest daughter of King Henrie the vij[th], an other from the Duke of Somerset, the thyrd from a daughter of Edmond Ironsyde before the Conquest.

Genethliacon of hir soon[2] printed, intituled *Prince of England, Scotland and Ireland.* Diverse bookes printed in France to that end.

The opinion of the Queen's ill subiectes owt of the realme, callynge the Queen nowe 'pretensed' and 'the late

Queene', and the Scottish Queene: 'our Queene': *videlicet* the Duchesse of Feria, the Countesse of Northumberland, Chamberlayne and others.|

The second — Sekyng a mariage with the Duke of Norfolke to advaunce that title in possession.

Part of the matters wherof the Duke of Norfolke was indicted, arrayned and condemned; whiche was alleaged as proffe sufficient. Hir advise to performe the mariage by force.   f.249v

The thyrd — The procurement of the late rebellion in the north.[1]

By messages continually to and fro between hir and the Erle of Northumberland, sent by John Leviston, a Scott, Thomas Bushoppe and his soon,[2] and by Hamlyn.

Oswold Wilkinson sent to the Spanishe ambassador, and brought to him by the Bushoppe of Rosse hir ambassador to whome he was directed to procure ayde of men and money for the rebellion.

The feare shee had and sorow, when shee heard the Erle of Sussex had taken the Erle of Northumberland, for combrynge of fryndes as she writte to the Duke of Norfolke.

The fourth — The releevyng of the rebelles after they fled.

She procured 20200 crownes from the Pope, whereof 6000 by hir order weare distributed, *videlicet* as to the Erle of Westmorland 2000, to the Countesse of Northumberland 2000, and to Dacres, Norton, Markenfild and the rest in Flanders 2000.

The receavyng and intertaynment of the rebelles in Scotland at their fyrst fliyng, by her frends only.|

Hir long lettre in cyphre to the Bushoppe of Rosse wherein shee discoursethe hir estate, and shewyng manie cawses not to trust uppon England, Scotland, nor Fraunce: resteth at the last uppon Spayne.   f.250

Hir opinion to send an expresse messinger to sollicite the Pope and Kynge of Spayne *etc.* Hir choyce of Rodolphi, the Pope's secreate agent in England.

The goynge of Rodolphi accordingly fyrst to the Duke of Alba, then to the Pope, and after to Spain with instructions: whereunto weare privie the Duke of Norfolke, the Spanish ambassador and Bishop of Rosse.

The some of his message was to procure 10,000 men to arryve in England, and to ioyne with the Duke and his frends: the port was Harwiche in Essex for neernesse to Norfolke.

The fyfte — The practisyng of an invasion by strangers into England and Ireland, and of rebellion in bothe the realmes.

Rodolphi returneth answeare of his audience by the Duke of Alba, whoe dyd accept the request and promised to further the same.

---

1. 22 in the event (*EP*, I.247).   2. I.e. son.

Rodolphi writt iij lettres in cyphre, one to the Bishop of Rosse, one to the Duke intitled *40*, and one to the Lord Lumley entitled *30*, declarynge the Duke's answeare.

The Pope writt ij lettres, one to the Queen of Scots and one to the Duke in cyphre, promisyng ayde.

The Bishop of Rosse hathe confessed all this and the whole practise in a lettre which he sent to the Queen of Scots since he was in the Tower.

Hir practise with Rolleston, Hall, Sir Thomas Stanley and Sir Thomas Gerard for hir escape by force.

Rolleston's confession of their intent to proclame them after hir escape Kynge and Queen of England *etc.*

3. Points from Arthur Hall's speech, 15 May

Text from PRO SP Dom.Eliz.147/52, copy.
Printed. H. G. Wright, *The Life and Works of Arthur Hall of Grantham* (1919), 49.

SP Dom.Eliz.147/52 (first folio)

[Endorsed '*18*[1] *Elizabethe. A note of words uttered in Parliament by M*r *Hall.*']

1. When the Scottish Queene's title is cutt off, where is our assurance?
2. That the offence of the Duke is but private to her Majesty and toucheth not us, and so [we] are not to deale in it but leave it to her self.
3. To move the Howse to surcease dealing in the matter; he alleaged for perswasion, that the harme was not yet donne.
4. Yow will hasten the execucion of such whose feet hereafter yow would be glad to have againe to kisse.
5. Mr Norton speaketh of cutting downe of bushes, he meaneth of two great Princes, the Queen of Scottes and the Duke of Norfolk: when they be cutt downe, where is ever a bush to hyde us then?
6. The practizes wherein the Duke of Norffolk dealt such as peradventure were not hurtfull to the Queen or the realme.
7. He tearmed the execucion of the Duke extremity and rigour of lawe.

1. *Sic.*

4. Arguments against Mary Queen of Scots presented to Elizabeth by some of both Houses, 26 May (?)

i. Presented by the bishops.
Text from BL Cott. Titus FI, copy.
Other MSS. London: PRO SP Scotland (Mary Queen of Scots) 8/47, a shorter version (possibly an earlier draft) endorsed by Burghley '26 May, 1572. A wrytyng exhibited by the clergy of the highar howss to the Queen's Majesty at St James to move hir Majesty to assent to justice against the Scottish Quene'; BL Stowe 358 (copy of Cott. Titus FI), Cott. Caligula CII (as SP Scotland, incorporating amendments), Harl. 2194 (As Cott. Caligula CII). Cambridge: University Library Gg.iii.34 (as Cott. Titus FI, but stopping short).
Printed. D'Ewes, 207-12.
ii. Presented by the laymen.
Text from BL Cott. Titus FI, copy.
Other MSS. London: BL Stowe 358 (copy of Cott. Titus FI), Harl. 4314 (omitting section headed 'Civil reasons for doubt of answer'). Cambridge: University Library Gg.iii.34.
Printed. D'Ewes, 215-19.

Cott. Titus FI, fos. 172-86v

Parliamento anno 14[1] Elizabethae. Certeine argumentes collected out of the scriptures, out of the civill lawe and the common, exhibited to the Queene's Majestie by some of both howses againste the Queen of Scottes.

[i. Presented by the bishops]

Reasones to proove the Queen's Majestie bound in conscience to proceed with severitie in the case of the late Queene of Scottes.

The worde of God, which is the only director of consciences and a certein rule for all estates and offices, doth often and moste earnestly teach that godlye princes or magistrates not only in conscience safelie may but also in dutie towardes God ought severely and uprightly to adminester iustice: ffor this is one of the princepall causes for the which the providence and wisdome of God hath ordeined magistrates in common weales, that they might by justice and punishement, according to the greatnes of the offences, represse the wickednes of mankinde whereunto by coruption of nature they are inclined.

The magistrate (as St Paule saith) is the minester of God and the revenger of wrath towardes him that hath done evell *etc.* And St Peeter: be subiecte to the kinge as to the cheefe or to under ruleres as sente of him *ad vindictam nocentium*, to the punishement or revengemente of offenders and to the prais of them that doe well.

Romans 13

1 Peter 2

Yf the magistrate doe not this, God threatenethe heavie punishmente. 'When you were', saith Wisdom to princes, 'the minesteres of his kingdome, you have not executed judgmente rightly nor kepte the lawe, nor walked accordinge to his will; horrible / and right soone shall he appeare unto you, for an hard judgment shall they have that beare rule', *etc. Potentes potenter tormenta patientur.*

Sapientia, 6

f.172v

Now then, if the magistrate be the minester of God, in his name and authoretie to punishe the wicked accordinge to the measure of theire offences, and are threatened greivous punishmente yf they doe not, and on the other party the Scottish Queen hath offended in two higheste degrees, both concerninge Gode's religeon and the disheriting and distruction of our prince; we see not but her Majestie muste needes offend in conscience before God if she doe not punishe her accordinge to the measure of her offence in the higheste degree.

Small punishment for greate offences in respect of any person is parcialletie and slack iustice which God in all thinges in iudgemente forbiddeth. Consider not (saith God) the person of the poore[2] nor honor the countenance of the rich. Yt is not good (saith Salomon) to consider the person of the wicked, thereby to decline from the truth of iudgemente. And Jesus Syrach: Make no labor to be a iudge excepte thou have that stoutnes that thou mightely maieste put downe wickednes, for if thou stand in awe of the mightie thou canste not but faile in givinge sentence.

Leviticus 19

Proverbs 18

Ecclesiasticus 7

Wherefore whether the late Queene of Scottes be queene or subiecte, be stranger or cittizen, be kinne or not kinne, by Gode's word for soe great offences she should have the iuste deserved punishment and that in the highest degree.

When God by his iuste providence doth committ any greevous offendor in to the handes of a prince or maiestrate as to his minester to be punished, he / ought to feare the heavie displeasure of God if by any coulor he doe[3] omitt the same. *Non enim hominis iudicium est, sed Dei, et maledictus est qui facit opus Domini fraudulenter vel necligenter.* For God often tymes bringeth sinneres to punishment for other offences then those that are knowne and appeare to the world, and therefore hath he shewed himselfe greevouslye displeased when such by the coullor of mercye and pittie in princes have escaped iuste judgement.

The second reason

f.173

Because Saule spared Agage although he were a kinge, God tooke from the same Saule his good sperite and transferred the kingdom of Israell from him and from his heires for evere. When Achab spared Benadab, the Kinge of Syria, by his unreasonable clemencye, though he weare a greate prince. God willed the proffet to say unto him, 'Because thou hast lett escape out of thy handes the man that I would have had to dye thy life shalbe for his life and thy people for his people.'[5]

1 *Reges* 15[4]

1. MS reads '13'.
2. MS reads 'poores'; this reading from SP Scotland 8/47.
3. 'He doe' repeated in MS.
4. I.e. 1 Samuel.
5. 1 Kings, 20.

In these examples great pretence might be made for mercye for sparinge of them and greate reproch of bloudines and crueltye in the contrary; but we see howe God iudged in them.

The late Queene of Scottes beinge a greevous offender diveres wayes both[6] before she came into this lande and afterwarde, hath bene by Gode's especiall and mervilouse providence put into the Queene's Majestie's handes to be punished, and farre more nottable then Agage and Benadab were put into the handes of Saule and Achabb.

Therefore it is greatly to be feared if she escape, as Benadab did under pretence of mercye and honorable dealinge, that Gode's heavie displeasure will for the same

f.173v   light both upon the prince and the realme as it / did upon Achab and the Isralites shortely after.

This sentance of the profite (as it is for certeine reported) was spoken to Lord James, late Regente of Scotland,[7] when with too much lenitie he proceeded therin; it hath followed too true in him, the Lorde turne it from our gracious Soveraigne.

The third   Every good prince ought by Gode's comaundement to punishe even by death all
reason   such as doe seeke to seduce the people of God from his true worshippe unto supersticion and idolatrye, for that offence God hath alwaies moste greevously punished as committed against the first table. Deuteronomy 13. His wordes are these: 'If thy brother, the sonne of thy mother, or thine owne sonne or thy daughter or thy wyfe that lyeth within thy bosome, or thy freind which is as thie owne soule unto thee, entice thee, sainge "Let us goe and serve strange godes *etc.*", thou shalt not consent unto him nor harken unto him, thy eye shall not pittye him neither shalte thou have compassyon upon him, nor keepe him seacret but cause him to be slaine, thine own hand shalbe firste upon him to kill him *etc.*'; and afterwardes addeth, 'And all Israell shall feare to doe any more any such weckednes.' The resedue of that chapter afterwardes contayneth more greevouse matter, which we would wishe all them to reade that in greate offences under coullore of pittie are loth to have sharpe punishment used.

Here you may perceave that God willeth his magestrates not to spare either brother or sister or sonne or daughter or wife or freinde be he never soe nigh if he seeke to seduce the people of God from his true worshippe; much lesse is an ennemye and traitor to be spared, yea and he addeth the cause whie he would have such sharpe punishment used in such cases, that Israell may feare to do the like. /

f.174   But the late Queene of Scottes hath not only sought and wrought by all meanes she can to seduce the people of God in this realme from true religeon, but is the only hope of all the adversaries of God throwgh out all Ewrope and the instrumente whereby they truste to overthrowgh the gospell of Christe in all countries, and thearefoare if she have not that punishement which God in this place afore menc[i]oned appointeth, it is of all Christian hartes to be feared that Gode's iust plage will light both upon the magestrates and subiectes for that by our slacnesse and remisse iustyce we give occasion of the overthrowe of Gode's glorye and truth in his Church mercifully restored unto us in these latter daies.

Eusebius, *liber 2, De*   Constantinus[9] Magnus caused Licinius to be putt to death, beinge not his
Vita Constantini[8]   subiecte but his fellowe emperore, for that the said Licinius labored to subverte the

Christyan religeon, and the same Constantine[10] is for the same in all historyes highely comended; much more shall it be lawfull and honorable for the Queene's Majestie to execute this woman who besides the subversion[11] of religeon hath sought the life of the same oure gratious Soveraigne.

Yt is dangerous for any prince aswell for his owne state as also for that punishement which may come from Gode's hande, by slacknes of justyce in greate offences to give occasyon by hope of impunetie of the encrease of like wickednes.

The fourthe reason.

Joab beinge spared of David for murderinge of Abner killed Amasa also. Because Amnon was winked at by his father for comitting rape and inceste with his owne sister, Absolon under hope of like impunetie / was embouldened to murder his brother Amnon.

f.174v

But looke I praye you how greevously God puneshed that slacke iustyce of David, coulored with a tender hearte towarde his naturall children. Did he not suffer, yea and by his iuste judgmente raise one of his owne sons towardes whome he used that excessyve tendernes and pittye, to rebell againste him and drive him out of his owne kingdome?

The late Scottishe Queene hath heaped upp together all the sinnes of the licentious sonnes of David, adulterye, murdere, conspiracye, treasones, and blasphemyes againste God also, and if she scape with slight or noe punishment her Majestie in conscience oughte, as also good and faithefull subiectes, to feare that God will reserve her as an instrumente to put her from the royall seat of this kingdome and to plague the unthankefull and noughty subiectes, *quod omen ut Deus avertat precamur*. Shall we thinke that God will not plage it? Surelye our heartes doe greatly feare he will doe it greevouslye.

A prince ought in all conscience before God by all the meanes he can to see to the quietnes, safety and good estat of that people over which God hath appointed him governor. For in the proffytes often tymes[12] under the names of pastores and watchemen he threateneth greate punyshemente to princes and governores for the contrary, especiallie in Ezechiell the 33 and 34, and signefyeth that if his people perishe eith[er] in soule or bodie by slacknes in adminestringe iustice or by any other misgovernemente God will require theire blood at the prince's hande.

The fifte reason.

Ezechiell 33

Which places as they maie be applied to proffetes and teacheres so doe they not exclude but principally comprehend kinges and magestrates, as Hieronimus[13] noteth in Exechiell the 33; the / wordes of the profyte are these: 'Yf the watchman see the swoarde and blowe not the trumpet, so that the people is not warned, that the sword come then and take any man from amonge them, the same shalbe taken away in his owne sine from amonge them but his bloud will I require at the watchmane's hande.' And againe: 'Woe unto the shepperd that distroye and scatter my fflocke, saith the Lord,' *etc*; 'you scatter and thruste out of my flocke and doe

f.175

J[e]remia 23

---

6. 'Both' repeated in MS.
7. I.e. Murray.
8. I.e. ii.xviii.
9. MS reads 'Constantius'; this reading from SP Scotland 8/47.
10. MS reads 'Constancius'; this reading from

SP Scotland 8/47.
11. MS reads 'subertion'; this reading from SP Scotland 8/47.
12. 'Often tymes' repeated in MS.
13. I.e. St Jerome's *Commentaria in Ezechialem*.

not looke upon them, therefore will I visite the wickednes of[14] your imagenac[i]ones etc.'

By theis and such othere wordes in many places God signefyeth yf his people perishe either in soule or bodie by the slacke or remisse governement of them that are appoynted rulers over them and as it weare sheppardes and heardes men to keepe them from daunger, that he will require the blood of his people at their handes.

But if the late Scotishe Queen with her alies by the pretensed title and other develishe and traiterous devises and workinges is like to bringe confusion to this noble realme of Englande, as evedentley appereth to all faithfull and good subiectes, therfore the prince offendethe grevouslie before God yf for the saftie of hir people she do not cutt hir of.[15]

3 Reges 2[16]   Salamon, a wise and godlie prince, spared not his owne naturall, yea and his elder brother Adonias for suspicion and likelihood of treason and for a maryage purposed only, but did putt him to death for the same and that speedely and that without course of justyce, leaste by delaye trouble and daunger might have ensued not only to his owne person beinge prince and cheefe minester of God in that lande but also to that people over which he had charge and for saffetye whereof in conscyence he was bounde to deale. He would have thought it a greate burden to his conscyence if by the sparinge of one man's life, were he never so nighe of bloud unto him, he should have hasarded the seate in which God had placed him and the bloud of many thousandes of his people which by rebellyon might have bene spente. /

f.175v   But this woman and her greatelie desired husbande as she pretended have put farre more hainous matter in executyon, wherefor her case standinge as it doth there is no scruple in conscyence to proceede with severetie but great daunger in conscience for dealinge too mildlie and contrary to order of justyce, makynge the punishment lesse then the offence, with the evidente daunger of her Majestie's owne person, the hasarde of the realme and the subvertion of Gode's truthe.

The sixte   It is daungerouse for any Christyan prince and contrary to the worde of God with
reason.   coullor of mercy and pittie to doe that whereby he shall discourage and kill the hartes not only of his owne good subiectes and faithfull councellores but also of all other nac[i]ones faithfully protestynge Gode's religeon and his true worshippe, as it may well appeare in the example of David.

David havinge this infirmetye of too much pittie and indulgence towardes offenderes, which is not of any prince to be followed, did forbide that his traytorous sonne Absolon should be slaine; and when he was kylled, effemynatly he bewailed the same to the discouraginge of his people. But he was sharply rebuked by Jobe, his counseilore, sainge 'Thou haste shamed this daye the faces of thy servantes which have saved thie lyfe and the life of thy sonnes' *etc.* 'Thou loveste[17] those that hate thee, and thou hateste those that love thee, and thou sheweste this daye that thou passeste not for / thy captaynes and for thy servantes. And nowe I perceav yf
f.176   Absolon had lived and all we had ben slayne it would have pleased thee well.'

What inconvenience was like to followe unto David by this doinge and what other good direction maye be taken out of this historye well considered for brevitie sacke wee leave to the considerac[i]on of wise princes and governores.

But David was so much moved with these wordes that he was contentcd to take another course which turned both to the comforte of his subiectes and his owne benefyte: the applycac[i]on needeth not.

If David were moved thus to doe to the comforte of his owne subiectes only and the abashinge of his owne privat rebelles, howe much more have we to desire God to move the Queene's Majestie by the execution of this ladye to gladd the hartes of all true Christyanes in Ewrope and to abashe and dampe the mindes of all the ennemyes of God and friendes of antechriste.

Yt[18] maye be obiected that thus to proceed is not honorable for the Queene's Majestie. Obiection

The shaddowe of honor (as maye evidently appeare) deceaved upon like occasyon both Kinge Saule in sparing Agage, Kinge of Amelich, and Kinge Achab in receavinge to his mercye Kinge Benadab, as it is in the example in the second reason menc[i]oned, who did pretend great honore in savinge a kinge and though[t] dishonor in the contrarye that one kinge should kill an other; but mane's judgment and Gode's in such cases are farre diveres, for in deed execution of justyce upon any person whatsoever is and ever hath bene accompted honorable. Responce

Josue, a worthie prince and governor, put to death / at one tyme fyve kynges, and that as might appere rudly, causinge his souldieres to sett theire feete on their neckes and slaye them, and willed them to be stoute and not to feare to doe it. f.176v
Josue 10

We fynde also in the scriptures that in this zeale of iustice two wicked queenes, Jesabell and Athelia, both inferiore in mischeefe to this late Queene, have ben by Gode's magestrates executed and the same execucion comended in the scriptures.

Yt may be further obiected that the Queene's Majestie in so doinge should exceede the limites and boundes of mercie and clemencye. Obiection

In deed a prince should be mercifull, but he should be iuste also. It is said '*misericordia et veritas custodiunt regem*,' but in the next chapter it followeth, '*qui sequitur iusticiam et misericordiam inveniet vitam.*' The prince in governement must be like unto God himselfe who is not only amyable by[21] mercye, but terible also by iustyce, and therfore is called '*misericors et justus Dominus.*' Mercye oftentymes sheweth itselfe in the image of justyce, yea and iustice[22] in scriptures is in God called mercye. Psalme 136: who smot Egipte with thier fyrste borne, for his mercye endureth for ever. In that psalme[23] the smitynge of Egipte with terrible plagues, the distruction of Pharoe, the killinge of greate and mightie kinges, are caled the mercifull workes of God, as in deed they were, but mercy towardes the people of God and not towardes the ennemyes of God and of his people. *Respontio*[19]
Proverb 20[20]

---

14. 'Of' repeated in MS.
15. 'But if . . . cutt hir of' from Cott.Caligula C11.
16. I.e. 1 Kings, 2: this reference supplied from Cambridge Gg.iii.34.
17. MS reads 'loveuste'.
18. MS reads 'Yf'; this reading from Cott.Caligula C11.
19. '*Respontio*' supplied from Cott.Caligula

C11.
20. 'Proverb 20' supplied from Cott.Caligula C11.
21. MS reads 'but'; this reading from Cott.Caligula C11.
22. 'Yea and iustice': supplied from Cott.Caligula C11.
23. MS reads 'phalme'; this reading from Cott.Caligula C11.

Therefore as the Queene's Majestie in deed is mercifull so we[24] moste humblye desire her that she will open the lappes of her mercye towardes Gode's people and her good subiectes in dispatchinge those ennemyes that seeke the confusyon of

f.177 Gode's cause amonge us / and of this noble realme.

Yt maie also be said that to spare one person beinge an ennemye, a stranger, a professed member of antechriste, and convicted of so many haynous crimes, with the evidente perrill of so many thousandes of bodies and soules of good and faithefull subiectes, may iustly be termed *crudelis mise[r]icordis.*

'*Petiliano obijciente Deum non delectari humano sanguine, respondet: legimus multos a famulo Dei Moise misericorditer interfectos. Nunquid crudelis efectus est cum de monte des[c]endens tot milia iuberet occidi?*'

'*Saul et Josophat reges fuerunt populi Dei et dum misericordiam iis quos Deus oderat prestiterunt, Dei offensam in opere pietatis incurunt. E contrario Phinees filijque Levi graciam Dei humana caede et suorum paricidio meruerunt.*'

The same Hierome, *de origine animae,* saith the like sparinge of evell personses is *misericors inobedientia.*

St Augustyne also saith '*sicuti est misericordia puniens ita est etiam crudelitas parcens.*'

But happely it may be that some doe discredit theis reasones by the persones when they cannot by the matter, and will put in her Majestie's minde that we, in perswadinge her, respecte our owne daunger and feare of perrill comminge to us and not right and true iudgement, yea and that it maye appeare very unseemly and worthie sharpe reproofe in a bishoppe to excite a prince to crueltie and bloud contrary to her mercyfull inclinac[i]on.

As touchinge the firste branche, surely we see not any great contynuance of daunger likely to come to us more than to all good subiectes whill this / state standeth, and the state cannot lightly alter without the certayne perill both of our prince and countrye. Now if our daunger be ioyned with the daunger of our gracious Soveraigne and naturall countrye we see not howe we can be accompted godlie bishoppes or faithefull subiectes if in common perrill we should not crye and give warninge, or on the other side howe they can be thought to have true hartes towardes God and towardes theire prince and countrye that will mislyke with us so doinge and seeke therby to discredite us.

As touchinge the second braunch, God forbidde that we should be instrumentes to increase a mercifull prince to crueltie and bloudines, neither cann wee thinke well of them or iudge that they have true meaninge hartes that in the minester of God and offycere doe terme justice and right punishemente by the name of bloudines or crueltie; God I truste in tyme shall open her Majestie's eyes to see and espie theire cruell purposes under the cloke of extollinge mercye.

When the prince or magistrate is slacke in punishinge the sinnefull and wicked, the bishoppe and preacher is bounde in conscience before God to exhorte him to more dilligence therein, leaste the bloude both of prince and people be required at his handes.

Maye the profite be accompted cruell or to incite Ahabe to bloudiness which so sharpelye rebuked him for his clemencye shewed towardes Benadab? May Samuell be iustly named cruell because in like case he reproved Saule for sparinge the life of

---

Side notes (left margin):

Augustine, Contra Litteras Petiliani, liber 2, caput 86

Hieronymous

Obiectio

Respontio
f.177v

3 Reges 20

Kinge Agage and killed the said / Agage with his owne handes in the sighte of the   f.178
prince?

What shall wee saye of the prophet Elyas? Shall we calle him cruell because in the zeale of just[ice] he killed all the false prophetes of Baalle? Did not God approve this his facte with the miraculous sendinge of aboundance of raine after three years contynuall droughte? But to those men I thinke God himselfe and his angeles will seeme cruell and his justice crueltie that they under the coullor of mercye might be spared untyll tyme will serve to satisfy theire owne cruell heartes.

St Augustyne also saith '*sicuti est misericordia puniens ita est etiam crudelitas parcens*'.

An argumente perswadinge that the Queen's Majestie ought to have in conscience a great care of the safetie of her owne person.

Every prince beinge the minester of God and a publicke person ought by Gode's worde to have an especiall care of his owne safetie more then a private person, and cheefely when the case soe standeth that the safetie of his realme and country and the true worshippinge of God by Gode's disposytyone may seeme to depend on him.

But so it is in the Queene's Majestie: therefore in conscience ought she to have a singuler care of her safetie, if not for her selfe sake yet at the leaste for the furtherance of Gode's cause and stay of her countrye, to the maintenance whereof she is bounde before God.

Moses wished to be put out of the booke of life for the safegard of his people.   Exodus 32
Pawle wished to be anathema for his bretheren. / Codrus and diveres other   Romans 10   f.178v
heathenes gave awaye theire lives for the safetie of theire countryes. Contrarywise we wishe and are humble suitores that it may please her Majestie to preserve her owne lyfe, and to cutt away the daungeres thereof if not for her owne sacke, which happely her noble courage doth smally regarde, yet at the leaste wise for Gode's cause and for her faithfull and lovinge subiectes, whose lyfe and good estate dependeth on her.

It may be obiected that her Majestie reposeth her truste and confydence in the   Obiection
providence of God and therefore maketh light of all attemptes that her ennemyes cann worke againste her.

Surelie it muste needes be confessed that the same proceedeth both of a noble   Responce
courage and stronge faith and truste in God and ought in deede to be the bulwarke of helpe and comforte to all good and godly princes, but yet so farre as they seeme not with all to tempte God by leavinge that dilligence and those ordinary meanes whereby he useth to save and deliver.

David knewe him selfe to be anoynted and appointed Kinge of Israell by God himselfe yet he did not rashely caste himself into the handes of Saule his ennemye.   Paral lo: 32[25]
Josophat and Ezechias in theire greate distresses undoubtedly had theire cheefe truste and confydence in the providence of God, but they ceased not both to shonn and cutt of all those thinges whereby daunger might growe and to use all meanes whereby theire safetie might be holpen *etc.*

It is alledged by Christe, 'Thou shalt not tempte thy Lorde God', but surelie it

24. 'We' repeated in MS.

25. *Sic*, and in Cambridge Gg.iii.34; SP
    Scotland 8/47 has 'paralip 20 (2°?), 32.

The reference is to 2 Chronicles
(Paralipomenon), 32.

f.179   might have bene as safe for Christe without temptinge God to have / caste him selfe doune from the pinacle of the temple as for the Queene's Majestie to suffer in her bosom this poysoned serpente that ceaseth not continually to thruste the stinge of her venemous[26] workinge in to her Majestie's safetie and possessyon of her crowne.

It is well said 'Principum securitas paucorum vita redimenda est'.

There are diveres histories and examples of late tyme whereby it hath bene declared that the temptinge confydence of Gode's providence, not shuninge evidente occasiones of daunger, hath falne out to the extreame hurte of the parties and on such as hath depended on them; which we thinke not fitte to recite leaste they might seeme in this case *ominosa*, as God for his greate mercies' sake forbidde that they should be. Many reasones, aucthoritie, and examples moe besides theis may be taken out of the holie scriptures for confirmac[i]on of this purpose but for tediousnes we thought good to omitt them and to leave the resedue to God.

In the Leviticus, *caput* 20 there is much like matter and that in as earneste manor set forth, neither can anie in conscience thinke that this punishement was here by God appointed so greivous only for those that then seduced the people of God to gentillishe and heathen idollatrie, for idollatry and false worshepinge by whome soever it be begone, though they beare the name of the Church or of the people of God never soe much, it is a directe offence againste the first Table, and therefore in Gode's judgemente worthie no lesse punishemente. Yea, theire offence must needes be more haynous in the sight of God for that they have had greater oppertunetie to understande Gode's true worshippe.

f.179v   Shall any Christyan man thinke that the worship / of God appointed in his lawe beinge but the figure, was more acceptable and pleasante to God then this nowe his true worshippe in the faith of Jesue accordinge to the gospell of our redemption, or that the violatinge of the same or seducing of his people from it is in his iudgemente lesse displeasante or not so greevouslye to be punished as was then the breakinge of his lawe or the seducynge from it? Shall we thinke that the gatheringe of a fewe stickes on the Saboth daye is to be punished by death in a poore simple persone, and the seeking to subverte the gospelle of Christe and to drawe the people of God to that idollotrous doctrine that teacheth to impute the merites of Christe's blood and passyon to men's wicked devises, yea to stockes, to stones, to stickes, to water, to belles, *etc.*, shall not be worthie the punishemente of death in a noble person? God directe our iudgementes otherwise.

By theis wordes of God before recited, Deuteronomy, 13, if it be evident that God willed his magestrates to spare neither brother nor sister, nor sonne, nor daughter, nor wife, nor freind, though they were never so nighe, if he sought to seduce the people of God from his true worshipe, how muche lesse is an ennemye, a traytor and an adulterer to be spared.

[ii. Presented by the laymen]

An humble peticion to her Majestie and the reasones gathered out of civill lawe by certayne appointed by aucthoritie in Parleamente to proove that it doth stand, not only with iustice, but also with the Queene's Majestie's honor and safetie to proceed crimenally againte the pretensed Scottishe Queene.

We your Majestie's most humble and faithful subiectes / assembled in Parliamente   f.180
for preservacion of your royall person and estate doe highly acknolledge the greate goodnes of God that hath chosen and appointed suche a soveraigne to raigne over us as never subiectes by any record ever had a better, and therefore, our hartie praiores are daily and ever shalbe to almightie God longe to preserve your most exelente Majestie in all and most perfecte felicetie that ever creature had or might have upon earth. And where as the higheste and cheefeste states are ever more envied of all such as be the worste and greateste disturberes of Gode's monarchie and his annoynted iurisdiction, we cannot but with a care of minde and force of our bodies seeke to redresse what soevere shalbe thought hurtefull to your Majestie's safe quietnes and moste blessed governement.

A queene of late tyme and yet through her owne actes nowe iustely no queene, a nigh kineswoman of your Majestie's and yet a verie unnaturall sister, Lady Mary Stuarde, late Queene of Scottes, beinge driven through violence and force of otheres to take harburgh in your Majestie's realme for the safegarde of her life hath not only had your Majestie's moste gratious protection but also was saved within her owne realme by your Majestie's authoritie from executyone of death for her moste horible and unnaturall doinges there, knowne through out Ewrope to her perpetuall infamye and shame for ever. And albeit upon her first cominge, your Highnes might bothe by lawe and iustice have[27] delte with her iudicially for her attemptes made by writyinge and otherwise againste your crowne and dignetie and to the dishherison[28] of your moste royall person for ever, yet / your Majestie in   f.180v
consideracion of her longe dangerous troubles in her owne realme and in hope that such great adversetie would have bene good lessones for her amendemente hereafter, hath not used her in any such manor as she hath deserved; but rather forgettinge or forgivinge after a soart her former doinges, hath delte with her like a good and naturall sister. All which notwithstandinge this unnaturall ladie (beinge borne out of kinde as it should seeme) hath altogether forgotten God and all goodnes, abusinge herselfe as it appeareth moste treasonably againste your Majestie's person and state, seekinge and devisinge by all means possible not only to deprive your Majestie of all earthlie dignetie and livinges but also of your naturall life, which thinge is founde by evident proofes and by the judges of your realme declared to be moste horible and most wicked treason that ever was wrought againste any prince. For which her doinges your Majestie myndinge to touche her in honore esteemeth her a person unworthie of any hope of tytle, preheminence or dignetie within this your lande; and therefore not seekinge to deall with her according to her desertes is only contented to have her disabled as a person not capeable of princely honor. And thus your Majestie using this course thinketh it the meeteste waye to establishe your selfe and to quiet your dominyones hereafter, takinge awaye hereby the hope of such as doe depend upon the pretenced title and weakeninge the whole strength of that faction.

26. MS reads 'unimos'; this reading from   27. 'Have' supplied from Harl.2194.
    Cott.Caligula C11.   28. *Sic.*

And for further assurance of your Majestie's quietnes your Highnes doth not mislike to have greevous paines of highe treason laide upon all such as shall attempte

f.181   and maintaine her pretenced tytle by any / manor of waye.

Thus as evell men shalbe kepte backe from intermedlinge in the maintenance of this title so may your Majestie's true and faithful subiectes be muche emboldened to deale againste this pretenced queen and her adherentes, when your subiectes shall see a lawe set downe for your availe, and your enemys shall wante force and waxe weake thereby and your true subiectes greatly hardened for all defence.

Moreover if the said pretenced queene shall hereafter make any attempte of treason, the lawe so to rune that she shall suffer paines of death without further trouble of Parleament.

And if any shall enterprise to deliver her out of prison after her disablemente either in your Majestie's life or after, the same to be convicted imedyatly of highe treason and her selfe assenting thereunto to be likewise adiudged a traytor in lawe.

In all which proceedinges your Majestie thinketh to deale both saflye and honorablye as well for your selfe as for your state, for thereby it seemeth that neither shall shee nor any for her hereafter dare deall to doe harme, but also all forrayne princes and nac[i]ones will thinke much honor of such your mercifull proceedinges.

And lastelye, where as she hath fallen into your handes from the violence of otheres and so as a birde followed by a hauke seeketh succour at your Majestie's feete, your Highnes thinketh your selfe bounde in honour, for that she is your sister and a queene borne, not to proceed further with her but only to her disablemente, countynge it is stronge worke for your safetie. /

f.181v   These be the reasones which in parte may move your Majestie to take this course, as we doe conceave.

All which notwithstandinge if it might please your moste exelente Majestie to suffer your poore and faithfull subiectes to enter deepely upon good leasure into the serche of this cause and by waye of replye to make answere, which proceeding by iuste proofes for your Majestie's safetie we doubte not but with your Highnes' favorable acceptac[i]on all that which hetherunto have bene uttered is rather a declarac[i]one of that moste mild and gratious nature of yours then anye assurance of your person or state at all.

Reasones answeringe the formor argumentes.

Maie it therefore please your Majestie: whereas it is saide that it standeth to very good purpose to proceed only in disablinge of the Scottish Queene for any claime or title to the crowne we take it by your Majestie's favore that suche and especiallye disablinge of her by name is in effecte a speciall confirmac[i]on of a righte that she should have had, *quia privatio presupponit habitum.* And further we doe take it for a knowne truth that both by the lawes and statutes in this lande nowe in force she is alredie disabled, and therefore it is to small purpose *rem actam agere.* And for answere unto the premisses wee saye further that neither shall this weakn other that are evell mynded but rather strengthen them in their mischeefe and make them desperate where there is no other remedie. And a firebrand once kindled and findinge apte

f.182   matter to worke upon / will hardlie be quenched without great hasard.

Touchinge the greevous paines layde upon those that shall deale, it litle feareth the wicked, when hope of gaine maketh more boulde than hasard[29] dothe appaule. Beside naturallye givene to this nacion and all otheres that are under the moone maketh men often tymes sturre without cause and as Plato saith, '*Naturales sunt conversiones rerum publicorum.*'[30] Yet they that heretofore have borne armore as traitores not fearinge the lawe then in force which did as much restraine them as this or any lawe to be made can be hable, will such wicked rebelles be kepte backe from doinge evell by this newe devised statut? Desperac[i]on feareth no lawes, and where suche an instrumente is livinge by whom all attemptes are to be wroughte force overthroweth justyce till the cause of all mischeefe which is the hoped helpe be clene[31] taken awaye.

And where it is said that the makinge of a lawe for her disablinge embouldenth muche your subiectes to dealle againste her, we aunswere that no newe lawe needeth to encourage good and loyall subiectes againste such a person who hath broken all lawes of God and nature and is worthie to be out of your Majestie's protection because she seeketh still the disturbance of this noble state and usinge often her owne phrase threateneth that she will stirre coles.

Touchinge a lawe to be made againste her if she should attempte any evell hereafter, the experience of her former life is such that no lawe hath any force with her that is fully minded to take her advauntage upon any apte occasione offered. And to threaten her with death / yf she should seeme to make an escape hereafter is such a   f.182v
devise that she nothinge feareth, for besides that shee was tould at Louglewen there was noe waye but death with her[32] if she would not take her imprisonemente quietly and live without seekinge libertie, she notwithstandinge adventure herselfe with a yonge fellowe verie dishonorably to gett away in a boate, and now since her cominge into Englande she hath wrought diveres wayes to make an escape of your owne disloyall subiectes and occupied the heades of the cheefeste estates of Christendom for that purpose. Therefore manacinge and but threateninge wordes of lawe shall not keepe her back from her mallicious intente to subverte your Magestye and to give a pushe for the crowne com of her what will. And likely it is that shee may escape aswell as be taken for neither she wanteth witt nor conninge to make her waye. And we have learned that in matteres of great hazarde to be well advised and to take alwaies that ordere which may be for the beste. Now to bringe this her devise about, there will wante noe traitores to be alwaies redie to bringe this her devise aboute and to doe what they can for her libertie, and such as will not deale in meane matteres will adventure deepe for a kingdome because the rewarde is greate when the service is done.

But your Majestie hath regarde unto your honore as much as unto your safetie and thinketh that in takinge this course all princes will speake well of your Highnes. May it please your Majestie, wee your good subiectes doe well like of so honorable a meaninge but wee would be loath to see that / when you have such regarde of honore   f.183
you doe therby loose your state, and so your life, honor and all; ffor if it should fall

---

29. 'Hasard' supplied from Harl.2194.
30. Cf. *Republic*, 424A, 546.
31. MS reads claime'; this reading from

Harl.2194.
32. MS reads 'here', as does Cambridge Gg.iii.34.

out that the Scottish Queene escaped your handes, which Christe of his mercy sake forbid, all good princes would thinke great wante of judgmente and foresight firste in your Majestie, next in your counsaile, laste of all in all the whole nac[i]on, and such a greefe it would be to your Majestie and subiectes and to all other good Christyane princes thorough out Ewrope as non could be greater. Againe, such a matter of comforte and tryumphe it would be to the adversaries that they would counte her escape a miraculouse worke of God and that your Majestie had no power, though will, to kep[33] her safe. And when that daye should come, woe be to all true Christyanes uneversally; for upon her doe depende the cheefeste ennemyes of religeon and to this kingdome. May it please you, therefore, moste gratious Queene, to be well advised and to take sounde counsaile when it is given, knowinge this for certayne truth that evell foreseene and advisedlie looked unto doth evere the lesse harme.

But still your Majestie, consideringe the greate troubles that she hath had and forgettinge or not greatlie esteeminge what troubles she hath brought unto your realme, doth by a mercifull respecte to your most gracious nature rather bende to doe good to her then to seeke safegarde to yourselfe; and seinge[34] here your sister although unnaturall and also a queene by birth although not worthie of life cannot but rather[35] hazarde your owne selfe then deale with her according to her desertes.

This your Majestie's nature beinge thus knowne it behooveth all your good
f.183v   subiectes, moste gratious Soveraigne, / to call and crye to God for his hevenly assistance that his powere may be given unto you nexte aftere the advauncemente of his glory to seeke assuredly your owne safetye, which your Majestie cannot fully doe by this meanes that hath hetherto ben taken or hereafter to be used.

Therefore if[36] it would please your most exelente Majestie to give eare to the sounde reasones of your moste faithefull subiectes, and rather deale certainlye then by chaunce, there is no doubte but your Majestie shall avoyde all apparante daungeres and live in all safetie and honor to Gode's glorye and to the comforte of all good Christyan princes universallye.

Thus much againste the oppinion of disablinge the Scottishe Queene whereby it appeareth that it wilbe rather for her benefite then to her hurt and moste certayne it is that it wilbe daungerous for the state divers wayes, where as dealinge with her in the firste degree accordinge to her desertes, the same is lawfull, safe, necessarie and honorable for your Majestie and all Christendom besides. And because it may appeare that this speech is grounded upon lawe and reason there shalbe argumentes of lawe alledged suffytyently for this matter as the shortenes of tyme may serve.

Civell reasones for doubte of answere.

1. A confederate beinge in the country of his confederate is to be punished as though hee were a subiecte.
2. Everie person offendinge is to be tried in the place where he comitteth the crime
f.184   withoute / exception of privelidge.
3. A kinge passinge thorough an other kinge's realme or there residente, is but a privat person.
4. The dignetie of the person offendinge encreaseth the offence.
5. *Reatus omnem honorem excludit.*

6. A kinge deposed is not to be taken for a kinge and therefore Fredericke Kinge of Naples beinge deprived by the Kinge of Spaine was afterwardes judged to be no kinge by sentence.

7. A kinge though not deposed may comitte treason.

8. Diotaurus, a kinge confederated with the Romanes, was criminally iudged by Caius Julius Cesar for that he conspired to have slaine the said Julyus Cesare at the banquete.

9. Johane Queene of Naples was put to death for that she gave her consente to the murder of her husbande, and caused him to be hanged out at a windowe.

10. Henry the 7th Emperor did give a solempe judgmente of death at Pisa 1311 againste Robarte, Kinge of Cicell for that the said king had entered in to conspiracye with the subiectes of the Emperor, and yet was not the Kinge Robarte within the iurisdiction of the Emperore at the tyme of the conspiracie neither at the tyme of judgmente.

11. It standeth with the lawe of nature, which is immutable, for any person to proceede for the safetie of him selfe and his charge.

12. Greate offences in the higheste degree ought not to be unpunished for any affection of kinred.

13. Justice, equetie and the comon welth are to / be preferred before the affection of kinred *quia arctiora*[37] *sunt vincula virtutis quam sanguinis.*   f.184v

14. An offence in the higheste degree againste a prince beinge a heade of the politicall bodie is an offence to every member of the same and requireth sharpe punishemente for preservac[i]one of the wholl.

15. The intentes of offences in the higheste degree is punished with death although the intente doth not followe.

16. The benefite and privelidge of saufe conducte loste by any crime comitted after the graunte made thereof.

17. Administrac[i]on of justice cannot but be honorable.[38]

18. All iuste and honorable dealinges are pleasinge to God and proffitable to the prince and state.

19. Executione of justyce is voide of all iniurye.

20. It is daungerouse for the state to swarve from the minestrac[i]on of justyce and the due executione of lawe.

21. To spare offenderes in the higheste degree is an iniurye to the prince and state of the realme.

22. *Pena unius salus multorum.*

23. The losse of lyfe is the penaltye appointed for treason and the losse of landes and goodes with the possebilletie of tytle cometh but in consequence and accessarely.

24. Punishemente ought to be equall with the faulte, and he that minestreth lesse punishemente then the faulte deserveth doth not execute the lawe according to the rules of justice. /

33. 'Her escape . . . to kep' supplied from Harl.2194.

34. 'And seinge' repeated in MS.

35. 'Rather' supplied from Harl.2194.

36. 'If' supplied from Harl.2194.

37. MS reads '*arctiara*'; Cambridge has '*arctiora*'.

38. MS reads 'cannot be but honorable'.

f.185   Reasones to proove that it standeth not only with justyce but with the Queene's Majestie's honore and safetie to proceed criminally againste Mary Stuarde late Queene of Scottes for her treasones comitted againste her Majestie and this realme.

A confederate beinge in the countrye of his confederate for a crime comitted is there to be punished. *Codice de captivis et post lumino reversis, verba legis: at*[39] *si sunt apud nos rei ex civitatibus foederatis in eos damnatos animadvertimus.*[40] Therefore although the Scottishe Queene were a confederate yet she is to be used in like soarte as a subiecte.

Item there is no person of what degree soever he be but is there to be tried where the crime is comitted without exception of priviledg. *Codice ubi de criminibus agi oportet,*[41] *verba legis: quia*[42] *in provincia quis deliquit aut in qua pecuniarum aut criminum reus sit, et ubi iudicari debet et hoc ius perpetuum sit.*[43]

But the Scottishe Queene here hath offended. *Ergo:*

Item every person is to be condempned and adiudged equally. *In crimine laesae magestatis verba legis: in crimine lesae magiestatis equa est omnium conditio. Ad legem Juliam lesae magiestatis, l.4.*[44]

But she hath falne in *crimen lesae magestatis. Ergo.*

Item a kinge in an other kinge's realme may comitt treasons as an other privat
f.185v   persone. *Corcetus, de p[o]testate regia, nu. 90, verba: Quero | utrum rex non habens iustum titulum regni incidat*[45] *in crimen lesae maiestatis. Respondeo quod sic, secundum Bartolum in legem, lex duodecim*[46] *tabularum et in legem primam, f. de crimine lesae magestatis.*[47]

But the Scottishe Queene hath offended here in Englande. *Ergo.*

A kinge passinge thorough an other kinge's realme or there resiante is but a privat person. *Bartolus duodecimo*[48] *libro de dignitatibus, verba: sed tamen dubitatur si rex vel baro transit per alias partes extra regnum suum, utrum possit creare milites.*[49] *Et videtur quod non, quia ibi privatus est homo: f. de prefecto urbis. f. de officio praesidis: praeses in homines sua provinciae imperium habet et hoc dum est in provincia; nam si excesserit, privatus est. Lapus in allegacione,*[50] *91 coll., penultima verba: Quislibet rex extra suum territorium cencetur*[51] *ad instar*[52] *privati.*

But the Scottishe Queene beinge here in England is out of her territory. *Ergo* to be punished as a priv[a]te person.

Every person of what condic[i]on soever he be either superior or equall submittinge him selfe to the iurisdiction of an other to be iudged by him to whom he submitteth him selfe. *L. est receptum, f. de iudiciis, verba: est receptum eoque iure utimur ut si quis maior vel equalis subbiiciat se iurisdictioni alterius potest ei et adversus eum ius dici.*

But the Queene of Scottes although she were a queene and thereby equall, by comittinge of hainous treason hath submitted her selfe to the Queene's jurisdiction. |

f.186   *Paulus de Castro*[53] *in dictam legem est receptum, f. eo, verba eius etiam: maior vel equalis potest se subiicere iurisdictioni ordinariae*[54] *alterius iudicis minoris vel paris tacite si iudex unius territorii delinquat vel contrahat in teritorium alterius iudicis vel minoris vel paris, quia ratione delicti vel contractus sortitur ibi forum. Rato definitionibus*[55] *de iudiciis Illi delinquint per delinquium amisit merum imperium et sic factus est alius privatus et sic suus compar potest eum punire. Quilibet in suo territorio est maior Alexandro.*[56]

But the Scottishe Queene havinge comitted high treason within this realme hath by constructione of lawe submitted her selfe to this jurisdiction and therefore to be punished as an other privat person.

And although it be said that noe *subditus potest non comittere crimen lesae maiestatis* yet that sayinge is to be taken whereas the crime is committed out of the iurisdiction then they are to be punished. *Papa in Clementina*[57] *de sententia et re iudicata.*[58]

And albeit the Pope did reverse the same sentence, yet[59] he saith that if the partie had ben within the iurisdiction of the superior at the time of the crime comitted and iudgmente the partie iustely had ben condempned *etc. Verba Papae:*[60] *quod si rex infra districtum*[61] *imperiale fuisset inventus delinquens potuisset contra eum sententia dici.*

Loe here the Pope declareth plainly that she here offendinge may iustely here be punished *in pena capitis.*

Item a kinge deposed is not afterwardes to be taken for a kinge. | *Thomas de Terra*   f.186v
Cremata, definitione 65: Rex regni[62] *privatus non est amplius rex.*

But the Queene of Scottes is depriv[e]d. *Ergo.*

The benefite or privelidge of safeconducte is lost when any crime is comitted after the safeconduct graunted: *Angelus de maleficiis in verbo publica fama.*

But the Queene of Scottes hath comitted againste the safeconducte since her cominge into the realme. *Ergo.*

The will and mind in treasones is punished equally as the acte. *Codice ad legem Juliam lesae maiestatis, verba legis: in crimine lesae maiestatis voluntatem scelleris eque ac effectum puniri iura voluerunt.*[63]

39. MS reads '*ut*'; this reading from Harl.2194.
40. Cf. *Corpus Juris Civilis*, ed. P. Krueger et al. (1911/15), I.885.
41. MS reads '*operteat*'; this reading from Harl.2194.
42. MS reads '*qua*'; this reading from Harl.2194.
43. Cf. *Corpus Juris Civilis*, ed. cit., II.128/9.
44. Cf. *Corpus Juris Civilis*, ed. cit., II.373.
45. MS reads '*iudicat*'; this reading from Harl.2194.
46. MS reads '*duodecem*'; this reading from Harl.2194.
47. These references to the Digests or Pandects seem to be drawn chiefly from the commentaries by Bartolus, with additional comments by Paulus de Castro and Alexander de Imola (Tartagni) in particular. Several editions of Bartolus' commentaries were produced in the 1490s, and 'ff' (or 'f') was the conventionally adopted means of representing the Digests: I have preserved this symbol and the other abbreviations used in those incunabula and which appear in these citations.
48. MS reads '*duodecimus*'; this reading from Harl.2194.

49. MS reads '*crare militis*'; this reading from Harl.2194.
50. *Nam si . . . allegacione*' misplaced in MS after '*extra suum territorum*'; this reading from Harl.2194.
51. MS reads '*consertur*'; this reading from Harl.2194.
52. MS reads '*iustra*'; this reading from Harl.2194.
53. MS reads '*Costro*'; this reading from Cambridge Gg.iii.34.
54. MS reads '*ordinarit*'; this reading from Harl.2194.
55. MS reads '*de efitionibus*'.
56. MS reads '*Alexander*'.
57. MS reads '*Clementa*'; this reading from Harl.2194.
58. MS reads '*iuicata*'; this reading from Harl.2194.
59. MS reads '*yt*'; this reading from Harl.2194.
60. MS reads '*Papa*'; this reading from Harl.2194.
61. MS reads '*districtium*'; this reading from Harl.2194.
62. MS reads '*regno*'; this reading from Harl.2194.
63. Cf. *Corpus Juris Civilis*, ed. cit., II.373.

But the Scottishe Queene hath not only had the effectiones but hath notoriously proceeded to the accions. *Ergo.*

Nether is it any newe or rare thinge for kinges and queenes to be adiudged and condempned for treason, for Henry the seventh Emperor did give a solempe iudgemente of death at Pisa *anno Domini* 1311 againste Robarte, Kinge of Cicill. Diotorus was likewise condempned by Julius Casar, and Joane Queene of Naples for murderinge her husband and hanginge him out of a windowe.

Punishmentes ought to be equall to the offences comitted: *f. de penis.* But death is the penalty appointed for treason. *Ergo.*

5. *Committee's settlement between Francis Alford and others, 27 May*

Text from PRO SP Dom.Eliz.86/52, original.

SP Dom.Eliz.86/52

[Endorsed 'The ordre set downe by the knights and burgesses of Parlament committed to the hearing of the cause for the enrolling of the fraudulent conveiaunce of W[illiam] Porter to Ed[mund] Porter and for the canceling of the same, with there names subscribed with their owne hands.']

Vicesimo septimo die Maij anno regni domine nostra Elizabeth Regine quartodecimo.

Where Frauncis Alford[1] of London, gentleman, hath before this tyme bought and purchased to him and to his heires of one William Porter gentleman decessed, the mannor of Ashton under-Edge in the county of Gloucester,[2] as by a deede indented and enrolled in her Majestie's Courte of Chauncery more at large dothe appere. Since the making and enrollinge whereof, yt appereth by a deede indented bearinge date before the sayd assuraunce made unto the sayd Frauncis Alford the sayd William Porter had bargained and sold the sayd mannor unto one Edmund Porter, gentleman, his uncle and to his heires. Which sayd latter deede indented was not (by the confession of the sayd Edmund Porter uppon his othe and by the testymony of one or two more of very good credyte) enrolled by the space of a yere or two after the knowledge and *teste* thereof. Nevertheles by some undue practize and indyrect dealinge, the said latter indenture is nowe fownd enrolled, within the tyme lymyted by the statute for th'enrollment of suche writinges, as by th'enrollment thereof in the said Courte of Chauncery dothe also appere.[3] After which sayd latter enrollment so procured, the said Edmund Porter hathe (by the speciall labour, requeast and desire of Lodovike Grevill, esquire) bargained and sold the said mannor by deede indented enrolled in the sayd Courte of Chauncery, unto Thomas Watkyns and Humfrey Mytton[4] and to their heires, by force of which said assuraunce made unto the sayd Edmund Porter in forme aforesayd the sayd Frauncis Alford and his heires are disinherited and excluded from th'inheritaunce of the sayd mannor by the common lawes of this realme. For the reformacion whereof the said Frauncis Alford

1. See Thomas Cromwell's diary, f.19v, for Alford's raising of the issue in the second reading debate on the bill of fraudulent gifts.
2. Words printed in light type are insertions; words in square brackets are deletions. All the insertions are in a second contemporary hand, filling in the blank spaces left in the text or amending it.
3. 5 Eliz., c.26 (1562-3) in *SR*, IV.456.
4. Thomas Watkyns and Humfrey Mytton were servants of Grevill (SP Dom.Eliz.79/120).

hathe exhibited a bill into the Quene's Majestie's highe courte of Parlyament. And uppon openinge of his greif therein the right worshipfull the knightes, citizens and burgesses of the said Parliament, representing the whole estate of the commons of this realme, thought yt meete and convenyent to commytt and appointe th'examinacion of the trothe of the premisses unto sundry bothe of honour and worshipp members of the sayd Howse whose names appear in a scedule hereunto annexed, geivinge them authoritye to call aswell the sayd Frauncis Alford as the said Lodovike Grevill before them and to [take such ordre in the premisses as to their wisdomes shall seeme good] to here the said [? action] and to [? report] therof unto the said court of Parlament.[5] Which said commyttees according to the trust reposed in them, have cald the said parties before them ounce or twise. And uppon the full and delyberate hearinge of the matter, [they have with the full assent and consent of the sayd Frauncis Alford and Lodovyke Grevill ordered and determyned] the said parties by their mutual assentes in the presens of the said commytte are contented that this order be taken touching the sayd cause and controversye in manner and forme folowinge, *viz :*[t] that the sayd Frauncis Alford shall in the beginninge of the next terme, commonly called Trynity terme, exhibite into the sayd Courte of Chauncery unto the Lord Keper of the Great Seale a bill of complainte against the sayd Lodovike Grevill, Edmund Porter, Thomas Watkyns and Humfrey Mytton comprehendinge therein his matter of greif to the same effect he hathe done in the sayd bill exhibited to the sayd courte of Parlyament. And prayinge proces against the sayd Lodovike Grevill, Edmund Porter, Watkyns and Mytton for their apparaunce, and that thereuppon order may be taken in the said Courte of Chauncery that th'enrollment of the said severall indentures made to the sayd Edmund Porter and the sayd Watkyns and Mytton maye be cancelled and made voyde, and that also the sayd two indentures maye lykewise be brought into the courte and their cancelled; and that the sayd Edmund Porter and the sayd Watkyns and Mytton shall doe and suffer to be done all suche acte and actes as shalbe ordered and decreed by the sayd Courte of Chauncery for the extinguishment of suche right, tytle and interest as the said Edmund Porter and the said Watkyns and Mytton hathe in and to the sayd mannor, discharged or saved harmeles of all incombraunces had, made or done by them or any other clayminge by, from or under any of them, and at the costes and charges of the sayd Alford. Unto which bill the sayd Grevill hathe promised that bothe he and the sayd [Edmund Porter] Watkyns and Mytton shall appere and proces shalbe made agaynst the said Edmund Porter for the doyng of the like. And uppon ther answer thereunto dothe also promise unto the sayd commyttees that the sayd [Edmund Porter][6] Watkyns and Mytton shalbe contented and shall furder do his indevour that aswell the sayd deedes indented made unto the sayd Edmund Porter and from him to Watkyns and Mytton and th'enrollment of them shalbe brought into the sayd Courte of Chauncery; and there be cancelled and made voyde. And that [the sayd Edmund Porter][7] the said Watkyns and Mytton shall doe all suche actes, as the sayd Courte of Chauncery shall order and decree for th'extinguishment and release of all their right and tytle in and to the said mannor unto the sayd Frauncis Alford and his heires discharged or saved harmeles of all incombraunces in manner and forme as is aforesayd. In witness whereof aswell the sayd Frauncis Alford and the said

Lodovyke Grevill as sundry of the sayd commyttees have hereunto put their handes the daye and yere first above wrytten.

	By me	Francis Alford[8]	
		Lodowyk Grevill	
Jamys Croft		Morris Barkeley	John Thinne
Thomas Wylson		Rowland Hayward	Thomas Seynctpol
Henry Gate			

5. 'Action' and 'report' are suggested readings, not deletions.

6. 'Edmund Porter' underlined in MS: meant to be deleted?

7. 'The sayd Edmund Porter' underlined in MS: meant to be deleted?

8. All the signatures are originals.

6. Reasons for executing the Duke of Norfolk provided by Thomas Digges and Thomas Dannet, 31 May[1]

Text from BL Add.48023 (Yelverton 26), copy.
Other MS. Add.48027 (Yelverton 31).

Add.48023 (Yelverton 26), fos.159-162

Reasons provided by Thomas Digges to be exhibited in the parlament *xiiij°
Reginae Elizabethae* for the execution of the Duke of Norfolk, according to a motion
agreed upon in the House[2] that reasons shold be provided to furnish a petition to the
Queen to that effect bicause a general resolution with full assent was agreed upon that
the Queen could not otherwise be safe.

The honor of the
nobilitie touched.

His faction
encreased.

The prince's
persone in danger.

Great feare and
sorrow impressed in
the hartes of her
Majesty's faithfull
subiectes.

The prophetes of
this time
discredited.
Religion defaced.
f.159v

Reportes vulgarely spred that his peres have wrongfully contrarie to law and right
condemned him, and that the Quene knowing it is moved in conscience to kepe
him alyve.

 The nature of the multitude being prone to credit rumors, and favor such as are in
miserie, it can not be but this preserving of him augmenteth his well willers and
encreaseth his faction.

 This appereth by the consultation of those traiters Madder *etc.* whoe resolved there
was no way to save the Duke but to destroy her Maiestie, and the danger herof the
more to be feared bicause it is an opinion in many established that God will not
suffer the prince to touche him whome they think by her Maiestie's lenitie uniustly
condemned, and thereby may hope for God's help in such a villanous attempt.

 Feare to all such as dutiefully have endevored themselves to syft out his treasons or
zelously have in open speches shewed their hatred toward such villanous practises,
wherof there is no small number. Sorrow to see her Maiestie so uncarefull of her
owne safetie, being not her private case but the only pyller wheron God's Chirch in
Christendome at this day chefely leaneth, the only sheld of all faithfull and true
Christian English subiectes: yea and the decay being in all humane policie the utter
subversion of the imperiall crowne of England, specially the Scott lyving.

 The preachers have plentiefully poured out vehement reasons, urgent examples
and horrible menaces out of the sacred scriptures concerning the execution of iustice
and shonning of that sugred poison bearing in outward shew the countenance of
mylde pitie, wheras in dede being depely sounded by grave consideration it is found
grevous crueltie. The contemning of / these yeldeth unto God's adversaries great
cause of triumph in advaunting our religion to be wicked and our preachers false
prophetes. For I suppose there is no enemie so malicious as will affirme her Maiestie

irreligious or so hardened in hart that such vehement exhortations of true prophetes alleging the scripture of God shold not move to geve eare to the lamentable crye of her whole realme pronounced by the mouth of the Parlament, as it were craving only by iustice to be delivered from the mouth of the dragon that, norseled in blood, expecteth but his time to satiate with the blood of her true subiectes, God's people, his unsatiable revengefull appetite.

Considering God for the sinnes of the people on whome he meaneth to lay plages, hardeneth the hart of the prince, the prophetes of our time with one voice have cried 'Justice, Justice'. All true Christian English hartes *in amaritudine cordis* crave it: the whole realme by the mouth of the Parlament request it: if her Majestie's hart shold be still hardened, we are enforced with great terror to feare that horrible iugement of the prophet pronounced upon Achab for neglecting of iustice, 'Thy life for his life' *etc.*, which God turne from us.

That it may please her Maiestie vigilantly to beware of such syrens as seke to enchaunt her Highnes' eares and wisdome with the poisoned sound of mercie and mansuetude; and to emprint in memorie that divine sayeng of Plutarch, '*Principis in facinorosos lenitas, quid est aliud quam in bonos crudelitas*'?[3] They are the dredfull scorpions that fawningly embrace with their armes, when they in dede styng with most mortal poison. |

Reasons provided to the same purpose by [blank] Dannet.

The defense of true religion, the realme, and her Maiestie's owne persone, touche her bothe in honor and conscience. The execution of the Duke is proved to be the only safetie of all these. Therfore her Maiestie is bound to do execution bothe in honor and conscience.

Her Maiestie is bound to execution of iustice bothe in honor and conscience.

Plutarch rehearseth that Archidamidas, hearing one commend Charillus for his clemencie and merciefulnesse to all men, sayd thus, 'How can he in any wise be praiseworthy that sheweth mercie to the wicked: *principis enim in facinorosos lenitas, quid, aliud est quam in bonos crudelitas*?' Wherfore it may please her Maiestie to reache reward to eche man according to his desert: mercie in her loving subiectes that be worthy therof, and iustice to her disloyal subiectes to whome it is due.

Her Maiestie's enimies redy to interpret every thing in the worst sense will iudge this lack of execution to procede of feare, whereby not onely they shall be animated, and her best subiectes utterly discouraged, but also forein princes caused to forbeare to treate with her for dout of her enimies' indignation, the feare of whoes faction they will suppose to be the onely stay of execution.

Plutarch writeth that the Ephori of Lacedemon punished Sciraptudas for

Marginal notes:
The wrath of God iustly to be feared if he be longer spared.

An humble petition to her Majesty.

f.160

Defense of religion *etc.*

Justice.
Mercie.

Feare.

New rebellions.

---

1. There is no direct evidence that this paper was produced in Parliament on this day, though in view of Thomas Norton's own submission there is a good chance that it was circulating, at least among some of the members.
2. On 24 May (*CJ*, I.98).
3. Cf. *Moralia*, 218B (Sayings of the Spartans).

remitting a haynous crime committed, alleging that by bearing one iniurie he encouraged his enimies to an other. For, sayd they, '*si is qui primus laeserat, delatus dedisset poenas legibus, caeteri temperassent ab iniuria'*.[4] It may therfore please her Maiestie for the cutting of of new attemptes, treasons and rebellions, to punish according to iustice those that have allredy ben attempted.

Necessitie will cause her owne murder.
f.160v

Her Maiestie layeth a necessitie upon her enimies to murder her owne royal persone. For considering that there are but twoo waies for them to avoide danger of death and recover libertie: the one, rebellion, which now they will / never attempt bicause fourthwith the occasion of the rebellion shold be cutt of; the other, murder of her Majestie's owne persone: surely necessitie enforceth them to make choise of the later, as it did Laetus and Electus when they slew Commodus, and the embassadors of Tarentum their maister, Johannes Antonius Ursinus.

Here will be made 2 obiections.

The first: that her enimies will attempt nothing against her.

Her enimies' evell will still endureth encreasced, not diminished.

Wherunto I answer. That her enimies had a will to hurt her Maiestie, their horrible treasons plainely deciphered and iustly condemned have sufficiently testified to the whole world. If that will be now altered, the alteration procedeth of some cause either natural or accidental. Nature can never be altered, ffor, as sayth Horace, '*Naturam expellas furca licet, usque recurret*.'[5] Further, what good can be hoped for in a nature wheare ingratitude in the hyest degree is grafted, where the floodgates of ambition and the flames of impotent love have utterly either swallowed up or consumed all dutie of allegeance, all bondes of nature, all remembrance of benefites, all care of contrey, all regard of othes, religion and God himself? Specially when upon the back of these twoo untamed beastes, ambition and love, hell hath now placed the furie of revenge. If then nature thus corrupted can not possibly be amended, neither (though it could) any cause appeare to amend it but rather to empeire it, shal her Maiestie adventure her life upon an alteration of nature not onely unlikely but also impossible?

I come now to examine what accidental cause may work this alteration in her Maiestie's professed enimie.

It will be sayd that her goodnesse in saving his life hath wrought it in him.

Wherunto I answer that the old proverb sayth, '*Ingrato quod feceris peribit*'; which sayeng is also confirmed by infinite examples, for a taste wherof I will allege Leonidas, Domitius, Popilius Laenas, Lucius Sylla, Herennius, and Apollodorus, all the which murdered and attempted to murder the preservers of their lyves,

f.161

attributing their / safetie to their owne devises, and no whit to their goodnesse that shewed them this grace.

Againe, he can not accept his safetie of his life in place of a great benefit, considering his honor to be stayned without the which he made protestation of no desire of life.

Further, at his departure from the barre he uttered these wordes, that as for mercie he neither craved it neither hoped for it. Why then shold her Maiestie graunt him that he craveth not? Or how can he make accompt of that which he holdeth not worth the asking?

Last of all her Maiestie is now so farr entred into the processe of this cause that mercie hurteth, not helpeth; irritateth, not asswageth; empeireth, not amendeth. For wheras there are but twoo wayes for a prince to deliver him self of enimies, mercie and iustice: mercie is to be used as Vespasian and Octavian used it, that is, without open examination clerely to forgeve and forget the offense. But her Maiestie having taken a contrarie course, and touched the offender bothe in honor, blood and landes, must now of force procede to iustice. For the middle way which her Maiestie holdeth, if she do not iustice, can not be but dangerous to her, *neque enim amicos parat, neque inimicos tollit*, and will but the more irritate him, considering the ignominie allredy received *vivet enim semper in illius pectore quicquid praesens necessitas inusserit, neque ante multiplices poenas expetitas quiescere sinet*, as Livie gravely discourseth, *Deca.* 2,[6] *liber* 9, where he maketh mention of the peace concluded betwene the Romanes and Samnites *ad Caudinas furculas*, where Pontius holding the middle way undid bothe his contrey and himself.[7]

Thus is it sufficiently proved: ffirst that an unthankfull and ambitious nature can never be altered; secondly that her Maiestie's mercie not thought worth the asking can not be of force sufficient to work amendement; and lastly that her mercie comyng after honor stayned, irritateth rather than appeaseth. And so her enimies will to hurt continueth firme, by desire of revenge rather encreasced than by to late mercie any whit diminished.

The second obiection is: that her Maiestie's enimie can do her no harme. |

Wherunto I answer that notwithstanding he himself be emprisoned, yet is he of habilitie to work her Maiestie's destruction. And a hard case it were for her to bylde her preservation upon this feble piller, that neither England, Spaine, Italie, no, nor Rome (which bothe forgeth and dispenseth with all kinde of treasons) are hable to furnish one desperate persone that dare either by swerd or by poison attempt her Maiestie's destruction, specially seing the hystoires plentiefully make report of diverse princes that have ben some destroyed, some hurt and nere their destruction, even in open assemblies, by such desperate attemptes, as for example Philip of Macedione, Ferdinand of Spaine, Baiazet the Turk, Galeace of Millain, with diverse others. And what that wretch Madder attempted of late against her Maiestie his punishment hath published to the whole world.

Further, though her Maiestie's loving subiectes hope all those that are about her to be trusty and faithfull, yet the grate care her sayd subiectes have of her preservation enforceth them, as long as the cause of her destruction, to dout her life in all places, at all times, and among all persones, even as the riche man supposeth upon every noyse theves to be at hand redy to breake in and bereve him of his only ioy. Neither hath any her Maiestie's trusty servantes cause to misslike of this our dout, considering that in histories we finde record of diverse princes murdered by their nerest servantes, persones most dangerous for a prince if they be disloyall bicause they are seldome denyed accesse to the prince's presence. Of the number of such princes were Alexander, Caesar, Commodus, Caracalla, Numerianus, Domitianus, Dion-

f.161v
Her Majestie's enemie hath power diverse waies to do her harme.

4. Cf. *Moralia*, 239C (Ancient Customs of the Spartans).
5. Cf. *Epistolae,* I.x.24.
6. *Sic.*
7. Bk.9, 3, 13-15.

ysius, Dion, Ferdinandus Davalus, Harald King of Denmark, Swercher King of Gotland, with diverse others to long to rehearse. I could here also make mention of Cleander and Perennius against Commodus, Plautianus against Severus, Seianus against Tiberius, and Piso against Nero, all the which were very familiar, and withall hyely avanced by those princes whome they sought to bereve to their lyves. In the rehearsall of the which examples this is also to be considered, that the murderers of diverse of these princes above-rehearsed escaped the danger after the murder committed, the possibilitie also wherof is very great in this case (none remayning behinde to revenge her Maiestie's death), yet so / great as her loving subiectes without bleeding hartes can not entre into consideration therof.

f.162

Thus have I proved that her Maiestie's enemie still persevereth in will, and withall wanteth no power neither in Court nor contrey to do her harme. And where will and power marie, the act must nedes be brought fourth. God graunt that her Maiestie may provid for her owne safetie and not put her self to his curtesie.

Not executing will discredit her Maiestie's preachers, whoe have told her out of God's boke that after iugement she ought to do iustice.

It is also agreable to her Maiestie's zele in religion to do this execution, considering that the stay therof will shake the state of religion through all Christendome.

Not executing will dishonor the whole Parlament, if their resolution, which is that the death of the Duke is the safetie of religion and of her Maiestie's realme and persone, be reiected.

Not executing dishonoreth the nobles that have condemned him. For the people will say that in consideration of the wrong they have done him, her Maiestie stayeth the execution.

Her Maiestie refusing to putt us in safetie after her death by establishing succession, ought at the least to prolong our safetie as long as may be, by preservation of her owne life; wherof if she shal continue unmindefull, her true and faithfull subiectes despeiring of safetie by her meanes shalbe forced to seke protection ellswhere, to the end they be not alltogether destitute of defense.

Last of all, it may please her Maiestie to encline her gracious eares to the humble petition of her faithfull subiectes, least her Maiestie be recorded for the onely prince of this land with whome the subiectes therof could never prevaile in any one sute.

7. *A form of a petition for executing the Duke of Norfolk provided by Thomas Norton, 31 May*

Text from BL Add.48023 (Yelverton 26), copy.
Other MS. Add.48027 (Yelverton 31).

Add.48023 (Yelverton 26), fos.163–4v

A forme or platt for the ground and order of a petition to be framed to her Maiestie for executing of the Duke of Norfolk, provided by T[homas] N[orton].

After acknowleging of her Maiestie's benefites and graciousnesse, with offer of all love, obedience and dutie, trusting upon reciprocal good acceptation and favourable inclination to our sutes for her Majestie's safetie and our owne; to procede with declaring that:

Where over and above the ordinarie dutie of care that all good subiectes, specially those whome it hath pleased her Maiestie to call to her hye court of Parlament, ought to have for her Maiestie's safetie, to whome they are so hyely bounden, it hath further pleased her Maiestie to geve in special charge and commaundement to her subiectes in this parlament assembled, generally to consider and employ their consultations and endevors for the conservation of her Maiestie's persone and the preserving of this realme, the safeties wherof have by late most horrible attemptes ben most perilously assalted.

And where her sayd subiectes, according to their duties and her Highnes' commaundement, entring into the sayd consideration do call to mynde the most unnaturall and dangerous factes of the late Duke of Norfolk attempted against her Maiestie and the realme.

And where the sayd Duke of Norfolk, after due triall according to the due course of the lawes of this realme to him most honorably graunted, standeth by the law iustly convicted and attainted.

And where it hath pleased her Maiestie hetherto of her most abounding clemencie of nature to spare the execution of the sayd Duke.

And where the doinges of the sayd Duke have ben such bothe in his unnaturall and disloyal proceding, and in contempt of true religion to him knowen, and breache of his allegeance, submissions, attestations and othes, and practising new treasons even while the old were in pardoning, and in receiving communions before his atteynder with purpose to pursue the course of destroyeing the communion, and in receyving communions sins his atteynder bothe with obstinate conceling of the particularities of his treasons and confederates and other maters mete for the safetie of f.163v   her Majestie and / the realme to be reveled, and with manifestly untrue protestations of ungiltinesse in thinges notoriously knowen and by lawfull triall uninimbly[1] proved, that there is no meane left whereby in any possibilitie her Maiestie may herafter be assured of him.

And where sondry most wicked persones, wherof some have for the same ben duely executed, have conceived and uttered that there resteth no hope of his deliverance but her Maiestie's destruction.

And where the long sparing of him hath not only geven occasion to evell interpretations of her Maiestie's iugement concerning the iustice of his case, to the great sclander of his noble peres, but also continueth great peril to her Maiestie.

And where thereby groweth not only boldnesse in noughty persones to desperate attemptes, but also great danger and feare in other subiectes freely to employ themselves against treasons herafter.

There enforce the reasons that may prove expedience of his execution, not so much in respect of peine for offense past as of necessitie to be assured against peril to come : wherin is to be remembred the honor of iustice, the benefit of example, losse of opportunities, peril by avantage to the other side, by example, by irritating and encouraging the worst, by appalling and endangering the best, arming traitors with greater circumspection, with a multitude of like considerations.

And where it hath pleased her Maiestie, in respect of causes seming to her Highnes to touche honor and conscience, to respite the due proceding against the Scottish Quene longer than her Maiestie's safetie may well beare, and for that consideration and the danger of the realme and true religion longer than we her poore subiectes do think that honor or conscience or her Maiestie's most due cares do advise her, and so much longer than true men are glad to see. In which meane long season, while bothe the sayd dangerous persones do yet lyve, namely the sayd Scottish Quene and the Duke, her Maiestie and the realme do remaine in doble peril, to the great feare and discomfort of all her true subiectes, and much greater than if but one of them lyved.

And where sithe her Maiestie will not begine with the execution of the Scottish Quene, which her subiectes wold most gladly have seen, and do think to be rather than the other the most assured provision for her Highnes' safetie (if it had so pleased her), the execution of the Duke shall yet be a great abatement of the forces of the Scottish Queen to endanger the Queene's Maiestie, bothe bicause it is thought that

f.164   the Scottish Quene is in England / stronger by him than he by her, and for that his frendes being not onely withdrawen from her but also (bicause she is the cause of his destruction) brought to hate her and seke revenge against her, she shalbe made thereby odious bothe to nobilitie and commons, she shalbe lesse hable to hurt the Quene, so as it may be rightly sayd that the striking of of his hedd shalbe at the least half the cutting of of her neck, bicause though it cutteth not the wisant wherewith she breatheth, it shall yet cutt asonder the sinewes wherewith her hed moveth. And so by his death shal she be made either more easy to be brought to death, or lesse terrible if she live.

Now her Maiestie's true subiectes with great care and grefe considering the premisses and weyeing, according to her Highnes' commaundement, all the circumstances therof, have fully resolved in opinion and iugement that they think it of most important necessitie for the preservation of her Maiestie's persone and the realme (specially sins her Maiestie to the realme's great peril and sorrow hath determined to deferre the proceding against the Scottish Quene according to her deservinges) that execution be bothe for the present necessitie of the case and for eschuing of peril and perilous example, done upon the sayd Duke.

It may therfore please her Maiestie to accept in good part the true and faithfull advises of her faithfull subiectes, and not to putt of her most gracious affection of mercie, but to bend the same the right way, *vz.* to all her true nobilitie, clergie and commons, and to the whole multitude of her true subiectes in general and their posterities, and to this noble realme which can not be preserved without her, and to her Maiestie's perpetuall honor allredy largely shewed in her natural disposition to spare offenders, but now chefely to be extended in her Highnes' care to preserve innocentes, and so to yeld her Maiestie's affection to the safetie and humble petitions of her whole realme, and therfore to command execution to be done upon the sayd Duke during this session.

Whereby all her Maiestie's vertues shall have their severall shyning, namely her clemencie[2] and lothenesse to extend due peines, and yet her zele of religion, her care of her realme, / her magnanimitie against traitors' thretenings, her constant wisdome to eschue periles, her vertuous regard of her othe to England, and her reciprocall love to most loving subiectes exceding all other inclinations. And so shall her Maiestie not temptingly neglect God's provisions for her safetie, whoe hath not for nothing miraculously detected these treasons and guided her proceding so farr. And so may her Maiestie for a season somwhat the more safely use the sayd delay and temper of proceding against the Scottish Quene (which otherwise her Maiestie can not safely do) and her Highnes' subiectes shal more sincerely and boldly serve her.

f.164v

1. *Sic*; Add.48027 appears to read 'uninunbly'.

2. MS reads 'clementie'.

8. The bill which passed both Houses against the Queen of Scots, 25 June

(not including the proviso, which is noted in Fulk Onslow's record of the bill, fos.5 and v)

Text from BL Cott.Caligula BVIII, copy which notes amendments.
Other MSS. London: BL Cott.Titus F1 and its copy, Stowe 358.
Printed. Camden Society, 3rd ser., XVII.113⁄27 (from Cott.Caligula BVIII).

Cott.Caligula BVIII, fos.240⁄6v

[Endorsed in a later hand 'The bill exhibited by the lordes spirituall and temporall to her Majesty against the Scottish Queen.']¹

To the Queene's most excellent Majestie.

In their most humble wise beseeche your most royall Majestie your most humble, loving and faithfull subiectes the lordes spirituall and temporall, and all other your most humble and obedient subiectes the commons of your most highe courte of Parliament nowe assembled: that where Mary, daughter and heire of Jeames the Fifte late Kinge of Scottes, commonly called Queene of Scottes, most wickedly, falsely and uniustly hath claymed the present state and possession of your royall crowne of your realmes of England and Ireland, and most untruly and iniuriously usurped the style and armes of the said realmes, entytlinge her selfe the Queene of England and Ireland; which her wrongfull and false usurpation shee hath not hitherto revolked, allthoughe shee hath by sondrie lettres, messages and ambassages from your Majestie bene therunto often required, and notwithstanding the treatie and conclusion by her commissioners to that effecte agreed uppon, yet hath shee hitherto delayed and refused to ratifye the same treatie, and the same her said false and pretended tytle shee hath by her ministers and fautors from tyme to tyme practised sondrye wayes to preferre, sett forward, advaunce and publishe, to the great iniurye and dishonour of your most excellent Majestie and to the great inward greefe of all your good, naturall and loyall subiectes. And the said Mary continuing her said most uniust and malicious pretence and purpose to clayme your Majestie's most royall estate in the said realmes, and to dispossesse your Highnes of the same, after many trayterous and wicked practises against your Majestie's honour and safetie, and after her dismission of the crowne of Scottland for manifold and horrible crymes and disorders, wherwith shee was chardged in the said realme of Scottland, flying into this your Majestie's realme for succour, and here by your Majestie of most royall bountie received into your Highnes' protection and honorably used, forgetting all

duite, nature and kindnes, hath for th'advauncement of her said most uniust tytle
and usurpacion, and to atchieve the same by disherison and destruction of your most
excellent Majestie, sought by subtile and / craftye meanes to withdrawe the late   f.240v
Duke of Norfolke, nowe iustly attainted of highe treason, from his due and naturall
obedience to your Highnes, and against your Majestie's expresse prohibition to
couple her selfe in marriadge with the said Duke, to th'intent that ioyninge together
such strength and force as shee sought to have by meanes of the Pope and other her
forreyne confederates, and of some traytors subiectes within this your realme of
England, with such power as in her opinion the said Duke might have, being
advaunced to such greatnes of degree and estate in this realme and brought and
mainteyned in great creditt by your Majestie's speciall favour and calling, shee might
the soner attaine and bring to effecte your Majestie's deprivation and destruction, to
the utter discomforte, desolacion and subvertion of your realmes and true subiectes.
And for the prosequuting of the said trayterous purpose and intencion against your
Majestie the said Mary hath also by her ministers sollicited the said late Duke not
only to th'accomplishement of the said daungerous mariadge but also to bringe the
same to effecte with force; and for more hastie perfourmaunce of the said daungerous
mariadge, shee stirred and procured your most false and trayterous subiectes the Erles
of Northumberland and Westmorland, and other their confederates, false traytors,
to rebell and levye open warre against your Majestie in the north partes of this your
realme with purpose to overthrowe the sincere relligion of God and to depose your
Majestie and to place the said Mary in your royall seate. And to that ende promised
to the said rebells ayde of men and money to the maintenaunce of their rebellion and
to the furtheraunce of her said trayterous intentes; and did relieve them with
comfortable encouragmentes, and procuring of promise of forraine succours before
and in the tyme of the said rebellion. And after that by the grace of allmightie God
prospering the good and true service and duties of your most loyall and faithfull
subiectes, your Majestie's power did putt the said rebells to flight, diverse lordes and
others of Scottland, favourers of the said Mary and adhering to her faction, did by
her meanes and in respecte of her favour receave, succour and cherishe the said
unnaturall and trayterous rebelles with such supportacion and maintenaunce as they
were able. / Which said rebelles together with certaine Scottes of the parte and faction   f.241
of the said Mary in most cruell and warlike manner entred and invaded this your
Majestie's realme, for the which your Highness most iustly by force and open warre
under the conducte of the right noble and your good and faithfull subiecte Thomas,
Erle of Sussex, then your Lieutenaunt, did pursue the said rebelles and their
favourers and receavers within the realme of Scotland, where shee the said Mary
procured by her said favorers and adherentes the said rebelles to be defended and
kept in salfe and secret places from your Majestie's armye. And when the habilitie of
her said frendes in Scottland sufficed not to defende the said rebelles against your
Majestie's power, shee did by her ministers advise and procure them to departe and
flye into the Lowe Countries beyonde the seas, where shee procured unto them not

1. Cott. Titus F1 has the heading 'The bill   Scottishe Queene *Anno 13* [*sic*] *Regine*
   that passed both Houses againste the   Elizabeth.'

only reliefe of money but also lettres of encouragement from the great enimye of God and your Majestie and this your realme, the Pope of Rome. Wherby not only their presente necessities were relieved and holpen, but also they were encouraged and put in great hope to recover their former estates in England, and to prosequute their former trayterous attemptes.

Moreover the said Mary still continuinge her said most wicked purposes, hath both by her selfe and her ministers and by the said late Duke of Norffolke, whom shee hath incited therunto, practised to procure newe rebellion to be raysed within this realme, and to ioyne with the force of straungers to invade this your said realme. And for that intente (besides sondrye other her ministers) shee made choyce of one Robert Ridolphe, a merchaunte of Italye, then being secreatlye as the Pope's agent in this realme, and recommended to her from the Pope by lettres of creditte to be her instrument and messenger in that matter. Which Ridolphe by her speciall meanes and by commission from her and from the said late Duke of Norffolke for th'accomplishment of certaine instructions to him given for furtheraunce of her service and for th'advauncement of her said trayterous and most wicked conspiracies, devices and intentes, went unto the partes[2] beyond the sea to procure from the Pope and other forraine potentates men and money for / the speedy invasion of this your realme, and to ioyne with such force of rebells and traytors as might be raysed by her, her confederates and adherentes within this realme; uppon which ioyning of forces it was intended that shee shold have bene proclaimed Queene of England and Ireland. And the same Ridolphe being arrived in the partes beyond the seas sollicited the said wicked enterprises to the said Pope and others, with whom the said Ridolphe had good and favourable audience, and receaved great and large promises to the furtheraunce of the said wicked intentes, as he the said Ridolphe by lettres in cyphre signified to the said Duke of Norffolke and other his adherentes, from whom advertisement therof was given by means[3] to the said Mary. And further the said Ridolphe so sent by her and the said Duke of Norffolke as is aforesaid procured from the Pope lettres of comforte to her and the said Duke of Norffolk for the maintenaunce of forreyne force to invade this your realme. Which forreine force by devices wherunto the said Mary and her confederates were privy, was appoynted to have landed at a porte in your realme, and to have ioyned with a power of rebells that shold have trayterously levied warre in this your realme against your Highnes, if God had permitted prosperity to their most vyle, wicked and trayterous exterprises; which wicked attempte was stayed uppon the happy discovery of the treason aforesaid.

Over and above all which most vyle and trayterous practises abovesaid, the said Mary conspired with diverse of your unnaturall subiectes for her delivery out of your Highnes' custody and power, to this intent, that if their said enterprise had taken effecte, shee should have bene proclaymed Queene of England at one tyme in severall places of this realme; as by the confession of some of her complices attaynted of highe treason for that cause hath plainely and evidently appeared. And further the said Mary for the better bringing to passe of her said wicked attemptes, receaved sondry lettres from her said confederate the Pope and from his nuntio, amonge many other thinges conteyninge matter of restoring her to the Church of Rome, with promise to

f.241v

embrace her and hers *sicut gallina pullos suos*, and to dispense with all those that wold
in her favour rebell against your Majestie and to take them as *filios Ecclesiae*, | with   f.242
promise of ayde and supporte to the said Mary. For which ende also the said Pope
hath to her further succour, wherunto shee was privy, put in banke one hundreth
thousand crownes, to be employed uppon any that wold take uppon him the
enterprise for setting upp of popish relligion in this realme, by helping her to the
crowne of this realme.

And where the said Pope most vainely, impudently and falsely usurping and
taking to him selfe power at his will and pleasure to deprive princes of their states and
kingdomes, did publishe a most vyle, tyrannicall and seditious bull of deprivacion,
full of most false, horrible and uncomely sclaunders against your Majestie, your
nobility, realme and subiectes, the said bull was knowen to the said Mary. Uppon
which bull hath bene founded not only the most trayterous perswasion of your
Majestie's false and untrue rebells and other trayterous subiectes against your
Majestie's undoubted right to your most royall crowne and the maintenance of her
pretenced tytle to the same, but also actuall rebellion in some part of your dominions.

And for further hastening her said wicked purpose and intencion, some of the
ministers of the said Mary in her favour and furtheraunce moved and devised in the
tyme of your Majestie's last parliament holden in the xiij[th] yeare[4] of your most
blessed raigne, to have supprised your Majestie's courte by force, and to have broken
upp and disturbed your parliament, and seased your Majestie's royall person, to the
great perill and daunger of subvertion of this your realme. And for better setting
forward of all the said trayterous intencions and for seducing of your subiectes, and
withdrawing their loyaltie from your Highnes to the said Mary, certaine rebelles and
traytors to your Majestie abyding beyond the seas, and other the adherentes of the said
Mary, still continuing their trayterous purposes and practises in her behalfe, have
by bookes, writinges, lettres and open speeches playnely disclosed what accompt
shee and they make of your Highnes' most undoubted right, calling her by the name
of 'our Queene', and 'Queene of England and Ireland', with such like speeches to
her utterly undue, and terming your Majestie, being our undoubted soveraigne lady
and Queene, by the name of Elizabeth, present Governour, 'pretenced Queene',
and 'late Queene', | and such like, and have both in bookes and petigrees deduced   f.242v
unto the said Mary a false pretenced and colorable tytle by discent to your Majestie's
crowne, not only above your Majestie's iust tytle, but also above all your most noble
progenitors kinges of this realme since the Conquest, not only to the most uniust
clayme and chalenge of your most royall seate, but also to the utter confusion of the
whole state of this realme: which bookes have bene attempted to be printed within
this realme, and by good forsight being stayed here, have bene finished beyond the
seas, by the meanes of her ministers, and some of your trayterous subiectes in those
partes, and from thence have bene brought hither to be published in her favour.
And of the said petigrees sondrie copies have bene made and dispersed, and some of

2. MS reads 'parties'; this reading from
Cott.Titus F1.

3. *Sic*, and in Cott.Titus F1.

4. Cott.Titus F1 reads 'eighteenth yeare'
although the MS is headed 13 Elizabeth.

the same coppies together with especiall instructions advauncing her treasons, have bene lately founde in custody of some of her principall agentes. In which instructions also amonge other most wicked and sedicious matter, it was conteyned and sett forth that the said Mary was and is the lawfull Queene of England.

And the said Mary not thus contented, hath also since the late discovery of her said horrible factes proceaded by newe attemptes and sollicitacions to pursue and procure the continuance and renewinge of the said most wicked enterprise of invading this your realme, besides infinite other most ungodly and daungerous practises against your most royall Majestie and your said realme attempted both within your dominions and elswhere beyond the seas, which are lett passe.

All which her most seditious and detestable practises have by her owne lettres and instructions, and by the free, voluntary and plaine confessions of diverse her confederates and ministers most amply, truly and largely bene proved. And allthoughe your Majestie of your most aboundaunt goodnes hath hitherto above the common limittes and bondes of mercye, forborne to procead against the said Mary accordinge to her deservinges, and as by justice and equitye your Majestie might have done: yet nowe seing her malice to be nothing restrayned with due consideracion of your Majestie's goodnes, clemencye and kindnes towardes her, at whose handes shee hath receaved great and sondry benifittes and namely (amongest many other) the / salfegarde, and preservation of her lyfe, which should have bene taken from her in the realme of Scottland for sondry horrible crymes wherwith shee was then chardged, if your Highnes' most kinde, favourable and most earnest mediacion, as well by your speeche as by your lettres and messages on her behalfe had not wrought her salftye; and considering also the most wicked and malicious devices and practises of her and her confederates and fautors towardes your Majestie do not cease but dayly encrease to the great daunger of your Majestie's most royall person, and perill of subvertion of true relligion, and of the prosperous state of your realmes and dominions: wee therfor your true and obedient subiectes the lordes spirituall and temporall and the commons in this presente parliament assembled do most humbly beseeche your Majestie for the securitie and preservacion of your most royall person (whom allmightie God longe preserve and protecte from all perill and daunger; and especially from the most daungerous and perillous attemptes of the said Mary and her adherentes) and for the good peace, rest and tranquillitye of all your most loving and obedient subiectes and of their posterityes and for the continuance of the true service, religion and honour of Allmightye God, not to beare in vayne the swerde of justice committed to your Majestie, but by the justice of the lawes of your realme to punishe and correcte *(which your Majesty iustly and lawfully may do)*[5] all the treasons and wicked attemptes of the said Mary condignely accordinge to the demerites, as speedely and in such manner and forme as may stande with your Majestie's good will and pleasure. Unto which humble and earnest petition of your said loving and obedient subiectes, they assuredly hope your Majestie will have such princely regarde as the greatnes of the cause requireth: considering that theruppon in very deed dependeth the securitye of your Majestie's most royall person, the service and relligion of allmightie God, the common peace and tranquillitye of the whole realme, and the preservation of all th' estates therof in

f.243

their sevearall honours, estates and degrees. And yet nevertheless in the meane tyme, for asmuch as many of the frendes and fautors of the said Mary (besydes the treasons and practises attempted most uniustly / to have brought her into the presente possession of this your Majestie's crowne of England) have also conceaved an uncertaine[6] hope, that if it should fortune your Majestie (as God forbid) to decease without heires of your body; that then the said Mary should succeede your Majestie in the regall estate of this your Majestie's realme, and other your realmes, dominions and countryes. Uppon which hope, founded upon uncertaine and doubtfull causes, it hath well appeared that sondrye perilous and daungerous enterprises, and *false and trayterous* practises have bene attempted towardes your Highnes, and this your realme, and more may ensue to the utter discomforte, desolation and ruyne of your *Majesty and* [your] said subiectes and their posterityes, if the same be not providently forseene and remedied.

f.243v

May it nowe therfor please your Majestie at the further instance and most humble desyre and petition of your said subiectes to th'end that such *undue* causes and groundes of highe treasons and daungerous practises against your Majestie's person and this your realme arising and manifestly comming by the said doubtfull and uncertaine hope[7] of the said Mary and of her fautors and adherentes to the *possession or* succession of the crowne of this your Majestie's realme may be cleerly and utterly[8] cutt of, and in respecte of the said treasons, practises, conspirac[i]es and other kinde demeanors and doinges of the said Mary against your royall Majestie and for other the causes above remembred, and towardes some parte of the punishement and correction of her offences and misdemeanors:

That it may be enacted, ordeyned and declared by your Highnes, the lordes spirituall and temporall, and the commons in this presente parliament assembled that the said Mary, commonly called Queene of Scottes, be *in deede and shalbe* to all intentes and purposes deemed, adiudged and taken a person unable, unworthy and uncapable of, [and] shall not at any tyme have, hold, clayme, possesse or enioy the dignity and[9] tytle of the said crowne of England and of all[10] other your Majestie's realmes, dominions and[11] countries, and of all regall *and other* power, estate, dignitye, tytle and[12] preheminence within this your Majestie's realme / and all other your realmes, dominions and[13] countries, in such manner and forme to all intentes and purposes as thoughe the said Mary *had never lyved* or weare naturally dead; and that the said Mary shall not at any tyme herafter have, hold, clayme, possesse nor enioye th'estate, dignitie, tytle or interest of the crowne of this your Majestie's realme or of any other your Highnes' realmes, dominions or countryes.

f.244

5. The formulation of this critical bill produced extensive debate. The concern with verbal precision was intense, and in this instance the italicization of the manuscript's amendments has been preserved. Words printed in light type are those underlined in the MS.

6. Alternatively *'imagined a vaine and daungerous'*. Alternative readings appear in the margin of the MS.

7. Alternatively *'fawlse perswasion and hope'*.
8. Alternatively *'the rather'*.
9. Alternatively *'or'*.
10. Alternatively *'nor of any'*.
11. Alternatively *'or'*.
12. Alternatively *'or'*.
13. Alternatively *'or'*.

And further that it may be enacted and declared by your Majestie, the lordes spirituall and temporall and the commons in this presente parliament assembled, and by authoritye of the same, that if the said Mary shall or doe at any tyme herafter in your Majestie's lyfe make or pretende any chalendge, clayme, demaund, interest or tytle to the crowne of this your Majestie's realme of England, or of any other your realmes, dominions or countries, or shall procure, conspire, devise or consent to bringe *or to be brought* into this realme of England or the realme of Ireland, or any other your Majestie's dominions, any forreyne force or invasion, or to rayse or stirre any warre or rebellion within the said realme of England or Ireland, or that[14] any warre, rebellion or invasion shalbe made, or any warre shalbe denounced to your Majestie for any matter or cause in any wise touching or concerning the said Mary; or that[15] shee shall at any tyme herafter do, committ, devise, or consent to the doing, comitting or devising of any manner of matter, acte or thinge which in case semblable shold be deemed and taken treason in any naturall borne subiecte of this realme, doing, committing or devising the same:[16] that then and from thenceforth the said Mary shalbe deemed and taken a traytor to your Majestie and that all and every the offences and causes aforesaid by her and in her behalfe to be done, shalbe deemed, adiudged and taken highe treasons in the said Mary; and that shee being therof or of any of them indyted and convicted, shall suffer and have paynes of death as in cases of highe treason is due and accustomed by the lawes of this realme.

f.244v And to th'end some certaine knowledge and declaracion may be made aswell for a[17] *convenient* tryall of all such treasons which the said / Mary may herafter committ as also for the treasons by her hertofore done and committed against your Majestie, your crowne and dignitye: may it please your Highnes that it may be further enacted by authority aforesaid in respecte of the state, honour and dignitye which shee hath hertofore borne, that the said Mary aswell for the treasons aforsaid by her hertofore done and committed against your Majestie as also for all other treasons which herafter shee shall do or committe, shall and may in such manner and forme be indicted, arayned, tryed and adiudged therof as the wyfe of any the noblest peere of this realme should or ought to be indicted, arayned, tryed and adiudged by the lawes and statutes of this realme for any treason by the wyfe of any such peere of this realme committed or done.

And over this that it may be enacted by your Majestie, the lordes spirituall and temporall and the commons in this presente parliament assembled, and by th'authoritye of the same, that if the said Mary at any tyme after your Majestie's decease (whom allmightie God longe preserve) do or shall make any clayme, chalendge or tytle to the crowne of this realme of England, or of any other your Highnes' realmes, dominions or countries; or that any open warre *or warrlike force*[18] be raysed or levied in this realme of England for the cause, quarrell or pretence of the said Mary in that behalfe and to th'advauncement and preferment of her said pretenced clayme: that then and from thenceforth the said Mary and every such her fautor shalbe deemed, taken and used as an enimye to the realme and crowne of England; and utterly out of the protection of the lawes of this realme of England.

And over this that it may please your Majestie that it may be enacted by authoritye aforesaid, that if any person or persons shall at any tyme after thirtye dayes next after th'end of this presente session of Parliament by expresse speache, writinge or other matter advisedly and directly affirme, attribute or ascribe to the said Mary any manner of tytle or right or possibilitye of tytle or right to the crowne of this realme or of any other your Highnes' realmes, dominions or / countryes, to th'intent to further any such right, tytle or possibilitye; or if any person or persons shall at any tyme or tymes herafter during your Majestie's lyfe conspire, practise, devise or assent by any wayes or meanes with force or otherwise without your Majestie's licence or consent, to take the said Mary out of such custody and place where your Majestie hath appointed or herafter shall appoynte her to be kept; or if any person or persons whatsoever shall at any tyme or tymes herafter willingly by any wayes or meanes minister or give *or procure to be ministered or given* to the said Mary any ayde, comforte, succour, supporte or reliefe by any expresse wordes, writinge, open acte or deed, to th'intent therby to deliver her *or procure her deliveraunce* out of your Highnes' custody or possession without your Majestie's licence and consent, for th'advauncement of her said pretence *or otherwise*, or to th'intent therby to supporte, mainteyne or defend the said Mary in or to any thinge contrary to the tenor, effecte and true meaninge of this presente acte; or if any person of what estate, degree or nation soever he be at any tyme herafter within this realme shall or doe for him selfe or for any other person practise or procure (*or cause or assent to be practised or procured*) any thinge for the having or obteyninge of any mariadge or contracte of mariadge with the said Mary without your Majestie's licence and consent therunto first had and obteyned: that then every person so offending in any the premisses shalbe deemed, adiudged and taken a traytor, and his offence therin deemed, adiudged and taken to be highe treason; and being therof lawfully endicted and attainted, shall suffer, incurre and have such paynes of death, losses, penalties and forfeitures as in cases of highe treason is due by the lawes and statutes of this realme.

And for the better maintenaunce and sure continuaunce of this presente acte and every article and thinge therin conteyned: may it also please your Majestie that it may be likewise established by authoritye of this parliament, that it shall and may be lawfull to all persons aswell at this present tyme as also at every / tyme and tymes herafter, to mainteine, sett forth and defend to the uttermost of thier powers all and every thinge and thinges declared, expressed, intended or mentioned against the said Mary in this presente acte and statute, without incurring or susteyning of any losse, domage, penaltie or forfeiture; and that every person that hertofore hath or at any tyme herafter shall with force or otherwise stand to sett forth, mainteyne or defende all, any, every or any the thinges or matters which by this presente acte are declared, expressed or mentioned against the said Mary, shall not therfore in any wise be impeached, molested, imprisoned or troubled in body, landes or goodes, but shall therof stand cleerly dischardged without any manner of impeachment, any lawe or statute whatsoever to the contrarye notwithstanding.

And for asmuch as all the horrible treasons and conspiracies before in this acte

f.245

f.245v

---

14. Alternatively '*if*'.
15. Alternatively '*if*'.
16. Alternatively '*like*'.

17. Alternatively '*the*'.
18. '*Or warrlike force*' a marginal insertion.

mencioned have growen by the said Mary and other her adherantes chieffly for this cause and purpose, to bringe againe into this realme the detestable and usurped authoritye of the sea of Rome, and therby to subiecte the imperiall crowne of this realme, and the faithfull and loving subiectes of the same, to the bondage, tyrranny and thraldome of the said sea, and so to chaunge and alter the true and sincere relligion of God nowe established within this realme: may it therfore please your Majestie for th'avoydinge of such great daungers and perilles, as by any such wicked attemptes might ensue to this your Majestie's realme and the good subiectes of the same, that it may be enacted by th'authoritye of this presente parliament, that if any person or persons of what state or degree soever he or they be, shall at any tyme or tymes herafter willingly, advisedly and directly do, make or procure, or assent to be done, made or procured any acte or thinge to th'intent that therby the usurped power or any the pretenced jurisdiction or authoritie of the said sea of Rome, nowe by the lawes and statutes of this realme iustly abolished, / shall or may in any wyse be brought againe or used within this realme or within any your Majestie's dominions and[19] countries: that then every such offence and offences shalbe taken, iudged and deemed to be highe treason; and the offendors therin shalbe taken to be traytors, and being therof indicted and lawfully attainted and convicted according to the lawes of this realme shall suffer paynes of death, and also shall lose and forfeyte all his and their landes, tenementes, goodes and cattailles, as in cases of highe treason is used and accustomed. Provided allwayes, that if it shall happen herafter any peere of this realme to be endicted of any offence made treason by this acte, he shall have his tryall by his peeres as in other cases of treason is accustomed.[20]

f.246

And where diverse your Majestie's true subiectes conceyving by reason of the great enormityes of the said Mary and her daungerous practises against your Majestie a iust and due displeasure and hatred against the said Mary, have in detestation of her lewde lyfe and treasons and for good zeale to your most excellent Majestie uttred diverse speeches and done sondry actes to the defacement of the said Mary and of her factious pretence and trayterous clayme and doinges; and as it is most likely after the disclosing of her so many and manifold horrible offences in this acte mentioned, will conceave greater lothing and abhorring of her crymes: may it please your Majestie that it may be enacted and declared, that all speeches and doinges of your Majestie's subiectes, and every of them hertofore had, used or done against the said Mary or to her defacement or preiudice, shalbe to all intentes, constructions and purposes iudged and deemed good and lawfull doinges of honest, zelous and true subiectes to your Majestie; and that all speeches and doinges herafter to be done and[21] used according to the meaninge or to th'advauncement of th'intent of this acte or any part therof, or to the defacement of any clayme or chalendge that the said Mary hath pretended or shall pretende to the crowne, / style or dignitye of this realme, or of any other your Majestie's dominions, be declared and shalbe iudged lawfull doinges, and that no person shall ever be empeached, reprehended, convented or otherwise troubled for the same: any matter whatsoever to the contrary notwithstandinge.

f.246v

19. Alternatively '*or*'.   21. Alternatively '*or*'.
20. Cott. Titus F1 ends here.

1. *Fulk Onslow's journal, 24-31 May, 25 June*

Text from House of Lords MS 3186 (Braye MS), original, in the hand of Onslow, Clerk of the House of Commons.
Printed. HMC 10. vi. 125-7 (extracts only); *The Manuscripts of the House of Lords*, XI. 6-12.

[Saturday 24 May]
Meane time the Speaker to consider with himselfe the maner of his motion, and that as many of the lower house as were disposed should in the meane time bring suche causes to the Speaker in writing to inforce the cause.[1]

The House brake up, and was adiourned againe untill Wednesday morning.

Thursday 29 *Maii*.

1. A bill that the freemen of London, aswell those by birth as suche as serve for yeres as an apprentice, may inioye the liberties and privileges thereof.
2. The bill for partition[2] of landes betweene Sir Robert Wingfield, knight, and the Lorde Latimer was readde the second time, and putto ingrossing.
3. The bill for fraudulent conveyaunces of landes the second time read and putto ingrossing. Sir Robert Skot against the bill. Sir Nicholas Arnold against the bill for looking backward. Norton with the bill.
4. The bill against building of cottages in waste groundes and commons was read the second time, and by the whole House adiudged to be torne.
5. The bill for vagaboundes and roges, and reliefe of the poore, was read the thirde time,[3] and committed againe to be better considered of.

A burgesse bargained the bill for the liberties of the Marshalsie.

Samp[o]ll with the bill.

Fortescue against the whole bill. He devided his matter into three partes, and made a very good argument. /

The Lordes sent into the lower house a bill for the annexing of Examshire unto the countie of Northumberland.

Wilbraham argued against the bill of roges, and made an excellent argument both wise and eloquent.

Alford against the whole bill.

f.1v

1. The reference is to the nature of the petition about the Duke of Norfolk to be made to the Queen.
2. MS reads 'petition'.
3. The following words occur at this point in the MS, but are crossed out: 'And by the whole House adiudged to be torne.'

Sir Fraunces Knowles made a longe argument partlye with the bill and partly against it.

Mounson with the bill. Sir James Croftes against part of the bill.

Dannet argued onely against certaine textes of scriptures, which Fortescue alleaged, affirming that he had greatly abused God's word. And this ended the House brake up.

[Friday 30 May.]

Seintleger. 'Since the Queene's Maiestie's will and pleasure is that we should not proceede nor deale with the firste bill against the monstrous and huge dragon, and masse of the earth, the Queene of Skottes, yet my conscience urgeth and pricketh me to speake and move this House to be in hande with her Maiestie with the execution of the roaring lion, I meane the Duke of Norfolk. And although her Maiestie be lolled asleepe, and wrapped in the mantle of her owne perill, yet for my part I cannot be silent in uttering of my conscience'. And alleaged the text of wicked Hamon whom he applied to the Duke, and of the godly Queene Hester to the Queene's Maiestie.

A bill that whereas Sir William Harper, knight, alderman of London, being by reason of his great age and sicknes in decay of his memorie and wit, was by one / f.2 Prestwood and his wife persuaded or rather inforced to geve unto them by deede in writing all his goodes and cattelles without any consideration, that the saide deede might be revoked. The bill committed.

The bill for the inclosing of Plumsted Marshe the second time read and putto ingrossing.

The bill of fraudulent recoveries against tenaunt for life *etc.* being altered into another sort was the first time read, and putto ingrossing.

A bill to have the assises within the countie of Buckinghamshire to be kept and holden at Aylesburie.

The bill for the freemen of London to inioye the privileges of the citie, and putto ingrossing.

The bill for leasses made by corporations, which have not the verie apt wordes of the corporation, to be good: the second time read.

Sackford, Master of Requestes, against the bill. Fenner against part of the bill. Dalton against all the bill. Popham to have the bill reformed. Bedell against the bill in part. Sir Nicholas Arnold with the bill. More with the bill.

Sir Fraunces Knowles made report howe he with others had travelled in reforming part of the bill against vagaboundes which was read, wherein in the newe alteration of these wordes 'minstrelles', whether they shoulde be conteined within the saide bill or not, great argument rose, *viz.* Wilbraham to have them left out. Sir f.2v James Croftes to the same effect. Cromwell to have / them within the bill. Marshe to the same effect. Sir Owen Hopton with the minstrelles. Sir Fraunces Knowles neither with them nor against them. Sandes with the minstrelles. Snagge muche talk and to no purpose. Sir Nicholas Arnold against them. Sampoll against them.

Recorder of London, a longe tedious talke nothing towching the matter in question. He tooke a theame *Res ipsa dabit consilium*, wherupon he replied still but to litle purpose.

Sackford, Master of the Requestes, against them. St John, Gargrave, Mounson, Edgecombe, Popham against them. Aylworth to no purpose.

In the ende it was agreed by the more number they should be within the bill, and so the House brake up.

Saturday 31.

A bill against Waxchaundlers for the deceiptfull making of waxe, and that the masters and wardens of the Waxchaundlers in London shall have authoritie to searche within fortie miles of London.

A burges of Oxford, the Recorder and Snagge against the bill.

A bill for the chappell of Lerpoole[4] that the same may be a parish churche by the name of St Paule.

Snagge, Wilbraham and the Recorder against the bill. Sekerston and Sandes with the bill.

The bill against fraudulent recoveries had against tenaunt for terme of life, the second time read, and / put againe to be altered in certaine poyntes.   f.3

A private bill for the Erle of Kent against the Lorde Compton being reformed into another order was the first time by me read, and committed to those that were the committies in the other bill.

Peter Wentworth moved the House to go on for motion to the Queene for the execution of the Duke.

Snagge to the same effect.

Norton to the like effect. He brought forth a paper in writing wherein he had written certaine reasons which should be delivered to the Speaker to be considered of, and collect the best for his purpose.[5]

Ireland to have the Queene moved for the speedie execution during the session.

Digges that such causes as are put in writing might be committed to certaine to be allowed or disalowed of.

Snagge to have all the commons of the House to go to the Queene for th'execution of the Duke. Marshe to th'effect of Digges' motion.

Sir Fraunces Knowles. 'I perceave your intent is to make motion for th'execution of the Duke, which I perceave proceedeth of verie love and care you have to the Queene's person, which is the marke whereat all good subiectes shoote at. And although I doo knowe nothing more convenient and needefull then execution, and that with speede, yet I knowe the disposition of princes is rather of themselves to doo such thinges then by way of pressing and urging. It may be, and it is like / ynough,   f.3v
her Maiestie is of her selfe alreadie disposed sooner to doo it then you doo perhaps thinke or beleve. And I would not wishe we should attempt her of his hastie execution, for that I knowe alreadie her minde partly therein. Th'execution wilbe more honourable to her Maiestie if the doing thereof come of her free minde without our motion. The woordes that I speake, I speake upon good reason, and I would wishe you all to consider what moveth me thereunto, and what may cause me to have and use this speeche. I pray you all let us stay. I trust we shall not repent it. If

---

4. I.e. Liverpool.   5. See Doc.7.

you go on with this attempt alreadie in hande, you may perhaps delay the thing you seeke to further'.

Ireland to have the Queene moved with speede, which thing, saith he, 'shall rather further her minde if she be bent that way, as I doo greatly doubt to the contrarie, then any way to hinder it'.

Recorder not to have any thing brought in in writing.

Cromwell misliked to have any delay from so necessarie a motion.

Snagge to the same effect.

Paul Wentworth[6] to the same effect.

Sir James Croftes wisshed us to have more regard to the report of Sir Fraunces Knowles. Newdigate the like.

After much debating it was agreed in respect of the credite that the House gave to Sir Fraunces Knowles' persuasion, that this attempt to move the Queene for execution should be deferred untill Monday next, in hope to heare newes before that time. /

f.4   [Wednesday 25 June][7]

A briefe note of the acte concerning Marie, daughter of James the Fifth, late King of Scottes, called the Queene of Skottes.

The preamble.

'Forasmuch as heretofore she hath uniustly claimed the crowne of England, and the present possession therof;

'and also for that she hath withdrawen the Duke of Norffolk from his duetifull subiection by contracting mariage with him without the consent of the Queene's Maiestie, meaning thereby to bring his wicked purposes to effect;

'and also for that she procured the late rebellion in the north, promising ayde of men and money, which she performed by inciting of her frendes in Scotland to mainteine and helpe suche of them as fled into Scotland, and for suche of them as fled beyond the seas she procured maintenaunce and releife for them from the Duke of Alva, and by his meanes from others *etc.*;

'and also for that she did go about to procure a newe rebellion, that certaine straungers should arrive at Harwitche in Essex, against whose arrivall certaine undewtifull subiectes of this realme did go about for to have delivered her out of the Queene's Maiestie's custodie, and to have proclaimed her queene of this realme in divers places thereof upon one day;

'and also for that she caused certaine bookes to be published wherein her title f.4v   was made that she was lawfull queene of / this realme, and ought to have the present possession thereof, and that our moste dreade soveraigne ladie Elizabeth was but an usurper;

'and also for that she meant a disturbaunce of the last parliament holden 13 Elizabeth *regine*':

A petition.

'That for the offences aforesaid it would please the Queene's Maiestie's Highnes not to beare the sworde of justice in vaine but that hereafter when any oportunitie shall serve, the offender may be called to aunswere her offences, and receive therefore as she hath deserved. And moreover to take away the vaine hope of her adherentes and fawtors, who without all reason have conceyved vaine hope of her title in succession, that it may be enacted by th'aucthoritie of this present parliament, that whereas Marie commonly called Queene of Skottes hath bene manifestly convicted of all the treasons aforesaid, she may for that cause be made unable, unworthie and uncapable of all suche title and interest to the crowne of England as she with her adherentes upon a vaine and uncertaine hope founded upon uncertaine and doub[t]full causes should ymagine her to have.

'Item, if any person or persons shall hereafter by worde or writing, deede or consent, publikely or in secrete, set forth or advaunce any suche undue claime or title preiudiciall to the Queene's safetie, and to the crowne of England, that the same partie so committing shall forthwith be apprehended, and adiudged by lawe, and suffer / paine of death, as in cases of highe treason is accustomed.   f.5

'Item, if the saide Marie or any her adherentes shall hereafter devise or invent, procure, practize or set forth any kind of wayes to advaunce the saide fained claime or title, whereby our Soveraigne's safetie may be in daunger, and the realme indamaged, that then the saide Marie and her adherentes to abide suche triall of the lawe as the hainousnes of suche a facte should require.

'Provided alwayes that for the kinde of triall she shalbe tried and adiudged by the peeres of this realme, as the wife of any other noble man in the like case of treason.

'Be it further enacted, that if at any time it happen that for her sake and in her name there be raysed or procured any tumult or insurrection within this realme by any lewde and seditious persons, she not witting or consenting thereunto, yet notwithstanding she to abide the same triall of the lawe as if she had bene the firste author and deviser of the same, and so utterlie to be voide of all protection. Or if any person or persons shall attempt to dispatche and destroy her, for whom and by whom suche tumult was reysed, that then the saide partie so attempting or committing shall not be any kinde of wayes troubled or impeached for the same, but to be clerely quitt by the vertue and aucthoritie of this acte.

'Provided that nothing saide or done in this acte shalbe interpreted or expounded any kinde of wayes by implication to allowe or confirme any right, claime or interest / towching the succession of the crowne of England to anye person or persons   f.5v whatsoever, any thing in this act to the contrarie notwithstanding'.

Fraunces Alford. He founde himselfe agrieved with two thinges, wherein he made some scruple of conscience.

The firste, that if by lewde and seditious persons there should be any tumult reysed in this lande, she not witting nor consenting thereunto, should be towched in life, or condemned unheard.

The second, that it should be lawfull for any man, were he never so meane a subiect, to lay hande on her being wholly out of the Queene's protection, and thereby should have his warrant by this acte.

---

6. MS reads 'Wentford'.

7. The day on which the bill was read the third time.

He thought them both to be verie harde cases. For first we must consider what she is, and what we be that thus deale against her. 'Her I take to be a queene still *in esse*, although she be[8] deposed by her subiectes: a queene I meane in England, not of England, a Scottish queene prisoner that came hither for succour. We that deale against her are the Queene's Maiestie, whom God longe preserve, and the whole bodie of the realme assembled in the high court of Parliament, being the moste noble and honourable court that we have in this lande. And for my part, I thinke that to be safe done for the realme that may be honorablie done for the realme: yea, and it is seene that princes doo asmuche esteeme their honours as they doo their lives. I thinke

f.6 her / to be as vile and as naughtie a creature as ever the earth bare, and am as throughly persuaded of her lewde demeanour as any man in this companie, yet can I not see howe it can stande with the honour of England for the avoyding of forreine slaunder, either to condemne her unheard or to towche her in life for that she never knewe of. And this is the one poynt wherein I desire to be satisfied. For the other poynt, that it should be lawfull for the meanest subiect. *etc.*, I would not wishe any man to inure a subiecte's handes with prince's bloud. It is a perillous president and example. David being a king was lothe and afraide to lay handes of Saule, and yet was he king annoynted, and Saul deposed of his kingdome by the ordinaunce of God. There is another example of the Duke of Naples, who having a king prisoner in his custodie, and finding him to have practized treason against him caused his head to be chopped off, and immediately after the hangman himself to be put to death, to this intent, that he shoulde not vaunt himselfe to have beene the spiller of so noble bloud'.

Norton. This last clause did Norton wrest to a contrarie sense, and making the Queene and the whole parliament to be th'executioners of the Queene of Skottes, and thereby did inferre that Alford should meane to have the Queene and all the

f.6v parliament chopped / off, because they should not vaunt themselves to have spilled the bloud of so noble a queene.

Finis.

8. 'Be' repeated in MS.

2. Anonymous journal, 8 May-25 June

Text from Oxford: Bodley (10220), Tanner 393, copy.

Bodley, Tanner 393, fos. 45-64

Part of the procedinges in the parlament begonne at Westminster the viij[th] of *Maii anno Domini* 1572.

Thursdaie [8 May]

Three baronnes, as Compton, Cheney and Noreis, were at this parlament first called by writ, and a fourth, which was my Lord Seintichon,[1] sonne to the Marques of Winchester, whose father had ben first called by writ before, was nowe also called by writ. Eatch of them, accordinge to the auncientie of his callinge, havinge one his robes, was led into the upper house by two other baronnes, and brought first to the Lord Keaper to make delivery of the writ by which he was called, and after to the place wher he shold sit, and this was done before the Quene's cominge.

The Lord Keeper's speach tended somwhat to this ende. First, he spake to the time, that the Quene's Majestie did well consider how unseasonable a time of the yeare this was to have a concurse of her poeple out of all quarters of her realme, and yet the cause was so necessarie and so waightie as it colde not otherwise be. Next he proceded to declare the causes, which he mad to be two. The first and cheif was to devise lawes for the saftie of the Queen's Majestie, for sins the rebellious and traiterous conspiracies which of lat had ben reveled it was agreed both by the Queen's Privie Councell and by the wisest persons beside of her realme that it colde not stande with the saftie of her Majestie onlesse ther were mad some other provision by lawe than was at that present alredy mad. The seconde cause was ordinary and more generall, to cut of sutch lawes as were to burdenous for the subiect, to make sharper sutch as were to gentill, to take awaie superfluous lawes, and to establishe sutch newe as were neadfull. Lastly a warninge was given, that[2] when thei had once begonne to deale with matters for the Queen's saftie, thei shold as litle as might be intermeddle with other matters untill the dispatch of them. / Next the Lord Keaper, havinge awhile talked with the Queen, willed the commons to repaire to ther nether house and ther accordinge to ther accustomed maner to make choise of a Speaker, and him to present ther the Saterdaie folowinge to receive his allowaunce of the Queen's Majestie.

f.45v

Saterdaie [10 May]

Bell was chosen to be Speaker, who at the daie apointed beinge presented, spake to the disablinge of himself, and required the Queen's Majestie to graunt leave that a

---

1. I.e. St John.   2. MS reads 'than'.

newe choise might be mad. Then the Lord Keaper spake in his commendacion, and shewed the Queen's approbation of the choise.

The effect of the speach which Mr Bell next used rested mutch in this: first, in shewinge how and by whom parlamentes begane to be called, how great likinge ther was at the first of that kinde of government, how parlamentes were than called yeare by yeare, how parlamentes were called for privat and smal causes; and herupon concluded, that by great reason every man ought to thinke well of the callinge of this parlament, notwithstanding that an other had ben called the yeare before, because it was no newe thinge, because it was for no triflinge cause, but for the cheifest cause of all, that is, for the saftie of the Queen's Majestie. In the discurse herof he shewed how this error was crept into the heades of a number, that ther was a person in this lande whom no lawe colde toutch.

Secondaryly, he made a repetition of the benefittes which the subiectes of this realme had received sins the good government of the Queen's Majestie, and therby gathered how greatly bounden thei were to have care of her saftie. In the aunswere to this point the Queen's Majestie, by the mouth of the Lord Keaper, said that she wisshed those benefittes dubled, tripled, yea quadrupled.

f.46   The therd part of his tale contained ordinary matter, that is, 3 petitions. The first for libertie of speach only, and so omitted to speake for the libertie / of the House in other matters: and that was graunted, so that it were done in more seamly sort then had ben hertofore used. The seconde for accesse to her Majestie upon neadfull occasions, which was likwise graunted, so that he were not importunat in his suites, nor required accesse at unseamly seasons. The therd for pardon yf he misreported any message to her Majestie, and this pardon he required not, yf he willfully offended in any sort.

The 12 of Maie.

It was agreed aswell by the upper house as the nether that a certaine number sholde be chosen of both to mete together in the Starre Chamber, and ther to have conference with the Queen's councell and so to procede meanes for the Queen's saftie. Herupon occasion was taken by Robin Snagg to saie that it were good that certaine were apointed to be humble suters to the Queen's Majestie that, as she had alredy by ordinary course of lawe proceded to iudgment against certaine malefactors, so likwise she wolde procede further to the execution; for otherwise men wilbe afraid to speake what thei thinke, and so the Queen's saftie, for which meanes might be devised yf men durst speake ther mindes, shold be unprovided for. Upon this Arthur Hall, as he were moved, spake, that the Queen of her self beinge enclined to mercie, sholde not be stirred up to use the rigor of her lawes towarde any. Then an other offringe to aunswere, the Speaker staied the procedinge therin, and said that he thought better opportunitie sholde be after given for that motion, and so it ceassed.

13 [May]

This daie litle was done, for most part of the time was spent in callinge the House, and beside, the hole foornonne and afternonne was emploied to the conference had by the committes with the Lordes and the Queen's councell. /

14 [May]

f.46v

It was agreed by the committees that report of ther hole conference shold be mad to the House by Mr Wilbrome, who speakinge shewed that the somme of ther hole conference rested in this: thei had opened unto them by plaine and great proffes the undue dealinge of the Scottish Queen towarde the Queen's Majestie, and that stode upon v pointes.

1° Upon the challeng mad in Fraunce duringe the life of her husbande to the crowne of Englande.

2° Upon the procedinge for the mariage with the Duke of Norfolke.

3° Upon her dealinge with the northren rebellion.

4° Upon her favor shewed after the rebellion ended to the rebelles, being fled out of the realme.

5° Upon the treason that concerned Rodulphe's viage, which was for bringinge in forein aide to dispossesse the Queen's Majestie of her crowne.

1. Upon the discourse and profe of the first point, this I bare awaie. In the end almost of Queen Marie's raigne, commissioners were sent into Fraunce to treat of a leage, of which the Erle of Arundell and Doctor Wotton were two. Upon ther first entrance to treat accordinge to ther commission, worde was brought of the death of Queen Marie, and so ther authoritie was iudged to ceasse. Than the Erle of Arundell returninge, the Lord William Hawarde, Lord Chamberlein, was sent over with a newe commission. When thei came to entreat, it appeared that the commission of Fraunce ranne in these wordes, that ther commissioners shold treat for a leauge with 'the Queen of Englande', without any other name. To this exception was taken by the English commissioners, and in reasoninge of the matter it was affirmed by the French partie that the Scottish Queen was / rightfull heir to the crowne of Englande. Yet in the end ther commission was altered to these wordes, 'Elizabeth Queen of England', and than thei proceded. This treatie ended, Sir Nicholas Frogmorton is apointed imbassador for Fraunce, duringe whose beinge ther, the Scottish Quene quartereth the armes of Englande and taketh upon her this title and stile, 'Queen of Scotlande, of Englande and Irlande'. Sir Nicholas complaineth herof to the Constable, who aunswered, he wolde do what he colde to the staie of it, but it laie not in him to remedie it onlesse he had speciall commission to deale in the matter. Notwithstandinge this complaint mad, afterwardes at a soleme iustes and triumph upon the mariage (as I remembre) of the Duke of Savoy, the Scottish Queen diversly quartered the armes of Englande, as on her plat, on the furniture of her horses, on the clothes for the iudges of the iustes, on the ripear clothes, yea and on her barbar clothes. Sir Nicholas certefied the Queen's Majestie herof, and therupon commissioners were sent over to treat of this matter and others, and amongst the articles agreed upon, this was one: that the Scottish Queen sholde renounce her claime to the crowne of Englande, and shold no more quarter the armes of Englande, and that aswell the Queen of Englande as the Scottish Queen themselves shold ratefie those articles agreed upon. The Queen of Englande herself doth ratefie the agrement, and sendeth it into Fraunce by the Lord of Bedford with a request that the Scottish Quene sholde do the like. Excuse was mad, that she was

f.47

covert and yonge when she gave her assent to the agrement: yet with some adoe she promised at the cominge of the Lord James, who was than to retorne out of Scotlande, to make her ratification. But / at his cominge she said he had no commission from the stat in Scotlande to deale in any sutch matter, and therupon denied to do any thinge without the assent of her realme ther. After this she mad denizens by the title of Queen of Scotland, of England and Irlande; she graunted also annuities with the like stile. The profe of these thinges rested cheifly in lettres sent to and fro, which were shewed to the committes; ther was also shewed papers quarteringe the armes of Englande, which had bene set up in Fraunce. It was further opened how at her retorne into Scotlande, Tamworth was sent to require againe her ratification. Than she begane to take exceptions to the writinge, and especially to this word '*deinceps*', as though by that she had bene concluded to make any claime aswell after the Queen's time as duringe her life. The Queen's Majestie was content that a qualification sholde be therof. In the end, when all causes of more delaie were taken awaie, she utterly refused to do it onlesse the Queen's Majestie wolde entaile the crowne to her and to the Lady Linox. It folowed after that the Lord of Bedford, beinge sent into Scotland for the christeninge of the yong kinge, had (as I toke it) full instructions to deale for the ratification, but colde get nothinge done. Ther was at that present a boke set out by one Adames,[3] entituled *Genethliacon*.

[Here a space follows] /

f.48   2. For the profe of the seconde point, the greatest matter which I noted to be brought forth was the recorde of the enditment of the Duke, in which was contained the seakinge of him to marie with the Queen of Scottes, and that was founde by the peeres of the realme. Ther was no liklyhoode of his assent to the mariage of her without her assent to the mariage of him.

3. Ther was alledged for profe of the therd[4] matter a confession of one Christopher Rocby. This gentleman beinge traveled into Scotland was ther sought unto by one Lassels and Melvin a Scot, to be (as it seemed) of the Scottish faction. He not yeldinge at the first, asked advise of certaine persons whom he knewe to favor the Queen of England his mistres, what he were best to do. Ther councell was that he sholde not withdrawe him self for it might be he sholde get to understande that which wolde bringe benefit to his countrie. It fell out after that he so behaved himself as the Scottish Queen opened unto him her title to the crowne of Englande and her devises for attaininge the same. She tolde him of lettres sent to men in Englande, and of her purpose to cause warre and tumultes ther, besides how she had consulted with cunninge men, as sorcerers and coniurors, who tolde her that the Queen of Englande sholde not live three yeare to an ende. And all this was confessed by that Rockby. The Scottish Queen affirmed the Nortons to be trustie persons to her. She hearinge of a speech scaped a noble man, sought to staie the rebellion untill she might escape, and withall said that if she colde not escape, thei sholde therby growe nothinge the weaker, but the stronger. In the beginninge / of the rebellion one Wilkinson was sent to the Bishop of Rose and the Spanish ambassador to cause Duke Dalba[5] to sende men and mony to Todcaster. Vitelly, lyinge at Colbroke, sent this message bake, that horsmen were redy, only monie lackinge. Ther was no reason of the rebellion of the erles and the rest, but for the Scottish Quene.

4. The rebelles beinge fled into Scotlande were ther releived by the Scottish Queen and her faction. Thei beinge from thenc driven by the Queen's power into Flaunders, were ther also by her releived, and that was thus. The Pope havinge by the procurment of one Morton, a Lovainist, proceded with his usurped authoritie to the deprivation of the Queen's Majestie of her royall stat, sent a 100,000 crownes to be emploied (as I toke it) upon the charges of those which wolde take upon them actually to deprive her. The Scottish Queen toke upon her the bestowinge of 12000 crownes of that somme, and disposed them in this sort: 6000 she apointed to the use of her self here, the other 6000 she caused Rodolf to distribute thus, 2000 to the Lady of Northumberlande and her traine, likwise 2000 to the Lord of Westmorlande, and the other 2000 amonge the rest of the rebelles. It was tolde how one[6] a time the Earl of Shrewsbury tolde the Scottish Queen that the Earl of Northumberlande was taken by the Queen's Majestie, wherat she was wonderfully abasshed and as she herself wrot to the Duke of Norfolk she wept three daies for it, and mad this her reason, for fear of cumbringe freindes. |

5. As concerninge the fivth point, this was part of that which was uttered. Rodulph that Italian and a principall traitor to this realme, had lettres of credit from the Pope to the Queen of Scots to be her agent. This was confessed by the Bisshop of Rose and the Duke of Norfolke. The Pope by him sent over the bulles of the deprivation of the Queen's Majestie, one of which was geven to the Spanish Embassador, and that was it which was hanged on the Bishop of London's gat, and for which Felton was hanged. It was thought by the Pope that the Scottish Queen had neede of expiation for sufferinge protestans in her realme, and therfore he sent lettres unto her by which he did signifie her expiation, and withall promised to make of her and hers, *sicut gallina pullos*, and that he wolde receive sutche as wolde rebelle against the Queen of England *sicut filios ecclesiae*. The Scottish Queen was certefied by lettres from the nuntio of Paris of the aforsaid number of crownes left in Flaunders. She wrot a lettre to Rose the 7 of February 1570, to cause a cyphered lettre of hers to be delivered to the Duke, which was disciphered by Hicf[ord] and so by him confessed. This lettre was founde by hap under a mat in a place of the Duke's house here in London, when as search was mad for other thinges. It contained great discourses in matters of stat, more than womane's witt doth commonly reatch unto, and in the end referred the determination of all to the Duke him self. Therin she shewed how weake her freinds in Fraunce were growen, and how unhable to helpe her; she opened the ill disposition of the chiefest sort ther towarde her, and therin it appeared she had very secret intelligences; she shewed the ielosie betwene France and Spain toutchinge her self; she shewed what wolde become of her | yf she fled into her owne country; and in the ende concluded that it were best for her to go into some of King Philip's countrees, and rather into Spaine than into Flaunders, for she thought the presence of her person sholde move King Philip to the more pitie of her cause. She thought it good that one were sent skilfull of the estates to solicite these matters both to the Pope and King Philip, that she might knowe how welcome she

f.49

f.49v

3. I.e. Adamson.
4. MS reads 'thred'.

5. *Sic*, and throughout.
6. I.e. 'on'.

sholde be and what aide and succor she might accompt of. She for her part thought Rodulph the meetest man for the voyage, especially because he was in countenance a marchant, and therby might the better colour his goinge out of the realme and his cominge in. She affirmed that all the confidence she had in Englande was reposed in the catholikes. Upon this letter the Duke entereth into his lat practises, and together with Rodulph and Rose agree upon men and monie to be sent, monie from the Pope, men from King Philip, the number 10,000, and Harwitch to be the place of landinge. It was thought good that Rodulph, before he sholde take in hande this iorney, shold have lettres of credit. The Scottish Queen beinge a prisoner was iudged unmete to give them. The Duke was contented thei shold be geven under his name, so that thei were without his hande; for, he said, the Queen's Majestie had so secret intelligences from beyond the seas as yf his hande sholde be to any thinge, she sholde strait have worde of it. Thus then Rodulph procedeth on his iorney and first openeth the matter to Duke Dalba, who referreth him over to one Mr Curteiso, secretary to Dalba; he, after he had the practise opened unto him, reporteth it to Dalba, who liked of it and willed that the freindes in Englande sholde be in

f.50   redinesse. Rodulph, havinge had good audience at / Duke Dalba['s] handes, determined with him self to sende backe worde therof into Englande, and therupon drewe two lettres which he, meeting with Charles Bayle at Brussels cominge into England, willed him to put them in cyphers, and when thei were so done, Rodulph subscribed the one lettre with a figure of 40, and the other with the figure of 30. Note the Bisshop of Rose had two as it were underagentes for him, the one for Scottish affaires and his name was Cutbert, the other for French affaires, and that was this Bayle. This felow had bene sent before into Flaunders with certeine bookes which (it was thought) were penned by certaine[7] lewde lawiers here in the behalf of the Scottish title. The bookes were sent to Sir Francis Englefeilde, that he might cause them to be printed. This Bayle, when he met with Rodulph at Brussels, was in his retorne home with these printed bookes, mindinge at his cominge into England to have them scattered abrode in the realme. At the cominge of this Bayle into England he was apprehended both with his bookes and lettres, but through the fault of some the lettres were conveied awaie, and other of small moment put in ther place. Yet with mutch adoe, after, the contentes of them were knowen, and therby the whole treason disclosed. Rodulph havinge sent those lettres by Bayle, proceded in his voyage to the Pope at Rome, and thether he came in Maie. Then he solicited his cause, but did litle good, for the Pope colde for that yeare helpe with no mony. In the ende he was content to take lettres of comfort, and so caused two to be written from the Pope, the one to the Scottish Queen, the other to the Duke beginninge '*Dilecti fili*' etc. Thei were sent, the one by France, the other by Flaunders, that if it hapt the one were intercepted, the other might be delivered. /

f.50v   Rodulph staieth not thus, but procedeth on with his iorney into Spaine, wher (as it sholde seeme) he had both good audience and successe in his busines. For 6000 Spaniardes were in redines to have come under the conduct of the Duke of Medena Celi[8] to have invaded this lande, and ther landinge place accordinge to the first agrement sholde have ben Harwitch. Yea thei were in sutch redines as thei were all embarked, but the hearinge of the Duke's apprehension was the cause of ther staie. For though ther color was of cominge into Flaunders, and of the retorninge of Duke Dalba into Spain, yet sins it hath ben knowen that ther entent was to invade this realme. Upon the apprehention of the Duke the Bisshop of Rose was also laid fast, who beinge examined toutchinge the lettres brought by Charles Bayle his agent out of Flaunders, confessed the havinge of them, and beinge further examined to whom thei were sent and to whom delivered, said the one was sent and delivered to the Spanish Embassidor, th'other to the Scottish Queen. Thei beinge askt the question, denied utterly the receipt of any sutch lettres, wherby the falsshode of the Scottish bisshope was manefestly detected. Rose beinge urged with this false dealinge, and beside with the confession made by others, and seyinge no other remedie, bewrayeth the hole treason, and after desireth licence to writ to the Scottish Queen his mistress, wherin he excuseth his confession to be but so mutch as other before had confessed, and therin sheweth all the doinges of Rodulph. It was opened how Rose devised that duringe the last parlament holden 13 of this Quene, the Duke sholde have caused a sturre or tumulte to be mad, and that the Queen's Majestie sholde have bene apprehended, and so to have proceded. It was / further tolde how sins the publication of the Pope's bull, the evill subiectes of this realme sticke not to name the Queen of England the pretensed and lat Quene, and the Scottish Queen thei call our Quene. For this matter thei shewed of a lettre of the Duchess of Pherea to Stukley speakinge thus, 'though our Queen be never so close keapt', meaninge (as it appeared by the rest of the lettre) the Scottish Quene. One Chamberlein wrot the like, callinge the Queen of England 'the lat Quene'. Likwise Sir Francis Englefeilde in the bookes brought him by Bayle altered these wordes, 'Queen of England', to 'the pretensed Quene'. It was tolde how sins the Duke's apprehention [the] Scottish Queen willed Duke Dalba not to feare to pro[ceed] for any evill to her, for she wolde sturre coales yf any thinge were entended against her. It was opened how Roulston had a devise to bringe in 3000 in Lankeshire, 2000 in the north, 1000 in Scotland, and thus havinge raised severall forces, ther intent was to proclame the Queen of Scotland Kinge and Quene of England with purpose to conteine both the title of her sexe and crowne. Toutchinge the Lord Seton, the Scottish Queen's factor, who of lat escaped through this realme under the countenaunce of a poore marchant beinge driven by tempest to lande at Harwitch, this thei tolde, how lettres and other writinges were founde behind in his shipe, as notes or instructions to formalise the French King, the King of Spain and Duke Dalba for the Scottish Queen, naminge her the present Queen *come le sole levant*. Ther was also founde a pedegre conveiynge the Scottish Queen's [title] to this crowne 2 waies: 1. by Henry 7, callinge all reigninge sins in order kinges, but only Queen Elizabeth; 2. by one Irenside before the Conquest. /

f.51

When Mr Wilbrome had ended his tale it was thought good, because the time was far spent, that men sholde not than fall into talke to shewe ther opinions upon these doinges of the Scottish Queen [and] what were best to be done for the Queen's saftie, but that thei sholde staie untill the daie after, whenas every man sholde be hard to the full.

f.51v

7. MS reads 'certaie'.   8. MS reads 'Ceni'.

15 [May]

The men that spake this daie.

Galles. 'In great congregations and assemblees the custome hath alwaie ben that the pune doth begine to speake. I, though in age superior, yet in wisdom and understandinge am of this societie the most puine and inferior. But howsoever it standeth with me, I take it not my part, in this cause we have nowe in hande, to hold my peace. I have hard it opened how the Scottish Queen hath sought to dispossesse the Queen's Majestie of her crowne. I thought it not good yesterdaie that we sholde have slept untill provition had ben herin mad. Theophrastus: *Societas humano, preservatur beneficentia, honore et poena*. The last is iudged to be as necessarie as any of the rest. The Scottish Queen hath made so small accompt of the Queen's goodnes towarde her as she deserveth no favor. Her predecessors longe agoe vowed troth and alleageance to the kinges of Englande, as is testefied of Malcalmus, who offered up his gantlet at Yorke. She hath ben a killer of her husbande, an adulteresse, which doth consequently folowe murder, a common disturber of the peace of this realme, and for that to be dealt with as an ennemie, And therfor my advise is to cut of her heade and make no more adoe about her'. |

f.52   Sir Thomas Scot. He thinketh it not needfull to make any repetition of the Scottish Queen's procedinges, through whom this hole realme is like to be brought into great thraldome. He beginneth, as a good phisitian, with seakinge the cause of this. The causes he iudgeth to be two: 1. antechristian religion, which hath procured aswell the Scottish Queen as other popish princes to enter into most great confederacies; 2. the uncertaintie of estat, for the Duke, though he be ambitiously geven of him self, yet this hath caused both him and many men beside so greatly to hange of the Scottish partie. The waies for remedie he thinketh to be 3 : 1. by cuttinge of the heades of the Scottish Queen and the Duke; 2. by takinge awaie the Scottish Queen's title; 3. by the establishment of a certaine successor. Yf the Queen's Majestie do deale with the seconde remedie alone, no good will come of it, for triall in other matters sheweth that no sutch provition will healpe. In speakinge of the staie of the Duke's execution, he said that he feared some Sinon laie hid in the court, which did secretly seake the undoinge of his countrie; but he hoped the ende of sutch wolde be ther owne destruction.

Robert Snag. 'The Scottish Queen's doinges hath ben sutch as I maie well saie, *tam turpe dictu, quam foedum factu*. I colde never understande her title, but her faction, which is her force. Warninge hath alredy ben given her by statut, and no good folowed of it, and therfore the axe must give the next warninge. The factes wherwith she is charged want no profe. She hath ben put doune in Scotland, and shall we sit her up? She hath ther
f.52v   spared neither / bed nor borde, and so unworthie to be well used. She came not hether of her self, but was driven. She is here as a straunger borne out of the lande'. He seeth not but nature and reason alloweth her *poenam*, yf she do amisse. 'What have we to do with *ius gentium*, havinge lawe of our owne? Shall we saie our lawe is not able to provide for this mischeif? We might then saie it hath defect in the hiest degree. The affection of her faction causeth that sutch thinges as are alledged on her behalf be allowed for reason'. Gehu slewe a Queen's daughter and without any adoe mad, he only willed her to be

burned.[9] Here he ended with a petition to seake the cuttinge of that ill member.

Message. It is required by the Lordes that a certaine [number] might be strait appointed for present conference. The number before is sent up. Upon ther retorne it is tolde how the Lordes thinke it good that thei and the committees might ioyne in drawinge a plat of a bill toutchinge the great matter, and therby lesse expence of time sholde be.

Tresorer. He receiveth comfort by hearinge the zealous speach used for the Queen's saftie, but alloweth not of ther pollicie. For he thinketh it best that men sholde bridle ther desires onlesse thei were in hope of good to folowe therof. God ruleth the hartes of princes. *Non volentis nec currentis, sed miserentis est Dei.* The seakinge to have over many matters done, often overthroweth that good which maie be done. /

Norton. 'We ought in these our doinges to procede with reverence towarde the   f.53
Queen's Majestie. The matter we have in hande is a motion, by which it is not ment any thinge sholde be done without her deliberation, and upon that let us staie. Our admonition was generall, to care for her saftie, in the consideration wherof it is more meete to seake that she fall not, than yf she fall what shall become of us. I am sorie to speake particularly, yet I must and will suppress that sorowe under the saftie of the Queen's Majestie. Though many heades be ill, yet it is good to cut them of so fast as maie be.[10] The Duke's owne kindred are against him, have founde him giltie of his treasons, and therfore I am the more to be spared for fredome of speach. This matter for the Queen's saftie can not procede without execution of him. For ther is no waie left how the Queen maie be assured of his loyaltie. Mercie hath ben shewed him and no good folowed: submissions have not served, subscriptions have not served, othes have not served, protestations and detestations have not served, and receivinge of communions sins his attainder hath bene without repentence. Practises of lat hath ben by his freindes, though he free. The cause of that Italian practise (meaninge that of Mader and Barley[11]) was he; and therfore necessarie it is that sutch a cause sholde be taken awaie. I will speake of the evill to come, yf this mischeif be not remedied. It is greatly to be feared that he remaineth on life to put in execution that no lawe of this realme is able to binde that Scottish / woman. When that matter shall come in   f.53v
question, many a wise man shall not be a free man. It is knowen how papistrie dispenseth with othes. The example is ill, for men wilbe afraid to disclose treasons when traitors are not punished but are suffered to live for the revenge of those trewe subiectes who have bewrayed ther traiterous attemptes. Impunitie is a great encoragment to the evill, not to give over, but to procede in ther ill doinges. It is knowen how greatly bound the Duke was to the Queen's Majestie, and yet all by him forgotten, yea when he was in perill. So unquensable an evill is ambition. The Scottish Queen, which is termed the sonne risinge, is but a comet, which doth pronosticate the overthrowe of this realme. It hath bene saied that mercie is good in a prince. Mercie without her Majestie['s] saftie causeth miserie. It is knowen how

9. Cf. 2 Kings, 9 for Jehu.
10. *Sic.*

11. *Sic.* MS not clear at this point, and 'l' may have been altered, by another hand, to 'r'.

some vertues ther be which be planted in sutch a meane as thei sone growe to an excedinge.

Our Quene aboundeth in mercie, she is naturally enclined therto, and that her doinges do testefie; and therfor to perswade and move her to mercie causeth that which is a vertue to abound to mutch. The execution of the Scottish Queen is of necessitie, it lawfully maie be done, yea it maie be done by nature, for it is but *propulsare iniuriam.* A generall impunitie to commit treason was never permitted to any. A common person in warre maie kill a prince that is an ennemie; whie maie not then our Queen with iustice kill her, who is in a worse degre than any ennemie?

f.54   *Frustra legis auxilium implorat, qui | in lege peccat.* I thinke it our part to do this punishment upon her for treasons sins her cominge into England, and not for her horrible doinges in Scotlande. The necessitie of the prince caused the killinge of the prisoners at the feild of Egincourt. By sparinge of the Scottish Queen we spare not to endaunger greatly the Queen's Majestie; by executinge of her we seake the preservation of our Quene. Whatsoever goodnes ther is or ever was in the Scottish Queen, whatsoever giftes of nature ther be or ever were in her, thei abounde mutch more in Queen Elizabeth, so that thoug[h]e she be put to death, we therby keape on live one who is her superior in all goodnes.' In the ende he requireth the execution of the Duke be moved unto the Queen without indentinge.[12]

This speach of Norton beinge ended, wherin I omitted very mutch, Arthur Hall fell into the speach for which he was after called to aunswere.[13] The House misliked so mutch of his talke that with shoflinge of feet and halkinge thei had wellny barred him to be hard.

Alforde. 'I am very carfull how to use my self. It is not fit for a councell that a resolution be asked afore other be hard speake.' He craveth fredome of speach without murmoringes or other kinde of interruption, and desireth that every man maie speake his conscience. He mindeth to excuse no offenses. He urged that it was agreed that nothinge sholde be done in these before the Queen's pleasure knowen. He thinketh it best to staie untill the committes have drawen a plat.

This was aunswered by Dalton.[14]

16 [May]

f.54v   Selenger.[15] He begane to charge Hall with speaches used in the House and uttereth them, and moveth the House wether it were not fit he sholde be called to aunswere to them.

Herupon divers men spake diversly, some for the libertie of the House in free speach, some that the libertie must be used in reverent and seemly sort, and so presidentes were shewed one waie and other.

The privilidg was required for a man sommoned on a iury betwene the Queen and Rolston, who was arraihned of treason, and it was agreed that yf he had ben sommoned on any iury betwene common persons he sholde have had the priveledge, but forasmutch as it was for service of the Queen, and in so great matter, it was thought his presence ther was not so requisite but that it might be spared. And so ordered.

17 [May]

Fletwoode. He sheweth two presidentes toutchinge libertie of speach, and both of D[octor] Story. In Kinge Edwarde's daies in the parlament house he used these wordes, '*ve regno cui puer est rex*'. For this he was called to aunswere, and for it sent to the Tower, and discharged the House, and an other chosen in his rowme. In the first yeare of this Queen's raigne he likwise uttered these wordes, that yf his councell had ben folowed, the root and not the braunches had bene cut of in Queen Marie's time. The House was content that this speach sholde be put up, notwithstandinge it was very bolde and ill.[16] He thinketh it best that Hall be put to / aunswere sutch speach   f.55 as he used out of the House, and be suffered to explane his minde for his speach within the House.

Alforde. He sheweth his likinge of Fletwood's talke, and withall inferreth the example of Fabius Maximus, who, when it hapt on a time that a very unadvised speach scaped one in the senat house, said thus, '*nunquam quicquam dictum inconsideratius*'.[17] Yet his advice was that he sholde not be punished for it, but that it sholde be keapt in the secretes of the House. He wisheth Hall sholde be so dealt withall for his inconsiderat speach, and therfore perswadeth that he might be suffered to explane his mind, and in the end receive an admonition.

Sir Nicholas Arnol. When divers had spoken for the libertie of the House, Sir Nicholas Arnol saith, he thinketh that the libertie of the House is no waie impugned, though Hall be put to aunswere, and therby do satisfie the House by expoundinge his speach. He confesseth the libertie of the House to be great and that great matters maie be ther spoken of, but yet with reverence and regarde of semlynes, and therfore thinketh the wordes of Hall to be sutch as it was not fit thei sholde be put up without aunswere.

[19 May]

Upon the conference had by the committes toutchinge a plat of a bill for procedinge against the Scottish Queen, these two waies were propounded to the House to see which thei thought best of.

1. That the bill sholde containe a rehersall of her treasons in the preamble, with a petition that she might be attainted and disabled to take any dignitie of this realme upon her. /

2. That she sholde be iudged unable to enioye the crowne of this realme after the Queen's time, and yf she did procede to any attempt herafter, that then she sholde be   f.55v atteinted as a naturall borne subiect of this realme.

It seemed good unto the Queen that the House sholde procede in the seconde degre, remittinge the procedinge in the first untill a more convenient time were offered. Her reasons were these. She colde not with her honor procede to the attaintinge of the Scottish Queen without callinge her to aunswere. To sende downe

---

12. *Sic.*
13. See Doc. 3.
14. See Cromwell's diary, f.16.

15. St Leger.
16. See *EP*, I. 62.
17. Cf. Livy, 23, 22. 8-9.

a chosen number of the upper house and the nether to examine her and charge her with those thinges, wherwith she were to be charged, and to receive her aunswere, wolde aske no small time. The season of the yeare did not suffer that sutch an assemble of her subiectes sholder be longe together; it sholde not be for ther safties; ther charges sholde be great by so longe taryinge. Beside, she wished the ende of the parlament before the cominge of the French imbassador. Herto aswell the Lordes (as it was said) as the Commons aunswered that thei estemed more of her Majestie's saftie, which was especially provided for by the first bill, than of ther own safties and charges, how great soever thei were. The House holy enctininge to the procedinge in the first bill, it was moved that a question sholde be mad of it; and herupon Alford spake.

Alforde. He desireth favorable construction of that which he wolde saie. He promiseth to utter his conscience with respect of dutie towardes God and the

f.56 Queen's Majestie. / He wissheth time of deliberation for the matter in hand, consideringe all the members of the House understande how unwillinge the Queen is to procede against the Scottish Queen in the first degree. 'The Queen's Majestie is wise, she knoweth and considereth more than every one of us doth knowe or can consider. It is better in consultations to give credit to one wise person than a number of others. To condemme a kinge is a matter of great wait. To condemme the Scottish Queen to die for faultes, before she knewe thei were faultes and that she offended by doinge them, is a matter worthie of consideration. Of necessitie she must be harde, yf condemnation of death shalbe given against her.' He thinketh her a kinge, though she be deposed and have resigned. For it were perilous for princes, that the deposition of ther subiectes sholde make them no princes. Her resignation is as her deposition, for it can in no wise be thought to be voluntary. He remembreth a canon by which a forein[er] is not bounde to take notice of a statut, for time must be given to take notice of sutch lawes. He saieth the Queen is most gratious in not mindinge to put her to death. He bringeth in an example of an embassidor who together with certaine of that countrie to which he was sent in embassage, did conspire the overthrowe of the stat. This treason being disclosed, it was agreed that notwithstandinge the imbassidor had passed his imbassage, yet *per ius gentium* he

f.56v sholde be sent home, and the home traitors sholde be punished. / Yf the 2nd bill procede, the Queen's Majestie shalbe safe and the Scottish Queen shall receive warninge. He saith her offenses be rather of an ennemie than of a subiect. The House maie perhappes lease the seconde bill yf thei stike to mutch upon the first. He concludeth that upon mor advis better resolution maie be than hath bene hetherto.

Doctor Wilson. He wissheth Alforde had bene a committe for hearinge the Scottish Queen's doinges opened. For yf he had, he iudged that he wolde have bene better content with the procedinge of the first bill. No man coondemneth the Queen's opinion, nor thinketh her otherwise than wise: yet he douteth wether she so fully seeth her owne perill. The case of a kinge in deade is great, but yf thei do ill and be wicked, thei must be dealt withall. The Scottish Queen shalbe hard, and any man beside, that will offer to speake for her. It is marveiled at by forein princes that her offenses beinge so great and horrible, the Queen's Majestie suffereth her to live. A kinge cominge hether into Englande is no kinge here. For admit that the Emperor come into Englande, two of his men here fall at variance, the one killeth the other, no pardon by the Emperor will here serve, and it is lawfull for the kinge of Englande to punish that offence accordinge to his lawes. *Leg[es] de officio presid[ent]is.* A kinge dealinge with causes in foren countries is but a privat person. The Scottish Queen but a privat person with us. We have no recorde to prove her a Quene. The iustices' opinion is, that Marie Stywarde called Queen of Scottes is a traitor. Though examples prove / not, for *lege vivimus, non exemplis,* yet for the better aunsweringe of   f.57 Mr. Alforde he remembreth the example of Zenocrates in Livie,[18] who beinge an ambassidor was punished for lyinge, for *dignitas no tuetur legatum mendacem,* likewise the example of the Duke of Millan's imbassidor, who fell to treason, and was punished by death. The imbassador, representeth the person of the prince.

The name of a traitor is most properly geven to a person in subiection.

It was tolde how the opinion of the iudges for the Scottish Queen was this, that her doinges in any per[son], subiect or straunger was treason, and yf she be a kinge (which thei wolde neither affirme nor denie) thei thought it convenient and necessarie to have her attainted by Parlament, aswell for her honor as for that ther was no president of the like.

It was said, how the Scottish Queen was mutch stronger within this realme by the Duke then the Duke by her, and here in shewinge how weake the Scottish Quene sholde be by the execution of the Duke, these wordes were uttered: 'though yow cut not of her wesell[19] wherwith she bretheth, yet her sinowes be cut of wherby she moveth'.

No arguinge ought to be to any matter without a bill.

It was agreed by the House that Arthur Hall sholde be called to aunswere sutch speaches as he was charged withall, and to the ende the certeintie / of that wherwith   f.57v he sholde be charged might be had, thei further agreed that sutch as colde charge him sholde set it downe in writinge and Hall to aunswere to the speaches in article wise; and herupon the seriant was commaunded to will him to appeare at a daie.

The speaches wherwith he was charged, beinge drawen in writinge, were these:

1 'When the Scottish Queen's title is cut of, wher is our assurance?'

2 That the offence of the Duke is privat to the Queen's Majestie.

3 That the harme was not yet done.

4 'Ye hasten the execution of them whose feet ye wolde kisse to have againe when thei be gone.'

5 Norton havinge spoken about cuttinge downe of busshes (meaninge the Duke and the Scottish Queen), Hall said, 'Yf those busshes be cut downe, what bush have we to shadowe us?'

6 Perhappes the doinges of the Duke, yf thei had had successe, wold not have tended to an ill ende.

7 That the execution is extremitie and rigour of lawe.[20]

Hall was charged with these speaches, as uttered by him either in worde the same, or in effect the same; and he beinge asked after the readinge of them what he had to aunswere, said part of this in effect.

18. *Sic.*   20. See Doc.3.
19. *Sic.*

Hall. He saith the presence of the place maketh him astonied. He telleth what
f.58   goodwill[21] he beareth towarde the Queen's Majestie. He did urge mercie / because
he sawe the Queen enclined to mercie. He requireth the House to accept of his
submission, for it sholde otherwise be greatly to his discredit. He confesseth not the
articles, wherwith he was charged, but saith it might be he forgat himself in his
speach, for his interruption moved color in him, and so mad him speake, he now
forgetteth what. He moved that the House might be devided yf his submission be
not accepted.

Upon this aunswere of his, which was not so well liked, he was withdrawen, and
than it seemed good unto the House that every article sholde be severally read unto
him and he asked wether he spake sutch wordes and, yf he spake them, wether he
thought them well spoken and as it became him. Herupon he was called in againe
and aunswered to every article read unto him, that he did not remember he spake
those wordes, but yf he did, he thought them ill and unadvisedly spoken, and sutch
as became him not, and that he was sorie for it; and so said as mutch as thei wolde
have him. Upon this submission he was dismissed with an admonition by the
Speaker.

The Treasurer, movinge the House to allowe of Hall's submission, tolde how he
feared that he had the disease of his father, and upon that shewed how his father had
ben madd. *Lubricum linguae non timere debet trahi ad poenam.*

The greatest reasons of this favorable dealinge with Hall were these. 1. For
f.58v   fredome of the House in speach, lest otherwise it sholde seme to have / bene
impugned. 2. For the honor of the cause wherin the speach was used, that it maie not
herafter be said how men were barred of speach in the treatinge of that cause. For it
maie nowe iustly be saied that sutch favor was shewed to one speakinge in that cause
as sholde have bene permitted to none in any cause beside.

It was made a question in the House [16 May] wether the execution of the Duke
were for the saftie of the Queen's Majestie or no, and all aunswered yea, without any
negative voice. It was also agreed that this opinion of the House touchinge that
matter sholde come to the Queen's hearinge by bare report, and not by any message
sent.

Yf a bill upon the seconde readinge be not put to the engrossinge, it cannot after
be argued unto.

A bill toutchinge religion was this parlament preferred, and had received three
readinges, and than beinge like to have bene overthrowen, was committed, and
upon a conference a newe bill drawen, both which, as well the first as the last, were
sent for by the Queen's Majestie [22 May] and withall this message: that herafter no
bill of religion sholde be admitted into the House onlesse conference and allowance
of the bisshoppes therin were first had. This bill of religion which was preferred
tended somwhat to reformation, and was so mutch the more of the hier sort misliked.
Yet one thinge which was sought to be holpen by the bill, beinge opened to the
Queen, seemed to her worthie of redresse. It was shewed unto her how yf any godly
f.59   minister upon iust occasion alter the readinge of / any lesson, as in readinge one
chapter for another, or omit the readinge of any part of his service, as perhappes for
the havinge of a sermon, he incurreth the penaltie of lawe; and it was tolde her how

divers poore ministers had bene of lat by malitious persons upon these light causes trobled and vexed. Upon this she willed D[octor] Wilson to signefie to the House how her pleasure was that sutch as knewe any of those malitious vexers of her ministers, shold declare ther names to him; not utteringe what further sholde be done against them. The messag that forbad the bringinge of billes of religion into the House semed mutch to impugne the libertie of the House, but nothinge was saied unto it.

Together with that message it was told the House [23 May] how the Queen's Majestie, for matters toutchinge her both in honor and in conscience, required ther procedinge in the seconde bill. Upon this, divers spake, shewinge how mutch more convenient it was to procede in the first degree, and in the ende one Atkins spake.

Atkins. Silence giveth him corage to speake, yet he confesseth it more saftie for him self to holde his peace. He hath observed the procedinge of the House in this cause, and thinketh thei maie stande upon ther first resolution. He sheweth how in a petition these circumstances are to be considered; what is asked, wherfore the petition is mad, and by whom, what wilbe the sequell yf it be graunted. The thinge which is asked is the execution of the Scottish Queen, which is pronounced to be lawfull after the attainder of her, by the iudges of this realme, by the civillians, and by the spirituall persons. Wherfore is this petition mad? Aswell / for the honor of our Queen as for her saftie. For it maie truly be saied that this Scottish woman is the burden of the earth. It was spoken to the dishonor of Hanniball, *'vincere scis Hannibal, victoria uti nescis'*. It is the saiynge of Senecke, *'inconsiderati est spernere occasionem oblatam.'*[22] Is it perilous for the Queen's Majestie to take awaie her perilous ennemie? As for the persons which do crave the petition, thei be the Queen's naturall subiectes. He refuseth to take upon him to tell what a subiect maie crave of ther prince. The sequel, yf the petition be graunted, whilbe this: hartie praiers for the Queen's longe continuance, love of her subiectes and a dread to her ennemies. The Scottish Queen was the principall of the Holie Leage, who beinge taken awaie, the cheif partie is wiped awaie. The overthrowe of this woman will more shake the tipe[23] of the crowne of Rome than ever did assault mad against the walles of Rome. In the ende he concludeth that he thinketh it not best for the House to despaire of obtaininge the Queen's favor to procede in the first degre.

f.59v

After this it seemed good that a further conference sholde be had with the Lordes about this matter, which beinge had [24 May], it was by them agreed that every man sholde set downe in writinge sutch reasons as he thought were best able to move the Queen herin, and that first the bisshoppes sholde set downe reasons movinge the conscience, and next reasons for pollicie, in which *tacite* sholde be aunswered sutch obiections as the Queen were able to make for the not procedinge in the first bill. The civilians drewe reasons *oro et contra*. It was agreed that the most principall reasons shold be / chosen and thei alone set downe in the writing which sholde be presented to the Queen's Majestie. It was thought better that these reasons sholde be thus delivered by writinge rather than uttered by the mouth of any one person. For

f.60

21. MS reads 'goowill'.
22. But not in this form?
23. I.e. 'tip'.

though the one waie move more for the time, yet it is gone strait, and the reasons sone forgotten. Wheras the other waie thei are read with pawsinge and are considered upon, and so the better imprinted in the minde, and therby so mutch the more do move.

Upon one of the holidaies in Witsontide[24] these reasons were presented to the Queen by certaine of the upper house and the nether; but it seemed thei moved litle, for the aunswere brought to the nether house [28 May] was this.

Her Majestie willed that the commons sholde be thanked for ther carfull mindes toutchinge her saftie. She wolde not have them thinke but she was of opinion how ther devise was the safest waie; yet the consideration of the time and of other circumstances made her resolve at this present to leve the first waie of procedinge and to deale with the seconde. For the avoidinge of expence of time about devisinge how the bill sholde be framed, she willed it sholde be drawen by her counsell towarde the lawe. She wolde have no sutch wordes put in the bill as sholde give colour of title, one waie or other. She thought it necessary and fitt for us to consider, though we had not that we wolde, yet like wise men we sholde take that good we might. And lastly it was tolde how she willed that no entrance sholde be into disputation of the matter of the bill before the cominge in of it.

After this message ended, Snag moveth that certaine of the House might be sent up to the Quene together / with the Speaker, who as the mouth of the House sholde make petition to her Majestie for the execution of the Duke, as a thinge most neadfull for her saftie.

Litle was said to this motion at the first, and as it seemed after, the Speaker had very ill likinge of it.

A daie or two after it was moved againe by an other, and than agreed, that sutch reasons as sholde seme best to the House sholde be put in writinge and uttered by the mouth of the Speaker. Upon this the Speaker willed the House to put him in writinge what thei wolde have him utter. For more than thei put him in writinge, he wolde not speake.

Upon the Saterdaie in Whitson weake [31 May] this matter grewe so farre as the House without further dealie beganne wholy to encline to have committes apointed, which shold consult upon and drawe out the fittest reasons to be uttered by the Speaker. The Tresorer, belike havinge some incklinge that the execution of the Duke was towarde, moved the House to staie this ther procedinge for a time, and upon this the House sholde have bene devided, and manie spake for the division. To ease the House of this troble a newe question was mad, and that was, wether thei were content to staie their procedinge for that daie; and therto all almost consented.

The Mondaie folowinge, which was the seconde of June, strait after vij a cloke in the morninge, the Duke was executed, at whose death, because I was present, somwhat of that which I harde him speake I have here written.

Aftre he had used some wordes in disablinge him self, as how his bringinge up was not to speake in sutch an audience, he him self devideth his speech into 3 partes. First he promiseth to declare his offences, as his conscience moved him. He telleth, he / came not thether to iustifie him self, not to complaine of his peeres. He confesseth his dealinge with the Scottish Queen without the Queen's Majestie's assent, and

f.60v

f.61

that therin he did otherwise than he ought to have done. For this matter he sheweth how the Queen accepted his submission and how after, contrary to that his submission, he dealt againe in the Scottish matters, which (he said) toutched him very mutch, for he did augment his fault with this seconde delinge. He denieth the takinge of an othe, as the report went in the worlde he had. He fell to tell how ill a man Rodulph that Italian was, how apt to any treason, and how he never spake with him except once, which was for the discharge of a recognisance. Here he was interrupted by the shrive, yet he proceeded, and confessed how two lettres came to his hande, but denied the burninge of the cyphered lettre and the consent therto. Here, he beinge againe interrupted more boldly by Christopher[25] for that he went about to purge his self, he clereth his peeres, and breaketh of his speach for this part.

Cominge to his seconde part, he promiseth to open his conscience towarde God. Here he denieth ever to have bene a papist sins he knewe what religion ment, and yf by his trusting of papistes, or kepinge them neere about him, any offence have growen therby, he asketh God and man forgivnes. He renounceth the Pope. He findeth fault with his interruption nowe againe.

In the therde part he telleth how gratiously he is bounde to the Queen's Majestie for the mercie which of her self she hath shewed. He wissheth her long continuance to the maintenance of religion. He desireth her to be good to his orphans; some said, orphalein children were the wordes he used. He [wisheth]/ that there maie be a givinge over of factions, and telleth that no good will come of them. He wissheth that he might make an ende of all the trobles which were than. He bringeth in the sayinge of Latimer, that the ill life of the people caused the punishment of the kinge, and upon this praieth that the religion and life of the people might be sutch as might procure God's favor for the continuance of the Queen's Majestie amongst them. He desireth the poeple to praie for him, and in the ende biddeth God save the Quene.   f.61v

This speach, which was devided as afore, beinge ended, he wispereth a message in the eare of Sir Henry Lee to be done to the Queen, the ende wherof I hard, and it was that he wolde die as trewe a subiect as any her Majestie had, and that he wolde praie for her to his ende.

Next procedinge to his praiers, he knelinge with Mr Nowall[26] by him said the phsalme of *Misereri* with a great boldnes, and raisings of his voice many times, and than the pshalme, 'Rebuke me not O Lorde', and lastly certaine praiers which were in the ende of the booke he praied upon. He nowe risinge asketh all forgivnes, and forgiveth all. He shaketh divers on the skafolde by the hande, and than procedeth to the puttinge of his apparell, at which time I first noted the alteration of his countenance; and so to the execution. /

The Thursdaie folowing [5 June] the bill against the Scottish Queen havinge passed the upper house was sent downe to the nether with this message, that it sholde have a readinge than presently before the risinge of the House.   f.62

The daie after [6 June] about the middell part of the sitting of the House, Hatton

24. Probably 26 May (*EP*, I.273 and n.1.)
25. MS not clear at this point: there may be an 'H' after 'Christopher' (Hatton?), but the reference may simply be to the interruption by 'Mr Christopher, one of the officers': T. B. Howell, *State Trials* (1809-26), I.1033.
26. I.e. Dean of St Paul's.

cometh in and wispereth with the Speaker. By the sequell it was geassed he brought a message from the Quene for the readinge againe of the Scottish Queen's bill, for presently after the Speaker moved to have the bill read, wherat ther was mutch stickinge, for it was thought more hast than good spede that the matter beinge of so great wait and havinge received a readinge but the daie before, it sholde nowe procede to the seconde readinge. Yet at lenggth it was read, through the meanes of the Speaker especially. It was than moved[27] that the bill might be drawen into articles because it was so longe, and that every man might speak to every article and that by a man's speach to one article he might not be barred to speake to an other. For otherwise the length of the bill was sutch, and the occasions of speach therin so many, as two or three men speakinge might spende a whole foornowne. It seemed herupon good that certaine of the ripest wittes within the House sholde be apointed to have conference upon every point in the bill, and after upon the readinge of it by articles thei sholde utter ther opinions, as in shewinge what thei thought amisse, and

f.62v   what waie thei had devised for the helpinge of that which / was amisse, and so to leave it to the House to iudg upon. This resolution eased the House of mutch labor, and saved the expence of mutch time. Yet it was said by Alforde that to growe to a conference before debatment was not orderly procedinge. The occasion of speach against the bill grewe most upon wordes which implied a title in the Scottish Quene, for the full remedie wherof no waie colde be be devised, yet the best waie was thought to have a proviso added to the ende of the bill, wherby it sholde be enacted that no part of the bill sholde be construed by implication; and so it was agreed upon.

By reason of the receivinge of Duke Momorancie, the French imbassador, an adiornement of this cession of Parlament was from the 12 of June untill the 24 of the same.

Note that duringe this adiornement the priveledge of the House was enioyed. Yf any member of the parlament be arested either in cominge to the parlament or in retorninge from it, though the parlament be ended, he maie have a speciall writ out of the clerke of the Crowne's office for his discharge.

The seconde or therd daie after the sittinge agine of the parlament [25 June], the Scottish bill received the therd readinge. The bill had bene so fully argued unto before as it was thought ther wolde have bene no speach used against it; yet Alforde, mindinge as it seemed the overthrowe of the bill (for so in deede it fell out afterwarde); spake against two principall pointes of it. /

f.63   Alforde. After he had used many wordes in requiringe not to be mistaken,[28] he entered into the matter and shewed that it was enacted by the bill that yf any conspiracie or rebellion sholde herafter be raised, the Scottish Queen sholde be deemed a traitor, and might suffer the paines of treason. Herupon, he saied, it might very well fall out that rebellion might be raised within this realme, the Scottish Queen not privie therto, nothinge at all knowinge therof, and so not to be blamed therfore. Than to laie the paines of treason upon her for that in respect wherof no fault cold be adiudged in her, he thought it sholde be acompted the greatest iniustice in the worlde. For so she sholde receive punishment for the offence of an other. For the seconde matter, he opened how it was enacted that yf God sholde take awaie the

Queen's Majestie and the Scottish Queen sholde make any claime to the crowne, or sholde make any troble within this realme for the obtaininge of the same, she sholde be out of the protection of the lawe. Free libertie without any perill of lawe is given to every person for the killinge of sutch as be out of the protection of the lawe. He misliked of the punishment to adiudg her out of the protection of the lawe. He said that yf any common person did transgresse the lawe he sholde never be adiudged to die without beinge called iudically to aunswere, and to deale worse with her than with a straunger or common person, he thought it neither meet nor reasonable. Herupon he tooke occasion to tell / how princes ought to be dealt withall, how men ought not to laie handes upon the annointed of the Lorde, and for that brought out the example of David towardes Saule.   f.63v

Norton. 'Those which meane well nead not greatly to feare the mistakinge of ther speach. I confesse that no man in this companie hath more cause to feare mistakinge than my self. For I am suer that no man's speach hath ben oftener mistaken than myne. Yet this advantage I have of some men and that is that my speach tendeth not alwaies to the overthrowe of good matters, as some other men's doth. It hath bene saied we sholde do iniustice yf we sholde adiudg the punishment of treason to the Scottish Queen for every rebellion herafter raised within this realme, for so perhappes we might punish her for the offence of an other. The matter is greatly mistaken by the gentleman that thus spake. For yf any tumult or rebellion herafter growe, the paines of treason are laied upon her not for that rebellion, but for those treasons which she hath hetherto committed, for which, yf the Queen's Majestie's lenitie were not the greater, she might nowe iustly receive punishment. So that the iustice which is done unto her is this, that she hath not presently that punishment which yet perhappes herafter maie fall upon her. Besides it is not amisse to laie these paines upon her, (a punishment which she hath alredy deserved) to be a bridell and / let that no rebellion herafter growe. For at this present ther is no liklyhoode of any   f.64 rebellious attempt to be mad but in respect of her, through the procurment either of her self or of her favorers. For the other matter, to wishe she were not punished before she were iudically called to auns[wer], it were as good to wishe she were not punished at all. For any man of iudgment can easiely see how possible it is to bringe her to aunswere iudically, when she once maketh claime to the crowne. And to saie she is worse dealt with than a common person, is nothinge so; for at this present in this Court, which is the hiest and cheifest place we have of iudgment (a place fit to iudge of so great a cause), we iudically procede in iudgment against her. Further, that we ought to deale reverently with her because she is a prince and quene, to that I saie that it maie be doubted wether she be a quene at all (consideringe her owne resignation and the deposition of her subiectes), but suer I am she is no quene of ours, she is none of our anoynted. The examples of the Olde Testament be not fewe for the puttinge of wicked kinges to death'.

27. I.e. after some speeches (Cf. *EP*,I.283-5).   28. MS reads 'mistakinge'.

3. *Thomas Cromwell's journal, 8 May–30 June*[1]

Text from TCD, MS 1045, fos. 1–72, copy.

Trinity College, Dublin, MS 1045, fos. 1–72

Bodnam in Cornwall.

At the parliament began the viij[th] of May xiiij *Reginae Elizabethae.* The summe of the Lord Keeper's oration.

Hee declared how the Queene's Majestie had commaunded him to open unto them the causes wherefore it had pleased her to cause this parliament to be summoned at this present, which he was purposed to doe in as fewe wordes as he might, as well to avoyd teadiousness, as also for that to the wise fewe words will suffice to declare the intention of the speaker. But first he thought good to say something concerninge the tyme, whereof he declared that the Queene's Majestie hath not beene unmindfull nor inconsiderat what preiudice or perill might growe by so greate concourse of people towards the heate of the yeare, which as she confesseth to be greate, so if a greater danger had not depended upon delay, her Majestie would have forborne at this present to have called the same, and therefore wished them all to thinke that this calling was by necessity enforced. In respect thereof he advised the assembly to employ their whole endevour in matters of most moment and greatest weight, and then be trusted noe great perill should ensue, and so rested in themselves to make a speedy release unto themselves.

The causes he declared to be two specially, wherein first he shewed that sithence the last parliament God of his mercyfull providence had detected great treasons and notable conspiracies very perillouse to her Majestie's person and to the whole state of the realme, and that therefore yt was most necessary to provide for her safety and tranquility of the realme some present remedy. The seconde cause was an old common cause in all parliamentes which rested in consideration whither the lawes were to sharpe or to loose, whither craft or malice had devised any mischeife to supplant lawes, whither the superfluity of any lawes were over bounde or over doubtfull, these thinges most necessary to be considered to, but the first cause to be first dealt in, for that therein rested the present most imminent danger. |

f.1v   The realmes of England and Ireland and for [blank]

This oration ended the petitions for Gascoygne and Guyan *etc.* were red, and then the Lord Keeper did declare that her Majestie's pleasure was that the lower house should assemble themselves together to their accustomed place and there choose amongst themselves some wise and discreete person to their Speaker and to present him uppon the Saturday following.

Mr Treasurer. 'You have heard what charge hath beene given by the Queene's Majestie'. The gravity of the House therefore to consider therof and to choose such a person, as for discretion, learninge, wisedom and temperance were fit to supplie the roome of their Speaker, for which purpose he thought for his parte Mr Bell most fit, which agreed to by the whole House.

Mr Bell. 'If it shall please yow, right honnorable and right worshipfull, when I consider with my selfe what burden this is which is offered unto me I cannot but let yow understande my debility in bearing the same best knowne unto my selfe'. The assemblie in this place as being a member of the highest courte in this realme, ought to be and is most grave, and therefore is looked for at your handes to make such choice as is most fitt, off which sorte he knoweth a greate sorte amongst this company. The insufficiency of him that shalbe chosen, shalbe an accusation off greate improvidence in them all which were greatly to be respected in so grave an assemblie. Such person as were to occupie that roome whereto they offer to call him ought to have, as hath beene very well declared, wisdome, discretion, learning, temperance and gravity; himselfe wanted the most of them all. He thought himselfe beholding unto them, that would so iudge of him, but yet off necessity compelled to acknowledge his imperfection the rather at this present time then any other. The tyme of the calling considered, the suddainess of the calling weighed, the small tyme since the last parliament ended, being not yet / a ffull yeare, importeth the causes to be very weightie. Although he confesseth the prince may call parliamentes at all tymes, yet the premysses considered argueth greate causes. The greater causes, the greater care ought to be had; yf his want of ability should hinder the accomplishment of the same, it should be to him a perpetuall shame, to them all a greate offence. To make long speech among the wise and considerat, he meaneth not. It shall suffice that he declare that he findeth himslefe grieved, protesting unto them that if he thought himselfe sufficient, he would be loath to refuse any action whatsoever with what perill soever to him, so as he might doe the prince and his common weale service, but knowing best his owne imbecillity, and as he hath not knowne any in his memory chosen other then considerat, so wisheth nowe in the tyme by likelyhoode of greatest importance to make like choice which rested in them as yet to reforme by a newe election, whereto he wished them to proceede. But he was alowed of, and so brought to place of the Speaker by Mr Treasurer and Mr Controler.

f.2

Mr Bell's oration made in the higher house before the Queene's Majestie *x° Maij*.

'Your Majestie by the advise of your most wise and grave councell for diverse weightie and necessary causes have summoned a parliament, and [for] that purpose

1. This collection of the accounts for the four sessions during which Cromwell was a member has been bound out of sequence. The account of the last session, 1584/5, is placed second, and bears two notes on its back page (f.94v). They are: 'Mye bookes of the proceedings in all the sessions [of] Parliament in which I had anye entermedlinges (?)', and; 'I can not finde my booke of the xxiij^th yere of the Queene'. These are in the same hande as the account for the session of 1584/5, which may be Cromwell's own. The remaining accounts (1572, 1576, 1581) are clerks' copies, and renumbering has occurred in binding the separate parts of TCD MS 1045 together. The margin of f.84v bears the inscription 'Thomas Moxon his booke, 1689', and f.136 has 'This is written by Sir Robert Naunton, Secretary to King James': both hands appear to be non-clerical.

have directed forth your severall writes aswell to your Grace's lordes temporall and spirituall for their repaire to your Majestie as also to your shiers, cities and townes for the electing and sending up of knightes, cittizens and burdgienses for the same, retornable the viij^th of this present moneth of May, who according to the purporte of the same, have performed your Majestie's pleasure in that behalfe. And thereupon according to the auncient and laudable order your knightes, citizens and burdgionses have by your Majestie's commandement proceeded to the election of a

f.2v   Speaker and amongst diverse most worthie have chosen me most unworthie, / and doe here present the same before your Majestie to the end it might please yow to accept the same. I am therefore to beseech your Majestie to give me leave in fewe wordes to shewe unto yow my unability of occupieing the same roome. When I doe consider the greate and weighty causes, ffor which parliamentes be commonly called and for which specially this seemeth to be called, and when I doe consider what person ought to be Speaker in so grave an assemblie, and withall behould myne owne imperfections, I must of necessitie acknoweledge my unworthenes to deale in so high an office. It behooveth such person to be wise, learned, discreete, grave and temperat, and also to have ability of liveing to carrie the countenance of that vocation, wherein I must confess the trueth of myselfe, the which is, that which in any of these in me is most, is rather a tast and a shaddowe then a substance. If therefore I should presume to enter into the same it must needes be to the weightinesse of the causes some hindrance or at the least noe such furtherance as were convenient. I ame therefore, most gracious Sovereigne, most humblie to beseech your Majestie to disallowe of their said e[le]ction, which heitherto hath not receaved perfection but may by your Majestie bee revoked, and that it will please yow to comaunde the knightes, cittizens and burdgionses to reassemble themselves ffor the election of a more fit person whereof there is amongst them good store, and to accept this not as an excuse, but as a true declaracion of my unfitness'.

The Lord Keeper's answere in the name of the Queenes Majestie.

'Mr Bell, the Queene's Majestie hath heard how with all humblenes and reverence yow have debaced your selfe, whom her good subiectes of her lower house have named, elected and presented for their Speaker and hath also considered the efect off your request, that they might reassemble themselves to the choice of an other. For answer, her Majestie hath comaunded me to declare that for asmuch as she hath sufficiently heard of your trueth and fidelitie towardes her, and sithence also she understandeth your abilitie to accomplish the same, and sithence yow have beene chosen and presented by her good subiectes of her lower house, who shee doubteth not have used great circumspection therein, to whose opinion her Majestie

f.3   condescendeth / and to their iudgment giveth credit, and therefore cannot allow of your request, but doth approve, ratifie and confirme theire said election and doth receive yow for the Speaker, nothing doubting but your dealinges in this parliament shalbe such as shall not onlie satisfie her Majestie's expectacion and confirme that good opinion which she hath conceived of your former doings, but also increase the same with full declaracion of your faithfull harte to her Majestie'.

Mr Bell's second oration.

'Your Highnes' noble progenitors kings of this realme not many yeares after the Conquest did publish and set forth diverse ordinances and constitucions. But the same was not confirmed by Parliament, and therefore proved perillous as well in not sufficiently providing for those which deserved well nor sufficient authoritie for punishment of them which deserved contrarie. Whereupon King Henrie the Third finding noe such perfection therein as he did desire, by the mature deliberacion and grave advise of his lordes and councell did condiscende to walke in a newe course of goverment, in which he determyned that all things should be provided for by authoritie of Parliament; and shortlie after called two of the same, the first at Marton,[2] the second at Marlebridge[3] in which diverse things before set forth but by chartre were then confirmed and ratified by Parliament, which have sithence beene received and obaied; who after that experience had taught him the benefit thereof did prosecute the same all the tyme of the rest of his raigne. And King Edward the First did the like, who called a parliament for one only cause, which was for that temporall posessions were gathered together by abbotes and other spirituall persons and corporacions, to restraine the same from that tyme forwardes and to provide that they should live onlie of their spirituall promotions. I meane to note principally but two or three statutes for my purpose. / In the xiij[th] yeare of his raigne he called   f.3v another parliament for the punishment of fellonies and robberies done by vagabondes. In the xiiij[th] yeare of his raigne he called another parliament for the onlie cause of the releiffe of his marchauntes, called *statutum de mercatoribus*.[4] And after him his sonne King Edward the Second in the ix[th] yeare of his raigne called a parliament for the ending of a controversie betweene the spiritualtie and laitie concerning disciplin.[5] These fewe statutes I thought good to recite, whereby it may well appeare what diligent care your Majestie's progenitors had for reformation of every small cause, and what obedience was in the subiectes. Every parliament a cause by it selfe, and the successe thereof had good allowance in the tyme of King Edward the Third, for he finding by experience the benefit thereof, in the fourth yeare of his raigne procured it to be enacted that there should every yeare once at the least a parliament bee kept, and oftener if neede were.[6]

'I move this the rather because I thinke many marvell of the soddaine calling of this parliament this tyme of the yeare so shortlie after the end of the last. These fewe examples may answer such obiections and satisfie every man that it is their duties to attend. If the causes before remembred were allowed sufficient causes [to] call parliamentes, then let us weigh them in balances with the weight of those causes for which this parliament is called; and if for punishment of vagabondes were a sufficient cause to call a parliament, as it was in deede then greate and now not small; if the releiffe of marchauntes were a sufficient cause to call a parliament, if the determination of a controversie betweene the clergie and laitie were a sufficient cause,

---

2. *Sic.*   3. *Sic.*

4. Cf. 7 Ed.I (1279), 13 Ed.I (Winchester, 1285), 13 Ed.I., *stat.merc.*, in *SR* I.51, 96-100.

5. 9 Ed. II, *articuli cleri* (1315-16), in *SR*, I. 171-4.

6. 4 Ed.III, c.14 (1330), in *SR*, I.265.

let us indifferentlie consider whether now farre greater be offred unto us, I meane the preservation of the prince uppon which one onlie cause, who seeeth not that all these causes[7] and all other causes which may concerne this state doth depende. The want of good provision in one parliament may be an over throwe to the good meaning of all the rest. / I will not presume of any cause now for what or how many causes the parliament is now called, for that I have noe speciall commyssion or direction in the same. One onely I cannot omyt, for that the same hath beene proclaymed and published through the realme, for remedy whereof your loving subiectes doe long more then the chased deere disireth the soile for his refreshing, which is the preservation of your most royall person assaulted with so many trayterous conspiracies and seditious practises, that who soever longeth not for redresse of the same deserveth not the name of a true subiect. A common opinion receaved that such a person should be as noe lawe can touch, and then noe offence, and so may they safely practise and attempt what they will. A perillous matter to our state if it were true. It hath beene said of old that the common lawe should be common reason, but this I dare safelie avouch, that if any person of what state, condicion or nation whatsoever shall commytt any fellonie within this realme they shall die for the same. What reason then can allowe that seeking the destruction of your Majestie whom the almightie God long preserve, such offender should be without lawe? Sure it were much like as one should maintayne that a giver of a phipp should be punished and the murderer should goe scott-free.

'But though the lawe be sufficient in that behalf, yet two principall causes why such matter may best be dealt with in Parliament, first for satisfaction of the common error receaved, wherein as long as the worst sorte of people are not satisfied they cease not to continue their evill proceedings, secondarily in such an assemblie the whole circumstances of a cause may be best considered and further remedy provided. If all these therefore could not move us to remember our dutie, yet nature itselfe would stirre us to remembrance thereof by the benefittes we have receaved by your Majestie. I cannot forget in what state your Majestie founde us at such tyme as the mercifull providence of God first delivered the scepter and goverment of this nation to your Highnes. Yow found us in warre with forraigne nations, subiect to ignorant hipocrisie and unsound doctrine, the best sorte under greate persecution, some imprisoned, some / driven to exile for their conscience, the treasure although in parte amended, yet for the most parte corrupt. But it pleased the Almightie in delivery of your diadem to give yow both power and will to reforme all these enormyties, a myraculous chang and the more miraculous to be so easily atchieved. Insteade of warre we enjoyed present peace: hipocrisie gave place to the Gospell; the captives were set at libertie; the exiles were receaved and suffered; the bullen converted to pure silver. One benefit more I will recite, [in] my opinion not much inferior to some of the rest. God hath enclined your heart to be a defence to his afflicted Church throughout all Europe. These benefittes I doe remember at this present, besides many which I doe forget, and yet doe remember diverse other which I leave for tediousnes. If these be not sufficient to move any person to love, they are not to be moved. It is love that your subiectes obaye yow for, perhappes not all, but of those it maketh noe matter how fewe and of the other it maketh noe matter how many. This cause which

I have touched containeth all which I meane at this present to touch. Others most weighty for considerations I will omytt, nothing doubting but when your Majestie seeth your good tyme yow will have the same in rememberance, which God put into your harte.

'It remaineth now for two[8] parte brieflie to make unto your Majestie certaine ordinary petitions consisting in three pointes, aswell for the whole House as for my selfe. The first for libertie of speech to be freely had, due reverence allwayes used to your Majestie, without which it is impossible any greate matter be atchieved in any conference, for except the obiections on every parte be hearde, answered and confuted, the councell cannot be perfected. Some speech perhappes singlie and nakedly reported hath and may seeme odious, which the circumstances considered and well digested carieth noe cause of offence. The second petition, that I may have repaire unto your Majestie at such tyme as I shalbe sent in message from the lower house, having due consideration of the tyme and place. The third petitione, that if by my imperfection / I shall mistake and so misreporte any message either from the   f.5 House to your Majestie or from your Majestie to them that I may be receaved to repaire anew for the declaracion of the same. Yf willfully I shall offend in any thing I crave noe pardon. And this is the summe of that which I have to say at this present.'

The Lord Keeper's answer in the name of the Queene's Majestie to the same.

'Mr Speaker, the Queene's Majestie hath heard your discourse with greate reverenc very learnedly uttered containeing much good matter which may be reduced into three partes. In the first yow have made declaracion of the maner of proceeding of her Majestie's progenitors in the making of lawes, in the second the benefitts which her subiectes have receaved by her, in the third three petitions made to her Majestie.

'Upon the first yow framed an arguement *a maiore* that sithence for smaller causes parliamentes have beene called men should not grudge at the calling of this assemblie for so weightie matters, which yow have very well handled. And her pleasure is that the same may be an induction to your selfe to employ your endeavour to the furtherance of those weightie causes, for that her Majestie shalbe compelled by tyme of the yeare to dissolve and disperse this greate concourse of people as shortlie as she may; and noe privat bills to be receaved.

'To the second, she hath commaunded me to declare that as shee delighteth not in the recitall of such benefits, so are the same the worke of God, and to him the thanks due for the same, and wisheth the said benefits quadrubled, and as she hath not heretofore pretermytted her care [nor] her ability, so meaneth to performe the same hereafter to her power, and prayeth hartelie that her power and will may so concurre as it may be performed, to the advancment of the weale publike of her realme.

'To the petitions, the first was for free speech wherein her Majestie hath willed me to declare that it hath beene often moved and men often warned and yet not so greate regarde had as was convenient. She knoweth that speech fit for the state well placed and used in matters convenient is very necessary, which she graunteth unto yow. But there is a difference betweene / staring and starke blinde. Trifling digressions from   f.5v

7. MS reads 'causes all these'.   8. *Sic*: 'my'?

matters proponed, idle and long discourses her Majestie misliketh and condemneth, wherein she adviseth them to be more wary then they have beene heretofore. To the second petition, as her Majestie hopeth noe such neede shalbe, for that she hopeth yow will not mistake any message, yet not proceeding of malice she thinketh it reason yow be receaved.[9] To the third, for accesse, her Majestie is content, so as such message be void of importunity[10] and in needfull causes in such sorte as hath beene required, that is to say the convenientnesse of tyme and place regarded, her Majestie is contented.'

And so gave Mondy to begin.

This oration ended the Speaker was called for to the Queene's Majestie and kneeling her Majestie had a quarter of an houre's conference with him under the cloath of state.

After the coming into the lower house the Speaker was sworne anew although before sworne as a burgesse.

A bill read that speciall baylives should be founde by defendants in the Common Place[11] provided that pieres of the realme should finde none.

The xij[th] of May.

A bill read requiring that a declaration might be made of the acte of receivers and tellers *etc*[12] should not extende to assurances made *bona fide* upon g[o]od considerations.

Mr Norton moved good consideration to be had of the bill for that as it is now penned if tellers and receavers themselves purchase landes *bona fide*, their landes should be discharged, which were not reason. He moveth also by reason of a greate mischeife happened to a good bishopp being by statute a collector of the tenthes, that the landes of such persons as be bishops' deputes may be liable to the paimentes as well as the landes of the bishopps, for that they are compelled to make collectors.

A bill read for repeale of an act made *viij° Reginae Elizabethae* then provided that none but drapers of the towne of Shrewsbury should buy Welsh cloathes *etc*.[13] |

f.6   A bill read to enable the maior of Plimouthe's corporations to enioye their liberties and certaine landes heretofore given for releiffe of an almes house, therefore moved by reason that their evidence is burnte.

A bill that before utlaryes proclamacion may be made in the parish church where the partie outlawed doth inhabit, which was commytted; never returned for that thought more inconvenience would growe thereby then before.

All the House together with the Speaker was sent for to the Lordes where as my Lord Keeper declared the Queene's pleasure that certaine of the higher house and certaine of the lower house should meete and receave advertisment by her learned councell concerning the speciall cause of the calling of this parliament, which was declared to be the Queene of Scottes; and declaration made that they purposed to send vij prelates, vij earles and vij barons and wished xl[ty] of the lower house to be sent and to meete tomorowe at viij[th] of the clocke in the Star Chamber, but the lower house not thinking good to be directed in their number did choose xliiij for the same purpose.

Mr Robart Snag declareth that he hath a motion to make to the House which is that sithenc it is purposed that the Queene of Scotes should be dealt with for conspiracies, that a petition might be made to the Queene's Majestie to execute such uppon whom iudgement is already given because it giveth occasion of feare to men to proceed any farther with other persons, seeing if execution be not had revenge may be sought, and declareth that it is very perillous and dangerous both to her Majestie and our whole realme to use delay therein.

Mr Arthur Hall thought it not good to diswade the Queene's Majestie from using of mercy, which is sometymes to have place aswell as iustice at other tymes to be executed. /

Mr Speaker declareth that when the bill concerning the Queene of Scottes is come in, he thinketh would be a fitter occasion to deale in this matter then now, and so the motion stayed.

f.6v

The xiijth of May.

A bill read for the enlarging of a statute made *xiij° Reginae Elizabethae* concerninge fraudulent convayances that the same may also extende to such conveyances as be not of recorde, wherein by any privy convenantes leading the uses the commodityes of the landes are reserved to the parties or their heires that such assurance shall not defeate any sale after made *bona fide*.[14]

A bill read requiring that whereas King Edward the vjth did erecte three hospitalles in London, and by his letters patentes did enable the same to purchase landes, since which tyme certaine well disposed persons have convayed by feofment or will diverse landes unto them, and hereafter likewise may doe, and yet misse the right name of the corporation, that notwithstanding the saied assurances might be good in lawe.[15]

A bill read restraininge the carriing of any undied clothes over the sea after Michellmasse 1573; noe dier to inhabit but in cities, boroughs and market townes, none in the citie of London but such as shalbe alowed by the wardens of the company, none in other townes but such as are alowed by the chiefe officers; noe gall, vitriall or logewoode or other stuffe to be used in the dieing which will marre the same; noe wollen yearne wrought or unwrought to be carried over sea after Michellmasse next.

A bill to avoyd fraudes used in conveyances made by tenant for tearme of life, tenaunt by curtesie and tenaunt in dower to defeate remainders or revertions; explaining the statute of *xxxj et xxxij°* concerning the same.[16]

The bill of Plimouth the second tyme read.

2.[17]

A bill read declaring that where a patent was made of certaine landes in [blank]

9. Marginal comment here: 'The Lord Keeper took the 3^d cause for the 2^d, and the 2^d for the 3^d'.
10. MS reads 'importance'.
11. I.e. Common Pleas.
12. 13 Eliz., c.4 (1571), in *SR*, IV.535–7.
13. 8 Eliz., c.7 (1566), in *SR*, IV.489–90.
14. 13 Eliz., c.5 (1571), in *SR*, IV.537–8.
15. Christ's, St.Thomas', Bridewell – see W. K. Jordan, *Edward VI: The Threshold of Power* (1970), 214–23.
16. I.e. 32 Hen.VIII, c.31 (1540), in *SR*, III.787.
17. I.e. second reading.

given to Thomas Golding and [blank] now dispersed in diverse men's handes which was to them graunted to be held by fealty only of a maner whose name was left / out in patent and a space left for the same in which space the Queene's Majestie hath put 'Haveringe at Bower' and notwithstandinge tenure *in capite* is claymed and the same not amended in the recorde; requiringe that the same may be made firme by acte.

f.7

The xiiij[th] of May[18]

This bill tooke noe place by reason the Lordes dealt with another bill which passed with us the last yeare.

The bill for the releife of the poore and punishment of vagabondes, wherein first confirmation is made of the statuts made *22° Henrici 5[i]*,[19] *3° Edwardi 6[i], and 5° Reginae Elizabethae*, of soe much of every of the same as is not repugnant to this bill.[20] Wherein is prayed a view to be made by the iustices of peace of all the needy and impotent in the shier and a consideration made for a contribution to be had accordinge to *v° Reginae Elizabethae*, and an augmentation made if need require; the iustices, or 4 of them whereof 2 to be of the *quorum*, to have authoritie to examine all persons by all wayes and meanes of their abilitie, and to perswade each man towardes a releife, and whom they finde wilfull to assese and the churchwardens to distraine for the same after proclamacion made; all licences made by iustices of peace to be void and from thenceforward the constable bounde to apprehend all vagarant persons and them to cary to prison, and such person to be brought to the sessions and beinge founde to be a vagabonde within the meaning of this estatute, the offender to be whipped and a hole an inch broade cutt out of his eare, except some man assessed at the last subsidy before at v[li] in goodes or xx[s] in landes take him into service for a yeare, and enter into regognizance for his usadge; and for the seconde offence to suffer as a felon except some man will take him into service as before *etc.* The surplusage of the former collection to be employed uppon such as shalbe set a worke by the iustices' authoritie, who shall also have authoritie by discretion to punish such parentes as bringe up their childrin in idlenes. A proviso for mariners and soulders so they have pass-portes, make speedy returnes, or aske noe almes at anybodie's doore, but resorte to such as keepe the poore mans box at every towne. iii iustices in every shier to alter these orders by their discretion and to use any other forme soe they make noe strayghter punishments then is apointed by this statute. And this to continue to the next parliament. /

f.7v

Mr Treasurer for the committees declareth how they have heard by the Queene's learned councell the dealings of the Queene of Scotes, which held them the whole day, tending to the dispossessinge of the Queene's Majestie of the crowne; and because he cannot take uppon him to declare the circumstances thereof, desireth that Mr Wilbraham may doe the same.

Mr Wilbraham sayeth he is very soddainly taken. He tooke noe notes in writinge, onely certaine speciall he retaineth in memory, to him best liking; and therefore a full relation not to be looked for. He will omit nothing willingly, desiringe others may supplie his wants. Declareth how as well the Lordes as our commyttees being set, the Atorney and Solliciter declared the matter against the Scottish Queene, which he shewed to be devided into five partes: first her chalenge made to the present possession of the crowne of Englande and refusall to renounce the same; secondly, to bring it to passe, practised a mariadge with the Duke; thirdly practised a rebellion; fourthlie ioyned with the late rebells in the north; and fiftly ioyned with forraigne power meaning to bring them, and put downe the Queene.

Uppon the first, he declared howe in the end of Queene Marie's raigne the Earle of Arundell with others being then in Fraunce in treaty and heareinge of her death, returned home, and the Lord Chamberlin sent in his roome, the Queene of Scotes being then wife to the Dolphin, at which tyme they published her as Queene of Scotts, Englande and Irelande. At first refusall made to treate with them by force of commyssion from Queene Elizabeth, but at length concluded peace with Queene Elizabeth. At that tyme greate mariadges were in hande with the Emperour; soddainely the armes of Englande set out quarterly with the armes of Scotlande. Herewith Sir Nicholas Frogmorton being iustly agreived, / complained to the   f.8 Constable, was answered with dilatorie answers but founde noe remedy. The iniury the more because at the saied mariadges was an assemblie of the greatest protestantes of all Christendome or theire embassadors. The same tyme the stille of England set over the Queene of Scottes' gate they proceeded to their triumphes and iustes every thing almost in the field, uppon the armor, the furniture of the horse, auncientes, *etc.*, the armes of England quartered with Scotlande set out her plate, the furniture of her howse, uppon the judgment seate the like armes. All actes that were done were saide to be done for the Queene of Englande, meaning the Queene of Scotes. The ripier cloathes, yea the barbars signes, had uppon them the armes of Englande. Uppon breach of this peace commyssioners were apointed to meete for consideration. At the same tyme Fraunce and Scotlande both one commyssioners.[21] Uppon the meeting it was agreed that all these titles should be lost. Recompence was demaunded by the Queene of Englande's commyssioners, which was deffered over to a conference at London. It was agreed that this conclusion should be ratefied by the king's seales on all partes. The Queene sealed her parte; they would not receave it. In this meane tyme died Kinge Henry of Fraunce, and she then wife to Frauncis the French king. My Lord of Bedford with others sent over to Fraunce to have the articles ratefied. Shee would not ratefie the same. Shee wanted tyme to consider; she was covert baron. Shee was urged that the matter was very convenient to be donne. She answered she was young, her Councell absent; at the Lord James his cominge she would consider thereof. When the Lord / James was come then shee said he was   f.8v come for privat causes and affairs, but shee would shortly have consideration thereof. She addeth for her advauntadge, that which was donne was donne shee being covert and therefore not bounde to answere it when shee was French queene. They declared that those which be queenes of Fraunce have authoritie to doe certaine actes as unmaried persons, as to make freemen and graunte anuities; wherein was declared how by her letters patentes shee had made diverse free by the name of Queene of Englande, had graunted an anuytie to Patricke a priest her amner by the name of Queene of England. These matters he declared to be diverse wayes proved unto

18. This date placed at beginning of preceding paragraph in MS; this dating from *CJ*, I.95.

19. *Sic*; i.e. '8¹'.

20. Cf.*SR*, III.328-32; IV.115-17, 411-14; and see for example the Anonymous Journal of 1571, f.20 and v.

21. *Sic.*

them, by witnesses, by the armes shewed forth, and by letters. Mr Tomworth sent into Scotlande to her, shee then beinge sole and therefore such excuses avoyded; an instrument was sent over of refusall of such claime. The instrument she said was preiudiciall to her estate. She tooke certaine exceptions at this word, 'from thenceforth to renownce'. This shee said extended for everlasting. It was offered to be reformed, to be explained from thencforth during the Queene's Majestie's life or the issue of her bodie, with certaine assuraunce that during her Majestie's life nothing should be donne to preiudicat her claime in any parliament. Shee refused altogether except the crowne might be enteyled to her and so to the Ladie Linewxs. Shortly the Earle of Bedforde sent over with a larger commyssion into Scotlande, where he sawe a booke made of the Queene of Scottes hir sonne, wherein he was named '*filius serenissimae Reginae Scotie Anglie et Hibernie.*'

Concerning the mariadg he shewed there neede[d] noe long speech for that the same was proved to the full uppon the Duke's araignment, whereof he thought none of the Howse ignorant. On his parte, and all the world he doubteth not beleeve[d], the same could not be donne without her consent, yea speciall seeking. One thing herein he cannot omyt, that the Queene of Scottes did write a letter to Bishope Roose, and conffessed by him, to bring the same mariadg aboute, either by faire meanes or else by force.

Concerning the third pointe he declared how a gentleman called Christopher
f.9   Rooke fled into Scotland / ffor debt, where as Lassels and others practised with him and brought him in credit with the Queene of Scottes, shee discoursed with him of her petigrees drawne by some English men. She wrote letters to some, such as shee trusted in Englande, and sent some other blankes. She declared her purpose to incite and procure warre in Ireland and the same to invade England, and there to have beene proclaimed Queene. Declared how she had conferred with sorcerers and was by them ascertained the Queene should die within three yeares. This the foundation of the rebellion. She was expelled her owne countrie, fled into England, where she was better kept then in her owne countrie. Greate posting betweene her and the Earles of Northumberland[22] by Bishoppe Roose and others to knowe whither the Nortons were sure. She sent worde they were sure. Shortly after she was given to understande that if any rebellion grewe by her she should come shorte, and therefore she wrote her letters with speede desiring stay for xx dayes and in the meane season she would seeke to escape. This declared by Hambden. Oswold Wilkinson was sent to Bishope Roose and to the Spanish embassador. They came to the Spanish embassador declaring that the Earles were in the field; looked for forraigne ayd and for mony; none was ready. They should have landed at Hartepoole. Wilkinson was taken and this confessed. When the Earles fled they were receaved in her countrie by those of her faction. She procured releife unto them. The Pope had sent a hundred thowsande crownes. Order taken Rodulphe to have xij thousande thereof. The same by her apointment was divided, two thowsande for Westmorland and his company, 2 thousand for Northumberlande and his company, ij thowsande to certaine other gentlemen in Flaunders, and the other vj thowsande for her selfe to be employed in Englande. Rodulphe brought letters of credit from the Pope to the Queene of Scotes whom he made his agent, which letters were sent to her and the

Duke, at which tyme the Pope had deprived the Queene of her kingdome. At the /
sute of Moorton, and others fled into Flaunders, bulls of deprivation were procured. f.9v
Two of the same sent into Englande under seale, one to the Spanish embassador,
the other to Bishopp Roose her embassador. That sent to the embassador [of] Spaine
fixed uppon the Bishoppe his gate of London. Letters immediat sent from the Pope
to the Queene of Scottes wherein was declared that shee was to be purged because
corruption of religion was entered in her countrie, but notwithstanding he embraced
her *sicut gallina pullos*, and those which would seeke to depose the Queene's Majestie
he tearmed *filios ecclesiae*. Letters from the nuncio were sent that a hundred
thowsande crownes should be sent to them which would rebell against the Queene's
Majestie. In Februarie was twelve month a letter was sent unto the Duke from the
Queene of Scotes which was deciphered by Hickford, and the Duke confessed it,
soe did Hickford, the Bishope of Roose and Banaster,[23] wherein she shewed the
order of proceeding she liked, wishing the Duke to proceede. Shee shewed that shee
had Fraunce in ielousy, in Scotland daungerous to entermedle, her faction there very
doubtfull; in Spain and Flaunders was her trust. Necessary a man of credit to be sent
that knowes the state of England and Scotland. She thought Rodulph most fit, but
referred all to the Duke how she might atcheive the crowne, but all her hope was in
the catholickes. Hereuppon was enforced she knewe all that followed. Roose
proceeds to conference with the Duke. Power for men and money from beyonde the
sea required to the number of x thowsande whereof three thowsande to be horsmen,
the men from Spaine, money from the Pope. The Duke's letters of credit were
thought most fit, but he would not agree but wrote onely that he gave credit to the
bearer; the Spanish embassador he writeth that what soever the bearer shall affirme
the Duke will performe the same. These letters are written to the King of Spaine, to
the Pope, and to the Duke of Alva. Uppon treaty had with the Duke of Alva, he
having good liking of the advise, referreth the consideration of the matter to
Courtevile. It is / finaly determined the Duke of Alva will provid a power, the same f.10
should lande at Harwich, the English men should be ready in the meane season and
lie betweene them and the Queene in some place that they be not disturbed in their
landing. Charles Bayly now in the Tower was sent over into Flaunders with
certaine seditious bookes made concerning the title of the Queene of Scottes to the
crowne of Englande by some towards the lawe in this realme. In the same sometymes
was the name of Queene Elizabeth, but uppon the print was altered and named
Elizabeth being Henrie the viij[th] daughter or King Edwarde's or Queene Marie's
sister; never named Queene. There was her title set out from before the Conquest as
though the Queene should be an usurper. He in his returne met with Rodulph at
Brisels and was there desired to put certaine letters in ciphers containing this matter,
who did soe accordingly. Thus the matter knowne to Charles. The letters were
directed to '*Trente*' and '*Quaranta*'; the meaning of the signification of those persons
was not declared. Charles was then taken, confessed the matter, all that he knew, not
to whom the letters were directed. Rodulph went from thence to Rome, the Pope
writeth his letters to the Queene of Scotes and to the Duke. The Duke is saluted in

22. *Sic.*   23. MS reads 'Ranaster'.

the letters by the name of '*Dilecte fili*' etc. The contentes were he was not able to disburse present money this yeare, but advised them to goe forwardes in his interprise and to comforte himselfe he should shortly have releif. This appered to come to the handes of Roose. He confessed the receipt of the same, but said he had burnt both, but at length perceiving it confessed by others did likewise confesse it. Hereuppon he desired licence to write a lettre to his misteris the Queene of Scotes which was graunted, wherein he first excuseth himselfe / in that he had confessed diverse things because the same had beene before confessed by others, secondarily declareth what he hath confessed to the ende they might agree in a tale, but finaly by the same he sheweth her to be the principall in all the action. These letters were delivered and sent by Floyde, a priest. In the last parliament, when there was some communication of the matter, Roose devised that some stirre should be made to the end the parliament might thereby be dissolved.

f.10v

The Queene's learned councell did farther set out what great reckining the evill subiectes of England made of her, calling the Queene's Majestie the pretensed Queene and the Queene of Scotes the Queene. So did the Duchesse of Northumberlande in her letters to Stukely, the Countesse of Ferry writing to him of the Queene of Scotes calleth her our Queene, Chamberline tearmeth the Queene's Majestie the late Queene. The Lord Seyton had beene in the meane season sent also into Spaine, retourned through England and passed into Scotland, there making his braggs of his doings. Intelligence was given to the Queene, search is made at the portes, his page was taken, his instructions and notes were founde howse shold for malize[24] the King of Spaine soe termed, meaning what course he should take with him. Rolston he should bring three thowsande straungers into Lankashier; to them a ciphere delivered. He confesseth the Queene of Scotes should have ben proclaimed King and Queene of Englande. vj thowsande men were ready in Spaine to have come in under the Duke of Medena Celi.[25] This knowne, the Duke was aprehended and commytted and soe stay made of all these matters.

Mr Dalton putteth in rememberance how in one of her letters she wisheth the Duke to proceede and not to feare her though shee were prisoner for she would stirre coles if any thing were atempted.

Others put in rememberance of a petigree shewed forth from King Henry the vij[th], also from the Earle of Sommerset, but declared that she could conveye from Edmond Ironside before the Conquest and so destroyes the Queene's title; and all this founde with the Lord Seaton's page. /

f.11

The Lord of Shrewsbury once declared unto her that the Earle of Northumberland was taken. Hereuppon she entered into great sorrow, but after understanding that it was not true shee wrote her letters to the Duke declaring how she was mocked, and that by meanes thereof she wept bitterly three dayes for sorrow of cumbering of freindes.

Mr Speaker. 'Yow have heard the reporte of the proceeding in this case. It resteth now for yow to consider in what sorte to provide for remedy, and whither yow will hereof talke with the Lordes, or first amongst your selves.'

Mr Treasurer. Thinketh best every man consider hereof untill the morninge and after conference had here, to move a conference with the Lords, which was agreed to.

A bill read that the defendent may have a *tales* aswell as the pleintiff.
The bill of tellers the seconde tyme read and commytted.

The xv^th of May.

Mr Galeise, taking occasion to shewe that in wise and grave councell the puisne or yongest hath used to speake first, declareth that he as one though eldest in age, yet thinking himself otherwise yonge, purposeth to deale first in this weighty cause and to shew his sentence in the same, and though wisdome in some men's opinions would he should give place to others, he cannot be silent. He noted uppon the declaration made in this House of the Queene of Scotes three things specially touched of her: that she was an usurper of the crowne, a disturber of the whole state, and a dispossesser of the Queene in will and desire. The particularitie of her doings he cannot recite, which when harde he thought it not good to have delayed her punishment to this tyme. Theophrastus sayeth well '*Societas humana in tribus, beneficentia, honnore, et poena*': beneficience is shewed by one to another, honor to be distributed to such as deserve the same, and by that good philosopher punishment was thought worthie to be ioyned with the rest as without which noe good society could continue. So now it rested to consider what punishment was due to so abhominable a person. He declared / that the Scotes by right are subiect to the crowne of Englande. He sheweth that Malcolm King of Scotes did his homadge for the same at Yorke and in token thereof offered his gauntlet at the alter, and there made an othe[26] for him and his successors for ever after and that if they did rebell against the King of England, to be deposed. And soe the Queene of Scotes in right a subiect and then ought not to be usurpe[r]: if she doe, worthy to receave condigne punishment. But though she were noe subiect, being under the Queene's protection and having receaved such benefites of her, ought to be true. He compared to Clitemnestra, a killer of her husbande and an adulteresse, and therefore put downe. Having then here in England proceeded soe farre where she founde grace, to set the subiect against the Queene and to dispossesse a rightfull Queene from her crowne, he thinketh noe punishment to harde. If this had beene donne in armes she might have beene killed. Being as it is he wisheth she may have her heade cutt of and noe more harme done to her.

f.11v

Sir Thomas Scot. Declareth that he meaneth not to make any repetition of the Queene of Scotes doings, for that the same hath beene excellently, sufficiently and truely declared already, even from the first coming of the Queene's Majestie to her crowne to this present day. He seeth to playnely the Queene in daunger, the nobility in perill, and the whole state of the realme in a most doubtfull estate. The disease therefore is deadly; the more neede to have remedy applied in tyme. A good phisician before he ministereth his medicin seeketh out the cause of the disease, whose order herein he meaneth to follow. Papestrie the principall which hath produced rebellion. He seeth the papistes placed in authoritie in all places, in commyssion of peace, in seate of iudgement, in noble mene's howses, in the court,

24. *Sic.*
25. MS reads 'Medina Creli'.

26. MS reads 'other'.

f.12   yea about the Queene's owne person. This encoradged / the Queene of Scotes to make this attempt thinking the parte to be strong, this encurradged the Pope to send out his bulls hoping the papistes were able and would maintaine it, this encurradged the rebels to rise, the King of Spaine and Duke of Alva to ioyne in their asistance. The second cause the uncertainty of our state. This procured the noble men and gentlemen, seeing her pretend title to the crowne and seing likelyhoode she should prevayle, to ioyne with the Queene of Scotes. This sore hath two heades, both very greate, yea such as if they be not cutt of will eat up our heades. Now to the remedy; the same he devided into three pointes. If all or one of two be provided for it may doe good, but one of the three without the rest he feareth wilbe but a shaddowe to a further evill. The first in executing the Queene of Scotes, the seconde disabling her title, the third the establishment of the crowne which is the principall, and giveth assurance to the subiect which loveth her Majestie. If the title be disabled and not her heade cutt of the wished frute will not follow. If lawes would serve, there was a statute made in King Henry viij[th] tyme and a watch this last parliament, but it would not serve.[27] The Queene's Majestie hath now taried so long she can tarie noe longer. It remaineth onely, if she doe, her nobility to be spoyled, her realme conquered, and her selfe deposed. But he feareth Sinon hath prevayled and herse be receaved,[28] and prayeth to God that Eneas and Anthenor be founde true. An humble sute he wisheth to be made to the Queene's Majestie that all two or one of the best of these may be performed.

   Mr Snage. That he meaneth not to shewe any more concerning the Queene of Scotes' person then [has] beene shewed, since it hath beene declared by one whose wisdome and knowledg is to every man knowne and to whose lif noe man can except; only he will say concerning[29] *tam fedum est factu quod turpe est dictu.* Her title he

f.12v   meaneth / not to call in question for that he thinketh she hath none at all, whereof he hath considered as advisedly as he could aswell by himselfe as others and could never finde it out. Yt is her faction which he feareth. Cut of her faction and let her title alone, for if she would come to clayme yt by lawe her feareth it not, for that then he might answere againe by lawe. When she shall offer to come she will seeke it by conquest and then wilbe pleading at the barre with a buckler. Noe statute can stay them in the field. He can say nothing to Edmond Ironside's title; he can not looke so farr backe. He will not call King Henry the viij[th]['s] tytle in controversie, nor Queene Elizabethe's possession to debate. It is the fact onely he respecteth and what punishment is due. She[30] hath already beene considered of by xxj noble men and xliiij of the best of our Howse — himselfe should have but xij godfathers if he had made like offence — and a true reporte hath beene made. To her person, whither she be such a one as may be dealt with: they have put her downe in Scotlande; shall wee receave and succor such an enemy in England? She hath not spared her nobility, neither her bed nor boorde. A sower of sedition in Fraunce, heither she came, not as an enemy but worse, as a dissembling freind, and under freindshipe hath sought the distruction of the Queene's Majestie. Surely he thinketh him not worthie to have a heade which would seeke to save her heade. She is now noe prince since deposed; of our nobilitie she is none; then it resteth she is but a common person. But it wilbe said she is a straunger. As much as is necessary to be alowed to straungers. Straungers may take leases and being put out shall have remedy; if an English man kill any of them he shall suffer; he hath lately seene the experience thereof uppon the death of a Duch man. 'If th'offence were commytted towardes me I should have remedy. Against a straunger they are protected, and shall we make a question whither they shalbe ruled and chastened. Is yt reason one both sides to have remedy for a subiect, and deffect in the lawe for the principall? *Lex summa ratio*, and shall we punish all in particular cases and / not punish in the generall case? Noe man can gainsay this except f.13 either affection on the one side doe drawe him or feare one the other side doe withdrawe him, as doubting the streinght of the factor and that he shall speake in vaine. But ye will say, spare her for curtesie because she is a king's daughter. But that sparing is daungerous, and therefore good to execute her for iustice and then bury her honno[r]ablie for her parentes' sake'. A petition to be made that she may be iustely iudged. He would offer noe wronge to any, and withall would have right offered her, that her selfe offereth noe right to any.

Mr Treasurer. It is very comfortable to see the good devotion had to the safetie of the Queene, and since noe remedy is thought good but the punishment of the offendors he liketh well their zeale and policie, but he would not have it caried to other matters which may be a hinderance to that which is in conference. He himselfe wisheth the establishment of the crowne, but since it is not to be obtained as yet, and that all our doings be in vaine without the consent of the Queene's Majestie, he would not have it soe urged. Former parliamentes have sufficientlie declared it. If this had beene thus moved by some, he must have thought it donne of purpose to destrube[31] the purposed proceeding, but in him that was the speaker he knoweth it proceeded of zeale. He wisheth us herein to depend uppon God, and pray to him to put it in the Queene's harte, and in the meane tyme be satisfied *quod non est volentis neque currentis sed miserentis Dei*. He would not have us hinder that which we would further; besides, the matter so intricate as requireth a longer tyme then now can be had for determinacion thereuppon.

This done, by messadge from the Lordes certaine of the Howse were required to come to those lords which were last commyttees in this matter, and so the last commyttees of the lower howse sent up accordingly. /

A bill read confirming all ould statutes made of weightes and measures through 1 f.13v Englande as farre forth as the same is not repugnant to this estatute, with certaine additions and new penalties to the same.

Then was declared by Mr Treasurer the Lordes' request onely to be for a meeting at two of the clocke in the after none in the Star Chamber.

Mr Norton. Liketh well the motion offered by the first man that the meanest should speake first and the gravest to come after in the approving of the same or the contrary as occasion should serve; and soe he as one of the meanest would shewe his minde. Touching the succession he sheweth it was onely moved and not urged, and there wisheth it to stay and therein to expecte her Highnesse' pleasure, who he

27. I.e. the 1571 Treason Act; and Scott is presumably referring to the 1543 Act of Succession (cf. *SR*, III.957-8).
28. *Sic.*
29. *Sic.*
30. MS reads 'he'.
31. *Sic.*

doubteth not in good tyme will provide for the same. In the meane season to strike downe the bushes which lie in the way. He remembreth uppon deliverie of the Queene's mind unto us, we receaved in generall tearmes a charge to make provission for the Queene's safety, without any speciall direction how and wherein particulerly. To this pointe he would have our consultation directed, and to remedy all things which may be letes thereof. Meete now to looke how to provide that she may stande, and not what shall become of us. If she fall he wisheth any head of rather then hers, yea though his owne, and yet a greate many others rather then his owne. Execution is the thing he specially moveth; lawes already very good. He liketh well of the motion made the last day by a gentleman who moved a request to be made first to have execution of those which are already condemned by lawe, before proceeding to the condemnation of moe. He said he was sorry he must needes speake particulerlie, but he will suppresse all sorrow for her safety, uppon whom all wee depende, and lay all care away under her feete. He sorroweth as he said before the noble man's fall, but he reioyceth to see that all his kinsfolke at this tyme were found trusty to the Queene, /

f.14   and that the Duke had noe truste in his owne kindred. He hath of him two consideracions; first, respect of treasons commytted, which though they be horrible, he could like the forbearing of due punishment and thinke it honnorable and a mercyfull acte, but when he considereth the perill which is to come in sparing of execution, he is driven to put all feare aside and to utter his conscience, and since he cannot devise how the Queene's Majestie may be assured in his life, he thinketh yt necessary she be assured in his death. Alwayes and meanes have been attempt, none lefte to be tried, whereby any hope may be he[32] should ever be a good subiect. The benefites which he hath receaved by the Queene such as might have drawne any man to love, but yt could doe noe good in him; her mercye towardes him hath beene unmeasurable, and even when the mercy was in shewing he practised new rebellions and conspiracies; submissions offered have beene receaved, but they were but *ore tenus*; subscriptions have beene made to promysses and seales fixed, but noe performanc hath followed; othes have beene solemly made, but faith hath not beene kept; uniting hath beene in religion, but a shorte disserverance hath followed; protestations have beene forgotten, communion hath beene receaved, but all would not serve. 'I knowe not what resteth to be attempted that may give hope of trueth. But if trueth were to be hoped for in him, all will not serve: the opinion conceaved by others cannot soe be stopped. Experience hath taught – and some latly executed for the same, the matter confessed – the Duke's faction liked, and noe way thought lefte to procure his liberty, but the death of the Queene's Majestie. Such perill must needes be mett with. Take him away uppon whom the hope resteth, that safety may follow.' He feareth else Italian practizes which he would not have harbored in England. The cause therefore to be removed. Publicacions have beene made; the papistes bounde to noe lawes. Libertie of speech he wisheth to be free against all men but the prince. Oathes will not serve them: experience by Gardiner who, haveing

f.14v   made his oath to King Henrie, King Edward said / they were Herod's oathes; they are persuaded the Pope can dispense with the same, and soe oathes taken in Parliamente will not serve. Besides, the examples of immunitie in this case will incuradge others to newe rebellions and treasons. 'It will also discoradge the revealers if it be more perillous to disclose then to doe treason; not that I thinke the Queene's grave councell have brought the disclosers in perill, but that the common multitude will iudge by actions, and by not executing will condemne the condemners. Surely the humer of ambicion is unquenchable which hath brought him to such adventures to chaunge so good a state as he hath chaunged. If this have beene adventured whilest he was in awe, what would be offered when bye libertie feare shalbe removed?' There is honnor yet hoped to the sunne rising, but it is but a comet. The Scot harde to be removed without this execution. They are knitt together soe as while the one liveth the faction is stronge. Take the one away and weaken the other by all his freindes. Mercy is good in some cases, but woe worth that mercy which bringeth misery. Mercy as farr as it may cary her safety, he aloweth; all mercy hindering the same he condemneth. Heat[33] and moisture are both necessary in every person; if either doe abounde it is perillous. 'I knowe her Majestie hath used severity, mercy, magnanimytie and lowlynesse to diverse persons uppon occasions, and all are commendable vertues in a prince; and yet if any of these should exceede, the nature is changed. Whosoever increaseth the humor of mercy in one naturaly enclined to mercy offendeth pernicioussly, and hath noe regard to her safety. Let us onely foresee that she be and wilbe honnorable, she wilbe good. If a noble man had a leprosie which cannot be cured but with the blood of a greate number of innocentes and the very hart bloode of the Queene, though it were a mercyfull acte to releive the / sicke yet were it not lawfull to minister such medicine.'   f.15

Now to the Queene of Scotes. He thinketh it unreasonable the prince should not be as well provided for as other common subiectes. If a subiect of another prince in another realme should offende mortally against her Majestie, she might either execute the offendor or procure his prince to execute. The Queene of Scotes hath noe prince by whome she may bee compeinte[34] be executed. Therefore the Queene her selfe in whose realme she is ought to doe it, for there ought to be noe immunitie for treason. He is not of opinion to deale with her as with a subiect of Scotlande, for that there our lawes doe not governe. She to be dealt with for offences here. If a king invade this realme the meanest souldier by lawe of armes may kill him: why not in cause of iustice? The souldier shall doe it suddainly, and not[35] the Queene with mature deliberation? It wilbe aledged she hath beene receaved under protection; but she hath beene noe true prisoner. Every protection carrieth conditions, which being broken, the protection dispensed with. *Frustra legis petit auxilium quo in legem peccat.* A man robbes a church, he shall not have the priviledge of the Church. 'If I take a prisoner I may by the lawe of armes choose whyther I will kill him or take him to mercy; but if I receave him to mercy I may not kill him, but then he must keepe faith or else I am at libertie'. And yet example may be shewed when such prisoners have beene executed. At the battell of Agincourte many prisoners taken, but yet uppon a new assault in case of necessitie, and for avoiding a greater daunger, by commaundement the prisoners were killed. Loe here the like necessitie. If she die not, the Queene endaungered, the succession never established with the Queene's safetie,

32. MS reads 'she'.
33. MS reads 'heath'.

34. *Sic*; 'by complaint'?
35. *Sic*; 'may not'?

for, an heier apparent named, if kept lowe it[36] shall never be able to prevaile against the Scotish faction, if it be made over stronge for the Scot, daungerous to the

f.15v Queene. But / the Scot removed, a low porte[37] may carie after the Queene, and her Majestie safe in the meane season. 'Yow will say she is a queene's daughter and therefore to be spared; nay then spare the Queene's Majestie that is a king's daughter and our Queene. If yow respect any qualities or vertues in her, they are not comparable to our Queene's. Let us with greate expectacion for the rest thinke only nowe how she may be in safetie. The person I spake of first, toucheth nearest the Lords. If yow like of my motion wee may declare it to the Lords'. And here making a pawse, a great number said 'Yea, yea'; and then he proceeded declaring he had shewed his opinion and wished the Speaker with some of the House might move the Lords therein, and uppon their agreement, the same to be declared to the Queene and so referred to her iudgement.

Mr Hall. Understandeth very well how two bushes have beene dealt with, and by the same was meante two princes. He thinketh it not convenient we direct the Queene's Majestie, or make any petition to her for execution of him whose practises peradventure should not be preiudiciall to the state. What if she be determined to pardon, or but to stay for a time? Her minde not to be searched. The cause touched the Queene only; if it touched our selves wee might deale. [If] both the bushes were removed, where is our assurrance? And therefore good to deale with the succession. And although the Duke's offence be to the common wealth, we have yet receaved noe harme. If others had beene meate with the same rod of iustice, diverse had not beene which nowe be. The nature of the lion not to devoure the prostrate.

Mr Alford. That he is very carefull how to use himselfe in this matter. Resolutions asked in cawses before they be hearde disputed on the other side. Declared that the person of the speaker may occassion one selfe-same thinge to be diversly construed. These interpretacions makes him doubtfull, for he seeth the old saying verefied, 'better some man steale a horse then other to looke over / a hedge'. He

f.16 craveth free speech, which was graunted by the Queene and therefore to be enioyed. Here it seemeth to be denied. He meaneth not to dispute whyther it be good to execute both or no: he hath heard diversitie of opinions and will beleeve the best. That every one hath spoke according to his conscience. The Lordes have apointed a meeting: good to follow their plot. And though some thinke it lawfull, he never read president of such dealing with kings, although he could alowe it if there were noe other remedy for the prince's preservation; but that is good to be considered. He trusteth he may be suffered to speake his minde: all here present knightes and burdgesses, and the voice of one as free as of another.

Mr Dalton. The last speaker hath mistaken the last save one before him. Not moved by him as a resolution presentlie to be moved to the Queene, but that since a conference is to be had with the Lordes, they might knowe how this Howse is affected in the mocion, and to see howe it standeth with the Queene's safetie. This to be declared to the Lordes as a matter in devising, not devised; and the mocion more necessarie since they are to go to the Lords. And it did him good to here the good liking of the motion.

xvj° die Maij.

Mr Sellenger. Had a question to move unto the Howse, whether he that shall saie that a practise pretended which peradventure might not be hurtfull to this realme, meaning the Duke's treasons, be a fit member to be one of this House. He for his owne parte doth thinke that his maladie is so greate and his leprosie so perillous as it is incurable; for, having hard soe many treasons and conspiracies opened and proved by the Queene of Scotes and the Duke, to see a direct purpose to overronne the realme, to usurpe the crowne, to distroy the Queene's Majestie's person, and to doubt whether this be hurtfull, is a manifest declaracion himselfe to be of the faction and therefore not to be aiudged a determinor of the cause, but comitted to some surer place. Speech / ought to be contained in boundes, cankers not to be suffered: it is not f.16v fit in iudgement, especiallie in the highest courtes.

Mr Fennor. Liketh well of the zeale of him which made the last mocion, but he wisheth libertie of speech without restraint. To the matter which is now in question. He verelie beleeveth that the necessitie is such at this present as execution ought to follow, and although that the practises have not come to effect, yet the mercie ought not to be the more. They proceeded as farrforth as they might: if they had performed their desires punishment could not have followed, for that themselves should have governed. So not otherwise giltles of fact onlie but *quia non successerunt*. We enioy the Queene's Majestie, we enioy our religion, but it was *quia non successerunt*. Socrates, talking of untrulie[38] persons when at a tyme such a one came unto him and gave him a box on the eare and then ranne away, he was demaunded by his freind why he did suffer it. He answered, the fault was not his which gave the box of the eare, but his owne, that had not before put on a sallet, meaning hereby that it was the parte of wise men to provide in tyme to prevent perills to come. The question nowe in hande whether iustice or mercy be most fit; and surelie he thinketh iustice most necessarie. He confesseth that both iustice and mercie be vertues, but it is wisedom to foresee which of the two is to be chosen. Ambition surely is unsatiable, never satisfied with inough, and not contented with too much. Mercie to be exercised when the falle is by ignorance, but not so when it is by malice. To use mercie when there is noe cause to save and great cause to spill were crueltie, and no mercie. Three causes he hath heard wherefore iustice is to be used: for / example to others, for a punishment for the f.17 offence, and for a terror that the offender offend noe more. If th'offence be so greate as the innocent cannot be in safetie without the loss of the nocent, it is better the nocent to die then the innocent to be in perill. *Quando plus timetur quam condemnatur*, then mercie hath noe place. Surelie he feareth more the signell of that which is to come then the harme that is past. He remembreth uppon the declaration made of the Queene of Scotes' doings, amongst other things was shewed that when the Earle of Shrewsburie had declared unto the Queene of Scotes that the Earle of Northumberlande should be taken by the Earle of Sussex, she writing hereof to the Duke did aledge that she did weepe bitterlie; and whie? For feare of opening of freindes. A maniefest proofe that she hath welwillers. Lacketh but drie stickes to

36. I.e. the heir apparent.   38. *Sic*; 'unruly'.
37. *Sic*.

kindle the fier. He will showe some examples in such persons as had cause to showe mercie in some respectes, and yet executed iustice. It must needes be confessed that it is greate cause of mercie to be shewed by the father towardes the sonne, and by on kinsman towardes another. Alexander Severus for offences to the common weale banished his owne kinsman, saying, '*carior est mihi patria*'. A wise senator executed iudgement uppon his owne sonne for offences to the common weale, saing, 'I begot thee a sonne, not a pariscede'. A wise king, having made a lawe that whosoever were taken in adultrie should have both his eies put out, it happened his owne sonne to bee first taken in the offence. The father yet executed the iudgement uppon his owne sonne in parte and the rest upon himselfe, putting out one of his son's eis and one of his owne, and so shewed both iustice and mercie. A wise captaine sent his sonne before with an armie, meaning to follow himselfe with a greater power, with

f.17v   commaundement in the meane season that the sone should not / fight with the adversarie. The sonne was yonge and adventerous and gave the charge uppon [the] adversarie and overthrewe them in the field and retorned the victor. Notwithstanding, uppon his retorne, forasmuch as he had adventured the estate and disobaied the commaundement, he was punished and not rewarded. He hath read likewise of a request made by one to an emperor to have soe much grounde as he could till in circuit in a daie, but the wise emperor answered that he would have noe such subiect as desired more than was fit for a subiect. So he thinketh in the present case: sithence persons could not be content to live as subiectes, they are not worthie to live at all. And therefore humble suite to be made to the Queene's Majestie to have execution done.

A case of liberties of the House

A man retorned of a iurie requireth priveledge of the Howse, and being understoode that it was in cases of treason, thought best he might goe, because therein he might doe the prince good service.

Mr French. The treasons notorious, religion subverted, the state to be trobled, the prince overthrowne, confedracies with the Pope, the King of Spaine and the Duke of Alva, the realme invaded and the crowne plucked from the Queene's Majestie's heade. This considered, noe doubt to be made as he thinketh that mercie is not to be shewed but execution to be done. Saule saved Agag, King of the Amelites, conntrie[39] to the comaundement of God, but Samuell a merciefull prophet did execution and Saule lost his kin[g]dome. It was said here the last daie that this case was a privat case, it touched the Queene's Majestie onlie, and therefore whie should wee stirr her to iustice. He thinketh it good that he that soe said were caused to declare whie the offence is not as well to the whole state as to her Majestie. /

f.18   Mr Peter Wentworth. The bill that remaineth to be made is for one not yet condempned by lawe. This treatie concerneth one alreadie condempned, the execution of whom would be such a cooling carde to the favorers of the other that it shalbe easilie obteined, a lawe to punish the other. One[40] the contrarie, a traitor proved to be preserved would give occasion of feare of proceeding in the other. He thinketh good that the Lordes be ioyned in mocion with them to the Queene for execution. Abinadabe warred agen Achab and the Israelites. Abinadab had a greate armie, but received the overthrowe. Abinadab fled. Councell was given him to goe to King Achab to when[41] it was declared that in him he should finde mercie.

Abinadab did so. Achab did receive him. Therefore the prophet said, 'Because thou hast not taken the life of Abinadab, therefore thy life shalbe taken awaie from thee.' It is noe mercie to save the life of Abinadab. He sheweth that by Achab he meaneth the Queene's Majestie, by the Israelites her good subiectes, and by Abinadab the Queene of Scotes, and the Ducke for the assistaunte of Abinadab.

Mr Treasurer. 'It may be gessed that I arrogate authoritie to my selfe by reason of my often speaches, and it may be called in question whether I was ignorant in my speech, or he that spake it of me arroganet. It was said preemynence ought not to prevaile in this place, and that there was equalitie amongst us, which I doe confesse, and yet was bold to speake in a matter of my owne knowledge uppon some talke offered of the succession. I said that I was in feare that this matter might be to much urged in some by zeale and of good affection, in others by coging,[42] meaning to overthrowe the proceeding of the cause in hand. This I spake to that / end that to one it might be a caveat, and to th'other an admonicion, to leave the same, least they might hinder that which they desired to further. If I rubbed any man one the galle, let him heale the sore, the rubbing wilnot hurt him. I will not denie but both of us maie lie and both may plaie the knaves. But I knowe I speake this the rather because I am nowe to move the like matter wherein I will speake myne opinion the rather for that I have cause to knowe something of the same. I doe reioyce to see the good zeale of the House in this matter, and the thing is to be wished.' But some circumstaunces perhappes are worthie of consideracion. He will shewe his opinion, which is that this matter were better to come to the Queene's Majestie by waie of opinion then request. As it is spoken it cannot be hid from her. To urge it he doubteth may doe harme. If it would doe more good it were good to be used, but modestie he thinketh wilbe better liked, since urged or pressed it cannot be.

f.18v

Mr Alford. That he hath a litle to saie for exposicion of himselfe. 'A gentleman here the last day told a tale, and suddenly there was a greate murmor, spitting, and coughing. Hereuppon, thinking it a greate disorder and an infamie to the gravitie of this Howse, I said there was equalitie amongst us all in the Howse, as knightes and burdgionses.' For the other pointe, hereing it said that some one speech might be diverslie interpreted in consideracion of the speaker, he misliked of the same, that harder opinion should be conceaved of one then of another. And wisheth that if too meanings maie be gathered, to take the best in all persons. No man knoweth the harte of man but God onlie. For lieing / or being a knave, he thinketh it not spoken by him, for that he is sure he is non. Difference of opinions must needes be, and then would the matter bee confuted and not the person of anie man blemished, ells he cannot speake with such circumspection as may be void from carping. His opinion is that they which would speake for the Queene of Scotes might be comforted and be heard at full, so as it might be said for the honnor of England, that as much hath beene said for her as shee could have said for her selfe if she had been here present.

f.19

Mr Speaker. 'This controversie must have an end and therefore I will put it to a question whether the Howse thinke it good this matter come to the Queene by opinion or by request'. Which was done, and agreed to be done by opinion; and

39. I.e. 'contrary'.
40. *Sic*; 'on'.
41. *Sic*.
42. I.e. cogging, or cheating.

here the Speaker gave a caveat that though it had been aledged by some that the Queene of Scotes was a subiect or feedarye, that the same is not to be taken as alowed, for that the law was not soe.

Mr Norton. Two resolucions are alreadie made; first that the Duk's death is to be wished; secondarilie this to be brought to the Queene as an opinion. It resteth to be considered, how this opinion shall come to the Queene, whether by the mouth of the Speaker, by communicating it to the Lordes, or by the Privie Councell. And he thinketh by the Privie Counsell.

Mr Treasurer. This is contrarie to that which is alreadie agreed, because this were to make it a message.

1   A bill read concerning the lande given to the foundacion of chauntries *etc.*, graunted to King Edward the Sixt by Parliament.[43] /

f.19v 2   A bill read to enlarge the statute of fraudulent guiftes, that it may extende also to make good the seconde sale, where a former fraudulent sale is made to his use or to the use of his childrin or kinsmen. The second tyme read.

Mr Thomas Scot. That the matter touicheth a privat person, and desireth he may be heard.

Mr Snagge. This bill would drawe every conveyaunce in question. This left out the last parliament willinglie which now is sought to be put in.

Mr Dalton. The bill the last parliament came from the Lords and being good was not thought neede to be altered. This bill meeteth onlie with fraude[s] which are not worthie to be favored, and if remedie be not had noe purchases can safelie be made. The Lord Keeper and Lord Cheife Iustice of England themselves deceaved by such like practises.

Mr St. John. Moveth that the bill maie be made to extend to a fraude done to infantes.

Mr Alford. Declareth of a notable fraude done to him by Lodowicke Grivell, and requireth remedie either by this bill or by another.

Mr Recorder. That Chawcer, sometimes a Speaker in this parliament howse, said well, '*Elecet nos per implere omnem iustitiam*'. The act which was made in the time of King Edward Third that a parliament should be kept every yeare once, speciallie for remedie for such secondarie causes. Deceiptes hath alwaies ben provided for. xix[th] of Edward the Third John Delarue practised to bye a debt which himselfe had before receaved. The matter but of an hundred poundes weight. Complaint was made in Parliament and put over to the King's Bench. There John Delarue was indicted

f.20 and arrayned, iudgement given. The partie had / his amendes. John Delarue committed to perpetuall imprisonment and all his goodes confiscat. In the xliij[th] yeare of Edward the Third the Lumbardes, meaning to deceave the people and to bring wolle to a lowe prise, bruted that there was warres in hand, and so bought greate quantitie of wolles iiij[?][44] under the prise in a lodde. They were likewise indicted at the King's Bench, and received like iudgement.[45] In the iiij[th] yeare of Henry 4, by the lawe of counters, two conspiring the death of a iustice of peace were condempned to perpetuall imprisonment, although the fact was not executed.

Mr Mounson. Moved for good advise to be taken in the passage of the bill; what shalbe said a fraudulent conveyance doubtfull.

Mr Norton. That Mr Alford may make his bill and be holpen. Better many litle billes then one long bill, least by doing to many good thinges at once, one good thing may not goe forwardes. The bill committed.

xvij° Maij.[46]

A bill requiring that the statute of uniformitie of praier made *primo Regine Elizabete* may extende onelie to such as shall saie anie papisticall service, and that it may be lawfull to the ministerie to saie such service as is used in the reformed churches allowed in the Douch and French Church by the bishop's consent, and to forbeare the wearing of such attire as limyted by the said former statute.

A new bill requiring that the landes and goodes of bishoppes' under-collectors may be extended to the answering of the Queene's x[tes] aswell as the landes of tellors, receavors *etc.* |

Mr Honywoode. Declareth he is to renewe a mocion made the last day by a   f.20v gentelman concerning certaine wordes spoken in this Howse. He sheweth that uppon every iurye the sheriffe is commaunded to retorne *probos et legales homines.* He trusteth much rather those which are to deale in making of lawes ought to be such persons. There was one, treating of the Duke's practizes, said, which peradventure should not be hurtfull to this realme. Such person he thinketh not fit for the Howse, sithence the Duke hath beene indicted, arrayned and founde giltie of such notorious treasons, by such and so many noble personages, to the dirogation of whose honnor it seemeth to tende, besides an utter condempnacion to all this Howse which have given forth for opinion to be declared unto the Queene's Majestie that it were convenient that he were executed. And therefore desired he may be called to answere to the premises.

Mr Treasurer. That he is loath to offende any that so zealouselie seeketh the preservacion of the Queene's Majestie. He sheweth that he wisheth speech in the Howse to be free, and that he had rather knowe men by their speech then not to knowe them by their scilence. He would have all blockes removed from the perverse, who otherwise would saie that they were denied speech, that they were able to answere but durst not. Therefore give them scope, let them speake their fill. We are not to be wonne from this course, nor to be abused by their sayinges.

Mr Ireland. Trusteth the libertie of this Howse wilnot permit a man to speake treason. Theise wordes, as he thinketh, tende to treason. And therefore desireth they may be considered of by some of the learned of the Howse. |

Mr Sampolle. That he never knewe in any parliament libertie of speech so freelie   f.21 graunted that a man might saie what he listed. These wordes call in question the proceedings of the Lordes and overthroweth the resolucion of this Howse. In *xxiiii*[to][47] of Henrie the viij[th] (as he remembreth) certaine lawes being made for abbolishing of supersticion, the Bishope of Rochester said in Parliament, 'There is

43. I Ed.VI, c.14 (1547), in *SR*, IV.24-33.
44. MS unclear: possibly 'iii[s].'
45. For Delarue and the Lombards see Fleetwood's speech in 1571 in the

Anonymous journal, fos.20v-21, *supra* p. 220.
46. MS reads '*xviij Maij*'.
47. MS reads '*xixiiij*[to]'.

nowe nothing but downe with the Church'.[48] Because theis wordes tended to the condempnation of the resolucion of the Howse, he was put to answer. In Edward the 4th his tyme, the Duke of Clarence and the Earle of Oxeford were sclaundered. The sclaunder[er]s therefore were put to answer. This man in other places aswell as in the Howse giveth forth speech and sclaunder of the nobilitie and of the whole state, and seemeth to him at the least to be an abetter of a traitor.

Mr Greenefild. That in the cawse of the Queene of Scotes he was a commyttee, where for her abhominable factes he was fullie satisfied, and heard such nothorious treasons as more could not bee except they were felt. *Equa condicio in crimine lesae majestatis.* Whosoever therefore in any treasons worketh as a meane, is in like fault with the traitor. I remember the same gentleman said, 'Quod differtur non aufertur, but *mora trahit periculum*.' Temeris apprehending his sonne and an other woman in adultrie cut of both their heades and then caused a coyne to be made of two heades issueing out of one, for a perpetuall monument of their adultrie. He would have the like to be done with the Queene of Scotes and the Duke, and some perpetuall memorie made for rememberance of the vilaines of their actes. Without this be

f.21v   executed he thinketh we labor in vaine, and bring ourselves / in daunger. 'If a man would bid us to be merie this weecke for the next weecke wee should die, I thinke we should hardlie be merie. Such is our case without execution.' And therefore he cannot be scilent. *In bona causa prestat quam cedere.*

Mr Norton. Liketh well we should have *sine acerbitate discentionem.* Men may be mistaken or may speake unadvisedlie that which they meane not. It were good the gentleman were called to answer, and to here howe he can explicat his owne meaning.

Mr Recorder. That he heard not the matter, but taketh it according as it is nowe called in question. He saieth that in all cases the tyme, place and person ought to bee considered. Doctor Storie in the time of King Edward the Sixt said in Parliament, '*Ve regno cui puer est rex*', and for the same wordes was put to anser in the Howse for iudgeing the same, and comytted to the Tower. The same Doctor Storie *anno primo regine Elizabethe*, uppon treatie in Parliament in cawses of religion, used theise wordes, that in Queene Marie's tyme they stroake at the braunches, but if they would have followed his advise they should have stricken downe the roote her selfe, and not it selfe. This cawse was consideratlie heard in the Howse. Storie had his wanton wordes and passed without punishment.[49] This wrought uppon one person by diversitie of tyme. Mr Coppley[50] wished to provide for my Lady Elizabeth: she was heire apparant to the crowne. He was brought to the barre and arreigned for the same. We have nowe great matters in hande and the arreignement of a queene; and therefore he would have the speech to be more liberalie suffered within the Howse. Let them aledge for her what thay can, they shalbe answered. But here is mencion of speech without the Howse: nowe the case is changed. He that saieth a iudge giveth a

f.22   wrongefull iudgement / is to be punished. He must use the remedie which is given him, which is by writ of error. Complaint was made in the Star Chamber against a iudge of this realme, by an inferior person. It was received and allowed. The same man spake but the same wordes uppon his alebenche: the iudge brought against him an action of his case and it will lie. So words tollerable in this Howse are not sufferable at Blunte's table.

Mr Alforde. The wordes he confesseth inconsiderat, but he heard not the same. The reportes thereof diverse: worthie of consideracion where the wordes were spoken. Surelie he would have much borne within the Howse. Kings' titles have beene here examined and a bill preferred against a king in possession, and by acte of revercion after his death given from him. He had rather be a bead[51] then a spider. Enimies will take advantadges of trifles. He is jeleous of the liberties of the Howse. If the wordes were spoken out of the Howse, let him be called to answer.

Mr Snagge. Noe libertie to be graunted to licentiousness. That the Howse may deale with examining of titles he doubteth not, but this speech was sclaunderous. For the wordes he is noe such Didimus to doubte of them, since he heard the same: he said, peradventure it might be to our safetie. If this be suffered let seditions be sowen. Touching Storie, God miraculouslie delivered withence, and hath receaved his demerites. /

Mr Marsh. A request was made to consider whither there were treason in the   f.22v wordes, which were good to be donne. That it was also required to knowe whither traiterous wordes might be spoaken: to that he answereth the Howse hath noe such libertie. But to his per[a]dventure if his peradventure were true, without peradventure the Lordes have uniustlie condemned the Duke.

Mr Fennor. Infinite the estimation of libertie. An emperor having most traiterous wordes spoaken to him by an embassador, answered, 'Thou hast not so much impudencie as I can beare with modestie'. The like he would have donn concerning this man. Let the libertie of the Howse be maintained and him be held as a mad man.

Sir Nicholas Arnolde. That he may well be called to answer by the Howse without infringing the libertie of the same.

Mr Speaker. Reciteth the severall mocions and bringeth the same to questions, and finalie it was agreed he should be here uppon Monday to answer to such matters as should be obiected.

Mr Newdigate. Moveth that for full resolucion of the opinion of the Howse concerning the Duke's execution, it might be put to question; which was donn soe and agreed unto, and passed without any negative voice. /

A bill read for avoiding of fraudulent conveiances, requiring that every assurance   f.23 made hereafter, the same should be knowledged before two iustices and the clarke of the peace, or else at London before a iudge and a clarke apointed. A note to be made in writing of the landes passed, the tyme and person, with a shorte note [of] incomborances, the clarke to make a note on the backe side of the deede, all the knowledges made in the countrie to be certefied within vj monthes to the chiefe officer in London. The fee of the iudge for the enrolement 3^s 4^d, of a iustice of peace xij^d and clarke xij^d, the search for every yeare $iiij^d$. If lande passe in diverse counties then the knowledge to be made before the iustices of assise. The chiefe officer to have the like authoritie for landes in cities and townes corporat. All assurances not thus entered to be void against the purchasor.

48. This is presumably a reference to Fisher's speech in 1529 (rather than 1533 as suggested here). Hall (*Chronicle*, 766) claims that Audley urged Henry to induce Fisher to moderate his attitude toward the Commons.

49. See *EP*, I.62, and references cited there.
50. MS reads 'Soppley'.
51. *Sic*.

A bill read that wherein [blank] Henrie viij[52] it was enacted that by the taking of a ij^d benefice the first should be void, that from thencforth no advantadge should be taken by the bishop or archbishope by lapse untill vj monthes after notice.

A bill by Mr Alford declaring that in *v Regine Elizabethe* he purchassed certaine landes in Aston Underich of William Porter who had made before a fraudulent conveiance to one Edmond Porter without any consideration, the landes convayed by bargaine and sale, the indentures knowledged but not enroled before the xij^th[month], and then meanes founde to get the same enroled as within vj monthes. Lodowicke Gryvill hath procured a conveiance to Thomas Walkin[53] his servante to his use without consideracion hereof. He desireth remedie. /

f.23v   A bill that in consideracion that one Giles Lambert hath devised to bring oyle for cloathes from xl^li the towne[54] to xx^li or under that he may for xxx yeares have of every broade cloath a peny and every cearsie a halfpenny.

xix° Maij.

A bill desiring libertie for the towne of Worcester to bring the water of Severne to Worcester, compounding with the owners of the grownde thorough which it should be brought for the same: first read.

A new bill brought in against fraudulent conveyances, that all assurances made to the intent to defraude any person shall be void against the ij^d bargaine, they that shall defend any such interest to leese a yeare's value of the lande: first read.

A bill that every iuror of Middlesex appearing for matters donne in other counties to have xvj^d for his charges: first read.

The bill of Shrewsburie for repeale of a former acte made *viij° Reginae Elizabethae*: the second tyme read; agreed to be engrossed.

The bill for explanation of a statute made *xxxij° Henrici viij^i* that the [act] might extend to all assurances by recoveries or other wise had from tenaunt for tearme of life, tenaunt in dower, or tenaunt by curtesie: the second tyme read and commytted.

The bill that patrones should not leese their[55] presentacions by lapse where the first benefice becomes void by taking of a ij^d, untill vj monthes after notice given: the 2 time read, agreed to be engroassed. /

f.24   The bill that the statute made *primo Reginae Elizabethae* concerning the prescise observation of the Booke of Common Praier should extend onlie to the saiers of papisticall or supersticious service, and that it should be lawfull by consent of the bishope to use such service as is authorised and set out in print to be used in the Duch and French Church: the second tyme read.

Mr Alforde. Zeale and science good when they meete together. He speaketh this for that he thinketh the preferrers of this bill had a zeale but noe science. He thinketh the matter longeth best to divines, and therefore would have the matter first treated of in the Convocacion howse. Greate strifes he knoweth hath beene aboute trifles, yet the things necessarie to be observed, for avoiding of scismes untill a farther generall order be taken, not to be lefte to the particuler order of every curat or bishope; neither we to follow the example of other realmes, having more learned men in England then any other dominion which he hath beene in.

Mr Snagge. Noe honest man would disable those he knoweth not. It hathe beene said we have noe authoritie to deale in matters of divinitie. If he considered the bill well, the substance of the service not dealt with, but affirmed in all pointes. It ought therefore to be remedied because the division aboute so smale matters is lamentable. It is malice that maketh many to troble honest preachers about such trifles. Some crie out they cannot pray because there is such babling in pulpites, onely becawse they mislike the doctrine. He thinketh every church in England in daunger by the statute. But nothing in this bill required unreasonable, nothing allowed / but that which shalbe alowed by the bishoppe and doth agree with the service used in the Duch and French Church, which is also in print and therfore wilfull ignorance not to knowe it.   f.24v

Mr Pistor. *Tempus rerum magistra.* It grieveth him to here any mislike so good a bill. If the speaker against the bill were a sheepe of the good shephard, he could not mislike that which is so referred to the bishopps. But he trusteth the speech of one cannot withdrawe the Howse. He hath noe doubt of the Queene's Majestie's or bishoppes' good enclinacion to the furtherance of this bill.

Agreed the same to be engrossed.

A bill from the Lordes to make it misprision of treason to counterfeit any coigne not currant in this realme: ones read.

The bill that the landes of bishopps under-collectors of the tenthes may be liable, as farr as the same will extend, to the payment of the Queene's Majestie of such summes as they shall gather: the second tyme read, agreed to be engrossed.

The bill that the defendant may have a *tales de circumstantibus* aswell as the pleyntiff: the second tyme read, agreed to be engroassed.

A bill that noe woode should be bestowed in coale or ther wise for making of iron within xx miles of London.

A bill that it should be lawfull for any English man or denizon, taking any kind of fish, to sell the same to any except the Quene's enimies.[56]

This bill, preferred by Suffolke men, an undoing to the towne of Yormouth, who by the King's patent have a speciall priviledge for herings. The maintenance of the haven in fewe yeares / hath stoode them in twelve thowsande poundes, which would   f.25 utterly [blank] if this bill passe. He hath heard many be made [blank] in this bill, but he trusteth the wisedom of the Howse is such as will indifferentlie consider of the same. The preferrers of the bill use none but smale boates, not fit for the navigation. Yormouth payeth 1^{li} fee ferme to the Queene by reason of this commoditie, they pay also 1^{li} feeferme for a roade where the fish is usually delivered.

A bill by William Chaterton to requier the disablement of Thomas Chaterton   An order from being of the Howse, aswell for that he is proclaimed a rebell for disobeiing of orders in the Chauncerie onelie for his safegard.

Mr Wilbraham. Declareth the order of their proceeding with the Lords concerning the Queene of Scotes. The last meeting the commytees of both Howses thought good to have the resolucion of the iudges concerning the factes, who did

52. I.e. 21 Hen.VIII, c.13 (1529), in *SR*, III.293.

53. I.e. Watkins.

54. I.e. 'ton/tun'?

55. MS reads 'these'.

56. Not mentioned in *CJ* (I.96).

agree to the facts sufficientlie proved by the Queen of Scotes to be treason in the highest degree in any person, straunger or other. The factes in her treason likewise; but for order of triall thereof, her estate considered, they thought the parliament most fit. He declareth hereuppon that two bills are drawne reciting the trueth of the factes, the one variing from the other only in the varietie of the punishment. The first extendeth that Mary Steward late Queene of Scots should be atainted of high treason, and to suffer as in cases of high treason, and to be also disabled from any claime to the crowne, and the alower of her title to be a traitor. The other extendeth but to the

f.25v   disablement, the affirmer / off any title in her to be a traitor, and if she hereafter shall clayme any title to be held *ipso facto* a traytor. Theise declared to the Queene's Majestie, she liked best of the last which she thought stoode best with her honner, not reiecting the first, but onelie staying the proceeding therein till a further proceeding, because it would aske long tyme, she to be called to the answere of the same, which could not now convenientlie be don, aswell by reason of perill in this tyme of the yeare; yt would also be chargeable to us as she said; besides, Memoransie[57] shortlie looked for. We that were commyttees thought not good to hazarde the Queene so longe.

Mr Norton. Noe perill to be respected of the Queene's Majestie's safety. Both billes will aske tyme. There is also perill in the person already condemned. Good to move the Queene for execution of him in the meane season.

Mr Snage. The last to ease a salve for so greate a sore. To the Duke he hath said asmuch as he can and can not so much as he would. The greater punishmentes he thinketh litle enough, since the lawe will beare it. For sickness he would wish us to referre it to God, who he trusteth will further soe good an attempt.

Mr Dalton. The ij[d] by noe meanes to be receaved. It will rather doe hurt then good. First, the perill thereby not avoided. Besides, to give so smale a punishment

f.26   were to affirme the offences to be / smale. It might rather seeme to affirme a title in her. Every common person, withdrawing but his homadge, shall leese his enheritance; she but for tearme of life. It should in effect establish a succession, which never to be graunted unto. He desireth at the least it to be left as *res integra*. Noe daunger to her but uppon new attemptes. The[58] *ipso facto* must have a triall, which asketh tyme, in which tyme what will she not attempt? Deliberacion therefore perillous in a matter of soe greate importance. Noe danger of sicknes can countervaile the danger of distruction depending aswell uppon our selves. Charges not to be considered nor weighed. And surelie for his parte he would follow the Queene uppon his knees to any place, rather then leave the thinge undone.

Mr Alforde. Desireth to be well thought of by the Howse. He hoped to have had a further tyme to have considered of it, and as the speech is suddaine, so if any thinge passe him rashly the same to be weighed as a suddaine speech. It hath alwayes beene his maner to credit more one wise man's opinion then of many others, and therefore he is moved to like best the Queene's opinion. Her opinion also likest to take effect. We, treating of the other, may delay tyme and so endanger her Majestie. Not convenient to passe to the condemnation of a queene without calling her to answere. He unfit person to deale in the iudgement of a queene. The iudges by deliberacion

f.26v   did determine we not to / proceede rashlie. He would have us consider the Queene's safetie with her honner. She remaineth a queene not withstanding her deposytion. The contrarie opinion not alowable in subiectes for feare of president. He confesseth he[59] hath done lewdlie and wickedlie and is sorie she wanted grace. A straunger not bounde to take notice of a statute *nisie per morum*, although of the common law. She, although have had continuance, hath beene emprisoned and so could not take notice. He sheweth that certaine embassadors, coming to Rome to demaunde the goodes of the Tarquines, the same was graunted and a tyme to carie the same away. The embassaders in the meane season conspired treason and thereuppon apprehended. Agreed they had passed their commyssion. They were iudged enimies and no farther proceedinge against them. Besides, the later bill followeth neerest the punishment of such a person. She a feodarye. No subiect hath withdrawen her homadge. Let her forfet her estate, not her life. Deprive her of name, title, dignitie and state, and so weigh of the offences as of an enimie, noe traitor. |

Mr Wilson. Wisheth Mr Alford had beene a commyttee in the cause, for that then he doubteth not he should have beene satisfied. The Queene he declareth made noe determinacion, onely shewed her inclination to mercy. He trusteth she will iudge well of us, and though she desireth to proceede more mildely, not seeing the danger she standeth in, which we weepe to see and therefore desire to proceede more safely, it is else to be feared many monthes will not pass before we feele it. Kings' cases must needes be rare, becawse there is but fewe kings. It is not meant to be denied but she shall be hearde by her counsell, and since the Queene's mercy is such as is admirable, we ought importunatly to cry for iustice, iustice. A king of another nation noe king in this realme, for that here no iurisdiction. The emperour cannot pardon here, though he were in Englande, any fact don in the realme. *Presull extra territorium privatie locum habet.* Robart of Cicylie seeking the inheritance of Henry the vij[th] Emperour was proclaimed traitor. The factes of the Queene of Scotes notorious, the iudges resolved she is a traitor. *Legibus non exemplis res probanda.* The lawe sayeth that dignity defendes not him which liveth unhonestly. *Mendacem legatum dignitas non tuetur.* The Duke of Melleynes executed embassadors sent from Florence for treason; and yet the embassador represented the person of a king. |

Mr Mounson. That the statute of *xxv° Edwardi iij^i* referreth doubtfull cases in treasons into the parliament.[60]

Finally agreed request to be made to have the first bill.

Mr Norton. That a present mocion may be made for execution in the meane season of the Duke, which he knoweth the Lordes like well of. This hath beene don in an acte of Parliament *xxxiij° Henrici viij^i*, in a queene's case, and executed during the Parliament.[61]

Mr Arthur Hall being brought to the barre, was charged with vij articles. First, that he should say, 'When the Scotish Queene's title is cut of where is then our assurance?' Secondlie, that the offence of the Duke was a privat offence to the Queene's Majestie and apertained not to us. Thirdlie, meaninge to move the Howse to forbeare execution, said the harme was not yet donne. Fourthlie, 'Yow will hasten

f.27

f.27v

57. I.e. Montmorency.
58. *Sic*: 'she'?
59. *Sic*: 'she'?

60. Cf. *SR*, I.320.
61. 33 Hen.VIII, c.21 (1541-2), in *SR*, III.857-60.

the execution of those whose feete yow would be glade hereafter to kisse'. Fiftlie, 'Mr Norton spake of the cutting downe of two bushes, meaning the Queene of Scots and the Duke. When they are gon where shall wee have ever a bushe to hide us?' Sixtlie, treating of their treasons, tearmed there practises, which peradventure would be preiudiciall to the Queene or realme. Seaventhlie, termed the execucion of the Duke riger extremytie of the lawe. Hereto answered he must confesse great folie in his

f.28 utterance. He desireth the Howse to / thinke that it amazeth him to be brought to answere in such an assemblie and that it takes away his harte. He beleeveth he hath here some enemies, but is a solamen[62] to him to thinke he hath many indifferent herers. He moved mercy because he knewe the Queene inclined to mercy. He desireth he may not be wounded, but that his submyssion may be accepted without particuler answere to the questions. He spake he knewe not what, the disturbance offered moved him to anger and he was *homo* and knewe not certainlie what he had said.

The Speaker demaunded whither he submytted himselfe generally to the Howse, to the which he answered 'Yea', and then was seperated for a tyme.

Mr Treasurer. Thinketh he lacketh discretion and therefore wise men may the rather beare with him. His father before him some what inclined to madness. By his owne confession appeareth to be subiect to passions. He would have him condemned for a rashe head and foole. But he liketh not his accussation of any as enemies, which he would have him unsay.

Mr Wilbraham. Would have him charged, not whither he spake the wordes but whither if he or any other had spoaken them, whither he thinketh [them] to be evill, rashelie and foolishelie spoaken. Which was donne accordingly and thereuppon renunciation also made and condemnacion also of his last wordes in terminge some of the Howse enemies. He was pardoned, receiving a good admonition to beware hereafter of such undutifull speeches, and to beware also he seemed not to iustefie himselfe by this favour shewed, least he might by that meanes double his faulte. /

f.28v   *xx^mo die* [*Maij*].

The bill of vagabondes from the Lordes, first read.

Segarston. The bill very parciall. London and other greate cities provided for. But no provision for Lirpoole and other smale boroughes. A greate enormitie that bishoppe and other lordes and gentlemen keepe so fewe servantes, which breedeth vagabondes. A gentleman's apparrell shall nowe be worth a 100 *lis* and but a boy to attende him. Besides bishopps and other priestes troble us with their childrine. And as for courteors they care not for us, nor we care not for them. He desired the Howse to beare with him; if they will not they may choose.

Mr Sampole. Moveth for the amendement of one fault as he thinketh. Roges generally appointed to prison without baile or mainprise, which he thinketh not reasonable, considering there is diversitie in roges. Smale fellons may be bailed, but so may not great. Another thing he noteth. The cariage of roges appointed to be donne by the townes where they be taken, at their owne costes and charges. This he doubteth will discorage the townes from taking of them. And therefore wisheth the charge to be generall and not particuler.

Mr St. John. Many roges increased by building of cottages uppon commons, having noe groundes belonging unto them. He would therefore from hencforth noe cotage to be builded unles it have three or foure ackers of grounde belonging unto it. /

Mr Norton. Where as libertie given to a man taxed at c^s in the subsidy booke, for avoiding of the first punishment of a roge, to take him into service, he would have the like libertie given unto any honest howse houlder. Mynstrolls by the bill appointed roges though they goe not aboute, 'which I would have reformed'. Besides, this statute saith also, 'and can yeeld a reckoning howe he laieth'; that 'and' should be an 'or', as he thinketh, for that the same alone were a sufficient cause to excuse a man from [being] deemed a roge.   f.29

Mr Treasurer. Wisheth that so good a bill be not hindered for smale scruples. And although the same provide not sufficientlie for all mischeifes, it is no cause to hinder the bill. Better to doe some good then by desiring to [do] all good to doe no good. The bill the rather to be liked, becawse the last parliament it went from us, and is nowe retourned to use by the Lordes. This ridiculous jesting he liketh not in the Howse, meaning by Segarston.

Mr Sergiant Loveles. Of all people vagabondes the worse. Impietie to give them any thinge. They have such devises to deceive men, and their clamors be so greate, as it moveth many to pitie them, and yet most of them none other but theeves. Sufficientlie proved by experience in Worstershier, by removing of whom it is fallen[63] out there by experience, that this last assises was no fellon to be executed, and yet is the shier verie populous. This / there brought aboute especiallie by the appointing one speciall person to search for them. He goeth to all faires and marketes, where if he finde any he carrieth them to the iusticers at his owne costes and charges, he seeth that they receive condigne punishment, and at his like costes and charges seeth them placed according to the statute, and findeth meanes that they be from tyme to tyme set on worke sometymes by one, sometymes by another. And for the [same] hath a competent living allowed him in the shier. And so concludeth that he wisheth the like provicion to be made in this estatute.   f.29v

Mr Sackford. The iustices alreadie have sufficient authoritie by their discrecion to doe this by force of this estatute. He would not have the statute presentlie hindred. It is to have continuance for seaven yeares, in which tyme experience will finde out all mischeifes, which then may be remedied.

Mr Slege. Every country knoweth best his owne estate. No one order can serve them. He wisheth like authoritie to be given to boroughe townes to those which be rulers of the same as is given to iustices of peace in the countrie. He would have those minstrels onely punished which wander abroade, not which keepe a continuall habitation.

The bill that a *tales de circumstantibus* might be paied and had by the defendant, the second tyme read, with an addicion that the like may be don uppon common reformacions. Agreed to be engrossed. /

The bill charging the landes of bishopps under-collectors, the third tyme read and passed the Howse.   f.30

---

62. *Sic*: 'solace'.   63. MS reads 'falles'.

The bill of Shrewsbury the third tyme read and passed the Howse.

The bill concerning rites and seremonies the third tyme read.

Mr Treasurer. Declareth that diverse mischeifes grewe by the straitness of the statute for uniformitie of common prayer made *primo Regine*. This bill offereth remedie of the same, but he wisheth reformacion of the preamble for that the same seemeth to much to derogat from the Booke, to the end it may have the better passag.

Mr Digs. The bill specially made for helpe of those which refuse the wearing of the apparrell apointed to the ministery, which he would have plainelie and not covertlie donn, neither allowed to every minister to use what service he list at his pleasure.

Mr Dalton. Liketh not the relacion to the Duch and French Church. The same a derogacion to the learned men of Englande. This libertie would cause diverse services and diverse sacramentes in Englande, which were a dissonancy. He wisheth the imperfections in the former Booke to be supplied. The best universall he liketh, but noe best particuler. The Duch Church may alter their service. /

f.30v   Mr Audley. Exceptions have beene taken by some to the preamble of the bill, by others to the bodie of the same. He thinketh both irreformable. Nothinge in the preamble but a trueth, neither any infamy to those which made the former acte to suffer some small matters according to the weakness of the tyme. The Apostells themselves in the begining made a lawe for strangled hoode, and whereof after they made reformacion. To that which hath beene [said] that the referring of the service to Duch Church were to the sclaunder of the learned of this realme, he shewed if it be true, as it is taken, yt were the greatest derogacion to the death of Christ which might be. But this bill onely referreth us to it as to a service printed and alowed, not to be followed becawse the Duch or French use it, but to one particuler for certainty. The bill, although not directly from the bishopps, yet hath beene considered by very grave learned men. Neither is it referred to the Duch Church service which may be used, but that which is used. Conformyty not alwayes necessary. The Jewes and Gentills did vary. It hath beene said the[64] matters trifles: the cheife matter of this bill, not for apparell but for a mischeife – that punishment of the good is so common for reading one chapter insteede of another. He thinketh the former law verie

f.31   unequall, to measure by one rod the obstinat despiser of the whole service / there established, and the observer of the whole in substance varying onely a litle in the accidentes. Thus the weake unlearned offended and the learned burdened. Every consistorie[65] can best oversee itselfe, and his charge not referred to every curat to alter. The uncertaintie troble the some. It is in the bishopps to reforme. Some thinke it will breede factions; we hope, being referred to the bishoppes, they will suffer none such to growe.

Mr Gates. That uniformytie never hitherto obtained, nor ever to be looked for in the Church. Not possible any one meate could like the taste of all us here present. *Nihill hac equalitate inequalius*. Men not in all places not alike affected. Some may brooke that by perfection which others cannot beare. The preacher can not performe the statute though he would. It is an occasion that withdraweth many from study of divinitie by reason if they enter into the minestery they indanger themselves. Deytie[66] more then their livings will answer. The misaying or misreading, adding or diminishing of one worde, within the compasse of the lawe. This causeth so many lewde persons to enter into the ministerie. Where noe woode is men are driven to burne strawe and sometymes dunge.

Mr Bamleye. Liketh well that the punishment be diverse. The iustice which would punish the papiste and the offender in small matters with one punishment, worthie to be removed. This parte of the bill he liketh. The second parte / tendeth to   f.31v innovacion of rites and ceremonies: he confesseth trifles in their owne natures, yet those trifles have lately bread greate devision. Was well liked for xx yeares under the profession of the gospell. He beleeveth those to be neerer Judaisme that striveth for a ceremony then those which yeld to yt. Rites to be altered by publike authoritie. Fewe ceremonies in the Apostells' tyme, and so may also fewe be suffered in the Duch or French Church because they were not under any monarchie; but after that Christianitie grewe to kin[g]domes, then ceremonies necessarie. He would have one uniforme order through the realme. Innovacion of rites by the common people taken for innovation of religion.

Mr Pister. He is sory to see how aswell the last parliament as this we are slowe to further religion. He ascribeth it to the sins of the tyme and punishment for our iniquitie. The feare of the Lord the beginning of wisedome. They feare the Lord which desire reformacion of such things as are against God. How farre are we from thence, soe farre from Gode's blessings. This is not *primum querere regnum Dei*. He feareth the rod which hath yet but shaken us will shortely destroy us for our iniquitie, and that we shall not prevaile in any good attempt. The bill prayeth onely that preachers by the consent of the ordinarye may alter that which the worde of God hath alreadie warraunted. They are bidden to feed his flocke, which must be according to the knowledge of the worde. He wisheth the bill to have furtherance, / and we to give life to the bishopps. It shall come to their consideracion. He doubteth   f.32 not that which we have well begun, they will give perfection.

Mr Speaker. Loath the bill should come to the question as it is. Ministers nowe trobled by every lewde man. He wisheth some reformacion that it may have the freer passage. And so the bill commytted.

xxj° Maij.

A bill by the Earle of Kente requiring to make voyd a release made by Sir George Gascoigne to the Lord Cumpton of the manner of Rayly and other landes whereof he was infeffed to the use of him. Enteyle contrary to trust and confidence reposed in him by his auncesters. Agreed that a copie thereof should be delivered to the Lord Cumpton and the counsell of both sides hearde by certaine counsellers apointed by the Howse commyttees in the cause, being of counsell with neither parte.

A newe bill brought in restraygning the statute of *anno primo Regine* concerning the Booke of Common Prayer to extend to any persons saying or hereing any other service then paposticall or more superstitious service then the service apointed by the said Booke. All other persons useing any other service lefte to the discretion of the

64. 'The' repeated in MS.   66. I.e. duty.
65. MS reads 'consistopie'.

ordinary to leave any parte thereof by consent of most of the bishoppes.

The bill restrayning employing of any woode to the making of iron within twentie miles of London, the ij^d tyme read. /

f.32v   Mr Browne. Noe such scarcitie of woode wherby any such restreynt should be allowed to the impeyring of any man's inheritance.

Mr Lewknor. There is woodes in Sussex within xx milles of London, as Grimsby, which is never brought to London, and therefore noe cause why that woode should not be employed aboute the mills.

Mr Heywars [Heyward]. Billets within theise xxx yeares worth but 4^s viij^d a thowsande, nowe at the best chepe tyme at x^s and sometimes hath beene at xxv^s. A loade of coales is in the same tyme rysen from 9^s to 20^s, 30^s and xl^s. Sometyme the want of woode hath driven the Citie to make provision in such places as they have beene driven to cary it xij miles by lande besides the cariadge by water.

Mr Cooper. The title of the bill seemeth onely to provide for preservacion of timber, but in the bodie thereof a restreynte to burne coppes woode. The Citie sufficiently provided for by a statute made *anno primo Regine*, in which statute were certeyne exception for certeine places, which he would have likewise provided for by this bill, and the bill made to hinder some privat persons.[67]

Mr Oure.[68] That it is true it toucheth Mr Gage, who latelie made an yron mill which within fewe yeares wilbe occasion of great scarcitie of woode aboute London, which is a hinderance to the holle common wealth. Wheresoever they come, lewsters[69] driven away, as is alreadie by experience in London, who are very

f.33   necessary for the common weale, as making trees of saddles for horsemen. / Alreadie not one lefte in London.

Mr Norton. The bill toucheth us all aswell as the Citye of London, which provideth not onely for it selfe but for the Queene also and for all them which travell to the same, being noe small number. It is reason all privat devises give place to generall commodities. The raising of the price thereof will make all other things rise for company. It hath beene said it is no helpe for preservacion of timber, but experience shall shewe that if coppes woode be consumed the tymber trees must needes be cutt downe for provision of fuell for the Citie. If it touch but one, he not to be preferred before the holle Citie; and nowe best tyme to provide remedie. If we tary till xij mills be made, there wilbe mor cryers out and harder passadge. But it is noe newe thinge that newe inconveniences should have newe remedies.

Sir Henry Sidney. Other occasions of the dearth of woode, besides iron mills. Iron worthie to be much made of, as wee stande with other nations. He would wish them to be called to it, whom it doth concerne.

Agreed the bill to be engrossed.

Mr Ireland. Moveth that forasmuch as papistrie was the efficient cawse of this rebellion and occasion of the prince's peryll, none of this conspiracie but either by[70] papistes, atheistes, or apostates; and therefore wisheth a statute made by King Henry the viijth concluding all papistes under the degree of traytors, to be renewed.[71] That, he doubteth not, would keepe them under. /

f.33v   The bill of the *tales* to be had by defendants in actions and informacions, the iij^d tyme read and passed the Howse.

The bill newelie corrected for explanacion of the statute of *xxj°* of *Henrici viij*[i] that the making voyd of a former benefice by taking of a ij[d] shalbe understoode as voyd as in case of resignacion and not otherwise, twise reade.

The bill from the Lordes making it misprision of treason to counterfet monye not currant in this realme, the seconde tyme read.

Three bills sent up to the Lordes, one of the *tales* to be had by the defendant, the seconde for the charging of the landes[72] of bishoppes' under‑collectors of tenthes, the thirde touching the towne of Shrewsbury.

Mr Norton. Moveth that sythence tyme is to be used in triall of the Queene of Scotes, and that it is determined she shall come to her triall, it will occasion her to attempt what she may, for desperat necessitie dareth the uttermost mischiefe that can be devised; therefore necessary the Duke be executed in the meane season, which wilbe halfe an execution of the Queene of Scotes. Besides, it will give us some hope of execution of this statute wee are now in hande with. Good the Lordes to be made party to our opinion and conferred with whither they be of the same opinion, which if they be, meanes to be made that this opinion may be declared to her Majestie. This agreed to be don by the commyttees accordingly. /

A bill that it might be lawfull to the inhabitantes of Woodestocke to buye and   f.34
sell wolles and convert the same to clothes.

A bill requiring confirmacion of a corporacion and an hospitall at Ledbury, graunted to certeyne persons by the Queene's letters patentes.

Mr Sackeforde. Declareth how lothe the Queene's Majestie was to graunte the same and that she hath no meaninge to hinder any men's right. The lande he understandeth is in controversie; and therefore good to consider what confirmacion is made. They promised at the graunte thereof that if any bodie did strive for the same, they would noe farther deale.

A bill read requiring that if any man did kill any other man's conies in the night or did hunte with visard to have three monthes imprisonment and to be bounde to the good abearing for a yeare, and if any such hunter be killed by any letting the same, they to incurre noe daunger, it being donne in their owne defence; if the wariner to be confederat with any such, he to have a yeare's emprisonment.

xxij° Maij.

A bill by Robert Wykes against Richard and Walter Dennis complayning that he bought certeine landes of them, payed for the same 1800[li] and entred in bande for payment of more; and that the said Dennis sued him for the money and will make noe assurance of the lande; and that by occasion / hereof [by] a degree[73] passed with   f.34v
him in the Chauncherie he had a commyssion to certeyne knightes to put him in possession of the lande, who were resisted; and that he was after put in possession by

67. 1 Eliz., c.15 (1558‑9), in *SR*, IV.377.
68. *Sic*; 'Cure'? (and see f.35).
69. *Sic*.
70. *Sic*.
71. The reference is probably to 28 Hen. VIII, c.10 (1536), which provided death for

treason on *first* refusal of the oath denouncing the Pope's authority: *SR*, III.663‑6.
72. MS reads 'lordes'.
73. *Sic*.

a sergiant at armes, who with diverse others were endicted uppon a forcible entry, and so Denis got the possession agayne by a writ of restitution, and so having noe remedie by lawe prayeth the lande may be assured to him by Parliament, according to the decree untill he be satisfied of his money.

A bill for assurance of certeyne landes according to the will of Sir Thomas Woodehowse to the which the Lord Keeper, my Lady Woodehowse and Mr Henry Woodehowse are all parties and did consent. Ons read.[74]

A bill requiring that noe musketes, daggs or calivers should be brought from beyonde the seas by way of merchaundize; all made within the realme to be marked with the armorers' marke; none to make any but such as are alowed by certeyne of the science.

Mr Treasurer. The most pieces which come from beyonde the seas are falsely made. He liketh well the same should be marked by the armorers, but he misliketh that all others should be restrayned to make the same, except such as should be by them alowed, for that then they will allowe very fewe and that for money; and so it tendeth to a monopoly. /

f.35   Mr Owre. To the same effect, and that by this meanes none should be made out of London, which were not reasonable since there is as good made in diverse other places.

Sir Nicholas Arnolde. Good to be considered who doe make the same in Englande, whither English men or strangers. Good also to see howe they are able to serve us: promyses very seldome performed. If they be not able to make enough, the prince in tyme of neede shall wante. Besides, he doubteth it will raise the prices and then men will be loath to buy, and forraigne countries, finding want of utterance with us, will seeke newe trades and restraine sale here for ever.

And so the bill commytted.

The bill of vagabondes the seconde tyme reade.

Mr Speaker. Declareth that the Queene's Majestie's pleasure is that before wee preferre any bills of religion to the Howse, conference be had with the bishopps and that her pleasure is to see the bills which be already preferred.

Mr Selinger. Moveth that those which are to deliver the same to the Queene's Majestie may require that there bee noe skanning of wordes, but the meaning of the bill to be onely considered.

A bill that noe lease be made hereafter of any cotadge without iij acres of severall grounde or vj acres in the common fieldes.[75] /

f.35v *Ordo*   An order agreed uppon that in all privat cawses indifferent commyttees be apointed first to examine the state of the cause, by informacion of both partes; and after, both the parties and their counsell heard openly in the Howse.

The bill ageinst fradulent conveyances the iij^d tyme reade; agreed to be engroassed.[76]

p.p.[77]   The bill making it misprison of treason to counterfet any coigne not currant in this realme, the third tyme read and passed the Howse.

2.   The bill of the freeholders of Middlesexe to have xvj^d apeece for their apparance in every action layed in their sheere and not being there, the seconde tyme read.

Mr Gente. A bill rather to be made forbidding any action to be served but where the fact was commytted, and then Middlesex shall have noe cause to complayne. The alowing them this money may cawse favor of the iurors and under pretence hereof they may receave a greate deale more.

Mr Popham. The troble to that county but by two occasions: by forraigne actions and forraigne pleas. Both may be holpen if noe forraigne plea be receaved without oath.

Mr Snage. The receapt of the money in no wise dangerouse, for that the same is not payable untill after triall. /

Mr Newdigate. This bill will not helpe the shier. They never likely lye lesse then a   f.36 night at charge, and therefore have alwayes their charges alowed by them on whose side the verdect goeth, which is more then xvij^d.[78]

Mr Wrothe. The xvj^d due when they doe appear and the jury taketh not.

And so the bill commytted.

xxiij° Maij.

The bill for Worster.

This day I was away from the reading of some bills.

Mr Controlar. Declareth how the Queene's Majestie hath shewed that she thought that never prince was more bounde to subiectes then her selfe. It had beene declared unto her Majestie that of the two bills purposed to be offered to the Howse, as well the Lords as wee had agreed in one minde, which was to deale with that bill which tended to the punishment of the Queene of Scotes in the highest degree, whereto her Majestie would not presently condiscend, partlie for honor, partlie for conscience, for her cawses to her selfe knowne; wishing therefore for the present to deale with the latter, not meaning to reiect the first, but in tyme convenient to deale also therewith.

Mr Ireland. As wee all are most bounden to her Majestie to thinke so well of us, so can we not but iustly lament she hath so small regarde unto her selfe. Our state therefore most miserable. Greate questions stir abroad, and great execution of newes. King / Philipe of Macedony being in hande with greate matters which were   f.36v slowly followed, Demostenes therefore being demaunded what newes *etc.*, said, 'Masters, ye goe up and downe to knowe newes; what greater newes can yow have then a barbarous nation shall subdue your common wealth?' The like he looketh for in England. Wee shall become subiectes to a trayterous generation. We have no Alexander to[79] revenge us. Hee meaneth not to provide for himselfe in Mary Stewarde's courte. 'Yow that be of her Majestie's Privy Counsell, thinke yt your dueties to incite and stirre her Majestie in this behalfe, else yow doe not the duties of good subiectes'. He for his parte had as lieve be hanged in resisting the Queene of Scotes as hunt after.

Mr Norton. Looketh to have parte of the payment and therefore will be bold to shewe his opinion. The cause hath beene well debated in the House, a good

74. *CJ* has second reading, first reading on 20 May (*CJ*, I.96).
75. Cf. f.28v and *CJ*, I.97.
76. *CJ*, I.97: second reading, and see f.46v

and *CJ*, I.99, for engrossment.
77. I.e. passed.
78. *Sic*: 'xvi^d'?
79. MS reads 'no'.

proceeding purposed, and nowe an obstacle offered. He is nowe persuaded the first is the worste, not for that it is so in his[80] owne nature, but for that he seeth no likelihoode of execution. They are both nowe dangerous. He seeth nowe no remedie but to make humble suite for execution of the Duke, soe though the will of the Queene of Scotes be verie greate we shall abate her power. Those that labor to save the Duke doe yt surely with intente to be themselves saved by the Duke in whom they have expectacion. No cause to let us proceede herein, for though heretofore we did agree the resolucion of the House should come to the Queene's Majestie by way of opinion that was *pro re et tempore.* Nowe that course is offered, execution of /

f.37　necessitie is to be required during the session. No hope to be had of him. Hee hath lately receaved communion with protestations of his faith, and yet most fained. And therefore wee to urge this importunately, either ioyntly with the Lordes or by our Speaker without them; else the parliament may seeme to be called to the end we should reveale our selves to be hanged hereafter.

Mr Hussey. This cause very weightie now called in question. Two queenes, the one our soveraigne lady Elizabeth, the other a Scot, an enemie to England, a[n] adulterous woman, a homicide, a traitor to the Queene, a subvertor of the state, an underminer of titles. The parliament called nowe by great advise. The sodainess thereof, the tyme of the yeare doth declare [it]; the Queene's Majestie her selfe by the mouth of my Lord Keeper hath pronounced it and the same to be called for very necessary consideracions, he trusteth not meant that it should passe without doyng of any thing. He hath hytherto forborne to speake, expecting [a] bill whereof to treate. He is now urged to speak and to yeld to the greatest reasons, which is that of the last: no good can follow. He would have the Queene's Majestie take example by the contention between Yorke and Lancaster, betweene two kings as this is betweene two queenes. Yorke made his claime in Parliament was established heire apparant.[81] He would not tary then for the crowne. Such wilbe the sequell of the

f.37v　Queene of Scotes. / This disabling shalbe an enabling, and that will shee put in practise ere it be long. Greate have beene the victories which the Queene's Majestie hath had in spite of the Pope. He would have her aswell to use victorie as to get victory, else the gotten victorie in vaine. Let the Queene therefore, while she hath such an enemie in hand, execute her, least heereafter herselfe come to be executed by her.

Mr Snag. No man more sorie to heere such a resolucion then hee. Hee trusteth hee may in dutie of his zeale to the Queene's Majestie compare with any man without arr[o]guncy. If her Majestie should command him to doe any thing which may tende to her safety he would doe it with adventure of his life. If her Majestie's pleasure were to commaunde to doe nothing he would lay his handes under her feete. But to deale with this second bill were not to doe nothing but to doe starke nought. Hee hath concerning her title hearde the wisest in this lande conferr with great diligence who could make nothing of her title. He noted well upon the messadge delivered, it was said that that which hath beene declared was her Majestie's dispossition, not her determinacion. Soe hee knoweth no cause but wee may proceed in the first. The first bill he shall not neede to perswade, since it was so learned don and so generally receaved without any no. He called hyther for two causes: one as a counceller to consider causes of the common wealth, for that unfit; secondly as a petitioner, which he may take upon him. Henry the iiij^th thought himselfe never in safety / while Richard the Second had his head upon his shoulders. If the enemie live and be able, the controversie wilbe desided by the sworde. Henry the vij^th being banished founde more ayde by his secrete freindes in England then by the power he brought with him. Archiophel's folly will be embraced: they will say rise with the yong king. No determynation of Parliament can restrayne the ambicious mynd. Hee is not willing to hinder the present state or empaier any person's title. This a greate coradge to traytors to attempt any thing in hope to obtaine. If they faille, yet she is a mercifull Queene, she will not execute us. A most dangerouse state when traytors live more surely then true men. He wisheth wee may proceede to incyte her Majestie. He is in hope she may chaunge her opinion. An auncient learned father of the Church hath donn so before her. St Augustine sometimes held that it was not lawfull to execute any man for his conscience: when he sawe heresies swarme, he chaunged his opinion. This except she doe, he looketh for the shorte distruction of the state. It is a sore to the minde, no wound to the bodie, that is to be cured. This sore hath two heads, the one in the arme hole, the other at the heart: he meaneth the one in the north, the other in London. The sores eyther to be cut out or the holle body to be lost. From hencforwardes we shall not be troubled with agues, to have a good and a bad day, but it resteth every day to expect our / ffinall destruction. He trusteth we were not called hyther for nought. In vayne to make a law alreadie made. The statute made the last parliament will that if any person *etc*. He doubteth not she is a person. He would she were none, upon condition that we might treate all this parliament of nought. The Duke of Alva by her meanes since the last parliament should [have] entered this realme: the cause wherefore, apparant. Some condemned as traytors for the same, and so claymed the crowne and therefore lost her title alreadie. If ye will allow it for no claime before she get the crowne, surely he will not resiste her but he will put his head betweene the Queene's Majestie's necke and the hatchet, for that wilbe the end of us both. The bill which is nowe desired to be dealt with purposeth as he remembreth that she should be thought unworthie of the succession of the crowne. Surely this might bee determined of the best king christened, being not heire to the same. 'Surely I thinke neyther the King of Fraunce, Spaine, or Emperor worthye of the crowne of Englande, for I thinke none worthie but the heire. Shall wee say or doe no more to a traytor? This were very iniurious. *Remota causa removetur affectus*'. He will never by implication affirme any bodie's title to the iniurie of a true title. Non but cirenes wilbe against the Queene's safety. It is come to a common voyce the Duke a true man, a greate freind to the common weale, sought to be destroyed by some of the nobility who have uniustely / condemned him; her Majestie will not for halfe her revenue execute him. He prayeth to God there be not those in London which if they durst would pluck him out of the Tower, and the like in the north which would set her at libertie. He can say noe more, but he looketh shortely for it if better remedie bee not provided.

f.38

f.38v

f.39

80. *Sic.*
81. See B. Wilkinson, *Constitutional History of*

England in the Fifteenth Century (1964), 138-9.

Mr Newdigate. The reporth[82] hath apawled him. He looketh nowe for no good. He that iudgeth well of either the Queene of Scotes or the Duke must needes be a traytor to the Queene. He sorroweth to see so small care in the Queene's Majestie of her selfe. He feareth she depend to much upon God's providence, refusing the meanes now miraculously by God offered unto her. Mary Steward by nature a Scote, enemies to England by nature. William Conqueror when he first invaded England made a surmized title to the crowne. Herolen[83] consented he should have the crowne after Edward the Confessor, but after he had atcheived the same, he then claymed it as a conquest. What followed? He deposed all the English nobilitie, placed Normans, changeth counsellers, magisterates and all kind of governers, disheriteth every man, altereth the holle state, and finally the realme brought to such miserie that it was counted detestable to be counted an English man. He looketh for no ther in[84] but to follow this paterne. Though she pretend a title for the present, yf she may prevaile / shee will clayme by conquest and then all our landes be lost, all our goodes forfet. This most gainefull to her and fittest for her honnor. Therefore now not onely to be deposed, but her head cut off whilst shee is in our handes, that wee may seeme to embrace so great a benefit offered us. Since the Queene in respect of her owne safety is not to bee induced hereunto, let us make petition shee will doe it in respect of our safety. 'I have hearde shee delighteth to bee called our mother. Let us desire her to be pitifull over us her childrene who have not deserved death'. The act of Parliament will doe no good. If shee attayne the possession, every king calleth newe parliamentes and frustrat the old.

f.39v

Mr Pole Wentworth. Wisheth it may be put to the question of the Howse whither wee should call for an axe or an acte.

Mr Atkins. The greate silience now in the Howse giveth him courage to speake, though happely it were more safe to be silent. Since his cominge to this parliament he hath beene to his ability a greate observer of the speaches uttered in this cause nowe in question. He hath weighed aswell the resolucions as the reasons of the same. He hath harkened how the same could be answered, and hitherto hath heard nothing[85] concerning any the reasons alledged in confirmacion of that opinion which hath passed this Howse without any nay. He is therefore put in hope it may be atc[h]ieved. The determination carieth with it all equiety. In every petition theise consideracions to be had: what it is that is desired, who desireth the same, the convenientness of the desire desired, and the end wherefore it is desired. To the first, nothing is desired but that which is lawfull and iust. The cause with greate consideracion hath beene considered by the common lawyers, the civillians, and divines. They all uppon matture deliberacion have agreed / that by every of the said lawes it is both iust and convenient, and greate reasons and notable examples shewed for the same; proved also that it may be by the law of nature and by the lawe of nations. To her Majestie it shalbe honnorable to suppress Gode's enemies, and to save her owne people surely farr more honnorable then ever was conquest. The Queene of Scotes the burthen of the earth. If Hanniball had taken his tyme after he had subdued Canubis, it had not beene said unto him '*Vincere ter bene scis, uti victoria nescis*'. The French men haveing gotten the capitoll entered into conference. Camollus stept up and overthrewe all their purposes. Tyme surely very precious and

f.40

to bee taken when it is offered. Scipio said well, '*Incogitantis est oblatum occassionem* [blank] *negligere*.' He said farther, '*Deiecti animi spernere spes securitatis talis consideratio offert extremum exitium*'.[86] No man can deny but it is most perillous to expect tyme except they thinke it perillous to take away the Queene's enemie in tyme. No enemie to all Christendome more to be feared then the Pope. The beheading of her will shake the type of his crowne and wilbe a terror to all other the papistes in Christendome. No forraigne prince to be feared, she being deiected. He hopeth the papistes wilbe against any offering to come in as a conqueror, for that then their landes and goodes are to be lost. It is one that pretendeth title only [is able] to undoe us and like to finde ayde. Nowe to the persons: he wisheth that her Majestie with her motherly pitie had beheld the fatherly eyes which he yesterday sawe shed salte teares for her Majestie upon reporte of this / messadge. We cannot but love her, haveing receaved such benefites by her. We are a company called together by her Majestie to consider how shee might bee preserved. Wee have with greate care considered and determyned that: let us proceede to offer it. 'I trust shee will receave it. I will not enter to declaracion what a subiect may iustly crave of his prince. Shee must trust to us protestantes if ought be offered her: the papestes sure will not protect her'. For the third pointe: it is not now disputable. Since it is determined it remayneth onely therefore to consider the end what will ensue. But he must not tary so long to tell yt. The Queene's Majestie shall by this meanes establish pure religion, be a terror to all her enemies, a fortresse to Christianity. The Queene of Scotes the whole hope of that called holly, but indeede unholy league of Trent. Her head being cutt of, their hope frustrate. He concludeth therefore wee should proceede without despaire to be let by no prohibition, cry out incessantly '*sepe Deus cessat sed tandem surgit et audit*'. 'Let us with perseverance proceede, especially yow that be counsellers. Shewe yourselves nowe to be true counsellers and farther so necessary a motion'.

f.40v

Mr Controler. Sheweth that he is sorry it was his chaunce to be the bringer of so uncomfortable a messadge. He would be glade if he could take away the cause of dispaier. He wisheth the order purposed might be proceeded in to gather the reasons of our refusall into writing. The same he hopeth will move her Majestie.

Mr Treasurer. Sithence he perceaveth all our purposes remaine firm and no alteracion; and sithence the Queene's disposition hath beene declared and not liked to be followed, it should be vaine now to use any longer speeches and so to let other thinges in proceeding. The order therefore of proceeding in this cause only to be considered. It resteth therefore to be considered / whyther the House thinke best of themselves to make petition by the mouth of their Speaker to her Majestie, or to move the Lordes to ioyne with us in our motions aswell touching the Queene of Scotes as the Duke. He liketh best to move the Lordes to ioyne with us: the request shalbe more effectuall. And surely to the Duke, hee would wish him deade though he were his brother. He is alyed unto him and neere of kin to his children. He hath knowne many living wickedly, dye godly. If he live, many practizes may be attempted to his

f.41

---

82. *Sic.*
83. *Sic.*
84. *Sic*: 'for nothing'?
85. MS has 'in' after 'nothing'.

86. *Sic*: there is a lengthy blank in the first 'quotation', and something is obviously wrong with the second.

perill, which perhappes may move him to desperacion. The Queene resolved that at least she would never advaunce him, so no good eyther worldly or heavenly to be looked for. He hath long agoe told more to the Duke in this matter then hee will tell us; but this amongst other things hee told him, that if hee atempted this mariadge that the realme must eyther destroy him or he destroy us. The reasons of our resolucions he wisheth to be made in readinesse that the same may bee presented.

Mr Speaker. 'Yow have heard the effect of the Queene's messadge, yow have heard diverse very learnedly shewe cause why her disposition in the same is misliked. I have heard none shewe any liking thereof, so as by silence they have all confirmed that which hath beene said by others. It remaineth yow grow to resolucion for the order of your proceeding. Yow knowe it must finally proceede from the prince'. Good he thinketh to knowe of the Lordes whyther they remayne in opinion as before and will ioyne in this motion, and so orderly to proceede in our doyngs that all that is said be not lost; which was agreed unto and the commyttees sent up to the Lordes for that purpose.

A bill read that landes given to any place reputed[87] or taken for a chauntery might be deemed in King Edward the vj[th] by force of the statute then made thereof. /

f.41v   Mr Boyer. This bill offered to the preiudice of the Deane of Paule's, and prayeth his counsell may be hearde.

Mr Snage. He thinketh the bill offered not to touch any man particulerly, for that it were more tollerable being hurtfull but to one; but the statute is generall, and as it is generally made so he generally misliketh of the same. At such tyme as the statute was made landes were superstitiously used. It was never meant to give the king any other landes then those which were so used. This word, 'accepted reputed or taken', very perillous to many men's states he knoweth, dover[88] reputed so, that were given to good uses, and greate pity to take the same away. And so the bill reiected.

2.   The bill of the landes graunted to Thomas Golding and Walter Selye for ratificacion of the patent where the name of the manor of which the landes should bee held was omytted, the seconde tyme read, agreed to be engrossed.

A bill requireing more yeares for the ininge of Plomsted marsh with leike conditions as in the former act therof made.[89]

The bill that weightes and measures of corne, beere, ale and wyne to be one thorough England and concerning the clarke of the market, the second tyme read.

Mr Greenefield moveth for a proviso for the universities who have a clarke of the market of their owne.

Mr Snage. That the same be not made to hinder any man's charter or liberties.

Mr [Blank]. The clarke of the market not to deal but for defaute of other men doing their duties.

Mr Recorder. Good to save all men's rightes where the Queene's progenitors have by their charters graunted liberties.

Sir Owen Hopton. Moveth that certaine corne is given yearly to certaine poore men that they may receave by the greatest bushels heretofore used. /

f.42   Mr Treasurer. Touching the bills required yesterday by the Queene's Majestie, sheweth that her Majestie did very much mislike the first and the bringer in thereof and did also mislike in us that wee did accept the same. He sheweth [he] did the messadg apointed by the House, which was, if any thinge were contayned therein to be misliked, not to attribute the same to the Howse who had made reformacion thereof; if any thing were in the other to thinke it to be of zeale to reforme the mischiefes and inconveniences growne to her good subiectes for diverse small causes, and not of malice. 'I shewed the order dayly broken aswell in her owne chappell as in her closset. Her Majestie hereuppon gave very good wordes of the good opinion shee had of the Howse, and will take the good protestantes to her protection and is desirous to knowe if it be true that such inditementes have beene preferred against any, yea or no, as is declared in the preamble of the bill'.

Mr Wilson. Declareth that he was commaunded to enquire the truth of the same and to bring word to her Majestie of the names of them which were so indited, who preferred the inditement and what iudges or iustices did receave the same; and this done it shalbe seene that since it appeareth to be don of malice it shalbe knowne to the world that, as shee is tearmed the deffender of the faith, so she wilbe founde the protector of true protestantes. Hee is doubtfull to utter some other speech passed. Shee said farther shee heard it had beene given abroad that shee could or would do nothing; but it should appeare ere long that shee both is able and will punish offendors according to our desires. 'It pleased her to demaunde of me what matters were now in the Howse. I desired pardon, for that the same were matters of / secrecy. Shee was important.[90] I declared how uppon declaracion of her messadge yesterday I sawe greate mourning and lamenting, yea to the shedding of teares, that her Majestie would leave so notorious treasons and conspiracies unpunished. Shee confessed the offence was haynous: so she thought the disablment would be a greate punishment to her. I replyed, if farther proceeding were not, noe safety could follow, the protestant in greate daunger. Finally shee concluded shee had but advised, not debarred us to use any other way; and for the protestantes, they should finde that, as shee hath founde them true, so will she be their defence.'

A bill read desiring to frustrat a forged lease claymed [by] Andrewe Fisher in certayne landes wherof Sir Andrewe Judde did infeffe Henry Fisher, his father, to the use of an hospitall in Tunbridge. Agreed to be commytted and the said Andrewe Fisher called to answere the same.

The bill that leases made by corporacions should be good although the true names of the corporations were omytted.

[xx]iiij° Maij.

The bill concerning the assurance between Mr Woodhouse and my Lady Woodhowse, the third tyme read and passed.

A bill that after triall or confession in any action the iudgement shall not be stayed or reversed but for errors in the verdict or iudgement; if any demurror be, noe advantage shalbe taken but causes assigned. /

A bill that no fine or recovery shalbe reversed for any imperfection except the writ of eror be sued within one yeare after the desolucion of this parliament of those

f.42v

p.

f.43

---

87. MS reads 'repaired'?
88. *Sic*: 'never'?

89. Private Act of 1566 noted in *SR*, IV.484.
90. *Sic*: 'importunate'?

already knowledged, and for others within a yeare after the knowledge.

A bill for avoyding delayes of vouchers: none allowed without shewing the cause and alledging the lien the plantife received to pleade; the same state to be made by covin.

A bill against taxations made by the City of London uppon others inhabiting out of the city, and likewise for strangers, denizens taxed where they dwell and not where they worke.

Mr Recorder. This bill sclanderous to the City. If they doe so, it is extortion and worthy to be punished. And so the bill commytted.

p.p.   Three bills from the Lordes, of which one passed before from us, *vz.*, the *tales* for the defendant.

The second against conspirers to enlarg any prisoner.

The third against detainers of any forte with force against the Queene.

Certaine additions being read to the bill of vagabondes, in one parte was required to exemte the iustices of peace from any forfeiture.

Mr Treasurer. Liketh better the iustices remayne subiect to punishment, for that else the evill iustice will not doe it. Besides, it shalbe a good excuse for a good iustice why [he] should shew no favor, for that he should thereby incurre a payne, which otherwise of pity many tymes by intercession would leave iustice undonne. /

f.43v   Mr Sampole. The execution of lawe the life of the lawe. Leave out the punishment, and the negligence will take away the severytie of others. Noe new thing to impose punishment uppon them. By the statute of forcible entry they may forfeit a 100^{li}, likewise for not certefieing of recognizances, with others.[91]

Mr Ireland. The office an office of charge and no commodity, and therefore no reason to impose such punishment. He would have, leese his office if he doe not his duty.

p.   The bill expounding how the statute of *xxj° Henrici viij^i* should be expounded, the being void but in kind of resignation. The third [time] read and passed the Howse.

p.   The bill concerning Thomas Golding's patent the third [time] read and passed.

The bill against converting wood to the making of iron within xx miles of London the third [time] read and passed.

Mr Wilson. Sheweth that he and the rest have examined Mr Grivell's case and finde fraude in his dealing. The said Mr Gryvell refused to answere, alledging that he had not brought his counsell, for that he was promysed to be heard openly in the Howse, which he requireth.

Mr Dalton. Thinketh him not worthy to be heard because of his contumacy. It may be an evill president for the Queene of Scotes.

Ordo   Mr Recorder. That Mr Alforde now not to be a iudge in his owne cause, but to be removed for the tyme, which was don accordingly.[92]

Mr Treasurer. The whole Howse not to be troubled with examination of the old[93] cause; the commyttees in that behalfe to be trusted. It was agreed he should ones againe be warned to answere to the commyttees, and after to be heard in the Howse. /

f.44   Certaine of the Howse were sent to the Lordes for answere of their determinacion concerning the Queene of Scotes and the Duke. To the first they answered they were contented to ioyne with us in petition to the Queene's Majestie, *vz.*, for the furtherance of the first bill against the Queene of Scotes. For the second, concerning the Duke, there was reason why they should not ioyne, for that a greate parte of them had beene triers of him, and therefore not convenient to require execution of that which themselves had adiudged; besides, their opinion in that matter sufficiently declared by their verdict given. Notwithstanding, had no mislikeing but we might proceede in the same by our selves.

After, the Lordes sent to us to meete for the same purpose, requiring certaine commyttees to be sent, sufficiently authorised to treate of the cause, with power to selecte certaine of themselves to atende the Queene's Majestie when they might have oportunitie; which was agreed unto.

Mr Wentworth. It remayneth yet to be considered for our petition to the Queene for execution of the Duke. It was determined the petition should be made by Mr Speaker. He to thinke of the matter betwene this and Wednesday, and every man that list in the meane season to bring such allegations as they thinke necessary to the Speaker, the same to be considered uppon Wednesday, and then to determine farther of our proceeding. In the meane season to adiorne the courte.

xxviij° Maij.

A burgesse of Southwarke desireth priviledg for a servant of his arested by a constable by the warrant of a iustice of peace at Camerwell. Agreed a wryt of priviledg should be made, and that aswell the iustice of peace / as constable should be sent for to be examined. And there Ferris' case alleadged: set at liberty uppon an execution, and both the sheriffe of London and serieant committed to the Tower.

A bill that the transporters of lether over the sea should forfeit the lether caried or the value thereof and to be set uppon the pillory for the first offence, and for the second offence to suffer as in case of fellony.

A bill that the inha[bi]tantes of Cogeshall and Bocking[94] should only use the signe of the cocke in their broad clothes called 'handewarpe cloathes' uppon [pain] of loss of the same.

The bill that the statute of *xxxij° Henrici viij* might be expounded aswell to extend to estates mad or suffered by the feffees or diseases[95] of tenaunt for life by curtesye or in dower to defeating of remainders or revertions as to states made by themselves to such intente. The bill commytted.

Mr Treasurer. Sheweth that they have receaved for answere from the Queene's Majestie concerning the mocion of the Howse for proceeding according to the first bill, that she taketh in very acceptable harte our carefullnesse for her safety and that she did confesse that it were more safe for her to follow the same; notwithstanding, weighing her estate in other respectes, the tyme present and other circumstances, she is purposed to deffere the doying thereof untill some other tyme. For the present is

Priviledg

f.44v

---

91. Cf.8 Hen.VI, c.9 (1429), in *SR*, II.244-6.
92. See Doc.5 for Alford.
93. *Sic*: 'whole'?
94. MS reads 'Godeshall' and 'Borking'.
95. MS unclear: could read 'difeases', i.e. 'defeasances'?

resolved we proceed in another cause[96] according to the meaning of the second bill, which she liketh best to bee drawne by her learned councell and to be so penned as neyther any title may seeme to be implicatively to have beene or not to have beene in her or to be in any other person; and in the same bill also provision to be made for the safety of such as have agreed so earnestly against her title; wishing us, although we have not for the present so much as we desire, to be content / with that wee may have and to forbeare farther treatie therof untill the bill come.

f.45

Mr Snage. That he submitteth himselfe to her Majestie's pleasure, glade that her Majestie would be content to proceed in the same if tyme would serve. It resteth notwithstanding to provide something for her safety. And since the calling us together at this tyme hath admonished us that in this tyme it is to be donne, he would we did seeme[97] good and therefore necessary in the meane season to cut of the heades of other her enemies which are already condemned by lawe and for whom no such excuse can be made, since now it is to be looked for that they will hasten their mischiefes, for otherwise they are to despaire, and desperation will dare any thinge. Experience that desperat men have killed themselves, and much rather would adventure to kill the Queene. Dags have already beene taken in the court, and that which hath beene may be. The Duke therefore to be executed in tyme, least in tyme the Queene and we our selves be destroyed. This request he wisheth us to make as children to her our mother, desiring her to shewe mercy uppon us. He trusteth she will not be offended with our importunatnesse, although for maydenly modesty she drawe backe. Those that have perswaded with the Queene to stay the former proceeding never to be liked of: to doe one thing here openly and perswade another secretly.

Mr Wentworth. Would have us hunger as we ought after righteousnesse. He must needes be plaine. This message very sorrowfull unto him. He is not satisfied to see the Queene forsake the better, which she seeth, and follow the worse, to the

f.45v

danger of her person, subversion of religion, destruction / of the realme and all her good subiectes. For this he can give no thankes. He thinketh them to be liked of which wilbe plaine with the Queene to her preservation, then such as dissemble with her to her destruction. It remaineth, since she will not alwholy provide for remedie hereof, that at least it be don in parte, in executing of the Duke, and so cut of halfe her head; and wisheth wee forbeare to deale in any other matter untill this be determined. Otherwise words of comfort to be given to us in vayne, to say 'Eate, eate, drinke and be mery'; but it wilbe said unto us iustely, 'O foole, this night shall thy life be taken from thee'. This petition to be made by the Speaker with the whole Howse.

Mr Treasurer. Loath to have much tyme spent. Agreed uppon already that petition should be made, and that the Speaker should make the same. The order how it should be made resteth to be considered, and whyther the whole Howse should goe with the Speaker or but certaine specially apointed. He thinketh best certaine specially apointed, for that noe one place is well able to receave all.

Mr Speaker. Moved whyther it were convenient to proceede in this sorte, since it was ones agreed it should come to the Queene but by way of opinion.

Mr Recordor. That wee ought to deale modestly when we deale with them that cary the sword. He will onely talke of orders and forme, and would not have his speech drawne to any other purpose. In Edward the iiij[th]['s] tyme certaine mummers desired to come to him, meaning to doe him a mischiefe in their mummery. Petitions have beene made by the Speaker in the name of the Howse in kings' dayes for small causes. In King Edward the Thirde's tyme a petition made to remove some of his Councell, and the king agreed to the same.[98] In the tyme of Henry the iv[th] the [? Speaker] sent to desire the King to advaunce his sonnes to honnor.[99] In Henry the vj[th] his tyme / a like petition made to advaunce the Earle of Somerset to the marqueshipe of Dorset for his good service.[100] A petition another tyme made in the behalfe of the Lord Powes that, where proclamation had beene made that whosoever could take Sir John Oldcastle should have a 100[li] for his labour who tooke him, that he might have same 100[li] payed accordingly.[101] Another petition in King Henry the vj[th] his tyme that the Duke of Chester might be made protector.[102] In Edward the iiij[th] his tyme a petition made that whereas all grauntes made by Henry the vj[th] were by Parliament made voyd, that Eaten College might enioy the landes given to the same. The King graunted the request for the one halfe and kept still the other.[103] It was graunted by Parliament to Henry the vij[th] to restore any man in blood by his prerogative, and yet after uppon a petition he was content to departe with his prerogative. And to all theise petitions was said *le Roy voet*. There was talke also of opinion. Opinion he thinketh is nothing; may change every day. Now whyther it may be changed he doubteth not whatsoever it were it might be altered during the session: it is all but one day. The iudges during the same tearme ordinarilly amend any thing. There was ones a bill of wines came to this Howse, brought to the question in an afternoone and the bill overthrowne. The same bill the next morning brought newly to the question and passed the Howse and remaines a good act at this day. In the bill of Cambridge this last parliament an error happened in putting the bill to the question, certaine wordes then altered not being thrise read. The Howse was in dividinge for triall for voyces. The error being found / was remedied and the bill put to the question anew and passed.[104] He misliketh this word 'opinion', and would have it brought to a resolucion, for that the gravitie of this Howse is not to deale with opinions but to make conclusions. Another pointe moved, whyther the whole Howse or but certaine should be sent with the Speaker.

f.46

f.46v

96. *Sic*: 'course'?
97. *Sic.*
98. I.e. May 1376.
99. 1399: *Rot. Parl.*, III.426–8.
100. See *Cal.Charter Rolls*, VI.37 for creation 'by authority of Parliament' and *Rot.Parl.*, V.446 for a grant of lands made at the request of Parliament.
101. Edward Lord Cherleton (of Powis) in 1417 (*Rot. Parl.*, IV.111).
102. There was no dukedom of Chester. The reference appears to be to the Duke of York, and the Commons pressed for his second Protectorate in 1455 (*Rot.Parl*, V.284–9). However, in 1460, soon after being recognized as heir apparent and protector, he was granted the county of Chester among other lands, and it has sometimes been assumed that he became Earl of Chester (GEC, III.174).
103. *Rot.Parl.*, V.523, 606; VI.79, for exemptions from Acts of Resumption, and of Sir Wasey Sterry, *The Eton College Register, 1441–1698* (1943), xxiv; *Rot.Parl.*, VI.526, for 19 Hen.VII.
104. See *CJ*, I.92; *CJ*, I.25–6, has four readings for the 1553 bill of wines, including an engrossment the afternoon before being passed, but no record of rejection.

He thinketh best but certaine, for else the Speaker seemeth not to bee sent but brought. This alwayes the use of the Howse. He knoweth the Speaker and the whole Howse have beene sent for by King Henry the vij^th and likewise by King Henry the viij^th, but never otherwise except sent for.

This matter was put to the question anew by way of resolution for mocion for execution of the Duke, and passed with one only negative voice, and agreed provision to be made for the same purpose.

xxix° Maij.

A bill that freemen of London may enioye their liberties.

A bill for particion of lande betweene the Lord Latimer and Sir Robart Wingfield.

The bill against fraudulent conveyances, the second tyme read. Agreed to be engrossed.

A bill that no man should erect or let any cotage without iij acres of severall or vj acres of common.

The bill for vagabondes the third tyme read.

Much argument *pro et contra* was made aboute minstrels, and the bill commytted.

xxx Maij.

This day I was absent, the most parte whereof bestowed aboute the bill of vagabondes. /

f.47   Ultimo Maij.

A bill that no man not having beene prentice for seven yeares or exercised trade of merchandise for twelve yeares should transporte any merchandise beyonde the seas.

Mr Recorder. This bill a monopoly. And so reiected.

A bill that the Waxechaundlers of London might oversee all waxe made within xx^thi myles of the same, and to burne that which is nought, *etc.*

A bill that the chappell of Lirpoole might be made a parish church by the name of 'St. Paule's church', Richard Mullenax and his successors to be patrons, the person of Walton who is now parson to have the tithes during his life.

Mr Snage. No provision here made for the successor of the person, who cannot speake for himselfe.

Mr Segerston. The chappell fairer then the church. No iniury offered to any. He that is patron shalbe patron still, shall have two patronadges having now but one. Lirpoole being a greate towne ioy[n]ing uppon the sea shalbe mainteined. The other shall have sufficient.

The bill against recoveries suffered by the graunte of tenaunte for life, the ij^d time read and commytted.[105]

The Earle's of Kente's bill being altered, newly read.

Mr Petter Wentworth. Moveth for execution of the Duke, that order may be taken for the petition.

After long disputation it was moved by Mr Treasurer to make stay for a tyme. He trusted execution would follow without sute. At lenght the Howse agreed to stay proceeding untill the next sitting. /

A bill that whosoever should attempt to set at libertie any prisoner committed for   f.47v
treason should incurre the danger of misprison of treason. If the person be commytted for treason to the Queene's person, then to be fellony; if [   ][106] of treason then to be treason.

A bill that the withholder of any castell from the Queene after proclamation should be deemed a traitor.

A bill to unite Hexam and Hexamshyer to the countie of Northumberlande.

ij° Junij.

The bill against recoveries had against tenaunte for tearme of life, to defeate remainders or reversions, the ij^d tyme read. Agreed to be engrossed.[107]

The bill for making of good callivers, being altered, first read.

The bill against the caring of lether beyond the seas, the second tyme read and to be engrossed.

The bill of vagabondes the third tyme read and passed.

iij° Junij.[108]

The bill for the schoole of Tunbridg, twise read. Agreed to be engrossed.

A byll that it may be lawfull to the Queene's Majestie to restraine the bringing in of any forraigne wares from any country where and during the tyme that our wares are forbidden in the same country.

A bill that the inhabitantes of the Citie and Soke of Winchester may occupie clothing and take prentises although they have not beene prentizes to the occupation vij yeares.

A bill that no curseye should containe above xviij^th yards.[109]

A bill that the wardens of the Waxechaundlers should have the search for the true making of all waxe in the Citie and suburbes and within xx miles of London and in Sturbridg faier, and where they find any defective to burne the same.[110] /

A bill for the well making of callivers, the ij^d tyme read.   f.48

Mr Winter. The pieces that be of less bullet more commodious. Expendeth less leade and the souldier may carrie more of the same aboute him. The lesser bullet will perse better and fly as farre.

Mr Page. The armerers not the fittest persons to have the profe of the same. Better the Liuetenaunt of the Ordinaunce should have the oversight thereof. Agreed the bill should be engrossed.

The bill against transporting of lether beyond the seas. The third tyme read.

A proviso was offered for such hides as are brought out of Scotlande to Berwicke.

105. The first reading of this new bill was on 30 May while Cromwell was away (*CJ*, I.99).

106. There is a short unintelligible word at this point.

107. This new bill had two readings on this day (*CJ*, I.99).

108. MS reads '*Maij*'. The entry '*iii° Junij*' comes at the top of f. 48v.

109. MS reads 'yeares'.

110. Cf. *CJ*, I.100.

Mr Segerston. The lawe very perillous. All against merchauntes who are not the authors of the dearth of shooes. He would the gentlemen which sell the hides so deere at first might be hanged. A provision might be made that all the hides which are now caried out of Ireland to Fraunce might be brought hither, which uttereth to Fraunce a thousand dicker in a yeare. Licences againe very hurtfull. My Lord Admirall hath one of them. And under colloure of every licence a greate many more are caried then the licence will extende to. Indorsed in many partes; harde to knowe when the number is past.

Mr Marsh. The cariadge over sea the cause of the dearth; else should not the gentleman sell it so deare. No merchaunte should seeke his living to the spoile of his country. No reason we to seeke ayd of Irelande, having store of our owne. Licences cannot doe so much hurt as the generall carying by everybody. The licences although they be hurtfull cannot be denied to the prince; but he wisheth it were well looked to, such persons as have licences did not soe deceave both the Queene and realme. Agreed to be engrossed. /

f.48v   The bill against recoveries by tenaunte for tearme of life, the third tyme read and passed the Howse.

Three billes were sent from the Lordes, of the which one we sent to them, *vz.*, concerninge the danger of lapse untill notice; a second for the severance of the sherivewycke of Cambridge and Huntingtonsheere; a third that the iustice of assise might sit at Stafford.

The bill against fraudulent conveiances to defraud purchases, the third tyme read.[111]

Mr Birkit. The bill very necessarie; only to avoyd fraudes which the common lawe hath always condemned. The cause not privat but almost every man's case who hath any landes. Very necessarie to looke backe to doe good and to punish fraude. He thinketh it good reason that he which selleth lande and knoweth it to be encombered with such former conveiance and will covenaunte to discharge the lande of encombrances should inccure the danger. He would rather such a seller were punished as a fellon. Good cause why the purchaser be provided for. The realme cannot stand without chevizunce.

Mr Edgecombe. The lawe dangerous, for as he taketh it a man, having made a good assurance to his child, if after he shall mislike him, may take it away, alleadging the first estate was uppon covin, who is like to be soonest credited.

Mr Lovelesse. The number of clientes which come to him, being greatly endangered and almost undon hereby, occasioneth him to speake. The bill toucheth no estate made with consideration, nor any except it be fraudulent and covenous. This from the beginning hath beene, as occasions of fraude did arise, beene[112]

f.49   remedied by estatutes, whereof he shewed / diverse examples. He wisheth that those which will not agree to have the statute to looke backwardes, that it were their owne case. The considerations which are not to be allowed to be good cannot possibly be expressed.

Mr Sampole. That it would take away many sutes. Men understanding that fraudes would not serve, would leave to use fraude. The evill being so common, very necessary to helpe purchasers. More dishonest sellers then purchasors. The purchasor ought rather to [be] holpen then the sonn in such case. The sonn would have it for nothing; the purchasor payeth deare for it to the father of the child, whom the child is bounde by reciprocate love to ayd. And as the father gave it freely, so he in conscience bounde to disburden his father or make amendes for his wrongs. Unworthy of the father's landes, who will defile his father's nest. The intente can never be proved by the second purchasor. The first purchasor may easily prove the consideration.

Mr Bromleye. A greate inconvenience to bring every man's conveyance in question, which now is like to fall out, if greate circumspection be not used. He would have the bill better considered.

iiij° Junij.

The bill that landes given to the hospitalles erected by King Edward the vj[th] in London should not be made voyd by the heires of the donors by misnaming the name of the foundation. Agreed to be engrossed.

A bill that every man for every v kids should reare one calfe for a yeare.

Mr St. John. In some places the nature of the soile is such as will not keepe the calfes, and therefore the lawe cannot be universall.

Mr Treasurer. Every countrie therein to doe according to the nature of the soile. Cheese as necessary for the common weale for the furniture of shippes. /

Mr Grimston. This no new presidente. The like before made aswell in the tyme   f.49v
of King Henry the viij[th] as in the tyme of Queene Marye.[113] The scarsity of beefes at this day very greate, which had neede be provided for and remedied. He would be glade if other countries mislike of [it], that it might be a lawe for his owne countrie.

A bill restraining the bruing of double double ale or doble double beere within the Citie or iij miles thereof, and no beere to be sould above 4[s] the barrell the strongest and 2[s] the single beere, and uttered in tipling howses after the gallane the best[114] and ij[d] the gallande the single.[115]

A bill that it may be lawfull for the Queene's Majestie by proclamacion to restraine the bringing in of any wares from any countrie where our wares be restrained.

Mr Segerston. This bill made for the benefite of Handeborough which we have noe more cause to favour then other places.

Mr Treasurer. The King of Spaine taketh all our goodes which he can catch. Our men conveye away our goodes thither to the reliefe of our enemy, and yet hee restraineth our wares. Reason the Queene doe the like, and to encourage such merchauntes as trade to such places with whom the Queene is in amytie.

A bill offered by Serieant Manwoode for explanation of a cause in the statute of fugitives made the last parliament, that any man not returning at such tyme as his

111. *CJ*, I.100 records that the committees on this bill were to meet on this day, the third reading having been given the day before.

112. *Sic.*

113. 21 Hen. VIII, c.8 (1529), in *SR*,

III.289-90; 2 & 3 Ph.& M., c.3 (1555), in *SR*, IV.274-5. The Henrician statute merely sought to control the slaughter of young calves.

114. *Sic.*

115. Not in *CJ*.

licence doth expire may be deemed to departe with such meaning.[116] /

f.50   A bill that leases made by corporations should be good, notwithstanding the corporation by mysnamed.

The bill of the City and Soke of Winchester, the ij^d tyme read.

Mr Fennor. Declareth that he and other of the commyttees have mett and uppon[117] the Earle's of Kinte's bill and that they and their councell have with them[118] and that iij exceptions were offered to the bill by the Lord Cumton's councell. First, that he doth not absolutely confesse that the release which the Earle of Kente desireth to frustrate doth take away his estate but sayeth it is doubtfull. To this the Earle of Kente's councell answered that he hath another title and therefore would be loath to preiudice the same. Secondly, was obiected that he had a bill in the Chauncery against him for the same matter. To that answere on the other parte that the Chauncery hath no authoritie to frustrate the release. Thirdly, that he had an action at the common law against him for landes which depende uppon the same title. To that was answered that it is doubtfull what title the Earle of Kente will make to the same. Finally, awarded that the Lord Cumpton should answere the bill and so was sent for to come in and receave such answere, and willed to make ready for the same and had day given till tomorowe.

A bill was sent from the Lordes against transporting of lether beyond the seas. /

f.50v   The bill for the making of callivers, the iij^d time read.

Sir Nicholas Arnolde. Would not have the makers bounde to make such bulletes as twenthie should be made of a pounde, but xx or xxx, for that he thinketh the peece which shooteth the smaller bullet cannot be spared.

Mr Treasurer. If the bill should be so made the whole scope thereof were overthrowne. A necessitie that one only kind of bullet should be used, that one souldier in tyme of neede might supply the wante of another. The store alreadie provided by the Queene is of that bullet, which neede to be observed or else that store lost. The souldier which hath other already may occupie the same notwithstandinge.

Mr Winter. The peeces which shoote lesser bulletes more necessarie; the peece the lighter for cariage; fewer bulletes kept in less roome; less expense of powder; the force the greater.

Mr Digs. As it is true that the peece which shooteth the greate bullet occupieth more leade and powder, so doth one shote of the same more harme to the enemye then foure of th'other, if both be alike well made. Finally the bill passed.

The bill for Tunebridge Schoole, the iij^d tyme read and passed.

The bill from the Lordes for division of the sherivewike of Cambridge and Huntington.

The bill from the Lordes against retainers of castells and shipps from the Queene's Majestie.

Mr Norton. That the bill may be made to extend likwise to the razers of any of the Queene's castells, or burners of her shipps.

The bill against such persons as shall practize to set at libertie any commytted to prison for treason, the second time read. /

f.51   The bill for annexing Hexam and Hexamshier to the countie of Northumberland, the second tyme reade.

v° Junij.

A bill for the severance of the sherivewike of Sussex and Surie.

A bill that every person inhabiting within v miles of Oxford having a yard land should vj dayes betweene this and Michellmas worke and finde one wayne for reparation of the wayes and bridges within one mile of Oxforde, and every other howsholder to finde a laborer to worke.

A bill that every borough towne might have a chamberleine for the kepeing of the goodes and chateles given by any person to any orphanes, in like sorte as is in the Citye of London.

A bill for partition of certaine landes betweene the Lord Latimer and Sir Robart Wingfield, the iij^d tyme read and passed.

A bill giving a longer tyme for th'inning of Plumsted marsh.

A bill against retainers of the Queene's fortes or shipps from the Lordes the third tyme read and passed.

A bill from the Lordes for the punishment of such as shall attempte to set any person at libertie commytted to prison for treason.

The bill for the towne of Worcester, that it should be lawfull for them to make a cute from the river of Severne to the towne *etc.*, the third tyme read.

Mr Newdigate. Liketh not that any man's inheritance should be taken from them against the wills of the owners, especially for so small a commodity as increase of water, the rather for that the river cometh already on the one side of the towne and although some meane be apointed for recompense, he liketh not / that   f.51v commyssioners should set price of other men's landes.

Sir Nicholas Arnolde. The river alreadie gathereth many shelves which would decaye the whole river and in small tyme stoppe the passadg of the water, to the undoing of the townes which be uppon the river. The towne unable to make recompence for such harmes. Their collour of their request for water, which they may have for the tenth parte of the charge eyther by conductes or horse. He thinketh their meaning is to make mills there.

Mr Snage. The most parte of the lande thorough which the cutt should go is my Lord of Worcester, who for the benefit of the towne is contented therewith, and thinketh it would prove beneficiall also to the country adioy[n]ing; besides, the viij commyssioners being indifferently chosen would indifferently make the price of the lande. There is such provision in the bill as they would never attempte the making of the cut if it should be preiudicall to any; else were there greate foly in them since they are bound at their owne costes both to stopp up the cut and make recompence, which were to leese an infinit charge, and the cut being stopped up the water must needes come to his ould course.

Mr Controller. Cannot agree that any person should make value of his landes. He hath some not worth xx yeares' purchase, which he would not give for lx.

Mr Atkins. A greate matter to alter the course of a streame. He suspecteth they

---

116. 13 Eliz., c.3 (1571), in *SR*, IV.531-4.   117. *Sic.*   118. *Sic.*

would not be at so greate charge for so small a commodity as water. He feareth their mean[ing] to make a leystowe[119] there and so a monopoly. The river already being in some places but two foote, water would now be much less, and so in small tyme the whole passadg stoped. And so the bill put to the question and overthrown.

The byll that landes given to hospitalls may be to them notwithstanding the misnaming of the foundation, the third tyme read and passed. /

f.52   Mr Townsende. Desireth to have some consideration of the bill for that he doubteth it may touch his inheritance: which[120] was agreed unto.

A bill from the Lordes for annexing Hexam and Hexamshyer to the county of Northumberlande, the third tyme read and passed.

[*vi Junij*]

A bill for making of handwarpe clothes in Cotteshall and Bocking, that no man should use their marke. The third tyme read and passed.[121]

The bill that Woodstocke may make clothes, the second tyme read.

A bill for severance of the sherivewike of Surrey and Sussex, the second tyme read.

A bill restraining the bringing in of any wares of any country in which our wares are forbidden, the third tyme read.

Segerston. This bill altogether for benefit of the City. They may bring from Handborough what they will. Other merchauntes of other countries which are not able to travell to Handborough not suffered to doe the like out of Fraunce. There is some Spanish wares which we cannot wante, as iron and oyle.

Mr Ap[p]ley. Handborough to farr a passadg for all his country and therefore of necessity compelled to buy Spanish wares in Fraunce. They cannot come to London for their provision.

Mr Marsh. Greate cause the trade of Handborough be mainteyned. In Spaine and Flaunders there is very straight execution that no English wares be solde there but the same are confiscate. Reason they be served with the measure. This they put in execution though the goods came from Rome. If our merchauntes goe to Handborough with their wolles and have no returne home, they shalbe undonn.

Mr Snage. That it is reason no man fetch any wares out of Spaine; but not restrayned to bring Spanish wares out of other countryes with which we are in amyty, and would have the bill penned accordingly.

Mr Controler. Moveth that the bill may be stayed and not put to the question.

A new bill against fraudulent conveyances. /

f.52v   The bill concerning Mary commonly called Queene of Scotes, wherein, reciting her treasons, conspiracies and clayme made to the crowne aswell in possession as reversion, is desired by the lord[s] spirituall and temporall,[122] *etc.*

Mr Yelverton. Englande the spectacle of religion thorough all Christendome, but some what dimmed in hope of alteracion. He wisheth this bill to be well and advisedly considered and not to make more hast therein then good speed. He looked not to have hearde the same read at this present, neyther would have it treated uppon at any tyme, but warning should be given thereof the day before. More fit for the beginning of a parliament then to be speedly passed in the end thereof. It toucheth very much the Queene's Majestie, the whole state in generall, and every man in particular. As he taketh it now uppon hearing thereof, it is in many things very iniuryous. He speaketh advisedly and not rashely. The Queene of Scotes hath no title, neyther in possession or reversion, to the crowne. If any man thinke otherwise, let him prove her title: he shalbe answered. And yet he feareth the contrary is coverdly caried in the bill. After recitall made in the bill of the Queene of Scotes' treasons, is declared that her fauters be great uppon 'uncertaine hope'[123] receaved of her title. These wordes he liketh not. Men hope of that whereto they have right, and yet uncertainly, for that untill it be had, the evente is not certaine. He would have [it] termed, a vayne and dangerous hope. In the proceeding thereof it saieth farther, 'founded[124] uppon uncertaine and doubtfull causes'.[125] He would have it striken out and have relation to the former tearmes. Some wordes have beene uttered this parliament terming her feodary and thinking she might be punished as a feodary, wherein they greatly erred. She to be punished as a stranger offending within the realme and not otherwise. In the proceeding of the bill, is farther required that in parte of punishment she may be declared 'unworthy, unable and uncapable'[126] of the crowne. So a punishment confessed, but no punishment is in truth except the person, landes and goodes be touched. If none of these, noe punishment. Consider well then of these wordes, and we shall seeme to declare the opinion of the whole parliament to allow that she hath title to the crowne, which we nowe take away; or else take away nothing, and then no punishment. The worde 'unworthy', he likewise / misliketh. A disobedient childe is unworthy of his father's patrimony, and yet hath right to the same. In the proceeding of the bill is desired to the end 'some certaine knowledg' of triall may be had hereafter: hereupon may very reasonably be inferred that there is nowe no certaine. This he also misliketh, for that he is thoroughly perswaded there is as certaine a triall for her as for any other person. He hath beene alwayes, and is of opinion she is a traytor, and then it were very impertinente to say shee cannot be tryed. But for certaine she is to be tryed as a subiect of another nation. She is here no queene, although she had never resigned the same. A duke of another nation is to be tried here by a common iury, for that he is here no duke. He would rather the wordes to be, 'for convenientnesse of tryall'. He noteth farther in the bill that if after the death of the Queene's Majestie shee should leave an 'open warre' or 'rebellion': he doubteth whither eyther of the tearmes will serve when no prince vested; whither it may be tearmed rebellion, not for that he thinketh the prince no prince before coronation, for he thinketh the coronation onely a ceremony. He noteth also that it is said if any person shall conspire without the Queene's consent to set at libertie the said Mary: these, 'without the Queene's consent', he liketh not, for that no conspiracie can be with the Queene's consent. He misliketh also the immunyty offered to speake or write against her. It may carye a

f.53

119. *Sic.*
120. MS reads 'was'.
121. *CJ*, I.100: second reading; Cromwell has a third reading for this bill on 10 June (f.60v) as does *CJ* I.101.
122. MS reads 'corporall': this is the second reading, the first on 5 June (*CJ*, I.100) not being noted by Cromwell.
123. See Doc.8, f.243v.
124. MS reads 'founder'.
125. See Doc.8, f.243v.
126. See Doc.8, f.243v.

doubtfullnesse that before it was not lawfull, and he would have all doubtes removed. He will never clayme benefit of this immunyty; he doubteth not but it is already lawfull and hath alwayes beene, yea even when she was in her best state. He noteth also it is said, that if at any tyme after the Queene's death she attempt to aspire to the crowne, that she should be out of protection: he would have everybody which shall take her parte to be in the same predicament. /

f.53v   Mr Snage. That he can never agree to have any tacite implication made of any title in there.[127] The wordes of the bill make her title stronger then before. The recitall of the factes, treasons and divellish practises will not touch her if shee hape the crowne. The whole factes purged by dignytie. The polytyke body confounds the property of a naturall body. Agreed in the tyme of Henry the vij^th that the Lordes and Commons must be purged, but the king purged *ipso facto*. He liketh not the apointment of this triall, which giveth a more honorable tryall then is due to her before: a presumption we meane to honour and not punish her. He thinketh surely if himselfe should commyt treason and be condemned of fellony, it were iniury offered unto him. He would have her also out of protection for any fact commytted in the Queene's life tyme. He would have every man which is absent likewise to declare their consent as we have don, and therefore requireth a generall oth. This don by King Henry the viij^th, and a speciall prayer made against the tiranny of the Bishoppe of Rome and all his enormyties.

Mr Norton. Will not be longe, neyther measured nor heard. This parliament called for matters of greate necessitie, and therefore not good to do nothing, much worse to doe starke naught. We require that in the meane tyme the Queene will enact: he feareth that this meane tyme wilbee to long a tyme. He would have all wordes of implicacion strikine out: the bill remaineth good without them. He would also have a proviso declaring that the meaning of the Howse is not to affirme any title in her. A bill preferred the last parliament for the Queene's safety, but it caryed nothinge. Additions were offered of farther provision: the Queene misinformed uppon the same that successions was sought to be established to the Queene's perill, whereas authority was given by the same to cut of all successions. He knoweth not what reliques remaines of that faction. He would therefore every man to make protestation, he meaneth not to advaunce any title, and yet to speake freely of the bill.

Fisher was called to the barre for misinforming the Lordes that we had passed a bill as consented unto by him, whereas he had given no such consent. And was commyted to the serieant.[128] /

f.54   *vij° Junii.*

A bill for making of clothes in Woodstocke, the seconde tyme read, to be engrossed.
A bill for the Waxechaundelers, the second tyme read, to be engrossed.[129]
A bill that no merchante not being set in subsidye at 500^li should purchase more then one house, one garden and one orchard, if so set not above li^li lande, if an alderman not above 100^li lande.
A bill for explanacion of two branches of the statute of fugitives made *xiij° Reginae Elizabethae*, declaring that the Queene should not onely have *vestucam*[130]

terram of such persons, but also let set and make such copies as tenaunt *pur termee dantre*[131] *vie* may doe; and secondly that every person departing by licence and not returning at the expiration of the same should be expounded to be in the compasse of the estatute. The seconde tyme read; to be engrossed.

A bill that the assises should be kept at Alesbury, with a proviso that the iustices of assise which nowe be may during their lives pointe the assises ones every yeare where they liste.[132]

A bill that Winchester and the Soke may make clothes and take printises, the third tyme read and passed.

The bill against fraudulent vouchers, to be engrossed.

A bill for Sir William Harper against Prestwoode and Beatrice his wife.[133]

Now to the bill of the late Queene of Scotes.

Mr St John. Moveth that she should not be called daughter and heire to James King of Scotes.

Mr Norton. That in the petition it might be added, where request is made for punishment, 'as your Majestie lawfully may doe'.[134]

Mr Alforde. Sheweth he is growne in double suspicion in the Howse: aswell in religion as for fancy and affection. He denieth both and desireth to be thought of to have a plaine and simple mynde. The stile he thinketh not to be altered, for that it is true she is daughter and heire to James. The bill not to be altered because made by the consent of the Queene's Majestie uppon greate deliberacion, not rash, with like consideration of the Lordes as she may lawfully do. He liketh not it carieth a common tryall, whereas afterwardes a speciall tryall by pieres is apointed / unto her; and so some contrarytye. The commyttees an advauntadge of us for that they have hearde the opinion of the iudges in all matters. He is therefore perswaded that it is iustely donn because all have agreed thereto, but yet he would not have the wordes used.

Mr Wilbraham. That he will not strive for the title. 'Justely charged'[135] he thinketh not good to use in matters forraigne, because we cannot take direct notice of the same. The petition cannot be turned to an act for that it hath already beene denied. The wordes 'as she may lawfully do' being moved cannot be omytted. It may breed a greate scruple. No doubt to be made to put it in. He for his parte will never desire any unlawfull thing of the Queene's Majestie, neyther can the Lordes mislike of the addicion, for he knoweth they beleeve it to be lawfull, else were it shame to them to desire it. And so agreed the wordes to be put in.

Sir Thomas Scot. We desire the Queene's Majestie to do execution. He feareth if she protracte tyme she shalbe unable to do it. She is a stronge enemy, shall have the

f.54v

---

127. *Sic*: 'her'?
128. Cf. *CJ*, I.101, for Fisher.
129. *CJ*, I.101, has 'twice read' and engrossed, though recording that the new bill had its first reading on 3 June (*CJ*, I.100).
130. *Sic*.
131. Or '*dautre*'?

132. I.e. the second reading, the first on 30 May when Cromwell was away from the House (*CJ*, I.99).
133. This is a new bill, the first reading of the original bill being on 30 May (*CJ*, I.99).
134. See Doc.8, f.243.
135. See Doc.8, f.243.

assistance of the papistes of England and of Scotland, the Pope, the King of Spaine, the Duke of Alva, and the Guysiance of Fraunce. He misliketh the place of her imprisoonment, and would in the meane season have her kept in safer garde. She now kept in the north neere the rebells which would be readie to asist her, neare also to her owne country where if she do escape she shall soone be receaved. He humbly desireth those which be of the Queene's Majestie's Privy Councell or that have access to her Majestie earnestly to incite her in this matter. The request being reasonable, he trusteth easy to be obtayned.

It was agreed also that the wordes, 'uncerteyne hope', and the wordes, 'founded uppon uncertaine and doubtfull causes arising' *etc.*, all to be put out, and insteede of 'clearly extinguished', to say the rather 'extinguished'; and also to put out 'in parte of punishment', and 'to the discoragement of her fauters and adherentes'.[136]

Mr Flowrdewe. Against the wordes, 'as if she were naturally dead',[137] for that the same may imply a title if she were alive. /

f.55   Mr Berkin.[138] Would have the word 'unworthy'[139] in, but not in that sorte. He would have it said unworthy though she were capable. He would also have it enacted that no papist should succeede the Queene's Majestie. No common weale can stande where sin is not punished. In his country in the north, a greate deale more dangerouse to be a protestant then a papist. He liketh well of Sir Thomas Scote's mocion, and as men are more carefull of theire posterity then of themselves, so wisheth the Queene's Majestie would doe the like.

Mr Dannet. That the wordes of 'unable' and 'uncapable' may very well stande. We say very well of a horse that he is uncapable of reason, and yet that implieth not that the horse ever had reason. We may say that the French king is uncapable of the crowne of Englande, and yet no implication that ever he was capable.

Mr Fennor. That it may well be saidd she is unable or uncapable of the crowne, but to enacte it so must needes implicatively affirme an ability before, because the acte seemeth to be the cause of the disabilitie.

Serieant Manwoode. This clawse of necessity to be very advisedly considered. It is the very marry[140] of the statute. The wordes 'as if she were naturally dead' not to be suffered, for that it directly implieth a deprivation for life.

Mr Loveleyse. The wordes onely to be considered according to the lawyers' phrase and not to any logicall sence. 'Unabilitie' in diverse cases diversely taken in pleading to an action brought by an outlawe or an excommunicate person if unabilitie in those causes be chalenged by the defendant. There it implyeth an abilitie. Otherwise when the like plea is made to an alien: there 'unabilitie' is meant always 'unable'. So the sense doubtfull, and therefore not used, *quia qua dubites ne feceris.* /

f.55v   Mr Wilson. Thinketh the wordes very fit. Philipus Verbarius being an emperor was deposed for that he was a slave borne, and the wordes pronounced that he was uncapable, and meante always uncapable. The like of a woman promoted to a benefice. She shalbe denounced uncapable *ratione sexus.* So of the Scotish Queene because a stranger.

Sir Walter Myldney.[141] This sentence would be tryed like drammes of gold. To be considered how in our lawe, not how by the civell lawe or in logique. The fewer causes, the lesser implication. He would have every commyttee and every lawyer to have a copie and to study it.

[Afternoon]

A bill that no man serving any subiect should be iustice of peace or high constable in any shier of Englande.

A bill for mending the bridges and high wayes within a mile of Oxford.

Mr St John. The suggestion that the inhabiters within v miles of Oxford receave such commodity by the City not true, and therefore the country not to be charged with such double charge.

Mr Treasurer. That he is knight for the shier and yet misliketh not the bill. The thing required beneficiall to them which should be charged, which have accesse to the market. The demaunde very small: onely asistance with cariadge for vj dayes for a common use.

Mr Controler. No reason to burden them more then other countries. Besides, yf they make the bridges ones, they shall alwayes be charged with it. Some parte standeth in Barkesheere within v myles of Oxforde.

Mr Wykes and Mr Dennis being brought in for their case, the same was declared by Mr Townsende.[142]

Mr Perham. That it were not reasonable to confirme the decree, for that decrees be often made and undon, sometymes by others, sometymes [by those?] which made it; yf it were confirmed here, it should be perpetuall. The proceeding of / the   f.56 Chauncery contrarye unto lawe, which will that no man be foreiudged of his lande but by the common lawe. No disobedience to be layd to Mr Dennis notwithstandinge any resistance, because he did obey that which is war[a]unted by lawe, *vz.*, emprisonment, which is the uttermost proceeding allowed to the Courte. The forces or ryotes, if they be forces, punishable in the Starr Chamber. The suggestion of the bill untrue supposing the bargaine to be made for the manors of Sison onely, where in truth it was for Sison and Pucklichurch. Sison alone valued at fowre thousand two hundred poundes. He would have it for a m:viii^c pounde. The decree proceedeth also that every person clayminge by Dennis should make such assurance to Wykes as he would require, which is not reasonable. He farther [says] he ys not without remedie, for Wikes hath a statute of two thowsande poundes. So remedie sufficient by lawe and Dennis still contented to make assurance according to his bargaine.

Mr Kerle. The request not to have the maner in per[pe]twyty but according to the decree, which is untill the money be payed. The punishment of the riotes no matter required.

Mr Watslowe. The Courte not to finde a statute uppon untrue surmises. Recited one untruth, that any bargeine was made for one maner onely; a second untruth, that Mr Dennis did refuse to make assurance according to the bargeine; a third untrueth, that Mr Dennis should contemptuously rebell, for he was commytted to prison. It hath beene confessed that Dennis was contente to make any assurance which the

---

136. See Doc.8, f.243v for these points.
137. See Doc.8, f.244.
138. *Sic.*
139. Doc.8, f.243v.
140. *Sic:* 'marrow'?

141. *Sic.*
142. During the hearing the parties may be represented by counsel and the House will therefore be addressed by men who are not elected members (*CJ*, I.101).

councell of Wikes could devise. Mr Dennis got the morgage to ioyne in assurance and Wikes would have none of yt.

The Earle of Kente and the Lord Cumpton brought in.

Mr Serieant Barrow. Declared the contentes of the bill and the deceipt used by the feffes of trust in making the release contrary to promise.

Mr Solliciter. Being layd in this sorte as doubtfull whither the release be a barre or no. In any other courte it would be reiected. The Earle / hath likewise actions at the common lawe and actions in the Chauncery for the same, so if eyther lawe or conscience will serve he may have remedie. He thinketh also it were very harde to worke any man's disherisenc contrary to lawe. The bill many untruethes and in some pointes iniurious; the matter very intricate and long, a greate [deal] depending uppon witnesses whereas the parliament was summoned *pro rebus arduis*; the title of necessitie to be enquired of. It is to decide demurrers, and they to be iudges which are not charged with oath. That the first recovery was to an use entayle, which is not true, for the first use was in fee simple. The will made v yeares after the same, onely nuncupative, and the witnesses for the same examined xxij yeares after. Hard for them to remember the wordes so longe. The release obtayned by others and not by the Lord Cumpton. The bill sayeth further that the release was gotten by undue meanes without sheweing by whom; and so uncertaine. The request iniuryous, in that it desireth all other leases to be made voyd whyther made by covin or no. The release generally required to be made frustrate, which goeth to the fee simple, whereas the Earle hath but a state tayle; and so iniuryous also. The release may also concerne other landes wherein the Earle hath no state. Besides, the order of pleading would be a very strange metamorphosis: the Earle of Kente to use his owne name and the Lord Cumpton answere as to the feffee. Besides, the Lord Cumpton allowed to make defence, but the Courte not warranted to accept yt. No warraunty alowed us against Mr Gascoygne: another iniury.[143] Innocentes may be touched. The lande continued this fifty yeares out of the Earle's auncesters. Two discentes had in the meane tyme many leases and copies made. The[y] being innocentes should all be punished. The will must needes be first examined because else no cause how the Earle should be entitled, and so the release not to be discharged. No fraude in the Lord Cumpton to seeke it having continued in his auncestors and being sought at their handes who had authoritie to make it. The Lord Audley the first buyer. And a recovery uppon the same, how that will enure, a doubtfull question. The deposytions which / would [serve] the Lord Cumptone's turne embesilled out of the Chauncery.

Mr Fetiplace. To that which is alledged that the first use was a fee simple. The word doubtfull put in because of another title. The bill onely saieth the state was made to certaine uses of a will. The remedie here desired, not because the matter wanteth conscience, but because the Chauncery hath not authority to frustrate the release but only to punish the person by imprisonment, and that doubted also in a noble man's case. No rare matter to relieve or deale in private cases. A greate [blank][144] it hath beene sayed. Our meaning not to call the whole circumstance of the matter in question, not to make the will better then it is; only we desire the release to be voyd. The will, if it be good, no desire to be relieved for any landes but for those

f.56v

f.57

for which the will is made. The fee simple barred alreadie by *iiij° Ricardi iij*.[145] No cause of warranty where fraude and covin ys. The metamorphosis no new thing: given generally to every body by *27° Henrici 8ⁱ* to *cesti qui use*.[146] He thinketh it very inconvenient that the use of the lande should be in the Earle and the use of the action in the feffee. This release unduely procured in truste, notice and covin. First, the feffee falsefied his trust, who had notice thereof and before persons of greate honor promised he would make noe such release. The Earle of Bedford a witnes. The Lord Cumpton had likwise notice, for his sollicitor was told of it. They had writings which shewe it. And no greater covin can be then to falsefie a truste and to take money for it, and by evill arte and engin, so contrary to good conscience. *7 Edwardi 4* an estate being made to use of the woman, she tooke a husbande, the feffees sold the lande by consente of the husbande and the wife; and notwithstanding adiudged a covin in feffees because they ought to have considered that being maryed she was to doe her husbande's pleasure; and hereuppon, the husbande being dead, processe was made against the vendee and he made to answere it.[147]

Mr Solliciter. Desireth the Courte to consider that the Lord Cumpton hath no remedy if the bill be reiected. And so not indifferent: a remedie for the pleintiff and none for the defendant. Besides, the bill being by a pier against a pier, more fit to be / begun in the higher howse: errors they may reverse without this Courte.   f.57v

ix° Junij.[148]

A bill that no subiecte's servant should be iustice of peace or high constable, the customer of Barnes, twise read, to be engrossed.

A bill that no subiecte's servant should be iustice of peace or high constable, the second tyme read, to be engrossed.

The bill from the Lordes against convaying of lether beyond the seas to be fellony, ones read.

A proviso offered to the bill of Mary Steward, that no imparticular wordes should be expounded to affirme any title in succession in any person.

Mr Marsh. Experience hath alreadie shewed that law will do no good.

The bill for explanation of two branches in the statute [of] fugitives, the third tyme read and passed.

The bill against delayes by covenous vouchers, the third tyme read, but the question differed to a farther arguement.

Certaine articles of the bill against Mary commonly called Queene of Scotes were   N.[149] read.

Mr Snage. We have long desired the best provisyon for the greatest sore, which

143. See *CJ*, I.101.

144. 'Pity'?

145. Clearly an error: perhaps 1 Rich.III, c.1 (1483/4), in *SR*, II.477/8, is intended, though as Mr J. Barton points out it is interesting that the speaker appears to think that it is applicable to a trust of the freehold.

146. 27 Hen.VIII, c.10 (1535/6), in *SR*, III.539/42.

147. Trin.7 Ed., IV, 14, pl.8. I owe this reference to Mr J. Barton.

148. This dating from *CJ*; MS gives the date later, at the bill for the explanation of the statute of fugitives.

149. 'Nota'? Or '*Nova*' for reading of proviso?

since we cannot obteyne, so would he be contente with any salve but not with any medicine which caryeth poyson. The nature of actes, some to explane, some to abridge fro or adde to old lawes, and some to make new lawes. 'I am perswaded there is already a lawe which condemneth the Scots title', but if hee were but doubtfull he would not iudge. He would the wordes should be declared and not enacted, for in enacting we shall affirme that there was no lawe before the proviso offered; but a kind of protestation which[150] cannot be meere contrary to an acte. He would likewise it should be declared that Mary is uncapable, in the present tense; and not be, in the future. 'As shee were naturally dead', he would have left out: it may seeme to helpe her sonn to the succession.

Mr Dalton. With the proviso. Liketh of the bill and thinketh no contrarity betweene them. /

f.58   Mr Recorder. In Queene Marye's tyme men were not suffered to write what was saied. This matter we now treate of a very weighty cause, concerning the crowne of Englande. He is amazed with a sentence of Tully. Yf breach of lawes a man should undertake, then breake them boldly for kingdome's sake. Causes of kingdomes cannot be pleaded by way of estopell. If any person happe the crowne, he doubteth what exposytion they would make. *Tempora mutantur et nos mutamur in illis.* How we will expound this statute he knoweth but how others in another king's dayes would expound it he knoweth not. He hath heard it notoriously argued that those which are borne in Scotlande are English borne; but their error is greate. It is iudicially adiudged in the tyme of Richard the 2, that the Scotes bee *accolini non incolini.*[151] The allegations concerning Anguish and Frevill not proofs to the contrary, for they then inhabiting in that parte of Scotlande which was under the king's government. The lawe of the crowne made *25º Edwardi 3ⁱ* hath declared yt.[152]

Mr Mounson. Thinketh cleerly the proviso will take away all implicacions. The like president in the statute of Wedensdayes and holpen by proviso.[153]

Mr Colby. That every man may speake his fill. Corne, the more it is grouned, the meale wilbe the finer. He specially misliketh of the wordes, 'as yf she were naturally dead'.

Mr Norton. Corne to long grouned makes burnte meale. He would not have wordes lately spoaken by the Recorder to be mistaken, in speaking of the lawes of the Crowne. That no man should thereby implye other but the common lawes and statute lawes concerning the Crowne: no other particular lawe of the Crowne varying from these.

Mr Wentworth. That he had rather comytt some foly in speech then doe iniury by silence. All learned men in Englande not of one opinion concerning the statute of *xxvº Edwardi 3ⁱ*. Some hold opinion, yea a iudge of this realme pronounced it, that the said estatute concerning king's childrene borne out of the king's obeysance should be expounded to the xᵗʰ degree. He would therefore that if any implicacions must be of necessitite, that since the Scottish faction is most dangerous, such wordes should rather be used which may implye to her disadvauntage then any one implication to her advantage. Better in case of necessitye of tempest to touch on the sandes then on the rocke. /

f.58v   Mr Popham. The iudge did not make any such affirmation uppon the sayed estatute of xxv° as affirmatively of himselfe for his owne opinion, but only said some were of such opinion; which he would not have to be mistaken. He thinketh there is a difference betweene implicacions directe and implicacions by intendement. Against any direct affirmation a proviso will not serve, and therefore the wordes 'in parte of punishment' cannot be in. The proviso will not serve: they are meare contrary. The rest of the article implyeth but by intendement: there the proviso will serve. The word 'enacting' carrieth an implicacion on the one side, the word 'declared' carrieth an implicacion on the other side. The proviso carrieth it even.

Mr Bedell. Thinketh many would speake more liberally if it were not for feare. He thinketh it as necessary to provide for the feete as the head, for if the feete be taken away the head is in daunger. The wordes 'in such manner and forme as if she were naturally dead', he thinketh of necessity must implye that if she were alive she had title; and the proviso disalloweth nothing.

Mr Wilbraham. The Scottish Queene the chiefest danger, and therefore he would in any case we should use as heavy wordes as may be against, not loose wordes. Crownes will not away in cloudes. Implicacions he confesseth must be of necessity in the wordes; but the proviso doth set all streight.
In the afternoone.

The bill for division of the sherivewike of Sussex and Surrey, the third tyme read and passed.

The bill for keeping the assises Alesbury, the third tyme read and passed.

The bill concerning the confirmacion of a lease from the Deane and Chapiter of Paule's to Mr Smyth, the customer, the third tyme read and passed.

To the greate byll.

Sir Thomas Scote. The wordes concerning the extolling of the Pope's authority would extend to all idolatrous religion.

Mr St John. For an oath to be taken for maintenance of this estatute.

Mr Dalton. Liketh well of it, but the Queene having already denied it, he is out of hope thereof. He would also that some addition might be made for a publique notification hereof to [the] realme, and also that whosoever should / be slayne in battell on the parte of the late Queene of Scotes, the heire should leese the enheritance and the wife the dower. f.59

The Erle of Kente and Lord Cumpton came to the barre, having the Earle of Bedford and Lord Cumpton for witnesses.

A mocion made whyther the Earle of Bedford should come into the House as a witnesse, or some of the Howse sent to him because he claymed such priviledge in respect of his calling. Agreed he should come in and declared that the Duke of Norfolke and the Lord Paget did the like in Queene Marye's tyme.[154] Ordo

The Earle of Bedford in the said case, first making protestation of his honor to do

150. *Sic*: superfluous? The MS' own punctuation is problematic here, though the meaning is reasonably clear.
151. See Fitzherbert's *Abridgement*, f.180: Continuall Claime, 8 Rich.II.
152. 25 Ed.III, stat.1. (1350-1), in *SR*, I.310.

153. Presumably section 23 of 5 Eliz., c.5, in *SR*, IV.427, which tried to prevent misconstruction of this intent of the statute.
154. See *CJ*, I.32, for Norfolk.

uprightly without affection rather to declare lesse then truth then more, sheweth that Sir John Gascoygne had declared unto him that he was feffee of trust to the use of the nowe Earle of Kente and that he was much bounde unto him and had beene his father's officer, and therefore bounde to pleasure the Earle all that he might; how at another tyme the nowe Earle charged the said Sir John Gasgoigne with such his promyses and that the said Sir John Gascoigne then saied he had evidence of the said Earles, and had beene dealt withall on ther side against the Earle, but would doe nothing which might be to his preiudice, for that he was bounde in conscience so to doe. And that the Earle of Pembrooke had said unto him that the release might be traveyled for well enough without offence.

The Lord Cumpton desireth to knowe of the Earle of Bedford whyther the Earle of Kente did ever affirme unto him that the Earle of Northumberlande was a feffee in the like matter. The Earle answereth 'No'; but he hath heard so by others. He asked farther of the said Earle whither the Earle of Pembrooke ever told him that he procured the release. He confesseth that the Earle of Pembrooke said unto him that he was a procurer, but that proveth not there was no mo procurers. /

f.59v   The Lord St John, with like protestation made, delivered in certaine depositions taken before him, Mr Lewes Dyve, and Mr Apsley, which he affirmeth to be the depositions of such persons as were then named, sheweth that it was by commyssion but not certefied by reason of the death of Sir John Gascoigne.

Mr Solliciter. Deposytions would be commytted to writing because memory may faile.

Mr Speaker. Profe alowed by oath, but no examiner apointed.

Mr Solliciter. How shall we then except against witnesses without tyme.

Mr Speaker. Lesse tyme in other courtes uppon issues tryed.

Mr Cobbe and Mr Gascoigne were sworne.

Mr Cobbe sheweth that he did prosecute a write of entry in the *per et cui* in the Earle of Kente's name against the Lord Cumpton, which proceeded so farre as the view was graunted, and that shortly after a like action was brought in the name of Sir John Gascoigne against the said Lord Cumpton, and that the Lord Cumpton's solliciter talked with him of the same, and he demaunding of the said solliciter whyther the said Sir John Gascoigne pretended any title to the lande, he said the action was brought to the Earle of Kente's use.

Mr Gascoygne. That he heard of the writ. He sheweth farther that the Earle brought a bill against his father in the Chauncery and that before the release procured he was sent for to my Lord Cumpton's howse and that the Earle of Pembrooke did perswade him to move his father to surcease the action against the Lord Cumpton, and that he promised to write to his father aswell to forbeare as to prosequte any action as to release to the Lord Cumpton, and that at his cominge to London he would bring him to the Earle of Pembrooke and that afterwardes, meeting his father going towardes a mariadge to Sir Anthony Browne's, he advised him to doe nothing for either parte otherwise then compelled. Such earnest meanes notwithstanding was made as he understoode he meante to release the lettre he wrote. He hath st[udied] and remembreth the contentes. Amongst other things in the same, he advised his father not to esteeme money. He desired in the end of his letter to have his lettre sent him againe, but his father sent it not. The release was afterwardes / brought to his father in Milke Streete, but it was not then sealed, being misliked. He f.60 sawe at the same tyme money in a bagge ready to be paid for the same, but afterwardes he saw it sealed and delivered to certaine feffees. The Lord Cumpton brought it to him to subscribe as a witnesse, which he refused to doe untill his father commaunded him to doe it, and then he wrote it ill-favoredly and the Lord Cumpton complayned of the same to his father, and then he sawe the same bagge brought in againe.

Uppon the foresaid deposytions inference being made of the profe of the making of the release, that the same was donn by fraude, that the Lord Cumpton was privy and partye to it, the money paied for it, he sawe no cause but the Howse was to proceede in the cawse.

Mr Solliciter. He perceaveth by the Howse that the bill was to be amended, and then was the same a suggestion, no bill, and so should answere to nothing. Secondly, that the release cannot be dealt in without consideration first had of the title, for yf no title in the Earle.[155] And uppon these pointes he desireth to be resolved before he answere to the matter. He trusteth the deposytions in by my Lord St Johne shall not be read because, not being ever certefied, the[y] are now *rerum non iudice* and as though they had never beene received.

Mr Gascoigne came in againe and declared that the Lord Cumpton did move him to be a meane to procure the release.

A motion made whyther the said deposytiones delivered by my Lord St John should be read, yea or no.

Mr Popham. Thinketh they may be read to informe our consciences the sayings of witnesses examined. He some mayor of some corporacion have beene certefied under seale to courtes,[156] oathes taken that papers are true copies of deposytions, yea letters shewed forth in profe from noble men; much rather theise deposytions.

Mr Bedell. The same of as greate credit before the certificate as after. The certificate but a matter of forme.

Hereuppon agreed the same should be read, which was don accordingly. And upon reading of the same it did purporte that Raynsford did pay / certaine mony to f.60v Sir John Gascoigne. What the summe was he certainly knoweth not, for that it was in a bagge, but by the quant[it]y, if it were all silver, it seemed to be lx^{li}. Neyther can certainly tell wherefore the same was payed.

x° Junij.[157]

A bill that no curseyes should be longer then xviij yardes, to be engrossed.

A bill that no servant to any subiect be iustice of peace or high constable, the third tyme read and passed.

A bill that Cockeshall and Bocking should onely make clothes called handwarpe clothes, marked with the signe of the cocke. The third tyme read and passed.

---

155. *Sic.*
156. *Sic.*

157. MS reads '*ix° Junij*', placed after next entry.

A bill that Woodstocke may buy and sell wolle and yarne, the third tyme read and passed.

A bill that the wardens of the Waxechaundlers in London should have the search of waxe in London, the suburbes, and within xx^ty miles of the same, and in Sturbridge faire. The third tyme read.

Mr Slege. To deale in Sturbridge fayre an iniury both to the university and the towne.

Mr Hayward. Yf unskillfull men have the search, no helpe will growe.

Mr Snage. No reason to give London such iurisdiction. No reason it should be burnte, though evill. Some good, he thinketh, might be picked out and given to the poore. Besides, he thinketh it very [un]reasonable that they which are to burne the waxe should have the forfeyture, since when it is burnte no tryall can be made whyther the waxe were good or no; so that one selfesame persons may burne good waxe, take a forfeyture of the owner of the waxe, and no man to controle them. And so uppon the question the bill reiected.

The bill for severance of the sherivewike of Huntingdon and Cambridge, the third tyme read and passed.

Sir Nicholas Arnold. Sheweth that uppon Saturday last he was summoned upon an ateynt and, attending here in this Howse, was amercyed x^li; and prayeth the priviledge of the Howse for discharge of the same, which was graunted. /

f.61   The bill of lether from the Lordes, the second tyme read.

Segerston. The dearth of the commodities of this realme more beneficiall to the common wealth then to have the same cheape, as of wolle; and though our lether goe forth they have it not for nothing. Good mony is returned for the same. The gentleman cawseth the dearth; that is, by selling the hides so deare, and therefore no reason to buy shooes good cheape.

The bill against conveying of lether, the third tyme read and passed.

[Afternoon]

A bill that all corporat townes might have a chamberleyne to keepe the goodes and chattelles of orphanes, the second tyme read.

This day I was away parte of the day uppon a commyttye of the greate bill.

Mr Heyward. In some townes the best of the towne is of small abilitie and so the orphanes shalbe utterly deceaved.

Mr Segerston. There never cam so good a bill in the Howse, and therefore yf it passe not he never looketh for any good bill.

Mr Knevit. Wisheth some good order be taken that the chamberline do not abuse the orphanes. They will many tymes sell them to such as will release to them the greatest parte of the goodes. And so the bill commytted.

A bill that leases from corporacions should be good notwithstanding the misnamer, the second tyme read, to be engrossed.

A bill that Lirpoole chapell might be made a church, the ij^d tyme read.

Mr Selinger. Liketh not yt should beare the name of St Paule; good also to have consideracion of the living which if it be small cannot be devided.

Mr Greenefield. The person of Walton must needes be hindered hereby, for a parte of the personadge shalbe taken from him and he paye tenthes and first fruites as before. And so the bill commytted.

A bill against evill tanning of lether, first read.

[xi] Junij.

A bill that meeses[158] and lande in Excyter might discende according to the course of the common law and not to be divided amongst the heires males and females.

A bill that one measure of corne, ale, beere, and wine may be observed thorough the realme, and the clarke of the market to make search for the same. /

Mr Galeyse. The statute needlesse. Lawe sufficient already in force for amendment of the same in cities and townes corporates best looked unto; the officers there sworne to do their duties. He liketh not that iustices of peace should intromyt there, since maiors deale not in the countie. Yf the maior and citisens do not their dutie they shall leese their liberties, which is punishment sufficient.   f.61v

Mr Grimston. The clerkes of the market leese their offices to diverse evill persons. They trouble the holle countrie. Although the measures be marked before, yet they will take two pence apeece for looking uppon the same.

Mr Browning. Yf this estatute should be executed it would be a mervellous trouble to such as use bargeyning, that have used to buy and sell in diverse places and knowe how to make and divide their cariadges according to the measures.

Mr Husseye. Declareth the Lord Cumpton hath t[h]reatened Mr Gascoigne since his deposytion made here in this Howse and therefore desireth the Lord Cumpton might be spoake with in that behalfe.

Mr Snage. That he is to desire the Howse to ayde him [in] that which he hath honestly donne. He declareth that uppon a speech uttered by him, occasion hath beene taken by some to make a wrongfull and uniust information to the Lordes, that he should utter speech tending to that end that they had not to doe with the common wealth, but that we in the common howse had onely the care thereof; they cam for their owne persons only. This he knoweth hath beene raysed uppon this occasion: hee moved the Howse for a generall oath to be taken thoroughe the realme for the approving of the Acte of Parliament made against Mary commonly called Queene of Scotes. Hereuppon he sheweth that he declared as it were the state of Parliament, that in the same the Queene and the noble men represented their owne voices only, the knightes and burgesses of the lower howse represented all the commynalty of the realme: and notwithstanding voices thus given by us in their names did binde them, yet he thought it not sufficient except they did confirme it by oath in their owne voyces. 'I desired at the same tyme I might be heard with indifferent eares and conceaved with indifferent iudgement'. This was not without some feare, which now is fallen out not to be without cause. Hereupon / hath beene gathered by meanes   f.62 of sinister[159] reportes that to the greate dishonnor of the nobilitie they were made shaddowes, unable to deale in matters of common weale. He desireth to be purged herein, and that some of the House may be sent up with him to answere for him.

Mr Wentworth. The freedome of the House taken away by tale tellers, and therefore very necessary to search them out and to sende to the Lordes to knowe from whence the information was receaved.

Mr Speaker. Thinketh it very necessary to be considered of, for that [it]

---

158. *Sic.*   159. MS reads 'sinisters'.

impeacheth the credit of the House that we should suffer such speeches unreproved. It had beene his dutie, if no man else had don it, to have reproved such speech. The speech uttered he remembreth very well and tended to such end as hath beene declared; that the Lordes represented themselves onely, the commynalty represented here, as it were by atornies.

Mr Yelverton. Considering the first institution of parliamentes and considering how the same are used at this present, he cannot but thinke greate iniury to be offered in theise late parliaments; and as the like hath beene offered to diverse heretofore, so the suggestion be true, the member of our House which now complaineth hath beene very much abused. The speech uttered he remembereth to[160] have beene such as hath beene declared, and the same as it was used was truly said. Then to have a contrary informacion made is not to be leafte unpunished. And looke how much the informacion may seeme to deserve offence of the Lordes towardes us, as yf it had beene true; so much the informer, not being true, deserveth evill of us all which be members of the House. He thinketh it very necessary a petition be made to the Lordes that he may be knowne which made the petition. If the wordes were never said, then is the offence the greater; but if said, not pardonable. He thinketh it not lawfull for any member of this House to utter out of the Howse any speech which may tende to the reproach of another member of the same. Zeale may cary a man sometime in speech in weighty causes beyonde discretion; yet were it not honest the wordes should be reported, beleeved, or revenged. It may breede disgrace to the whole parliament. What can be a more detestable acte then to set discention and debate or to procure displeasure betweene the Queene, the nobilitie, and us which represent the commynalty? This kinde of offence hath beene to common a burden, /

f.62v but no amendement groweth because none hath beene punished for the same. He would have it taken that no man can speake offencively. For his parte, he thinketh it more convenient to beare with offence then to breede dumme silence, and then bad lawes are to be looked for. Very necessary therefore an humble sute be made unto the Lordes that he or they which made the informacion might be knowne. It is not to slipe least we might seeme to confesse it. A noble man's good or evill countenance may farther or hinder any of us. He moveth likewise that examination be made by whome the charge of the House with bribery did first springe.

Mr Digs. For the first matter, agreeth in opinion with the last man: for the last matter, as he was the first utterer thereof in the House, so was he not the deviser thereof, but was warraunted to say mor then he did.

Mr Recorder. That he was here at the utterance of the speech whereof mencion is here made. Men's phrases be diverse aswell as their garmentes; and certeinly the speech caried such sence as hath beene uttered, in what kinde of phrase soever it was spoaken. Reporters speake what they list to the reproach of others, and by that occasion many good men cannot speake for evill reporters. By the way he declareth that the order of the House was not that noblemen should be brought in as witnesses in any cause, but that certaine commyttees should be sente to them to receave their sayings uppon their honnor and to make reporte of the same to the House; and therefore would that in[161] president were taken of the Earle of Bedford's coming in the laste day for that purpose. A noble man came in here ones to the detriment of the crowne. Theise tale tellers very ripe in Queene Marye's tyme. It was the practise of papistes, and they were traiters. Some of them be dead since and some of them walke nowe in Westminster Hall. Messadges were sent to the House, greate trouble grewe; some men troubled by speaking, some men by silence, and generally every man offend[ed]. He is assured, whensoever the tale teller is founde, it shall appeare he is an errant papist that seeke to set discention. Himselfe hath beene in like sorte used. God forgive him, one Flower, a Speaker in this House, for tale telling out of this House, was taken out of his chaire and committed to the Tower.[162] Thompson in like sorte used. Some such punishmentes in theise dayes would make better parliamentes. Surely it is greate treason to set discention betweene [the Lordes] and this House. Surely this matter would be searched *omnibus vi[i]s et modis.* / In the like case   f.63 heretofore order hath beene taken and entered of recorde that neyther he nor any of his name should ever after be of any parliament.

Mr Mounson. This cause of very greate moment. Concerneth not one particular person but all the whole House and every member of the same. That we should beare such speeches enough to breede an uproare betweene the Lordes and us, and so a publique cause, and therefore to be generally moved. Misreportes have beene made of diverse. He hath tasted thereof and is fully resolved they be papistes. Yf the mover hereof be sure that the Lordes have so conceaved, it is necessary publique meanes be used least by silence we may seeme to condemne our selves.

Mr Honywoode. That yester night he supped at my Lord Wentworth's, whereas my Lord at supper tyme uttered such speech as hath beene declared, not meaning who should be the speaker, but affirming that reporte was made that one of the Howse had spoaken it; and did further advise him that the party which spake it might be rebuked if it were true. If not, he thought it very necessary he did purge himselfe. Theise wordes were spoaken in the presence of Mr Pooly, another member of this House, and as for the present he did answere the same, so he thinketh it not his dutie to conceale it.

Mr Pooley. Affirmed the same to be true.

Sir Raph Sadler. That it is too true that such informacion hath beene made to some of the nobilitie. He hath beene told so by some of verie good calling. And so finally agreed a messadge with request to be made [to] that effect: which was donne accordingly by Mr Treasurer.

A bill against fraudulent conveyances, the third tyme read and passed.[163]

A bill to us from the Lordes for sea markes, and another bill for continuance of certaine estatutes.

Mr Treasurer. Sheweth that he hath declared our message, and uppon which my Lord Keeper shewed that he hath heard nothing thereof, but afterwardes two or three lordes came unto them who confessed they had receaved such informacion and that the speech should be spoaken by diverse, but the names of the informers they

160. 'To' repeated in MS.
161. *Sic*; 'no'?
162. Cf. J. S. Roskell, *The Commons and their Speakers in English Parliaments* (1965), for

Roger Flore.
163. The second reading was on 10 June while Cromwell was away from the House (*CJ*, I.102).

would not declare; and did desire that yf no such speech were spoaken it might be passed over with silence. /

f.63v   After, uppon farther mocions made, it was agreed that it should be declared unto the Lordes that the House could not bee so satisfied, but did humbly desire to knowe the informer of the same, with declaracion that otherwise it would be an occasion the House to be put to farther circumstances in trying out the truth. But before the coming of the message the Lordes were up and so no farther proceeding could be therein.

A bill that leases made by corporations should bee good notwithstanding the misnaming of the corporation, the third tyme read and passed.

This donne, the parliament by the mouth of the Speaker[164] was adiorned untill Tuesday sennight following, being the xxiiij[th] of this moneth of June.

At the second session, beginning the xxiiij[th] of June *anno predicto.*

A bill that landes in Exciter might discende according to the course of the comon lawe, and not according to the custome of the towne: the second tyme read; to be engrossed.

A bill that the assises for Staffordsheere should be kept at the towne of Stafford and not elsewhere, except in tyme of plague; the second tyme read.

A bill that no sea markes should be destroyed and that no crosse sayle or smacke sayle should passe the seas.

A bill for the true dying of cloth and to restraine dying in all places, except cities, boroughes, townes corporat and market, and to restraine cariadg of undyed cloathes out of the realme.

Mr Marsh. The whole bill to be overthrowne, the innovation so great and so perillous to the state. The comodities of England nowe distributed thorough Chirstendome; tryall sufficient that we wante no vente as they be now used. What vente wilbe when the clothes be dyed and coloured very doubtfull. Besides, we have not that wherewith we should dye in our owne realme, but must be holpen by others; of our ode from Fraunce, with whom we have not assurance of peace. It is very doubtfull, being died, how they shall be liked in other countries. Not like we shall make col[our] to please all nationes, and then they wilbe unbought, and clothiers and carsey men driven to give over their occupationes, and wolle will waxe

f.64   cheape, which is not for the / commoditie of Englande. For good dyeing there is already a good acte in force. There is also other townes more fit for cloathing then eyther borough townes or market townes. They must needes be died where there is plenty of woode. The procuring of licences to carie cloathes over sea undressed hath cost a marveillous masse of money. Yt would now cost much more when they must also be dyed. Such monopoly to the undoyng of the whole state he cannot alowe.

Mr Hastinges. That he is very sory to here such speech of so great a person, the hinderance of the proceeding of a bill which carieth, as he thinketh, no such preiudice as is supposed. By the byll good provision is made that cloathes should be aswell and as cheape made as in any place, and then he thinketh it more reason our country reape the profite as strangers. The commodytie of the holle realme preferred before the commodytie of the Citie of London. Three hundered thousand caried over every yeare to Flaunders for dyeing of cloathes, and yet the ode not from thence, but from Burdeuxs, where we might have it aswell as they. Undyed clothes notwithstanding may be fetched. They may be caried to any place in certaine number. Wolle shalbe solde both to the [blank] and to the workeman. Experience already hath beene had that our duye is as good as others by a cloth cut in twayne, the one halfe dyed in England and the other beyond the seas. Greate number hereby shalbe set aworke, which wilbe a good provision for vagaboundes.

Mr Treasurer. This bill toucheth the vente of the greatest richesse in Englande. He confesseth that being dyed the clothes wilbe the richer, if we had assurance of a good vente. It hath beene a long question betweene the dressers of cloathes and venters of the same before the Councell and likewise with the dier. He is privy. The merchauntes have given many thousand poundes to carie them undressed. This would they not doe if the vente were good being dressed and died. If the merchaunte wante utterance, the clothier must give over, and the[n] an infinit number must begge. The chiefe gaine to us is in converting wolle to cloathes. If we hinder our trade outwardes we shall have litle come in. Let the duyers of clothes first get them credit by well duyinge.

Mr Atkins. Liketh well of so much of the bill as is for well dyeing of cloathes. The rest he liketh not, yea he thinketh it impossible to be executed. The clothiers already complaine that there is / not ode inough to be gotten in Englande as will die   f.64v
fiftie threedes in every cloath. There also lacketh wodde to die all the cloathes made in England, whereof there is already to much scarsitie. And so the bill reiected.

The bill of jeofeyles the second tyme reade.

xxv⁰ Junij.

The bill for continuance of certaine statutes from the Lordes, ones read.

The bill for sea markes and that no hoye or smacke should crosse the seas, the second tyme read.

The byll against Mary Queene of Scotes, the third tyme read.

Mr Alford. Desireth all men to marke his wordes, and that if any parte of his speech be misliked he may be charged while his speech is best in remembrance. The cause concerneth a queene and a state of enheritance, which occasioneth him to say so much as he meaneth to speake at this present. *Regum efflicta fortuna magis trahit nos ad commyserationem quam aliorum.* The offences of the Queene of Scotes the cause of this bill, and a iudge is to iudge *secundum allegata et probata*, yea though himselfe knew the contrary. There is in the bill one article, that if any warre be levyed for her, whyther with her consent or no, she shalbe held a traitor. This article he cannot condiscende unto. All disablementes he alloweth of, but not to touch her in life unhearde. Yf xxᵗʰʸ lewd men should proclaime her Queene, she shalbe condemned. This a hard dealing with a queene, for so he must needes accompt of her, as of a Scottish queene in Englande; and we ought not to touch God's annoynted. This he thinketh should be against the honnor of England, and wee ought not to consent to any thing dishonorable to the realme. It wilbe talked of in all Christendome. He therefore very

164. 'The parliament' repeated here in MS.

scruplous in this matter. Another pointe of the bill is that if after the Queene's death she should make any clayme, then to be out of protection and held as an enemy. This he thinketh very unreasonable in any, much more in her, for that the greater the person the greater ought to be the compassion. David's advoutry was pardoned. She shalbe killed without tryall, for it is to late to make tryall when she is dead. King Salomon would not execute Adonias because he was a king, *quia unctus Domini.*

f.65   The Emperour Charles caused to be executed the Duke of Bavier and the Duke of Austria, and afterwardes considering what the hangman / had don in executing so noble personadge, the Emperor commaunded the hangman to be beheaded, least he should at any tyme after boast of the distruction of so noble personadges. He wisheth rather that the subiect which shall ayd or assiste her should in this case be out of protection.

Mr Norton. As much neede as any man to crave favourable construction. The cause wherefore after the death of the Queene's Majestie the said Mary should be out of protection is for that there is then lefte no other remedy to punish her by lawe, and therefore to be deemed as an enemy. Why she should be counted a queene he knoweth not. We may as well take notice of her dismission of the crowne as of her having the crowne, since both are matters forraigne. But to all the world appeareth manifestly she is a very unnaturall person, and no repentance found in her; and mercy hath no place where there is no repentance. Yf ye wilbe mercyfull extend mercy to the best prince that liveth, and not extende mercy to the worste to the daunger and distruction of the best. Let mercy be shewed to the good Christianes whom she seeketh to destroy; be mercyfull to our selves, *charitas incipit a se ipso.* It hath beene said she is not heard, but it is well knowne she hath beene largely heard. To give away a crowne from her he is content without hearing, but her life. He knoweth not what might induce him to the one rather then the other. But what yf she will not be hearde or not before a certayne tyme? Shall wee in the meane season leave the Queene's Majestie and the whole realme in daunger, and provide no remedy untill a new mischiefe or treason be wrought, and then provide remedy when it is to late, she living to the daunger of our Queene dayly? Proofes sufficient against her have beene hearde. Adonias at first not executed by Salomon, it is true, neyther yet pardoned but uppon good behaviour: uppon a second offence commytted was put to death. Such the Queene of Scotes case. Yf warre be offered for her sake it must needes be by her meanes. What followeth? She shall dye for the first treasons whereof she is already culpable and hath deserved death; and that very reasonable. It hath beene said not reason to leese so noble and honorable a queene; it should not be honorable. But he thinketh lawe and iustice to be always honorable. The matter hath beene considered by the bishoppes according to the word of God, by the civilians and by the iudges of the common lawe, and all have agreed that it is

f.65v   iust and / lawfull. God forbidd we should preferre the vaine name of honor before the safety of the Queene's Majestie. The example of David can not serve. He did repente, and yet David was punished, and choose himselfe to be rather punished then his people. The lawe shall protecte her as longe as she is obedient to lawe. But, her title being taken away, if she clayme the crowne she comes eyther as an enemy or a conqueror, and then by lawe may be killed. The example alledged of Charles the

Emperour commaunding the hangman of the Duke of Bavier to be executed when he had before executed the Duke, he knoweth not to what purpose it should be alledged, except it were meant that all we of the Parliament House should be put to death for making of this lawe; and that he thinketh not reasonable. But he will say he meante him that should kill the Scote, for that he is the hangman. But who set him aworke but the whole parliament, the Queene's Majestie, the Lordes, and our selves. He requireth that our Speaker in his oration may declare to the Queene's Majestie that this bill is no perfect safety for the Queene's Majestie, but that it will be necessary for her Majestie to proceede farther to execucion, or otherwise that both she and we shall continue in perill.

Mr Sampoole. The death of her, for warres attempted for her, very necessary. A good meanes for the Queene's safety when the Scottish fautors shall knowe that to stirre for her shall worke the destruction of her whom they love. Henry the vj^{th} lost his crowne because the Queene stirred warre, and yet he no evill disposed prince. Dalba the emperor in case of extremity executed two without lawe. De la Poole executed by King Henry the viij^{th}. And so the bill passed without any 'No'.

[Afternoon]

A bill for the severance of the sherivewike of Bedford and Buckingham, to be engrossed.

A bill that landes in Exciter may discende according to the course of the common lawe, the third tyme read and passed.

A bill that carseyes should not contayne above xix yardes, the third tyme read and passed.

A bill for keeping the assises at Stafford onely and not else where, the third tyme read.

Mr Segerston. Stafford the head towne of the shier scitu[ate] in the midest of the same, had neede of reliefe. /

Mr Bedell. Unreasonable to bynd the iustices of assise to a place certaine. The commyssion is *ad certos diem et ad locum quem ad hoc provideritis*. If sicknesse should happen to himselfe he cannot alter the place and so no assises. Besides, the bill extendeth to all sessions of enquiry, whereas forcible entries ought to be enquired of as neere the place as may be. Stafford already pilleth and poleth: if it be tyed to that place certaine it will pill and pole more.

Mr Snage. Would have an exception for the present iustices of assise according to a former president of Aylesbury at the least. Besides, sickness or no sicknesse, shall call every man's *nisi prius* in question.

Mr Yelverton. The iustices of assise had neede to be favored. They compelled to that office; never voluntarily take it. Whyther the minde or bodie be respected, their trouble importable; a labour besides without commodity. The meanest councellor gaineth more then they have allowance for their travell. For the most parte not iudges before they be old. He knoweth some which would give liberally to be discharged. The assises apointed for the ease of the country and trouble of the iudge. Before, all matters tryed at Westminster. And therefore not to encroch to much of favor shewed. Sicknesse in Stafford onely respected, without consideracion if sicknesse should be in any place neere adiacente.

f.66

Mr Lockwoode. This bill hath heretofore passed the parliament.[165] Now preferred by the Earle of Essex, the Lord Stafford, and the Lord Paget, and by the holle shiere. The bill sheweth also that is commodious to the Queene, for that the towne is hers. The iustices of assises already come thither for the most parte, and therefore cannot much offende them to be brought to that which already they doe voluntarily.

Mr Recorder. Against the old cabelist to name any person. The law of Locris would have them hanged that moveth anything whereof cometh no benefit. *Legibus vivimus non exemplis. Sapiens pro republica nullum vitabit periculum.* And therefore he to have more respect to the country, which is a multitude, then particular persons. He wisheth a proviso for the Lord Chiefe Barron during his life. And so the bill put to the question and passed. /

f.66v   *xxvj° Junij.*

A bill for the well making and sealing of tanned lether, the third tyme read and passed.

A bill fo[r] the well watring of hempe and that no dew dried hempe should be put in cables, hawsers, or cariadges; twise read.

A bill for the severance of the sherivewike of Bedford and Buckingham, the third tyme read and passed.

The bill of jeofeyles, the third tyme read, to the reading whereof one French lord was permytted enter the Howse and to sit by Mr Treasurer, certaine others to stande at the barre; which was argued in their presence by Mr Yelverton against the bill and Mr Recorder with the bill.

xxvij° Junij.

The bill for sea markes and hoyes, the third tyme read and passed.

Mr Boyes. Moveth that the Lord Warden of Cinque Portes may [have] forfetures forfeited within the iurisdiction of the same, according to their patentes mad in that behalfe.

Mr Colbrahan. That it were greate iniury to take away from men their plats and hoyes. The hoyes very necessary; in many cases will abide the seas when other shipps will not. He wisheth a lawe to be made or other provision had for restrainte of cariadge of timber beyond the seas. A thousand ton every yeare caried out of this country. There is one man which hath made a bargeine for xv hundered thousande tonn yet to be caried over.

Segerston. Liketh not that the forfeitures should be to the Trinity House. Lancasheer, Cheshier have speciall priviledge. Every man now seeketh all commodities to come to London, as though all the knightes and burgesses of the rest of the realme come in vayne.

Mr Treasurer. If this lawe were reiected, all sea markes will [be] cut downe and then greate danger to all travellers, life and goodes. Plattes and hoyes may still passe along the seas, or by using crosse sayles may also crosse the seas.

Mr Recorder. His commyssion to speake to Gode's glory, the preservacion [of] the Queene's Majestie and the profit of the common weale. Lancas[hire] hath of very old tyme enioyed many priviledges and in the Duke of Gaunte's tyme made a county palantine and so [have] jurisdiction and tryall of all matters. They goe tole free [in] London. The first male child of the king by birth born Duke of Lancaster and Earle of Chester. Prince of Wales is by creation. And therefore he trusteth that the Howse / will not agree to hinder the inheritance of the heir of the Crowne, when so ever God shall [send] such a one. For the benefit of the Trinitie he would not have them seeke to incroch so much of other men's liberties.   f.67

Mr Snage. Aloweth well that the Countye Palantine have all the forfeitures within their liberties, and would have the like to V Portes, and the like in a greate many. Shippes may perish if a tempest overthrowe the sea markes before notice shall come to them to take order for the setting up of newe.

Hereuppon a proviso was added and the bill passed.

Note. After the passing of this bill, it was amended and brought to the question anewe.

A bill for recontinuance of certaine estatutes, the third tyme read and passed.

Mr Tompest. Desireth the priviledg of the Howse for a servant of his arrested uppon an execution.   Case of priviledg

Mr Bedell. Being uppon an execution we should seeme to doe uniustly to set him at liberty, for that then the debt should be lost and the sherive charged with the gainement of the same, for he cannot be twyse put in execution.

Mr Sampole. That Ferris was set at liberty, being imprisoned upon an execution, and that the sherive and serieant commytted to the Tower, and the debt never sithence payed. At the least the arrester is to be sent for and punished by the discretion of the Howse.

Mr Norton. No question but the priviledge is grauntable and every man bounde to take notice at his perill, for that a parliament is a matter notoriously knowne.

Mr Gargrave. Declareth that he hath heard that the execucion is by force of a *capias utlagatum*.

Mr Recorder. There is 2 statutes concerning the priviledges of the parliament which they ought to have aswell for themselves as their servants in cominge, during their aboad, and in their returne: as may amongst other estatutes may[166] appeare *8° Henrici 6^i, caput 1° ;*[167] and if any such be arrested by the waye a man shall have a speciall writ from the Clerke of the / Crowne for their discharge. But the case   f.67v necessary to be considered: yf the party be outlawed, no fit person to be protected. And so, for that it appeared he was in by force of an utlarie, the priviledge denied.

xxviij° Junij.

The bill of fugitives being before twise at the question was againe amended and the third tyme brought to question and passed after it had come from the Lordes, being before sente to them by us.

Mr French. To the bill of jeofeyles. That he misliketh most the second parte of the

---

165. See *CJ*, I.57-8 (1558).
166. *Sic.*
167. 8 Hen.VI, c.1 (1429), in *SR*, II.238 (for the clergy in Convocation); the other statute mentioned here is probably 5 Hen.IV, c.6 (1403-4), in *SR*, II.144, concerning Richard Cheddre.

bill which forbiddeth any iudgement to be given uppon any other causes then those which be published and declared uppon the demurrer tendered, and so it may fall out that iudgement shalbe given contrary to the very substance and matter, the same being not shewed as no man doth at the beginning see all causes of demurrer.

Mr Snage. That as this bill offereth to remedy some mischeifes, so it offereth greater mischiefes then before. Now men's enheritance may be overthrowne where a good title was before had. Before, the mischiefe only in delayes. Iudgement shalbe given although the matter will not beare it, and the iudge saying it, compelled to give iudgement contrary to his conscience.

The bill of fugitives ones more amended and in a proviso offered by us, and the fourth tyme brought to the question.

Mr Dalton. To the former bill. It may be that sometymes issue may be ioyned of not culpable, whereas the declaracion itself was insufficient in matter, and so iudgement given contrary [to] a man's cause; which were not reasonable. Besides, a verdicte sometymes unduely procured, in which case it were reasonable such advantages were lefte or else the party shall have ha[?rd] remedy. This will also marre all pleading, for no counsell shall neede to use diligence, and then every botcher shalbe a counsellor.

Mr Fennor. The bill very necessary. Offered for avoyding of delays of sutes, so common a mischiefe as requireth necessary provision. Indirect verdictes have beene obiected. No reason in respect of a fewe of those to over throwe or endaunger all direct verdictes. Neyther is any man concluded by any such indirecte verdicte. The remedy of ateynte is lefte him in / such case, which is most convenient to punish that which is the cause of the griefe. The same already lawe for barres, replicacions *etc.*, in which commonly a man's matter is set out and but seldome uppon the declaracion. To the seconde matter. It hath beene said the matter it selfe may be omytted uppon the demurrer, and that a man should be bounde to one matter. But the truth is the bill offereth not to binde a man to any one cause. He may shewe as many as he liste; and knowing a man bounde to the causes which be shewed, he were unworthy to be a counseller which would omytt the principall. The demurrer already peremptory to both partes if it be in such action where title of lande is to be recovered; and he thinketh it more reason a man be bounde by an oversight whereof he was forewarned, then for matters whereof he never thought. Neyther is the judge restrained to amende any thing for satisfaction of himselfe, onely that he shall not hinder the parties thereby.

Mr Sampole. No liking to the bill and lesse to the proviso. An action uppon the case may be brought against a man for calling him a promoter. The defendant will plead not culpable. The yssue passeth for the pleyntiff. In this case though the very wordes give no cause of such action, yet the iudge compelled to give iudgement against the defendant, which were not reasonable. The remedy of ateynt a hard remedy, a greate trouble to the country, and seldome passeth. This will cause new demurrers dayly. The proviso most unnecessary. Diverse actions, as common trespasses and actions of debt, wherein heretofore was not neede to use a counseller, now a man compelled to get a counseller's hande and so driven to greater charges then ever before. He mistrusteth that the bill was brought in to get the proviso.

Serieant Manwood. This bill hath had diverse obiections. Some have thought the same to be offered for increase of gaine to the lawyers, others that it will decrease knowledg. Both these errors being removed, truth will remayne truth. The lawe apointeth two solemne trialles for all causes, one by the country, the other by demurrer. Liberty given to eyther party, as occasion serveth, to use which of theise he liste. Tryall by battell he speaketh not of because the case is rare, and we specially to regarde dayly griefs. If this bill corrupt neyther of the said trialls / but amende them, it is to be liked. The greatest commodity in all trialls is convenient expedicion. That by this bill greatly furthered. The experience to common that a man, as the lawe nowe standeth, hath had foure or five recoveries, and yet the same still reversed by some errors which have growne by over sight eyther of the counseller, atorney, or clarke of some office; and so a man [can] scant get an end of a sute in his life. Besides, if all theise doe their duties and no oversight happen, after iudgement given he may be a yeare delayed of execution by writ of error. This mischiefe foreseene longe agoe, and therefore about xxxij yeares passed a remedy provided for such oversightes in all the rest of the pleading except the declaracion and the wryt, and by the said xxxij yeares' experience hath beene founde necessary lawe.[168] No learned iudge will deny it. All the obiections made against this bill might then be made against that bill. This but a handmayde to the former. The body reformed by the former estatute; this requireth the head may be also set straight, which in a deformed person is as necessary [as] reformacion of any parte of the body. Now to the fainte[169] reasons. Cases have beene put where yssue hath beene taken uppon insufficient declaracions founde against the defendant and the iudge compelled to give iudgement against him. This is reasonable: *volento non fit iniuriae*. He had a tyme to have iustefied; he had his election, if he will chose the worse. It hath also beene obiected that indirecte verdicts be often procured. The party hath his remedy by ataynte or wryt of right. Let the partie which hath recovered have his fee, which is iudgement. This wounde fou[nd] xxiiij yeares agoe by as learned iudges as ever were, and the bill drawne by them, though hindered often of passage. Now to the demurrer. A vaine cause commonly she[?wn]; the demurrer is intered; it standeth uppon title of la[nd]; a blind cinq[?ue] manes; a good causest shall leese my land.[170] A greate deale more reasonable to adventure a losse w[?here] the cause is shewed then to have it so often. Nowe to the obiection of decrease of learning. He seeth no[t] but that learning shalbe in as good estimacion as ever / it was. Men will goe to such as can iudge whyther the causes be sufficient for demurrers, yea or no, and men driven to as much study as ever they were, to the end they may iudge. The matter in substance can never be omytted. He unworthie to be a counseller that should forget the principall cause, knowing the undoing of his client and his owne discredit to depende thereon. The proviso he confesseth may bring gaine to the lawyer. The same not offered by him, but cometh in he knoweth not howe.

Mr Dalton. The former lawe not so large as this. It extendeth only to matters in forme, this generally to all matters. Who will regard learning when his adversary

f.68v

f.69

---

168. 32 Hen. VIII, c.30 (1540), in *SR*, III.786-7.

169. *Sic*: 'feigned'?

170. *Sic*.

shall put it in his mouth? Besides, who will study without gaine? No marvell if they which have already gained enough and doe deale with more then they can dispatch, can be content to spare the proviso.

And so the bill put to the question and passed.

Ultimo Junij.

Mr Honywood. Declareth that his horses being coming for him towardes London, are taken at Gravesende for the Frenchmen, and requireth priviledge and that the takers may be sent for and punished; but had no remedy.

Mr Norton. Declared the indirecte and false dealings of Fisher, and his practises used to get a proviso added to the bill of Tundbridge, with will that the acte should not preiudice the validity of his deede against Alderman Rivers.[171] Requireth that a memorandum might be entered into the clarke's booke that the forgery wherewith Fisher was charged was left out of the acte by reason that he did submyt himselfe to them. Which, after longe disputation, was agreed unto; and after a convenient pause, a new motion made to have it againe brought to the question uppon a surmise that the 'No' was greater. But in the end, for that it did appeare that diverse were gon out of the House and others entered in the meane season, it was agreed that it should not be brought to any new question.

The bill for Sir William Harper, the third tyme read, and concerning the avoyding of a deede of gift to Prestward, and passed.[172] |

f.69v   In the after noone this day the Queene's Majestie came to the Howse, who being sat under her cloath of estate in her robes, all the lordes being likewise in their robes, the Speaker came in, accompanied with the residue of the Howse, and made an oration to this effect following.

'It hath pleased your excellent Majestie to [call] this parliament especially and principally for one only cause, and the same the weightiest that I have knowne any parliament called in my tyme, the whereof[173] hath given cause of greate consultation aswell to the Lordes as also to her Majesti's loving subiectes of the lower howse, by whose grave and deliberat advise a bill hath beene drawne against Mary Stewarde commonly called Queene of Scotes, whereto the common consent of both the Howses hath beene given to the end it might be enacted; containing diverse and sundery horribly[174] factes, seditious practises, forraigne conspiracies, and domesticall treasons attempted, furthered and procured by the said Mary and her complices against your royall person, to the destruction of the same, overthrowe of religion, and utter subversion of the generall estate of this comon weale; which recitall, as it is to true, so hath it beene proved by good circumstances. In this bill such provision is made as this tyme doth suffer, the suddainnesse of the cause and other circumstances considered. Notwithstanding, weighing the same to the full, although your Majestie hath thought good at this present to stay us from farther proceeding in the cause, yet we all have receaved hope[175] that lacke of tyme only hath staied your Majestie, for such farther correction were more correspondente to the qualities of the crimes. We therefore most humbly beseech your Highness that, as we confidently trust yow will have consideracion hereof, so it may please your Highnesse speedily to proceede to the execution thereof accordingly, sith long tracte of tyme may not only renewe the former haza[rd] but increase courage and boldnes to newe attemptes more perilouse then the former.

'It hath beene an old and true saying, "Hapie are they that can take heed by others' harmes," or rather by former harmes towardes themselves to shun like harmes which may hape to themselves. On the contrary, unhapie be they which / neyther by   f.70 the examples of others nor by former perill to themselves wilbe warned to prevent perills to come. Examples hereof amongst subiectes very common, amongst princes rare. I will therefore by your Majestie's patience make a shorte collection of an example or two. Methrodates King of Armenia receaved into his favour Rothrodistus. The said Rothrodistus used diverse practises for the distruction of Methrodates. This well knowne to the King of Armenia, and he notwithstanding, deluded by faire wordes and smooth promises, receaved him into favour and used him in all pointes as a king's sonn. Rothrodistus notwithstanding practised anewe against Methrodates, first robbed him of his subiectes, after rise in armes against him, tooke the King and most miserably and ceytifly destroyed him. Isathius, Emperour of Constantinople, having to brother Alexius, the said Alexius wrought many conspiracies against his brother. Notwithstanding Isathius did beare with him, whereby being emboldned proceeded under disimulation to newe practises and being pardoned never would give over untill he had deposed his brother, committed and kept him long tyme in prison, where he most miserably dyed. The like example betweene Davide and Absolon his sonn, although his life cut of for the same. I will add hereto a shorte fable of Isope, who maketh mention that a man traveyling on his way found a serpent honge in a snare or gin. The serpent, not knowing how to get liberty, complained to the man with pitifull moane and lamentation, made large promises of recompence. The man hereby being perswaded, set the serpent at libertie, who immediately sought to devour and destroye the man, who charged the serpent of ingratitude. The lion by chaunce passing by and having the complaintes on both partes, was made iudge. He determined for conclusion he could render no good iudgement except the serpent were newely entangled in the snare, in such sorte as he was before he was set at libertie; which being donn accordingly, the lion greatly blamed the man for giving so light credit to such a beast, in whome never was founde other then deceipt, and now bad him choose whyther, having had tryall sufficient of the serpente's nature, he would set him at liberty. To avoyd tedyousnesse I will forbeare the applications of theise histories. /

'This notwithstanding I must say, that when your Majestie's good subiectes   f.70v consider the greate benefits they have receaved of your Grace, they cannot but thinke your Majestie will nowe likewise have care for their preservation, being in greate danger without diligent providence, which they are compelled to feare seing the imminent daunger to your person and therein the utter ruine and subversion of the state and the present perill and destruction of your people, who love yow as dutifully as this your knowne enemy doth horribly hate yow. We therefore, representing the

171. See *CJ*, I.103.   174. *Sic.*
172. *Sic.*   175. MS reads 'hape'.
173. *Sic.*

state of your people, do make continuell intercession to your Majestie with motherly pitye to beholde your afflicted children, whereby yow may the rather take a iust occasion to prevent this perill, aswell towardes your Majestie as us, by due punishment, and give a iust cause to us continually to reioyce in the memory of your most happie raigne, which God long continue over us, and withall leave a perpetuall monument in perpetuyty of your providence, love and zeale borne to your people, which except the ioyes of heaven is the greatest glory which can be to any prince. And be [it] spoaken under your Highnesse' allowance, if your noble progenitors had not practised and put in ure to prevent imminent mischiefes with present remedies, they had not raigned so long tyme as they did; of the which, notwithstanding, some for wante of prudent prevention tasted of the chaunce of fortune, or rather of the mighty hande of God. The neglecting to provide remedy in tyme against such persons hath already bred your Majestie some perills, and it is not to be doubted theire cankred malice ceas[es] not, but as it hath heretofore, so continueth still their hope in the destruction of your royall Majestie; whose secrete practises are farre more dangerouse then any forraigne hostility against whom preparacion may be made; against the other no remedy after the mischiefe donne. The meanest subiect of this lande, being assaulted by f[orce] and violence, may defende himselfe and hath priviledge rather to kill then to be killed. Why then should not your Majestie execute that by iudgement which both the lawes of God and of your realme doe permit and suffer? Your Majestie beareth the name of pitye, and not unworthyly. Our h[olle] prayer is it be not extended to your destruction.

f.71 And / since your Majestie will needes exersise the same, apply it to us your lovinge subiectes to whom it is due, and not to such as meane to deprive soe loving subiectes of so good a princesse to the destruction of both in one. Blame us not, most mighty soveriagne lady, although we use importunity in a matter of greate importance, for we, considering the benefites we have receaved and hope to receave by your Majestie, knowing also that uppon your prosperouse raigne standeth the event of our state, in such sorte as [except] in your Majestie's life we have no assurance for the fruytion of our religion, the quietnesse of our consciences, the enioying of lands and goodes, nor for the preservation of the lives of ourselves, our wives and children and famyly, must needes be loth to make a chaunge, to so greate perill; and therefore yf importunity were ever alowable in any cause, we now may iustly use it. But what availeth our perswasion except the mighty hande of God mollifie your princely hearte, since the hartes of kings and princes are in his handes and subiect to his providence? But I feare our demerites and deservings be such and so contrary to our professions that God reserveth it for a vengeance of our offences. Hereof then we ourselves [are] the causes and your Majestie discharged. Thus much touching this greate bill.

'The rest of the lawes framed by us for the better order of the comon weale as also the said principall bill, although as well the Lordes as we have given our consentes, lacke that life which is to make them perfect lawes, your Majestie's power affirmative or negative to every of the same, in the meane season rest of no force or validyty. And therefore most humbly crave of your Majestie to add your royall assent to such and so many of the same as to your Majestie shall seeme to stande with your honorable pleasure and the preservation of this your state, crowne and dignity. And therewithall rendering our dutyfull thankes unto your Highnesse for calling this parliament especially for such a cause of so great moment and comforte to us all. And although the same be not a sufficient provision for your safety, we trust your Majestie will shortly proceede farther, to the better finishing of a worke so well begun, so farre forth in every degree as is our duties to crave and for your Majestie in honnor to graunte; for whose longe preservacion we all most hartely pray. Thus I will conclude with one petition more to your excellent Majestie, that it may please your Highnesse to conceave that we all, subiects of the lower howse, most lovingly and entirely with all humylity, honor and tender your Highnesse' preservation, without any will to offende in any small cause, whatsoever hath beene or shall be reported to the contrarye.' |

This oration thus ended, the Lord Keeper, after the Queene's Majestie's pleasure f.71v to him in that behalfe declared in her Majestie's name, answered to this effecte following.

'Mr Speaker, the Queene's Majestie hath and doth well understande your petition, for thereuppon in effect resteth the summe of your speech. But afore I enter thereunto, her Majestie hath thought good and commaunded me to let yow all understande, first the Lordes and then yow her good subiectes of the lower howse, that your labour and travell employed aswell aboute matters of the common wealth as also especially aboute the preservation of her person, is most acceptable to her Highnesse, which she cannot but take in thankefull parte, as things proceeding of so tender zeale as are in no wise to be forgotten or passed in oblivion; and therefore commaunded me from her owne mouth to give unto yow as harty thankes as I could devise, adding farther that neyther I nor any other can by speech utter howe thankfully shee accepteth the same, with promise of recompense to her power; and sheweth that her love towardes yow is as tender as yours towardes her, for whose preservacion she will not be unmindefull while she liveth. The last petition by yow made seemeth to her very strange and carieth an implicacion that yow all or some of yow conceave the reportes and messadges should be told to her Highnesse to the drawing of her misliking to some of the Howse; which she thinketh a shrewd presumption in those which have so donne, since, as she openly protesteth unto yow all, is not true and, if they were knowne to her Majestie which have so reported, shee would take order for the due punishment of them accordinge to theire demerits; and being untrue, she must needes thinke that eyther to much suspition or malice hath procured it. Her Majestie hath farther willed me to give in charge to all those of yow which be in commyssion, each of yow severally in your shieres to employ all your travell and indeavor well, iustly and effectually to execute aswell the lawes which shalbe concluded uppon at this present as all other good lawes heretofore made; and as cheife[176] has beene made of diverse of yow, uppon greate trust and confidence in yow reposed, that yow defraude not her Majestie of her expectation in this behalfe, which if yow shall doe so effectually as by oa[th] and office yow rest bounde, this greate charge in making newe lawes might be avoyded, to your owne greate ease and commodity. As touching your petition for her assente / to the bills passed by both the f.72

176. *Sic.*

Howses, the Clearke as they be read shall signifie her pleasure in that behalfe'.

This oration ended, the bills were read and to those which the Queene alowed the Clearke pronounced uppon the reading of the titles, '*Le Roigne le voit*'; to the other whereto she gave not her consent the Clearke said '*Le Roigne se avisera*'; and lastly the title of the bill against Mary commonly called Queene of Scots was read, before any answere made whereto the Queene's Majestie called the Lord Keeper unto her, who thereuppon pronounced thus much in effect following.

'The Queene's Highnesse' pleasure is, I wish yow not to be moved though uppon a strange occasion a strange answere have beene made'. Here the Queene enterrupted him and told him that no answere at all was made as yet. He then proceeded, turning his speech to the answere which should be made, which was '*Le Roigne se avisera*'; wishing them not to take the same in such sense as it hath heretofore beene commonly understoode, applied, and taken. That manner of speech in tymes past taken as reiecting of a bill; which she meaneth not to reiect or refuse, she liketh so well of the substance thereof. Some pointes notwithstanding are contayned in the same whereof she is not yet fully resolved, some things so excluded, some so concluded as hath not as yet her whole and perfect liking. But the greatest parte thereof is to her contentation, and therefore, the tyme of the yeare considered, she is compelled to prolonge the performance thereof to a farther deliberacion. And for that purpose her pleasure is the parliament be prorogued[177] untill the feast of All Saints next ensuing, when as her pleasure is, yow repaire hither againe for the farther accomplishment of her pleasure. In the meane season every of yow to departe, except such as be or shalbe commaunded to farther attendance.

---

177. MS reads 'purged'.

THE FOURTH PARLIAMENT
SECOND SESSION
8 FEBRUARY ⁄ 15 MARCH 1576

Documents

Without the major task of providing for the Queen's safety Parliament managed to consider a fuller legislative load this session. In 31 working days, the Commons dealt with over 100 bills in various stages, and Elizabeth was pleased to give her assent to no less than 37, of which a good third seem to have been private.[1] Her generosity on this occasion probably owed something to the fact that, despite the Wentworth incident, there was no major attempt to cajole her into taking an unpalatable course of action as there had been in 1572 over Mary Stuart; and in addition Parliament had not defied the Queen's ban on private bills, since she had issued none.

Compared with 1572, our sources of information from private journals are meagre. There is a copy of the brief notes made by some unknown person: it is a random selection of observations and occurrences during debates which in some cases are so brief as to make it impossible to link them directly with specific days or bills. The problem of the extent of the privilege of freedom from arrest in Arthur Hall's case predominates, and most of the other entries concern the limits of various forms of authorities and jurisdictions. The recorded decision about amendments to bills, coming as it does in 1576, is of particular interest.[2] Thomas Cromwell's journal for 1576 is by no means as thorough as its predecessor for, while covering the whole session, he confined himself largely to registering bills coming before the House. It may be that committee work was now taking its toll: on 23 February, for example, he missed the reading of eight of the 12 bills heard that day because he was away from the House serving on the committee for the bill of promoters; and on other occasions, whether involved in committee work or not, he failed to notice bills which appear in the *Commons Journals* – three on 17 February, six of some 20 on the busy day of 5 March, four on 10 March and three on 12 March. These are only the most notable instances, and at other times his view on the progress of bills is at variance with that of the *Journals*, while on 6/7 March he recorded three bills which do not appear in the official account (enclosing salt marshes, college fellowships, and Stourton's bill, the last of which he subsequently placed correctly). Although Cromwell redressed the balance in other cases by giving a fuller description of bills than is to be found in the *Journals*, there is little of the enthusiastic interest for extensive accounts of debates which was evident in 1572.[3] A fuller report of Mr

1. *SR*, IV.606/7.
2. Oxford: Bodley, Tanner 393, f.67.
3. E.g., 21 February: prisoners in KB jurisdiction; 24 February: denizens; 6 March: oils.

Croke's motion that the Queen, now in her forty-third year, should marry might have been illuminating, for we know little of the precise reaction this prompted in the House, or of any debate surrounding it. How much was made of the point that heirs of Elizabeth's body would place men in some surety 'to what parte to leane'? Does it explain Elizabeth's conjuring up the spectre of factional division again when she addressed the House on 15 March?

One of the matters Cromwell reported in much condensed form was that part of Peter Wentworth's speech which led to his being silenced and denied admission to Parliament until 12 March, when he came to acknowledge his fault before the House [Doc.1]. On his own showing, he had written the speech long before the session had been summoned, no doubt little imagining that Parliament would stand prorogued for some three and a half years.[4] The passion of the famous speech is clearly a response to the widespread uneasiness about speaking which men felt in 1572, and should be seen as a plea for the removal of the causes.[5] If Wentworth's draft survives, it has not come to light, and the copies at our disposal were probably made well into the seventeenth century, being defective in at least one respect since they omit the section in which Wentworth had made scathing reference to Mary Stuart.[6] The style has a fine resonance, even arrogant defiance, and it is easy to understand the amazement it stimulated. In the afternoon of the same day he maintained his position before a committee of the House dominated by Privy Councillors, emerging – not surprisingly, since he wrote the account himself – as the clear moral victor [Doc.2]. In any event, the problem of loyalty, which here goes hand in hand with that of the Commons' liberties, is emphasized: on the fundamental issue of Elizabeth's handling of the bills against Mary in the previous session, the committee appears to have been in agreement with Wentworth, though he 'might have uttered yt in better termes'.[7]

Two days after Wentworth's dismissal the government set about the main business of the session. It was launched by Sir Walter Mildmay, Chancellor of the Exchequer, who was very prominent during these weeks, both on behalf of the Commons in committee, and for the Queen as one of her ministers. In his justification of further taxation in time of peace Mildmay provided yet another summary of Elizabeth's virtues as a monarch who had brought and maintained peaceful order out of chaos [Doc.3],[8] and in so doing he provided about as clear and succinct an analysis of the problems of foreign policy and finance as one could hope to find in so short a space. He took evident pride in revealing to the Commons the measure of success achieved by 1574 in the reorganization of the finances, and in particular, the pattern of government borrowing.[9] Before the end of February the Commons had passed the subsidy bill, which then went to the Lords and received its third reading on 1 March. Meanwhile, Pistor and various puritan elements in the Commons had secured the appointment of a committee to draft a document on Church discipline for presentation to Elizabeth after consultation with the Lords. The Commons' petition — called a bill in the *Journals*[10] — was read to the House on 2 March: its appeal was to a broadly-based, moderate anti-clericalism, and it emphasized the advantages for the civil government which would flow from a healthy, preaching Church, and the wisdom of maintaining all those virtues of which

Mildmay had spoken so highly. Elizabeth's answer, reported to the Commons on 9 March by Mildmay, probably surprised nobody [Doc.4]. The petition had demanded little more than an assurance from Elizabeth that reform would be undertaken in consultation with the bishops, so the Queen could make a short, and sweet, reply, not even commenting on the rather negatively expressed idea that reformation of this sort was a matter for parliamentary legislation.[11] Three days later, when Wentworth was released, Mildmay reiterated Elizabeth's virtues and the respect they commanded of members [Doc.6], though the statement is at the same time a carefully constructed argument in favour of Elizabeth's respect of Parliament's discreet exercise of the privilege of freedom of speech, particularly along lines that Bell and others had become concerned about in 1572.[12]

Documents 5 and 7 are accounts, possibly written originally by Sir Walter Mildmay, of negotiations in the bills of forests and apparel respectively, and they offer good opportunities of seeing the Commons committees at work under the direction of the House. In both cases, the bills had emanated from the Lords and encountered considerable opposition from the lower house; and in neither instance were the differences resolved before the session ended. The subject matter of both bills proved to be too contentious for the Commons to allow through as it stood, and the objections are retailed to the Lords are eloquent upon the nature of lawmaking, law enforcement, the nature of local government and society, and fears for the future which seem to have been the yardstick by which the Commons judged the merits and demerits of proposed legislation. Part of the difficulty came to be the vexed question of the relative jurisdictions of the two Houses *vis-à-vis* one another; and the protracted and complex dealings over lord Stourton's bill, as described in Document 8, show very clearly the Commons' fears that their liberties had been infringed. But some members of the House had obviously been roused to cast a critical eye upon the bill because of the inadequate provisions regarding security of land title, and indeed, because the Lords had already nullified previous Commons measures to eradicate such insecurities and uncertainties.[13]

Bacon's last closing speech [Doc.9] followed unexceptional lines, conveyed the Queen's great pleasure that the session had been so even-tempered, and therefore prorogued rather than dissolved Parliament. The first version printed here probably finds its origin in an account written by Bacon himself, for there is a mention of the point at which Elizabeth herself unexpectedly arose to speak, so putting a stop to his own lengthy, and presumably prepared, peroration: fortunately, we are told what 'I entended to have saide if I had not bynn countermaunded'.[14] Elizabeth's

4. Inner Temple, Petyt 538/17, fos.252, 255 and v.
5. *Ibid.*, f.252v.
6. *Ibid.*, f.254.
7. *Ibid.*, f.255.
8. *CJ*, I.104.
9. Cf. R. B. Outhwaite, 'The trials of foreign borrowing: the English Crown and the Antwerp money market in the mid-sixteenth century', *EcHR*, 2nd ser.,

xix (1966), and 'Royal borrowing in the reign of Elizabeth: the aftermath of Antwerp', *EHR*, LXXXVI (1971).
10. *CJ*, I.110.
11. BL Add.33271, f.14.
12. BL Sloane 326, fos.41v and 42.
13. *Ibid.*, f.34.
14. Corpus Christi College, Cambridge, 543, f.28v.

contentment had not apparently been dulled by the Commons' reiteration of their suit for her marriage, which was again dealt with in the Queen's customary manner. There then followed an extensive homily on the need to execute the laws fully, thanks for the subsidy, granted with 'universalitie of consent', and comments on the need to collect it efficiently.[15] The second version, in note form, differs in minor respects, and may reflect the extent to which Bacon departed from a prepared text in his delivery. When Elizabeth halted Bacon, it was not immediately obvious that she intended to speak herself as there had been no announcement that she was to depart from normal practice; and when she rose, members of the Commons were already streaming away. The Wentworth incident on the one hand, and the relatively easy atmosphere surrounding the petitions for Church reform and marriage on the other, may have prompted this retrospective analysis of her government [Doc.10]. Two versions are included, the second a cruder, more condensed account, but both show Elizabeth's enduring, and surely calculated, enigmatism which she tried to dismiss as a fabrication of 'ripe and divers wits'. The essence of the whole speech, which supported her stand on marriage and the succession, was a vindication of a divinely guided monarchy blessed with peace for 17 years, even though it had pursued the politics of 'truth' rather than taking the easy road of leagues and alliances.

15. *Ibid.*, f.28.

1. Peter Wentworth's speech, 8 February

Text from Inner Temple, Petyt 538/17, copy.
Other MSS. London: BL Stowe 302; PRO SP Dom.Eliz.107/30 (two
extracts only), SP Dom.Eliz.46/166 (Petyt).
Printed. D'Ewes, 236-41.

Petyt 538/17, fos.1-6

Mr Peter Wentworth his speech in the parliament house *anno* 1576 for which he was
put into the Tower.

Mr Speaker, I find written in a little volume these words in effect, 'Sweet indeed is
the name of libertye and the thing it selfe a value beyond all inestimable treasure': soe
much the more it behoveth us to take heed least we, contenting our selves with the
sweetness of the name onely, doe not loose and forgoe the value of the thing; and the
greatest value that can come unto this noble realme by the inestimable treasure is the
use of it in this House, for unto it it is due. And therefore I doe think it needfull to
put yow in remembrance that this honourable assembly (to the great charges of the
whole realme) are assembled and come together here in this place for 3 speciall
causes of most waighty and great importance.

The first and principall is to make and abrogate such lawes as may be most for the
preservacion of our noble Soveraigne.[1]

The second is to make or abrogate such lawes as may be most for the preservacion
of our noble Soveraigne.

The 3^d is to make or abrogate such lawes as may be to the chiefest comodity,
surety, safekeeping and inrichment of this noble realme of England, soe that I doe
think that the part of a faithfull hearted subject to doe his endeavour, to remove all
stumbling blocks out of the way that may impare or any manner of way hinder these
good and godly causes of this our comming together. I was never of Parliament but
the last and the last session, at both which times I saw the libertye of free speech, the
which is the onely salve to heale all the sores of this common wealth, soe much and
soe many wayes infringed and soe many abuses offered to this honourable counsell
(whereby the prince and state are most chiefly mayntained), that my mynde (when I
have many times since thought thereof) hath not been a little agreeved even of very
conscience and love to my prince and state. Wherefore to avoyd the like I doe think
it expedient to open the commodityes that grow to the prince and whole state by free
speech used in this place, at the least soe much as my symple wytt can gather of itt,
the which is very little, in respect of that, that wyse heades can say therein, and soe it
is of the more force.

---

1. *Sic*, and in all copies except SP   most advance God's honor and glorie.'
Dom.46/166 which reads: '. . . as may

First, all matters that concerne God's honour through free speech shall be propagated here and sett forward and all things that doe hinder it removed, repulsed, and taken away.

Next, there is noe thing comodious, profitable or any way benificiall for the prince or state but faithfull and loving subjects will offer it in this place.

Thirdly, all things discomodious, perilous or hurtfull to the prince or state shall be prevented even soe much as seemeth good to our mercifull God to put into our mindes, the which we need not[2] doubt shall be sufficient if wee doe earnestly call upon him and feare him. For Solomon sayth the feare of God is the begining of wisdome.[3] Wisdom / (sayth he) breatheth life into her children, releiveth[4] them that seeke her, and will goe beside them in the way of righteousness. Soe that our mindes shall be directed to all good nedfull and necessary things yf wee call upon God with faithfull hearts.

f.1v

Fourthly, if the envious doe offer anything hurtfull or perilous to the prince or state in this place, what incomodity doth grow thereby? Verily I think none;[5] nay, will you have me to say my simple opinion therein? Much good cometh thereof. How forsooth? For by the darkness of the night the brightness of[6] the sunn sheweth more excellent and cleare, and how can the truth appeare and conquer untill falsehood and all subtillties that should shadow and darken it be found out? For it is offered in this place as a piece of fine needle worke unto them that are most skillfull therein, for there cannot be a false stiche (God ayding us) but wilbe found out.

5ly, this good cometh thereof: a wicked purpose may the easier be prevented when it is knowne.

6ly, an evill man can doe the less harme when he is knowne.

7ly, sometime it happeneth that a good man will in this place (for argument['s] sake) prefer an evill cause both for that he would have a doubtfull trewth to be opened and manifested and allsoe the evill prevented; soe that to this point I conclude that in this House which is tearmed a place of free speech there is nothing soe necessary for the preservacion of the prince and state as free speech, and without it it is a scorne and mockery to call it a parliament house for in truth it is none, but a very schoole of flattery and dissimulacion and soe a fitt place to serve the Devill and his angells in and not to glorifye God and benefitt the comonwealth.

Now to the impediments thereof to which by God's grace and the little expedience[7] I have I will utter plainly and faithfully. I will use the words of Eliha,[8] 'Behold, I am as the new wine which hath noe vent and bursteth the new vessells in sunder'; therefore I will speake that I may have a vent, I will open my lipps and make answer, I will regard noe manner of person, noe man wyll I spare, for yf I should goe aboute to please men I know not how soone my maker wyll take me away. My text is vement,[9] the which by God's sufferance I meane to observe, hopeing therwith to offend none for that of very justice none ought to be offended for seeking to doe good and saying of the trewth.

Amongst other, Mr Speaker, two things doe very[10] great hurt in this place of the which I doe meane to speake. The one is a rumour that runneth about the Howse, and this it is: 'take heed what yow doe, the Queen's Majestie liketh not of[11] such a matter; whosoever preferreth it, she will be much[12] offended with him'. Or the

contrary: 'Her Majestie liketh of such a matter, whosoever speaketh against it she will be much offended with him'. / The other is,[13] sometimes a message is brought   f.2
into the House either of commandinge or inhibiting, very injurious unto the freedome of speech and consultacion. I would to God, Mr Speaker, that these two were buryed in Hell, I meane rumours and messages, for wicked undoubtedly they are: the reason is, the Divill was the first author of them, from whome proceedeth nothing but wickednes.

Now I will sett downe reasons to prove them wicked. First if we be in hand with any thing for the advancement of God's glory, were it not wicked to say the Queen's Majestie liketh not of it, or commanding[14] that we shall not deale in it? Greatly were these speaches to her Majestie's dishonour. And an hard opinion were it, Mr Speaker, thus to conceive of the Queen's Majestie. And hardest of all were it, Mr Speaker, that these things should enter into her Majestie's thought. Much more wicked and unnaturall were it that her Majestie should like or command any thinge against God or hurtfull to her selfe and the state. The Lord grant this thing may be farre from her Majestie's heart. Here this may be objected, that if the Queen's Majestie should have intelligence of any thing perillous or beneficiall to her Majestie's person or the state, would yow not have her Majestie give knowledge thereof in this House whereby her perill may be prevented and her benefit provided for? God forbid, for then were her Majestie in worse case then any of her subjects and in the beginning of our speech I showed it to be a speciall cause of our assembly. But my intent is that nothing should be done to God's dishonour, to her Majestie's perill or to the perrell of the state. And therefore I will showe the inconveniences that growe of these two.

First, if we follow not the prince's minde. Solomon sayth the king's displeasure is a messenger of death.[15] This is a terrible thing to the weake nature of frayle flesh. Why soe? For who is able to abyde the fearce countenance of his prince? But if we will discharge our consciences and be true to God, our prince, and[16] state we must have due consideration of the place and the occasion of our coming together, and especially have regard unto the matter, wherein we shall both serve God and our prince and state faithfully and not dissembling as eye pleasers, and soe justly avoyd all displeasures both to God and our prince. For Solomon sayth in the way of the righteous there is life; as for any other way, it is the path to death.[17] Soe that to avoyd everlasting death and condempnacion with the high and mighty God we ought to

2. 'Need not' supplied from an insertion in Stowe 302.
3. Proverbs 1.7.
4. MS reads 'receaveth'; this reading from Stowe 302.
5. MS reads 'noe', corrected in Stowe 302 to this reading.
6. 'Of' repeated in MS
7. *Sic.*
8. I.e. Elihu; cf. Job 32.19.
9. Stowe 302 reads 'venient'.
10. 'Very' supplied from SP

11. MS reads 'as'; this reading from SP Dom.Eliz.107/30.
12. 'Much' supplied from SP Dom.Eliz.107/30.
13. 'Is' supplied from SP Dom.Eliz.107/30.
14. *Sic.*
15. Proverbs 16.14.
16. MS reads 'or'; this reading from Stowe 302.
17. Proverbs 12.28.

proceed in every cause according to the matter and not according to the prince's mynde. And now I will shew yow a reason to prove it perillous always to follow the prince's minde. Many times it falleth out that the prince may favour a cause perillous to himselfe and the whole state. What are we then if we follow the prince's minde? Are we not unfaithfull unto God, our prince and state? Yes, truely, for wee are chosen of the whole realme of a speciall trust and confidence by them reposed in us to forsee all such / inconveniences. Then I will sett downe my opinion herein: that is, he that dissembleth to her Majestie's perill is to be counted[18] as an hatefull enemy for that he giveth unto her Majestie a detestable Judas his kisse. And he that contraryeth her minde to her preservacion, yea, though her Majestie would be much offended with him, is to be adjudged an approved lover. For faithfull are the wounds of a lover, sayth Solomon, but the kisses of an enemy are deceitfull.[19] And it is better, sayth Anthisthenes, to fall amongst ravens then amongst flatterers, for ravens doe devour but the dead corps, but flatterers doe devour the liveing.[20] And it is both trayterous and hellish through flattery to seeke to devoure our naturall prince; and that doth flatterers, therefore lett them leave it with shame. Enough.

f.2v

Now I will shew yow a president of the last parliament to prove it a perillous rumour and much more perillous to give place unto it. It was forseene by divers of this House that if the supposed title of the Scottish King or Queen to the crowne of England were not by act of Parliament overthrowne and manifested to the whole realme that it had possessed such number of trayterous hearts, that it would one day breake out to the danger of the prince and state. For of the wicked Esai[ah] saith they weave the spider's webb and breake[21] cockatrice's egges.[22] And what falleth out of it? Truely they long to see their good brood hatched. Even soe this wicked brood of Scottish hearts in English bodyes, a detestable and unnaturall thing, Mr Speaker: what webbe did they weave and what brood did they breed? (I may truely say doe they weave or breede, for ill brood hath not yet had such soe ill hatching as I doe wish unto them.) Forsooth, the spider's webbe and cockatrice egg, even abhominable treason: namely the life of our noble prince, whome God long preserve, was and I doe feare is yett sought for, and the subversion of the whole state, as the one cannot be without the other. But praysed be our loveing and mercifull Father which never deceiveth them that feare and put their trust in him, according to the saying of Jesus the son of Sirach: 'Now I see', sayth he, 'they that feare the Lord have the right spirit, for their hope standeth in him that can helpe them'.[23] For things as I have heard have beene revealed beyond the expectacion of man, yea, even when the greatest traytours stood upon their deliverance, who hath since, blessed be our Lord, received condigne punishment for his[24] deserts to the terrour[25] of all the rest. If this be a true president, as it is very well knowne to be unto many here present, I heartily beseech yow all to examine every matter exactly before yow give your voyces either affirmative or negative; and soe shall yow discharge your consciences and dutyes first towards God, next to our noble Queen, then to the whole realme who have put us in trust with all matters concerning the advancement of God's honour, the safety of our prince and the commodity of the whole state.

Now to another great matter that riseth of this grievous rumour. What is it? Forsooth, what soever thou art that pronounceth it thou dost pronounce thy owne

discreditt. / Why soe? For that thou dost what lyeth in the[e] to pronounce the   f.3
prince to be perjured, the which we neyther may nor will believe, for we ought not
without too too[26] manifest proofe to creditt any such dishonour to our anoynted.
No, we ought not without it to thinke any evill of her Majestie but rather to hold him
a lyer, what creditt soever he be of. For the Queen's Majestie is the head of the law
and must of necessity mainteyne the lawe, for by the law her Majestie is made justly
our Queen and by it she is most chiefly mainteyned. Hereunto agreeth the most
excellent words of Bracton, who sayth the king hath noe pear nor equall in his   *Bracton, De Legibus*
kingdome. He hath noe equall for otherwise he might loose his authority of   *Angliae,*
commanding, sithence that an equall hath noe rule of commandmentes over his   *liber 1, c.7.*[27]
equall. The king ought not to be under man but under God and under the law,
because the law maketh him a king. Lett the king therefore attribute that unto the
law which the law attributeth unto him, that is, dominion and power. For he is not
a king in whome will and not the law doth rule, and therefore he ought to be under
the law. I pray yow marke the reason why my authority sayth the king ought to be
under the law. For, sayth he, he is God's vicegerent here upon earth: that is, his
lievetenant to execute and doe his will, the which is law, or justice. And thereunto
was her Majestie sworne at her coronacion, as I have heard learned men in this place
sundry times affirme, unto the which I doubt not but her Majestie will for her
honour and conscience sake have speciall regard. For free speech and conscience in
this place are granted by a speciall law as that without the which the prince and state
cannot be preserved or mayntayned. Soe that I would wish every man that feareth
God, regardeth the prince's honour or esteemeth his owne creditt to feare at all tymes
hereafter to pronounce any such horrible or terrible[28] speach soe much to the prince's
dishonour, for in soe doing he sheweth himselfe an open enemy to her Majestie and
soe worthy to be contemned of all faithfull hearts.

    Yet there is another inconvenience that riseth of this wicked rumour. The utterers
thereof seemeth to putt into our heads that the Queen's Majestie hath conceived an
evill opinion, diffidence and mistrust in us her faithfull and loving subjects. For if
she had not her Majestie would then wish that all things dangerous to her selfe
should be layd open before us, affirming[29] herselfe that soe loving subjects as we are
would without schooling and direccion, with carefull mindes, to our powers
prevent and withstand all perrells that might happen unto her Majestie. And this
opinion I doubt not but her Majestie hath conceived of us, for undoubtedly there
was never prince that had faithfuller hearts then her Majestie hath here; and surely
there were never subjects had more cause hartily to love their prince for her quiett
goverment then wee have. Soe that he that raiseth this rumour still / increaseth but   f.3v

18. MS reads 'committed'; corrected in Stowe   25. MS reads 'traytour'; corrected in Stowe
    302 to this reading.   302 to this reading.
19. Proverbs 27.6.   26. *Sic.*
20. Diogenes Laertius, 'Antisthenes', vi.4.   27. I.e. '8'.
21. I.e. 'hatch'.   28. MS reads 'tirable'; this reading from Stowe
22. Isaiah 59.5.   302.
23. Ecclesiasticus 34.13.   29. *Sic.*
24. *Sic.*

this discreditt in seking to sowe sedition, as much as lyeth in him betweene our mercifull Queen and us her most loving and faithfull subjects: the which by God's grace shall never lye in power, lett him spitt out all his venome and therewithall shew[30] out his malicious heart. Yet I have collected sundry reasons to prove this a hatefull and detestable rumour and the utterer thereof to be a very Judas to our noble Queen: therefore lett any hereafter take heed how he publish it, for as very Judas unto her Majestie and enemy unto the whole state wee ought to accept[31] him.

Now the other. There was a message, Mr Speaker, brought the last session[32] into the House that we should not deale in any matters of religion but first to receive it from the bishopps. Surely this was a dolefull message for it was as much to say as 'Sirs, yee shall not deale in God's causes; noe, yee shall in noe wise seeke to advance his glory. And in recompence of your unkindnes God in his wrath will soe looke upon your doeings that the chiefe and only cause that yee are called together for, the which is the preservacion of the[33] prince, shall have noe good successe.' If some one of this House had presently made this interpretation of the said message had he not seemed to have the spirit of prophesie? Yes, truely, I assure yow, Mr Speaker, there were divers of this House that said with grievous hearts immediately upon the message that God of his justice could not prosper the session. And lett it be holden for a principall, Mr Speaker: that counsell that cometh not together in God's name cannot prosper. For God sayth, 'When two or three are gathered together in my[34] name there am I in the midst among them'. Well God, even the great and mighty God, whose name is the Lord of hostes, great in counsayle and infinite in thought, and who is the onely good[35] director of all hearts, was the last session shutt out of the doores. But what fell out of it? Forsooth his great indignacion was therefore powred upon this House. How so?[36] For he did put into the Queen's Majestie's heart to refuse good and wholsome lawes for her owne preservacion, the which caused many faithfull hearts for griefe to burst out with sorrowfull tears and moved all papists, trayters to God and her Majestie and every[37] good Christian goverment, in their sleeves to laugh all the whole parliament house to scorne. And shall I passe over this weighty matter so lightly or[38] soe slightly? May[39] I discharge my conscience and dutye to God, my prince and country soe? Certaine it is, Mr Speaker, that none is without fault, noe, not our noble Queen. Since then that her Majestie hath committed great faultes,[40] yea dangerous faultes to her selfe and the state[41] / love, even perfit love voyd of dissimulacion, will not suffer me to hide them to her Majestie's perill but to utter them to her Majestie's safetye. And these they are. It is a dangerous thing in a prince unkindly to intreat and[42] abuse his or her nobility and people as her Majestie did the last parlament;[43] and it is a dangerous thing in a prince to oppose or bend her selfe against her nobility and people, yea, against most loving and faithfull nobility and people. And how could any prince more unkindly intreate, abuse and oppose[44] her selfe against her nobility and people then her Majestie did the last parliament? Did shee not call it of purpose to prevent trayterous perills to her person and for noe other cause? Did not her Majestie send unto us two billes, willing to make a choyce of that we liked best for her safety and therof to make a law, promising her Majestie's royall consent thereto?[45] And did wee not first chuse the one and her Majestie refused it, yielding noe reason, nay, yielding great reasons

f.4

why she ought to have yielded to it? Yet did not we never the lesse receive the other and agreeing to make a law thereof did not her Majestie in the end refuse all our travells? And did not wee, her Majestie's faithfull nobility and subjects, plainely and openly decipher our selfes unto her Majestie and our hatefull enemy? And hath not her Majesty left us all to her open revenge? Is this a just recompence in our Christian Queen for our faithfull dealings? The heathen doe requite good for good; then how much more is it dutifull in a Christian prince? And will not this her Majestie's handling, thinke yow Mr Speaker, make cold dealing in many of her Majestye's subjects toward her? Againe, I feare it will. And hath it not caused many all ready, think yow, Mr Speaker, to seeke a salve for the head that they have broken? I feare it hath. And many more will doe the like if it be not prevented in tyme. And hath it not marvelously rejoyced and incouraged the hollow hearts of her Majestie's hatefull enemyes and trayterous subjects? Noe doubt but it hath. And I beseech God that her Majestie may doe all things that may grieve the hearts of all her enemyes and may joy the hearts of all that unfeignedly love her Majestie. And I beseech the same God to endue her Majestie with his wisedome wherby she may discerne faithfull advice from trayterous sugred speeches, and to send her Majestie a melting yeilding heart unto sound counsell, that will may not stand for a reason. And then her Majestie [will] stand when her enemyes are fallen, for noe estate can stand where the prince will not be governed by advice. And I doubt not but that some of her Majestie's counsell have dealt plainely and faithfully / with her Majestie herein: if any have, let   f.4v it be a sure token to her Majestie to know them for approved lovers. And whatsoever they be that did perswade her Majestie soe unkindly to intreat, abuse and oppose her selfe against her nobilitye and people or comend her Majestye for soe doeing, let it be a sure token to her Majestye to know them for sure traytors and undermyners of her Majestie's[46] life and safety: God remove them even for his mercye's sake out of her Majestie's presence and favour and either to turne their hearts or to send them their just rewards, for the more cuning they are the more dangerous are they unto her Majestye. But was this all? Noe, for God would not vouchsafe that his Holy Spirit should all that session descend upon our bishops, soe that the session nothing was done to the advancement of his glory. I have heard of old parliament men that the

30. *Sic.*

31. *Sic.*

32. MS reads 'sessions'; this reading from Stowe 302.

33. MS reads 'their'; this reading from Stowe 302.

34. MS reads 'his'; this reading from SP Dom.Eliz.107/30.

35. MS reads 'God'; this reading from SP Dom.Eliz.107/30.

36. 'How so' supplied from SP Dom.Eliz.107/30.

37. MS reads 'envie'; this reading from SP Dom.Eliz.107/30.

38. 'So lightly or' supplied from SP Dom.Eliz.107/30.

39. MS reads 'nay'; this reading from SP Dom.Eliz.107/30.

40. MS reads 'fault'; this reading from SP Dom.Eliz.107/30.

41. 'And the state' supplied from SP Dom.Eliz.107/30.

42. 'Intreat and' supplied from SP Dom.Eliz.107/30.

43. 'As . . . parlament' supplied from SP Dom.Eliz.107/30.

44. 'And' supplied from SP Dom.Eliz.107/30.

45. It was at about this point that Wentworth was stopped (Cromwell's diary, f.117v).

46. MS reads 'our Majestie's'; corrected in Stowe 302 to 'of her Majestie's'.

banishment of the Pope and popery and the restoring of true religion had there begining from this Howse, and not from the bishopps, and I have heard that few lawes for religion had their foundacion from them; and I doe surely think, before God I speake it, that the bishops were the cause of that dolefull message and I will show you what moveth me soe to think. I was amongst others the last parliament sent unto the Bishopp of Canterbury for the articles of religion that then passed this House.[47] He asked us why we did put out of the booke the articles for the homilyes consecrateing of bishopps, and such like. 'Surely, Sir', said I, 'because wee were soe occupied in other matters that wee had noe time to examine them how they agreed with the word of God.' 'What', said he, 'surely yow mistooke the matter; yow will referr your selves wholly to us therein.' 'Noe, by the faith I beare to God', said I, 'wee will pass nothing before we understand what it is, for that were but to make yow popes; make yow popes who list', said I, 'for we will make yow none'. And sure Mr Speaker, the speech seemed to me to be a very popelike speech and I feare least our bishopps do attribute this of the Pope's canons unto themselves, *Papa non protest errare*; for surely if they did not they would reforme things amiss and not to spurre[48] against God's people for writeing their minde therein as they doe. But I can tell them newes: they doe but kick against the prick, for undoubtedly they both have and doe erre, and God reveale[s] his truth maugre the hearts of them and all his enemyes, for great is the truth and it will prevayle; and to say the truth, it is an error to think that God's spirit is tyed onely to them, for the heavenly spirit sayth, 'First seek the kingdome of God and the righteousness thereof and all these things' – meaning temporall – 'shall be given yow'.[49] These words were not spoken to the bishopps only / but to all, and the writt, Mr Speaker, that wee are called up by is chiefly to deale in God's cause, soe that our comission both from God and our prince is to deale in God's causes. Therefore the accepting of such messages and takeing them in good parte doth highly offend God and is the acceptac[i]on of the breach of the libertyes of this honourable counsayle. For is it not all one thing to say, 'Syres, yow shall deale in such matters onely', as to say, 'Yow shall not deale in such matters'? And soe as good to have fooles and flatterers in the House as men of wisedome, grave judgement, faythfull hearts and synceare consciences, for they being taught what they shall doe can give there consents as well as the others well.[50] 'He that hath an office', sayth Saynt Paule, 'let him waite on his office or give dilligent attendance uppon his office.'[51] It is a great and speciall part of our dewty and office, Mr Speaker, to mayntayne the freedome of consultacion and speech for by this are[52] good lawes that doe sett forth God's glorye and are for the preservac[i]on of the prince and state made. St Paull in the same place sayth, 'Hate that which is evill and cleave unto that which is good;[53] then with St Paule I doe advise yow all here present, yea, and heartily and earnestly I desire yow from the bothom of your hearts to hate all messengers, tale caryers, or any other thing whatsoever it be that any manner of way infringe the liberties of this honourable counsale. Yea, hate it or them, I say, as venomous and poyson unto our comon wealth, for they are venomous beasts that doe use it. Therefore I say againe and againe, hate that that is evell and cleave to that that is good. And this, loving and faithfull hearted, I doe wish to be conceaved in feare of God, and of love to our prince and state, for wee are incorporated into this

f.5

place to serve God and all England and not to be timeservers and[54] humour feeders, as cancers that would pearce the bone or as flatterers that would faine beguile all the world, and soe worthy to be condemned both of God and man; but lett us shew our selves to be a people endued with faith, I meane with a lively faith that bringeth forth good works and not a deade faith. And these good workes I wish to breake forth in this sorte not onely in hatting[55] the enemys before spoken against, but alsoe in open reproving them all enemys to God, our prince and state that doe use them, for they are soe. Therefore I would have none spared or forborne that shall from henceforth offend herein of what calling soever he be of, for the higher place he hath the more harme he may doe; therefore yf he wyll not eschew offences the higher I wish him hanged. I speake this in charitye, Mr Speaker, for it is better that one should be hanged then that this noble state should be subverted. Well, I pray God with all my heart to turne the hearts of all the enemys of our prince and state and to forgive them that wherein they have offended, yea, and to give them grace to offend therein noe more. Even soe I doe heartily beseech God to forgive us for holding our peaces when wee have heard any injurye offered to this honourable counsaill, for surely it is noe small offence, Mr Speaker, / for we offend therein against God, our prince and state　　f.5v and abuse the confidence by them reposed in us. Wherefore God for his great mercy['s] sake grant that wee may from henceforth shew our selves neither bastards nor dastards therein, but that as rightly begotten children we may sharply and bouldly reprove God's enemyes, our prince's and state's, and soe shall every one of us discharge our dutyes in this our high office wherin he hath placed us and shew ourselves haters of evill and cleavers to that that is good, to the setting forth of God's glory and honour and to the preservac[i]on of our noble Queen and common wealth: for these are the markes that we ought onely in this place to shoot at. I ame thusse earnest I take God to wittness for conscience['s] sake, love, love unto my prince and common wealth and for the advancement of justice; for justice, sayth an antient father, is the prince of all vertues, yea, the safe and faithfull guard of man's life, for by it emperors, kingdomes, people and cityes be governed, the which if it be taken away the societie of man cannot long endure. And a kyng, sayth Solomon, that sitteth in the throne of judgement and looketh well about him chaseth away all evill.[56] In the whych state and throne God for his greate mercy['s] sake grant that our noble Queen may be heartily vigilent and watchfull, for surely there was a great fault comitted both in the last parliament time and since allsoe; that was as faithfull hearts as any were unto the prince and state received most displeasure, the which is but an hard point in policie to encorage the enemye, to discourage the faithfull hearted who of fervent love cannot disemble but follow the rule of St Paule, who sayth, 'Let love be without dissimulacion.'[57]

47. Cf. *CJ*, I.86.
48. MS reads 'spurne'; this reading from Stowe 302.
49. Matthew 6.33.
50. *Sic.*
51. Romans 12.8.
52. MS reads 'as' corrected in Stowe 302 to this reading.
53. Romans 2.9.
54. MS reads 'as'; this reading from Stowe 302.
55. *Sic*; Stowe 302 has 'hateinge'.
56. Proverbs 20.8.
57. Romans 12.9.

Now to another great fault I found the last parliament comitted by some of this House alsoe, the which I would desire them all might be left. I have [seen] right good men in other causes, although I did mislike them in that doeing, sitt in an evill matter against which they had most earnestly spoken. I mused at it and asked what it meant, for I doe think it a shamefull thing to serve God, their prince or cuntry with the tongue onely and not with the heart and body. I was aunswered that it was comon policy in this Howse to marke the best sorte of the same and either to sitt or arise with them. That same common policy I would gladly have banished this House and have grafted in the stead thereof either to rise or sitt as the matter giveth[58] cause, for the eyes of the Lord behold all the earth to strengthen all the hearts of them that are whole with him. These be God's owne words, marke them well I heartily beseech
f.6 yow all, for God wyll not receive halfe parte, / he will have the whole; and againe he misliketh with two faced gentlemen and here be many eyes that will to there greate shame behold their duble dealing that uses it. Thus I have holden yow long with my rude speach, the which since it tendeth wholy with pure consciences to seek the advancement of God's glory, our honourables[59] soveraygne's safety and to the sure defence of this noble ile of England, and all by mayntaining the liberties of this honourable counsell, the fountayne from whence all these doe spring, my humble and hearty suite unto yow all is to accept my good will and that this that I have here spoken of conscience and great zeale unto my prince and state may not be buried in the pitt of oblivion and soe noe good come thereof.

Finis Finis

58. 'Giveth' repeated in MS.

59. *Sic*; 's' crossed off in Stowe 302.

2. Peter Wentworth's examination by committee, 8 February

Text from Inner Temple, Petyt 538/17, copy.
Other MSS. BL Harl.1877, Harl.161 (both defective).
Printed. D'Ewes, 241-4.

Petyt MS 538/17, fos.251-6

A true reporte of that which was layd to my charge in the Starre Chamber by the committees of the parliament house that same afternoone after that I had delivered my speech in the House, and my answer to the same.

'Where is your tale yow promised to deliver in writing?' Committees
'Here it is, and I deliver it upon 2 conditions. The first is that yow shall peruse it all Wentworth and if you finde any want of good will to my prince or state in any parte thereof lett me answere all as well[1] as if I had uttered all. The second is that yow shall deliver it unto the Queen's Majestie; if her Majesty or you of her Privie Councell can finde any want of love to her Majestie or the state therein lett me likewise answer it.'
'We will deale with noe more then yow uttered in the House.' Committees[2]
'Your honours cannot refuse to deliver it to her Majestie for I doe send it to her Wentworth Majestie as my heart and minde, knowing that it will doe her Majestie good. It will hurt noe man but my selfe.'
'Seing your desire is to have us deliver it to her Majestie wee will doe it.' Committees
'I humbly require your honours soe to doe.' Wentworth
Then the speech being read the[y] said, 'Here yow have uttered certaine rumers of Committees the Queen's Majestie: where or of whome heard yow them?' /

[in another hand] f.251v

'Yf your honours aske me as councellors to her Majesty, you shall pardon me, I Wentworth will make you no answere; I will doe noe such iniurie to the place from whence I came. For I am now no private person; I am a publicque and a councellor to the whole state in that place, where it is lawfull for me to speake my minde freely and not for you (as counsellors) to call me to accompt for any thing that I doe speake in the House. And therefore, if you aske me as counsellors to her Majesty, you shall pardon me; I will make noe answere. But if you aske me as committees from the House, I will then willingly make you the best answere I can.'
'We aske you as committees from the House.' Committees
'I will then answere you; and the willinglier for that mine answere will be in some Wentworth part imperfect as of necessitye it must be. Your question consisteth of these two

---

1. 'As well' repeated in MS. 2. 'Committees' supplied from Harl.1877.

points, where and of whom I heard these rumours. The place where I heard them, was the parliament house; but of whom I assure you I cannot tell.'

Committees
Wentworth

'This is no answere to say, you cannot tell of whom, neither will we take yt for any.'

'Surely, your honours must needes take it for an answer, when I cannot make you noe better.'

[the rest of this page — almost half — is left blank] /

f.252 [in the first hand]

Comitees

'Be like yow have heard some speeches in the towne of her Majestie's mislikeing of religion and succession and yow are loth to utter of whome. And did use speeches thereupon.'

Wentworth

'I assure your honours I can show you that speech at my owne howse written with my hand two or three yeares agoe, prepared against this time, soe that then you may thereby judge that I did not speake it of any thing that I heard since I came to the towne.'

Comitees

'You have answered that, but where herard[3] you it then?'

Wentworth

'If your honours thinke that I speake for excuse's sake lett this satisfie yow. I protest before the liveing God I cannot tell of whome I heard these rumours, yet I doe verily think that I heard them of 100 or 200 in the House.'[4]

Comitees

'Then of soe many you can name some.'

Wentworth

'Noe surely because it was soe generall[5] a speech I marked none, neither doe men marke speakers comonly when they are generall.[6] And I assure you if[7] I could tell I would not, for I will never utter any thing told me to the hurt of any man when I am not inforced thereunto as in this case I may choose. Yet I would deale plainly with yow, for I would tell your honours soe and if your honours doe not creditt me I will voluntarilie take an oath (if you offer me a booke) that I can not tell of whom I heard

f.252v

those rumers. / But if yow offer me an othe of your[8] authorityes I will refuse yt: I will doe noething to infringe the liberties of the House. But what need I to use these speeches? I will give you an instance where upon I heard those rumours to your satisfying, even such a one as if you will speake the truth yow shall confesse that you heard them as well as I.'

Comitees

'In soe doeing wee will be satisfied. What is that?'

Wentworth

'The last parlment he that is now Speaker uttered a very good speech for the calling in[9] of certaine licences granted to 4 courtiers to the utter undoing of 6 or 8000 of the Queen's Majestie's subjects.[10] This speech was soe disliked of some of the Counsell that he was sent for and soe hardly dealt with that he came into the House with such an amazed continnance that it daunted all the House in such sort that for 10, 12 or 16 dayes there was not one of the House that durst deale in any matter of importance, and in those simple matters that they dealt in they spent more words and time in their preamble requiring that they might not be mistaken then they did in the matter they

f.253

spake unto. This inconvenience grew unto the Howse by the Counsellors' / hard handling of the said good member, whereupon this rumoure grewe in the House: "Sirs, yow may not speake against licences, the Queen's Majesties[11] will be angry, the Counsell will bee too too angry." And this rumour I suppose there is not one of you here but yow herde it as well as I. I beseech your honours discharge your consciences herein as I doe.'

'Wee heard that, wee confesse yt, you have satisfied us in this. But how saye yow to   Comitees
the hard interpretation yow made of the message that was sent into the House?' The words were recited. 'I assure yow I never heard an harder an interpretation of a message.'

'I beseech your honours first, [what say yow to that?][12] was there not such a message   Wentworth
sent into the House?'

'Wee grant that there was. What say you to that?'   Comitees

'Then I trust you will beare me record that I made it not and I answer yow that soe   Wentworth
hard a message could not have too hard an interpretacion made by the wisest man in England. For can there (by any possible meanes) be sent a harder message to a counsell gathered together to serve God then to saie, yow shall not seeke to advance the glory[13] of God? I am of this opinion that there cannot be a more wicked message then yt was.'

'You maie not speake against messages for none sendeth / them but the Q[u]een's   Comitees
Majestie.'   f.253v

'If the message be against the glory of God, against the prince's safetye or against the   Wentworth
libertie of the parlment house whereby the state is maintayned, I neither may nor will hold my peace: I cannot (in soe doing) discharge my conscience, who soever doth send yt. And I say that I heartilye repent me for that I have hitherto held my peace in these causes and that I doe promise you all (if God forsake me not) that I will never during life hold my peace yf any message bee sent wherein God is dishonoured, the prince perilled or the liberties of the parliament house impeached. And everie one of yow here present ought to repent yow of these faults and to amend them.'

'It is noe new president to have the prince to send messages. There were 2 or 3   Comitees
messages recited sent by 2 or 3 princes.'

'Sir',[14] said I, 'yow doe verye evill.'[15] to alleadge your presidents in this order. You   Wentworth
oughto alleadge good presidents to comfort and ymbolden men in good doeing and not evill presidents to discourage and terrifie men to doe evill. Therein you doe verye evill, to alleadge wicked presidents to encourage men to doe wickedlye.'

'But what meant yow to make soe hard interpretac[i]ons of messages?'   Commitees

'Surely I marvaile what you meane by / asking this question. Have I not said soe   Wentworth f.254
hard a message could not have too hard an interpretation and have I not set downe the reason that moved me in my speech, that is to saie, that for the receiving and

3. *Sic.*	9. 'In' supplied from Harl.1877.
4. This paragraph repeated in MS.	10. I.e. Bell in 1571, Anonymous journal,
5. MS reads 'generally'; this reading from	f.7.
Harl.1877.	11. *Sic.*
6. MS reads 'generally'; this reading from	12. 'what say you to that?' crossed out.
Harl.1877.	13. MS reads 'grory'.
7. MS reads 'Iy'; this reading from	14. 'Sir' supplied from Harl.1877.
Harl.1877.	15. MS reads 'well'; this reading from
8. MS reads 'those'; this reading from	Harl.1877.
Harl.1877.	

accepting that message God his soe great indignation is now powred upon us that he put into the Queene's Majestie's heart to refuse God[16] and wholesome lawes for her owne preservacion, which caused many loving and faithfull hearts for greife to burst out with sorrowfull teares and moved all papists, traytors to God, to her Majesty and every good Christian government in their sleeves to laugh the whole parliament house to scorne; have I not this said and doe not your honours think it[17] did soe?'

[Committees] 'Yes, truely, and you have satisfyed us. But yow called the Scottish Queen Isabell[18]; what meant yow by that?'

Wentworth 'Did I not publish her openly in the last parlment to be the most notorious whore in all the world? And wherefore should I then be afraid to call her soe nowe againe?'

Committees 'She is a queen, yow ought to speake reverently of her.'

Wentworth 'Let him take her parte that list: I will speake the truth boldly']19

Committees 'How durst yow saye that the Queen's Majestie had unkindly abbused and opposed her selfe against he[r] nobility and people?'

f.254v Wentworth 'I beseech your honours tell me how far yow / can stretch these words of her unkindlye abusing and opposing her selfe against her Majestie's nobilitye and people. Can you applie them any further then I have applyed them (that is to say) in that her Majestie called the parlment of purpose to prevent traitorous perills to her person and for noe other cause; and in that her Majestye did send unto us 2 bills, willing us to take our choise of that we liked best for her Majestie's safetye, and thereof to make a lawe, promising her royall consent therunto. And did wee not first choose the one and her Majestie refused yt, yielding noe reason, nay we[20] yielding great reasons whie she ought to have yielded to it? Yet did not wee neverthelesse receave the other and agreeing to make a law thereof did not her Majestie in the end refuse all our travaills? And did not my Lord Keeper in her Majestie's presence in the beginning of the parliament shewe this to be the occasion that wee were called together; and did not her Majestie in th'end of the parliament refuse all our travaills? Is not this knowne to yow all here present and to all the parliament house alsoe? I beseeche your honours discharge your consciences herein and utter your knowledge simplie as I doe, for in truth herein her Majestie did abuse her nobilitye and subjects and did oppose her selfe against them by way of advice.'

Committee 'Surelye wee cannot denye it, you say the truth, she did soe indeed?'21

Wentworth 'Then I beseech your honours shew me if it were not dangerous doeing to her
f.255v22 Majestie in theis / two respectes: first in weakning, wounding and discouraging the hearts of her Majestie's loveing and faithful subjects, thereby to make them the lesse able or the more fearefull and unwilling to serve her Majestye another tyme; on the other side was it not a raysing up and encourageing the hearts of her Majestie's hatefull enemies to adventure anie desperate enterprise to her Majestie's perill and danger?'

Committees 'Wee cannot deny but that it was very dangerous to her Majestie in those respects.'

Wentworth 'And is it not a loveing parte of a subject to give her Majestie warnyng to avoid her danger?'

Committees 'Yt is soe.'

Wentworth 'Then why doe your honours aske how I dare telle a truthe to give the Queen's Majestye warning to avoyde her daunger? I answer yow this. I doe thank my Lord

God that I never found feare in my selfe to give the Queen's Majestie warning to avoid her danger. Be yow all affraid thereof if you will for I praise God I am not, and I hope never to live to see that day. And yet I will assure your honours that 20 times and more when I walked in my ground when I revolved this speech to prepare it against this day, mine owne fearefull conceipte did say unto me that this speech would carry me to the place whither I shall now goe and feare would have moved me to have put it out. Then I weighed whither in / conscience and the dutie of a faithfull subject I might keep my selfe out of prison and not to warne my prince from walking in a dangerouse course. My conscience said unto me that I could not be a faithfull subjecte if I did more respect to avoyd my owne danger then my prince's danger. Herewithall I was made bold and went forward as your honours heard. Yet when I uttered these words in the House, that there was none without fault, noe, not our noble Queen, I pawsed and beheld all your countenances and sawe plainlye that those words did amaze yow all. Then I was afraid with yow for company and feare bad me to put out those wordes that followed, ffor your countenances did assure me that not one of you would stay me of my journey. Yet the consideracion of a good conscience and of a faithfull subject did make me bould to utter that in such sorte as your honours heard; with this heart and mind I spake it and I prayse God for yt and, if it were to doe, I would with the same minde speake it againe.'

f.255[23]

'Yea, but might have uttered yt in better termes. Why did you not soe?'

Committees

'Would you have me to have done as you of her Majestie's Privie Counsell doe? To utter a waightye matter in such termes as she should not have understood to have made a fault? Then it would have done her Majesty noe good and my intent was to doe her good.'

Wentworth

'You have answered us, we are satisfyed.' /

Committees

[in the second hand]

f.256

'Then I praise God for yt.' And as I made a curtesie, an other spake theis wordes. 'Mr Wentworth will never acknowledge himself to make a fault nor sey that he is sorrie for any thing that he doth speake; you shall heare none of these thinges come out of his mouth.'

Wentworth
Sackford[24]

'Mr Sakford,[25] I will never confesse yt to be a fault to love the Queene's Majesty while I live, neither will I be sorrie for giving her Majesty warning to avoyd her daunger, while the breath is in my belly; yf you doe thinke it a fault to love her Majesty or to be sorrie that her Majesty should have warning to avoyd her daunger, sey soe, for I cannot; speake for your self Mr Sackford.'[26]

Wentworth

---

16. Sic, and in all MSS.
17. MS reads 'I'; this reading from Harl.1877.
18. *Sic.*
19. Passage in square brackets is crossed out in MS; in Harl.1877 and 161 the greater part is omitted altogether.
20. 'We' omitted in Harl.1877.
21. No question mark in Harl. 1877.
22. *Sic.*
23. *Sic.*
24. MS reads 'Sackvile'; Harl.1877 and 161 reads 'committees'.
25. MS reads 'Sackvile'; this reading from Harl.1877.
26. MS reads 'Sackvile'; this reading from Harl.1877.

3. *Sir Walter Mildmay's speech for supply,* *10 February*

Text from BL Sloane 326, copy.
Other MSS. London: BL Harl.6265. Oxford: Bodley, Rawlinson
C838.
Printed. D'Ewes 244/7.

Sloane 326, fos.1/8v

x^{mo} Februarii 1575. This session began *viii°* February 1575. In the common hous.

That in the beginyng of this our meeting such matters as be of importance may be thought on in tyme, I am bould with your favors to move you of one that in my opinion is both of moment and of necessity. To th'end that if you likewise finde the same to be so you may commytt it further to the consideracion of such as you shall thinke convenient.

And that you may the better iudge of that which I shall propone, it is requisite that I putt you in remembrance:

1. first how the Quene found the realme,

Praecipua 2. next how shee hath restored and conserved it,

Primi capitis 3. and thirdly how we stand now. /

f.1v *explicatio*   Touching the first, no man can be ignorant that our most gracious Quene, at her entry, found this noble realme, by reason of the evill goverment preceding, miserably overwhelmed with popery, dangerously afflicted with warr and greivously oppressed with debt. The burden of which three cannot be remembred without greife; specially if wee call to mynde how this kingdome being utterly

Papism delivered from the usurped tyranny of Rome, and that many yeres together, was nevertheles by the iniquity of the later tyme brought back agayne under the former captivity to the greate thraldome both of body and soule of all the people of this land.

A wretched tyme and wretched ministers to bring to passe so wicked and wretched an act. To strengthen this bondage of Rome, wee saw how that there was

Spaine brought hither a strange nation, to presse our necks agayne into the yoke; terrible this

f.2 was to all the inhabitants of this land and soe would / have proved if their abode had byn here so long as was to be feared. From them and by their occasion came the warr

Bellum that wee entred into with Fraunce and Scotland, not upon any quarrell of our owne,

Calys but to helpe them forwardes to their great advantage and our greate losse and shame.

Aes alienum   By meanes whereof, and of other disorders, the realme grew into great debt both at home and abrode, and soe was left to the intollerable charge of her Majestie and the State.

The realme being thus miserablie oppressed with popery, with warr and with   *2 capitis explicatio*
debt, the Queen our most gracious Sovereigne hath thus restored and conserved it.
She hath delivered us from the tyrannous yoke of Rome, and restored agayne the
most holy religion of the Gospell, not slacking any tyme therein, but even at the first
doing that which was for the honour of God to the inspeakable ioy of / all her good   f.2v
subiects; but adventuring thereby the malice of the mighty princes of the world her
neighbours, being enemyes of our religion, whereby did appeare how much she
preferred the glory of our God before her owne quietnes. This done, she made peace
with Fraunce and Scotland, th'one a mighty nation, th'other though not so potent,
yet in respect of their neirnes and of their habitacion with us upon one continent,
more dangerous. Which may easely appeare by consideracion of former tymes
wherein it hath byn seene how dangerous and costly the Scottish warrs have proved
to this realme, above thoes of any other nation.

But such hath byn the providence of our gracious Queen as the peace with
Scotland, which in tymes past was found always very tickle[1], is now become so
firme, as in no age there hath byn so long and so good peace betweene them and us. /

And that is brought to passe the rather for that her Majestie by two notable   f.3
jorneys with her forces, th'one to Lithe, and th'other to Edenburgh Castle, hath
both quieted that realme and taken away all occasions of hostility that might arrise
against this countrey also. By the first, delivering Scotland from the French which
had so greate a footing there as, without ayde from hence, they must needes in short
tyme have tyrannized over that countrey to their perpetuall servitude and to the perill
also of this countrey being so neire them, and they so ill neighbours to dwell by. And
by the second, ending and cleirely putting out the fyre of the civill warrs amongst
them to the preservacion of their young king, and the perpetuall quietnes of that
realm.

Both which as they have brought unto her Majesty great and ymortall honour and
renowne, and unto this countrey and that peace and surety, so you cannott but
thinke therewith upon the charges which necessarily / follow such two jorneys, so   f.3v
furnished by land and by sea, as for the atchieving of so great enterprizes was
requisite.

What her Majestie hath done besides for the repressing of a dangerous and
unnaturall rebellion practiced by the Pope, the most principall and malicious enemy
of this state, and putt in ure by certeyne unduetifull subiectes in the north partes of
this realme, was seene so late even in your view, as it needeth not to be remembred;
neither the charge that belongeth to a matter of such ymportance as did threaten utter
ruyne to our most gracious Sovereigne and to all the people of this land, if God in his
mercy had not prevented it.

Notwithstanding all which costly jorneys, both into Scotland and within the
realme, her Majestie hath most carefully and providently delivered this kingdome
from a greate and weighty debt wherewith it hath byn long burthened: a debt begon
/ ffowre yeres at the least before the death of King Henry the viij[th] and not cleired   f.4
untill within theis two yeres, and all that while runnyng upon interest, a cancre able

---

1. I.e. 'fickle'.

to eate upp not only private men and their patrimonyes, as by daily experience is too much seene, but also princes and their estates.[2]

But such hath byn the care of this tyme as her Majesty and the state is cleirely freed from that eating corsie.[3] The trueth whereof may be testifyed by the citizens of London, whoes bondes under the common seale of the Cittie for assurance of payment being usually given and renewed, and which have hanged so many yeres to their greate danger, and to the perill of the whole trafique, are now all discharged, cancelled and delivered into the Chamber of London to their owne handes.

f.4v   By meanes whereof not only the realme is acquited of this great / burden and the marchantes free[d], but also her Majestie's creditt thereby both at home and abroad greater then the creditt of any other prince for money if she hath need. And so in reason it ought to be, for that shee hath kept promyse with all men wherein other princes have often failed to the hindrance of many.

Lastly, for this poynt, how the justice of the realme is preserved and ministred to her people by her Majestie's politicall and just government is so well knowne to all men, as our enemyes are driven to confesse that justice, which is the band of all common wealthes, doth so tye and lincke together all degrees of persons within this land as there is suffered here no vyolence, none oppression, no respecte of persons in judgment but *ius equabile*, used to all indifferently. /

f.5 *3 capitis explicatio*   All which godly, provident and wise actes in goverment have brought forth theis effetes:

that we be in peace and all our neighbours in warr;

that wee bee in quietnes at home and safe inough from trowbles abroad;

that wee live in wealth and in all prosperity;

and that which is the greatest, wee enioy the freedome of our consciences delivered from the bondage of Rome, wherewith wee were so lately pressed.

And thus wee stand now.

Transitio   But for all this, as wise maryners in calme weather do then most diligently prepare their tackle and provide to withstand a tempest that may happen, even so, in this our blessed tyme of peace that wee enioy by the goodnes of God through the ministry of her Majestie, wee ought in tyme to make provision to prevent any storme that may

f.5v   arrise either / here or abroad; and neither to be too careles nor negligent, but to thinke that the tayle of thoes stormes which are so bitter and so boystrous in other countryes may reach us also before they be ended, specially if wee do not forgett the hatred that is borne us by the adversaryes of our religion, both for our profession, and for that also this realme is a mercifull sanctuary for such poore Christians as fly hither for succour.

So as now one of the most principall cares that wee ought to take in this great councell of the realme is both to consider aforehand the dangers that may come by the malice of enemyes and to provyde in tyme how to resist them.

And seeing that by thoes greate occasions which I have remembred you can

f.6 *Aerarium*   easelie understand how low her Majestie's cofers are brought, it is our partes here

restaurandum   franckly and willingly to offer / unto her Majestie such a contribucion as shalbe able to restore the same agayne in such sort as shee may be sufficiently furnished of treasure, to put in order and maynteyne her forces by land and by sea, to answere any thing that shalbe attempted against her and us.

And least it might seeme strange to some that her Majestie should want thus soone – considering that not long sithens ayd with granted by the realme – to that I answere that, albeit her Majestie is not to yield an accompt how she spendeth her treasure, yet for your satisfaccions I will lett you understand such thinges as are very trew, and which I dare affirme, having more knowledg thereof then some other in respect of the place that I hould in her Majestie's service.

*Anno xiij°
Regine*

First, how favorable the taxacions of subsidies be through the whole realme, cannot be unknowne to any, / whereby farr lesse cometh to her Majestie's cofers then by the law is granted, a matter now drawne to be so usuall as is hard to be reformed.

f.6v

Next the cleiring of all debtes that ran upon interest, to the insupportable charge of the realme.

Thirdly the charge in suppressing the rebellion in the north.

Fowerthly the free and honourable repayment of the last lone,[4] the like whereof was not seene before.

Fyvethly, the jorney to Edenburgh Castle, for the quieting of that countrey and this.

And lastly, the great and continuall charges in Ireland, by the evill disposition of the people there.

All which could not have byn performed by the last ayd, except it had pleased her Majestie to spare out of her owne revennewes great sommes of money for the supplyment of that which lacked, wherein she more respected / the realme then her owne particuler estate, lyving as you see in most temperate manner, without excesse either in building or other superfluous thinges of pleasure.

f.7

And like as theis be cawses sufficient to move you to devise how theis wantes may be repayred, so you ought the rather to do it, for that her Majestie lacketh and cannott [have] without greate inconvenience thoes helpes, which in the tymes of her ffather, her brother and her sister were used.

As:

the abasing of the coyne, which brought infinite sommes to them for the tyme, but wrought great damage to the whole realme which wee do yett feele and should do more, had not her Majestie to her perpetuall fame restored the same agayne, so much as the tyme could suffer;

the sale of land, whereof came likewise very great somes of / money. But that is not hereafter to be used, seeing that by the same the revennewes of the Crowne are greately deminished which it cann no more beare.

f.7v

The borrowing of money upon interest, the burden whereof the realme hath felt so heavy as that is never more to be done, if by any meanes it may be avoyded.

---

2. The reference must be to the loan raised in Antwerp in 1544, and Mildmay was thinking of rates of interest of the order of 14 per cent (see R. B. Outhwaite, 'The trials of foreign borrowing: the English Crown and the Antwerp money market in the mid-sixteenth century', *EcHR*, 2nd ser., xix (1966), 289, 301-2; 'Royal borrowing in the reign of Elizabeth: the aftermath of Antwerp', *EHR*, lxxvi (1971), 251, 254.

3. I.e. 'corrosive'.

4. MS reads 'love'.

And yett notwithstanding all thoes helpes, it is apparant that subsidies and ffifteenes were continually granted in thoes tymes.

If so then, much more now, when besides warr and other extraordinary charges that may happen, her Majestie's very ordinary charges which she cannott but susteyne, are farr greater by dearth of prizes and other occasions then in any former prince's dayes. /

f.8   As you may see by the ordinary and annuall charges of:

the Howsholde,

the navye,

the ordnance,

the armory,

the garrison of Barwick,

the standing garrison and officers within the realme of Ireland.

And whether theis are like to be more costly to her Majestie then in former tymes in respect of the prices of all thinges lett every man judge by the experience he hath of his private expences.

Peroratio   And so to draw to an end for avoyding of your trowble, I trust theis few thinges may suffice to remember us how her Majestie found the realme: how she hath restored, and preserved it, and how the present state is now. And therewith also may

f.8v   serve as reasons sufficient to perswade us to deale in / this necessary cause, as her Majestie being the head of the common wealth be not unfurnished of that which shalbe sufficient to maineteyne both her and us against the privy or open malice of enemyes; wherein lett us so proceed as her Majestie may fynde how much wee thinke our selves bound to God that hath given us so gracious a Quene to reigne over us, and shew thereby also such gratuity towardes her as she may performe the course of her government *cum alacritate*.

4. Petition of Commons for reform of church discipline, 2 March (petition read in Commons) and 9 March (Queen's reply reported to Commons by Sir Walter Mildmay)

Text from BL Add.33271, copy.
Other MSS. London: BL Add.48064 (Yelverton 70, heading and list of names omitted). Northants.: CRO, Fitzwilliam of Milton Political 162 (petition) and 181 (Queen's reply), both in Sir William Fitzwilliam's hand.

A petition of the lower howse unto the Queen's Majestie. *ij^do Martij* 1575. The first readinge.

The Lord Tresaurer
The Lord Steward
The Lord Chamberlaine
The Erle of Leicester

Upper howse

Mr Tresaurer
Mr Controller
Mr Chancelor of th'Exchequer.

Lower howse

'To the Queen's most excellent Majestie, our most sovereigne Ladye.

'In most humble wise besechinge your Highnes, your Majestie's most lovinge, faithfull and obedient subiectes the commons in this present parliament assembled, that whereas by the lack of the true discipline of the Churche amongest other abuses a greate number of men are admitted to occupie the place of ministers in the Churche of England, who are not only alto[ge]ther unfurnished of such guiftes as are by the word of God necessarelie and inseparablie required to be incident to theire callinge, but also are infamous in theire lives and conversac[i]ons. And also many of the ministery whome God hath endewed with habilitie to teache are by meane of non residences,[1] pluralities, and such like dispensacions so withdrawen from theire

Unlearned
ministers;
infamous ministers;
pluralities;
dispensac[i]ons.

___
1. MS reads 'non residentes'; this reading from Add.48064.

flockes that theire guiftes are almost altogeither become unprofitable, whereby an infinite numbre of your Majestie's subiectes for want of the prechinge of the word – the only ordinary meane of salvation of soules and th'only good meanes to teache your Majestie's subiectes to knowe theire true obedience to your Majestie and to the magistrates under you, and without the which the Lord God[2] hath pronounced that the people must needes perishe – have alreadye runne hedlonge into distruction, and many thowsand of the reasidue yet remaine in greate perill (yf speedy reamedye be not provided) daylie to faull into the diche and to dye in theire sinnes, to the greate daunger and chardge of those to whome the Lord God hath committed the care of provision for them in this behalf. And by meanes whereof the common blaspheaminge of the Lord's name, the most licenciousnes of lief, the abuse of excommunicacion, the greate numbre of athiestes, scismatiques, and heretiques daylie springing upp. And to conclude, the hinderaunce and increase of

Abuse of excom-
municacion;
commutacion of
penaunce;
the numbre of
scismatiques and
heretiques and
obstinate papiste.[4]

obstinate papistes, which ever[3] since your Majestie's sworne enemye the Pope did by his bulles pronounce deffinitive sentence againste your Highnes' person and prosedinges, have given evident testimonie of theire corrupte affection to him and of theire wilfull dissobedience to your Majestie in that they forbeare to participate with your Majestie's faithful subiectes in prayer and administracion of sacramentes, wherein they most manifestly declare that they carry very unsound and undutifull heartes unto your Majestie.

'In consideracion therefore of the premisses, havinge regard first and principally to the advauncement of the glory of God, next to the longe and most blessed continuaunce of your Majestie's reigne and safetie (which we most instantly beseech almightie God longe to preserve), then to the dischardge of our most bounden obedience, which in all dutie and reverence we beare unto your Majestie, besides beinge moved to pittifull consideracion of the most lamentable estate of so manie thowsandes of your Majestie's subiectes daylie in daunger to be lost for want of the foode of the worde and true discipline, and lastly respectinge the peace of our

f.14

consciences and the salvation of our soules, beinge at this presente / assembled by your Majestie's aucthoritie to open the greifes and to seeke the salvinge of the soares of oure cuntrie; and theis before remembred, beyond measure excedinge in greatenes all the reasidue which can be discloased in your Majestie's common wealth: we are most humblie to beseech your Highnes, seinge the same is of so greate importaunce, yf the parlament at this presente maye not be so longe continued as that, by good and godly lawes established in the same, provision maye be made for supplie and reformation of theis great wantes and grevous abuses, that yet by such other good meanes as to your Majestie's most godly wisdome shall seme beste, a perfecte redresse maye be had of the same; which doinge you shall doe such acceptable service to the Lord God which cannot but procure at his handes the sure establishment of your seate and scepter, and the number of your Majestie's most faithfull subiectes (the bonde of conscience beinge of all other most streightest) by meane of preachinge and discipline be so multiplied and the greate swarmes of malefactors, scismatiques, athiestes, anabaptistes and papistes, your most daungerous enemies, so weakened and diminished, that by the helpe and assistaunce of allmightie God, yf all popishe treasons and trayterous practizes should conspire togeither in one against your

Majestie, they should not be hable to shake the estate. And we your Majestie's most lovinge and obedient subiectes togeither with the remembraunce of those enestimable and innumerable benefittes which by your Majestie's means the Lord God hath alredy blessed us withall, farre beyond anie other of our neighbors round aboute us, shall not only be more and more stirred upp to dutifull thanckfullnes unto your Majestie and continuall and earnest prayer unto almightie God (which we will nevertheles) for the longe and prosperous continuaunce of your Majestie's reigne, but also both we and the reasidue of your Majestie's most faithfull subiectes and our posterities shalbe most bounden to continue in that obedient dutie which we owe to your most royall Majestie. And to conclude, your Majestie shalbe recomended to all posterities for such a paterne to be followed, that nothinge maye seme to be added to the perfection of your renowne.'

An answeare to the petition of the common house exhibited to her Majestie, delivered by her comaundement by the Lord Tresaurer and other lordes, and uttered in the House by Sir Walter Mildmay. *Anno 1575*

'The Queene's Majestie had of theis thinges consideracion before, in such sort as thoughe this motion had not bene, the[5] reformation thereof neverthelesse should have followed. And yet she alloweth well that her subiectes, beinge agreved therewith, have in such sort and discreet maner both opened theire greifes and remitted them to be reformed by her Majestie. And consideringe that reformation hereof is to be principally sought in the cleargie, and namely in the bisshopps and ordinaries, her Majestie did in the beginninge of her Convocation conferre with some of the principalls of them and such as she thought were best disposed to reforme[6] theis errors in the Churche; from whome yf she shall not finde some directe dealinges for the reformacion, then she will by her supreame aucthoritie with th'advise of her Councell directe them herself to amende; whereof her Majestie doubteth not but her people shall see that her Majestie will use that aucthoritie which she hath to the encrease of th'onour of God and to the reformation of th'abuses in the Churche.'

---

2. 'God' repeated in MS.
3. MS reads 'even'; this reading from Add.48064.
4. *Sic.*

5. MS reads 'ther'; this reading from Add.48064.
6. 'To reforme' repeated in MS.

5. Proceedings in the bill of forests, 8 and 9 March

Text from BL Sloane 326, copy.
Other MSS. London: BL Harl.6265. Oxford: Bodley, Rawlinson
C 838. Northants.: CRO, Fitzwilliam of Milton Political 124 (in Sir
William Fitzwilliam's hand). California: Huntington Library,
Ellesmere 2582.
Printed. D'Ewes, 255⁄7.

Sloane 326, fos.9⁄14v

Mense Martij 1575. The bill of forrests.

This bill passing the Lordes was by them sent to the common howse, and did conteyne an inlargement of the justices of the fforrestes' authority.

Th'effect whereof was that they should not be driven to keepe their justice seates in every fforrest, which the bill affyrmed was over chargable for men of their calling and a great delay of justice, butt might by authority of this act send for the swanimote bookes, and open them and proceed to the punishment of the offenderes as they should see cawse, according to the lawes, usages, customes and ordinaunces of the fforrestes.

The bill upon the second reading was greately impugned in the common howse, conteyning in the opinyons of divers men many thinges not meete to passe. /

f.9v   Whereupon it was comytted according to the usage in like cases. The committyes upon deliberate consideration of the partes and of the scope of the bill, found the same convenient to proceed, but in respect of the Lordes from whom it came the Howse thought it not amisse to offer their lordships conference, which they accepted; whereupon there did assemble in a place appoynted as commissioners for the Lordes, the Earle of Sussex, the Earle of Rutland, the Earle of Leycester, the Lord Gray of Wilton, and the Lord of Hunsdon, having for their assistance standing by the two Cheife Justices, and the Quene's Attorney Generall. Upon theis, the committies by order of the common howse gave their attendance and by one of them in the name and by consent of the rest, was said to the Lordes in effect as followeth: /

f.10   That whereas a bill touching the enlargement of the justices of fforrestes' authority had passed from their lordshipes and was sent to the common howse, the same had received there two readinges, and upon the second reading was greately impugned by many argumentes made against it. Nevertheless the respect they had to their lordships moved them to stay any further proceeding therein to the hazard of the bill, untill by some conference with their lordships the Howse in such thinges as were obiected might be satisfyed.

To that end he said the common howse had sent them to attend on their lordships. And so entering into the matter said, that of many thinges spoken to the hindrance of the bill, they would trowble their lordships but with some few, such as they had noted to be of most valew, by which he said that their lordships / should fynde that the common howse did take the bill as it was offered for a law to be

  f.10v

  unnecessary,
  chargeable,
  dangerous,
  obscure.

For the first. That whereas in the preamble of the bill it was pretended that one principall cawse of this act was that the justices of the fforrestes having none authority to sitt but within the severall fforrestes, which to execute in their owne persons could not be done, through the distance of the countyes, and through the great charges that would follow in expences if men of their calling should be driven to travell once every third yere to keepe their sittinges in so many severall places: by meanes whereof the justice seates were greately delayed and seldome holden, whereby th'offendors / either by generall pardons comyng betweene or by the death of the parties did escape unpunished. To that he said, all thoes defects were sufficiently holpen by lawes heretofore provided. For in the tyme of King Henry the viij[th] yt was enacted that both the justice of the fforrestes on this side Trent, and the justice of the fforrestes beyond Trent, might make in every fforrest a deputy that should in all thinges have like authority to themselves.[1] And therefore seing they had and usually did make deputyes, men of lesse degree then they are and most commonly inhabiting the countyes where the fforrestes do lye, there was no necessity that the justice in his owne person should ryde, but thoes his substitutes might very well performe the same service with a small charge. And so there appeared no cawse for that respect to make this law for that yt might be supplyed otherwise sufficiently. /

  Non necessarium

  f.11

For the second, he said that where[a]s by this new law the justice should have power to open the swanymote bookes at his pleasure and to convent before him th'offendors at such place and tyme as he thought good, the same must needes prove a very chargable matter to the subiectes. For men being compellable only to appeare and answere in the county where the fforrest lyeth and where for the most part they abide, and there to receive their tryall, if now they shalbe dryven to appeare and answere in any place and at any tyme where and when the justice shall appoynt them, it may easely be seene how farre greater charge this will breed to the subiectes, both in travaile, expence and losse of tyme, then heretofore hath byn used. Chargable besides it would be to such as should happen to by ympanelled upon juries for tryall of th'offences, if they should be dryven to come out of the fforrestes / to appeare before the justice in any place which he shall assigne, contrary to the ancient lawes heretofore ordeyned for such cawses.

  Inutile[2] f.11v

  f.12

For the third, he said that if the justice sending for the swanymote bookes and

  Periculosum[3]

---

1. 32 Hen. VIII, c.35 (1540) in *SR*, III.789. 3. '*Periculosum*' supplied from Harl.6265.
2. '*Inutile*' supplied from Harl.6265.

opening them, should proceed to the punishment of th'offendors according to such presentmentes as he should fynde there, that might prove very dangerous to the subiectes, and especially to such as dwell within or neire any fforrest; ffor those presentmentes being made by the oath of the keepers, do as often proceed upon suspition or upon malice as upon any good and sufficient ground. And then if they be so peremptory to th'offendors as some men thinke they are, or if the tryall be not very indifferent (which taken out of the county may be dowbted), it is easely seene how perillous that wilbe to the subiectes, ffor either the party shalbe forced to submitt

f.12v   himselfe / to the discretion of the justice, or ells abyde such tryall as he shall not be able to indure.

Besides, whereas the Quene most graciouslie doth use to grant oftentymes generall pardons by act of Parliament whereby the subiectes of the land are discharged of farr greater offences then theis, such as might happen to offend this way, or be brought in question for the same, should never be partakers of that grace, which all other subiectes do enioy, but by yerely vexacion be in danger of trowble and charge almost without hope to be released, although th'offences be (as often tymes they are) very small and slenderly proved; whereas now the justice cannott by the law keepe his seate but once in three yeres, and if a pardon come in the meane tyme all thoes offences are discharged.

Difficile[4]   Touching the fowerth and laste poynt, he said in making of lawes one principall
f.13   and speciall care is to be taken, that nothing passe in darke / wordes, but that all may be cleire and evident to the understanding of the makers, thereby to know to what they bynde themselves and their posterity. The contrary whereof was to be dowbted in this bill as it was penned, wherein authority should be given to the justices of the fforrestes to proceed in exeqution of punishmentes and other matters not only according to the lawes, but also according to the customes, usages and ordinances of the fforrestes: which later wordes are very obscure, and therefore dangerous to passe in that forme. For what the lawes of the fforestes are, such as be established by authority of Parliament are evident and open to all men, and every subiect is bound to take knowledge of them; but what the customes, usages and ordinances of the fforrestes be, and how farr theis wordes may extend, is very dowtfull and uncerteyne, the same being knowne only to the officers and ministers of

f.13v   the fforrestes and are so farr from the common knowledge / of other men as few or none that are learned in the lawes of the realme have any understanding in them; so as if any subiect of the land should be ympeached for an offence comytted in the fforrestes, he shall not be able to receive advise by councell in the law for his reasonable defence. And therefore under thoes generall wordes, to bynde the subiectes to thinges that neither they do nor may easely gett knowledge of, the common howse do thinke it a matter very inconvenient: and do also thinke that the fforrest lawes already established by Parliament are streight ynough and being put in due exeqution may suffice without any further addition to encrease the burden of them.

To theis fower obieccions, the Earle of Sussex, a wise man and of good understanding in fforrest matters, being justice of the fforrestes on this side Trent, said for answere in effect as followeth: /

To the first, confessing that by authority of Parliament the justices of the fforrestes   f.14
might appoynt their deputyes, said nevertheles that thoes also could not holde their
sittinges without greate charge, and their doinges should not be so obeyed nor
esteemed as the actes and proceedinges of the justices themselves, and therefore
thought this law necessary.

To the second, third, and fowerth, he said that there was no meaning by the
Lordes that passed the bill to bring upon the subiectes any of thoes inconveniences
that were noted by the comon howse: howsoever the bill might be penned contrary
to their intentions. And yett he thought, that the wordes were misconceyved, and
drawne to a harder sence then there was cawse. Nevertheles he said, the Lordes
could be well content that the comon howse should reforme such thinges in the bill,
touching thoes poyntes as they should fynde convenient, so as the same were done
with good consideracion and upon sufficient cawse; whereof they dowbted not. /

This, being the substance of the conference, was the next day reported by one of   f.14v
the committees to the neyther howse. Whereupon the Speaker moved the Howse to
appoynt some to amend thoes thinges which the Lordes had yeilded to have
reformed that so the bill might passe. But the whole Howse, a very few excepted,
said they would heare no more of it. And so yt stayed without any further
proceeding becawse it appeared the comon hows did not thinke their obieccions
sufficiently answered by the Lordes.

---

4. '*Difficile*' supplied from Harl.6265.

6. *Sir Walter Mildmay's speech on the return of Peter Wentworth, 12 March*

Text from BL Sloane 326, copy.
Other MSS. London: BL Harl.6265, Cott.Titus F1 and its copy,
Stowe 358. Oxford: Bodley, Rawlinson C838. Northants.: CRO,
Fitzwilliam of Milton Correspondence 60 (in Fitzwilliam's hand and
endorsed by him, 'Peter Wentwoorth in the parliament').
Printed. D'Ewes, 259.

Sloane 326, fos.40v‑43

xij[1] *Martij* 1575.

A gentleman being a burgesse of the common howse did the first day of this session
of Parliament, which was the viij[th] of February last, utter in a prepared speech divers
offensive matters touching her Majestie. For the which by iudgment of the whole
Howse he was comytted to the Tower, where he remayned till towardes th'end of the
session. At which tyme yt pleased her Majestie graciously to remytt her displeasure,
and to referr th'enlargement of the partie to the Howse. This being signifyed thither
by her Majestie's commandement and most thankfully accepted, it was after said
that by this whole action, and by her Majestie's dealing in this cause, we had iust
occasion to consider theis 3 thinges:

1. her Majestie's good and clement nature.
2. her respect to us.
3. and our duetyes towardes her.

f.41 Sir Walter Touching the first, that sovereigne princess placed by God are to be / honored
Mildmay[2] with all humble and duetifull reverence, both in word and deede, specially if they be
good and vertuous, such as our most gracious sovereigne is, a princesse that hath
governed this realme so many yeres, so quietly, so iustly, and so providently: which
being trew, as no man can deny, then see how greate an offence this was to reprove
and charge so gracious a Quene, so uniustly; and that not to be done by any comon
person abrode, but by a member of this Howse, and not in any private or secrett
place, but openly in this most honorable assembly of the parliament being the
highest court and councell of the realme. And thereby see also her gracious and good
nature, that so mercifully and so easely can remytt so great an offence, a thing rarely
found in princes[3] of so greate estate, that use commonly to thinke themselves touched
in honour if they should passe over smaller iniuryes so lightly: the greater is her
Majestie's comendacion, and the more are we bound to thanke God for her. /

f.41v Secondly, her Majestie's gracious respect towardes us, that notwithstanding the
iust cawse that was given her to punish severely so great an offence, yett the favour

that she had conceyved towardes us, proceeding from iust tryall of our duetifull affeccions towardes her, had so qualifyed her displeasure as she was contented for our sakes to pardon the whole, and that so freely as she[4] would not at any tyme thinke of yt agayne (for thoes were her wordes): a marvellous grace towardes us, and never on our partes to be forgotten. The rather for that the same proceeded merely from herselfe, thereby preventing the suyte which we in all humblenes might have made unto her.

Thirdly, that for this so gracious a dealing yt was our bounden duetyes to yeild unto her Majestie our most humble and hearty thankes, and to beseech the almighty Lord to enlarge her dayes as th'only stay of our felicity. And not only so, but to learne also by this example how to behave our selves hereafter, and not / under the pretence of liberty to forgett our bounden duety to so gracious a Queen. Trew yt is that nothing can be well concluded in any councell, but where there is allowed in debating of the cawses brought in deliberacion, liberty and freedome of speech. Otherwise, if in consultacions men be eyther interrupted, or terrifyed, so as they cannot, or dare not, speake their opinions freely – like as that councell cannott be reputed but for a servill councell – even so all the proceedinges therein shalbe rather to satisfy the will of a few, then to determyne that which shalbe iust and reasonable.   f.42

But herein we may not forgett to putt a difference betweene liberty of speech, and lycencious speech: ffor by th'one men deliver their opinions freely but with this caution, that all be spoken pertinently, modestly, reverently and discretly. Th'other contrary wise, utterreth all impertinently, rashly, arrogantly and irreverently without respect of person, tyme or place. / And though freedome of speech hath always byn used in this great councell of the parliament and is a thing most necessary to be preserved amongst us, yett the same was never, nor ought to be extended so farr as though a man in this Howse may speake what, and of whom he lyst: the contrary whereof both in our owne dayes and in the dayes of our predecessors, by the punishment of such inconsiderate and disorderly speakers, hath appeared. And so to returne. Lett this serve us for an example to beware that we offend not in the like hereafter, least that in forgetting our duetyes so farr, we may give iust cawse to our most gracious Sovereigne to thinke that this her clemency hath given occasion of further bouldnes, and thereby so much greive and provoke her as, contrary to her most gracious and milde disposition, she be constreyned to change her naturall clemency into necessary and iust severity; / a thing that he trusted should never happen amongst wise and duetifull men, such as the members of this Howse are thought alwayes to be.   f.42v   f.43

This done, the sergeaunt of armes that attendeth in the common howse by their commandment brought the partie to the barr within the Howse. And there, after the Speaker had declared to him both the greatnes of his offence and the greatnes of the Queen's mercy, and after his humble submission upon his knees acknowledging his fault and craving her Majestie's pardon and favour, he was receyved agayne into the Howse, and restored to his place to the greate contentment of all that were present.

1. MS reads 'xiiij', as does Rawlinson C838. Cott. Titus F1 reads '12 of Marche', the date given in the *Commons Journal*.
2. Marginal note from Cott. Titus F1.
3. MS reads 'a princes'.
4. MS reads 'we'; this reading from Cott. Titus F1.

7. Proceedings in the bill of apparel, 10-13 March

Text from BL Sloane 326, copy.
Other MSS. London: BL Harl.6265, Cott.Titus FII (misdated).
Oxford: Bodley, Rawlinson C838. Northants.: CRO, Fitzwilliam of
Milton Political 149 (in Fitzwilliam's hand). California: Huntington
Library, Ellesmere 2581.

Sloane 326, fos.15-18v

Mense Martij 1575. The bill of apparrell.

Th'effect of this bill was that the Quene's Majestie from tyme to tyme might by her
proclamacion appoynt what kynde of apparrell every degeree of persons within the
realme should weare, not exceeding for the punishment of th'offendors the penalty
lymitted in the bill.

This bill being passed from the Lordes, and comyng into the neyther howse, was
upon the second reading spoken against by divers that did alledge many argumentes
for the stay thereof. Nevertheles becawse disorder of apparrell is very greate in this
tyme, yt was thought good by the Howse to commytt the bill and to offer unto the
Lordes a conference, if it should please them to accept yt.

The committees after deliberate consideracion of every part of the bill at the last
f.15v agreed to attend upon the Lordes to conferr with such of them as / should be
appoynted by the upper Hous; and so did.

And to them by one of the same commyttees in the name and by consent of the
rest, was said in effect as followeth:

That the bill for reformacion of excesse in apparrell that came from their
lordshipps being upon the second reading much impugned in the common howse,
and rather likely to quaile then to proceed in that sort, they thought yt convenyent,
both in respect of the matter and in respect of their lordships that passed the bill, to
attend upon them to open such thinges as moved the misliking of the same: wherein
they ment not to trowble them with all that had byn obiected, but only with some
few thinges such as they could remember and such as they tooke to be of most
weight.

Some, he said, misliked the whole bill utterly, grounding themselves specially
f.16 upon this reason: that where the subiectes / of the land have not byn heretofore
bound to any thing but unto such as should be certeynly established by authority of
Parliament, this act proceeding, a proclamacion from the prince should take the
force of law, which might prove a dangerous precedent in tyme to come. For though
we live now in the tyme of a gracious sovereigne that will never offer us any thing

disagreeable from the nature and office of a good and mercifull princesse, yett what this may worke hereafter in more dangerous tymes, when the goverment shall not be so directed by justice and equity, is greately to be foreseene, least by this example the authority of proclamacions may extend to greater matters then theis are: a thing much to be considered both for our selves, and our posterity, the rather for that it is seene by daily experience that of precedentes greate hold is taken, specially in the case of princes.

Some other, he said, not thinking the matter to be so dangerous becawse the proclamacion is circumscribed within / certeyne lymittes, and the penalty sett downe expressly in the act, did nevertheles obiect against the bill as yt was penned theis iiij thinges: f.16v

1. the ordre of the proclamacions
2. the greatnes of the penalty
3. the manner of the exeqution
4. the continuance of the act.

Touching the first, he said, that whereas all other proclamacions are notefyed to   1 the people by open pronouncing of them in every county of the realme, and often in sundry places of the sheire, and a tyme appoynted for the subiectes to take heede how they offend the same, by th'order of this bill, if a proclamacion made for the redresse of theis disorders be published in any one place all the subiectes of the land are bound to take knowledge of it, which is impossible. Neither is there any tyme given for men to reforme themselves, but / ymediately upon the proclayming the penalty   f.17 lighteth upon them; both things very inconvenient and as they thought, not so ment by their lordshipps. Besides, the uncerteny that might grow if the proclamacions should be often altered.

For the second, he said that in punishmentes regard ought to be had that the   2. payne be not greater then th'offence; which they thought to be here, for besides the losse of the garment, to forfeyt also x^{li} a day was two heavy for the subiectes to beare: and therefore did thinke that the penalty mencioned in the statute of apparrell made in the xxiiijth yere of King Henry the viijth, which is losse of the garment and the forfeyture of tenn grotes by the day, was a punishment sufficient for such an offence.[1]

For the third, he said, whereas by the bill authority was given to any officer, were he never so inferior, to arrest any man whom he thought to offende and to take from his back the garment that in the opinyon of such officer he could not avow to weare, or ells to commytt him to warde except he put in surety to deliver to that officer the garment / within xxiiij howers: this manner of exeqution would prove very   f.17v comberous and quarrellous, and sometymes iniurious; ffor thoes officers may light upon men, though unknowne to them, yett of sufficient ability to iustify the wearing of thoes garmentes as they challenge, which must of necessity breed great contention and strife in all places, to the disquietnes both of themselves and of such as they shall ympeach. Better it were therefore, to rest upon the manner of exeqution mencioned in the said former act of King Henry the viijth, which is by informacion or accion,

1. 24 Hen. VIII, c.13 (1532-3), in *SR*, III.430-2.

an ordre agreeable to justice, when no man shall suffer the punishment of any law before he be heard and condempned by tryall.

For the forwerth and last, he said that this law being a new meane to reforme this disorder of apparrell and continuance of the act appoynted by the bill to be for vij yeres, this tyme was thought very long: and better yt were, as in such new cases is commonly used, to make tryall in some shorter tyme how the successe thereof will prove, that / if the same be not found so proffittable for the realme as is pretended it might cease the sooner.

f.18

To theis obiections answere was made by one of the Lordes, after consultacion amongest themselves, in effect thus:

To the first, that they agreed with the common hows in opinyon, thinking the same worthy of reformacion as a fault happening by the negligence of the drawers of the bill. For except the proclamac[i]on were published at the least in every county, and a tyme also of warning to such as might offend, they thought yt no reason that any man should be bound.

To the second, that yf the penalty were not greater then in that act of King Henry, the terror would be so small that the mischeif would not be reformed.

To the third, that without such an exeqution as was expressed in the bill they dowbted there would follow little good of this act. /

f.18v

To the fowerth, that they tooke the tyme of vij yeres to be little ynough for a tryall what this law would worke.

Nevertheles, they could like very well that the comon howse should reforme, or alter, any thing in the bill as they saw cawse, so as the substance were reteyned.

After this conference the committyes thought good to draw a new bill, wherein they remedied all thoes thinges that they found amisse in the poyntes before remembred; and that being presented to the common howse did orderly passe there, and so was sent upp to the Lordes with their owne bill as the custome is.

But of this came nothing, for the Lordes misliking the smallnes of the penalty, the manner of the exeqution, and certeyne other thinges in the new bill, gave yt only one reading, and that session of Parliament ending within two dayes after, the matter proceeded no further.

8. *Proceedings in Lord Stourton's bill, 10-14 March*

Text from BL Sloane 326, copy.
Other MSS. London: BL Harl.6265, Cott.Titus F1 and its copy
Stowe 358. Oxford: Bodley, Rawlinson C838. Northants.: CRO,
Fitzwilliam of Milton Political 152 (in Fitzwilliam's hand).
Printed. D'Ewes, 260 (short extract only).

Sloane 326, fos.33-40

Anno xviij° Regine Elizabethe et anno Domini 1575, mense Martii.
Notes of a case happeninge in the parliament by which the commons of the nether
howse thought their libertyes touched.

The occasion and proceeding whereof was in some as ffolloweth.

The Lord Sturton, whose ffather was atteynted of murder, and thereby his bloud
corrupted, made humble suyte to the Queen's Majestie to be restored in bloud by
authority of Parliament, which her Majestie graciously inclyned unto; and for
declaracion of her good liking thereof signed his bill, which being brought to the upper
howse did passe the lordes, and so was sent downe from them to the comons of the
nether hous as in such cases is used.

The bill in the nether howse upon the second reading was impugned by some in
misliking of the partie, that before this had given cause for men to thinke that he
would not hereafter be worthy of so much favour; and by some other, that there
wanted / in the bill sufficient provision for such as had byn purchasers from his
ffather, grandfather, or other his auncestors.   f.33v

To the first obiection yt was said in the Howse that seing her Majestie had so
graciously yeilded to his peticion, there was no dowbt but shee was well satisfyed in
all such thinges as might touch him; and therefore no cawse that this Howse should
mislike her gracious favour to be extended to any of her subiectes in such cases, but
rather to hope that he being a young noble man would prove a good servant to her
Majestie and the realme, as divers of his auncesters had don.

The second obiection was thought worthie of consideracion, that if the saving
which already was in the bill were not sufficient, there might be other provision
added; whereupon the bill was commytted. The commyttees reading deliberately
the bill and the whole contentes thereof, partly upon cawses / alledged in the Hous,   f.34
and partly upon cawses remembred amongst themselves, tooke the saving in the bill
not to be sufficient, but added a proviso unto yt; the speciall poynt whereof was to
barr the Lord Sturton that he should not take advantage of any error that might
happen to be in any fyne, recovery, or other conveyance passed by his ffather or other

his auncestors, but he should be in that respect as though his bloud were not restored, in which state he can bring to wrytt of error. Th'occasion of which proviso grew cheifely for that the Lords had within few dayes before in this session dashed a bill that passed in the comon howse for the helping of such errors.[1] Whereupon they thought yt dangerous to give that scope to any man that should be restored in bloud; and therefore they added such a proviso both to this bill, and to another bill of like tenor that did concerne one Maynye of Kent.[2]

f.34v   During the tyme of this conference with the comyttees, the Lord Stourton, being enformed how his case was ordered in / the nether howse, came to the place where the commyttees sate and desired that himselfe and his councell might be heard, which they allowed of their owne discresion without the privity of the Howse. His councell labored to shew to the commyttees that the saving in the bill was sufficient so that there needed none addition of any other proviso, but being answered to all that he said, he could not much reply but seemed to be satisfyed.

Nevertheles the Lord Stourton nothing contented therewithall, procured ymediately a message from the Lordes to the nether howse in his favour that the bill might passe in such sort as yt came downe without any alteracion or addition, which they thought could not be without her Majestie's assent: and this message was done streight after the comyttees had agreed on the proviso and made report of their doinges to the Howse.

The comon howse tooke this manner of dealing to be very strange, not f.35   having / heretofore received any such message from the Lordes, tending to prescribe them what they should do in the accions of that councell; and therefore notwithstanding this message meant to proceed as they had begonne.

This being, as yt seemed, knowne to the Lord Stourton, he procured the next day another earnest message from the Lordes in his behalfe, with this further request that the Howse would appoynt some to conferr with the Lordes for resolucion of such thinges as they dowbted of.

This message seemed strange to the Howse, and to be thus pressed in any such matter they thought preiudiciall to their libertyes.

And therefore they gave the bill a third reading and the proviso three readinges, as is used in like cases, and so passed the bill, sending up the same with the proviso annexed.

f.35v   Herewith the Lordes were greatly / moved, and thereupon sent a message to the common howse that some of them should come to speake with certeyne of the Lordes in such matter as they had to say to them from the higher howse.

According to which message certeyne of the nether howse were appoynted and did give attendance at the parliament chambre, sending in word by the ussher of their being there. The lordes, after a greate pawse, at the last came forth into the utter chamber. The numbre of them were many, and the persons of the principall noble men of that Howse. After they had taken their places at a long table and used some conference amongst themselves, they called for thoes of the nether howse, to whom the Lord Treasuror in the name of all the rest present and absent said in effect:

That the lordes of the upper howse could not but greately mislike the dealing of the common howse in the Lord Sturton's bill, specially for that they had passed the

bill with a proviso annexed notwithstanding their sundry / messages sent to them in   f.36
his favour, and lastly one message to have conference with them for resolucion of
such dowbtes as were moved; wherein they tooke themselves greatly touched in
honour and thought that the comon howse did not use that reverence towardes
them as they ought to do. The cawse besides, he said, was such, as they saw no
reason why the comon howse should proceed in that order. For the bill being signed
by her Majestie, he said none might presume to alter, or add any thing to yt, without
the assent of her Majestie, which they for their partes durst not do: and for proofe
hereof he shewed the comyttees sundry provisoes in King Henry the viij[th] his tyme
annexed to like billes signed by the King, inferring thereby that none might passe
otherwise. Moreover, he said that by the opinion of the judges which were in the upper
howse, the saving in the bill already was so sufficient as there needed none addition of
any such proviso as the comon howse had / annexed; and therefore required to know   f.36v
what reasons did leade them to proceed in this ordre. This and some larger and more
vehement[3] speech being utterred to that end, the comyttees answered that their
commission was only to heare what their Lordships would say: they would returne
and make report to the Howse, and so attend upon them agayne with answere.

When this was reported to the nether howse, yt moved them all greatly and gave
occasion of many argumentes and speeches, all generally misliking this kinde of
dealing with them, and thinking their libertyes much preiudiced in three poyntes:
one, that they might not alter or add to any bill signed by the Queen; an other, that
any conference should be looked for (the bill remayning with them), except
themselves saw cawse to require yt; and the third, to yeild a reason why they passed
the bill in that sort. After all theis thinges / were sufficiently debated, an answere was   f.37
agreed on to be retorned to the Lords by the same comyttees. And they gave their
attendance upon the same lordes in the former place, to whom was said in effect by   Sir Walter
one of the comyttees in the name and by the consent of the reste: Mildmay[4]

That they had delivered to the common howse the somme of that which their
lordships had said to them, which (as they had conceyved) did stand upon two
partes: one, the manner of their proceeding in this case of the Lord Sturton, and the
other the matter[5] wherein they had proceed[ed].

To both which they had commission from the Howse to make unto their
lordshipps this answere.

First, that they were very sorry that their lordshipps had conceyved such an
opinion of the Howse as though they had forgotten their duety to them, praying their
lordshipps to thinke that the nether howse did not want consideracion to thinke of
the superiority / of their estates in respect of their honourable calling, which they did   f.37v
acknowledge with all humblenes, protesting that they would yeild unto their
lordshipps all duetifull reverence so farr as the same were not preiudiciall to the
libertyes of their Howse, which yt behoved them to leave to their posterity in the same

1. *LJ*, I.740.
2. See *CJ*, I.111, 113-15 for progress of both
   bills in the Commons.
3. 'And more vehement' supplied from

Fitzwilliam of Milton Political 152.
4. Marginal note supplied from Cott. Titus
   F1.
5. 'Matter' supplied from Cott. Titus F1.

freedome they received them. And touching this perticuler case, the manner of their proceeding hath not byn, as they thinke, in any wise unduetifull or unsemely: ffor the bill being sent from their lordships to the nether howse receyved there within little space two readinges, and becawse upon the second reading some obiections were made to lett the course of the bill the Howse thought meete to commytt yt, which doth shew they had no disposition to overthrowe the bill, butt to further yt both in respect of her Majestie's signature and that yt came passed from their lordships. And whether the Lord Stourton had cawse or no to thinke himselfe favorably used in

f.38   being heard of the / comyttees with his learned councell, they referred to their lordships' judgmentes. That after the comyttees report of their doinges the Howse gave the bill a third reading, and so passed the same in such sort as now their lordships had yt, notwithstanding their sundry messages to the contrary, and lastly notwithstanding their request of conference: they said they could not have otherwise done without breach of their libertyes. For they take the order of the parliament to be that when a bill is passed in either Howse, and after sent from thence to th'other Howse, that Howse wherein the bill remayneth may require conference with the Howse that passed the bill, if they thinke good, but not otherwise. And so this bill passing from their lordships, the nether howse might if they had thought yt convenient, have required conference, but not their lordships of a bill passed from themselves. And thus much for the manner of their proceeding.

f.38v   Touching the / matter wherein they have proceeded in that they annexed a proviso to this bill, the same being signed with her Majestie's hand, they thought they might lawfully do yt without offence to her Majestie, taking her signature to be only a recommendation of the cawse to both the Howses, without which they could not treate of any bill of that nature; the Howses not being thereby concluded, but that they might alter or add any thing that should be thought meete, either for her Majestie or for her subiectes. Which proviso they have added upon good deliberacion, not hastely nor inconsiderately, but upon greate and sufficient reasons moving them, praying their lordships so to conceyve yt. Nevertheles to declare thoes reasons in perticuler to their lordships (as they required), in that parte the Howse desired their lordships to beare with them, for that were to yeild an accompt of their doinges and of thinges passed in their Howse, which they could not in any wise

f.39   agree / unto being so preiudiciall to their libertyes.

This speech finished, the comyttees were willed by the Lordes to retyre into the nether end of the chambre and so they did: and after some pawse and consultacion amongst the Lordes, they called agayne the comyttees, and to them was said by the Lord Treasorer that the Lordes had considered the answere which the comyttees had brought them from the comon howse. And touching the first part thereof, he said that albeit through such information as was given them they might have cawse to conceyve amisse in the manner of their proceeding, yett becawse themselves were the trewest reporters of their owne actions and the best interpretors of their owne meaninges, the Lordes did accept of their answere, and rested satisfied with the same.

f.39v   But touching the other parte he once agayne earnestly pressed / the commyttees to shew the reasons that moved the Howse to add that proviso which the Lords tooke to be superfluous, the bill, as he said, conteyning in yt already a saving that was sufficient for all cases that might happen.

To that was said by one of the commyttees that they humbly thanked their lordships that it pleased them so well to accept of their answere to the first part; butt for the second, which concerned the matter yt selfe and the reasons that moved the Howse, he said that the comyttees had no further authority to deale in, having only commission to deliver to their lordships the answere which they receyved from the Howse.

Whereupon the assembly brake, the lordes returning to the higher howse, and the commyttees to the nether howse: where at their comyng one of them reported their whole proceeding with the Lordes, wherewith the Howse was much satisfyed, seing / that so greate a storme was so well callmed and the libertyes of the Howse preserved, which otherwise in tyme to come might have byn preiudiced in thoes three poyntes before remembred, which are in deed, if they be well considered, of great weight and ymportance.   f.40

The bill as yt appeared after passed no further, the Lordes not liking of the proviso, nor the comon howse yeilding not to the provisoe's withdrawing, for the cawses afore declared.

9. Lord Keeper's speech at close of session, 15 March

i. Text from Corpus Christi College, Cambridge, 543, copy.
Other MSS. London: BL Cott. Titus F1 (ending at the point where the Queen interrupted).
Printed. D'Ewes, 232-5 (misdated 14 March; text as Cott. Titus F1).
ii. Text from Northants. CRO, Fitzwilliam of Milton Political 133: notes only, in Sir William Fitzwilliam's hand.

Corpus Christi College, Cambridge, 543, fos.25-9

A speach used in the end of the second session of the parliament begunn *anno quartodecimo Elilizabethae*[1] *Regine et anno Domini* 1571[2]: Mr Bell being Speaker, who was afterward Lord Cheife Baron of the Exchequer.

'Master Speaker, the Queene's most excellent Majestie our most dread and gratious Soveraigne hath heard and doth verie well understand your oracion full of good will and good matter, the summe wherof as I take yt may bee reduced into five partes: wherof the first conteineth a discourse of sundrie kindes of government from the begining untill this time; the second the comendacions of her Majestie's virtues and of her greate good and gratious goverment from the begining, with a remembrance of her Highnes' bountifull benefittes; the third conteineth your humble and earnest peticion moveing her Majestie to marriage; the fowerth is a declaracion of the lawes past in the nether howse, with an humble suite for her Highnes' royall assent to bee given to the same; the fift and last concerneth the presentacion of a subsidie granted in this session.

'As touching the first, which conteineth the discourse concerneing sundrie kindes of goverment, I see not that this time and place doth require any answere to bee given unto yt other then this: that yow, Mr Speaker, are much to bee commended for your diligent collecting and also for your apt compareing of the last parte of the same.

'And as to the second, which concerneth the comendacion of her Majestie's greate virtues and goverment with the remembrance of the manifolde benefittes that yow have received att her Highnes' handes, her Majesty hath commanded mee to say f.25v unto yow that she wisheth / of God with all her heart that all those royall virtues and princelie partes, togeather with the greate giftes of gratious goverment that you make mencion of, were soe perfectlie planted in her as best might serve to the maintenance of Gode's glorie (from whom her Highnes confesseth all goodnes to proceed), and best also might serve to the good governance of yow her good loveing and obedient subjectes; and withall prayeth yow with her and for her, to give God heartie thankes for those virtues and graces that it hath pleased God to blesse her withall, and also to pray for the continewance of them with such encrease as best shall like his divine Majesty. And besides this I may and dare certainely affirme unto yow from her Majestie's owne mouth that if all the virtues of all the princes in Europe were united within her Highnes' brest, shee would gladlie employe the same to the best of her power about the good governance of yow that bee so good and loveing unto her, so greate is her Highnes' heartie good will and inwarde affeccion towardes yow. Againe, true yt is that theise your loveing and reverent conceaveinges[3] of the virtues and good and gratious goverment of your Soveraigne is taken by her Majesty in very thankefull parte, as a spetiall and a peculier propertie perteineing to faithfull and loveing subjectes; neither will her Highnes pretermitt any occasion that may[4] move yow to conceive otherwise then yow have, neither doe I thinke that any man can devise any way more readie, or any perswasion more stronge, to move a princely nature to bee such towardes her subjectes as they would wish then by such good, reverend and loveing conceptions and conceiveings remembred by yow. To conclude as touching this point, I am to affirme unto yow from her Majesty that shee taketh your proceedeinges in this parliament, both in the begininge and in the middest and in the ending, so gratiously and in so thankefull parte that, if both art and nature did concurr in mee abundantly to make mee eloquente (as neither of them doe), yet I am sure I were not able to sett forth this pointe according to her Highnes' desire nor to the worthines of yt. And for the more manifestacion of this, and of the greate good likeing that her Majesty hath conceived of yow that bee of this parliament, her Highnes meaneth not to determine the same but / to proroge yt untill the next winter. And as to the agnizeinge[5] and recognizing of benefittes, her Majestie's pleasure and comandement is that I should declare unto yow that ther is none of those benefittes remembred by you but shee wisheth them treble in number and quadruple in greatnes and goodnes; and further her Highnes thinketh that the oft faithfull recogniseing of benefittes received is one of the greatest satisfaccions that a subject cann make to his soveraigne for them.

f.26

'And as to the third, which concerneth your humble and earnest peticion made to her Majesty concerneinge marriage, her Highnes' pleasure and comandement is that I should lett yow understand that her Highnes noteth therin three principall thinges. The first is that shee presentlie conceiveth that this your peticion proceedeth from your inwarde affeccions and benevolent mindes, founded and grounded uppon the greate good opinion that yow have conceived of her Majestie's most gratious goverment over yow, according to the declaracion made by yow: a matter greately moveing her Majesty the rather to allow of this your peticion. The second note importeth yet more then this, for therin shee conceiveth that this greate good opinion of this her blessed goverment is not conceived by yow, as yt appeareth by your owne declaracion, uppon any suddaine ground or cause, but hath growen

---

1. *Sic.*
2. *Sic* in MS; Cott.Titus F1 leaves a blank in the heading, but gives '18 Eliz' at the top of each page. The speech was made at the second session of the parliament of 1572, i.e. 15 March 1575/6.

3. MS reads 'conceiveing'; this reading from Cott.Titus F1.
4. 'May' supplied from Cott.Titus F1.
5. MS reads 'agnifieing'; this reading from Cott.Titus F1.

uppon the consideracion of her Highnes' governance dureing the raigne of seaventeen yeares now past, wherby yt is evident that this is a constant and setled opinion of youres, and therfore much the more moveing her Majestie to give a gratious eare unto this your peticion. And the third note exceedeth theis other two former, for in this noate shee conceiveth the abundance of your inward affeccions grounded uppon her good governance of yow to bee so greate that yt doth not only content yow to have her Majesty to raigne and governe over yow, but also you doe desire that some proceedeing of her Majestie's bodie might by perpetuall succession raigne over your posteritie also: a matter greately to move her Highnes, shee saith, to encline to this your suite. Besides her Highnes is not unmindfull of all the benefittes

f.26v   that will growe to / the realme by such a marriage, neither doth shee forgett any of the perills that are like to growe for want therof. All which matters considered, her Majesty hath called mee to say that albeit of her owne natureall disposicion shee is not disposed or inclined to marriage, neither would shee ever marrie if shee weare a private person, yet for your sakes and for the benefitt of the realme shee is contented to encline and dispose herselfe to the satisfaccion of your humble peticion so that all thinges convenient may concurr that bee meete for such a marriage, wherof ther bee verie many: some touching the estate of her most royall person, some the person of him whom God shall ioyne,[6] some touching the estate of the whole realme; theis thinges concurring and considered her Majesty hath assented as is before remembred. And thus much touching this matter.

'As to the fowerth parte which concerneth a declaracion of the lawes past in this session wherunto yow doe humbly pray that her Majesty would give her royall assent, her Majesty hath commanded mee to say unto yow that shee cannot but greatly commend your travaile and paines taken in deviseing of theis lawes, your consideracions and carefulnes in debateing and consulting, and your judgementes and determinacions in concludeing and passing of the same; and meaneth to give her royall assent to so many of them as her Majesty shall thinke meete and convenient to passe att this time. But heer I am to remember you that this is not all that her Highnes requireth in this pointe, for shee is desirous that the travailes, paines and great charges employed about the makeing of theis lawes should not bee lost, neither her Majestie's royall assent granted in vaine, which must needes come to pass excepte yow looke better to the execucion of lawes than heertofore yow have donne. For as I have before this time said, lawes without execucion bee nothing else but penn, inke and parchement, a countenance[7] of a thing and nothing indeed, cause without an effect; and doe serve as much to the good governance of a common wealth as a

f.27   rudder of a shipp doth serve to the governance of yt / without a governor, and doe serve to as good purpose to direct men's accions as torches doe serve to direct men's goeinges in the darke when their lightes bee putt out. Weare yt not a greate folly, trowe yow, yea a meere maddnes for a gardner to provide apt and handsome tooles and instrumentes to reforme and pruine his trees withall and then to lay them upp in faire boxes and bagges without use of them? And is it not as strang, trowe yee, to make lawes to reforme men's manners and to pruine away the ill braunches and members of the common wealth and then to lay upp those lawes in faire bookes or boxes without executeing of them? Surelie ther is small difference[8] betweene the cases; nay, yt weare much better to have noe new lawes made att all then to have lawes made and theise not executed, for the former doth but leave us in the state wee were in before the makeing of the new lawes; but to make lawes and not to execute them is to breed a contempt of lawes and law makers and of all magistrates which is the verie mother and nurse of disobedience. And what shee breedeth and bringeth forth I leave yt to yow to iudge. Now this offence of not executeing of lawes groweing so greate yt resteth to see in whose default this is, and who ought to beare the burthen of yt. First, certeine yt is that her Majesty leaveth nothing undonne meete for her to doe for th'execucion of lawes. For first, shee maketh choise of persons of most creditt and of best understanding throughout her whole realme to whom for the greate trust and fidelitie that shee reposeth in them shee giveth authoritie by commission to execute a greate parte of theis lawes, who also by oath bee bound to performe the same. Besides, the most spetiall and needfull laws her Highnes causeth them to bee proclaimed and published unto her people, and over this also, least men should bee forgettfull of their duties, shee causeth a number of her justices to bee called into publique place and ther to bee exhorted and admonished in her Majestie's name to see to the execucion of her lawes. And what cann bee heerin more devised for her Majestie to doe? Surelie in mine opinion nothing. Then falleth it out necessarily and consequently that the burthen / of all those enormities, absurdities and mischeifes that doe grow in the commonwealth for the not executeing of lawes must needes light uppon those persons that have authority from her Majestie to execute them and doe[9] yt not: which is a burthen over heavie for any person to beare beinge iustlie charged. For th'avoideing of this therfore, methinkes men being thus remembred should seeke with all dilligence and endeavor to satisfie for theire negligence and carelesnes by past, which, if they shall forgett to doe, her Majestie shalbee then driven cleane contrarie to her most gratious nature and inclinacion to appoint and assigne private men for profitt and gaine's sake to see her penall lawes to bee executed. The course her Majesty hath hitherto taken hath bynn to have theis lawes executed by men of creditt and estimacion for the love of iustice, uprightly and indifferently. But if they shall refuse so to doe, forgetting their dutie to God, their soveraigne and their countrie, then of necessitie rather then the lawes should bee unexecuted her Majestie shalbee driven, I say, to committ the execucion of them to those, who in respect of profitt and gaine, will see them executed with all extremitie: and what a burthen that will bring to the realme I leave yt to your consideracions. But it is to bee hoped that if the respectes before remembred will not move yow to see better to your charge, yet the feare of this greate inconvenience should constraine men that bee in comission to looke better to the execucion of lawes. And thus much touching the fowerth parte.

'Now as to the fift and last, which concerneth the grant of a subsidie, her Majesty hath commanded mee to say to yow that that grant is a manifest declaracion by deedes of that which before was declared by wordes, for how could such a grant bee

f.27v

6. *Sic.*
7. MS reads 'continewance'; this reading from Cott.Titus FI.
8. MS reads 'differences'; this reading from Cott.Titus FI.
9. MS reads 'doth'; this reading from Cott.Titus FI.

made, and in such manner granted and by such persons, but that of necessitie yt must proceed from the benevolent mindes and heartie affeccions of such loveing subjectes as be[10] before remembred? True yt is that her Majestie in theise your doinges hath noted three thinges principally, every of them tending much to the setting forth of your benevolence; the first who yt was that granted, / the second the manner of the granting, the third what it is that was granted.

f.28

'And as to the first, her Majesty cannot forgett how this grant is proceeded from the earnest affeccions and hearty good wills of her good loveing and obedient subjectes, wherof her Majesty maketh greater accompt then of tenn subsidies, and so shee hath comanded mee to say unto yow; againe her Majestie remembreth verie well that this grant is made, not by subjectes that never made the like before, but by subjectes that have bynn, and continew to bee, readie from time to time to contribute towardes the necessarie chardges and defence of the realme, which doth greatlie commend and sett forth, shee saith, this greate benevolence of yours.

'And as to the second which is the manner of granting, her Highnes noateth two thinges spetially. Th'one is universalitie of concent: and cann ther bee a more universall consent then wher all agree none denieing as this was? Nay, her Highnes knoweth that before her time this manner of grante passed not but with a great perswasion and many difficulties, wher this was offerred frankely without any perswasion or difficultie at all. Th'other is the readines in granting. It is written of benevolences that *bis dat qui cito dat*: which her Majestie saith may be iustlie applied to theis your proceedinges.

'And as to the third, which is the thing granted, shee taketh yt to bee as liberall as any heertofore hath bynn granted, and therfor hath comanded mee to yeild unto yow her most heartie and condigne thankes and withall to lett yow understand that her Majestie is as willing and desirous to yeald unto yow[11] this whole subsidie againe as yow have bynn readie and willing to grant, if the necessitie of the realme and your suertie would suffer yt. And thus much touching the granteing of this subsidie.

'Now as to the due and trew execucion of the same. I am to exhorte and also to admonish yow; and yet it may bee probably saide that persons that have thus bountefullie and readily made this grante, wherin and wherby their benevolent mindes and heartie affeccions have bynn so manifestly declared in graunting that, to those persons neither admonishement neither exhortacion is due for the true executeing of that graunte, noe more then / a spurr is to a horse tht runneth as swiftly as hee cann. Albeit this argument in reason carrieth probabilitie and likelihood with yt, yet because former experience hath taught that theis grantes have not bynn so duely and truly executed as they have bynn benevolentlie granted, . . .'

f.28v

Heere being comanded to cease I did forbeare to say that which I meant to say.

'Looe, my Lords and Masters, her Majestie's pleasure is that I shall forbeare any further to exhorte you, wherby yt may manifestly appeare unto yow that the trust and confidence which shee reposeth in your troathes and fidelities is so great that her Highnes thinketh it needles and a vaine matter to exhort men so willinglie and loveinglie disposed, and had rather hazard a part of the thing granted then to breed any suspicion in any of yow, by long exhorting and perswadeing, that shee is doubtfull of your faithfull and diligent dealeing and proceeding in this matter'.

Heerafter followeth that I entended to have saide if I had not bynn countermaunded:

and for that the most parte of you that have bynn privie to this grant are likely to bee used about the due execucion of the same, therfore meethinkes yt shall not bee amisse partelie to exhorte yow concerneing this matter. As first to remember yow what a greate offence yt is for a franke and benevolent grantor to become a remisse and negligent executor of his grante. If yow doe but imagine what a fault it is to have a common person verie willing and liberall to grant any thing to another, and afterwardes negligently and fraudulentlie doe[12] goe about to take away or withhold any parte of that which is granted: this offence amongst common persons that bee honest is detested. And if so, then what manner of offence will yt prove to [?be] when this is used by a subject to his soveragine, and in case that tendeth to the defence of the realme; a fault suerlie that every subject ought to abhorr. Againe, yt is to bee remembred that such persons as shalbee by her Majesty put in comission to see the due execucion of this graunte to bee persons spetially chosen / by her Majesty for the greate fidelitie and trust shee reposeth in them. Now if theis persons thus trusted shall satisfie this trust with negligence, or shall for favor or affeccion borne to any forgett unnatureally and ungratefully their dutie to her Majesty, yea their dutie to God and to their country, then cann yt not bee denied but they shall shew themselves to regard more the private commodities of themselves and their freindes then their dutie to God, their soveraigne and their country, and so never worthy to bee putt in trust after, to their perpetuall infamie and ignominie. And thus much touching the execucion of this subsidie.'

f.29

Fitzwilliam of Milton Political 133

xv[to] *Martii* 1575.
Notes of the oration made by the Lord Keper of the Greate Seale in the parlamentt chamber in the presence of the Queen's Majesty.

His speach was fframed as an aunsweare to an oration made the daie before in the same place and presence by Mr Bell, Speaker of the common house.

The sum wheareof was by his Lordship collected into five partes:	The first a discoorse of divers manner of governementtes. The seconde a declaration of hir Majestie's blessed and happie raine over hir subiectes: with an enumeration of hir vertues and of the greate and singuler benefittes that theie have and continuallie doo receive under hir governementt. The third an humble petition to move hir to marie. The fourth a petition that it might please hir Majesty by hir roiall assentt to consumatt such lawes as had beene agreed on by the Lords and Commons. The fift, and last, a presentasion of a subsidie and too fifteenes

10. MS reads 'bine'; this reading from Cott. Titus F1.

11. 'Yow' supplied from Cott. Titus F1.
12. *Sic.*

graunted by the temporaltie for the releefe of hir Majestie's
greate charge and the maintenance of the realme.

To everie of the which hee awnswered in effect as folloeth.

1.   To the first, that the same required onelie this awnsweare: that the Speaker havinge
verie well and at good lenghte expressed sundrie kindes of governementes whearebie
common welt[h]es are ruled (which weare *monarchia, aristo[c]ratia, democratia*),
deserveth much commendation for so diligentt a collection of the same.

2.   To the seconde: that hir Majesty did thanke God with them that hit had pleased
him in hir daies, and thorough hir minesterie, to bles this realme with that happines
which theie acqnoleged, humblie besechinge him, from whome onelie the same
procedeth, to continue so his favorable countenance over hir and them, as thease hir
greate and singuler bennifittes recited by the Speaker might in no time decrease.

Touchinge hir self, she wisshed of God that all the vertues which theie thought to
bee in hir weare so in deade, as thearebie she might bee the more able to governe well
so lovinge subiectes; and that hir desire was that theie shoulde praie to God dailie to
increase the same in hir, ffor she saith that if all the vertues of all the princes in Europe
weare in hir, she shoulde thinke them well bestoed uppon so good subiectes.

3.   In the third hee considered three thinges.

First, the good will of them from whome the petition cam, that is from most
lovinge and dutifull subiectes that in all times and in all thinges have sheued that
love and obedience to hir which a good prince maie in reason looke for.

Second, that this good will in them was constantt, without either alteration or
decaie after so longe continuance of hir raine by the space of xvij yeares and more,
not waveringe nor unthankefull, as is seene often in children towardes theire parentes
and in servantes towardes theire masters, whome nevertheles th'one by nature,
th'other by dutie thiei ough[t] to love and reverence with all humilitie.

Thirdlie, that theire good wills doo so abounde as thieie did not onelie desire the
longe continuance of hir Majestie's raine over them in hir owne person, but also after
hir daies the issue of hir most noble bodie might succede and menie other to rule in
hir place.

All which shee saide did greatelie move hir to accept in verie thankefull parte a
petition of that nature procedinge from so greate good wills of so good and lovinge
subiectes.

Neither was shee, hee saide, unmindefull of that which the Speaker had recited,
that was, both of the greate quietnes and greate bennifittes which theie received by
the goodnes of almightie God in thease daies of hir reine, and of the greate perrilles
that hoonge over them if God, by such honorable mach, should not raise up to them
seede of hirs to governe after hir.

And thearefore saide for awnsweare to that petition that, albeitt mariage
wheareunto thie moved hir is not the coorse of life that she coulde hitherunto in enie
wise incline hir hart unto (this estate of life whearein she nowe is best agreeing with
hir owne disposition), yeat in respect of them and in respect of the realme committed
to hir by God, the preservation wheareof she desireth above all thinges in the worlde,

she was not unwillinge to dispose hir self contrarie to hir owne affection, not to pas
hir daies in this sole life: so as all thinges might concure and bee awnswerable for hir
self in particular, and for them in generall.

To the fourth, hee saide that as the principall cause for assemblie in parliamenttes
is to consider of the sores and greefes of common welth, even so hir Majesty did verie
well like and alowe of the greate care and paines theie had taken in providinge of
good and sufficientt lawes to redresse those thinges that weare amis. Such as thieie
had passed she had considered and woulde assentt to so menie of them as she
thought at this time meete to take the force of lawe.

Uppon which occasion hee entred into a large exhortasion that lawes made with
so greate charge and with so greate paine might bee bettar exequted then hearetofore
theie had beene. For as no common wealth, saith hee, can bee governed withoute
lawes meete for the state and the time; and as that prince and people deserveth greate
commendation that carefullie provide good lawes, th'ende wheareof is to defende the
good and punish the evill: so, if the same after theie bee so well made doo lie still
withoute due execution, theie becoom utterlie unprofitable and the laboure in
makinge of them emploied in vaine.

In which respect a magistrate that suffereth his lawes to lie ded withoute practise
maie well bee compared to a gardenar that with care and cost prepareth a number of
good tooles, whearewith to proine[1] and clenge[2] the superfluus and wilde braunches
of his orcharde, thearebie to geve the more comforte to the good graftes to prosper:
but havinge thus provided thease so good and necessarie tooles, laieth them up
nevertheles in faire boxes and bagges withoute puttinge them in youse, wheareby his
treese growe so far loden with wilde bowes as theie yealde either none or verie bad
fruite.

And lawes thus made and thus neglected maie also, hee saide, bee likened to faire
torches withoute light, leesinge thearebi theire proper yeouse, which is to direct men
in darke waies for[3] stumblinge, as lawes doo the people in the crooked waies of
man's life for offendinge.

The fault, hee saide, was neither in the parlament that with so greate care did
provide lawes necessarie and sufficientt, neither in the Queen that not onelie by hir
proclemation did publish the same to hir subiectes, but also by commission did
commaunde the same to bee put in execution, apointinge for that poorpose in everie
countie men taken to bee of wisdom and integritie: but the fault indeade, hee saide,
was in those men so auctorised that, contrarie to the trust committed to them, either
of neclgence or affection did suffer the lawes to lie as ded creatures withoute life, not
remembringe theire conscience to God, the auctorised good lawes[4], theire dutie to
hir Majesty, hir supreame Majesty in the common wealth[5], nor the preservation of
the people in quietnes from iniurie and opression.

To this, hee said, greater regard must bee had then hearetofore hath beene,
otherwaies his Majesty shall bee forced not onelie to punish severelie such ministers

---

1. *Sic.*
2. *Sic.*
3. *Sic.*

4. *Sic.*
5. *Sic.*

as neglect so greatelie theire duties, but also to make choise of others that with more diligence and sinceritie will perfoorme theire functions.

5.   To the fift, and last, hee saide that hir Majesty did reaseave in verie gratious and thankefull parte theire gift; the rather for that in the same shee did consider thease 3 speciall thinges:

> the persons that gave it;
> the manner of the gevinge;
> the thinge geven.

1   And first, the persons to bee hir most lovinge and faithfull subiectes that weare so carefull for hir estate.

2   Second, in the manner of the gevinge she considered 3 thinges:

> universalitie – beinge doone with generall consent, withoute deniall of enie;
> willingnes – as doone most ffrancklie;
> redines – in assentinge to the same in the beginninge of the parlamentt withoute difficultie or delaie, whearein was verefied the oulde true saing, '*Bis dat qui cito dat.*'

3   Thirdlie, the thinge geven beinge a subsidie and too fifteenes, equale with the greatest that have beene graunted in anie former time.

6.   Lastlie, uppon this occasion hee saide that it was to bee well seene unto that this so willinge, so ffranke and so redie a gift, migh[t] not by necligence or affection, as hath beene hearetofore founde, becoom so smaule in valeue as it shoulde not awnsweare the good meaninge of the gevers, nor furnish the necessarie service of hir Majesty for the maintenance of the realm. Nevertheles hir Majesty was pleased to committ the same to the order and discreation of the lords and others that shoulde bee hir commissioners, not doughtinge but theie woulde bee as carefull as the matter did emporte.

And thus eftsoones rendringe hir Majesty's thankes to all the assemblie for theire good and painfull service in this session hee ended.

And after a particular speach used at that time by the Queen hir self to the Lords and Commons, touchinge hir mariage and the care she had for the quiett governement of the realme after hir, the Lord Keper by hir commaundementt did proroge the parlament untill the vth of November next 1576.

10. *Queen's speech at close of session, 15 March*

i. Text from Northants.: CRO Fitzwilliam of Milton Political 177 (in Fitzwilliam's hand).
Other MSS. London: BL Add.15891, Add.29975, Add.32379, Add.33271, Harl.787. Oxford: Bodley, Tanner 169.
Printed. Nugae Antiquae, ed. H. Harington and T. Park (1804), I.120-7.
ii. Text from Oxford: Exeter College, 92, copy.

Fitzwilliam of Milton Political 177

The speach uttered by hir Majestie in the parlament house at the eande of the session holden in March 1575, the xviij[th] of hir raine, uppon pointes both in the Speaker's oracion and also in the Lord Keper's.

Doo I see Gode's most sacred woorde and text of hollie writt drawen to so divers senses bee it never so presiselie taughte, and shall I hope that my speach can pas foorth thorowe so meanie eares withoute mistakinge, wheare so meanie ripe and divers wittes doo ofter bende to conster then attaine the true and perfect understandinge? If anie looke for eloquence, I shall deceave theire hope. If sum thinke I can mach theire guiftes that spake before, theie houlde an open heresie. I can not satisfie theire longinge thristes[1] that wach for thease delightes unles I shoulde affoorde them what my self had never in possession. If I shoulde saie that the sweetest toonge or eloquentest speach that evar was in man weare able to express that restles care which I have ever bent to governe for youre greatest weales, I shoulde most wronge myne entent and greatelie bate the meritt of my owne endevoure.

   I can not attribute thease happes and good succes to my device withoute detractinge much from the devine providence, nor chalenge to my privatt commendacion what is onelie due to his eternall glorie: my sex permittes it not; or if it might bee in this kinde, yeat finde I no impeachment whi to persons of more base estate the like proportion shoulde not bee alotted. One speciall favoure yeat must I neades confes I have good cause to vaunt of: that wheareas varietie and love of chaunge is ever so rife in servantes to theire masters, in children to theire parentes, and in privatt freindes one to an other — as though for one yeare, or perhapps for toowe, can content them selves to houlde theire coorse upright yeat after by mistrust or dowght of woorse theie ar dissevered, and in time wax wearie of theire woonted

Bennifittes that were mentioned by Mr Speaker to have happened in hir raine.[2]

---

1. *Sic.*
2. The marginal comments (in another hand) are against words which have been marked in the MS with a broken line; 'I can not . . . much from' is marked here.

likinge – yeat still I finde that assured zeale amonge my ffaithfull subiectes to my especiall comfort which was first declared to my greate encoragement. Can a prince that of necessitie must discontentt a number to delight and please a fewe (because the greatest parte ar oft not best enclined) continue a longe time withoute greate offence, much mischeefe, or common grudge? Or happes it often[3] that princes' actions ar taken in so good parte and favorablie interpreted? No, no, my lordes. Howe greate my fortune is in this respect I weare ingrate if I shoulde not acknoledge. And as for those rare and speciall bennifittes which have manie yeares followed and accompanied my happie raine, I attribute to God aloane the prince of rule, and count my self no better then his hand maide, rather brought up in a scoole to abide the ferula then traded in a kingdom to supporte the scepter.

Repeated by the Lord Keper.[4]

If pollicie had beene preferred before truth, woulde I, tro you, even at the first beginninge of my rule have turned upsidowne so greate affaires, or entred into tossinge of the greatest waves and billowes of the worlde that might, if I had sought my ease, have harbored and cast ancor in most seeminge securitie? It can not bee denied but worldlie wisdoome rather bad me knitt and mach my self in leage and fast aliance with greate princes to purchase ffrendes one everie side by worllie[5] meanes, and theare repose the trust of my strengh[6] wheare force coulde never wantt to geave assistance. Was I too seeke that by mane's outwarde iudgmentt this must needes bee thought the safest coorse?[7] No, I can never graunt my self so simple as not to see what all mene's eies discovered. But all thease meanes of leauges,[8] aliances and foreine strenghes I quite forsooke, and gave myself to seeke for truth withoute respect, reposinge my cheefe staie in Gode's most mightie grace. Thus I began, thus I did proceede, and thus I hope to eande. Thease 17 yeares God hath both prospered and protected you with good succes under my direction, and I dought not but the same maintaininge hand will guide you still and bringe you to ripenes of perfection. Consider with your selves the bitter stormes and trobles of your neighboures, the true cause wheareof I will not attribute to princes (God forbid I shoulde) seence thease misfortunes maie proceede as well from sinnes among the people: for want of plauges declare[s][9] not alwaise want of guilt, but rather proves God['s] mersie. I knowe besides that privatt persons maie rather finde a fault then mende a prince's state; and for my parte I graunt my self to guiltie to encrease the burden of others. Lett all men thearefore beare theire privatt faultes; my owne have waight inough for me to awnsweare for. The beast waie thearefore, I suppose, for you and me is by sum humble praieres to crave of God that not in weeninge,[10] but in perfect waight, in beeinge not in seeminge, wee maie wish the best and further it with oure habilitie. Nether can the finest witt, the scrapingest iudgment that can rake most deepelie and take up men's captious eares with pleasinge tales have greater care to guide you to the safest state, or woulde bee glad to establish you wheare you ought to thinke youre selves most sure and happi then she that telles you nowe this tale.

For want of heires of hir bodi, spoken of by Mr Speaker and recited by my Lorde Keper.[11]

And touchinge daungers cheeflie feared. To rehearse my meaninge latelye unfolded unto you by the Lord Keper it shall not neade, for that maie well suffice, though I must confes my owne mislike so much to strive against the matter as, if I weare a milkemaide with a paile one my arme – whearebie my privatt person might bee litell sett by – I woulde not forsake that single state to mach my self with the greatest monarch of the worlde. Not that I doo condeme the dooble knott or iudge amis of such as forced by necessitie can not dispose them selves to other life; but this I wish that none weare driven to chaunge but such as coulde not kepe within the boundes of honestie.[12] And yeat for your behoofe theare is no waie so difficile that maie withstande my private liking that I coulde not well content my self to like of, and in this case as willinglie to spoile myself quite out[13] of my self, as if I shoulde put of my upper garment when it wearieth me if the present state might not thearebie bee encoombered. I saie not this for my behoolf. I knowe I am but mortall, which good lesson Mr Speaker in his thirde devision of a vertuous prince's properties with reasone late remembered, and so theare whilest prepare myself with such contentmentt to reaseave death whensoever it shall please God to send it; as, if others woulde endevoure to perfoorme the like, it coulde not bee so bitter unto menie as it hath beene counted. My experience teacheth me to bee no fonder of thease vaine delightes then reason woulde, nether further to delight in thinges uncertaine then maie seeme convenient. But lett good heade bee taken least that reaching to far after future good you perrill not the presentt, or begine to quarrell or faule together by the eares by dispute before it maie bee well discided who shall weare my crowne. I will not denie but I might bee thought the most indifferent iudge in this respect in that I shall not bee when thease pointes bee fulfilled, which none beside my self can speake in all this companie. Misdeeme not my woordes as though I sought what hearetofore to others hath beene graunted. I entende it not; my braines be to thin to carie so tough a matter. Although I trust God will not in such hast cut of my daies, but accordinge to your owne desertes and my desire I maie provide sum good waie for your securitie. And thus as one that yealdeth you more thankes, both for your zeale to my self and service in this parlament, then nowe my toonge can utter, I recommende you to the assured garde and best kepinge of the Almightie, who will preserve you safe I trust, in all felicitie; and wish withall that each one of you had tasted sum dropps of Lethe's flud to deface and cancell thease speaches oute of your remembrance.

By avoidinge the unpleasinge state of mariag, or daunger of havinge children.[14]

By to gredi desire of mariage or certaine heire to be apointed, the one by endaungeringe hir life, th'other by causinge civill disention.[15]

To dispose the crowne by will.[16]

Exeter College, Oxford, 92, f.62 and v

Quene Elizabethe's answer to the lords and others in the parliament howse upon Thursday *xvᵒ Marcii*.1575

My lordes, doe I see the Scriptures, Gode's woorde, in so manye wayes enterpreted

3. 'Often' repeated in MS.
4. 'And as . . . benniffites which' marked in MS.
5. *Sic.*
6. *Sic.*
7. Add.32379: 'Was I to seeke that?' etc. Cf. *EP*, I.365.
8. *Sic.*
9. MS appears to read 'delai'; this reading from Add.32379.
10. 'Weyinge' in other MSS.

11. 'And touchinge . . . latelie unfolded' marked in MS.
12. Or 'kepe the chastest lymittes' (Add.32379).
13. 'Out' supplied from Add.32379.
14. 'I saie not . . . Mr Speaker' marked in MS.
15. 'But lett good . . . not the presentt' marked in MS.
16. 'Misdeeme not . . . beene graunted' marked in MS.

and wrested, accordinge to the diverse humours of the readers? And shall I thinke
that some fewe woordes of myne shall not be mysconstered as it shall please the
hearers? For eloquence, yf you looke for any I shall deceave yow: for I am farre from
hit. And I thinke none in suche an heresye as to imagyne yt. Thus I will saye that if I
had the most eloquent tongue in the world, and that I wold declare the care that I
have allwaies had of your welfare, I shold not come nere yt; neither do I thinke that
all these benefictes (which under me yow have enjoyed[1], and have sayed to proceade
from my good governement) can any wayes be attributed unto me, or that the
prosperous successe therof ought to be acknowledged to come from me, but from
God onlye. For my sex will not beare yt, neither hathe God gyven me any suche rare
and particuler giefte but that I do knowe a great meny of farre meaner callinge which
are able to exede me.

    This singuler beneficte only I do take upon me from him, or ells shold I be
unthankfull: that wheras we see all thinges subiect to chaunge, and that not only
famyliar ffrendes, but also children of ther parentes, yea servantes of ther masters, do
wax wery and discontented, no mene yeare but in lesse while; in me thies xvij[en]
yeares' government have confirmed and assured your affections to be subiect to no
chainge. And this must[2] doubtlesse be by the hand of God, that a prince shold see
all so well contented, that had suche diverse cawses to discontent so many: for by
whose pollityke head and fyne witt, or by what other meanes then by the assistaunce
of God, cold it have come to passe that a woman cominge rawlye, and as it weare
taken from the ferulue[3] to her kyngdome, and takinge a cleane contrary coursse from
that she founde, could so sodenlye (in despite of the mallice of so many) turne up sett
downe so great mattiers, and laye newe foundations, and yet her country and
subiectes preserved from that pestilence wherwith her nearest neighbours one every
syde have bene grevouslie infected? Neither is ther any of you that thinketh me so
f.62v   ignoraunt that / to compasse so great matters, pollicye wolde that I shold have bene
contented to matche with some greate prynce, who might have asisted me; I shold
have mad leagues, and not leafte any one prynce discontented with whome I shold
not have contracted league, and that no forrayne invasion might disturbe my platt at
home. But I symplye, withe a cleare conscience (to do nothinge but what shold be to
the glorye of God and wealthe of my subiectes), did allwayes commytt the whole
unto the providence of God, only trustinge and dependinge upon his goodnes: and
therfore doubt not but that the same God, which thies xvij[ten] yeares hathe governed
and prospered[4] me, will not nowe abandon me and foresake the worke that he hathe
begone in me. No thankes therfore dewe to my self, but all to God.

    Yet remayneth towchinge that my Lord Keaper answered in his third
parte — your suit I meane. I allowe your zeale, and withall aunswer you that no fyne
and scrapinge judgment or factioned head, that will see further into mattiers then
perchaunce is neade, not any of them, I saye, shall shewe him self more carefull to
provide for your saffetye and advoid inconveniences that may endanger you then I.
And yet I promise you that it is a course of lyef so farre from my disposition that, if
your good did not depend one yt, or that I had benne some pryvat mayede to live
with a payle, I wold not marrye to be the greattest kynge's wiefe; or were it that
nonne shold so doe, but suche as fownde provocation in them selves, I protest it

shold not be I this yeare to marry: not that I do discommend yt, beinge an ordynaunce of God for suche as cannot lyve without it. Onlye your well doinge, wherof none ought to be so carefull as I, for non of you then assured yt then to be but I.[5] I praye God that I may ever do that which in effect, and not in seeminge,[6] may be beneficiall unto yow, and not, by hopinge to eschewe a danger likely to ensue, willinglye to enter into any present perill — not a perill to my self I meane, for, althoughe Mr Speaker rehersed that I was mortall, I thanke God that althoughe fewe have greater cawses yet non I am suer I[7] have lesse desire to lyve then my self, and shall neade no preast. I meane not thies in respect of presente danger to my selfe so that you may enter into none more dangerous then that which you feare so moche, wherof no bodye ought to be so carefull as I becawse I only shall then be assured not to be.

Finis.

1. MS reads 'enyoyed'.
2. MS reads 'most'.
3. *Sic.*
4. MS reads 'prorspered'.
5. *Sic*: the original punctuation of the MS is

no help, and one or more words have probably been omitted from an already complex sentence.
6. MS appears to read 'shoinge'.
7. *Sic.*

1. *Thomas Cromwell's journal,*
8 February-15 March

Text from TCD MS 1045, copy.

TCD MS 1045, fos.116-35[1]

viij Februarij.

Memorandum: that this being a prorogation the Queene came not to the House.

First, the Speaker moved that for expedition['s] sake, uppon every motion made certaine might be apointed to consider whyther the matter moved were fit to bee commytted to bill before any argument should bee used of the matter.

A bill reade containing that every man upon whom any sclaunderouse wordes were spoken should, in the same county, lay his action and that the county might bee issuable.

Mr Peter Wentworth made a motion concerning the libertie of speach in the House shewing that greate commodities might growe thereby. In hindrance hereof he declared that certaine pesti[fe]rowse rumors were raysed, *vz.*, 'Take heede what yow doe, the Queene misliketh of such a matter', or, 'Take heede yow speake not against such a matter, for the Queene liketh of it.' Other some tymes messages were brought very greivous to the House, and odyous, and not [to] be suffered, as, amongst others, that the last parliament there was a message brought that wee should not deale with matters of religion. He said that this was an ungodly message and signified as much as wee might doe nothing tending to the glory of God; and so God, even the mightie God, was shote out of the doores. And therefore he that then

f.116v said that no good success could follow of that parliament might / seeme to speake with the spirit of prophecye, for he after put into her Majestie's harte to reiect the bill which was made with greate care and diligence for her safe[ty]; in reiecting of which bill her Majestie had commytted greate fautes in being so careless of her owne and our safety; that it was a dangerous thing for her Majestie to abuse her moste loveing subiectes of the lower house and to oppose her selfe against her nobilitie, considering the parliament was purposely called for that purpose. Two billes declared — Uppon theise wordes thus undutyfully pronounced against her Majestie, he was interrupted in his speech, secluded the House whilest these wordes might be considered of, and then agreed by the House to bee commytted to the custody of the serieant; and in the meane season certeyne apointed to take his examination.

ix° Februarij.

Mr Treasurer declared that upon examination he had confessed the whole matter and delivered the same to the commyttees in writing. Whereupon, his fact being considered, Mr Rowrmun would have the same to have beene brought within the statute [of] King Philipe and Queene Mary for raising seditious rumors, or else a lawe nowe to be made for the punishing of it.[2] In fine, uppon consideration of the matter it was agreed he should be comytted close prisoner to the Tower. And he being brought in to heare his iudgement, did there submitt himselfe to the censure of the House, acknowledging that he could not as much as thinke evill / of the same;   f.117 notwithstanding, desired that his rash speech might not be a cause of preiudice of the libertie of speech in other, protesting that what soever he had said, his faute did grow in abundance of zeale and love and good will to the Queene's Majestie, and that whensoever any service of hers were required, he would adventure himselfe with the formost, and desired the whole House to be suitors to the Queene's Majestie for him.

There was then a question moved whither the Lord Russell, being the last session of the parliament howse and now since being lord, should continue of the Howse; and agreed that he should, considering that he had no voice in the higher house, and shewed that the like president had beene before in his father.[3]

There was also another motion concerning a burgesse of the House now in execucion, whither he should continue burgesse or a new to be chosen; and agreed that neither for absence for sicknes, imprisonment, by reason of embassadage, or other accidentall cause, any alteration of the burgesse should bee made.[4]

A bill was read that no fine or common recovery should be reversed for matters of forme.

A bill read concerning an explanation of the statute made in the last parliament concerning roges,[5] with a new provision for the reliefe of the poore by having stockes in every parishes[6] and houses of correction in every shyer to sett some to worke and to punish others. /

A bill read that fines at the common lawe of landes in auncient demeasne[7] should   f.117v be of force, with a proviso; the landes still in other respectes to follow the nature of ancient demeasne.[8]

x° Februarij.

A bill for the better preservation of woodes, that no [blank] should be cutt downe before the same be xij inches square iiij foote from the ground; for every acre of timber cutt downe asmuch new grounde fit for timber to be inclosed; not trees to be cutt downe by force of commyssion within xl rod of any man's house.

A bill read that children borne after divorce should not inherit, except there[9] be a reconciliacion, and which children borne after reconciliacion to bee legitimate.

The bill concerning roges the second tyme read, which was referred to be argued unto the next sitting.

1. The numbering of the folios has been preserved as it appears in the MS, even though an error has occurred and f.116 ought properly to be f.117.
2. 1 & 2 Ph. & Mary, c.3 (1554-5), in *SR*, IV,240-1.
3. See *CJ*, I.15, 104 for both cases, and

GEC, II.75-7.
4. Cf.*CJ*, I.104.
5. 14 Eliz., c.5 (1572) in *SR*, IV.590-8.
6. *Sic.*
7. MS reads 'demeasure'.
8. MS reads 'demeasure'.
9. MS reads 'they'.

xi° Februarij.

A bill for the assurance of certeine landes from Sir John Spencer to Mr Hatton.

A bill for the sale of William Isley to be donn by certeine of the counsell and others for the payment of his debtes, to bee equally distributed and no advantage to bee taken by any body but of the principall debt.

The rest of the day bestowed in argument of the bill of roges and then commytted. /

xiij° Februarij.

A bill read that wolle and yarne may bee bought and sould in Woodstocke.

A bill that prentises of London and others being free of the Citie may exercise any trade after their freedome, notwithstanding a former act.[10]

A bill to enable the Deane and Chapiter of Paule's to make a lease to Mr Smyth, according to a former bargaine betweene them, in consideracion of other landes assured to them, and of a sermon to be preached at Paule's every Sunday, or else two schollers maynteined paying the accustomed rent.

The bill that the county in actions uppon the case for wordes might be traversable, the third tyme read.[11]

The bill that matters of forme should be no cause in wryttes of error to reverse any fine.

One indicted of felony not being convict, agreed that he might continue of the Howse.

This day one Johnson of the Inner Temple, having sit in the parliament howse one houer and a halfe being none of the same, was found out there, and therefore commytted to the ward of the serieant.

Mr Recorder shewed that 21 *Ricardi 2i* because some others besides those of the Howse had ioyned in the making of the lawes, all the actes / of the parliament were revoked, and so likewise the parliament held at Coventry in the tyme of King Henry the vjth in like sorte revoked for the same cause.[12]

Shadnell of Essex commytted to the Tower for speaking in this, which example he thought fit to bee followed.

A bill from the Lordes against such as shall empaier the Queene's coigne.

The bill concerning fines of landes in auncient demeasne,[13] the second tyme read and commytted.

xiiij° Februarij.

A bill read for the assurance of certeine landes in Northampton shier from Sir John Spencer to Mr Hatton, the [second] tyme read, agreed to be engrossed.

The bill that it should be lawefull to certaine persons to sell the landes of William Isley gentleman to the payment of his debtes, the second tyme read, agreed to be engrossed.

A bill concerning reformacion of the disorders of sherives, first read.

A bill that the Queene should have the landes of Edward Dakers notwithstandinge any secret convayance, first read.[14]

f.119   *xv° Februarij.*

A bill making it felony to cary any pistoll or dagg to the intent to kill any man; the shooting at any man with any pistoll to the intent aforesaid, the wounding of any man in the high way by way of assault, or in his howse to the intent to kill him, the giving of poyson to any to the intent to kill him to be likewise felony; first read.

A bill from the Lordes making it treason to empaier the Queene's coygne, first read.[15]

The bill for illegitimation of children borne after divorce, the second tyme read.

The bill concerning prentises in London, the second tyme read.

xvj° Februarij.

A bill concerning the making of clothes, first read.

The bill for a subsidy according to the rates of the last subsidye, first read.

[xvii February.]

The bill for the towne of Woodstocke, the second tyme read, agreed to be engrossed.

The bill authorising the Deane and Chapiter of Paule's to make a lease to Mr Smyth the customer of h.[16] Barnes, the second tyme read, agreed to be engrossed.

A bill that actions in Middlesex may be tryed in Westminster in the vacacion[17] tyme in nature of assises, first read.

A bill concerning butleradge and prisadge of wine, first read.

Note that the Queene had of every one which brought in ten tonn one tonn, and of twenty tonn 2 tonn, and no more, how much soever was brought, which was called 'butleradge'; and a certaine rate of every tunn which any stranger brought in under the number of ten tunn / is called 'prisage', and by this acte the Queene   f.119v should have d. tonn of every person bringing in v tonn.

The bill for remedy of errors in fines being amended by the commytees, first read.

A bill concerning the disorders of sherives, the second tyme read.

Serieant Jefferey made a motion whither he, being before a member of this Howse and now served with writt of attendance to attend upon the Lordes, should retaine his place here and attend at such tyme as he might be spared with them; and agreed that not having voice above, he was to retayne his [place] here.

xviij° Februuarij.

A bill read for the better making cable[18] ropes within the realme and for the ordering of the hempe, first read.

---

10. Cf.28 Hen.VIII, c.5 (1536), in *SR*, III.654.

11. *Sic*; second reading according to *CJ*, I.105.

12. 1 Hen.IV, c.3 (1399), in *SR*, II.112 repealing Acts of 21 Rich.11; 39 Hen.VI, c.1-2 (1460), in *SR*, II.378-9, repealing Acts of the Coventry Parliament of 38 Henry VI.

13. MS reads 'demeasure'.

14. First reading on 15 February, according to *CJ*, I.106.

15. Second reading according to *CJ*, I.106.

16. *Sic.*

17. MS reads 'rocacion'.

18. MS reads 'gable'.

A bill for the explanation of the statute of monasteries made *anno xxxj Henrici viijⁱ* that the same should not be expounded to extend to any colledge in Cambridge or Oxford, first read.[19]

A bill that where deprivacion is given by statutes *ipso facto* that no advantadge should grow by lapse until vj monthes after notice given to the patron, first read.

A bill for the better keping of the bookes in parishes of christenings and burialls, first read.

A bill for the intering of notes of all convayances here after to be made, to the intent that all purchasors may knowe whither the lande be incombered, first reade.[20] |

f.120   *xx Februiary.*

The bill of subsidye a second tyme read and agreed to be engrossed.

The bill that the statute of xxxj [Henry VIII] concerning monasteries should not extend to any colledge in Cambridge or Oxforde, the seconde tyme read and agreed to bee engrossed.

The bill that no advantadge should grow by lapse of benefices becoming voyd *ipso facto* by force of any statute untill vj monthes after notice given to the patron, the second tyme read, agreed to be engrossed.

Being nowe againe moved whither Mr Hall's man atending uppon his master being in execution should be set at libertie by this Howse, diverse argumentes were made what should be donn therein. Defaute was layd to the man for that he did not publish it to the serieant that his master was of the parliament howse; not proved also that the serieant had otherwise any knowledge him so to be. The mischeife was likewise shewed that by this meanes the sherives of London should be chargeable with the debt, who had not offended.

Mr Recorder. That in King Henry 5 and in 7 Richard 2 a request was made to the king that the knightes and burgesses of the Howse might enioye their auncient liberties, and graunted them. In the tyme of King Henry the vjth Thomas Thorpe during a prorogation tyme, being Speaker of the Howse, was commytted to prison for tresspaces to Richard Duke of Yorke. He receaved it by Mr Carell, Mr Carell from

f.120v   Mr Mordant by | tradicion that he was sett at libertie and brought home to be Speaker. In appeall of murder, [blank] or crimi[n]all causes no priviledge allowable, but his body ought to be free for debt. Ferris, being in execution in the tyme of King Henry the viijth, set at libertie. The cooke of the Temple when[21] the Lord Adley was Speaker at libertie uppon an execution in the higher howse. They have a writt of priviledge in the same. No exception for executions. In the *viij^o* of Henry the vjth the like priviledge graunted to bishopps as others called to Parliament had. In Edward the iij^{d's} tyme Gudshot commytted to the Tower for sclandering a member of the same. Men at their perill to take heede with whom they deale, whither they bee of the parliament howse. There is a recorde to which they may resorte to knowe.[22]

Mr Alford. That though the man claymed not the priviledg, yet the master doth who is to bee attended uppon. In the Queene's Howse, if any be imprisoned they use to[23] set the Queene's servant at libertie, though they after take order for the debt. The Livetenant of the Tower useth to arest any of the Citie if any of the Tower be arested in the Cittie and will not take any excuse of ignorance of the man. So in this case. |

Mr Sampole. *Volenti non fit iniuria.* Any man's preiudice not to be respected in   f.121
regard to the whole body of this Howse, who should be touched in their libertie and
priviledge. And he well understandeth that in the tyme of King Henry the vij[th] the
use was for the serieant to send to knowe whither they were of the Howse or attended
uppon any in the Howse.[24]

Finally, after many argumentes made on the contrary side that the lawe should
leave no man without remedy, which should happen yf the prisoner be now sett at
libertie, and that[25] therefore that the priviledge should not extend to executions (one
booke case vouched where the iudges had affirmed that the setting at libertie of one in
such a case was taken erronious by the iudges), advantage of the case was taken that
the same was another president, and the libertie of the Howse was best knowne by
presidentes. And the matter being put to the question, whither he should be set at
libertie or no, the Howse was devided and the yea prevailed, and order thereuppon
taken that the serieant should goe to the Counter with his man and fetch him out.

The xxj[th] of Februarie.

A bill to make leases and grauntes to and from the Deane and Chapiter of Norwich
aveylable notwithstanding the misnaming of the corporacion, first read.

A bill for the re-arest of Chaterton and Whytney and Cooke having broken
prison, being imprisoned uppon executions, and to make their bodies liable to the
executions, first read.[26] |

A bill that it may be lawfull for the Queene's Majestie, when any forreyne prince   f.121v
dealeth with her subiectes or their goodes by way of arest or restraint of the coming in
of the same, to doe the like with the said prince's subiectes and their goodes and
merchaundise, first read.

A bill for the better order of gold-smythes and their ware, first read.

A bill that children borne in England of both parentes straungiers should pay

19. 31 Hen. VIII, c.13 (1539), in *SR*,
    III.733-9.
20. Cf. *CJ*, I.105-6 for first and second
    readings of bill for open assurance of
    lands, the second reading being on 18
    February.
21. MS reads 'with'.
22. Fleetwood, at least as reported, seems to be
    relying on dubious allusions. The
    precedents cited in the first sentence, even
    allowing for incorrect reporting and/or
    copying, seem to be unlikely in view of
    J. S. Roskell's findings (*The Commons and
    their Speakers . . .*, 1965, 39-40).
    Fleetwood was mistaken about the
    outcome of Thorpe's case, though he had
    apparently reported otherwise in 1571,
    and the structure of the sentence here
    makes it unlikely that this has arisen from

the simple omission of a negative
(Roskell, *op.cit.*, 252-4). It is probably
impossible to identify Mr Carell and Mr
Mordant with any certainty, even if we
assume them to have been members of
Parliament. The reference to cooks came
in Henry VIII's speech to Parliament in
Ferrers' case in 1543 (J. Hatsell,
*Precedents of Proceedings in the House of
Commons*, 1818 edn, I.56-7) and 8
Hen. VI, c.1 (1429), in *SR*, II.238, refers
to the clergy in Convocation.
23. 'To' repeated in MS.
24. Cf. *EP*, I.336 where the notion is
    described as a fiction.
25. *Sic*.
26. I.e. bill for prisoners in execution escaped
    out of King's Bench (*CJ*, I.107).

subsidies and customes and in all other respectes to be as straungers, first read.

A bill from the Lordes ratefieing all assurances made to the Queene since the beginning of her raigne, or to be made for vij yeares to come, and for the same tyme confirming all letters patentes made or to be made from her Majestie; with a proviso notwithstanding that if any were rated for less then the rent which it was then letten for, that then for the overplus of the rent there should be xxx yeares' purchase payed; first read.

p.   Mr Hatton's bill the third tyme read and passed.

p.   The bill for wolle yarne *etc*. Woodstocke, the third tyme read and passed.

p.   The bill concerning prentizes and other free of London, the third tyme read and passed.

p.   The bill concerning the statute of xxxj [Henry VIII] not to extend to colledges in Cambridge and Oxford, the third tyme read and passed. /

f.122 p.   The bill that fines should not be reserved for matters of forme, the third tyme read and passed.

The bill for the sale of the landes of William Isley esq., for the payment of his debtes, the second tyme read, to be engrossed.

The bill for the manumising of the children of diverse English men borne beyond the seas, first read.

xxij[th] Febriuary.

A bill limiting what prentices every maker of hattes may keepe, and orders prescribed for the due workemanshippe of the same.

The newe bill for roges and vagabondes, first read.

p.   The bill for the sale of the landes of William Isley, the third time read and passed.

Priviledge   Mr Atorney of the Duchy[27] declared unto the Howse that uppon search in the Chauncery he hath founde a dozen presidentes of writtes which have beene made for the release of the imprisonment of knightes and burgesses, or their servantes, imprisoned in the parliament tyme and to stay sutes against them; and that the most presidentes which he sawe of the servant, the master tooke an oath that he was at the tyme of arest a servant attendant uppon him; but he sawe no president for any being in execution. Whereuppon it was agreed that the Speaker should make a certificat to my Lord Keper and Mr Hall to make his affidavit, and so to prey the writt and to bring the prisoner to the barr by the writt. /

f.122v   xxiij[th] Febriuary.

This morninge I was absent a good parte of the same by reason I was in a commyttee uppon the bill of promoters, but after my coming these bills were read:

p.   The bill that no benefit of lapse should incurre upon deprivations *ipso facto* before vj monthes after notice, the third tyme read and passed.

The bill for the better makeing of cables,[28] the second tyme read and reiected.

The bill for the making of a lease to Mr Smyth, Barnes, from the Deane and Chapiter of Pole's, the third tyme read; and because the same lease was for so many yeares and therefore thought to be greatly preiudiciall to the successor and against the statute of *anno xiij°*, the bill reiected.[29]

The bill from the Lordes making it treason to empaier by any meanes the Queene's coygne for filthy lucre or gaine's sake, the third tyme read and passed.

pp.

xxiiij[th] of Februarie.

A bill that no lord of any wast ground, being wood grounde wherein free holders have heretofore had common of estovers, shall take any more wood then he hath accustomed, and that the freeholders may take their parte; and where the lord hath used to sett out the freeholders' parte, yf the lord doe it not, the sherive may see it donn; first read. /

f.123

A bill that privy tithes should be payd in Reading according to the order of payment of tythes in London sett forth 37 Henry 8, first read.[30]

A bill to make the landes in Cringelforde dimisyble by coppie of court role, first read.

The bill for the naturalizing of the children of James Haryve and others, the second tyme read, to be engrossed.

A bill to give the Queene like authority over strangers as their king exercise towardes her subiectes, twise read.[31]

A bill touching jayle of Bury, the second tyme read, to bee engrossed.[32]

A bill that no lease heretofore or hereafter to be made by any spirituall person for any more yeares then xxj from the making of the same should bee good, first read.[33]

A bill that no moore should be burnt betweene the last of March and Michelmasse, twise read and reiected.[34]

A bill from the Lordes that every person clayming any landes by any secret convayance from any the rebelles of the north should bring in the same into the Exchequer within a twellvemonth, there to be enroled and make profes of the execution and perfecting of the assurances, or else the same to be voyd, if the same were made to the intent to defraude the Queene's Majestie of the forfeiture within 2 yeares before the rebellion; first read.

A bill from the Lordes concerning the maintenance of Chepstowe bridge, first read.

A bill that iurors in Midlesex for forreygne trialls should have xvj[d] of the party for whom the verdict is given, twise read.[35] /

A bill for a *nisi prius* to be had after the tearme for triall of matters layed in Middelsex, twise read.[36]

f.123v

A bill no wyre[37] but for virginalles and clevicolls should be brought from beyonde sea, twise[38] read and reiected.

---

27. George Bromley.
28. MS reads 'Gables'.
29. 13 Eliz., c.20 (1571), in *SR*, IV.556.
30. 37 Hen.VIII, 12 (1545), in *SR*, III.998-1000.
31. One of which readings was of a newly amended bill (*CJ*, I.108).
32. The first reading had been on 18 February

(*CJ*, I.108).
33. I.e. dilapidations and Thomas White in *CJ*, I.108, 111-12.
34. Only one reading according to *CJ*, I.108.
35. First reading according to *CJ*, I.108.
36. Second reading (*CJ*, I.108).
37. MS reads 'wyne'.
38. Second reading (*CJ*, I.108).

xxv° Februarij.

A bill that fines in Chester should not be reversed for matters in forme, first read.

The bill for payment of tithes in Reading, the third[39] time read, to be engrossed.

p.   The bill for naturalizing of James Harvy and others, the third tyme read and passed.

The bill of the rebells from the Lordes, ij[d] tyme read and commytted.

The bill for mayntenance of Rochester bridge from the Lords, first read.

The bill for confirmacion of letters patentes, the second tyme read.

The new bill for roges, the second tyme read.

xxvij° Februarij.

p.   The bill of subsidy, the third tyme read and passed.

Priviledg   This day it was agreed that since a writt for delivery of Mr Hall's men was denyed, he should be fetcht only by the mace.[40]

p.[41]   The bill of roges the second tyme read, agreed to be engrossed.

xxviij° Februarij.

A bill for naturalizing of Juna Sibilla now wife to the Lord Gray, daughter to Mr Morrizan, the second and third tyme read and passed.[42] |

f.124   A bill that the sessions for Middelsex and London at the tymes of the delivery of the iayle may be kept at Justice Hall in the Old Bayly, first read.

A bill from the Lords for the mayntenance of Rochester bridge, the second tyme read.

A bill from the Lordes for the mayntenance of Chepstowe bridge, the second tyme read.

A bill that no partriches should be taken in the night and that no man should shoote at any phesant, first read.

A bill concerning hatters, the second tyme read and commytted.

The bill against the abuses of sherives, first read.[43]

The bill for more indiffirency of trialls, first read.

Priviledg   This day Mr Hall's man was brought out of the Counter out of execution and delivered, and Smalley delivered to the custody of the serieant.

xxix° Februarij.

A bill that the inhabiters within vj myles of Oxford might bee charged for vj dayes in the yeare to helpe to mend the high wayes, first read.

A bill for naturalizing of [blank] and others, first read.[44]

pp.   A bill from the Lordes for the amendement of Chepstow bridge, the third tyme read and passed.

pp.   A bill from the Lordes for the mending of Rochester bridge, the third tyme read and passed.

p.   The bill that tythes may be payd in Reading according to the custome of London, the third tyme read and passed.

A bill concerning goldsmythes, the second tyme read and passed.[45]

Mr Bendbridge sheweth that one Williams, having had diverse unseemly speeches concerning the state, being rebuked by him, had striken him and drawen his dagger uppon him; uppon which it was agreed that he should be sent for by the mace, which was performed accordingly and he commytted to the custodye of the serieant. /

A bill for keeping of alayes in making of moneys and keeping the weight according to the standerd, first read.

The bill for butlerage and prisadge, first read.[46]

A bill from the Lordes concerning apparell, first read.

Mr Pister with greate zeale declared to the Howse the greate preiudice grewe to the realme by the unlearnednesse of the ministerie, abuse of excommunication, want of disciplin, dispensations and tollerations for not resiancye and such like: prayeth that an humble petition may be made to the Queene's Majestie for reformacion, and exhibited a supplicacion in writing for that purpose; which matter was well proseqwuted by Mr Snage, Mr Lewknor, and others, and in the end agreed that certaine commyttees might meete and consider of the same, and then those of the Privy Counsell of the Howse to conferre with the counsell of the Lordes' howse and so to deale farther with the Queene.

Primo Martij.

A bill from the Lordes for the assurance of the maner of Newhall to the Earle of Sussex, twise read.

A bill from the Lordes for the assurance of landes to Sir John Riviers, first read.

A bill from the Lordes there may be two iustices of assise in Wales in every county, first read.

A bill from the Lordes that where any dye holding landes of the Queene *in capite* in the Duchy or counties palatine, the transcriptes of the office should certifie into the Courte of Wardes; first read. /

Three billes concerning clothes and cloath making, requiring the repeale of certaine braunches of the statute made in the tyme of King Philipp and Queene Mary, and in the statute of King Edward the vj[th], first read.[47]

A bill to take away clergie in cases of rape, first read.

A bill against certaine abuses of promoters, first read.

The bill for errecting of stockes for the setting men to worke, and howses of correction, the iij[d] tyme read and passed.

f.124v

f.125

---

39. Second reading (*CJ*, I.108).
40. MS reads 'man'.
41. *Sic*; it had been given a second reading the day before, as Cromwell says, though the *Commons Journal* records no engrossment on that day.
42. First reading on 25 February (*CJ*, I.108).
43. I.e. a new bill (*CJ*, I.109).
44. I.e. a new bill, and passed according to

CJ, I.109.
45. I.e. a new bill (*CJ*, I.109).
46. I.e. a new bill (*CJ*, I.109).
47. See *CJ*, I.109:only one of these became law this session, i.e. 18 Eliz., c.16, in *SR*, IV.626-7, and it cites 4 & 5 Ph. & Mary, c.5 (1557-8) in *SR*, IV.323-6. The Edwardian statute appears to be 5 & 6 Ed.VI, c.6 (1551-2), in *SR*, IV.136-41.

ij° Martij.

A bill from the Lordes for the payment of tithes in Hallifax, first read.

A bill for the assurance of certaine landes to Sir John Rivers, the second tyme read.

A bill to make good fines with proclamations in Chester, notwithstanding certaine imperfections in the proclamations, and to make good deedes inroled being knowledged before the deputy of the clerke of the peace, first read.[48]

A bill to the like effect concerning fines with proclamations in Wales, first read.

A bill that recoveries, fines or other devises by tenant for terme of life should not be preiudiciall to them in remaynder, first read.

A bill that in all leases hereafter to be made by any colledge, whom[49] the rent hath been v^{li} or upwardes, the moyetye of the rent shalbe reserved in corne to be delivered at viij^s the quarter to the benefit of the howse, first read.[50] /

f.125v   A bill that nothing should be taken in any colledge for fellowshippes or schollershippes, first read.

A bill concerning ale howses and prices of ale and beere, first read.

Three bills concerning clothes in diverse counties, the second tyme read, to be engrossed.[51]

A bill for butlerage and prisadge, the ij^d tyme read.

3° Martij.

A bill for the [as]size of woode and coale within 3 myles of London, first read.

A bill for the maner of payment of tythes in Hallifax, the second tyme read.

A bill concerning tanners and cordweyners, first read.

A bill that there may be *nisi priuses* tried in Middelsex iij or iiij dayes after the terme, being amended, first read.[52]

A bill that children borne of both parentes straungiers should as strangers[53]; the second tyme read and reiected.[54]

A bill concerning fines in Chester, the ij^d tyme read.[55]

A bill concerning the length and bredth of clothes, the iij^d tyme read and reiected.

In the afternoone the same day.

pp.   A bill for the assurance of the manor of Newhall to the Earle of Sussex, the third tyme red and passed.

pp.   The bill for the payment of tythes in Hallifax, the third tyme read and passed.

pp.   The bill for the assurance of certeyne lands to Sir John Rivers, the third tyme read and passed.

pp.   The bill for the erecting of an hospitall in Lester and assurance of certeyne lands to the same, thrise read and passed. /

f.126   The bill concerning engrossing of barley, first read.[56]

The bill for the having of two iustices in Wales, the ij^d tyme read.

The bill for the assise of woode and colle within 3 myles of London, the second tyme read.

The bill concerning fines in Wales, the seconde tyme read.

The bill concerning tanners and cordweyners, the ij^d tyme read.

v° Martij.

A bill for the paving of the cittie of Chichester, first and second [time] read.

A bill for the naturalizing of Mr Whitnoll and others, second and third tyme   p.
read and passed.

A bill that a fine levyed by the Lady Waynman being tenaunt in dower, the
remaynder to Mr Francis Weynman, should be no forfeyture of her estate, first read.

A bill that the inhabitantes within v myles of Oxforde should helpe for vj dayes
for the mending of the high wayes within one myle of Oxforde, ij^d read.

A bill that no tythes should be payd for woodes being above xxx yeares growth
nor for toppes of trees, where tyth for the same hath not beene heretofore payed, first
read.

A bill concerning rowing and making of clothes in Glostersheere, Wilsheere and
Somersetsheere, the second[57] tyme read and passed.

A bill for the having of two iustices of assise in Wales, the second tyme read.[58]

A bill for ieofeyles, first and second tyme read.[59]

A bill for the jayle called Justice Hall in the Old Bayly to serve Middelsex, the
second tyme read.

A bill against the disorders of ale howses and of the prices of ale and [beer], the
second tyme read.

A bill against the abuse of promoter[s], the second tyme read, to be engrossed. /

A bill concerning goldsmythes, the second tyme read, to be engrossed.   f.126v

A bill concerning the making of money, the seconde tyme read and respited.

In the afternoone the same day.

A bill against the wearing of certaine weapons, the second tyme read.

A bill of ieofeyles the second tyme read, to be engrossed.[60]

A bill for more indifferent triall of iuries, the second tyme read, to be engrossed.

A bill against collaterall warranties and fines by tenaunt for tearme of life to the
preiudice of them in remaynder or revercyon, the second tyme read and commytted.

vi° Martij.

A bill that one Giles Lambert, in respect that he should discover a secret in making

---

48. Second reading; first reading on 25
    February (*CJ*, I.108-9).
49. *Sic*; 'where'?
50. Second reading (*CJ*, I.110).
51. Cf. *CJ*, I.110.
52. Second reading according to *CJ*, I.108,
    110.
53. *Sic*.
54. *CJ*, I.110 has 'committed' rather than
    'rejected'.
55. Third reading and passed (*CJ*, I.110).
56. Second reading (*CJ*, I.110).
57. *Sic*.
58. This reading had been given on 3 March:
    the bill was passed on 7 March (*CJ*,
    I.111.).
59. Cf. *CJ*, I.110.
60. Cf. *CJ*, I.111.

of oyle for clothing, should have a penny of every broad cloath transported and a halfepenny of every carzie, first[61] read and reiected.

A bill of petition by the Merchant Venterers against the merchauntes of London of remedy of certaine exactions raysed by them contrary to the forme of the statute of xij *Henrici vij*,[62] first read.

A bill against transporting of lether, first read.

p.   A bill for orders to be observed by tanners and cordweyners, the third tyme read and passed.

A bill against the inclosing salt marshes, first read.[63]

p.   A bill against the abuses of promoters, the third tyme read and passed.

p.   A bill of ieofeyles, the third tyme read and passed.

p.   A bill concerning goldsmythes, the iij^d tyme read and passed. |

f.127   *vij° Martij.*

A bill for the paving of Chichester, the iij^d tyme read and passed.

A bill that no lease in revertion by any ecclesiasticall person should be good except the old lease wer surrendered, cancelled or ended within 3 yeares, and none good for longer tyme then xxj yeares; first read.[64]

A bill that uppon all leases made by any colledge, being heretofore letten for v^{li}, that a third parte of the rent should be reserved in corne at a lowe rate; twise read, to be engrossed.

A bill that no master or president of any colledge should take any thing for any fellowshippe or schollershippe, twise read, to be engrossed.[65]

A bill that collaterall warrantyes should be no barre without an assets, first read.[66]

A bill for confirmacion of letters patents, the third tyme read and passed.

pp.   A bill for the restoring in blood of the Lord Sturton, thrise read and passed with two provisoes added.[67]

pp.   A bill for the assurance of the rebells' landes to the Queene's Majestie, the third tyme read and passed.

A bill taking away the clergie in cases of burglerie and rape, and for the discharge of clearkes convicte without oath; the third tyme read.

In the afternoone.

p.   A bill for the mending of the high wayes about Oxforde, the third tyme read and passed.

p.   A bill that Justice Hall in the Old Bayly might be the place of generall sessions for Middelsex, the third tyme read and passed. |

f.127v   This day was declared by the commyttees put in trust to take order concerning the debt for the which Smalley, Mr Hall's man, was in execution and delivered by the Howse, that they had heard the cause, and had agreed that Mr Hall should pay one hundred poundes to Mr Mollerye,[68] Mr Mallery to release to the sherives of London all advantadge he could have against them, and likewise to release Mr Hall of all actions *etc.*; which order was agreed to be confirmed by the Howse. Notwithstanding, because it appeared manifestly unto the Howse that there was greate cawtell used by Smalley, Mr[69] Hall's man, and abuse towardes the Howse (for that hee sought his owne imprisonment and then required the benefit of the priviledg), and likewise that another servant of Mr Hall's, being his scholemaster called Mathew Kirtelton, was privy to the same practise and did put on a citizen's gowne and in the name of the Malleryes required the arest of his fellow contrarie to the will of the Malleries, they were both adiudged to bee commytted to the Tower. Mr Hall himselfe was also vehemently presumed to be privy therto, and directly proved to have abused himselfe in calling some of the commyttees his enemyes and saying that others were of counsell against him and that hee had no indiffirencie. |

Note that the same day Mr Sampole declared that he had seene the record   f.128 concerning the delivery of Mr Thorpe in execution, and that at the same tyme all the iudges being[70] required to declare their opinions concerning his delivery, they answered that being iudges [they] could deliver none by lawe being in execution, but that of the priviledges of the parliament that they could not iudge.

Mr Alford the same day sayed that Mr Mallerie should say that those which gave iudgement for the setting of Mr Hall's man at libertie were but fethers.

viij° Martij.

A bill for a subsydye of the clergie at vj[s] the pound, first read.

A bill that the maior of Norwich might demise the landes in Cringellforde by   p. copie, and that the same might be alowed as auncyent copiehold, the third[71] tyme read and passed.

A bill that leases made by spirituall persons should not be good for xxj yeares except the old lease were surrendered, cancelled or ended within three yeares following; the second tyme read.

A bill against transportation of lether beyonde the seas, the second tyme read, to be engrossed.

A bill for corne to bee reserved to the benefit of the colledges uppon all leases   p. hereafter to be made of any landes letten heretofore for v[li] by the yeare; the third tyme read and passed. |

A bill for mending of high wayes, first read.   f.128v

A bill for the better order of such as have licence of the Queene's Majestie to transport any thing beyonde the seas, first read.

A bill for reformacion of alehowses, the third tyme read and reiected.

A bill that no master or governor of any colledge, hall, hospitall, deanry *etc.*   p. should take any thing of any person for any fellowshipe or scholershippe, prebende, besman *etc.*, the third tyme read and passed.

A bill from the Lordes that the iustice in ayre might have authoritie to examine

61. Cf. *CJ*, I.111.
62. 12 Hen.VII, c.6 (1496-7), in *SR*, II.638-9.
63. Cf. *CJ*, I.111.
64. I.e. the bill for the heirs of Thomas White (*CJ*, I.111).
65. Not included in *CJ*, and Cromwell missed the new bill for butlerage and prisage of wines (*CJ*, I.111).
66. Cf. *CJ*, I.111.
67. Incorrect: as Cromwell himself reports, the bill was read on 10 March. It came from the Lords on this day (*CJ*, I.111).
68. *Sic*.
69. MS reads 'in'.
70. 'Being' repeated in MS.
71. *Sic*; cf. 9 March.

all matters concerninge the forest and take order for the correction of them here above, the second tyme read.[72]

ix° Martij.

pp. A bill for the authorising the Lord Norris to perfect abilitie for the having of any lands by descent from any his ancestors, and to enlarg the word of restitution of his father being by former act; thrise read and passed.

A bill wherby the maior of Norwich is authorised to pass coppies of all theise landes in Cringelford and to make the same auncient coppihold, the third tyme read and passed.

pp. A bill for a subsydie of the clergie, the second and third tyme read and passed.

Mr Crooke with great earnestnes moved for a petition to be made to the Queene's Majestie to incline herselfe to mariage. /

f.129 A bill concerning the Lady Weynman for a comprimise to be ratefied by their assentes for a title of lande between [her] and Mr Francis Weynman her sonn, twise read, to be engrossed.

[Afternoon]

A bill for a sale of certeyne landes by the Lord Bindon, twise read.

A bill for the enroling of defeyances of statutes, first read.

p. A bill against taking of partriches by night and shooting at phesantes, the third tyme read and passed.

A bill for mending of high wayes, the second tyme read, to be engrossed.

x° Martij.

p. A bill that lessors in the borders of Scotland should take recognizances of their lessees to answere all matters of felonyes and treasons don by them *etc.*, the third tyme read and passed.

p. A bill against transporting of lether, tallow, or raw hides beyond the seas, the third tyme read and passed.

p. A bill restraining spirituall persons to make any new leases to any person except the old leases be expired, surrendered, cancelled or ended within 3 yeares after the taking of the new; the third tyme read and passed.[73]

A bill for reformacion of apparell, the second tyme red.

A bill for an arbitriment to be made betwene the Lady Weynman and Mr

f.129v Francis Weynman her sonn, for certeyne landes forfeited by her in leving of / a fine, shee having then estate but for terme of life; the third tyme read and passed.

[Afternoon]

A bill for butleradge and prisadge, the third[74] tyme read and reiected.

A bill for the restitution in blood of the Lord Sturton, twise read.

xij° Martij.

p. A bill that it might be lawefull to Lord Vicount Binden to sell certeyne landes towards the payment of his debts and his sonne's, and to assure certaine lands for the ioynture of his sonne's wife; the third tyme read and passed.

p. A bill for the mending of high wayes, the third tyme read and passed.

Mr Hatton declared to the Howse the greate good acceptation of the Queene's Majestie of the temperat usage of the Howse, and shewed that her Majestie had sent Mr Wentworth againe to the Howse, of whom, as shee[75] was absolutly perswaded that his speech proceeded of aboundance of zeale towardes her, so had shee not onely forgiven but also forgotten the inconsideratnes of the same, and did accept him to be in as good grace and favour as ever she did before. And so setting forth the greate blessings we had receaved under her, thought it necessary we should be thankefull for the same. Whereuppon it was agreed that the Speaker in all our names should render her Majestie thankes for the same; and upon a motion likewise prosequuted by Mr Crooke for her Majestie's mariadge, it was likewise agreed that humble suite should likewise be made to her by the Speaker to encline herselfe to a mariadge, / whereby shee f.130
having children, we might stande in some surety to what parte to leane.

Shortly after, Mr Wentworth came to the Howse.

In the afternoone.

A newe bill for reformation of excesse in apparell, first read.

A bill that a transcript might be sent into Court of Wardes[76] of all those which died seazed held by the knighte's service or in chiefe of the Queene in Durham and the county palatine;[77] the second tyme read.

A bill that the Queene might limit by commyssion at what wharfe in every county men might load and unloade, the second tyme read.

A bill from the Lordes to restore Anthony Meynye in blood, twise read.[78]

A bill from the Lordes concerning the make of goldsmythes' worke, first read.

xij° Martij.

A bill for restoring in bloode of Mr Anthony Meynye, the third tyme read and passed pp.
with a proviso added.[79]

A bill for apparell newly made, thrise read and passed.[80]

A bill for wharfes to be apointed in every porte, the second tyme read.[81]

A bill concerning goldsmythes, the second tyme read.

The Lord Sturton's bill the third tyme read and passed with 2 provisos added. pp.

[Afternoon]

A bill for personadges impropriat being in spiritu[a]ll persons' handes to [be] dismised to the vicars, twise read.

A bill that the defendantes uppon English billes being sclanderous should have doble costes and damages against the plaintife, first read.

A bill from the Lordes for certificates to be made of such as die in Durham and pp.
the countye palatine[82] holding landes by knighte's service or in chiefe of the

72. Cf. *CJ*, I.112 for two readings on this day.
73. Cf. *CJ*, I.113.
74. Second reading (*CJ*, I.113).
75. MS reads 'he shee'.
76. MS reads 'wordes'.
77. MS reads 'palantine'.
78. Cf. *CJ*, I.114.
79. Cf. *CJ*, I.114.
80. Cf. *CJ*, I.114–15.
81. *Sic*; third reading.
82. MS reads 'palantine'.

f.130v   Queene's Majestie, / the third tyme read and passed.

A bill for the towne of Gateshide to be annexed to Berwike, the second tyme read.[83]

This day motion was made by the Lordes for a conferenc concerning the Lord Sturton's bill for his restitution in bloode, being sent to our Howse from them. And the matter grewe in debate in the Howse whyther it were conven[i]ent to be yeilded unto or no; and in fine agreed that we being once possessed of a bill cannot by order of the [higher] howse be called to conference before the bill returned, for that were to yeild accompt of the meaning of our doyings, which be to ourselves unknowne untill they be past; besides the sayd Lordes cannot by ordinary meanes take notice of our doyings.

xiiijo[84] *Martij.*

This day was declared to our Howse by Sir Walter Mildmeye from the Lordes that they thought unkindnesse in us that, being so often desired to have conference concerning the Lord Sturton's bill, we had refused the same; besydes that they thought wee had dealt inconsideratly to add, diminish, or alter any thinge in the same bill or to ioyne thereto any proviso, considering the bill was subscribed with the Queene's hande, whereof they thought we had no president. Wherein the resolution of the Howse was required what was fitt to be answered, and the matter being longe debated diverse reasons were shewed why our doyings therein should be warranted: first, for that we had authority to dash any such bill, much more to alter;

f.131   also that diverse particular subiectes had / interest in land where one is ateynted of felony, whom wee did represent, and sitting as iudges ought not to see any man receave preiudice; that the Queene's subscription of the bill is but a commendacion thereof, as a matter which her Majestie is content should be treated of. Diverse presidentes also were recited in like cases, namely that to a bill prefered and subscribed by King Henry the viij[th] that it might be lawefull for him by proclamacion to make a law, that there was a proviso added by the Howse which tooke away the whole body of the act; a proviso likewise added for Mr St John and others in a bill signed with the hand of King Henry the viij[th] for the [blank] [blank]; *ijo* Mary in a bill subscribed with the Queene's hande there was a proviso added, and thrise read and put to the question whyther it should be added, and by the most voices the proviso disallowed of, without any question made whyther it might be added; *vo* of the Queene's Majestie in Mr Isleye's restitution a proviso added;[85] *xiijo* of the Queene in the bill signed with the Queene's hande for the Lady Barkleye's ioynture, a proviso was likewise added;[86] in this parliament to a bill specially commended to the Howse for Mr Isley diverse provisoes and alteracions made, and it was thought in our Howse that the Queene's subscription of the bill was no more but a recommendation. Lastly, that we had no president to the contrary. Finally it was agreed that Sir Walter Mildmey in the name of the whole Howse should signifie to the

f.131v   Lordes that we were very sorry they should conceave any / unkindness in our doyings, who meant all reverence unto them in all things convenient, otherwise then we thought it necessary to preserve the liberties of our House in not thinking it reasonable to be called to an accompt of our doyngs.

The bill of the Queene's generall pardon, once read and passed.   pp.

The bill for the better order of goldsmythes, the third tyme read and passed.   pp.

In the afternoone.

A bill for the apointing of wharfes by commyssion, the third tyme read and reiected.

Mr Treasurer moved according to old order that wee might end in love and amytye and for thankes to be rendered to our Speaker, which was don accordingly. And then a motion made to have something given to the poore, and thereuppon there was a gathering and the disposition thereof assigned to Mr Moore and Mr Harry Knowles the elder.

In this afternoone her Majestie resorted to the Howse, and being set in her robes under the cloath of estat and all the lordes likewise set in their robes, our Speaker came in having the bill of subsidy in his hande; and in his oration first he shewed the greate preiudice that grewe by diverse kindes of government, namely of *anarchia*, *democratia*, *aristocratia* and *monarchia*, shewed the diversity each of them and gave the laste the commendacion. He[87] shewed what a punishment / yt was to a nation to   f.132 have a tiranicall king and thereby what a blessing to have a verteouse, mild and mercyfull princesse, whereof we now had present tast of the benefit of the one and understood of the misery[88] of our neybours in France and Flanders for the other. He shewed the greate blessing we had receaved under her Majestie, namely the restoring of relligion, the delivery from forraigne tiranicall iurisdiction, our quiet and peace, the disburdening the realme of the greate mote of interest, the equall administration of iustice, the reliefe of Gode's afflicted Church thorough Christendome, the furniture with armor, munition and shippes, the fining of the coygne, with others. He shewed also that great travell had beene taken in making of lawes, which rested uppon her confirmation. He shewed farther that he had receaved in commaundement by our Howse to render thankes to her Highness, most humble thankes, for that it has pleased her to send so comfortable an answer to a petition made by us this parliament for reforming some abuses in matters of religion, which we desyred to [be] performed as soone as conveniently might be; that we also rendered to her Majestie like thankes for the thankefull acceptation of our services; and lastly for restoring to our Howse a member of the same comytted by us to the / Tower for irreverent speaches used of her Majestie, who slipped into the same   f.132v by infirmity not by malice, and uppon his knees had desired the Howse that his thankes might be rendered. He shewed that he had also a petition to make to her Majestie to encline herselfe to mariage, declaring the greate commodyties that grew by mariage, the commendation given thereto aswell by the word of God as also by diverse philosophers; by common experience shewed how willing every noble man and gentleman was to continue their line; desired her Majestie to consider in what case we should be left if her Majestie should die without yssue; to remember that she

83. I.e. 'Newcastle'; and first reading, not second (*CJ*, I.115).

84. MS reads 'xiij°'.

85. Private Act noted in *SR*, IV.402.

86. Private Act noted in *SR*, IV.526.

87. MS reads 'the'.

88. MS reads 'mistery'.

was mortall; how glad we would be to continue subiectes in that lineall dissent under which we had longe continued; desired her Majestie to consider that she was the last which could conveye lineally, and therefore besought her Majestie as shortly as conveniently might be to encline her selfe to mariadg. Lastely he presented the subsidy, desiring her Majestie in the acceptance thereof not to consider the value of the thing offered, but the gratfull mindes of the offerers, which was not so soone moved as willingly with full consent yeilded by all and every member of the Howse.

This oration ended, the parliament was adiourned to the next day at 3 of the clocke.

The xv^th of March the Queene returned to the Howse. |

f.133   The Lord Keeper, having receaved instructions from her Majestie, first deviding Mr Speaker's oration into v partes. The first parte he shewed to contayne[89] a discourse of the originall beginning of kingdomes, the diversities of kindes of goverment and the effectes of every of them. The second he shewed to contayne[90] diverse benefittes which her subiectes had enioyed under her goverment. The third a petition to her Majestie to incline her selfe to mariage. The fourth a declaration of the travell bestowed in making of lawes. The vth an offer of a subsidye.

To the first hee shewed that her Majestie's pleasure was he should say that the same needed no other answer then commendacion to the Speaker for his good declaration and collection made thereof. To the second that her Majestie most hartely wished that all those royall vertues recyted by the Speaker were so perfect in her as might best serve to the advauncement of Gode's glory, the profitt of the common wealth, and increase of the love of her most loving subiectes; and that she will not cease to employ her selfe, and pray God to graunt to her continuance and increase of the same. That her Majestie did most acceptably take those reverent conceptions of the Speaker and other her Majestie's subiectes; that shee thought all that she had don or could doe well employed uppon so loving subiectes; and that

f.133v   if / nature and art would give him eloquence, yet were he unable to declare what her Majestie had both sayd and conceaved of them. She wished her benefittes to be treble, which they had well deserved, since this theire doing was the greatest satisfacion which could be given to the best prince.

To the third parte, he sayd that her Majestie in discourse of the petition had noted three thinges which ought most specially to be noted: the harty good will of her subiectes; secondly, their good opinions conceaved after experience of her xvij yeares' raigne; the third that they were not content with the good likinge of her but did desire the continuance of goverment of her progeny and issue of her body. This shee conceaved to be a marvelous liking. She noted very well the perills whereto they accompted themselves subiect after her death, whereof she was not unmyndfull. But

f.134   in answer to the petition she had willed him to declare that in respect of her selfe / she neyther had disposition nor liking to yeld thereunto; notwithstanding, in respect of so loving subjectes, so as thinges necessary to be considered in her person might frame to her expectation and all things concurre incidente to the same, she was enclined to give eare and to yeld to the petition.

To the fourth parte, he shewed that her pleasure was he should declare that her Majestie had considered the greate paynes taken in the making of those lawes, theire descreete proceeding and modest dealing in this session of Parliament, which she did most thankefully accept; and though one member thereof had overslipped himselfe, yet uppon his humble submission declared, shee cannot but hope he wilbe a profitable member of his common weale. Her assent to the lawes offered should uppon the reading thereof be declared. That her Majestie farther requireth that this labour and charge bestowed in the makeing of theise lawes be not lost for want of execution, for that then they should be as causes without effect, as torches unlight caried in the darke, much like to a gardiner that shall provide tooles necessary for gardining and then lay them upp in a bagg and not occupie the same. That in this behalfe her Majestie had donn all that hath beene in her from tyme to tyme by admonishment, by / commyssions, by proclamacions. The defaute therefore in those whome she had put in trust, wherein if they should still continue remisse, shee should most unwillingly be driven to take another course and commytt them to private persons. f.134v

To the last parte, he shewed that her Majestie in most thankefull parte did accept the offer of the subsidy, wherein she respected three things: the persons of the givers, the maner of the giving, and the thinge given. That in respect of the persons and maner of the giving, she esteemed it more then tenn subsidies, since she understood of the universalitye of the consent, where no man sayd no. A matter which other princes heretofore earnestly requiring had with greate difficulty obtayned, to bee given to her frankly, freely, voluntarily, without perswasion, she could not but most thankefully accept. That she could say not more, but that *bis dat qui cito dat*. For the thing given she yeildes most harty thankes. There remayned no more. Smale exhortation needed to such persons to see this subsydie duely answered. It were but to offer the spurre to a willing horse in running in the middest of his course. Yet hee thought good to require them to looke well and have regard that a subsydy so freely given were not to much impayred in the maner of assesment, / which had heretofore beene donn, and – but as he was entering to the matter, the Queene interrupted him, whereuppon he sayd he would proceede no farther, since her Majestie had declared unto him that in that point she neyther would have them exhorted nor admonished; and so he ended. f.135

This oration thus ended, the billes were read, of the which to some the Queene gave her royall assent, and of others was advised. Which being donn the parliament was proroged untill the vth of November next.

Hereuppon the greatest company went forth, and after her Majestie made an oration, but I could not here the same, scant one word of xx^ty, no one perfect sentence.

89. MS reads 'certayne'.   90. MS reads 'certayne'.

2. Notes of occurrences in Parliament

Text from Oxford: Bodley (10220), Tanner 393, copy in same hand as 1572 Anonymous Journal in this volume.

Tanner 393, f.67 and v

Session 2   Some notes of thinges passed and spoken in the parliament held xviij of the reigne of Queen Elizabeth from the viij of February unto the xv of Martch 1575.

It was greatly douted wether a leasse mad for terme of yeares out of the Exchequer were good, for that it is not the prince's seale. But out of the Dutchie otherwise, which hath authoritie given by an old act.[1]

Wordes of amendmentes of a bill must be twise read, and so engrossed, and then to the question; and this order is to be folowed wher the bill first passed.[2]

In the statute for setting idle persons of work, a proviso was sent into the House to make him in the degre of felonie that willingly and wittingly marieth two wifes.

One Arthur Hall, burgesse for Grauntom in Lincolnshire, having his servaunt in the beginning of this session of Parliament arrested in London upon an execution for det, demaunded the priviledg for him, and with mutch ado (the House being first devided therupon) it was graunted. The graunt of this priviledg bread often disputations upon sondry occasions, and an end therof was not until iiij daies of the end of the parliament. /

f.67v   An alderman within his warde is but *conservator pacis*.

The imperfection of the iudgment given in Halle's servaunte's case was bewraied when the same begane to be put in execution. For the Speaker directeth a warraunt to the Lord Keaper in the nature of a petition from the commons house for graunting a writ to discharg Hall's man of execution. The Lord Keaper directeth his lettres, one to the vj clerkes of the Chauncery, the other to the cursitors and secondaries of the same, that thei shold seartch ther presidents and conferre together for the forme of a writ to be graunted in this case. Thei retorne aunswer that upon seartch of their presidentes, thei can find no sutch forme of writ. The Lord Keaper sending for the Speaker delivereth unto him the lettres he wrote to the officers of the Chauncery and ther aunswere, which being read in the commons house, the question grewe how the iudgment shold be executed.

1. The reference is probably to the letters patent presented in Parliament on 19 November 1414, which among other things authorised the use of the Duchy seal for Duchy affairs (R. Somerville, *Duchy of Lancaster*, I, 1953, 177-8).

2. Cf. *HC*, 372; H. Scobell, *Memorials of the Method and Manner of Proceedings in Parliament in Passing Bills* (1670), 52; W. Hakewell, *Modus Tenendi Parliamentum* (1671), 148-9.

THE FOURTH PARLIAMENT
THIRD SESSION
16 JANUARY⁄18 MARCH 1581

Documents

The need to take precautions against the new dangers of Roman Catholicism provided the main work for this session, and when Sir Walter Mildmay explained the urgent need for more taxation he stressed the role of the Jesuits, 'a rable of vagrant fryers', whose subversive activities had to be resisted [Doc.1]. Since the realm was being corrupted with false doctrine and attempts were being made to foster rebellion, new laws were needed to see that men 'yeild their open obedience at the least to her Majestie in cawses of religion'.[1] This is a clear statement of the level of conformity required at law from Catholics, but Mildmay also expressed some regret that the 'mild and clement' settlement had failed to win them over, and had apparently encouraged their arrogant and contemptuous approach to the English Church.[2]

On 4 February, a week or so after Mildmay's speech, Thomas Norton pointed out that Arthur Hall had slandered Parliament in a further pamphlet publication about the quarrel with Mallory which had occasioned the dispute over privilege in 1576. The Privy Council had already taken action over the pamphlet, and Mildmay told the House that the work was 'dangerous'.[3] Against this background the Commons called Hall to account, and coming before them on 6 and 14 February, he answered the charges so unsatisfactorily that members voted not only to fine him, but to dismiss him from the House and secure a new election at Grantham. A copy of these charges exists among the State Papers, and it explains the severity of Hall's sentence [Doc.2]. The eleventh count in particular reveals the Commons' sensitivity about its own standing; but Hall's persistent offensive conduct over a number of years and his refusal to let matters rest was bound to invite retaliation. He had flouted the Privy Council's instructions by re-issuing his pamphlet after offering 'some forme of submission', and publishing details of parliamentary proceedings had long been a serious offence by any standards.

But Arthur Hall's case was not the only reminder of the previous session. On 3 March motions were put before the House reminiscent of the Commons' petition of 1576 about religious matters, and four Privy Councillors (mostly sympathetic) were commissioned to approach the bishops in order to exert pressure on Elizabeth. The Queen's answer followed by now well-established lines, but the usual assertion of her own supremacy in these matters was accompanied by an expression of regret that the bishops had failed to act as she had wanted in 1576. She would now ensure that this was remedied. The articles for ecclesiastical causes were, as the endorsement

1. BL Sloane 326, f.24v.   3. *EP.*, I.407.
2. *Ibid.*, f.24.

indicates, offered to the Commons by some of its members, and it may be that they are evidence of a prepared Puritan campaign to secure what had been started five years before [Doc.3]. The Queen promised action, and Mildmay successfully urged the House to rest content with this, and with an instruction to the Speaker to remind her of the matter at the end of the session. When that time came, Popham thanked Elizabeth for her promise and urged her to fulfil it 'without delayes, which the necessitye of the thinges did require' [Doc.4]. In addition to this nagging reiteration of the House's request, Mildmay himself was unwilling to allow the Queen to forget the issue. He made sure that the articles were brought to her notice after Parliament had dispersed, and in due course they were examined by Sandys and several bishops. Burghley's copy of the articles is printed here, together with the bishops' answers.[4]

Cromwell's diary covers the whole session from 16 January to 18 March. It is a concise account of nine weeks' work, again illustrating very well the range of topics falling under the Commons' scrutiny in addition to the important bills concerning Catholics and seditious activity: much time was clearly spent on the adjustment of the statutory regulation of the cloth trade in the localities. Cromwell's record reflects the attitude of the seasoned man of affairs he had by now become. In common with other members he was concerned about the two most important bills of the session, yet he reveals an overriding sense of proportion in the attention he gave to other matters, taking time to note in some detail the substance of many bills, but especially those dealing with slander of the nobility and officers of state, armour in the City of London, and the activities of attorneys.[5] In some cases this may have owed much to the fact that his participation in committees was by now so extensive as to give him a close working knowledge of Parliament's legislative activities.[6] But while this kept him close to some affairs, it naturally cut him off from others, and on 22 February he noted that he had missed the reading of two bills for paving of certain streets 'by reason I was in a commytee'.[7]

Cromwell's interest in procedural points was maintained in this session. Although he says, somewhat surprisingly, that the debate of 19 January on by-elections was inconclusive, he did record the eventual outcome two months later. In January, Thomas Norton had argued that members newly elected in place of sick men should not be admitted, for although sick members might be replaced, 'that ought not to be done upon a suggestion in the Chancery'. At this stage the House did not take Norton's point and refused to exclude the members elected on the Chancery's initiative; but on 18 March this decision was reversed.[8] By this time it had already taken the first step to the position where it could expel members and see to the election of replacements in its own right. On 14 February Arthur Hall's case had reached its climax. His unbending demeanour resulted in his being 'dismembred the [House] and a warrant to be made to the towne of Grantham for election of a new burgesse'.[9]

There are signs in 1581 of some tension between the Lords and Commons over the scope of their respective powers. Norton successfully convinced the Commons of the need to instruct committees conferring with the Lords to deal only with what the Commons had agreed to, and to emphasize the fact that they had no power to negotiate beyond that point.[10] In this way the House guarded sensibly against being committed to anything not discussed in full assembly; and it also took exception to being asked to agree to matters which the Lords had altered so as to run contrary to the already expressed view of the House. The Lords' sedition bill was the obvious case in question, the Commons refusing to agree to the quashing of their own amendments and returning the bill to the Lords with the message that the lower house was unable to deal with it. The following day it was back with the Commons having been rejected by the Lords in their turn; and it was hardly surprising that in the afternoon the Lords themselves should retaliate and complain to the Commons for replacing one of *their* measures without due conference. Needless to say, in both cases there were those who were ready to come forward with precedents to show that the Commons were not acting in either an illegal or novel way.[11]

Despite his obvious interest in procedure, Cromwell appears sometimes to be curiously unforthcoming. He records no surprise that Popham made a formal request for Commons privileges, despite the fact that a new parliament was not being opened;[12] and his account of the debates on public fasts and the articles concerning ecclesiastical matters is very brief. There are grounds for the view that Norton's overall contribution this session was considerable, yet in a number of instances – by-elections and the subsidy bill being the most obvious – Cromwell does not mention him by name or note the arguments he pursued.[13] Was his imagination not caught by the notion that the House should authorize new elections and expel members? And when Norton moved for a committee to draw up the subsidy bill, why did he not show some appreciation of the fact that Norton was trying, in Neale's words, to 'steal the legislative initiative for the House'? Cromwell's silence must be taken seriously, if only because it seems to challenge the currently accepted picture; but the deeper issue at stake is the enduring problem of analysis which private journals, or diaries, seem in particular to present to the historian. It would be easy to assume that the 'failure' of Cromwell's record at this point indicates a failure of perception, but that would be a rash assumption unless we could be sure that he intended this to be a complete record, possibly for eyes other than his own. We cannot know that, and the fact that there is no mention of his opening the debate on foreigners' children seems to point the other way, for the omission could hardly be due to a lapse of memory or perception.[14] If in this case, as in others, we have at our disposal an essentially *private* notebook, then there is little sense in regretting the absence, for example, of any coverage of what was probably an interesting naval debate, and every reason to be thankful for the information which has been left behind.[15]

4. *EP*, I.398–404.
5. TCD MS 1045, fos.102 and v, 110.
6. *Ibid.*, f.101 and v.
7. *Ibid.*, f.109.
8. *Ibid.*, fos.96v, 114 and v; D'Ewes, 281–2, 307–08; *EP*, I.375–6.
9. TCD MS 1045, f.107v.

10. *Ibid.*, f.104v.
11. *Ibid.*, fos.112v–13v.
12. *EP*, I.376.
13. *Ibid.*, I.375–6, 385.
14. TCD MS 1045, f.99v; *EP*, I.412.
15. TCD MS 1045, f.115.

1. Sir Walter Mildmay's speech for supply, 25 January

Text from BL Sloane 326, copy.
Other MSS. London: BL Harl.6265, Cott.Titus F1 and its copy,
Stowe 358. Oxford: Bodley, Rawlinson C838. California:
Huntington Library, Ellesmere 2583.
Printed. D'Ewes, 285⁄8.

Sloane 326, fos.19⁄29v

xxv^{to} *Januarij* 1580 In the common hous.

The principall cawse of our assembly here being to consult of matters that do concerne the realme, I have thought good, with your pacience, to remember you of such thinges as for the weight and necessity of them I take to be worthy of your consideracions, wherein I meane to note unto you what I have conceyved:

Capita praecipua.   First, of the present state that we be in; next, of the dangers that we may iustly be in dowbt of; and last, what provision ought to be made to prevent or resist them.

This shewed as briefly as the matters will suffer, I leave them to your iudgementes to proceed further as you shall fynde yet expedient.

Status: 1   That our most gracious Quene, even at her first entry, did loosen us from
f.19v   the / yoke of Rome and did restore unto this realme the most pure and holy religion of the Gospell, which for a tyme was overshadowed with popery, is knowne to all the world and fealt of us to our singular comfortes.

But from hence as from the roote hath sprong that inplacable malice of the Pope and his confederates against her, whereby they have, and do seeke not only to trowble, but if they could to bring the realme agayne into thraldome.

The rather for that they hold this as a firme and settled opinion, that England is th'only sovereigne monarchie that most doth mainteyne and countnance religion, being the cheif sanctuary for the afflicted members of the Church that fly hither from the tyranny of Rome, as men that be in danger of shippwrack do from a raging and tempesteous sea to a calme and quiet haven. /

f.20   This being so, what hath not the Pope assayed to annoy the Quene, and her state, thereby as he thinketh to remove this greate obstacle that standeth betweene him and th'overflowing of the world agayne with popery?

For proofe whereof theis may suffise:

Anno 1569   the northerne rebellion stirred upp by the Pope, and the quarell for popery; the mayntenance sithence of thoes rebells, and other fugitives;

Anno 1570   the publishing of a most impudent, blasphemous and malicious bull against our most rightfull Quene;

the invasion into Ireland by James Fitzmorrice with the assistance of some English rebells;

the raising of a dangerous rebellion in Ireland by the Earle of Desmond and others intending thereby to make a generall revolt of that whole realme;

the late invasion of strangers into Ireland, and their fortifying at Smirwick. | The Pope turning thus the venom of his courses,[1] and the penns of his malicious parasites, into men of warr and weapons to wyn that by force which otherwise he could not do.

And though all theis are said to be done by the Pope, and in his name, yet who seeth not that they be maynteyned underhand by some other princes his confederates? And if any man be in dowbt of that, lett him but note from whence the last invasion into Ireland came, of what countrey the shipps, and of what nation the most part of the souldiers were, and by the direccion of whose ministers they receyved their victuall and furnyture.

For the Pope of himselfe at this present is farr unable to make warr upon any prince of that estate which her Majestie is of, having lost as you know many yeres by the preaching of the Gospell thoes infinite revenues which he was wont to have out of England, Scotland, Germany, Swyzerland, Denmarke and | others, and now of late out of Fraunce and the Lowe Countreys, so as wee are to thinke that his name only is used, and all or the most part of the charge borne by other.

The Quene nevertheles by the almighty power of God, standeth fast maulgre the Pope and all his freindes, having hitherto resisted all attemptes against her, to her greate honour and their greate shame, as:

the rebellion in the north suppressed without effusion of bloud, wherein her Majestie might say as Cesar did, *veni, vidi, vici,* so expedite and so honorable was the victory that God did give hir, by the diligence and valure of thoes noble men that had the conducting thereof;

th'enterprize of James Fitzmorrice defeated and himselfe slayne;

The Italians and Spaniardes pull'd out by the eares[2] at Smirwick in Ireland and cutt in peeces by the notable service of a noble capteyne[3] and valiaunt souldiers. | Neyther theis, nor any other threatninges or feare of danger, hath or doth make her once to stagger or relent in the cawse of religion, but like a constant Christian princesse she holdeth fast the profession of the Gospell that hath so long upholden her and made us to lyve in peace xxij[tie] yeres and more under her moste gracious goverment, free from thoes trowbles that our neighboures have felt.

So as now this seameth to be our present state, a blissed, peaceable and happy tyme, for the which wee are most bound to God, and to pray to him for continuance thereof.

But yet notwithstanding, seing our enemyes sleepe not, it behoveth us also not to be careles, as though all were past, but rather to thinke that there is but a peece of the storme over, and that the greater part of the tempest remayneth behinde and is like to fall upon us by:

---

1. Harl.6265 reads 'curses'.
2. Corrected in the margin from 'yeres'.
3. Arthur, Lord Grey de Wilton.

f.22 the malice of the Pope, the most capitall enemy of the Quene and this state; the determynac[i]ons of the Councell of Trent; / and by the combynacion with the Pope of other monarches and princes devoted unto Rome.

Assuring ourselves that if their powers be answerable to their wills, this realme shall fynde at their handes all the miseryes and extremyties that they can bring upon yt.

And though by the late good successe which God hath given in Ireland theis lewd and malicious enterprizes seeme for a tyme to be as yt were at a stand, yett lett us be assured that neither their attempt upon Ireland, neither the mischeif intended against England will cease thus, but if they fynd as negligent they will be revived with greater forces then have byn yett seene.

The certeyne determynacion which the Pope and his combyned freindes have to roote out the religion of the Gospell in all places, and to begyn here as their greatest f.22v ympediment, is cawse sufficient to make us the more / vigilant, and to have a more wary eye to their doinges and preparacions how smoothly soever they speake and dissemble their frendshipps for a tyme.

For lett us thinke surely that they have ioyned their handes together against us. And that if they can, they will procure the sparkes of the flames, that have byn so terrible in other countreys, to fly over into England and to kindle as greate a fyer here.

And as the Pope by open hostility as you see, hath shewed himselfe against her Majestie so the better to answere in tyme the purposes that he hath sett downe, in the meane season till they may come to ripenes he hath and doth by secrett practizes within this realme leave nothing unproved, embouldning many unduetyfull subiectes to stand fast in their disobedience to her Majestie and her lawes.

For albeit the pure religion of the Gospell hath had a free course and hath byn f.23 freely preached now many / yeres within this realme, by the proteccion of her Majestie's most Christian goverment, yet such have byn the practizes of the Pope and his secrett min[i]sters as th'obstinate and stiff-necked papist is so farr from being reformed as he hath gotten stomack to go backwardes and to shew his disobedience not only in arrogant wordes but also in contemptuous deedes.

To confirme them herein, and to increase their nombers, you see how the Pope hath and doth comfort their hollow heartes with absoluc[i]ons, dispensations, reconciliations, and such other thinges of Rome, you see how lately he hath sent hither a sort of hipocrites naming themselves Jesuites, a rable of vagarant fryers newly sprung upp and comyng through the world to trowble the Church of God, whoes principall errand is, by creeping into the howses and familiarityes of men of behaviour and reputacion, not only to corrupt the realme with false doctrine, but also under that pretence to stirr sedition to the perill of her Majestie and her good f.23v subiectes. /

How thoes practizes of the Pope have wrought in the disobedient subiectes of this land, is both evident and lamentable to consider. For such ympression hath th'estimacion of the Pope's authority made in them, as not only thoes which from the beginyng have refused to obey but many, yea very many, of those which divers yeres together did yeild and conforme[4] themselves in their open accions, sithence the decrees of that unholy Councell of Trent, and sithence the publishing and denouncing of that blasphemous bull against her Majestie, and sithence thoes secrett absoluc[i]ons and reconciliacions and the swarming hither of a nomber of popish preistes and monkish Jesuites, have and do utturly refuse to be of our Church or to resort to our preachings and prayers. The sequele whereof must needes prove dangerous to the whole state of this common wealth.

By this you see what cawse we have iustly to dowbt great mischeif threatned to this realme. And therewith you may easely see also how for the preventing and withstanding of the same, it behoveth her Majestie not only in tyme to provyde / sufficient lawes for the continuance of this peaceable goverment but also to be ready with forces to represse all attemptes that may be enterprized either by enemyes abroade, or by evill subiectes at home.

f.24
Remedia: 3[5]

What difference there is betweene the Pope's persecuting Church and the milde Church of the Gospell hath byn seene in all ages, and specially in the late goverment compared with her Majestie's mercifull reigne, the continuance of which clemency is also to be wished so farr as may stand with Godde's glory and the safety of the realme.

Pro pace
[*conser*]*venda*

But when by long proofe wee finde that this favorable and gentle manner of dealing with the disobedient contempnors of religion, to wynn them by faire meanes if yt were posible, hath done no good, but hath bredd in them a more arrogant and contemptuous spirit, so as they have presumed not only to disobey the lawes and orders of the realme, but also to accept from Rome secrett absolucions, reconciliacions and such like; and that by the handes of lewde / runagate preistes and Jesuites, harboring and interteyning them even in their howses, thereby shewing an obedience to the Pope, and by their direccion also nourishing and trayning up their children and kinsfolkes, not only at home but also abroade in the seminaryes of popery: now I say, yt is tyme for us to looke more narrowly and streightly to them least that as they be corrupt, so they prove dangerous members too much borne with in the entrailes of our common wealth.

f.24v

And seeing that the lenytie of the tyme and the mildnes of the lawes heretofore made are one greate cawse of their arrogant disobedience, yt is necessary that we here make provision of lawes more streight and more severe, to constreyne them to yeild their open obedience at the least to her Majestie in cawses of religion, and not to live as they list to the perillous example of other, and to th'encouraging of their owne evill affected myndes.

But if they will needes submytt themselves to the benediccion of the / Pope, they may feele how little his curses can hurt us, and how little his blessinges can save them from that punishment which wee are able to lay upon them; letting them also fynde how dangerous yt shalbe for them to deale with the Pope or any thinges of his, or with thoes Romish preistes and Jesuites, and therewith also how perillous it shalbe for those seditious runagates to enter into this land, to draw away from her Majestie that obedience which by the lawes of God and man is due unto her.

f.25

This then is one of the provisions that we ought to take care of in this councell,

---

4. MS reads 'confirme'; this reading from Harl.6265.

5. Number supplied from Harl.6265.

whereby both wee may enioy still that happy peace we lyve in, and the Pope take the lesse boldnes to trowble us by any favorers that he shall fynde here.

Pro bello propulsando

The next is provision of forces sufficient to answere any vyolence that may be offered, either here or abroade, for the which you know yt is requisite that her Majestie do make preparacion / both by sea and by land.

f.25v

Copia maritime

God hath placed this kingdome in an island environned with the sea as with a naturall and strong wall, whereby we are not subiect to thoes sudden invasions and incursions which other frontier[6] countreys bee; one of our greatest defences therefore standing by sea, the nom[b]er of good shipps are of the most ymportance for us.

What the Queen's navy is, how many notable shipps, and how farr beyond the navy of any other prince, is knowne to all men. And therewith also yt may easely be considered how great charges be incident to the same.

Copiae terrestres

Necessary also yt is that her Majestie have forces by land sufficient to chastize the rebells in Ireland and to represse any forreyne attempt, either there or here. /

f.26

For which services either by land or by sea her Majestie needeth not, as other princes are fayne to doe, to enterteyne mercenary souldiers of forreigne countryes, hardly gotten, costly and dangerously kept, and in th'end little or no service done by them; but may bring sufficient forces of her owne naturall subiectes, ready and easie to be levyed, that carry with them willing, valiaunt, and faithfull myndes, such as few nations may easely compare with.

Pecunia comparanda

But theis forces, with their munycion and furniture, can neyther be prepared nor maynteyned to have continuance without provision of treasure[7] sufficient to beare the charge, being as you know termed of the old *nervus belli*.

This belongeth to us to consider and that in tyme, that there be not lacke of the synnews that must hold together the strength of our body.

And because, through the malice of our enemyes, her Majestie is driven to keepe

f.26v

at / this present greate forces in Ireland for the utter suppressing of that rebellion to her exceeding charge; and for that also it is uncerteyne how sodeyne or how greate other attemptes may be: therefore in reason our supply of that mayntenance ought to be the more, specially the warrs being at this day so costly, as every man in his private expence may easely judge.

But least peradventure some may thinke that the contribuc[i]on granted by us now fyve yeres past both franckly and duetifully might suffice for many yeres without any new, I dare assure you for the acquaintance I have (though I be unworthie) with thoes her Majestie's affayres, that the same hath not byn sufficient to answere th'extraordinary charges happened sythence, (specially thoes of Ireland,) by th'one halfe; but her Majestie hath supplyed the rest of her owne revennewes, sparing from herselfe to serve the necessity of the realme, and shunnyng thereby loanes upon

f.27

interest / as a most pestilent cancre, that is able to devowre even the estates[8] of princes. Which being so, as it is most trew, we are not to thinke upon the charge that is past, but upon the good that we have receyved by yt, being by that provision well and honorably defended against the malice of our enemyes.

And therefore considering the greate benefitt we have received by the last payment (being easely taxed and easely borne whereby we have kept all the rest in peace) lett us, as provident councellors of this state, prepare agayne in tyme that which may be able to withstand the mischeife intended against her and us.

To do this willingly and liberally our duetyes to our Quene and countrey and our owne safetyes ought to move us. /

The love and duety that we owe to our most gracious Quene, by whoes ministry God hath done so greate thinges for us, even such as be wonderfull in the eyes of the world, ought to make us more carefull for her preservacion and security then for our owne: a princesse knowne by longe experience to be a principall patron of the Gospell, vertuous, wise, faithfull, just, unspotted in word or deed, mercifull, temperate, a mainteynor of peace and justice amongst her people without respect of persons; a Quene besides of this realme our native countrey renouned through the world, which our enemyes daily gape to overrunne, if by force or sleight they could do yt. *Honestum* f.27v
Pium

For such a Queen and such a countrey and for the defence of the honour and / surety of them both, nothing ought to be so deare unto us, that with most willing heartes we should not spend and adventure freely. f.28

The same love and duety that we owe to our most gracious sovereigne, and to this our native countrey, ought to make us all so thinke upon the realme of Ireland as upon a principall member of this Crowne, having so continued 400 yeres and more. To loose that land or any part thereof, which the enemyes seeke, would not only bring with it shame and dishonour but also prove a thing most dangerous to England, considering the neirenes of that realme to this, and the goodnes of so many notable havens as be there. Agayne, to reforme that nation by planting there of religion and justice, which the enemyes labour to interrupt, is most godly and necessary. The neglecting whereof hath and will continue that people in all irreligion and disorder, to the great / offence of God, and to the infinite charge of this realme. f.28v

Finally, lett us be myndfull also of our owne safetyes, thereby to avoyd so greate dangers, not seene a farr of but imynent even over our heades. The quietnes that we have by the peaceable goverment of her Majestie doth make us to enioy all that is ours in more freedome then any nation under the sunne at this day. But lett that not breed in us a careles security, as though this cleiresome light[9] could never be darkned. But lett us thinke certeynely that the Pope and his favourers do both envy our felicity, and leave no practice unsought to overthrow the same. *Necessarium*

And if any man be so dull, as I trust there be none here, that he cannott conceive the blessednes of theis our tymes / and the golden peace we now enioy, except he felt the lacke of yt: lett him but cast his eyes over the seas into our neighbour countreys, and there beholde what trowble the Pope and his ministers have stirred against such as professe the same religion of Jesus Christ as we doe. f.29

There he may fynde depopulac[i]ons and devastacions of whole provinces and countreyes, overthrowing, spoyling, and sacking of cittyes and townes, ymprisoning, rannsoming and murthering of all kinde of people, besides other *Comentarium rerum*
Gallicarum et
Belgicarum

6. 'frontier' omitted in Harl.6265.
7. 'Treasure' in large capitals in MS.
8. MS reads 'thestes'; this reading from

Harl.6265.

9. Harl.6265 reads 'cleare sunne light'.

infynite calamityes which the insolency of warre doth usually bring with yt. From theis God in his mercy hath delyvered us, but this nevertheles is the state and condicion that our enemyes would see us in, if by any devise they could bring it to passe. And to that end be you assured they will spare for no cost, nor leave any meane unassayed. /

Therefore to conclude, seing the malice of the Pope and his confederates is so notorious unto us, and seing the dangers be so greate, so evident and so imynent, and seing that preparac[i]on to withstand them cannott be made without support of the realme; and seing that our duetyes to God, our Quene and countrey, and the necessity that hangeth upon our owne safegardes, be reasons sufficient to perswade us: lett us thinke upon theis matters as the weight of them deserveth, and so provyde in tyme both by lawes to restreyne and correct the evill affected subiect, and by provis[i]on of that which shalbe requisite for the mayntenance of forces, as our enemyes fynding our myndes so willing, and our handes so ready to keepe in order our countrey and to furnish her Majestie of all that shalbe necessary, may either be discouraged to attempt any thing against us, or yf they do they may fynde such resistance as shall bring confusion to themselves, honour to our most gracious Queen and safety to us all.

2. Charges brought against Arthur Hall, 14 February

Text from PRO SP Dom.Eliz.147/52 (second folio), copy.

SP Dom.Eliz.147/52 (second folio)[1]

1. That the last session being commanded to appeare, he departed in contempt of the court, and testified that wilfull contempt by an uncomely lettre.
2. That he hath published the conferences of the Howse in print.
3. That he published the same as a libell, with counterfeit name of the author and no name of the printer.
4. That he hath therin published matter of infamy to the whole assembly.
5. That he hath published matter of infamy to sundry members of the Howse.
6. That he hath untruly reported the orders of the Howse.
7. That he hath affirmed that he knoweth that the Howse hath *de facto* affirmed and iudged untruly.
8. That he hath uniustly defamed the memory of the late Speaker.
9. That he hath impugned the authorytie of the Howse in appointing committees without his consent.
10. That in defaming the credit of the body and members of the Howse, he hath practized to deface and discredit the authorytie of the lawes and the proceedinges in the parlament.
11. That in impugning the authorytie of the Howse, he hath sought to impayre the honourable and ancient order touching the government of the realme and the rytes of the comon howse and the form in making of the lawes, wherby the subiectes of this realme are ruled and governed.
12. That since he was called before the lordes of the Councell for this offence and there receyved rebuke, and offered some forme of submission, he hath newely and lately againe published the same book.
13. That being examined in the Howse, he said that he had but one of those bookes, where it is proved that he had xij or xiij, and six of them since his calling before the lordes of the Councell.

1. The two pamphlets largely responsible for provoking these charges were *An Account of a Quarrel between Arthur Hall Esq. and Melchisidech Mallorie, Gent.* and *An Admonition by the Father of F.A. to him being a Burgesse of the Parliament for his better Behaviour therein.* The case is fully covered in *EP*, I.407-10, and cf. H. G. Wright, *Arthur Hall of Grantham* (1919).

3. Articles for ecclesiastical causes, with the bishops' reply

Text from BL Lansdowne 30, copy, endorsed by Burghley.
Other MSS. London: Inner Temple, Petyt 538/54, text as Lansdowne, endorsed by Whitgift 'An answere to certaine articles exhibited in Parlament when I was Bishop of Wigorn' and amended by him.
Articles only. London: BL Add.29546, Add.48064 (Yelverton 70), Cott. Cleopatra F11. Northants.: CRO, Fitzwilliam of Milton Political 148, headed '1580. Articles concerninge ministers and excommunycatyon, which things were touched in Mr Speaker's oracyon to the Queene after the session ended and delivered by Sir Water Mildmay to Mr Secretory Walsingham for him to treat therof with hir Majesty that they might be enacted at the next parlament holden whensoever'. (The last three MSS omit the sixth and seventh articles concerning ministers.)
Reply only. London: St Paul's Add.vii.34,* an independent text in the hand of the writer of the marginal answers to 'Motions for a conference, 1589', in Longleat lxxvi; St Paul's Add.vii.30,* draft in Whitgift's hand of the answer to the fourth article concerning ministers (points 9‑12 of Lansdowne do not appear; Whitgift's amendments are incorporated in Lansdowne 30); Inner Temple Petyt 538/38, passage from the section 'Touching the execution by men of no calling in the church', with some additional paragraphs.
Printed. J. Strype, *Whitgift* (1822 edn), III.47‑63 (from Lansdowne 30); *Annals of the Reformation* (1824 edn), III.ii.302‑17 (? from Petyt; dated 1584).
Articles only. J. Strype, *Grindal* (1821 edn), 591‑5 (from Cott. Cleopatra F11, with an additional final sentence; dated 1586).
Reply only (in part). J. Strype, *Grindal*, 589‑591 (from Petyt).

*Note. I have retained these citations, together with details of the MSS, which appear in the transcriptions originally made for Neale, but I have been unable to trace the MSS themselves. Some St Paul's MSS were acquired in and after 1963 by Lambeth Palace Library, though those cited here were not among them: I am currently trying to trace their whereabouts. – T.E.H.

Lansdowne 30, fos.203-10

[Two endorsements:
1. in Burghley's hand 'A book of articles offred to the last session of Parlement *anno* 23 for ecclesiasticall causes', with an addition in another hand 'with an answere to the same from the bishopps'.
2. in a third hand 'The copie of certen articles exhibited by some of the lower house, the last parliament. And the aunswere unto them. For the tyme: but not as yet delivered to any'.]

Concerninge ministers.

The firste article.
That it maie be enacted that none be admitted to be minister of the woord and sacramentes but in a benefice havinge cure of soule then vacant in the diocese of suche a bishop as is to admitt him.

The answere to the first article.
This cannot possiblye be performed without alteracion of the whole state of the Churche of England:

ffirste because there must be curates, and that of necessitie.   1.

because their are other ecclesiasticall livinges which require ministers of the worde   2.
and sacramentes aswell as benefices with cure, as deneries, prebends, mastershipps and ffellowshipps in the universities, pettycannons in cathedrall churges.

This article is grownded upon a false principle of T[homas] C[artwright] agaynst ministers having no pastorall cure, which neyther he nor any mann ells is able to mayntayne eyther by the worde of God, or auncient aucthoritie. For by *ministerium vagum* the old Counsells and cannons did alwayes understand suche as were ordayned *sine patrimonio aut titulo*, that is, not havinge any staye of lyvinge, as it is manifest in the Councell of Chalcedon.

Suche as have great cures shalbe overburdened with sayinge of service, preachinge, ministringe of sacramentes, all them selves, for they shalbe destitute of a curate to helpe them to saie service, to visitt the sicke, to minister the sacramentes, to cathechise *etc*. By this meanes fellowshipps in colleges which by their statutes must be within orders are overthrowne.

The seconde article.
That before th'admission of suche mynistre, the bishop shall geve publicke notice by wrytinge under his seale to be fixed on the churche dore the[n] destitute of a pastor, upon some Sondaye or holydaye in the tyme of divyne service, signifienge the name of the partie presented to that churche or thereto to be admitted, with intimacion that suche as within xx^ti dayes after will obiect agaynste his admission shall appeare at a place certayne before him and alleadge suche matter as shall onlye concerne his conversacion of lyfe, and thereby his insufficiencie for that place.

The thirde article.
That the bishop shall not procead to th'admission of any to be minister of the worde and sacramentes before due certificate be made, in aucthenticke forme and publicke

place by him to be assigned, that his processe of notice and intimacion was executed in forme aforesaid, nor before th'expiracion of the saide xx^ty dayes, nor without caulinge for, and hearinge of suche as uppon retorne of the said processe shall and will obiecte as is aforesaid.

The answeare to the second and thirde articles.
This is unnecessarye, and in vayne, unlesse he that is to be admitted had been dwellinge in that parishe before, which will happen verye seldome.

The writinge and sendinge to the benefice voide and the retorne thereof in aucthenticke forme wilbe very chargeable to the minister especially where the place is farre from the bishop's mansion house.

It also protracteth tyme, and will minister occasion of quarrelinge.

The charges and delaye wilbe alsoe encreased, yf the partie to be admitted doe stande uppon the purgacions of the obiections layde agaynst him. |

f.203v   This testimony required of the parishioners lackinge their pastor is an introduction to bringe the patronage to the people, and to sett a fier amongst them for testifienge or not testifyinge, and that many tymes of a person they knowe not.

The obiectinge of the people will fall out many tymes to be of malice, whereby immortall hatred will rise amongste them.

The person had neede be a very evell mann that a nomber of the parishe will come a longe jorney to the ordinarie on their owne cost to obiect agaynst him that is to be admitted.

What yf the parishe wilbe negligent, and will not retorne: shall they lacke a pastor still? The patrone yf he be mightie maie eyther lett the retorne, or procure suche as he shall lyke of, and whoe and howe many of the parishe shall retorne.

The fourth article.
It is here to be provided that, where in certayne colleges and cathedrall and collegiat churches the ffoundacion or statutes require suche as are there placed to be ministers, it shalbe lawfull for suche as are knowne to professe the studye of dyvinitie, or otherwise be lawfully dispensed withall, to retayne as before this acte they might any ffellowship [or] prebend within the said colleges, notwithstandinge they be noe ministers.

The answere to the fourthe article.[1]
1. This utterlye overthroweth the fowndacion and statutes of almost all the colleges in Cambridge and Oxford, beinge fownded principally for the studye of dyvinitie and encrease of the nomber of learned preachers and ministers, and therefor not only the Master, Provost, Warden, President, *etc.* by the saide fowndac[i]ons and statutes [are] bounden to be ministers but dyvers others also of suche societies are lykewise bounden to enter into the ministery by a certayne tyme or ells to yelde there places to others.
2. It will deprive the Churche of England of the worthieste, best learned and wysest mynisters and preachers, for there is noe comparison betwixt suche mynisters and preachers as the universities continually yeld in the respect of suche fowndacions and statutes and others beinge noe universitie menn, or not entringe into the ministerie

whiles they remayned there: as at this daye it is notorius. For althoughe there are divers that cann preache *etc.*, yit they have noe substaunce of learninge in them, neyther are they able to stand with th'adversarie eyther in pulpett or disputacion, a thinge aswell required in a minister as exhortacion is.

3. Yf this devise take place, where the universities yeld nowe yerely great nomber of preachers and ministers they would not then yelde one for twentie, and soe the nomber of preachers, which nowe are thought to be very fewe, would then be muche lesse, and at length the utter decaye of the studye of divinitie and the very next waie to bringe in poperie and ignoraunce agayne. /

4. It overthroweth the degrees of the universities which are taken in divinitie, as the bachelershipp and doctorshipp, for even sythens the firste ffoundacion of them bothe it hathe ben perpetually used, and it is by statute requyred, that none should take any of theis degrees but suche as are in the ministerie. And in deed it is bothe inconvenient and absurde that it should be otherwise.

f.204

5. At this daye there are in the universitie of Cambridge 100 preachers at the lest very worthye menn, and not many lesse in the universitie of Oxforde, and the nomber daylye encreaseth in bothe to the great benifitt of the Churche. But yf this might take place, within theis vij yeres there would not be v ministers in eyther of them.

6. It would cause men all their lyfe tyme to remayne in the universities, soe that there should be noe succession.[2]

7. It alsoe overthrowethe the foundacion and statutes of all cathedrall and collegiat churches, and takethe away the cheife and principall reward for learned preachers, for the best lyvinges for worthie men ar in suche churches.

8. It takethe away the wisest, best learned and gravest divines suche as bothe doe and are most able to withstand not only papistes, but other sectaries also.

9.[3] Everye one, to kepe theis places, would openly professe the studye of divinitie and secretly study the one lawe or th'other, or phisicke, or some tryflynge studye all his lyfe longe.

10. There wilbe noe care of profitinge when theire is noe triall thereof, which is most especiall by open preachinge, which were absurde to be done by noe ministers.

11. Any which hathe bene a student maie under pretence of studyenge dyvinitie without any triall obtayne deaneries, provostshipps, prebends *etc.* and beinge a laye man maie lyve idlely on the spoyle of the Churche all his lyfe, except he take a benefice.

12. There shall want sufficient triall of the abilities of preachinge of suche as are to be bysshopps excepte they be chosen from some benefice: which breadeth smale experience for government.

13.[4] It would greatly dyminishe the nomber of preachers and sermons which the

---

1. St Paul's vii.30 is Whitgift's draft answer to the fourth article 'concerning ministers', the alterations being incorporated into Lansdowne 30.
2. This point is a marginal comment by Whitgift in St Paul's vii.30.
3. Points 9-12 are not in St Paul's vii.30.
4. Number 8 in St Paul's vii.30, which finishes at number 10 (number 15 here). St Paul's vii.30 reads '. . . which these churchs yeald in everie countrie in this respectes that those . . .'.

universities, colleges, and cathedrall churches doe yeld bothe at home and abroade in every cuntrie, in the respect that those which nowe have the lyvinges are bounde to be ministers.

14. It taketh awaie dailie service used in theis churches (which were impietie) unlesse it might be said or songe by suche as are noe ministers, which is absurde.

15. To conclude, it will breede a beggerlye, unlearned and contemptible clergie and ministerie. It is the very waie to overthrowe all colleges, cathedrall churches and places of learninge. It will extinguishe the studye of divinitie, diminishe the nomber of preachers, and breede a great confusion and alteracion in the Churche and common welthe. And it is a pece of T[homas] C[artwright] his platforme.[5] |

f.204v 16. By this the rewarde of divinitie wilbe taken awaie and the divine thrust to a benefice of xl^{li}. This is covertly to shove at the Gosspell to place the lawyer and others as they please.

17. Note that here they woulde have dispensacions to take place agaynst the statutes of colleges and cathedrall churches.

The vth article.
That none be made mynister but uppon some Sondaye publickly in the cathedrall churche of the dioces where the minister is admitted.

The answere to the vth article.
4. [6]That he be made publickly it is not amysse, but to observe the precise place of the cathedrall churche it cannot be, because dyvers bysshopps dwell farr from their cathedrall churches. |

f.205 ## The sixth article.
That the bishop make noe minister but suche as be of his owne diocese and have there contynued by the space of one whole yere, except suche only as come from the universities and bringe testimoniall of their meetenesse under the universitie seale.

The vijth article.
That suche as be of the bishop's owne diocese shall bringe with them suche a testimoniall as is lymyted in the statute of *anno 13° Elizabethae*[7]

[The answer to the sixth and seventh articles.]
1. Theis are very expedient and necessarie and even soe provided for by the lawe.
2. It were most meete also that theis two were observed when patrons present to a benefice and that as the testimonialls doe witnesse their conversacion, so the bishop should without any impeachement of *quare impedit etc.* be judge of their abilitie in respect of the cure which they desire.

The viijth article.
That after the receipte of the said testimoniall, the bishop shall not procead to the makinge of the person minister which bringeth that testimoniall before he shall declare, before the deane and chapter of his cathedrall churche, that he well knoweth the persons by whome the testimoniall is made to be suche as is by the saide statute expressed.

The answere to the viij^th article.
This is unnecessarie and altogether needelesse, neyther can it be performed.

The ix^th article.
That he shall not make any minister but suche as shall by the deane and chapiter or the more parte of them, or vj learned preachers of the diocese then present, be allowed for a man meete and sufficient by subscription of their hands to some writinge declaringe their assent in allowinge of him.

The answere to the ix^th article.
1. It will breed great troble and not worke that effect which is looked for, neyther can it in all places be performed. /
2. It would alsoe be very chargeable uppon the absence of the most of the chapitre, yf the partie should procure the hands of vj preachers dwellinge dispersed.

f.205v

The xth article.
That none shall have a benefice with cure, beinge of the value of xx^li yerely in the Quene's bookes, except he be a Master of Arte or preacher allowed, notwithstandinge that he be made a ministre before of some meane cure.

The answere to the xth article.
It is to be lyked of, so that diligent heede be taken that none be admitted preachers but suche as be worthye. /

Concerninge Excomunicacion

f.206

The first article.
Excommunicacion is at this tyme the payne of contumacie, and hathe place where a mann appeareth not uppon processe, or satisfieth not some order prescribed by the judge, as not takinge some othe or not payinge legacies, tythes, *etc.*

The second article.
The offences that growe by the practise hereof in this manner ar great. One, that beinge the highest censure leafte to the Churche of God, it is prophaned by applyenge it to temporall and civell causes.

An other, that it is executed by men that have noe caulinge in the Churche, as chauncellors, officials, *etc.*

Agayne, for as muche as the Churche maie not be leafte without this censure of excommunicacion, it is to be provyded that for enormious crimes, as adultery and suche other, the same be executed eyther by the bishopps them selves with th'assistaunce of grave persons or ells by other persons of callinge in the Churche with the lyke assistaunce, and not by chauncellors and officials as hath bene used.

[The answer to the first and second articles.]
Excommunicacion hathe bene used by th'exclesiasticall[8] judge ever sythens there

5. St Paul's vii.30 finishes here.
6. *Sic.*

7. 13 Eliz., c.12 (1571), in *SR*, IV.546-7.
8. *Sic.*

hathe bene eyther discipline in the Churche or jurisdiction in the ecclesiasticall magistrate, and is the only punishemente thereof. For the auncient lawe makers, thinkinge that bloud and bodyly paine ought to be farr from ecclesiasticall magistrates, have geven them this myld spirituall sworde to devide that person from the ecclesiasticall body that refusethe to doe his ecclesiasticall duties and to obaye the ecclesiasticall judge, not excomunicatinge[9] every mann for two penny causes (as is surmised, thoughe in deed there be asmuche right in ij pence as in CC^li) but excommunicatinge[10] them for not obeying the order, decree and sentence of the judge accordinge to her Majestie's ecclesiasticall lawes, even as in a temporall cause of ij^d the partie is outlawed and consequently his goods and fruictes of his lands at the prince's pleasure yf he appeare not or obey not, and yit it is not to be said that a mann is owtlawed for ij^d but for not obeyinge the lawe, processe and judge in a ij^d matter: for the smaler the matter is the greater is the faulte of contumacie and disobedience saythe the lawe.

Excommunicacion for processe, order not obeyed, takinge some othe *etc.* is not for civell causes but theis causes ar ecclesiasticall. And what cann be more agaynst the Churche then when menn will not be ordered by it nor obey it? In God's lawe suche as would not be ordered by their judge or hie preist were stoned.

There is no lawe nor function in this world voyd of exception and imperfection, and to have it void thereof *est optandum magis quam sperandum* as in Platoe's Common Welthe *etc.*

If excomunicacion be either taken away or changed, the whole course of the common lawes of the realme concerninge thatt matter and towchinge the write of *excomunicato capiendo* must be changed, wherein manie thinges (not yet thought of) maie happen, and in steede thereof some convenient temporall penaltye must be devised, which howe unliking and unplawsible it will be and howe full of difficulties the wise can consider. /

f.206v   And if excommunicacion be thought fittest to contynewe (for that there wilbe as many inconveniences or more in tyme fownde in other thinges as in that) and that for the better creadit of the proceadinge therein the bishop him selfe be arcted[11] to sitt in consistory, his whole lyfe wilbe spente in his jurisdiccion and in study of lawe, for that he must be able to decearne whether the processe be accordinge to lawe before he inflecte the censure; which wilbe as great a decaye of preachinge as it hath be[en] in fore tyme, for that jurisdiction alone requireth *totum et integrum hominem.*

Touchinge the execucion by menn of noe caulinge in the Churche.
The jurisdiction in the beginninge was ioyntly in the bishop, deane and chapter, which bread so many opinions, suche impeachementes and confusion in proceadinge that by the generall custome of the worlde generally the jurisdiction was thought convenient to be exercised by the bisshopp alone; which growinge great as the Churche and ecclesiasticall causes encreased and consequently caulinge the bishop from his function, the lawe and constitucions ordered that the officiall or vicar generall of a bishop or archebishop should have the same consistory and jurisdiction that the archebisshopp or bisshopp had, and the same aucthoritie to excomunicate, which by the statutes of this realme is also allowed to doctors of the

lawe, for that in latter tymes dyvines have wholy employed them selves to divinitie and not to the procedinges and studdy of the lawe, whereunto in fore tymes the clargie was more addicted then to divinitie in respect of the gayne and offices exercised under bisshopps, archedeacons, and other ecclesiasticall caulinges, which drewe them wholy from dyvinitie.

The excommunicacion by lawe was never used nor coulde be used as a punishemente of any cryme savinge of notorious heresie, usury, symonye, pyracie, conspiracie agaynste the person of the prince, of his state, dignitie and crowne, perturbers of the common peace and quietnes of the Churche or realme, wilfull murderers, sacrilegers, periurers and incorrigible and notoriuse committers of incest and adultery, false witnesse and suborners thereof, violent layers of hands uppon ecclesiasticall persons and suche other great and horrible crimes which were cauled *sentencie canonum* : wherin, besids the particuler penaunces that the bishops and their officers ded[12] impose, it was for more terror provided by aunciant canons that there should be a generall open denunciacion of the excommunicacion in every cathedrall churche and parishe churche twise in the yere.

For other light faultes there was noe excommunicacion permitted or used as a punishment, other then for manifest and wilfull contumacie or disobedience in not appearinge when persons were cauled and somoned for a cause ecclesiasticall, or when any sentence or decree of the bishop or his officer beinge deliberatly made was wilfully disobeyed or not performed. /

Suche wilfull contumacie and disobedience to aucthoritie is in the lawe accompted soe great that it is cauled a contempte of that *quod est in jurisdictione extremum*, that is to saie, yf the judge cannot have apparaunce of the parties or execucion of his judgementes, he is at the wall and can goe noe further.

f.207

Of very aunciant tyme this was the manner of proceadinge in this realme and the only meanes of reducinge obstinate persons to the obedience of the lawe.

It maie appeare by the aunciant statute or acte of Parliament in the ix[th] yeare of Edward the Second, that it was the olde custome and usage of the realme longe before that tyme. The words are theis:

Si aliqui propter suam contumaciam manifestam excommunicentur ac post 40[ta] dies pro eorum captione scribatur ac pretendunt se privilegiatos et sic denegatur breve regium pro captione corporum : responsio regis, nunquam fuit negatum nec negabitur in futur[um].[13]

It is to be considered whither this manifest contumacie and wilfull disobedience to the magistrate, and aucthoritie, be not as well punishable when the originall cause or matter is light as waightie, the difference whereof dothe nothinge alter the nature of the disobedience.

In this our realme of very aunciant tyme it hathe bene observed from tyme to tyme that there was never alteracion made of any lawe ecclesiasticall, althoughe it had apparaunce to benifitte the state of the clergye, but that it turned ever to some notable preiudice.

9. MS reads 'excomnicatinge'.
10. MS reads 'excomnicatinge'.
11. I.e. constrained.

12. *Sic.*
13. 9 Ed. II, stat.1, *articuli cleri*, xii (1315/16), in *SR*, I.173.

Concerninge commutacion of penaunce.
That there be no commutacion of penaunce for synne but by the order and appoyntement of the bishop with th'assent of the deane and chapter or the most parte of them, or with the assent of vj preachers of that diocese.

The answere.
1. The bishop is sufficient for this matter.
2. It were good to inhibite justices of peace to commute: but to permitt them only to punishe corporally. And yit notwithstandinge the parties offendinge not to be receyved into the Churche till they have done suche penaunce whereby the congregacion maie be satisfied. /

f.207v   Concerninge dispensacions.

The first article.
The ffaculties which did the greatest hurte in the Churche of God were three, *viz.* dispensacion *de non promovendo*, dispensacion for pluralitie of benefices and dispensacion for non residence.

The second article.
Theis two last named faculties have bredd the disorder of makinge vage ministers whereof hathe ensued ij great incommodities. One and the cheifest of all, that the people is not taught. Th'other that the ministers placed in benefices where the pastor is absent and havinge for the most parte smale allowaunce, doe post from place to place for their better prefermente, and restinge noe where, respect neyther their lyfe ne increase in knowledge, for men be carefull for their conversacion where they are to have continuaunce and smale accompte cann be taken how he profiteth that abydethe no where longe.

[The answer to the first and second articles.]
The ffacultie *de non promovendo*[14] is soe rare as by the present archebishop there was never any graunted, and by the last archebishop never any yelded unto but by speciall request and warrant from my lords of her Majestie's Counsell, and that to menn qualified in her Majestie's service or otherwise greatly imployed in the common welth; and therefor it needeth noe further provision by lawe.

The facultie of non residence is alsoe so rare and graunted in suche respectes as sythens the tyme of this archebishop there hathe not bene above one graunted, and that to a man of lxxx yeare old with whome the lawe it selfe dispenseth; besides that the statute of the realme provideth so sharpe a penaltie for non residence by the forfeyture of x^{li} a moneth to be recovered in the Exchequor as noe man carethe to sue for that facultie and yf they doe, it profiteth nothinge, for that the statute inflicteth the punishment all faculties and dispensacions notwithstandinge and a more severe punishement cannot well be devised.[15]

Towchinge the facultie of pluralities the grounde thereof is this: men of excellent giftes and extraordinarie vertue oft tymes eyther have noe lyvinges or very smale lyvinges, and when they cannot obtayne so great as there qualitie deserveth the

f.208   pollicie of the Churche hath thought fitt to graunte / to suche an one twoe lyvinges as an extraordinarie rewarde for extraordinarie vertue. For yf all menn could be made fitt for all lyvinges or all livinges for all manner of menn there should have needed noe dispensacion of pluralities; but for as muche as that cannot bee, it is lawfull in suche case of necessitie and for suche extraordinarie causes to receed from the streight and common course of the lawe and soe hath it bene used in all ages, neyther can it be better polliced or more restrayned then of late it hathe beene in respecte both of distaunce of places and the valewe of their persons, with great caution bothe for their hospitalitie and preachinges. Beesides that the lawes beinge positive, that forbid pluralities, the difference in reason is very smale betwene ij litle benefices not farr distant, and one great benefice; and therefore noe strange thinge yf by lyke positive lawe there be admitted by dispensac[i]on a mitigacion of the rigour of lawe.

Moreover the nomber of benefices in England beinge about xviij thowsand and the universities not able to ffurnishe the third parte of them with sufficient menn, it is better that one worthie mann hath ij benefices then to be unfurnished of lyvinge or obscurely placed in a small parishe and pore lyvinge, or the same ij benefices comitted to two unlearned menn.[16]

The third article.
That noe chapleyne have two cures, yf bothe amounte above xl^{li} in the Quene's bookes or be twentie myles distaunte.

The ffourth article.
That none enhabled to have twoe cures shall enioye the same unlesse they be under the value aforesaid and within xx^{ti} miles distaunce and be resident upon one of them.

The answere to the 3 and 4 articles.
1. The distaunce of miles is not to be mislyked, but the limitinge of the valewe is unreasonable and tendeth only to the impoverishinge of the ministerye, beinge a state as worthie or lyvinge in many respectes as others of other caulinge whatsoever in respecte of their caling.
2. The best giftes deserve the best rewards and therfore it were better to make a lymitacion what degrees of schooles shall only be enhabled for the best lyvinges.
3. Dignities, prebends and places in colleges (as before) are required by dispensacion for lay menn; here the divine is sett at his xl^{li}. If a man would deale covertly to pull awaye religion howe could he doe it better? /

The vth article.   f.208v
That noe deane of cathedrall churche, prebendarie or other havinge dignitie shall have more then one benefice with cure besids his dignitie *etc.*

The vjth article.
That noe one have moe dignities or prebends then ij.

The answere to the vth and vith articles.
1. It is very unreasonable and tendethe to the same end with the third and fourth

14. MS reads '*residendo*'; altered by Whitgift in
    Petyt to this reading.
15. 21 Hen. VIII, c.13, sect.15 (1529), in

SR, III.294-5.
16. MS reads 'meen'.

articles and will discourage menn from the ministery and make a beggerly clergie far unapte to geve hospitalitie or to doe many other thinges required of them and looked for at their hands.

2. It is also very inconvenient for most of theis dignitaties[17] are decayed within theis last 50 yeres very muche, greater impositions for the service of the realme are layed uppon them, every thinge to be required at double or treble pryce in respect of that which it was then at; and yet as great or greater hospitalitie looked for.

The vij^th article.
That they which maie have chaplens shall advaunce noe more then their number till the advaunced dye, or otherwise one of [the] ij benefices become voide.

The answere to the vij^th article.
1. This is not to be myslyked unlesse the partie be otherwise qualified then by his chaplenshipp.
2. And yit inconvenience maie arise of it. For yf a chaplen doe not behave him selfe as appertayneth, noe reason he should be retayned in service. And it were hard not to allowe another in suche a case. /

f.209   The viij^th article.
That none shalbe chaplen enhabled to two benefices unlesse he be Master of Arte, or allowed by the ordynary as sufficient.

The answere to the viij^th article.
It is very convenient.

The ix^th article.
That none shalbe non resident but suche as be continually attendant in the houses of suche as they be chaplens unto.

The answere to the ix^th article.
1. To be attendaunt the greater parte of the yere were sufficient; for the other parte of the yere they maie be at their cure. And besides, some have chaplens which attend by course which is very convenient.
2. This is very preiudiciall to grave menn, required for governmente in the universities, which maie very well dischardge bothe duties.
3. This overthroweth residence in cathedrall churches, colleges, deaneries, so that they cannot be attendaunt there excepte they will leave their benefice thoughe it be but one.

The xth article.
That they shall preache in person yerely two sermons and iiij^or sermons besides *per se vel per alium.*

The answere to the 10 article.
1. It is too too easie: it is requisite they should preache moe sermons even in their owne persons.

The xj^th article.
Lastly, to consider whether it were not meete to abate the nombers of the chaplens of

archbusshops and other under that degree that maie by the statute kepe more then one chaplen.

The answere to the xjth article.
It is not meete: ffor those of the clargie that have chaplens allowed, the statute setteth downe a good consideracion, and there are not many suche. Besids, it is looked for that they should have preachers about them to furnishe the want that is in most dioceses. /

The xijth article.
That in cases of pluralities and non residentes the bishop shall have the allowinge of the minister that shall serve the cure in th'absence of the incumbent. And the stipend of the said minister to be appoynted by the bishop accordinge to the sufficiencie of the ministre, so that the same stipend doe not exceade the thirde parte of the clere yearely valewe of the benefice.

The answere to the 12th article.
This is very reasonable and accordinge to lawe.

The xiijth article.
Their is one facultie of great inconvenience graunted not only by the Courte of Faculties but by the chauncellor of every diocese, *vz.* the dispensacion for marriage without banes askinge. By occasion whereof children make disordered matches without the assent of their parentes, and orphanes are lefte to the spoyle of unthriftie persons.

The answere to the xiijth article.
1. It maie be soe qualified that noe inconvenience shall ensue thereof.
2. Their be divers reasonable occasions that dayly happen which maie hinder the thrise askinge of banes, which causes are meete to be considered of and allowed by the ordinarie or his deputie.
3. The inconvenience that is proposed is in most dioceses already mett withall by puttinge theis condicions in the ffacultie, *viz.* that they have their governors' consent, that there is noe sute for matrimonye dependinge, noe precontracte nor noe other impediment which the partie is by a bond with suerties bounde unto. Soe that by this meanes this inconvenience is better mett withall then by askinge the banes thryse, which maie be done and yit theis impedimentes remayne.
4. And since the bonds have bene qualified as is abovesaid, beinge about one twelve monethes past, experience dothe teache that none of the pretended inconveniences have happened. /

A generall answere to all the articles of excommunicacion, comutacion and dispensacion.
Generally this alteracion, confusion and abridgement of exercise of that jurisdiction will shortly decaye the profession of the cannon lawe and civell lawe together, whereby divers nowe are bred upp in learninge, in languages and in studye, soe that they are inhabled to serve the realme in any forrayne service aswell as any sorte of learned menn in the realme besides.
17. *Sic.*

4. *Speaker's speech at close of Parliament,*
18 March

Text from Northants.: CRO, Fitzwilliam of Milton Political 148, copy.

Fitzwilliam of Milton Political 148

xviij[th] *Martii* 1580 *Die Sabbato.*
A note of the cheife heds touched by John Popham esquier, Speaker of the perlament, in his oracyon before the Queene.

In makinge of lawes he said three thinges were specyally to be considered:
1. First, that they shoold be to the honor of God and to th'advauncement of his true religion.
2. Next, to the safetye of hir Majestie's person and state.
3. And last, to the publicke benefitte of the subiects of the realme.

Everye of which partes he handled severallye, notinge in the first two thinges requisite: one, the diligent and sinceare preaching of the woorde by the bishopps and ministers of the same, whiche he tearmed to be the wateringe and refreshinge of the soules and consciences of men as gardens were refreshed with sweete showres to make them bringe foorthe plenty of good fruites; and the other by discypline, for th'exterpacyon of heresies and reformacyon of mannors as in gardens weedes are rooted out, least the good plantes bee choked upp or hindred.

In the second he remembred the great benefitts and blessings that we receyve of almightye God thorowe the ministerye of our most gracyous Queene, that so manye yeares together hath maynteyned us in so great pease and wealthe, together with hir singular vertues, justice and mercye, seene and deeply felt of all her people, being causes sufficient to make us carefull to provide by all meanes for the honor and safetye of hir, by whom we all live and enioye that we have.

And in the third parte he noted how necessary it was to provide lawes tendinge[1] not onely to the maintenance and encrease of the wealthe of the subiects of the lande, beinge the strength and glorye of the Queene, but also to the refreshinge and correctinge of those ill members which, by indirect meanes and of private respect to them selves, woold any wise procure the detriment of the common wealthe.

Uppon which occasion he made peticyon to the Queene that seinge all such lawes as had passed booth Howses to th'ends aforesaid remayned yet unperfect, without his Majestie gave life unto them: that therfore it might please hir to geve hir royall assent so as therby they might take the force of lawes.

This doone he remembred a peticyon made by the Common Howse the last session of Parliament to the Queene's Majestie for redresse to be hadd of certaine enormityes in the Chirche which he noted to be theise: the admittinge of unlearned and insufficient ministers; next, th'abbuse of excommunicatyon used in things of small momente; thirdlye the commutacyon of pennance into monye even in the greatest offences; and lastlye, the great inconveniences growen by reason of pluralyties and dispensatyons.

Wherunto hir Majesty made them a most gracyous awnswere, that she had and woold geve ordre therin, ffor the which he rendred to hir most humble and dutyfull thanckes. He remembered lickewise that bycause those thinges for lack of time were not fullye refoormed the House had eftsoones this session presumed to put hir Majestie in mynde therof agayne, wherunto also as to the former they received a gracyous answere, that those matters belonginge to hir as incydente to that supreame authorytie which she hathe over the cleargie and state ecclesiasticall, she woold geve such directyon therin as all the disorders shoold be reformed so farr as shoold be necessarye. For the which answere also he rendred the like most humble thancks, besechinge hir Majestie in the name of the whole commons that it might please hir to commaunde that to be doone without delaye which the necessitye of the thinges did require.

Finallye he presented unto hir a subsidie[2] and two fiveteenes graunted by bothe the Houses towardes the mayntenance of hir great charges: most humbly besechinge hir not to wey the smalnes of the guifte, being farr lesse then was nedefull, but the good wills and mindes of the gevers, who beside this woold be ever redye according to their most bounden[3] dutyes to employe all the rest which theye have and their lives also for the service of hir Majestie and the realme.

Thus much in effect beinge uttred by the Speaker, the Lord Chauncelor[4] made answere in hir Majestie's name particularlye to everye pointe, declaringe hir good acceptatyon of the paines and travayles of boothe the Howses; and so concludinge with hir Majestie's thankes, pronounced a prorogacyon of the parlament untill the xxiij[th] of Aprill next.

---

1. MS reads 'tendringe'.
2. MS reads 'subsidue'.
3. MS reads 'bound'.
4. Sir Thomas Bromley.

1. Thomas Cromwell's journal, 16 January-18 March

Text from TCD MS 1045, copy.

TCD MS 1045, fos.96-115v

At the parliament held by prorogation and beginning the xvj[th] of January in the xxiij[th] yeare of the raygne of our soveraigne lady Queene Elizabeth.

Ordo The said xvj[th] day, considering that we were destitute of a Speaker by the death of Sir Robart Bell, it was moved that the Privy Counsell and certeyne other of [the] House should goe to the Lordes and desire them to ioyne with us in motion to the Queene's Majestie that it might please her to give us licence to chuse a Speaker. Which was don accordingly, and the Lordes agreed that certeyne of them with foure of the Privy Counsell, being of our Howse, should move her Majestie therein, and so notifie to the Howse her Majestie's answer.

The xvij[th] of January nothinge was don save onely notefied by Mr Treasurer that the next day wee should understande the Queene's pleasure.

Ordo The xviij[th], certeyne of our Howse went up to the Lordes, whereas there was a commyssion read under the Greate Seale by which her Majestie did licence the Howse to proceed to the choice of a Speaker. And after their returne,[1] certeyne of our Howse were sent up againe to the Lordes to notefye unto them that Mr Popham, being her Majestie's Solliciter Generall, was a member of our Howse, and that [we] were desirous to have him ioyne with us in the election of our Speaker; who shortely after came downe accordingly. And then we being ready to proceede to the election of our Speaker, Mr Lewknor moved that, considering prayer was necessary to be used in all such actions, that we might all ioyne in prayer to God to directe us in our

f.96v doyngs; offered a prayer for that purpose, which was read by our clearke. And / after the prayer ended, the Lorde's prayer sayed by the whole Howse.

And then we proceeded to the election of our Speaker. Mr Treasurer for his parte commended Mr Solliciter, who was also aproved by some other voices, the rest saying nothing which was taken for a consent. And so he brought to [the] Speaker's chayer by Mr Treasurer and Mr Controler,[2] and presently agreed that fouer of the Privy Counsell of our Howse and should notefie to the Queene's Majestie, and so to understande her farther pleasure.

The xix[th], Mr Treasurer declared to the Howse that they had advertised her Majestie of our election, and that the next day we should understande her Highness' pleasure.

Ordo This day also was moved that certeyne were nowe returned as burgesses in place of persons which were alive, and certeyne others in place of some employed in her

Majestie's service beyond the seas. Whyther this might be or no was debated *pro et contra* by diverse of the Howse, and was not agreed uppon in the ende.

The xx[th], her Majestie came to the Lordes' howse and being sett in her robes with all her lords, our Speaker, the rest of the lower howse atending him, came to the barre, and after iij solemne curtesyes made, Mr Popham declared that the commons of the lower howse amongst many worthie had chosen him unworthie to be their Speaker, and did there present him to her Majestie. Notwithstanding, considering the weight / of the office and the giftes, knowledge and experience requisite to   f.97 apertaine to such a person as were to supply that function, he which knewe himselfe best, founde himselfe uterly unable to performe the same, in respecte whereof, it being in her Majestie to disalowe of the election and to apoynt the Howse to reassemble themselves for choise of a person more able, he humbly besought her Majestie to apointe them to doe soe accordingly. So might her Majestie be better served, and the expectation of the Howse better satisfied.

To this request, after instructions given in that behalfe by her Majestie to the Lord Chauncelor, he declared that her Majestie for three causes would not condisend to his request. First, in respect of the good opinion she had of the Howse; secondly, in respect of his faythfull service, whereof she had heretofore had tryall; thirdly, for that by disabling himselfe and the maner thereof, it appeared to her Majestie that he was very well able to performe the function. And therefore did ratifie and confirme the election.

This answer receaved, Mr Popham, being now Speaker, declared that in auncient use it had beene used that such as were Speakers should enter into discourses of common wealthes, which he acknowledged himselfe unable to performe, having so litle knowledge and experience. This common wealth, notwithstanding, he could not but commend greatly in comparison of others, in which iustice was so orderly administred, mingle[d] with a meane measure of mercie. Here / also he entered into comparison of our happie estate with forraigne   f.97v govermentes, most unhappie. He proceeded in comparing of this common wealth to a naturall body, whereof each parte and member is assistant to other, and all governed and guided by the head; which body, if it should have two heads or no head were a monster. And[3] each particular member had their severall functions in the common weale. The common rusticall persons he likened to the feete, without whose travell and labour notwithstanding it could not have have continueance. The martiall men he likened to the handes, by whose prowesse the realme ought to be deffended. Those which be neere unto her Majestie, some of them to the eyes and some to the eares, namely those of the nobilitie present, the counsell of estate the harte, the prelates to the minde, who ought to asist her Majestie with counsell of God's booke, preaching disciplin, administracion of the sacramentes, and reliefe of the poore. The meanes to preserve the common weale is to have men well furnished with armor, whereof he feareth there is greate wante. He seeth also greate hurte to the realme by our excesse, wherein is greate neede of reformation; and yf we continue thus in expences of forraygne commodities, it cannot be without overthrowe of the

1. MS reads 'returne to'.   3. MS reads 'and as'.
2. Sir James Croft.

common wealth. Religion, he seeth that there is many seduced, some by papistes, some by sectaries, which except they reforme themselves would be servered and cutt

f.98   of from the rest of / the body lest they procure farther infection.

This donn, he made the three ordinary petitions:[4] one for the priviledge of the persons of the knightes, cittizens and burgesses of the Howse, their servantes and their goodes; the second for libertie of speech in the Howse; the third for his accesse to the Queene's Majestie when he should be sent by the Howse, and explanacion of himselfe if he should mistake any thing, and generally that all wordes spoaken by [him] or any member of the Howse might be expounded with favour and the meaninge of the parties considered and not the wordes.

My Lord Chaunclor, after instructions taken of her Majestie, declareth that his learned discourse and fitt comparison made betweene the common wealth and a naturall bodie needeth no answere. Touchinge the petitions he sheweth that concerning freedome of speech her Majestie graunteth it as liberally as it hath at any tyme heretofore [been] graunted, notwithstanding would have them to knowe that it is alwayes tyed within limittes, *vz.* not to deale with her estate, which he sheweth to be intended aswell touching her prerogative as also in religion. Touching the priviledge of our bodies, she likewise graunteth, but she would not have any purposely become of the Howse or certayne[5] servantes indebted to defraude other crediters of their due debtes. Touching the Speaker's accesse, she also condiscendeth unto [it], respect being used to conveniencie of tyme; and for his explanacion of

f.98v   himselfe shee hopeth it shall not neede. The / reasonable interpretacion of men's speeches according to their meanings she aloweth of.

This donn wee went to the Howse, where was one bill read, *vz.* that rente charges graunted by tenaunte in tayle in remaynder should not be hurtfull [to] the purchasor.

The xxi[th][6] of January.

A bill read for the order of the clerke of the market, that he should make noe deputy except he might dispend xx[li] by yeare, and that he should notifie the dayes of his courtes to two iustices of peace and they to be present, and to keepe but two courtes by the yeare.

This day Mr Pole Wentworth mad a mocion for a publique fast to the end that it might please God to blesse us in our actions better then we had beene heretofore, and for a sermon to be had every morning; which was longe argued[7] to, and some wishing the faste to be private every bodie to himselfe, in the end a question was made whither the Howse would have the same to be privat in that sorte or else apointe a publique place of meeting for as many members of our Howse as would. *In fine* the Howse divided, and cxv were with the faste publique for the Howse and one hundred with the privat. The Temple church agreed for the place and the preachers to be named and procured by the Privy Counsell.

Ordo   A motion whither one indicted of felony might continue in the Howse; agreed that he might, not being convict.[8] /

f.99   The xxiij[th], nothing was donn but onely the prayer sayd, by reason Mr Speake[r] all the forenoone atended uppon her Majestie; onely came to the Howse and read the prayer as afore is sayd and no bill read.

One William Hanny, being none of the Howse, was taken in the Howse, who submitting himselfe was pardoned.[9]

The xxiiij[th] of January.

A bill read that the childrene of strangers should not be accompted English, first read.

A bill requiring it to be made felony to counterfet commyssions or other writings under seales of offices or other courtes or seales of corporations, first read.

A bill that actions of the case for sclaunders and assumptions should be layed in the place where the sclaunder or assumption was made and that the county may be traversed in that case, first read.

This day Mr Speaker declared her Majestie's greate mislike of our proceeding in agreeing to the publique faste, and that wee contrary to her commaundement had intermedled in causes of religion; desired the Howse from thenceforth to forbeare to inter into such accions as were not fitt for them to beare and such as himselfe could not beare; declared that of ould tyme there was foure of the Howse apointed to consider of all billes offered, and none to be read but such as they thought convenient.[10] This order he wished nowe to be observed, and no mocions to be made but for priviledges or good order.

Afterwardes Mr Vicechamberlain[11] declared that he was to declare a message to the Howse from her Majestie, which was how greatly shee misliked the maner of our proceeding in the former accion, how much wee had offended her in breaking her commaundement, how her Majestie her selfe liked well of fasting, prayer and sermons, but disliked our disorderly proceeding therein of our selves, that vouched St Paule's saying that good things must / also be well donn. Noe publique fast could bee apointed but by her, and therefore [it] empeached her iurisdiction. How her Majestie, notwithstanding, accepted the faute as of an acte of zeale, inconsideratly;[12] wisheth us to consider how fit it were in all actions to consider the end before we begin. How loath we ought to be to offende so good a Queene, and therefore thought it necessary to acknoweledge our offences and to desire her Majestie of pardon. And then he converted his speech to the Speaker and declared that as her Majestie liked well that [he] was against the action, so did she mislike in him that he would make a question and to suffer the Howse to be divided uppon such a matter, being noe bill.

This matter was prosequuted by diverse, and in the end agreed that Mr Vicechamberlain should in our names deliver to her Majestie how sorry we were for her conceaved offence, and that we acknoweledged and desired her to thinke the same not to be of malice but inconsideratnesse.

f.99v

4. Cf. *EP*, I.376-7.
5. *Sic*: 'retain'?
6. MS reads 'xxij[th]' which was Sunday. *CJ* gives these entries under 21 January.
7. MS reads 'agreed'.
8. Cf. *CJ*, I.118 where the man was not named, but the possibility of the House 'amoving' him was raised and dealt with by the Lord Chancellor.

9. In the MS this entry appears in the margin for the previous day; *CJ*, has it under 23 January. Hanny was a servant of Antony Kirle of Middle Temple (*CJ*, I.118, 120; D'Ewes, 283, 288-9).
10. This seems unlikely (cf. *HC*, 383, 392-4).
11. Sir Christopher Hatton.
12. *Sic*.

Mr Carelon[13] was desirous to speake, but Mr Speaker [did] rise and would not tary.

xxvij⁰ Januarij.

A bill that straungiers' children borne since the first yeare of the Queene's raygne should in all respectes be deemed as aliens, the second tyme read.

This bill was much impugned, first as being against charitie, against the lawe [of] nature, an imposition of punishment for the fathers' no offence[14], and lastly very perilous to all, a thing that might be obiected to our children after two or three discentes and call every man's enheritance in question; finally, that under f.100 pretense / of providing for the Queene's custome it would doe much harme. Agreed to be committed and to be better considered.

This donn, Mr Vicechamberlayne made reporte how thankefull[y] her Majestie accepted the submission made by our Howse and howe tenderly she deemed of us, and wished all men, yf any speech grew of the matter, to reporte a truth, that the maner not the matter of the purpose was misliked, for that her Majestie very well liked both of fasting, prayer and sermons.

Sir Walter Mildmey made a motion that considering the outragious dealings and hatred of the papistes to the prince and government appeareth so playnly by diverse circumstances, *vz.* the rebellion of the north, the mayntaining of certaine of the rebells being fled, the publishing of a bull of absolucion, the dealing of James FitzJames in Ireland, the invasion of strangiers, knowne whose souldiers they were and whence maintained, and rebellion of the Desmonde, they nowe withdrawing themselves from the Church, the publique dealing of the Jesuites and then such sectes; it is needfull first to provide for the more streight holding of them in by providing lawes for them, that they may knowe — which they cannot but see — how litle the Pope's bulls can availe, and that they may all knowe that her Majestie still upholdeth that gospell which hath so longe upheld her, and that since in so long mercie they are not won to be loyall subiectes to her Majestie, if they would needes be subiect to the Pope's benediction that they may withall taste of such punishment as is f.100v fit for such persons as withdrawe theire dew obedience from their soveraigne. / And that likewise as it hath pleased God to make her victoriouse in all former attemptes, and to weaken the power of all her adversaries, which hath not beene without[15] greate charges, so is it needefull wee relieve her Majestie with a subsidy, the better to enable her to resist violence to come; which is greatly to bee feared, not in respect of the Pope himselfe, but in respect of so many princes which iustely be doubted to be his confederates. This mocion was very well liked and committees presently named for drawing of bills to this purpose.

xxvj⁰ Januarij.

The bill against counterfetting of seales of offices *etc.*, the second tyme read and committed. The xxviij[th] apointed for meeting of the committees whereof my selfe am one.

The bill that rente charges and leasses by tenaunt in remaynder or revertion depending uppon a particular estate of inheritance should not hinder the purchasor of him that had the inheritance, the second tyme read and committed.

The bill that in actions uppon the case for sclaunderous wordes and uppon assumptions the county may bee traversable, the second tyme read and many inconveniences showed which may grow thereby, and therefore committed.

xxvij° Januarij.

A bill that every meane processe may be returned the next returne after the returne of the originall, and no writ of error sued after verdict or confession of an action, first read.

A bill that no iron milles be erected within xxij miles of London or the Tems, first read. /

A bill that noe woode shalbe converted to tillage, medowe or pasture upon paine   f.101
to forfeite v^{li} for every aker, no cattell but swine put into any coppes uppon paine of ij^s for every beast, noe common coppes enclosed for ix yeares to be felled for a xj yeares following, a priviso for the in[16] the wildes of Suffolke, Surrey and Kent; first read.

A bill that dephezances be made on the backe side of the statutes and the sayed dephezances to be also enroled in a booke in the office where the statutes be enroled with a space left for the fee, the booke left to him which shall next have the office, uppon payne of a hundered poundes; first read.

A bill that conveyances or writings made to or from corporacions, or reputed corporations, shalbe good notwithstanding the misnaming of the corporation, and such reputed corporations to be corporat by this bill; first read.

A bill for the assise of woode brought to London and Westminister to be overseene by such persons as hath the oversight of the woode in place where the same is brought, and against forestalling of coales; first read.

The bill concerning the clarke of the market, the seconde tyme read.

xxviij° Januarij.

A bill against such persons as under colour of clayming right in wreckes doe seaze the goodes of diverse persons, having no right thereto, that they may answer doble damadges; first read.

A bill that the taker of a ij^d wife, living the first wife, not being lawefully divorced from her, shalbe deemed a felon; first read.

The bill concerning the preserving woodes fensed, the second tyme read and committed to my selfe and others. /

The bill against burning of coales for yron mylles, the second tyme read and   f.101v
commytted to my selfe and others.

The bill for expedition of personall actions, the second tyme read, agreed to be engrossed.

The bill for enrolment of dephezances, the second tyme read and commytted.

A bill for the assise of woode and oversight thereof, and against forestalling of coales, the second tyme read, commytted to myselfe and others.

13. I.e. Carlton.
14. *Sic.*

15. MS reads 'with the'.
16. *Sic.*

xxx January.

The bill concerning abusinge of wreckes, the second tyme read and commytted.

A bill for reformacion of trialles by iuries and concerning sherives' fees for executions and for damadges cleere, first read.

A bill concerning the lenght and bredth of clothes in Suffolke,[17] repealing that parte of the statute of King Edward the vj[th][18] which apointeth another lenght and bredth to the same, first read.

The bill for expedition of processe in actions of debt and for avoiding of writes of error where the action is confessed or passed by verdict, the third tyme read and passed.

The bill that rent charges and leasses made by one in remaynder depending uppon a particular estate of inheritance should not binde the purchasor after recovery suffered, the third tyme read and passed.

xxxj January. /

f.102   A bill from the Lords that the speaker of sclaunderous wordes against the Queene's Majestie should be sett uppon the pillorie, leese his eares, and suffer imprisonement at the Queene's pleasure; if uppon reporte of another, leese one of his eares and a yeare's imprisonement; and for the second offence felony; if by writing, printing, *etc.*, felony at the first; and that cal[cul]ating the Queene's death or concerning the succession, or utter prophecies or will her death, felony; the indictment for wordes to be by two sufficient witnesses and within the yeare: first read.

A bill that the spreaders of slaunderous wordes against greate officers, bishoppes, noble men, their wifes and children, being convict in the Starr Chamber, shall make fine at the discretion of the courte, be sett uppon the pillory and imprisoned and his oath noe more to be receaved; yf uppon a knight, serieant at lawe or iustice of peace, fined as before, emprisoned for three monethes and sett uppon the pillorie and his oath reiected; the knower and not revealer to leese xx[li], the discloser of such offender to have the moytie of the fine; the offender to answer uppon his oath if he be no pier to suffer three monethes imprisonment though it be true: first read.

Nota.[19]   The bill for expedition of processe in actions of debt which passed the Howse yesterday, being mistaken in some wordes, was amended, the amendementes thrise read and againe passed.

f.102v   A bill that all armor brought in shalbe viewed by the officers of the Citie and that it shalbe lawfull for the Maior to viewe all the armor in London / and to see that the same be cleane, and furnish[20] and to inter the same into a booke, and to have of every one x[li] lande or a C[li] in goodes j[d], and every other charged by lawe *ob.*; no stranger to bring any armore to London or within three miles thereof before it be marked by the wardens of the armorers, the armor to be left alwayes to the heyer; the like for gunns *etc.*, the same to be viewed by the wardens of the armorors and the wardens of the ioyners: first read.

The bill against taking a ij[d] wife, living the first and[21] second tyme read and commytted.

Primo Februarij.

A bill requiring a partition made betweene the Earle of Northumberland, Sir Thomas Cicile, Sir John Davers, Sir Anthony Winkfield and Mr William Cornwall is in the right of their wives to be confirmed by act of Parliament, saving strangers' rightes; first read.

A bill that ij of every x white Devonshier clothes sent over should be wrought in England and five of every x pieces of carsie and every coloured cloath to be wrought in England, and that the wardens of the clothiers may make deputies to over see it.

The bill against counterfeiting of counsellors' hands or of seales of offices *etc.*, or counterfeiting writtings under seales of office, being amended was returned to the Howse, and first read.

A bill for hopps brought from beyond sea to be truely pakt without mixture of drosse, sand or leaves, and the seller therof should in / like sorte sell none except they   f.103
be cleane as aforesaid; first read.

The bill from the Lordes against sclaunderous words and libels against the Queene and against calculating concerning her life; the second tyme read and commytted.

The porters of Serieantes Inn for refusing to let Mr Norton in were sent for by the   *Nota*
serieant, who were brought in and commytted to the serieante's custody; the[22] next day uppon submission were forgiven.[23]

A bill for explanation of the statute made in the vth yeare of Queene Elizabeth[24] to extend to razers, adders, subtracters and alterers of wordes in writings in such degree as if the whole writing had beene forged; first read.

A bill that noe person should keepe any inn or common alehowse except he be authorised by the iustice of assise, first read and reiected.

3° Februarij.

A bill containing an addition to a former statute[25] for the paving and mending of certaine wayes aboute Aldersgate by charging the owners of the howses and groundes adiacent, first read.

The bill of disabling strangers' children borne in England, newely come in from the commyttees, first read.

A bill that none sell wolle but of his owne sheepe or tyth except lockes, nor any yarne to be sould but of one sorte of spinning, first read.

The bill from the Lordes prescribing a new forme of oath to the sherives and undersherives and their deputies, that noe iuror be returned without an addition nor any returned but duely warned; first read. /

A bill that Devonshier carzeies called dozens shall coming out of the weaver's   f.103v
loome wey xv[li] and containe xv yardes at the least, and the searchers and enawlers of London to make noe search at clothiers coming to faiers and markets, and none to

17. *Sic*; Somerset.
18. 5 & 6 Ed.VI, c.6 (1551-2), in *SR*, IV.136.
19. MS reads '*nata*'.
20. ?MS reads 'fuonish'.
21. *Sic*.
22. MS reads 'there'.
23. See *CJ*, I.121; D'Ewes, 290-1.
24. 5 Eliz., c.14 (1562-3), in *SR*, IV.443-5.
25. 13 Eliz., c.23 (1571), in *SR*, IV.558-9.

make of the said carzeies except he have beene seaven yeares printice; first read.

A bill restrayning the bringing in or using of any log wood for dwyers which make the false colours in clothes, and to have an eye of blewe first in all colours except blacke; first read.

A bill from the Lordes against sclaunderous libells, ij^d read, impugned for many cawses and at last commytted.

A bill that of erronyous iudgementes given in the Kinge's Bench a writt of error might be swed and might be examined by the iudges of the Common Place and Barrons of the Exchequer, so as no writ of error be sued uppon a former writ of error; first read.

iiij° Februarij.

A bill that the unlawfull taking of conyes by 2 or more in the day uppon paine of xx^s, if by night uppon paine of xl^s, and commytted to the jayle for a quarter of a yeare and bound to the good abearing for two yeares; if with a net, the paine v^li, the second offence doble; if examined of the offence they conceale their company, the paine v^li.

A bill for the lenght, breadth and weight of Somersetshier clothes called Tauntons and Bridgewaters, for qualification of a former lawe[26] made in that behalfe, aledging that it should be to the undoing of the country to observe the rates of the former statute; ij° read, commytted. /

f.104   A bill against counterfeiting of counsellers' hands and of seales of offices to writings, or of counterfet writings under such true seales; twise read, to be engrossed.

A bill that strangiers' children borne in England should no longer enioye their births right then they shalbe dwelling in England and continue their solle obedience to the Queene of England; twise read, to be engrossed.

The bill from the Lords concerning sherives ij° read and commytted.

Ordo   This day was moved that Mr Arthur Hall, having set forth a booke in printe under the name of F.A., greatly to the slaunder of the parliament howse, might be called to answer his offence, whereuppon it was ordered that the serieant should arest, and Sir Thomas Scott and Sir [Thomas] Browne were required to ayd the said serieant; and the printer likewise to be sent for. Certaine of the Howse apointed to examine the matter.

vj° Februarij.

A bill to confirme an award betweene the deane and chapiter of Worster and certaine his tenaunts, twise[27] read and commytted to myselfe and others.

A bill for the particion of the lands of the late Lord Latimer according to an agreement made betweene those who have maried the co-heires, twise read and commytted to myselfe and others.[28]

This day Mr Arthur Hall was brought to the barre to answer his offence in publishing, cawsing the booke to be printed, for which he was before apointed to be atached. The cawsing of the booke to be printed he confessed, but would not by any meanes be induced to confesse that he had offended or given cawse of offence in the doing thereof, only he sayd, / if he had offended he desired the Howse to be good

f.104v

unto him. He also denyed the publishing or having any more of the said bookes then one, and that himselfe had also restrained the publishing thereof. But uppon examination of the printer of the booke it fell out that he had xiij of the same, of the which one at the first, six in Michellmas terme was twe[l]vemoneth, and vj in Michelmasse terme last, and that he had also cawsed one to be delivered forth this parliament tyme.

Walter Vaghain esq., outlawed, being a burgesse of this Howse, it is referred to examination what shalbe donn; viij Februiary, agreed that he should continue of the Howse.   *Nota*[29]

viij° Februarij.

The bill concerning the search of clothes and limiting what number shalbe wrought in England before they be transported, the second tyme read and commytted.

A bill concerning straungers' children, being the third tyme read, uppon diverse great imperfections shewed was againe commytted to certeine commyttees.

Uppon a motion by Mr Norton it is agreed that commyttees may make the best reasons they can to the Lords in maintenance of things passed the Howse, but not to consent to any new matter.   *Nota*[30]

viij° Februarij.

A bill concerning Gringelford [Cringleford] in the county of Norfolke to make good coppieholds graunte by the lord by the assent of the parties, first read.

A bill for a collection for the building of Gradiffe [Cardiff] bridge, first read. |
A bill concerning Devonshier carzeyes called doozens, ij° read.   f.105

A bill that reconcillers of the Queene's subiectes to the sea of Roome by shrift or like perswasion by Jesuites and seminary priests shalbe in like state of punishments as those which doth the same effect by bulls, the parties so reconciled in like predicament, the procurers, counsellors and abettors in like degree as procurers, counsellers and abettors by bulles, the conceallers of the offence in like degree as concealers of bulls, every papist acknoweledging the sea of Roome, saying or singing Masse adiudged a felon, every such person hearing Masse to pay CC markes and a yeare's imprisonment, for the second offence *praemunire*; every person suspected to be a papist and alowing of the Church of Roome as it now is, refusing to come to church and to heare the devine service and preaching by the space of a moneth, to forfeit xx^{li}, for the second moneth x^{li}[31] and six monethes' imprisonment, for the third moneth a C^{li} and a yeare's imprisonment, for the fourth moneth *praemunire*; warning to be given by the curat uppon paine of x^{li}; if any counseller towards the law absent himselfe in such sorte or refuse the oath of the Queene's

26. See 5 & 6 Ed. VI, c.6 (1551-2), 4 & 5 Ph. & M., c.5 (1557-8), in *SR*, IV.136-41, 323-6.

27. Cf. *CJ*, I.121-2: first reading on Saturday 4 Feb.

28. Cf. *CJ*, I.122: 'twise' may mean 'second',

but there is no record of a first reading here, nor in *CJ*.

29. MS reads '*nata*'.

30. MS reads '*nata*'.

31. *Sic*; the Act has £40.

supremacy, to be disabled to be a counseller and from thence forth reputed a mayntainer; if any officer offend [in] such case he to be sequestered from his office untill he be reconcilled; all schoolemasters shall in like sorte take the same oath or els to be disabled to be shoolemasters and suffer two yeares' imprisonment, the keper of such schoolemaster leese x^l; all students of the Inns of Courts to take the oath or els disabled to be of any howse of court and chauncery; the sufferers of any Masse to be

f.105v said in their howse, knowing / thereof and not revealing the same, in like payne as the hearers of the Masse; the wife of every person refusing to come to church to be imprisoned, yet baylable at the discretion of two iustices of peace, whereof one to be of the *quorum*; if she be not reconcilled in the life[32] tyme of hir husband, to leese her dower, ioynture, and all other livings during her life after the death of her husbande, and disabled to be capable of any legacy; all bonnds for assuring any of the premisses to her use to be void; all offences not being treason or *praemunire* enquyrable by the iustices of peace and by them also determinable; treasons and *praemunires* enquirable also before them; any person reconcilling himselfe beefore indictment to save the penalty, if attainted uppon the *praemunire* uppon reconcilliation to be restored to his living from thenceforth; the offendor unable to pay the penaltie stand uppon the pillorie with a miter uppon his head, and a yeare's imprisonment; this statute and all other made against like offenders to be expounded most beneficially to the Queene; no landes lost but for life, no corruption of blood, disheriting of any heir, no forfeiture of any dower for the husband's offence, neither shall it be lawfull to kill any ateynted of the *praemunire*. All other persons refusing to come to church to forfeit for the first moneth x^{li}, for the second xx^{li}, for the third xl^{li}, and all covenous conveyances made since the first day of this session of Parliament to be void: first read. /

f.106   A bill explaining the statute of limitation of prescription to extend to copieholdes first read.[33]

A bill that the seasen of lx yeares shalbe a sufficient possession uppon fermedowns[34] in discender, first read.

A bill against alowance of depositions examined by any corporation concerning any landes not lying within the libertie of the corporacion, first read.

ix° Februarij.

The bill against the unlawfull killing of conyes, ij° read and commytted.

The bill concerning ratifiing of copieholdes passed betweene the lord and tenauntes in Gringelfield in the countie of Norfolke, ij° read, to be engrossed.

A bill that the taking of any thing or promisse of any thing for execution of any office, or for any favour to be shewed therein above ordinary fees, to pay xx^{li} for a fine and damages doble to the partie, first read.

A bill for the paving of diverse streetes and mending of diverse wayes aboute Bishoppesgate[35] and the fieldes there, ij° read and commytted.

The Lords this day sent a bill unto us touching the erection of an hospitall.

The bill that no money should be given or sent to fugitives not returning uppon proclamation, by way of exchaunge or otherwise, and to make void all bonnds made to them or any other to their benefit for such purpose, other then such as be to the Queene; first read.

The bill that the statute of forgerie may be explaned to extend to razures and alterations in writings, twise read, to be engrossed. /

A bill that the not discloser of any person uppon examination knowne to have forged any writing should receave like degree of punishment as the forger himselfe.[36]

The bill against counterfeiting of counsellers' hands to writings and counterfetters of seales of any office or corporation, being engrossed, the third tyme read; long disputed of the punishment of the offendors as felons especially for corporations, much misliked by many and put over to a farther argument.

xº Februarij.

A bill that certeyne gavelkind land in Exceter may be made inheritable according to the course of the common lawe, first reade.

A bill to ratefie an awarde made betweene Dorrell and Hide and after confirmed by decree in the Starr Chamber, first read.

A bill that paines layed by former statutes uppon markes of clothes shalbe uppon them in whose hands the clothes be found; the like for stretching and straining of clothes; and that carzeyes likewise missmade should be forfeited in whose hands they be found; first read.

A bill that the Lord President, Vicepresident or counsell of Yorke may appointe officers to view all cloth made in Yorkeshier before the awlneger deale therewith; this officer to forfeit xˢ [?] for every cloth alowed to be saleable not being so; if the sea[r]cher of London unpacke the cloth after and they be founde to be well, he to forfeite xˢ for every cloth: first read.

A bill for alteration of the length and bredth of Kentish cloth and other such like clothes, first read.

The bill of subsidie, first read. /

xjº Februarij.

A bill for alteration of the lenght and bredht of Kentish clothes the third[37] tyme read and reiected.

The bill transfferring punishment from makers of cloth to them in whose possession the cloth is founde, and concerning stretching and straining of clothes, ijº read and commytted.

The bill for explaining of the statute of forgery t[o] extend to razures, additions and subtractions of words and letters in writings, iijº read and passed.

Overthrowne by the Lords

xiijº Februarij.

A bill that atorneyes and clerkes of the Common Place should take no larger fees then their due, and that no iudge's servant or retainor should be atorney, nor any

f.106v

f.107

---

32. MS reads 'like'.
33. 32 Hen. VIII, c.2 (1540), in *SR*, III.747-8.
34. I.e. formedons.

35. *Sic*: Aldgate.
36. Not in *CJ*.
37. *Sic*; *CJ*, I.124 has 'second' correctly.

more atorneyes alowed then doble the number heretofore alowed by statute, the rest if they shall deale or if any lende his name to another, to be reputed a maintainer; first read.

A bill that no atorny should be swed for not putting in his warrant but within the yeare, first read.

A bill against the taking of pheaszantes and partriches by nets, and against hawking before Bartholowmetide and against the common keeping of hawkes; first read.

The bill that none should sell woll but of his owne and that there should be but one sorte of yarne spun, ij° read and commytted.

The bill for the ratification of the award betweene the deane of Worster and his tenauntes, twise read and agreed to be engrossed.[38]

xiiij° Februarij.

A bill for ratifieing of an award confirmed by decree in the Starr Chamber betweene Hide and Dorrell, ij° read and commytted.

The bill concerning the enabling of coppies to be made of the demeasne[39] lands of Gringelforde, thrice read and passed.

A bill that the statute of xxxij *Henrici viij* for limitation of prescription betweene coppieholders may extend to coppiehold lands, twise read and commytted to my selfe and others. /

f.107v *Ordo*　This day reporte was made by the commyttees concerning Mr Arthur Hall's booke, and long debating what punishment should be inflicted uppon him for the same. The conclusion was adiudged to be dismembred the [House] and a warrant to be made to the towne of Grantham for election of a new burgesse; farther adiudged to the Tower for vj monethes and so long after untill by writing hee condemne his former booke and acknowledge the same to be erronious and sclaunderous; and beside to paye five hundred markes to the Queene for a fine.

xv° Februarij.

A bill for the punishment of corrupt making and melting of wax, that the makers should set their markes uppon the wax they make and the likewise the sellers of vessells of honye; first read.

A bill that the professors of the Famylye of Love may for the first offence be whipped and for the second branded with this lettre H.N.,[40] and the third tyme adiudged a felon; first read.

A bill for the relieffe of the creditors of Sir Thomas Gresham first read.

The bill of subsydie, twise read, to be engrossed.

xvj February.

A bill against the favorers of the doctrine commonly called the Famylie of Love, twise read and commytted.

The bill from the Lords that [for] the better fortification on the borders, a commyssion might be awarded to commyssioners for reformacion of such lords as by enhauncing rentes and fines disable their tenauntes to be serviceable, and for the reedefying of howses there; first read.

A new bill brought in against counterfettors of counsellers' hands or seales, and the old ingrossed and no further proceeded in; and was twise read.

A bill to make the gavelkind land in Exceter enheritable according to the course of the common law, twise read, to be engrossed.

A bill for ratification of the awarde betweene the deane and chapiter of Worster and his tenauntes, thrise read and passed. /

xvij° Februarie.   f.108

A bill to exempt the citie of Yorke out of the statute of 8[41] Elizabeth 4 concerning the maner of the taking of prentices, as London and Norwich was before in the sayd estatute excepted; first read.

A bill adding a farther penalty of v[li] to the offendors contrary to the statute made 8 Elizabeth concerning hatt makers to be given to the informer, and that no hatt maker should have more prentices then two nor take any prentice for any fewer yeares then vij, appointing a forme of search, and that none should set up the said art except he have used the trade for vij yeares and that only in corporat townes; first read.[42]

A bill to exempt Hartfordshire out of the statute[43] made for sowing of flax and hempe, first read.

A bill for reformation of certaine abuses concerning atorneyes, twise read and commytted.

The bill concerning straungers' children and denizens, thrise read and passed, being reformed in diverse pointes.[44]   Not liked of by the Lordes.

xviij° Februarij.

A bill against deceitefull winding of woll and that none shall winde any woll except alowed; first read.

A bill for repealing of a braunch of a statute made in the tyme of King Edward the vj concerning clothes, first read and commytted.

A bill for denization of certaine persons, first read.

A bill for the strayning of clothes, first read and commytted.

A bill for preservation of pheazants and partriches, twise read and commytted.

A bill against the unlawfull killing of conyes, twise read and reiected.

The bill for punishment of Jesuites and obstinat priests and others refusing to come to church was nowe returned altered in mater in fewe pointtes, save that there is a penaltie of xx[li] layd uppon the wife refusing to come to church and authoritie given to make search in howses for Jesuites and like offendors.

38. Cf. *CJ*, I.125: 'Mr. Crumwell bringeth in the bill with the amendment of one letter in a man's name, *viz.* Dallowe for Ballowe.'

39. MS reads 'demeasure'.

40. I.e. Hendrik Niclaus: there had been a proclamation against the sect in 1580 (*Tudor Royal Proclamations*, ed. P. L.

Hughes and J. F. Larkin, 1964-9, II.474-5).

41. *Sic*; 5 Eliz., c.4 (1562-3), in *SR*, IV.414-22.

42. 8 Eliz., c.11 (1566), in *SR*, IV.494-5.

43. 5 Eliz., c.5, sect.19 (1562-3), in *SR*, IV.424-6.

44. Cf. *CJ*, I.127: a fourth reading given.

xx February. /

f.108v   A bill for denization of diverse persons begotten beyond the seas by English fathers, twise read, to be engrossed.

A bill against the burning of moores in the counties of Yorke, Northumberland, Cumberland and Westmerland betweene the end of March and October.

A bill for the better paving of diverse streetes and mending of diverse wayes about Algate, thrise read and passed.

A bill that th'inhabitantes of the countie of Mungumory in Wales should within two yeares repaier the bridge of Cardiffe; for the charges the countrie to beare four partes and the towne of Cardiffe the vth parte.[45]

A bill for ratification of a decree made in the Starr Chamber betweene Hide and Dorrell by their assentes, the third tyme read and passed.[46]

The bill against seditious rumors against the Queene's Majestie with diverse amendments and one addition, that affirming that the doctrin established by lawe in the Church of England should bee hereticall or schismaticall shalbe taken for seditious rumors; the third tyme read and passed.

A bill from the Lords to confirme an award mad in the Excheqer concerning an hospitall at Ledbery, first read.

A bill for the payment of Sir Thomas Gresham's debtes, twise read and commytted to my selfe and others.

A bill for the making of clothe in Sussex and Essex repealing al former lawes concerning the same, first read and commytted.

xxj February.

This day there were two billes read that I heard not.[47]

The bill concerning the ratifying of the particion betweene the heires of the Lord Latimer was brought in by the commyttees with two provisoes, the one for the Earle of Oxforde, the other for Sir Thomas Tindall; agreed to be ingrossed.

A bill reviving an estatute made 12 Henry 7 concerning the intercourse betweene us and the howse of Burgundy for traffique of wolls, first read.[48] /

f.109   A bill to repeale the late acte made for the same for Woodstocke concerning the buying and selling of wolle and yarne, restrayning that straungers may buy and sell the same uppon the market day and th'inhabitaunts only at other tymes; first read.[49]

Reiected by the   The bill against counterfeitting of seales and counsellers' hands, thrise read and
Lords.   passed.[50]

The bill for ratification of the decree betweene Hide and Dorrell, thrise read, passed.

The bill against the Famylie of Love, first read.[51]

A bill that iij[d] should be given of every tunn passing thorough the narrow seas towardes the reedefying of Dover pier, first read.

xxij° Februarij.

Two billes for paving of certaine streetes were read before my coming, by reason I was in a commyttee.[52]

A bill to enlarge a statute made concerning hatts and capps and requiring that noe straunger use the trad of hatting nor any to keepe any more then one apprentise except he have beene a howseholder by the space of four yeares, twise read and commytted.

A bill for the punishment of the Famylie of Love, twise read and long argwed whether paines of death might be inflicted to an heretique. Agreed to be further argued the next day.

xxiij° Februarij.

A bill for exemption of Hartfordshier from sowing[53] of hempe and flax, twise read and commytted to me and others.

A bill concerning the preservation of wood, being long since commytted, was brought in and reformed in diverse pointes, first read.

A bill for the better packing of wolle and for the punishment of the packer who suffereth any drosse, lockes, sande or such like amongst the woll; twise read and commytted.

xxiiij° Februarij.

A bill for Woodstocke twise read, agreed to be engrossed. /

A bill against converting of wood to coales for yron milles within a certaine distance of the Themes or London, being amended by the commyttees, first read.   f.109v

A bill requiring like authoritie to be given to xcvj to be chosen in Cornewall and they, or the most parte of them, may have authoritie to make lawes as they doe in Devonshier for the Stannery[54] for the ordering of their tin-workes, first read.

A bill for the true melting of wax and against corrupt mixture thereof, and for the well ordering of honey, first read.[55]

The bill from the Lords concerning the new oath prescribed to the sherive, and for ayd of iurors in their isswes, thrise read and commytted for farther amendments.

A new bill for more indifferencie of tryalles by iury, first read.[56]

xxv° Februarij.

A bill for particion of the lands betweene the coheires of the late Lord Latimer, thrise read and passed.

A bill from the Lords requiring authoritie to be given to commissioners to take order betweene the lord and the tenauntes concerning provision of armor, horse and munition in the countie of Northumberland, twise read and commytted.

45. Second reading.
46. *Sic*; but *CJ*, I.128 reads: 'the amendment twice read, the bill is ordered to be engrossed'.
47. Bills for Coventry & Carlisle (*CJ*, I.128).
48. 12 Hen. VII, c.6 (1496-7), in *SR*, II.638-9.
49. 18 Eliz., c.21 (1576), in *SR* IV.632.
50. cf. *CJ*, I.128: fourth reading.
51. I.e. a new bill.
52. See *CJ*, I.129.
53. MS reads 'showing'.
54. MS reads 'Stamery'.
55. I.e. second reading, the first on 15 February.
56. Cf. *CJ*, I.129 for this and previous bill.

xxvij° Februarij.

A bill that examinations taken in corporat townes for matters out of their iurisdictions shall not be read as any evidence, twise read, to be engrossed.

A bill concerning a schoole erected in Coventree by John Hales with an hospitall there, first read.[57]

A bill that those which bring formedowns in discender shall not be admytted to the same except they can aledge season in their auncestors within lx yeares, twise read being brought in by the commyttees and againe commytted.

A bill for the buying of woll and yarne in Woodstocke, *tercio* read and reiected. |

f.110   A bill that tenaunt in teyle may have libertie to make leases for three lives one after another and also for yeares determinable uppon three lives, twise read and commytted to me and others.

A bill against conveying of fells and skins and such like into Scottland from Berwicke and Carlile and other places adioyning, and that it may be lawfull for the persons there inhabiting to seaze the same; twise read and commytted.

A bill against the Famylie of Love, brought in by the commyttees and againe commytted.

xxviij° Februarij.

The bill of wreckes brought in by the comyttees, twise read.

The bill concerning narrow clothes and carzeyes in Sussex and Surrey and Hamshier brought in by commyttees, first read.

A bill concerning clothes called Tawntons and Bridgewater brought in by the commyttees, wherin the weight is decreased six pound from the old statute; twise read and agreed to be engrossed.[58]

A bill against taking of pa[r]tritches by night and restrayning hawkeing uppon grounds uppon which corne is standing, without the licence of the owner, brought in by the commyttees, twise read, agreed to be engrossed.

A bill restrayning any person belonging to any judge to be atornye in the court where the partie is judge or baron, and restrayning any person belonging to any judge to be an intreator or soliciter, or take any thing to entreate or solicite the iudge in the behalfe of any person, restrayning also any person to be an atorney except he have practised atornyshipp by the space of v yeares; none hereafter to be admytted except he have writen in some office of the court or beene of some howse of court or chauncerie five yeares, all others to be counted mayntainors; none of the sayd atorneyes to suffer any other to use their name: brought in by the commyttees, first read. |

f.110v   A bill against burning of moores in the north during the summer, twise read, agreed to be engrossed.

A bill against the admittance of depositions taken in any corporat townes concerning any lands being out of the same townes, thrise read and passed.

Primo Martij.

A bill against dressing of lether like to Spanish or buffe lether by any not traded therein for vij yeares, first read.

A bill against false packing of hopps and selling of corrupt hopps, twise read, to be engrossed.

A bill of the subsydie iij° read and passed

2° Martij.

A bill for the clerke of the market brought in by the commyttees, first read.

A bill against the use of logwoode and blockwoode in dying and for making of blew eyes in mathered blacke clothes, brought in by the commyttees, twise read.[59]

A bill concerning a schoole erected in Coventrie by John Hales, iij° read and passed.

A bill for making lawes of the Stannery[60] in Cornwale, twise read and commytted.

A bill for the better execution of a statute made in [blank] of Henry the vij[th] concerning Merchaunt Adventurers, twis read and commytted.

3° Martij.

A bill for the assurance of Chippingnorton to the Lord Cumpton with diverse enteyles to his children, and for the passing of diverse lands and tenements in Bashole in the parish of Mitton from the Lord Cumpton to Mr Thomas Talbot; first read.[61]

A bill for preservation of woodes, being brought in by the commyttees, twise read, againe commytted.

A bill against the corruption of hony and wax, being brought in by the commyttees, twise read. /

A bill for limitation of prescription in formedowns, iij° read and passed.[62]   f.111

4° Martij.

A bill of wreckes brought in by the commyttees, twise read, agreed to be engrossed.

A bill for denization of certaine persons, iij° read and passed.

The bill concerning absovellers, persons absolved to Roome, massing priests, and recusantes to come to church, twise read, agreed to be engrossed.

A bill concerning leases by teneunt[63] in teyle to be made in succession, *tercie*[64] read and passed.

A bill for the tinners in Cornewall, *tercio* read and passed.

A bill against the using of logwoode by dyers, iij° read and passed.

A bill concerning clothes called Tawntons and Bridgewaters to be abated six pound in the weight of every cloth, iij° read and passed.
In the afternoone the same day.

The bill of Dover pier, ij° read and commytted.

---

57. Second reading; the first reading was on 21 February, when Cromwell says he missed two bills.
58. Cf. *CJ*. I.130.
59. And engrossed (*CJ*, I.130).
60. MS reads 'Stamery'.
61. Not in *CJ*.
62. This bill under 2 March in *CJ*, I.130.
63. *Sic*.
64. *Sic*.

The bill from the Lords concerning the hospital of Ledbery to confirme a decree made in the Excheqwer concerning the same, ijᵒ [read] and commytted.

A bill from the Lords restrayning the buying of any saltefish or salte hering from beyond sea, and buying of any such of straungers, and against the killing of any flesh betweene Sherovetide and the Twesday before Easter, and against the selling of flesh to any not having licence to eat; first read.

A bill of carzeyes in Sussex and Surrey and Hamshier, twise read, to be engrossed.

A bill to give remedy uppon hwe and crie against other hundreds besides that wherein the felony is commytted, first read.

vjᵒ Martij.

25. pp.[65]   A bill of the subsidie of the clergie, once read and passed.

26. pp.   A bill for punishment of reconcillers and persons reconcilled, sayers and hearers of Masse, and refuserers to come to church; twise[66] read and passed. /

f.111v   A bill for Dover pier brought in by the commyttees, twise read and againe commytted.

vijᵒ Martij.

A bill for the ayd of vendees against persons clayming by secret conveyances made without consideration, first read.

A bill to explane a statute made *ijᵒ Edwardi iiijⁱ*[67] concerning merchaundises at Berwicke to extend in all respectes as largly to Carlile, first read.

A bill for reedefying of howses and maintenance of horse and armor uppon the borders of Scotland in the counties of Northumberland, Westmerland and Cumberlande and the bishoppricke of Derham, brought in by the commyttees in place of a bill which came from the Lordes, with alteration of the meanes from the abatment of rents and fines to paines and bondes; twise read, to be engrossed.

This day reporte was made by Sir Walter Mildmey of the proceeding of himselfe and certaine other of the Counsell concerning the petition made the last parliament touching the ministerie and such like, which was that her Majestie would appointe commissioners who should see her regall authoritie executed for reformation of the disorders; and hereuppon after long speech, agreed that the Speaker in his oration should farther, in the name of all the Howse, earnestly move her Majestie for the execution thereof accordingly.

viijᵒ Martij.

A bill concerning the inning of Plumsted marshe, requiring two yeares more to be given to John Baptista Castalion and others for finishing the same, first read and commytted.

A bill from the Lords for the assurance of a rent charge of lxxxijˡⁱ by the yeare from Edward Fisher to the Bishopp of Lichfield and Coventrie, first read and commytted. /

f.112   A bill from the Lords for the avoyding of errors in fines, first read.

A bill for provision against iron mills within xxij miles of London, twise read, to be engrossed.   27. pp.

A new bill brought in by the commyttees for reliefe of Sir Thomas Gresham, first read.

A bill for preservation of pheazantes and pa[r]tritches, iij° read and passed.[68]   28. pp.

ix° Martij.

A bill that Devonshier carzeyes called dozens being wet should containe xv yardes and weigh fifteene pounde, uppon paine uppon the weaver, brought in by the commyttees, twise read, to be engrossed.

The bill concerning the Bishoppe of Lichfield and Coventrie, twise read.

The bill concerning Plamsted marsh, twise read.

The bill for maintenance of Dover pier brought in by the commyttees, twyse read, to be engrossed.

x° Martii.

A bill for restoring in blood of Anthony Meynie esq., twyse read.

A bill from the Lords for the Lord Shouch to make an exemplification of a tenor of a recorde, altered since the exemplification thereof, to stande and be alowed for the record; first read.

A bill that owners of impropriations may assigne parte of the personage impropriat or some rent thereout to the augmentation of the living of the curat and that spirituall persons having such impropriation where the vicaradg is not worth xx^{li} by the yeare, having xx^{ty} howsesholdes, shall alowe so much as shall make it so worth, and that they shall not let the same but to the curat; first read.

A bill for the alowance of iij^d in the tonn in every vessell passing or returning out of and into England, for the making of Dover haven; iij° read and passed.   pp.10.

A bill for the better making of hony and wax iij° read and passed. /   pp.11.

A bill of errors in fines, ij° read.   f.112v

xj Martij.

A bill for the restitution in blood of the Earle of Arundell, first read.

A bill for reliefe of the hundred in which a felony is commytted uppon hue and crie pursewed by them and omytted in another hundred or county, ij° read, to be engrossed.

A bill for the almes howse of Ledberie with a saving added, iij° read and passed.   pp.12.

A bill for restoring in blood of Anthony Meynie, iij° read and passed.   pp.13.

A bill for the more indifferencie of triall by iuries, ij° read, to be engrossed.

A bill for the inning of Plamstead marsh, iij° read and passed.   pp.14.

65. All the bills marked with a number and a 'pp' became Acts this session, the number presumably indicating the order in which Cromwell considered they completed the process: they do not correspond with the order of their enrolment.

66. I.e. third reading.

67. *Sic*: 22 Ed.IV, c.8 (1482/3), in *SR*, II.475/6.

68. Not in *CJ*.

The bill against slaunderous words against the Queene's Majestie, having before passed from the Lords to us and returned to them with diverse amendmentes and an addition, was returned to us againe; uppon reading whereof it did appeare that the Lords dissented from diverse of our amendmentes, namely where we appointed in diverse places that it should be added 'intending the sclaunder and dishonor of the Queene's Majestie', they altered the same to 'tending to the sclaunder and dishonour of the Queene's Majestie'; and in one place without any addition had stricke out the amendment and let the bill stande as it was; in another place, where in the bill we appointed theise words to be stricken out 'or other unlawfull art or meanes whatsoever', they had let the bill stande as it was; besides, in our addition, by diverse amendments offered by them, both diverse partes of our amendments were to be stricken out and also the very substance of the sence altered. Uppon deliberat consideration whereof it was agreed that by this act we were disabled to deale with the bill, since, directly disalowinge of our amendments, we could not undoe that which we had donn; added unto our amendments, it was resolved they might, but not directly to impugne it; concerning our addition, entirely added of our selves, there was diversitie / of opinions, some thought they myght in any sorte make alterations therein as in a new bill, others thought they might add thereto but not put out any thing. Examples were alledged that in viij° of the Queene's Majestie, uppon a bill sent from us, the worde 'wines' being added by the Lords and the bill returned, our Howse disalowing of the worde 'wines', the bill was held and overthrowne.[69] Likewise shewe that in xiiij° uppon the bill against Marie commonly called Queene of Scotts, uppon alterations made by the Lords to the bill which passed with us, we grieving that we could not chaunge of any of their amendments, were fayne to add a proviso.[70] And so concluded, that the bill should be returned to the Lords with a message that we founde it so dealt with as we could not by lawe proceede any farther thereuppon.

f.113

The bill of fines iij° read and passed.

xiij Martij.

This day according to the order made the xj^th of March the bill of sclaunderous wordes was sent up to the Lords, but they refused the receipt thereof and therefore the same was brought backe againe to our Howse.

The bill for the payment of Sir Thomas Gresham's debts, the third tyme read and passed.

A bill for restitution in blood of the Earle of Arundell, ij° read.

A bill for assurance of a rent charge to the bishopp of Coventrie from Edward Fisher, *tercie* read and passed.

The bill for the Lord Sowch against the amendment of a role, ij° read, agreed that his counsell should be hard the next day.

The Lord Cumpton's bill ij° read.

This day the Lords required a conference concerning the bill made for strengthning of the borders, which in the afternoone was had accordingly, uppon which conference the Lords alledged that there was greate faulte in us that had made a new bill for the same, reiecting theirs and sending it to them againe without any

conference / first had;[71] wherein we alledged that we had donn nothing but we   f.113v
thought we might lawefully doe, and shewed that the like was donn *xviij°*
Elizabethae uppon a bill of apparell, and since we might dash a bill we might also
make a newe.[72] Then they proceeded to shewe some things wherein they wished
amendment.

xiiij° Martij.

A bill from the Lords to make bankeroutes' goods liable to straungers debtes
aswell as the debtes of our owne countrie, first read.

The Lord Cumpton's bill with amendment iij° read and passed.

A bill against secret conveyances made to men's freinds of lands after sould, ij°
read.

A bill touching hue and crye iij° read, to be in some poinctes amended.

This day the Lord Sowch came to the barre with his counsell and was harde.

This day also Mr Vicechamberlaine moved that a new bill might be made
against sclaunderous words against her Majestie, to the intent we might shewe our
selves carefull of her estate.

The Lord of Arundell's bill iij° read and passed.

xv Martij.

A bill against procuring any straungier to bring salted fish from beyond sea and
against killing of any flesh betweene Shrovetide and the Twesday before Ester, ij°
read and commytted.

A bill to extend the statute of banckeroutes[73] to strangiers aswell as to English, ij°
read.

A bill for restoring in bloode of John and Dudley Sentliger, iij° read and passed.

A bill for more indifferent tryall by iuries, *tercio* read and reiected. /

A newe bill against raysing of seditious rumors against the Queene's Majestie,   f.114
twyse read, agreed to be engrossed.

xvj° Martij.

A bill concerning the search of clothes, first read.

A bill that Suffolke and Kentish clothes may be caried as other clothes be, first
read.

A bill extending the statute of banckeroutes to strangiers aswell as to English, iij°
read and reiected.

A newe bill against sclaunderous words of her Majestie, *tercio* read and passed.

xviij°[74] Martij.

The bill against using of logwoode by dwyers was sent from the Lords with

69. *CJ*, I.76,8?
70. This sequence of events does not accord
    with what we knew of the bill of 1572,
    though perhaps the treasons bill of 1571
    (13 Elizabeth) is intended (*EP*, I.225,34,
    283,90).

71. MS reads 'read'.
72. Cf. Doc.7, 1576.
73. 13 Eliz., c.7 (1571), in *SR*, IV.539,41.
74. MS reads 'xvij°; this reading from *CJ*.

amendimentes, which amendiments were thrise read and passed.

Ordo   This day also were the names of vj persons read, come in this session in place of vj others returned to be sicke, two in place of two others employed in the Queene's service, and one returned to come in place of another affirmed to be dead yet being in truth alive. Uppon consideration whereof it was agreed by the Howse that the persons which heretofore occupied the place should continue their service and those now newly come in to be removed, being fully resolved that neither of the said cawses were sufficient for remove of the former burgesses. Notwithstanding, for that Serieant Flowrdewe was before returned for Rising and nowe returned for Norwich, it was agreed he should remayne for Rising and not for Norwich. Concerning Norwich, the Howse being enformed that Thomas Beomont in whose place Serieant Flowrdew was chosen was sicke of a disease which was continuall, it was agreed that a warrant should be made to the clerke of the crowne to make a writt for choyse

f.114v   of a new one. John Leveson esquier was / also returned in place of Charles Mathew, made a minister, which was alowed of in respect that it was thought necessarie the minister should atende his cure.

This day also was an order penned read in the Howse concerning Mr Arthur Hall and alowed of by the Howse, and for that the said Mr Hall had not during the session of the parliament acknowledged his offences according to the order nor condemned his booke, Mr Treasurer, Mr Controlor, the two Secretaries, Mr Vice-chamberlaine, the Chauncelors of the Duchie and Excheqwer, or three of them, were named by the Howse to consider of and to have the alowance of his said submission during the vacacion tyme, without which made in writing to their liking he is ordered not to be delivered after the vj monethes.

There were also certaine which uppon calling of the Howse appeared to have beene absent during the whole session of Parliament; as many of which as were knightes for the shier had xx^{li} fine set uppon their head, and the burgesses x^{li}; some others had atended parte of the session, which for this tyme were pardoned. Agreed that it should be mor streightly looked to hereafter, and deeper fines set in both cases.

An order [a]greed uppon that noe knight or burgesse shall departe without licence of the Howse or Speaker.[75]

In the afternoone the same day.

The Queene's generall pardon, once read and passed.

Aboute v of the clocke in the afternoone the Queene's Majestie came to the higher howse and being set under the cloth of estate, the Speaker came to the Howse accompanied with the rest of the lower howse, bringing with him the subsydie and pardon, and came to his usuall place, where after his three solemne congies made, hee made an oration wherein he amplified at large the cawses to be respected in making of lawes, namely the honor of God, the safety of the prince, and

f.115   goverment / of the common wealth. After, he declared that in this behalfe diverse matters to all these effectes had beene treated of this parliament. He specially recommended three: one made against disloyall sub[je]ctes, the second against sclaunderous words of her Majestie, the third for increase of the navye. Afterwardes he declared that he had receaved in charge to put her Majestie in mynde of a petition, made by our Howse the last session of Parliament, of reformation of the unlearned and unfit ministers, for provission against commutation[76] of penance and against the abuse of excommunication and against dispensation for pluralities and such like; and giving thankes for her Majestie's answer made, that she would have a care thereof, yet earnestly requiring that it might be effectually performed, shewing that which was donn hitherto was no sufficient provision. After, offered the subsidie and then gave humble thankes for the pardon and delivered them in. Finally, desired her Majestie's alowance of such billes as wer to her Highnes' liking.

This donn, her Majestie called the Lord Chauncellor to [her] who, after instructions receaved, having recited brieflie the effect of the Speaker's oration, he declared that her Majestie commended our diligence in the making of the lawes. Concerning the lawe made against disobedient subiects, she meant to see it put in execution. Concerning the second, she nothing doub[t]eth her safetie though no lawe were made therefor, yet considering their request, she will consent thereto, and rendereth thankes for the care of the Howse therin; yet in those thankes comprehendeth not some in the lower howse who forgot themselves. Concerning the petition, she sayeth it needed not any such reiteration. The Howse might have beene satisfied with her answer before made. It should be founde she would deale effectually with her bishopps therein, and if that served not, should use her supreame authoritie graunted to her Highnesse by Parliament in those cawses. Concerning the subsidie, / shee thankefully accepted the same, which if it were not for other cawses   f.115v then her owne particular, she would refuse. Concerning the bill[s] passed, uppon reading of the titles her consent or dissent should be declared. And so the same were commaunded to be read, of the which the Queene alowed of all but onely one against corrupt hopps, of which the answer was that she would be advised.

And this donn, my Lord Chauncelor declared that her Majestie's pleasure was that for this tyme they might departe, keeping their day againe the xxiiij[th] of Apperill next, untill which tyme the parliament was now proroged.

---

75. Cf. *HC*, 413-15.   76. MS reads 'commulation'.

Indexes

Note

I have divided the index into three parts: persons (and principal officers); bills, arranged session by session; and a general index of main subjects, where the matters covered by the bills will of course appear again alphabetically. Precise identification of members may be problematic and sometimes ultimately impossible: the diarists do not usually attribute Christian names to the speakers they report, surnames may be common to more than one member, and the *Returns of Members of Parliament* (1878) is not wholly reliable. I have supplied Christian names in parentheses in some cases, but in others I have simply listed speakers as they appear in the MS, that is as 'Mr'. The invaluable work undertaken by the research team of the forthcoming Elizabethan section of *The History of Parliament* will doubtless solve many of the difficulties here.

GENERAL INDEX

INDEX OF BILLS
House of Commons Bills

House of Lords Bills

INDEX OF PERSONS
(including principal officers)

Detail from Anthonis van den Wyngaerde's 'Panorama of London from a point in Southwark', showing the Palace of Westminster in 1558 (Ashmolean Museum, Oxford).

This Book must be returned to
the Library on, or before the
last date shown below